Basic Bankruptcy Law
for Paralegals

PARALEGAL SERIES

Basic Bankruptcy Law for Paralegals

Tenth Edition

David L. Buchbinder

Wolters Kluwer

Wolters Kluwer Legal & Regulatory U.S. serves customers worldwide with CCH, Aspen Publishers, and Kluwer Law International products. (www.WKLegaledu.com)

To contact Customer Service, e-mail customer.service@ wolterskluwer.com, call 1-800-234-1660, fax 1-800-901-9075, or mail correspondence to:

> Wolters Kluwer
> Attn: Order Department
> PO Box 990
> Frederick, MD 21705

Printed in the United States of America.

1 2 3 4 5 6 7 8 9 0

ISBN 978-1-4548-7340-2

Library of Congress Cataloging-in-Publication Data

Names: Buchbinder, David L., author.
Title: Basic bankruptcy law for paralegals / David L. Buchbinder.
Description: Tenth edition. | New York : Wolters Kluwer, 2017. | Includes
   index.
Identifiers: LCCN 2017000925| ISBN 9781454873402 | ISBN 145487340X
Subjects: LCSH: Bankruptcy—United States. | Legal
   assistants—United States—Handbooks, manuals, etc.
Classification: LCC KF1524.85 .B758 2017 | DDC 346.7307/8—dc23 LC record available at https://lccn.loc.gov/2017000925

About Wolters Kluwer Legal & Regulatory U.S.

Wolters Kluwer Legal & Regulatory U.S. delivers expert content and solutions in the areas of law, corporate compliance, health compliance, reimbursement, and legal education. Its practical solutions help customers successfully navigate the demands of a changing environment to drive their daily activities, enhance decision quality and inspire confident outcomes.

Serving customers worldwide, its legal and regulatory portfolio includes products under the Aspen Publishers, CCH Incorporated, Kluwer Law International, ftwilliam.com and MediRegs names. They are regarded as exceptional and trusted resources for general legal and practice-specific knowledge, compliance and risk management, dynamic workflow solutions, and expert commentary.

Summary of Contents

Contents

Note on forms: The text occasionally refers to a Forms Disk. The forms are now available for download, rather than on a stand-alone CD. The forms can be accessed at the companion website to accompany this text at http://www.aspenlawschool.com/books/Buchbinder_BankruptcyPara10e/. All references to forms are to these materials.

Preface

This book evolved from a need to develop a nuts-and-bolts description of the bankruptcy system written in a manner that could be easily understood by nonlawyers.

My primary intent has been to design this text as a basic primer for legal assistants or paralegal students to help them grasp the practical aspects of representing debtors or creditors within the bankruptcy system. To meet this challenge, I have explained practice and theory together in as concise a format as possible. I have chosen this approach because practice is almost always dictated by the underlying theory, and it is easier to learn a practice when one has been provided with the basic theory behind the practice.

In subsequent editions I have listened to the many thoughtful comments of paralegal instructors and students from all over the country, some of whom have gone to exceptional effort to hunt me down, to enhance the practical nature of the text, and to further simplify the subtleties and nuances of the Bankruptcy Code and system. Each new edition updates and revises the text to keep abreast of all statutory, case law, and rule changes that regularly take place.

Along with the now standard Practice Pointers and Practice Exercises features, this Tenth Edition incorporates several innovations unique to this text and this edition, as well as utilizing the most up-to-date revisions to the Official Bankruptcy Forms and the most current dollar amount adjustments. The major revisions begin with a new chapter 3, Understanding the Client, where client interview skills are introduced along with the interview process. In this new chapter, there is presented a detailed fact pattern designed almost like a short story to both develop the interview concept and also to provide reference points for the instruction to come. In conjunction with this "story", throughout the book you will find "Fact Pattern" references to tie the material on a given page back to the fact pattern in chapter 3. The hope is that this new design will help to facilitate the learning process for students as you can tie the new material presented in each subsequent chapter back to the underlying fact pattern. This edition is also the first to include the new Official Bankruptcy Forms adopted by Congress as part of the Forms Modernization Project beginning in December 2015, up to and including December 2016. In addition, this revised edition includes the most up-to-date statutory adjustment of dollar amounts, as revised triennially, most recently on April 1, 2016, to the exemption amounts and other provisions in the Code. Combined, these innovations and revisions represent the cutting edge in bankruptcy education.

Paralegals are invaluable in the bankruptcy system. Under proper legal supervision, paralegals can efficiently perform various tasks for clients at a substantial savings. Because much of bankruptcy practice is routine, presenting these routines and the reasons for them will help a paralegal be properly prepared to assist in a debtor or creditor bankruptcy practice. The introduction describes the role of paralegals in the bankruptcy system. The student should read the introduction twice, once at the beginning of the course and again at the end. In this way, the material will act as both an introduction and final review of the course.

It has not been my intent to analyze the complex subtleties of the Bankruptcy Code and its attendant case law interpretation, but rather to describe the routine events that occur in all bankruptcy proceedings, events that normally occur without dispute or litigation. These events account for a majority of bankruptcy practice, much of which is not problematic. Thus, law students and nonbankruptcy attorneys may also find this text a useful reference tool for finding the answers to common bankruptcy questions.

For example, by reading chapter 4 of the text and the forms accompanying chapter 4 in the forms disk, any student or practitioner can quickly learn the basic principles of providing notices to creditors or parties in interest in bankruptcy proceedings, and learn about the documents and timing involved, while receiving some guidance as to the existence of applicable local rules in a given district.

My philosophical goal in undertaking this work has been to describe the Bankruptcy Code as a comprehensive system of debtor relief and debt collection, as well as the organization and practical functioning of this system. I am honored to have been given the opportunity to evolve the original work from the laboratory of time and use.

Upon completing this undertaking I have reached the inescapable conclusion that the Bankruptcy Code exists first and foremost as a tool of debt collection and not of debtor relief. Conversely, the debtor relief provided by the Bankruptcy Code is among the most liberal relief that has existed in the evolution of bankruptcy laws in Western civilization. Nonetheless, the 2005 legislation has been perceived by many to restrict debtor relief while enhancing the debt collection aspects of the Code, particularly in consumer bankruptcy cases.

This book has also been prepared with the secondary purpose of aiding creditor representatives in understanding how the bankruptcy system may be properly utilized as a debt collection device to increase overall recovery rates.

I am optimistic that having described the Bankruptcy Code in this manner I may aid, however slightly, in enhancing the efficiency of the system.

Finally, please note that the text occasionally refers to a forms disk. For this edition, the forms are now available for download, rather than on a stand-alone CD. All forms can be accessed at the companion website to accompany this text at http://www.aspenlawschool.com/books/Buchbinder_BankruptcyPara10e/.

David L. Buchbinder

January 2017

Acknowledgments

Acknowledgments to the First Edition

In early 1987, my associate Lauren Austin made a wild suggestion that I tape-record my legal-assistant bankruptcy course at the University of San Diego and then transform the spoken word into a written text. After some thought, I decided to give it a whirl. My legal assistant at the time, Vicki Johnson, assisted me in the recording of my class during the spring of 1987.

Some 3,000 hours, 28 months, and five drafts later I take pleasure in gratefully acknowledging the encouragement and assistance of the many people who have aided me in this project.

My loyal long-distance typist, Joan Jackson, has been invaluable from the beginning of this project. She has been ably assisted by Lynn Williamson, Julie Rasmussen, and Mary Lou Staight, particularly in connection with the final manuscript draft. Numerous members of my staff have offered aid and sustenance with the footnotes and citation checking. Among them are Flora Calem, Beth Sandler, Adam Nach, and my friend and colleague, Mark R. Nims. Mr. Nims's comments were particularly instructive in helping me prepare a teacher's manual to accompany the text.

Susan Sullivan of the University of San Diego Legal Assistant Program has been a positive and encouraging force throughout. Indeed, but for her giving me an initial opportunity to teach, this book would never have been written.

Many of my colleagues, too numerous to mention individually, have also offered helpful advice and suggestions. I would particularly like to thank Kathryn Infante and Ted Simmons, estate administrators for the United States Bankruptcy Court for the Southern District of California, for their assistance. Ms. Infante provided me with the address of every Bankruptcy Court in the United States so the data resulting in the appendices could be obtained. Mr. Simmons regularly provided me with the statistical data contained in the footnotes regarding the numbers of annual bankruptcy filings nationwide. Mr. Larry Ramey of the United

States Trustee Office provided me with this data for 1988. (In 2008, anyone can access all of this data on the Internet 24 hours a day, but that's not how it was in the "old days.")

The appendices turned out to be a project within a project. Ms. Austin rendered services above and beyond the call of duty in obtaining local rules from throughout the United States. Then she prepared preliminary tables from her own review of every set of rules. The effort involved has been considerable, and the appendices would likely not exist but for her important contributions. Judge Keith M. Lundin of the Middle District of Tennessee gave me considerable encouragement when he caused an early draft of chapter 1, A Short History of Bankruptcy, to be published in the November 1988 issue of the Norton Bankruptcy Advisor.

The editorial staff at Little, Brown and Company has been most pleasant to work with. Richard Heuser, Elizabeth Kenny, Cathryn Capra, and Alistair Nevius have ably guided me through the actual publication preparation and process.

Finally, my thanks and love to my wife Deborah and my son Rafe for tolerating the many evening and weekend hours that have been devoted to this book.

Acknowledgments to the Second, Third, Fourth, and Fifth Editions

I would like to thank those whose continuing support and encouragement have helped me bring to fruition the subsequent editions of Practical Guide, now known as Basic Bankruptcy Law for Paralegals.

Lynn Williamson, Julie Rasmussen, and Catherine Forrest provided many skillful services in the manuscript preparation and updating of the appendices for the second edition. Kristen DiPaolo was invaluable in helping me redraft the tutorial for the third edition.

Carolyn O'Sullivan, Betsy Kenny, Carol McGeehan, Jessica Barmack, Anne Starr, and Pat Wakeley of Little, Brown and Company have always been a pleasure to work with.

For the fourth edition, I would like to thank Betsy Kenny for her continuing supervision, and Curt Berkowitz and Barbara Rappaport for their time and care in bringing this edition to press on an expedited basis.

For the fifth edition, I have continued to be ably supervised by Betsy Kenny, Cathi Reinfelder, and Elsie Starbecker in the production process. I have also received invaluable editorial assistance from my friends Mark Gallagher and William Hanafee III.

I am also grateful for the many constructive comments from instructors and students throughout the country who have kindly taken time to provide me with their thoughts on improving the text. I have made my best efforts to incorporate your suggestions into these latter editions.

Finally, my thanks and love to Deborah and Rafe for their continuing patience for the time it takes to keep these materials up-to-date.

Acknowledgments to the Sixth Edition

The sixth edition has been daunting. Hard on the heels of the publication of the fifth edition in November 2004, Congress passed the Bankruptcy Abuse Prevention and Consumer Protection Act of 2005, the most radical and sweeping modifications to the Bankruptcy Code since its adoption in 1978. This has required the most thorough revision of this text in record time. I have been most ably assisted in this process through these many months by Betsy Kenny. In the final production, I have been further ably assisted in this rush process by Carmen Corral-Reid. Finally, my thanks and love to Rafe for putting up with me.

Acknowledgments to the Seventh Edition

The seventh edition incorporates the evolution of the BAPCPA statute in case law and actual practice. This is particularly the case in the new area of "means testing," in which case law evolution would be necessary to flesh out the words in the statute. In addition, the means testing form has evolved, along with attendant case law, which now permits a meaningful means testing tutorial chapter.

The seventh edition also incorporates innovations made to the text in development of an abridged edition. The Practice Pointers and Practice Exercises are the invaluable contribution of the abridged edition co-author Robert Cooper. Thank you, Robert, so very much. Robert also contributed extensively to many of the text revisions.

Betsy Kenny and I have been working on this material together for almost 20 years. That speaks for itself. Thank you, Betsy.

Acknowledgments to the Eighth and Ninth Editions

I would like to thank Betsy Kenny at Aspen Publishing for her eternal editorial assistance. I would also like to thank Robert Cooper for his contributions to the work through the Abridged Edition. I would like to thank Jay Harward at Newgen for his tutelage during the production stage of this edition.

Acknowledgments to the Tenth Edition

I would like to thank Kaesmene Banks at Wolters-Kluwers for her guidance and assistance during the publication process, and Christine Becker at Progressive Publishing Services, who guided us through the actual publication process. Colleague David Gerardi deserves particular thanks for his assistance in assembling the forms for this edition. Most of all, I would like to thank Robert Cooper for his continuing invaluable contribution to the success and longevity of these materials. Finally, I would like to thank the many instructors and students who have thought and think highly enough of this work to give me the continuing honor and privilege to say thank you. I hope that in the process I have made a valuable contribution to the bankruptcy system. Little could I have imagined way back in 1986 when I began this project, and that 30 years later I would be preparing a tenth edition. I have been truly blessed.

Introduction

Paralegals and the Bankruptcy System

The use of paralegals to assist counsel engaged in bankruptcy practice has grown commensurate with the growth and acceptance of paralegals within the legal system in general. As in other areas of legal practice, bankruptcy paralegals can provide competent assistance to counsel in the areas of legal research, document preparation, fact investigation, and litigation support.

The Bankruptcy Courts that have examined the use of paralegals in bankruptcy practice overwhelmingly favor the concept. Many basic services can be provided to clients at a substantial cost savings because of the low hourly billing rates of paralegals compared to associate or partner attorneys. The services of paralegals can normally be compensated for under the bankruptcy system's fee application process described in chapter 7 infra. The Bankruptcy Courts' view of paralegal activity is best summed up in the following quotation:

> In effect, the goal of the paralegal is to perform a supervised legal function for a client at considerably less expense to the client. The concept is an efficient idea in today's legal market where attorney costs are escalating beyond the approach of clients in need of legal assistance.[1]

This is not to suggest, however, that a paralegal may operate independently of counsel in providing bankruptcy-related services to clients. The Bankruptcy Courts examining this issue have invariably and correctly found such independent activities to constitute the unauthorized practice of law.[2] In many states the unauthorized practice of law can be prosecuted as a misdemeanor. The paralegal must always tread cautiously in the face

---

1. In re Bonds Lucky Foods, Inc., No. 1, 76 B.R. 664, 671 (Bankr. E.D. Ark. 1986).
2. In re Caise, 359 B.R. 152, 155 (Bankr. E.D. Ky. 2006) ("the paralegal must work under the supervision and direction of a licensed lawyer"). See chapters 7 and 9 infra.

of clients who will invariably seek to pressure the paralegal to provide legal advice.

This text focuses on the theory, practice, and substantive law used by any member of the legal profession engaged in activity within the bankruptcy system, emphasizing the perspective of a paralegal working under the supervision of counsel. This introduction to the Full Edition will clarify the role and most useful functions that paralegals can provide to counsel in consumer bankruptcy practice. The authors suggest that students read this introduction both at the beginning and at the end of the course. The second reading will serve as a concise review of the course.

A. ROLE OF THE PARALEGAL

The role of paralegals in bankruptcy practice is similar to that of paralegals in other areas of legal practice. Research assistance, document preparation, and litigation support comprise the core of activity performed by paralegals in bankruptcy practice.

In the area of legal research, paralegals will be required to research specific legal issues based on counsel's factual analysis of a matter. The research activity may be as simple as verifying the existence and amount of a particular exemption, as described in chapter 10 of this text, or the research assignment might involve complex issues of adequate protection in relief from stay motions in chapter 13 of this text. Exemptions are items of property that individual debtors may keep after filing bankruptcy. Motions for relief from the automatic stay typically concern an effort by a secured creditor to repossess or foreclose the debtor's property, such as a car or a home. All of these issues are critical to the rights of debtors and creditors in bankruptcy proceedings. Paralegals can participate in many aspects of these activities. This course will illustrate and amplify these activities. Nonetheless, regardless of the simplicity or complexity of a research assignment, the basic research methodology presented in chapter 32 will allow many issues to be competently researched in minimal time.

In the area of document preparation, paralegals aiding in bankruptcy practice will often provide substantial assistance to counsel in preparing Statements and Schedules and the Statement of Current Monthly Income for a debtor or proofs of claim for a creditor. In these two areas, bankruptcy paralegals will likely render a majority of their services. Chapters 30 and 31 of this text are tutorials about the preparation of a debtor's schedules and Statement of Current Monthly Income.

In smaller firms, paralegals may also be asked to prepare preliminary drafts of motions for relief from stay (see chapter 13 infra), complaints objecting to the dischargeability of a debt or the discharge of a debtor (see chapter 14 infra), and motions to sell property (see chapter 19 infra). In addition, paralegals may assist in preparing preliminary drafts of all or a portion of briefs or memoranda in support of or in opposition to motions in any area of bankruptcy law.

In the realm of bankruptcy litigation, a paralegal will provide litigation support services similar to those performed in other areas of legal practice. Preparing digests of depositions, assembling and marking exhibits for a trial or evidentiary hearing, compiling factual data for counsel to prepare or respond to discovery requests, and making charts or other demonstrative aids are all activities that occur in bankruptcy practice.

B. COMMON ACTIVITIES

A summary of the activities most commonly performed by paralegals in bankruptcy practice will help the student to synthesize many of the materials found later in this text. This summary may also serve as a useful guide to practitioners, particularly those who do not regularly practice bankruptcy law.

When representing debtors, the most common activity performed by a paralegal is assisting counsel in the preparation of the basic documents required to be filed in a bankruptcy proceeding as described in chapters 4 and 8 of this text with regard to Chapter 7 proceedings, or as described in chapter 24 of this text with regard to a Chapter 13 proceeding, respectively. The checklists and forms accompanying these text chapters will serve as useful practice aids for students in class and for practicing paralegals.

The most important basic documents in any proceeding, the Statements and Schedules and the Statement of Current Monthly Income, are very often prepared by paralegals in draft form from data provided by counsel. The tutorials in chapters 30 and 31 have been designed to educate and assist students in the effective preparation and reading of these materials, as well as to explain the reason or reasons for the required data and its organization.

When representing creditors, paralegals will perform a number of basic tasks. Preparing a proof of claim, as described in chapter 22 infra, is by far the most common. Providing support to counsel in the preparation and prosecution of a motion for relief from the automatic stay, as described in chapter 13 infra, is another common activity performed by paralegals for creditor clients.

Obtaining a copy and providing a preliminary report to counsel concerning the information contained in a debtor's Statements and Schedules is a task that is also regularly performed by paralegals for creditor clients. The analysis provided in chapter 30 has also been designed to assist paralegals in performing this preliminary review. Because this analysis will always help a creditor's counsel or a trustee to determine the initial likelihood of a recovery for the creditors, the importance of this review cannot be overemphasized. Any creditor client will need to know this information in order to determine how much effort to expend in attempting to recover a dividend from a bankruptcy estate.

Regardless of the party represented, a paralegal will always provide invaluable litigation support. This support may involve the performing of services in connection with any of the various motions or adversary proceedings described throughout this text. Other than legal issues involving specific application of the Bankruptcy Code or Federal Rules of Bankruptcy Procedure, the types of activity conducted will not vary from those in any other litigation: Facts and documents have to be investigated and organized, discovery may take place, depositions will have to be digested, briefs and motions may have to be written, and finally, the matter may have to be prepared for trial and actually tried. The value of paralegals to counsel in assisting with these services is well proven.

Basic Bankruptcy Law
for Paralegals

PART I

History and Introduction

1

A Short History of Bankruptcy

Learning Objectives

- Trace the evolution of bankruptcy law in the United States
- Introduce the concepts of debtor relief and debt collection
- Identify the foundational terms and concepts necessary to approach a study of the bankruptcy system

A. ORIGINS OF BANKRUPTCY SYSTEMS

Throughout history, financial crisis has affected the lives and relationships of individuals and businesses. Regardless of the era, unemployment, illness, unforeseen disaster, and technological advance have all caused financial failure. The methods developed by societies to resolve the effects of financial crisis are known as **bankruptcy systems**. Bankruptcy systems exist in any society where there are debtors (those who owe) and creditors (those who are owed). Bankruptcy systems have existed in some form from the first moment that a tribal chieftain or village elder ordered the seizure of a debtor's possessions and their distribution to multiple creditors in full or partial satisfaction of the creditors' claims.

Creditors have always sought to collect debts and debtors have always sought relief from debt. These contrasting concepts of debt collection and debtor relief are the foundation of any bankruptcy system. The primary focus of the **debt collection** features of bankruptcy systems has always been to formulate a body of rules ". . . to provide for the collection of assets of a debtor and the equitable distribution of the proceeds of those

Bankruptcy systems: the methods developed by societies to resolve the effects of financial crises between debtors and creditors

Debt collection: the process of collecting a debt

3

Debtor relief:
what an individual
filing personal
bankruptcy seeks:
a discharge, ex-
emptions, and the
benefits of the
automatic stay

assets among . . . multiple creditors."[1] The primary focus of the **debtor relief** features of bankruptcy systems has vacillated throughout history from one extreme to another, from punishment to forgiveness. Bankruptcy systems containing liberal debtor relief provisions have existed primarily in sophisticated economies, where a continual reconciliation of accounts has been an economic necessity. Simpler economies have tended to contain more conservative debtor relief concepts, the mere sparing of life sometimes being considered revolutionary. The one exception to this pattern appears to be ancient Israel, in which liberal debtor relief concepts prevailed in a simple agricultural economy.

While the historical trend of debtor relief has favored punishment rather than forgiveness, our present United States Bankruptcy Code departs from this trend in its liberal treatment of debtor relief. In many respects the U.S. Bankruptcy Code is perhaps the most liberal debtor relief bankruptcy system to come into existence since the jubilee year of the Old Testament.[2]

The jubilee year occurred every 50 years. (Every seventh year was a sabbatical year in which some limited form of debtor relief was provided.[3]) The essence of the jubilee year is contained in the biblical verse: "And ye shall hallow the fiftieth year, and proclaim liberty throughout the land unto all the inhabitants thereof; it shall be a jubilee unto you; and ye shall return every man unto his possession, and ye shall return every man unto his family."[4] In the jubilee year, all debts would be discharged, some mortgages released, and all indentured servants or slaves freed (the concept of **discharge**, legal relief from debt, is the most basic element of debtor relief). During the intervening years any family member had the right to redeem, by payment, any property or persons that had been seized or given in satisfaction of a debt.[5]

Discharge: legal
relief from perso-
nal obligation to
satisfy a debt

The debtor relief provided for in the Old Testament most likely derived from even earlier regulations that existed in ancient Mesopotamia, from where the early Hebrews migrated to the region that became Israel. In the eighteenth century B.C., section 48 of the Code of Hammurabi releases debts in a year where crops are destroyed by storm. A century

---

1. Merrick, A Thumbnail Sketch of Bankruptcy History, ABI Newsletter (July/Aug./Sept. 1987).
2. 11 U.S.C. The Bankruptcy Abuse Prevention and Consumer Protection Act of 2005 ("BAPCPA"), Pub. L. No. 109-8, 119 Stat. 23 (2005), limits and restricts the scope of debtor relief as it has existed in American Bankruptcy practice from 1979 through 2005. BAPCPA demonstrates the pendulum-like nature of the treatment of debtor relief throughout history.
3. Leviticus 25:1-8.
4. Leviticus 25:10. If a portion of this verse seems familiar, it is because the phrase "proclaim liberty throughout the land unto all the inhabitants thereof" is the inscription on the Liberty Bell in Philadelphia.
5. Leviticus 25:11-55. The purpose of the jubilee year was to give debtors a second chance or fresh start. The "fresh start" concept is an essential feature of the United States Bankruptcy Code.

later, King Ammi-Saduqa of Babylonia issued decrees freeing private debts in barley and silver and releasing people from debt slavery in an effort to resolve economic difficulties in his kingdom. These are the earliest recorded evidences of some form of debtor relief from which bankruptcy systems have evolved.[6]

Unlike in ancient Israel, second chances were not generally given to debtors in the other ancient civilizations of the Mediterranean basin. Early Greek law did not seek to discharge debtors or reconcile accounts: A debt was always collectible. In the fifth century B.C., the Twelve Tables regulated only the procedures for selling an individual into slavery to satisfy a debt.[7]

The commentators concur that death, slavery, mutilation, imprisonment, or exile were often the only prospects for debtors in ancient Greece and also in republican Rome.[8] Roman republican law also provided that multiple creditors could, upon exhibiting a debtor in the forum for three days, divide the debtor up into pieces in satisfaction of the debts. Evidence exists suggesting that multiple creditors could also seize a deceased debtor's corpse and hold it for ransom from the debtor's heirs until the debts were satisfied.[9] This practice would make sense in Roman culture since the body had to remain whole if it were to commence a successful journey into the afterlife. The religious significance given to the satisfaction of a debt thus acted as an incentive for repayment. This appears to have been the state of insolvency law, as such, during the Roman Republic.

In the course of the Empire, Roman debtor relief and collection law evolved in the direction of debtor relief.[10] By approximately the second century A.D., debtor slavery had been abolished. Debtor imprisonment continued to exist, but this was distinguishable from slavery in that creditors could not use the services of an imprisoned debtor. The debtor could be held for ransom only until friends or family of the debtor paid the debt.[11] (Debtor imprisonment has existed throughout history, including the twentieth century.)

The Roman Empire encompassed much of present-day Europe, North Africa, and the Middle East. This vast area, comparable in size to the United States, developed a sophisticated commercial economy permitting free

---

6. Gwendolyn Leick, Mesopotamia: The Invention of the City (Penguin Books 2001), at page 187. Code of Hammurabi, Section 48.
7. Vern Countryman, Bankruptcy and the Individual Debtor — and a Modest Proposal to Return to the Seventeenth Century, 32 Cath. U. L. Rev. 809 (1983). Under the Twelve Tables a creditor had to provide a 60-day redemption period before a debtor could be sold into slavery. Payment of the debt within this period would prevent sale into slavery.
8. Id. See also Radin, Debt, 5 Ency. Soc. Sci. 33-34 (1931); Ford, Imprisonment for Debt, 25 Mich. L. Rev. 24 (1926).
9. Countryman, supra n.7; Radin, supra n.8; Ford, supra n.8.
10. Merrick, supra n.1; Radin, supra n.8; Ford, supra n.8.
11. Radin, supra n.8.

Exemption:
statutorily defined
property that an
individual debtor
may protect from
administration by
a bankruptcy
estate

trade throughout its territories in a civilization without motor vehicles, aircraft, computers, the internet, or any other form of instant long-distance communication. In this environment, Rome developed an insolvency system that permitted exemptions (an **exemption** is property that a debtor may protect from seizure by creditors) and restrained personal execution.[12] This restraint took the form of a debtor's ceding all assets for distribution to creditors. Although this act would not discharge those debts that were not fully repaid, it did act to prohibit creditors from killing, mutilating, or selling the debtor into bondage. This procedure was known as *cessio bonorum*.[13] The assets so surrendered were distributed according to statutory priorities similar to modern United States bankruptcy law.[14] To a modern American observer this procedure would appear similar to a Chapter 7 liquidation proceeding. A form of composition agreement in which a discharge could be granted also came into use as the economy grew in sophistication.[15] A **composition agreement** is an agreement between a debtor and multiple creditors for the repayment of debt. These procedures would be recognizable today as the reorganization proceedings known as Chapter 11 and Chapter 13.

Composition agreement: an agreement between a debtor and multiple creditors for the repayment of debt

When the Western Roman Empire dissolved in the fifth century A.D., the then-existing economy of Western Europe also collapsed. Whereas for approximately five centuries it had been possible to trade between London and Constantinople (modern Istanbul) with identical currency, trade practices, laws, and language, this commonality ceased to exist. The rise of the Dark Ages caused a corresponding devolution of bankruptcy laws.

B.   BANKRUPTCY IN THE MIDDLE AGES

During the Dark Ages the financial system of Western Europe receded as an important factor of daily life. Debtor imprisonment returned to vogue, prevailing throughout the period.[16] The Christian Church proclaimed debt and insolvency sinful. Debtors were subject to excommunication

12. Radin, supra n.8 at 34, 37.
13. Merrick, supra n.1.
14. Riesenfeld, Evolution of Modern Bankruptcy Law, 31 Minn. L. Rev. 401, 432 (1947).
15. Id. at 439, citing Code of Justinian VII.71.8. Justinian reigned as emperor of the Eastern Empire during the sixth century A.D. Although after the final collapse of the Western Empire, which most historians date at A.D. 476, the Code of Justinian is generally accepted to be a codification of law as it existed during the Empire period. Justinian's Codes, therefore, demonstrate the evolution of bankruptcy law from the Republic to the Empire.
     A *composition* is an agreement between a debtor and two or more creditors that satisfies the debts for less than payment in full. See chapters 2, 24-28 infra.
16. Ford, supra n.8 at 25; Radin, supra n.8 at 34.

while alive or denial of a Christian burial upon death.[17] As had been the case in early Rome, religious sanctions were once again utilized as an incentive to debt repayment.

The debtor punishments of the Dark Ages were not radically different from the earlier practices of the Roman Republic. They were consistent with a simpler society in which there once again existed few entities with multiple creditors. In the Dark Ages, a serf would generally be beholden to only two creditors: the feudal lord and the Church. Neither institution could or would tolerate an unsatisfied debt from a subservient soul.

The punishment of debtors was necessary to assist the land-owning and religious ruling classes to maintain their power. Forgiveness became a radical idea in this stratified economic structure. The lack of a commercial economy also eliminated any practical need for a reconciliation of accounts or balancing of books after an extended period of time.

International commerce and trade began its resurgence in the tenth century. As trade recommenced, the credit system resumed.[18] As the number of debtors with multiple creditors increased, the bankruptcy system began its renaissance.

The first bankruptcy laws that arose in the late Middle Ages were to a large degree reenactments of the *cessio bonorum* of the Roman Empire.[19] The focus of such statutes was twofold: the prevention of fraud upon creditors stemming from an inequitable distribution of assets and the protection of the debtor from imprisonment. If all assets were surrendered for distribution to creditors there would be no imprisonment. A discharge was not given or contemplated. These statutes were limited to use only by merchants. Loss of a trading place or bench (*banca*) in the local market would befall a debtor who fraudulently concealed or transferred assets while not paying his or her just debts. In Italy this was known as *banca rotta* and in France as *banquerotte*. This is the etymology of the English word *bankrupt*.[20] The composition agreement began to reappear in Western European law as early as 1256 in Spain.[21] A composition agreement provided some form of debtor relief in that a debtor could be released from the debts due those creditors who agreed to the composition. By the seventeenth century, the composition agreement existed throughout Western Europe with the exception of England, where such statutes did not come into regular existence until after 1705.[22]

---

17. Ford, supra n.8 at 25.
18. Radin, supra n.8 at 34.
19. Merrick, supra n.1.
20. Countryman, supra n.7 at 810.
21. Riesenfeld, supra n.14 at 439-440.
22. Countryman, supra n.7 at 811-812. See infra this chapter.

C.   EARLY ENGLISH INSOLVENCY LAWS

The emphasis of early English insolvency law was on punishment. Forgiveness was rarely known to English debtors prior to 1705. This is an important point to recognize in any study of American bankruptcy law because the law of England as it existed in 1776 is the direct legal antecedent of American bankruptcy law.

Anglo-Saxon England practiced debtor imprisonment, although the sale of a debtor into slavery or debtor dissection was probably not permitted.[23] The first statute akin to a bankruptcy statute was enacted in 1283. The Statute of Acton Burnell authorized the seizure of a debtor's assets to satisfy debt. If the assets seized were insufficient to satisfy the debt then the debtor would be imprisoned until the debt was paid.[24] We recognize at least part of this procedure today as a "writ of attachment," a common state law collection device.

From the thirteenth to fifteenth centuries, debtor imprisonment in England evolved under two related writs, *capias ad respondendum* and *capias ad satisfaciendum*. The former allowed a creditor to "attach" a debtor to ensure appearance at trial. The latter allowed a creditor to imprison a debtor in satisfaction of a judgment until the debt was actually paid.[25] Some form of debtor imprisonment existed in England until the twentieth century.[26] The first true insolvency law in England was not enacted until 1543.[27] This delay, in contrast to the rest of Western Europe, is attributable to England's lack of substantial involvement in international trade until the sixteenth century.[28] The statute of 1543 permitted the seizure and distribution of a debtor's assets to creditors and imprisonment of the debtor if the debts remained unsatisfied. The proceeding applied only to merchants and was initiated by creditors. There was no discharge for the debtor.[29] To the extent that this proceeding was creditor initiated, it was similar to the present-day American involuntary petition.[30] In 1571 the Statute of Elizabeth further refined the system of asset

---

23. Id. at 810-811. Ford, supra n.8 at 26.
24. 11 Edw. (1283). Countryman, supra n.7 at 811.
25. Countryman, supra n.7 at 811; Ford, supra n.8 at 27-28. A writ of *capias ad satisfaciendum* was used in 1989 in New Jersey to place a debtor into custody. A Bankruptcy Court refused to abrogate the writ. See 76 A.B.A. J. 28 (Feb. 1990); In re Bona, 110 B.R. 1012 (Bankr. S.D.N.Y. 1990). The use of a writ of *capias ad satisfaciendum* was affirmed by the New Jersey state courts as recently as 2000 in Marshall v. Matthei, 744 A.2d 209 (N.J. App. Div. 2000).
26. Ford, supra n.8 at 31. Ford points out that in 1921, 424 contract debtors were held imprisoned in England.
27. 34 & 35 Henry VII, ch. 4 (1543).
28. Merrick, supra n.1 at 12.
29. Countryman, supra n.7 at 811-812; Merrick, supra n.1 at 13.
30. See chapter 3 infra.

distribution to creditors. This statute defined fraudulent transfers as acts of bankruptcy. Transactions deemed fraudulent that occurred within a fixed time prior to the bankruptcy filing were considered void. For instance, concealing property from creditors would be one such act.[31] This statute is a likely basis of today's concept of an avoidable transfer, which is a major feature of our Bankruptcy Code.[32] Composition agreements made their appearance in England rather late in comparison to the rest of Western Europe. When they did, compositions were permitted only in the Chancery Courts and only during a relatively short period of time (approximately 1583-1621). Another statute authorizing compositions existed for only one year, 1697-1698.[33] Because a discharge, legal relief from debt, could occur only as a result of a composition, punishment prevailed over forgiveness in early English bankruptcy law.

In 1705 England enacted a statute in which a composition with creditors could effectuate a full discharge of all debt.[34] The Statute of Anne appears to be the first law to recognize a full discharge or legal relief of debt by a debtor since the jubilee year of the Old Testament. Otherwise, the Statute of Anne is remarkably similar in appearance to the bankruptcy system as it existed at the height of the Roman Empire.

Under the Statute of Anne a debtor would receive a full discharge and be able to retain exempt property provided that certain conditions were complied with. The conditions were that a minimum dividend of eight shillings per pound be paid to creditors and that no act in fraud of creditors had taken place prior to the bankruptcy. If a lesser dividend were to be paid, a commissioner would determine the debtor's exemptions.[35] In 1732, the Statute of George added the consent by four-fifths of the creditor body as a requirement of the debtor receiving a discharge.[36] These statutes compose the formal roots of American bankruptcy law.

D. BANKRUPTCY IN THE UNITED STATES

America is a nation of debtors: "[I]t is stated that nearly half our total white immigration came over under indenture."[37] Indentured servitude acted

---

31. 13 Eliz., ch. 7 (1571); Riesenfeld, supra n.14 at 422.
32. See chapters 16-18 infra.
33. Riesenfeld, supra n.14 at 442-443.
34. 4 Anne, ch. 17 (1705).
35. Countryman, supra n.7 at 812.
36. 5 Geo. II, ch. 30 (1732); Countryman, supra n.7 at 812.
37. Countryman, supra n.7 at 813.

as an alternative to debtor prison in some colonies.[38] Georgia was originally settled by indentured servants. In general, colonial bankruptcy law corresponded to that of England in the eighteenth century.[39] One goal of the Constitutional Convention was to establish the free flow of trade and commerce between the various states. In an effort to achieve this goal, the framers reserved for Congress the power "to establish . . . uniform laws on the subject of Bankruptcies throughout the United States."[40] By virtue of the Supremacy Clause, which provides that federal law is the supreme law of the land, the enactment of a federal bankruptcy law preempts the states from so acting and acts as the supreme law of the land.[41]

The power granted Congress to enact federal law on the various subjects, including bankruptcy, that are described in Article I, Section 8, of the Constitution, does not, however, require congressional action within a described area. Thus, although Congress has the power to enact bankruptcy laws, it is not required to do so. Accordingly, there is no constitutional requirement that there be a federal bankruptcy law. Bankruptcy laws were only in effect in the United States for short periods of time during the nineteenth century. However, a federal bankruptcy law has been continuously in effect since 1898.

Debtor imprisonment continued to be a prevalent practice in the United States until after 1830. After this date a movement toward debtor relief began and individual state constitutions began to abolish debtor imprisonment.[42] While debtor imprisonment lasted, however, there were periods of time during which substantially more debtors occupied prisons than convicted criminals.[43]

The first United States Bankruptcy Act was in effect from 1800 to 1803. This statute was virtually identical in its features to the law in England as it existed after 1732 as described above.[44]

The second United States Bankruptcy Act was enacted in 1841, effective in 1842, and repealed in 1843. This statute permitted voluntary proceedings and applied to nonmerchants as well as merchants. A voluntary proceeding was one initiated by a debtor seeking relief. Exemptions were

---

38. Countryman, supra n.7 at 813.
39. Ford, supra n.8 at 28. See also, Central Virginia Community College v. Katz, 546 U.S. 356 (2006), in which the Supreme Court discusses the evolution of American Bankruptcy Law from the early English Statutes.
40. U.S. Const., Art. I, §8.
41. U.S. Const., Art. VI.
42. Ford, supra n.8 at 32-33.
43. Ford, supra n.8 at 29, reports that in Pennsylvania, New York, Massachusetts, and Maryland there were three to five times as many persons imprisoned for debt as for crime. Countryman, supra n.7 at 814, cites statistics indicating that debtors constituted approximately 20% of all prisoners in Boston during the 1820s.
44. 2 Stat. 19 (1800). Countryman, supra n.7 at 813; Riesenfeld, supra n.14 at 407. See also notes 34-36 supra.

expanded to include "necessaries of life" in addition to clothing. A discharge was granted with creditor consent. Certain transactions were void in fraud of creditors and some debts would not be affected by a discharge.[45]

The third Bankruptcy Act was in effect during Reconstruction, 1867 to 1878.[46] This act expanded upon the scope of debtor relief provided for in the 1841 law by permitting state exemptions to be claimed by a debtor and by permitting, for the first time in a bankruptcy law since the Old Testament, a full discharge without creditor consent or payment of a dividend. Additionally, the 1867 Bankruptcy Act contained provisions permitting an "arrangement," or composition. These arrangements are the genesis of the present-day reorganization proceedings of Chapter 11, 12, and 13.[47]

A fourth Bankruptcy Act was enacted in 1898 and remained in effect, with amendments, until October 1, 1979, when the present Bankruptcy Code became law.[48] The 1898 Act contained all of the basic elements that are present in today's Bankruptcy Code. An amendment enacted in 1938 contained provisions creating Chapters XI and XIII, the reorganization proceedings that still exist under the Bankruptcy Code.[49] The Supreme Court described the Act's liberal debtor relief provisions as providing a "fresh start" to debtors in their financial affairs.[50] In 1970 Congress authorized a commission to determine the desirability of reforming the Bankruptcy Act. In 1973 the Commission reported that modernization and recodification of the Bankruptcy Act was in order.[51] The report was accepted, and the Bankruptcy Code of 1978 was the result. An analysis of this Code in its present form, along with practical descriptions to aid in conducting many routine bankruptcy procedures, is the subject matter of this text.

Thus, the substantive foundations of our current United States Bankruptcy Code are rooted deep within the history of Western civilization. For individual debtors, the Bankruptcy Code emphasizes the discharge of debt and the allowance of exemptions, thus giving a fresh start to the debtor. Such liberal treatment of debtor relief has not existed since the jubilee and sabbatical years of ancient Israel. For creditors, the Bankruptcy Code emphasizes the orderly and consistent liquidation of assets and

---

45. 5 Stat. 440 (1841); 5 Stat. 614 (1843); Countryman, supra n.7 at 814-815; Riesenfeld, supra n.14 at 407, 423.
46. 14 Stat. 517 (1867); 20 Stat. 99 (1878).
47. Countryman, supra n.7 at 815-816; Riesenfeld, supra n.14 at 409, 423, 446-447.
48. 30 Stat. 541 (1898). See chapter 2 infra.
49. 52 Stat. 541 (1938). Countryman, supra n.7 at 817; Riesenfeld, supra n.14 at 408. See chapters 23-27 infra.
50. Local Loan Co. v. Hunt, 292 U.S. 234 (1934).
51. Countryman, supra n.7 at 818; Report of the Commission on the Bankruptcy Laws of the United States, H.R. Doc. No. 137, 82d Cong., 1st Sess., pt. I, ch. 17 (1973).

distribution of dividends. In various forms, this collection process has existed in sophisticated commercial economies since the Roman Empire.[52] Finally, the formal and stylistic aspects of the United States Bankruptcy Code began their evolution with the 1705 English Statute of Anne.

Summary

Bankruptcy systems exist in any society where there are debtors (those who owe) and creditors (those who are owed). The practice of the jubilee year in ancient Israel provided debtors a discharge or legal relief from debt.

In other ancient Mediterranean civilizations, debtors were punished and not legally forgiven from debt. During the later Roman Empire, a bankruptcy system developed in a sophisticated commercial economy. In this system, debtors were allowed to protect property from creditors. This concept was and is known as exemptions.

The United States Bankruptcy Code evolved from eighteenth-century English bankruptcy law. Our Bankruptcy Code provides for debtor relief in the form of a discharge and also permits debtors to protect exempt property. The Bankruptcy Code provides creditors with an orderly process to liquidate the debtor's nonexempt assets and to distribute the proceeds as dividends. An analysis of the Code, in its present form, along with practical descriptions to aid in conducting many routine bankruptcy procedures is the subject of this text.

KEY TERMS

bankruptcy systems	debtor relief
composition agreement	discharge
debt collection	exemptions

---

52. Globalization has spawned a corresponding growth of bankruptcy statutes throughout the world bearing many similarities to Chapter 11 of the United States Bankruptcy Code. Chinese Bankruptcy Law permits liquidations and reorganizations of business entities. See The Enterprise Bankruptcy Law of the People's Republic of China, Bankruptcy Strategist, Volume 25, Number 9 (July 2008). In 1991 Hungary became the first former Warsaw Pact country to enact a bankruptcy law. See ABI Newsletter (November/December 1991). A law permitting business bankruptcies became effective in Russia in 1993. See ABI Journal, April 1993. Polish bankruptcy law contains a statute similar to Chapter 11. See Bankruptcy Court Decisions Newsletter, June 10, 2003, LRP Publications: "Poland to enact new insolvency law to aid economy."

DISCUSSION QUESTIONS

1. Why do individuals or businesses seek bankruptcy relief?

2. What distinguishes debtor relief from debt collection in a bankruptcy system?

3. How does the concept of debtor relief in modern American bankruptcy law compare with debtor relief found in England before the American Revolution? The Roman Empire? Medieval Europe?

4. What is the etymology of the term *bankruptcy*?

2

Introduction to the Bankruptcy Code

Learning Objectives

- Provide an organizational overview of the Bankruptcy Code

- Define fundamental bankruptcy terms, including creditor, debtor, and trustee

- Identify the two basic types of bankruptcy proceedings: liquidations and reorganizations

- Explain the purpose of a composition agreement and how it is an alternative to bankruptcy

A.   ORGANIZATION OF THE BANKRUPTCY CODE AND A NOTE ON THE TEXT

The Bankruptcy Code was enacted into law in 1978 and became effective on October 1, 1979.[1] It has since been significantly amended four times, in 1984, 1986, 1994, and 2005.[2] The bankruptcy law is now properly referred

---

1. Pub. L. No. 95-598, (92 Stat. 2549 1978).
2. The 1984 amendments are commonly known as BAFJA (the Bankruptcy Amendments and Federal Judgeship Act of 1984), Pub. L. No. 98-353 (July 10, 1984). The 1986 amendments are known as the Bankruptcy Judges, United States Trustees, and Family Farmer Bankruptcy Act of 1986, Pub. L. No. 99-554 (Oct. 27, 1986). The 1994 amendments are known as the Bankruptcy Reform Act of 1994, Pub. L. No. 103-394 (Oct. 26, 1994). The National Bankruptcy Review Commission, created in the 1994 amendments, delivered an 1,100-page report to Congress in late 1997. The document made 170 recommendations for changes or additions to the Code. The Bankruptcy Abuse Prevention and Consumer Protection Act of 2005, Pub. L.

to as the Bankruptcy Code. The law prior to 1979 was known as the Bankruptcy Act. Any reference to the present law as the Bankruptcy Act is incorrect. Where the Bankruptcy Act used Roman numerals to identify its Chapters, the Bankruptcy Code uses Arabic numerals. This will explain references in older cases, for example, to Chapter XIII of the Bankruptcy Act.

The Bankruptcy Code is divided into nine Chapters.[3] In essence, it is primarily a self-contained system designed to resolve the financial affairs of a debtor. The Code's basic structure can be easily illustrated and briefly described in a flow chart. This description also serves as a useful guide to understanding the organization of this text. Since the Bankruptcy Code is a system, it is best analyzed and described in a similar format. We have attempted to use a "building block" approach, working from the simpler to the more complex concepts as the text progresses. This may necessitate some reference in earlier chapters of this text to concepts not discussed in detail until a later chapter. Where this occurs, an effort has been made to briefly define the concept that will be described in greater detail later. Reference back to the chart or to the glossary at the end of the text may help simplify this initial learning process. This same chart will also serve as a capsule review of the entire text when it has been completed.

The provisions found in Code Chapters 1, 3, and 5 apply in all bankruptcy proceedings. These three Code Chapters contain the statutes dealing with the fundamental debtor relief features of discharge, exemptions, and the automatic stay. These Chapters also contain the general provisions regulating the debt collection features of claims and their priority of distribution.[4] These are the basic issues affecting debtors and creditors in a bankruptcy proceeding.

The remaining Code Chapters (7, 9, 11, 12, 13, and 15) comprise the specific types of bankruptcy proceedings that are available to debtors. The most common proceedings are Chapters 7, 11, and 13.[5] These three

---

109-8, 119 Stat. 23 (April 20, 2005) has its genesis in pro-credit-industry legislation introduced in reaction to the Commission Report. Throughout this text these amendments shall be referred to as BAPCPA.

3. All Chapters enacted in 1978 bore odd numbers (1, 3, 5, 7, 9, 11, and 13). Although apocryphal, it is believed Congress adopted this format so it could fill in other chapters later. In 1986, Congress did enact Chapter 12, the family farmer reorganization proceeding. A second reason for only enacting odd-numbered chapters may have been so that the various types of bankruptcy proceedings would still retain their common identities of Chapter 7 (VII), Chapter 11 (XI), and Chapter 13 (XIII). Chapter 15 was added to the Code in 2005 by BAPCPA.

4. See chapters 8, 10, 12, 14 and 22 infra.

5. For the fiscal year ending September 30, 2016, 805,580 bankruptcies were filed nationwide and 61.9% or 498,367 cases were under Chapter 7, less than 1% or 7,450 were Chapter 11, 458 were Chapter 12, and 37.1% or 299,150 were under Chapter 13. The remainder were Chapter 9 and Chapter 15 filings. The annual number of filings is contrasted to the pre-BAPCPA numbers for the 2005 calendar year, which included a record 2,078,415 filings, of which 80% or 1,659,017 were under Chapter 7, <1% or 6,800 were under Chapter 11, 380

proceedings comprise in excess of 95 percent of all bankruptcies filed. Normally, the provisions contained in each of these Code Chapters will apply only to the specific Chapter proceeding that has actually been filed.[6]

BANKRUPTCY CODE FLOW CHART

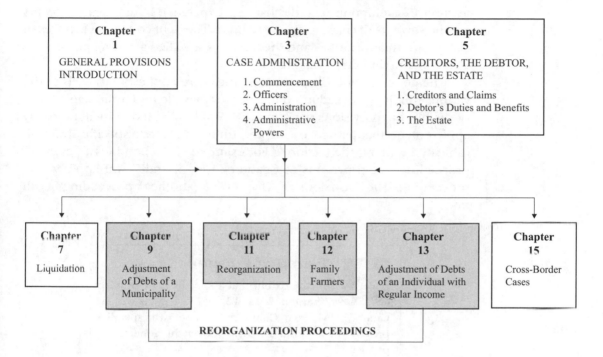

B. OVERVIEW OF THE BANKRUPTCY CODE

Chapter 1 contains definitions and general procedural rules applicable to all bankruptcy proceedings.

This Chapter can also be referred to as the "Introduction" to the bankruptcy process. The provisions of Code Chapter 1 are described in chapters 4 and 6 of this text.

Code Chapter 3 contains various rules pertaining to the administration of bankruptcy estates, including rules relating to professionals and to such issues as the regulation of professional fees in bankruptcy

---

were under Chapter 12, and approximately 20% or 412,130 were under Chapter 13. See Bankruptcy Statistics at www.uscourts.gov.
6. 11 U.S.C. §103.

proceedings.[7] This is part of the subject of chapter 7 of this text. Among the other rules of Chapter 3 are rules relating to the automatic stay and executory contracts.[8]

Code Chapter 5 contains rules governing creditors and claims, the debtor, and the estate. The core of the debtor relief and debt collection provisions is contained in this Code Chapter. The primary debtor relief features of exemptions and discharge are included here. These concepts are the subjects of chapters 9 and 12 infra. The debt collection features of claims and their priorities and the trustee's so-called avoiding powers are also contained in Code Chapter 5.[9]

The general Code Chapters 1, 3, and 5 are applicable to each of the various Chapter proceedings that a debtor may file under the Bankruptcy Code, but the provisions of Chapters 7, 9, 11, 12, 13, or 15 will normally apply only to that particular Chapter, unless it is made specifically applicable by another Code section.[10] For example, if a debtor files a Chapter 7 proceeding, the provisions of Chapters 1, 3, 5, and 7 will apply to the proceeding. The provisions of Chapter 11 (another "proceeding") will not.

Practice Pointer

To the extent that a specific provision of Chapters 7, 11, 12, or 13 conflicts with a general provision in Chapters 1, 3, and 5, the specific provision will generally control over the general provision.

Chapter 7 is the most common type of bankruptcy proceeding. It may be described in one word: liquidation. The majority of all bankruptcies filed are Chapter 7 proceedings.[11] In a **liquidation** proceeding, the anticipation is that all of the debtor's nonexempt assets will be sold. The proceeds are then distributed to the creditors according to their priority. The basic details of Chapter 7 proceedings are the specific subjects of chapters 8, 8, 11, and 19 through 23 of this text.

Liquidation: the sale of an estate's assets to repay creditors

---

7. 11 U.S.C. §§326, 327, 330, 331. See chapter 7 infra.
8. 11 U.S.C. §§362, 365. See chapters 11 and 15 infra.
9. 11 U.S.C. §§501-510, 522, 523-524, 541-559. See chapters 10, 15-18, and 22-23 infra.
10. 11 U.S.C. §103.
11. Chapter 7 cases comprised approximately 61.9% of the filings for the fiscal year ending September 30, 2016.

Chapter 13 is the second most common proceeding filed under the code. Chapter 13 is a reorganization proceeding for individuals with regular income where a qualified individual seeks expedited and summary approval of a repayment plan for a small consumer estate. Approximately 37 percent of all cases filed are Chapter 13 proceedings.[12] Chapter 13 is the subject of chapter 24 of this text.

A third type of proceeding is Chapter 11, which is commonly known as the "Reorganization" Chapter. Approximately 0.9 percent of all proceedings filed are filed under Chapter 11.[13] Chapter 11 is the most complex, time-consuming, and expensive type of bankruptcy proceeding. In a **reorganization** proceeding, a debtor seeks to avoid liquidation by proposing a viable plan of reorganization to the creditors that can be successfully confirmed and performed. Chapter 11 is described later in this text in chapters 25-27.

Reorganization: a bankruptcy proceeding where a debtor seeks confirmation of a plan that will repay creditors while permitting the debtor to retain assets or continue in business.

Both Chapter 11 and Chapter 13 are reorganization proceedings and, as a result, have many similarities. In a Chapter 11 case, a business or individual debtor proposes a plan to reorganize its business and avoid liquidation. The business may be Joe's Donut Shop down at the corner or it may be a large public company like American Airlines, which reorganized in 2014. Similarly, in a Chapter 13 case, an individual debtor proposes a plan to repay debt over a period of time, thus reorganizing the individual's affairs. To this extent, the goals of a Chapter 11 and a Chapter 13 are identical.

Chapter 9, Chapter 12, and Chapter 15 comprise the three remaining available bankruptcy proceedings. Chapter 9 is a reorganization proceeding limited to municipal corporations — such as a city. Municipal corporations seeking reorganization have been provided with a special reorganization proceeding because in addition to being business entities, a Chapter 9 debtor is typically a political entity. The provisions of Chapter 9 attempt to account for the special considerations that can arise when a political entity is also a debtor. Chapter 9 filings are rare. For example, in 2013, Detroit, Michigan, filed a widely publicized Chapter 9 to restructure its pension obligations. In the 12 months ending on September 30, 2016, there were only five Chapter 9 cases filed.

Chapter 12 was added to the Code in November 1986.[14] Chapter 12 is entitled the "Adjustment of Debts of a Family Farmer or Fisherman with

---

12. Chapter 13 cases comprised approximately 37.1% of the filings for the fiscal year ending September 30, 2016.
13. Chapter 11 cases comprised approximately 0.9% of the filings for the fiscal year ending September 30, 2016. The vast majority of large Chapter 11 cases are filed in the Southern District of New York, the Central District of California or the District of Delaware.
14. Pub. L. 99-554. Section 1001 of BAPCPA made Chapter 12 a permanent addition to the Bankruptcy Code.

Regular Annual Income." A hybrid of Chapters 11 and 13, Chapter 12 was enacted as an experiment to assist financially distressed family farmers and fishermen who desire to reorganize their affairs. Chapter 12 provides these specialized debtors the essential benefits and cost savings of a Chapter 13 case in what would otherwise have to be a Chapter 11 proceeding. Code Chapter 12 is described in chapter 28 of this text.

Chapter 15 was added to the Code in 2005. Entitled "Ancillary and Other Cross-Border Cases," it was intended "to incorporate the Model Law on Cross-Border Insolvency."[15] Chapter 15 exists to help resolve insolvency issues arising from globalization.

C.   THE BANKRUPTCY SYSTEM

The Bankruptcy Code is designed to function as a system. This point cannot be overemphasized. It is the key to understanding how the Bankruptcy Code works to resolve the financial affairs of a debtor. This understanding will aid the paralegal in providing realistic and practical results for either debtor or creditor clients. For unlike many other areas of the law, a specific provision of the Bankruptcy Code is often best understood in the context of its role within the entire system and not as an isolated statute. When approached in this manner, many aspects of the Code that may at first appear illogical will become logical, rational, and understandable.

Bankruptcy Code: the name of the bankruptcy laws in effect in the United States since October 1, 1979

The systems approach also helps in understanding the practical nature of the Code. In this context, the **Bankruptcy Code** is a largely self-contained legal, economic, and accounting system designed to reconcile all financial affairs of a debtor as they exist at the time of filing. All assets and liabilities are disclosed. Assets that are not exempt are available for liquidation and distribution to creditors according to a list of priorities designated by the Code. Most debts will be subject to the debtor's discharge. This is the most basic description of a bankruptcy proceeding. The specific details of this basic process, the documents involved and how to prepare them, are the subject matter of chapters 8, 30, and 31 of the text.

Bankruptcy proceedings appear and feel different than traditional litigation. For example, a Chapter filing of any type is best referred to as a proceeding. This distinguishes the bankruptcy proceeding itself from the

---

15. 11 U.S.C. §1501(a). In the 12 months ending on September 30, 2016, 150 Chapter 15 cases had been filed.

various types of litigation or motions that may take place within the proceeding. For instance, a Chapter 7 proceeding may have activity occurring within it that constitutes independent litigation or other activity that will occur only by way of a motion. This semantic distinction will also help the reader to understand bankruptcy jurisdiction in simple terms.[16] The text will describe some suggested methods for presenting issues to the Bankruptcy Court either by way of motion or through litigation.

There are normally no plaintiffs or defendants in a bankruptcy proceeding. There is a debtor, a trustee, and creditors. Sometimes a debtor may have only one or two creditors, and sometimes a debtor may have several hundred or thousands of creditors. But the major players will always be the debtor, a trustee, and the creditors. The **debtor** is the entity that is bankrupt and owes the debts. The **creditors** are the entities to whom the debts are owed. The **trustee** is an independent third party who liquidates the estate's assets and distributes the dividends to the creditors. Trustees are described in chapter 10 of this text.

The traditional adversarial approach is often not the most practical way to approach a bankruptcy problem. The bankruptcy system generally functions most efficiently when the debtor, creditors, and trustee cooperate. All of the major players, particularly in a reorganization proceeding, share a similar goal: satisfaction of debts while preserving the business. Litigation will not necessarily resolve a debtor's problems or even define their solutions. In bankruptcy practice, one must always be aware of the likely ultimate result and act on the basis of prudent economics. This philosophy will always aid in giving a reorganization proceeding the greatest chance for success. This philosophy also assists in the Chapter 7 effort to maximize returns to unsecured creditors. From the creditor perspective this is the practical goal of Chapter 7, to "squeeze blood out of a turnip."

If there is any other area of law that is comparable to the bankruptcy system, it is the probate system.[17] In probate, an estate is liquidated and the proceeds distributed first to creditors and then to the beneficiaries of the estate according to distributive priorities set by state law. Similarly, in bankruptcy an estate is liquidated, the proceeds are distributed to creditors by federal statutory priorities, and then any remaining proceeds are returned to the debtor's shareholders or to the debtor.

Debtor: an entity that owes a debt

Creditor: an entity with a claim arising before the filing of a bankruptcy petition

Trustee: a fiduciary appointed by the United States Trustee to administer a bankruptcy estate

---

16. See chapter 29 infra.
17. In In re Pacific Forest Industries, Inc., 95 B.R. 740, 744 (Bankr. C.D. Cal. 1989), the court said: "There is no other practice of law which is identical in nature to bankruptcy practice, but the Court believes that probate practice has some of the same elements. The attorney is dealing with a fiduciary, who he must advise. The decisions made by the Court may affect creditors who are not even yet known. There is a limited 'res' that will be dealt with and distributed."

D. COMPOSITION AGREEMENTS —
A BANKRUPTCY ALTERNATIVE

A possible alternative to a bankruptcy proceeding in consumer bankruptcy cases is the common law vehicle of the composition agreement. Any transaction in which an individual and a creditor agree to a revision of their legal obligations to one another is a form of composition. Picking up the telephone and getting an extra month to pay a bill is a form of composition. Debt consolidations are a form of composition. A formal **composition agreement** comes into being when an individual and multiple creditors agree to a revision of existing obligations.

Composition agreement: an agreement between a debtor and multiple creditors for the repayment of debt

When an individual has a number of unpaid creditors, there is no prohibition against the person entering into a joint repayment plan simultaneously with multiple creditors. A composition agreement is therefore an agreement between a person and two or more creditors to extend repayment terms or to accept less than full payment in discharge of debts. An accepted composition agreement is a new contract between the person and the consenting creditors. A written document, defining all of the terms of repayment and signed by all the involved parties, is sufficient to be a valid composition agreement.

BAPCPA added two provisions to the Bankruptcy Code that encourage the use of composition agreements in consumer bankruptcy cases. First, a debtor can object to a creditor's claim and reduce it by 20 percent if a debtor can show by clear and convincing evidence that the debtor made, at least 60 days prior to the bankruptcy filing, an offer to repay at least 60 percent of a debt over a period "not to exceed the repayment period of the loan, or a reasonable extension thereof" and the debt is otherwise dischargeable.[18] Second, any creditor receiving payments pursuant to such a payment plan, so long as the plan is created by an approved credit counseling agency, will not be subject to having to return the payment to a bankruptcy trustee as a preference.[19] These provisions are intended to encourage composition agreements in consumer cases. In the first instance, debtors are given an incentive to propose out of court 60 percent repayment plans, and creditors are subject to penalties in Bankruptcy Court for unreasonably refusing acceptance. The clear import of the provision is to encourage debtors to propose 60 percent or more composition agreements and for creditors to accept them. In the second

---

18. 11 U.S.C. §502(k). See chapter 22 infra.
19. 11 U.S.C. §547(h). See chapter 17 infra.

instance, insulating approved composition agreement payments received by creditors from the trustee's preference powers acts as a further incentive for creditors to accept consumer composition proposals.

Summary

The United States Bankruptcy Code is primarily a self-contained system designed to resolve the financial affairs of a debtor. The Bankruptcy Code is organized into Chapters. There are currently nine such Chapters. Three Chapters (1, 3, and 5) contain rules that apply in all of the various Chapter proceedings. The provisions in these three Chapters include the basic features of debtor relief, discharge, exemptions, and the automatic stay, as well as the basic features of debt collection, claims, and their priority of distribution.

The remaining six Chapters of the Bankruptcy Code (7, 9, 11, 12, 13, and 15) comprise the various types of bankruptcy proceedings available to debtors. The different proceedings may be categorized as either "liquidation" or "reorganization" proceedings.

In a liquidation, a debtor's nonexempt assets are sold by a trustee and the proceeds are distributed to the creditors. In a reorganization, the debtor will seek approval of a repayment plan that will avoid liquidation.

Chapter 7 is a liquidation proceeding. Chapters 9, 11, 12, and 13 are reorganization proceedings that apply to specific types of debtors. Chapters 11 and 13 are the most common reorganization proceedings. A Chapter 11 is primarily a business reorganization. A Chapter 13 is a consumer reorganization. Chapter 9 applies only to Municipal Corporations. Chapter 12 is a reorganization proceeding for family farmers and fishermen.

Chapter 15 applies only to cross-border bankruptcies and may be either liquidations or reorganizations.

A composition agreement is an agreement between a person and one or more creditors for the repayment of existing debt. Two provisions of BAPCPA are intended to encourage individual consumers in proposing debt repayment plans.

KEY TERMS

Bankruptcy Code	**liquidation**
composition agreement	**reorganization**
creditor	**trustee**
debtor	

DISCUSSION QUESTIONS

1.   What is a liquidation proceeding?

2.   What is a reorganization proceeding?

3.   Identify:

    (a)   Those Chapters of the Bankruptcy Code applicable to all bankruptcy proceedings;

    (b)   Those Chapters of the Bankruptcy Code applicable to liquidation proceedings;

    (c)   Those Chapters of the Bankruptcy Code applicable to reorganization proceedings.

4.   Identify the major parties in a bankruptcy proceeding.

5.   How can a consumer debtor negotiate a composition agreement with creditors? What are the advantages of doing this? Should counsel for a consumer debtor attempt to negotiate the composition agreement?

3

Understanding the Client

Learning Objectives

- Recognize the interpersonal skills needed to conduct a client interview
- Review the objectives for an initial client interview
- Begin to categorize the responses given in a client interview

While many authors and/or text books may ignore or gloss over client interaction, in the end, it is the most important component of the bankruptcy process. Understanding the Bankruptcy Code and the various federal and local rules of bankruptcy practice enables an attorney to provide the best possible legal advice to help a client. However, as important as the statutes and rules are, they have no application without a case to analyze to better grasp a basic understanding of the bankruptcy process. Each client must be approached uniquely. While the statute may be the same, the application of the law to the particular circumstances of each case may dictate a different result. In order to understand how to help a prospective client, you must understand not only the law, but also your client. The only way to do that is to interact with the client.

A.   THE CLIENT INTERVIEW

In order to file a bankruptcy petition for an individual, someone must first meet with a prospective client and gather the necessary information: the facts. Whether your firm is a small bankruptcy boutique or a larger law firm, filing bankruptcy for every client that walks through the door is not always the correct answer. Bankruptcy filings do not occur in a vacuum. Instead, prospective clients come to your office with many issues, sometimes in the form of bills and collection letters, often accompanied with emotional stress and trauma. Sometimes it is one unanticipated crisis that forces an individual to consider filing bankruptcy, but in many cases there is a long history or buildup until an event takes place precipitating the need to consider bankruptcy. More often than not, you will not always learn the full or complete story as to what brought your client to this point in his or her life. The contributing history often gets lost in the process, particularly where the focus is on the next steps to take, and not reliving the steps that led the client to your door.

There are several different ways the interview process may be initiated. Every firm has its own approach to initiating a relationship with prospective bankruptcy clients. For some, the initial contact may be by telephone, Internet, or through an "intake" interview that may or may not be conducted by a paralegal. Some basic document production and gathering of information can be accomplished at this stage. Before an actual attorney client relationship can be created, the attorney will need to meet with the prospective client in person. While the client may or may not have some general understanding of the bankruptcy process, it is at this meeting that the attorney will explain the different options available and provide a general understanding of how the bankruptcy laws work.

1. Intake

Intake may be handled differently depending on firm practice. In some cases, paralegals may be required to gather basic contact information: name, address, telephone number, list of major creditors, etc. In other situations, paralegals may work from a list of questions to help gather the necessary documentation and information regarding the prospective client's assets and liabilities. Many firms provide the client with a list of items for the client to bring to an initial interview. The client may not always think to bring financial documentation with them or be aware of what paperwork will be necessary. A paralegal plays a critical role in the process by aiding in collecting the facts. This process can take place over the telephone or through computer resources. Occasionally the gathering of information takes place in the office.

2. The Interview

The initial client interview usually takes place at your work or firm location and serves as a way to develop an initial rapport with the client. It creates an opportunity to gather information about the client's financial situation, and provides the attorney with a time and place to listen, advise, and counsel the client. The initial meeting is an important opportunity to allow you to understand the circumstances that led the client to seek bankruptcy assistance. At this stage of the process, counseling requires empathetic communication, characterized by concern, helpfulness, a desire for understanding and agreement, and a dispassionate overview. This meeting is not scheduled solely so that the information necessary to complete a bankruptcy petition can be gathered. It is to gain an understanding of the client's situation so that the available courses of action can be recommended to the client, whether a bankruptcy is necessary or if it can be avoided. If bankruptcy is the recommendation, the question then becomes whether to file a Chapter 7 liquidation or an appropriate reorganization proceeding, typically Chapter 13 for individual debtors.

It is important to set the client at ease. You should remember that for most clients this is a very traumatic experience. This may be the first time that this client has approached an attorney for help. At the beginning of the initial interview, the client should be met with courtesy, consideration, and warmth. If there is some delay in beginning the interview, you should consider introducing yourself, assuming it does not violate your firm's policies, and do your best to reduce the client's general anxiety. Remember to always address the client by their surname unless they encourage you to do otherwise. There will generally be rooms set aside for the interview process which may or may not be large. It may only be the client, the attorney and yourself in the initial client meeting. It is important to make sure to minimize an otherwise potentially intimidating situation, by not over-whelming the client. Make the client comfortable.

The attorney will explain to the client who you are, who anyone else in the room is, the purpose of the initial meeting, and how it is intended to apply to the client's situation. The attorney will conduct the interview, but you should be familiar with the process in order to keep track of what was disclosed and what will be needed later.

Note taking and writing in general may tend to be both intimidating and distracting. Determine beforehand how information will be gath-ered and notes taken. If the interviewing attorney is not taking notes, it may help to more clearly hear the client's concerns and adjust the interview process in response to the client's answers. Otherwise, some questions may be missed or the client may forget some details during the interview as both the questioning and conversation slow down to accommodate the note taking. It is appropriate for the attorney or the paralegal, depending on firm practice, to bring up points that may have been missed or not clear from the initial questions as the

initial interview nears its end. Remember also that there is no requirement that all of the questions be asked within that first interview. It is
common practice to allow for follow up meetings that can be scheduled
at a later date with appropriate notice.

During the interview you should try to maintain a professional
demeanor by being cordial and respectful. But you should also always
try to just be yourself. Do not try to "act" like an attorney. Clients are
often uncomfortable and defensive in these types of situations. You
should try to convey an attitude of both patience and understanding.
Remember, the clients are often scared and worried about both their
creditors and the system in general. Try not to be judgmental, disapprov-
ing, or condescending in listening to or discussing the client's actions. The
clients can often read your sincerity from both your verbal and nonverbal
body language. The potential client will never become an actual client
unless their trust and confidence is gained at the initial interview. It is not
your task to judge the causes that led the client to your firm. It is your
firm's task to help the client out of the circumstances that brought them to
you. It is often said in personal injury practice that "you take your plaintiffs
as you find them." Likewise, in bankruptcy practice, you take your debtor
clients as you find them.

When the interview begins, most attorneys will not start by asking the
client a list of prepared questions. Instead, they allow the client the opportunity to briefly explain their situation. They may ask: "How may we help
you today?" "What seems to be the problem that has brought you here?"
"Please tell me about your problem and we can then discuss how we may
be able to help." The discussion should generally begin with the areas
chosen by the client. Letting the client talk first to tell you what brought
them to you will help set the client at ease by letting him or her tell you
their story in their own words first.

Most firms have a filing checklist and a list of standard questions. It
will be necessary to complete all of the items on the checklist, and to
ask all relevant questions on the list. However, there is no one right way
to approach the questions that must be asked. The course of the
interview will often be dictated by the rapport established with the
client from the initial introduction. The client's responses will often
lead to the next question. Although you should avoid getting into a
mechanical reading of one question after another, to a certain degree,
this is often unavoidable. Remember, the client's direct answers may
also imply other indirect information. Repeating a question another way
later in the interview process may help to clarify an earlier answer or to
identify any gaps or inconsistencies. It is important that you do not
make any assumptions as to the client's answers. For example, do
not assume that just because the client is living at or near the poverty
level that he/she has no possessions, no entitlement to a trust, or is not

the potential beneficiary to a life insurance policy or other inheritance. You will not know unless you ask.

Once the attorney understands the basic facts of the client's position, then it becomes possible to evaluate the alternatives available to help this particular client. The answer is not always: "we can file a Chapter 7 petition for you." There may be other nonbankruptcy remedies that are more appropriate. The attorney will take the lead in this area of the interview. By discussing the client's alternatives, a required part of the bankruptcy process, the client will be more focused upon their situation and may be able to offer additional information. This process will also allow the client to feel that they are part of a team, and that the firm is there to help them. It is not your job, however, to make their decisions for them. You should also be careful to respect and understand the attorney-client privilege and the nature of the business relationship with the client. The important thing to remember is that it is ultimately the client's case.

B.   THE FACT PATTERN

Bankruptcy does not suddenly spring itself upon you without any warning or notice. Although there may be a triggering event, there is usually a long history of actions or inactions, sometimes tragic, leading up to the need to file for bankruptcy protection. The full story or picture is often obfuscated by your client's poor recollection, a sketchy paper trail, the time between events, and/or simple miscommunication. To assist you in understanding how the facts of a particular client's case can influence the application of the various bankruptcy statutes and rules, all of the examples in this textbook will be driven by one underlying hypothetical fact pattern: "Cash on the Rocks." Rather than listing all of the facts in order at one time, which is unrealistic, we will instead paint for you some of the backstory of your prospective clients so that you can develop a feel for how they ended up in your office.

The goal here is to show you what you might not have known otherwise and to hopefully get you thinking about questions that could be asked during the interview process and different ways that you will need to "connect the dots" to understand how your clients got where they are and how you can best help them to move forward. It will also serve to illustrate the various facts that may be shared that may have nothing to do with a bankruptcy filing. Sifting through all of the information provided and shared by the client can also be a challenging part of the process. We will begin with the "story" and then transition to the interview.

C.   "CASH ON THE ROCKS"

Owen Cash was an entrepreneur from birth who saw promising ideas to make money anywhere and everywhere. As the only child of a traveling salesman, he was always industrious, selling lemonade, delivering newspapers, babysitting, dog walking, cutting grass and shoveling snow. He picked up cans and bottles and collected scrap metal and carried everything to the nearest scrap recycling center for money. He was always looking for a way to make a buck. Unfortunately, as quickly as money found its way into his pocket, it soon found its way back out.

Owen's father, Lester Cash, known as Les by his friends, was a salesman by trade and a hoarder by choice. He loved to be on the road and he loved to collect things. You name it and he collected it. He was captivated by the thrill of the hunt. He loved to go to flea markets, auctions, and yard and estate sales. He often took on extra jobs to clean out homes, offices, and buildings, keeping the contents as part of his payment. Les loved to collect, but rarely sold what he collected. To Les, each item had a story and a history that he cherished. He would often regale Owen with tales of how he found particular items and why they were so valuable to him. He was particularly proud of a confederate officer's sword that he had obtained twenty years ago while in Virginia from a collector for $500, but that he considered to be priceless. The provenance was questionable, but Les was good at spinning the ever-changing story of how a confederate colonel had stormed a Union defensive position to rescue his soldiers. Les gave the sword to Owen for his 18th birthday. Les also had a Springfield Model 1861 rifle in very good condition. He often talked about firing it, but somehow never got around to it. He gifted the rifle to Owen on Owen's 21st birthday. Over time, Lester's collection gradually took over the family home, expanding from the basement to the den, and from there overflowing into every room in the house including the garage. After the garage was full, Les filled several trailers that he kept in the backyard.

When Les was not on sales trips, he often took Owen with him on shopping trips and it wasn't long before Owen also caught the collecting bug. In the beginning, it started simply as a bonding time for Owen and his often absent father. At first, Owen was focused mainly on items with a deposit value, such as bottles and cans, or items that had scrap value based on their weight and that he could get money for right away. He met other pickers during his excursions with his father and he was always anxious to hear their stories of their big finds or their search for the holy grail of garage or barn sales. Gradually, Owen began to learn the difference between scrap value and collectability, although he rarely kept an item that he found or bought, preferring instead for the quick conversion to cash. Still, he began his own stockpile of items that spilled over from his bedroom to various nooks and crannies around the family home that Les had not already filled.

When his father left home on sales trips, Owen often went picking alone and he had soon scoured the nearby neighborhoods of everything remotely of any value left out for trash or alongside the road. Frustrated one night after an unprofitable spin around the area, Owen discovered online sales and auctions. Surfing the net at all hours, Owen gave himself a crash course in advertising and sales. He began offering some small, relatively inexpensive items online and was surprised at how much some people would pay for items that he thought were worthless. While most of his sales were legitimately earned, he quickly realized that he could make real money describing his wares as "antiques" and selling them to unsuspecting customers. He made $1,000 in his first week and was immediately hooked.

Before starting his online sales, Owen had always drifted from part-time job to part-time job, although he had always had an affinity for lawn care. Among other things, working in people's yards gave him a chance to look for and take their discarded junk to add to his collection. His outgoing personality made it easy for him to talk with customers and he started to create a customer base. With the seed money from his online sales, Owen purchased a riding mower for $2,000 and entered into a seven year purchase plan with A to Z Motors for a 2013 Ford F150 pickup truck with an attached plow at $500 a month. His fledgling lawn care business was a go.

Shortly after graduating high school, Owen had started dating Helen Wlells and the couple soon had a baby girl Charlotte, Lottie or Lotta for short. The couple's relationship was rocky at best, with money usually being the source of discord, and soon the couple split up. Owen agreed to a court order to provide child support of $125 a week for Charlotte, although he rarely saw his daughter. However, payments were sporadic and he often had to make lump sum payments to stay reasonably current. Owen still lived at home, and he had big plans to buy the family home. Refocused on his fledgling businesses, Owen never noticed the decline in his father.

Lester had scaled back his traveling as he approached retirement. Collecting took over more and more of his time. When his wife unexpectedly passed away, Lester's life went into a tailspin. He stopped working altogether and his health began to decline. His bills began to pile up, and he failed for the first time ever to file his state and federal tax returns. Lester had always taken care of the family's finances and he had naturally started filing Owen's returns for him as well. Owen simply signed his name and forgot about it each year, at least until his tax refund came in. With his mind firmly entrenched in the future, filing tax returns never crossed Owen's mind. Unbeknownst to Owen, his dad also failed to file Owen's tax returns.

Around this time, two major things happened in Owen's life. He jumped "all in" to get his lawn care business up and running, and he met and married Robin Banks. Using a form he had discovered online, Owen set up a sole proprietorship that he called "The Lawn Cuttery" and jazzed up his letterhead with a fancy new logo. He opened a bank account in the business name and printed flyers and had a magnetic sign designed for his truck. With his naturally gregarious personality and go-getter attitude, Owen's business quickly grew beyond what he could easily service on his own. Finding high school or college-age employees was easy, but with the additional work and employees came a need for bookkeeping, additional trucks and more equipment. Turning again to the internet for answers, Owen came across a model financial statement that he began to modify for his new business. Lacking traditional inventory or collateral, sitting at the dining room table one night amidst all of the piles of "collectibles," Owen mentally began converting the mounds into fictitious equipment and supplies to provide the basis for his company, at least on paper. He planned to use this imagined inventory as collateral for a bank loan, thinking to himself that at worst he could always sell the junk when necessary to cover his debt.

Working backwards from an estimate of the cost for the vehicles and equipment he needed to purchase for his growing company, Owen made up a financial statement and created a paper trail suggesting a viable entity. Searching online, he quickly located First American Trust & Loan Co. and using his fictitious financial statement, successfully obtained a personal business loan for $50,000. With the money safely in the bank and his new letterhead and logo in hand, Owen returned to A to Z Motors and purchased three used pickup trucks for his business, entering into 72 month payment plans for each. Stopping next at Pathway Equipment Co., he entered into lease agreements for several riding motors, aerators, and spray equipment. After posting a couple of flyers, he hired half a dozen employees, agreeing to pay them under the table for both his and their benefit. Owen's expanding business was off and running.

Robin Banks was a junior at the local college, Breckinridge School of Nursing. Buried in student loans and credit card debt, Robin was hoping to make it to graduation before her bill collectors caught up with her. Robin lived in a condominium struggling to keep up with her condo association fees. She and her brother had inherited the condo when her mother passed away. They agreed that she would move in and stay there while in school. She used to have roommates, but they had graduated before her, leaving her name alone on the agreement. She relied on cash advances and small purchases on her credit cards to live day to day, and on student loans to pay for her schooling. At nearly $10,000 a semester, the school was expensive, but it had a good graduation and job placement rate. The loans were provided through a program at the school and offered reasonable interest rates and repayment plans. Robin also wait-ressed part-time to help make ends meet, but sometimes work and school clashed. Like many other students, Robin received credit card applications in the mail and online through email regularly. Applying for one card soon led to two and finally twelve different cards. Robin became a pro at jug-gling the minimum payments to keep the credit card companies happy, but the interest was piling up. Because she had to tap the cards occasion-ally for rent, she was quickly sliding into more debt than she could handle and slowly but surely she was approaching the credit limit on some of the cards. Sometimes she wrote checks she knew could not be cashed. She always made sure to put a future date on the checks to protect herself. By the time she met Owen, Robin estimated that she owed almost $45,000 on her various credit cards, $50,000 on her student loans, and at least $2,000 to the condo association.

Robin met Owen one day at the restaurant where she worked and they quickly hit it off. She was impressed by his drive and business acumen and he was amazed by her intelligence and work ethic. A whirlwind courtship led to a courthouse wedding. Owen found a wedding band in his collec-tion and gave it to Robin as a gift, promising to one day get her the engagement ring that she deserved. Due to the demands of Owen's new business and Robin's upcoming exams, their honeymoon was over a weekend at a local hotel. Robin quit her job and moved into Owen's parents' home, which Lester promised to gift to them. Unfortunately, Robin could not sell her condominium and she was no longer able to make the continuing monthly rental payments of $650 since she had quit working. So she simply stopped making any payments at all. After a year of wedded bliss with the newlyweds learning to get along, juggling new and old bills, navigating the hoard in the house, and dealing with Lester's growing depression, the quicksand of their new life became the perfect storm.

Owen's business was seasonal, the lawn care portion running from March 1st to December 1st. He would lay off his employees in December until the following March. Occasionally he would bring some of them back to help with street plowing and snow blowing during particularly bad winters. After an abnormally dry summer, Owen's business was running in the red. He became three payments behind on each of his trucks and he had not made a lease payment on his equipment in six months. Although he was usually able to talk his way through problems, Owen's creditors were losing their patience. With the building stress at home, Robin Cash went to visit her mother for a few days. Meanwhile Les Cash continued his downward spiral, now often exhibiting signs of dementia. After a bad fall in their home, Les broke his hip and leg and was not found until several hours later, confused and in pain. Physical therapy took its toll on him and Owen was forced to make the difficult decision to move him into an assisted living facility. Owen came back to a home empty of people but filled to the brim with "stuff." A week later, Les took a turn for the worse and Owen was informed that his father might only have a couple of months or perhaps weeks to live.

Following a particularly bad day at work, when five customers refused to pay him for rendering, in their opinion, unnecessary services, Owen lost his patience on his last stop of the day when he pulled up to the property of a regular customer, Frank Stein, only to find another lawn care company on site. In this case, Mr. Stein had agreed to retain Owen's company for the year, but had never actually signed a contract or made a payment. Relying only on his customer's promises to sign and pay, Owen had continued to provide his services, expecting to get paid at some point. Finding another lawn care business at the customer's home, Owen exchanged words and threatened lawsuits, and finally peeled out of his now ex-customer's driveway. Stopping at his favorite bar on the way home, Owen poured out his life story to the bartender, who poured drink after drink for his new friend.

After three hours of heavy drinking, Owen was still furious about not getting paid and getting dumped by his customer. Dropping money on the bar, he stormed out of the building and jumped into his truck. Driving back to his now ex-customer's property, Owen lowered the plow on the front of his truck and proceeded to scrape the top four inches of grass and topsoil off of his ex-customer's front lawn, depositing it in the pool in his former customer's backyard. When the lights came on in the house, Owen sped away, taking out a chain link fence in the backyard as he fled.

Afraid to go home, Owen returned to the bar to lay low for a couple of hours. Either because of the alcohol or as time passed with no sound of sirens, Owen began to feel more comfortable. Staggering out of the place at nearly two o'clock in the morning, Owen headed home. After getting off the wrong exit of the highway because of unexpected road construction and being somewhat inebriated, Owen found himself in an unfamiliar residential area. Attempting to make a U-turn at the next intersection, Owen clipped a mail box and scraped along several parked cars, removing paint, side mirrors and anything in his way. Heading the wrong way down a one-way street, Owen briefly panicked when he saw several headlights headed his way. Swerving off of the road and through a line of hedges, Owen finally came to a stop on a stranger's front lawn. Dropping his head to the steering wheel, Owen passed out, stirring only once when the homeowner's sprinkler system turned on, spraying him and the inside of his truck through an open window. He awoke in the morning to the sound of a policeman tapping on his driver's side window.

Thankfully, Les Cash was well enough to post bail for his son and Owen returned home where he was all alone amidst the hoard of collectibles. Seeking solace, Owen made a few sales online and then his interest began to wander. He eventually found himself on a couple of online gambling sites. Initial "wins" of $50 and $100 had him hooked. Ten hours later, he owed over $10,000 to King's Online Casino before he was cut off by the site. The online casino refused to extend him additional credit until he could produce reasonable collateral. After wallowing in self-pity for a few minutes, Owen began searching through his father's papers.

Two hours later, Owen discovered his father's will, the deed to the house, and papers captioned at the top, "An Assignment of Interest," transferring the house to him. The papers were dated a year ago, but were unsigned. Owen considered using the information to unlock his online casino accounts, but by this time, the novelty and excitement had worn off.

Talking with his bartender friend the next day, Owen was told that the papers did not mean anything if they were never signed or filed. His new friend put him in touch with a court clerk, who informed Owen that there were no mortgages on the house and that if the assignment was filed, the property would transfer to him. Gazing around the house packed with "collectibles," Owen began to formulate a plan. In his mind, this transfer could be the answer to all of his problems.

The next morning, Owen drove to visit his father at the nursing facility under the pretense of getting him to pay some bills and with the intent of also getting Les to sign the assignment and a power of attorney. Stopping at the nursing station, Owen discovered that his father's medical bills were quickly piling up. Owen got his father to sign some checks to cover some outstanding bills at home and even managed to sneak the power of attorney through with the other papers. He felt too guilty however to get his father to sign the assignment. Owen tried instead to convince his father to part with his growing hoard at home. When this failed, Owen tried a new tack instead. He offered to buy the house from his dad to help pay his medical bills. Les reluctantly agreed with the understanding that he could continue to live there. Using an online property appraisal website, Owen estimated the home to be worth $140,000. Two hours later, Owen was able to obtain a loan for $100,000 to purchase Les' house by granting a mortgage on the home to Second American Trust & Loan Co. Using the power of attorney and the internet once again, Owen gave himself a $40,000 loan from his father to cover the remaining cost of the house, using the house as collateral. Owen planned to record the loan from his father in a few days, but first he also applied for and obtained a line of credit for $25,000 from Third American Trust & Loan Co. By that evening, Owen was back online gambling, having provided proof of his new line of credit. Before long, Owen owed another $15,000 to King's Online Casino.

Flush with the knowledge of the cash in his line of credit, the next day Owen decided to go on a short spending spree. In no time at all, Owen was the proud owner of a $5,000 72-inch television and surround sound system, a desktop computer, laptop, tablet, and new cellphone, totaling $4,000, and an online time share condominium in Ocean City, Maryland, for $10,000. Thinking of his strained marriage, he booked a three-week stay in Cancun for two months from now to make up for their missed honeymoon at a cost of $5,000, and he purchased a $5,000 custom-made engagement ring for Robin, paying $1,000 down with the remainder to be paid over two years.

Returning to the bar after an early lunch, Owen was feeling pretty good about himself. That did not last. While there, Owen was served with a complaint for the property damage to his ex-customer. This was followed by three more complaints alleging fraudulent Internet sales. Before he could fully process what was happening, Owen was also served with divorce papers. A week later, notice of an IRS audit was received. Owen tried to keep his head above water, but he seemed to run into problems every other day. His missed payments on his equipment resulted in three lawn mowers and an aerator being repossessed. While he was on the phone with Pathway Equipment, two of his work trucks were also repossessed. Eating dinner later that evening, his electricity was turned off because he had failed to pay his electric bill for the last six months. His life was going from bad to worse.

Crying his financial woes at the bar, Owen's bartender friend referred him to Jimmy Bold, of Bold Messenger Service. The bartender heard that Jimmy helped people file for bankruptcy. Owen later met with Jimmy who helped him to fill out a bankruptcy petition, but who did not want his name or information included in the petition. Bold recommended that Owen file a Chapter 13 to save his house and agreed to be paid on the side for his assistance. He explained that Owen would get more sympathy from the court if he filed *pro se* without an attorney and if he also filed a joint petition with his wife. Although most of the documents were missing or incomplete, Jimmy explained that Owen did not need to worry about it until the court told him to fix it. Jimmy also stated that there was no fee to file for bankruptcy if you filed *pro se*.

After speaking with Jimmy, Owen saw the writing on the wall. Knowing that his work season was scheduled to end soon, Owen decided that he was going to have to file for bankruptcy. Before the bubble burst though, Owen decided to squirrel away as much money as he could. In a final attempt to reconcile, Owen met with Robin and explained his bankruptcy plan to her, telling her she could get out from under her student loans and condo expenses, and hiding most everything else from her. Feeling better about their finances, the two decided to take the Cancun trip together, but Owen kept the existence of the new engagement ring a secret from Robin. Robin happily signed the bank-ruptcy petition that Owen promised to complete later.

Owen then stopped at several ATM machines, carefully withdrawing only $800 from each of his five credit cards, to avoid the fraud limit that he remembered Jimmy telling him about. To complete his prebankruptcy plan, Owen closed his checking account, withdrawing the remaining $10,000 and placing it in his father's old safety deposit box. Going through a checklist in his head, Owen realized that he was now six months behind in his child support obligations, and although he was in the habit of making lump sum payments to his ex-girlfriend to cover missed payments, he remembered Jimmy telling him he could discharge this debt since he had never married Lotta's mother, Helen.

Completing the petition to the best of his ability, Owen signed it and placed it in the mail. As he was leaving for Cancun, he decided to leave his dad a quick note stating that he was returning the confederate officer's sword and the Civil War era rifle to him for safekeeping. Stopping in a local convenience store on the way to the airport, Owen purchased multistate jackpot lottery tickets for the next three months of drawings. Feeling much better about his situation, he picked up his wife and they left for their trip. That very day, Robin Cash received in the mail notice of a complaint for passing bad checks and also a judgment for possession of her condominium. The day after they left, the Cash bankruptcy petition was received by the court. Because it was incomplete, it was listed for dismissal. When Owen and Robin failed to respond or appear before the court, their petition was subsequently dismissed before they returned home. On their answering machine were several messages from the nursing home telling them that Les' health was rapidly deteriorating.

After returning home with new tans and a fresh outlook on life, Owen and Robin discovered overflowing voicemail, a mail box full of collection letters, and the utilities turned off at their home. Unable to reach his bartender friend or to get Jimmy Bond to return his calls, Owen stopped in an Internet café to search online for help. It was here that he discovered your bankruptcy firm.

Noting that your firm specializes in business reorganizations as well as individual filings, Owen for the first time begins to consider filing bank-ruptcy for his company, The Lawn Cuttery. Taking the first step, he quickly locates model articles of incorporation online and navigates to his state's government website. Less than two hours and $100 later, his company is incorporated and registered with his state and the IRS. He named Lester and Robin as officers but retained all of the shares in his name only. He quickly transferred all of the equipment and business inventory to the "new" business in his computer records.

D.   INITIAL INTERVIEW

Owen scheduled an initial interview with your firm and he was set up with the intake department who compiled some initial information. Next, sitting down with an attorney, Owen and Robin were encouraged to summarize the main reasons for their visit. The following are a few selected snippets from this conversation:

"Why are we here? Great question! Owen, I thought you took care of this before we left!" began Robin.

"I did, it was. For some reason we got a notice in the mail saying our case was dismissed. I tried to reach the guy who helped me file the first time, but he doesn't answer," Owen replied. *"After looking on the Internet, I think maybe I made a mistake listening to Jimmy."*

"Well, we will need to talk about that first case, and I see that we have a copy of the documents that you filed here in our file, but first let's focus on the main reasons you believe that you should file for bankruptcy," explains the interviewing attorney.

"Where to start . . . ," began Owen. *"How about with what you told me?"* interjected Robin. *"I am swimming in credit card debt, student loans, and a condo that I can't afford. You said this would all go away by the time we got back from our trip."*

"I thought it would. I trusted Jimmy. I just need everyone to leave me alone so that I can focus. I need the power turned back on and I need to somehow save my dad's house. Well, my house now. Dad's in bad shape and he really can't handle hearing that we may lose the house. Plus, for some reason, I'm being audited by the IRS and like I told the intake person, I have several people suing me. I thought that bankruptcy stops everybody from harassing me and then I can make different payments or not pay them at all," Owen explained.

"Your house? You mean our house, right? What lawsuits? What are you talking about? Why am I just now hearing about all of this?" said Robin, her voice rising with each sentence.

. . .

"How about my condo? Can I just sign over my interest to my brother and be done with it?" asked Robin. *"Your interest? I thought you said it was still in your mom's name,"* stressed Owen.

. . .

"Everything is crazy right now and I really need to focus on my dad. They are saying he might have six months or it can be any day. I need to be with him," said Owen.

. . .

"Let me ask you something. Will it matter if we're divorced before we file for bankruptcy, or can we do it during, or do I have to wait until it's over?" Robin asked. *"What?!"* yelped Owen.

. . .

"So can I just sign this petition thing now and have you fill in all of the other information later? I understand you said once we filed that stay thing starts. I need that now because I really need to pick up some supplies for my lawn care business but the vendors won't talk to me until my credit card balances are back down to zero," said Owen.

Although it was a lengthy interview, it was clear by the end of the session that a follow-up meeting would need to be scheduled with the Cashes. While Robin went outside to get the truck, Owen stayed behind and asked some additional questions:

"As I mentioned, I have a lawn business. I just incorporated the company. If I understood you correctly, my business would not be protected if I just file an individual bankruptcy. Can you file a business bankruptcy for me?"

"I don't have a business credit card yet, but I am going to get one after I get home. I want to pick up some inventory before the new season starts. Can we work on the timing to file a bankruptcy for the business after I do that?"

. . .

"The big thing is I need to get my trucks and equipment back so that we can start work on time. I don't think I got the best financing deals and I'm wondering now if you can help me to change them."

. . .

"Robin is listed as an officer, but it is more like a silent officer thing. I needed to have three people on the form and she's not really involved with the business end of things," Owen explained.

DISCUSSION QUESTIONS

1. Which interviewing approach do you think would be most effective to set the Cashes at ease and maximize the amount of information they will provide?

2. There seems to be some information that the Cashes have not shared with one another. How would you best address those issues if the parties do not want each other to know certain facts?

3. If Robin elects to move forward with her divorce proceeding, how will the timing affect the bankruptcy case?

4. Assuming you only have a small understanding of how bankruptcy works, would you think that bankruptcy will help Robin? Will it help Owen?

5. How would you prioritize the relief sought by the Cashes?

6. What red flags or hot issues were identified during the interview conversation with the Cashes?

4

Filing a Petition

Learning Objectives

- Describe the "gatekeeper" provisions in individual bankruptcy cases

- Understand how a bankruptcy is initiated, by filing a voluntary or involuntary petition

- Define prepetition credit counseling

- Describe how a voluntary bankruptcy petition is filed by a debtor

- Describe how an involuntary petition is filed by creditors

- Define an "order of relief"

The first step in initiating any bankruptcy proceeding is to file a petition. If it is filed by the debtor, the petition is called a **voluntary petition**.[1] If the petition is filed by the debtor's creditors (to place the debtor into bankruptcy), it is referred to as an **involuntary petition**.[2] The debtor in an involuntary proceeding is known as an **alleged debtor** and is not generally considered to be bankrupt in a practical or legal sense until the court enters an order for relief.[3] Generally speaking, each person or entity in bankruptcy must file their own separate bankruptcy petition. A married couple, however, may be joint debtors in either a voluntary or an involuntary proceeding.[4] Other related debtors must have separate petitions filed by or against them, although the Federal Rules of Bankruptcy

Voluntary petition: a bankruptcy proceeding initiated by a debtor filing a petition for relief; most bankruptcy proceedings are voluntary

Involuntary petition: a bankruptcy proceeding initiated by one or more creditors (or general partners of a partnership) by filing a petition seeking the entry of an order for relief, a judgment that the debtor is bankrupt

---

1. 11 U.S.C. §301; Bankruptcy Rule 1002.
2. 11 U.S.C. §303.
3. 11 U.S.C. §303(f), (h).
4. 11 U.S.C. §302; 1 U.S.C. §7.

41

Alleged debtor:
the debtor in an
involuntary pro-
ceeding

Procedure do permit procedural or substantive consolidation of proceed-ings in appropriate circumstances.[5]

FACT PATTERN

Owen and Robin could file separate cases or one joint filing.

A. GATEKEEPER PROVISIONS IN INDIVIDUAL BANKRUPTCIES

1. Prepetition Credit Counseling

There are a number of provisions in the Bankruptcy Code that an individual debtor, or the debtor's legal representative, must actually com-ply with prior to filing a bankruptcy petition. These provisions may best be understood as gatekeeper provisions or prerequisites to an individual bankruptcy filing, because if they are not complied with, a filing may not take place, may be subject to dismissal, or the legal representative may be subject to sanctions or penalties.

Prepetition credit counseling: counseling that a debtor must receive from a credit counseling agency as a prerequisite to seeking individual bankruptcy relief

Section 109(h) of the Bankruptcy Code requires **prepetition credit counseling** as a prerequisite to an individual debtor seeking bankruptcy relief. Corporations and partnerships are not subject to this requirement. An individual seeking bankruptcy relief must participate in an individual or group credit counseling session provided by an approved credit counseling agency within the 180-day period ending on the date that the debtor files his or her petition.[6] The debtor must also provide proof of participation in the program by filing with the court, at the time the petition is filed, a certificate from the credit counseling agency that provided the services along with a copy of any debt repayment plan developed by the agency.[7] If the debtor fails to comply with these provi-sions, it may result in the dismissal of the case.[8] There are three exceptions to the prepetition credit counseling requirement. First, the Code provides that the United States Trustee may exempt a district from the requirement if the United States Trustee determines that approved credit counseling

---

5. Bankruptcy Rule 1015. See infra this chapter for a more detailed description.
6. 11 U.S.C. §109(h); 11 U.S.C. §111. The United States Trustee, a division of the Department of Justice, designates approved credit counseling agencies. The role and function of the United States Trustee is discussed at chapter 11 infra.
7. 11 U.S.C. §521(b).
8. 11 U.S.C. §109(h)(3)(B).

services in a district are not reasonably able to provide counseling services to individuals.[9] For example, the United States Trustee could determine that certain large rural districts are exempt from this requirement. However, with the availability of credit counseling services over the telephone and through the Internet, such exemptions are virtually nonexistent.

If the Cashes have not already completed credit counseling, they will need to do so in order to file another bankruptcy proceeding.

FACT PATTERN

Second, a debtor may file a certification with the court at the time of filing stating that "exigent circumstances" merit a waiver of the rule, provided that the debtor made a request for counseling services and could not obtain them within seven days of making a request from a counseling agency. A debtor seeking a waiver for exigent circumstances must still obtain the required credit counseling within 30 days from filing the petition, except that the court, for cause, may allow an additional 15 days.[10] Ultimately, failure of a debtor to comply with the requirement to obtain prepetition counseling and to file the certificate with the Bankruptcy Court will be sufficient grounds for dismissal of the case if the documents are not filed within the time periods provided for under the statute.

Practice Pointer

It is important to check the local rules for your jurisdiction. Some courts will dismiss the case automatically without a hearing if the certification seeking a waiver is not filed with the petition.

The third exception to the prepetition credit counseling requirement arises if, after notice and a hearing, the court finds that a debtor is not able to comply with the requirement due to mental incapacity, physical disability, or active military service in a military combat zone.[11]

---

9. 11 U.S.C. §109(h)(2)(A).
10. 11 U.S.C. §109(h)(3)(B).
11. 11 U.S.C. §109(h)(4).

This provision could come into play if Owen's father, Les, has to file for bankruptcy protection.

Requiring individual debtors to obtain approved credit counseling as a prerequisite to file a petition is an entirely new concept in bankruptcy practice, raising questions and concerns that will have to be resolved by the courts. For example, what is an "exigent circumstance?" Is an imminent repossession, foreclosure, sheriff's sale, eviction, or termination of utility service an exigent circumstance? In any event, the seven-day waiting period appears to be mandatory if the exigent circumstances exception is to apply. Since many debtors wait until the last minute to consult with a professional about their financial affairs, the seven-day waiting period may increase foreclosures and repossessions, thereby depriving some debtors of the ability to save their homes or cars by seeking bankruptcy relief.[12]

Bankruptcy Code Section 111 provides the guidelines necessary for the approval of the budget and credit counseling agencies required to provide both the prepetition credit counseling mandated by Section 109(h) and the financial management course now required as a condition to receive a Chapter 7 discharge (§727(a)(11)) or a Chapter 13 discharge (§1328(g)). (See chapters 8 and 23 infra.) The United States Trustee is charged with establishing the requirements to approve these agencies and to evaluate them on a regular basis. Although the agencies may charge a fee, the services are required to be provided without consideration of the ability to pay the fee. Prepetition credit counseling focuses upon the debtor's ability to qualify for bankruptcy relief, the types of chapters available, and whether or not the debtor has the ability to propose a reasonable nonbankruptcy repayment plan to creditors. In this regard, if a debtor proposes to repay at least 60 percent over the loan repayment period, and the creditor unreasonably refuses, this may constitute a ground to object to at least 20 percent of the claim in a bankruptcy case pursuant to

---

12. Opinions are diverse. Some courts find imminent foreclosure to be an exigent circumstance. See, e.g., In re Giambrone, 365 B.R. 386 (Bankr. W.D.N.Y. 2007). Some find that imminent foreclosure is not an exigent circumstance. See, e.g., In re Hedquist, 342 B.R. 295 (8th Cir. BAP 2006). Some cases have found that obtaining credit counseling on the filing date is not sufficient. See, e.g., In re Shaw, 2014 WL 6980478 (Bankr. D.D.C. Dec. 9, 2014) (dismissing a case where the counseling was obtained approximately four and a half hours after the petition was filed); In re Francisco, 390 B.R. 700 (Bankr. D.N.M. 2008).

new Section 502(k). Additionally, payments made to creditors pursuant to such a repayment plan are not considered preferential pursuant to new Section 547(h).

2. Debt Relief Agency Provisions

A second group of gatekeeper provisions added to the Code by BAPCPA establishes additional responsibilities for any "**debt relief agency**" providing "**bankruptcy assistance**" to an "assisted person." A debt relief agency, as defined under Section 101(12A), is any person, including a bankruptcy petition preparer, providing "bankruptcy assistance," as defined under Section 101(4A) to an "**assisted person**," defined under Section 101(3) as a person whose debts are primarily consumer debts and whose nonexempt property has a value of less than $192,450.

> ### *Practice Pointer*
> The Supreme Court has ruled that a bankruptcy attorney qualifies as a "debt relief agency" for purposes of Section 101(12A). Milavetz, Gallop & Milavetz, P.A. v. United States, 559 U.S. 229 (2010).

Would Jimmy Bond qualify as a debt relief agency under this definition?

FACT PATTERN

Section 527 requires a debt relief agency to provide written notice to the debtor, as provided for in Section 342(b), describing the various chapters available to individual debtors along with a brief description of bankruptcy in general. Form 8.7 on the Forms Disk is a sample form. This notice is to be given within three business days of offering to provide assistance to the assisted person, along with an additional notice advising the assisted person that they have a duty to be truthful, to accurately disclose all assets and liabilities, and to provide current monthly income. The notice will also state that their petition is subject to random audit. Section 527(b) requires that a statement be given to assisted persons about the obligations of the debt relief agency. This section sets forth the specific terms that must be included in this statement.

Debt relief agency: a bankruptcy attorney or bankruptcy petition preparer and any person providing bankruptcy assistance to assisted persons for money or other valuable consideration pursuant to 11 U.S.C. §101(12A)

Bankruptcy assistance: goods or services provided to an assisted person for the purpose of providing advice, counsel, document preparation, or court appearance in a bankruptcy proceeding; section 101(4A) of the Bankruptcy Code defines bankruptcy assistance

Assisted person: any person whose debts are primarily consumer debts and whose nonexempt assets are less than $192,450 pursuant to 11 U.S.C. §101(3); assisted persons are entitled to written retainer agreements and prepetition written disclosures from Debt Relief Agencies pursuant to 11 U.S.C. §§527 and 528

Section 528 requires written retainer agreements between debtors and all debt relief agencies within five business days of first rendering services to an assisted person. The written retainer agreement must clearly and conspicuously explain the services to be rendered, the fees to be charged, and any payment terms to be assigned. Section 528 further requires that any advertising must make clear that any services being advertised are for bankruptcy services and clearly and conspicuously state: "We are a debt relief agency. We help people file for bankruptcy relief under the Bankruptcy Code," or a substantially similar statement. The purpose of these new provisions is to ensure that potential debtors will understand that the assistance they are receiving involves bankruptcy relief and not simply debt counseling or some other form of debt relief.

Section 526 enforces compliance with Sections 527 and 528. Section 526 requires a debt relief agency to perform all the services they promise to provide to an assisted person. These provisions of Sections 527 and 528 may not be waived. Failure to comply with any of the provisions in Section 526, 527, or 528 will make the debt relief agency liable for all damages and a refund of any fees paid. Additionally, state attorneys general, the court, and the United States Trustee are given authority to enforce these provisions, including the authority to seek an injunction against a debt relief agency that repeatedly violates these provisions.

FACT PATTERN

The nature of the agreement with Jimmy Bond likely violates sections 527 and 528, potentially making him liable for damages to Owen Cash.

In Milavetz, Gallop & Milavetz, P.A. v. United States, 559 U.S. 229 (2010), a law firm challenged the constitutionality of the definition of "debt relief agency" at 11 U.S.C. §101(12A) and contended it should not apply to attorneys. The plaintiffs asserted that 11 U.S.C. §526(a)(4), barring advice to assisted persons to ". . . incur more debt in contemplation of such person filing . . ." bankruptcy, violates the First Amendment, and claimed that 11 U.S.C. §528, requiring disclosure as a debt relief agency in advertising, violates the First Amendment. The Supreme Court held that a law firm is a debt relief agency and that the regulation of speech contained in the debt relief agency provisions is otherwise constitutional.

With respect to the first point, the Court held the plain meaning of the Code to foreclose a ". . . reading of 'debt relief agency' excluding attorneys. A law firm representing consumer bankruptcy debtors is a debt relief agency." The Court then turned to the constitutionality of the remaining provisions. As to Section 526(a)(4), the Court found the phrase ". . . in contemplation of . . ." means advice ". . . most naturally read to forbid

only advice to undertake actions to abuse the bankruptcy system." Incurring debt for a "valid purpose" will not violate the provision. The lower
courts will be left to determine a valid purpose. Since Section 528 requires
disclosure that a debt relief agency helps people file for bankruptcy relief
under the Bankruptcy Code, disclosures directed at misleading
commercial speech will pass scrutiny if they are reasonably related to
the State's interest in preventing deception of consumers. The Court
found Section 528 to be just such a provision.

B.   VOLUNTARY PETITIONS

A debtor initiates a voluntary proceeding by filing a petition conforming to
the appropriate official form depending upon whether the debtor is or is
not an individual.[13] The form is for the most part self-explanatory. The
purpose of the various representations contained within the petition is to
establish that the debtor is qualified to be a debtor under the particular
Chapter commenced and that the proceeding has been filed in the district
with the proper venue.[14] The debtor's involvement in related or prior
bankruptcy proceedings must also be disclosed in the petition.

Venue is the proper Bankruptcy Court (federal judicial district) in
which to commence a proceeding. A proceeding may be commenced in
any district meeting one of the following qualifications: (1) the district in
which the petitioner is domiciled, resides, or has its principal place of
business; (2) the district in which the debtor's principal United States
assets are located; or (3) the district in which the debtor has complied
with either of the above for the greatest portion of the 180 days preceding
the petition's filing.[15] As a practical matter, this means that venue is appropriate if either requirement 1 or 2 is met for at least 91 days preceding the
filing of the petition. If a debtor has been in existence for less than 91 days,
it will still qualify under either basic requirement because there will be no
other location possible for establishing venue. Improper venue does not
invalidate the effect of filing a petition.[16]

Venue: the proper Bankruptcy Court (federal district) in which a bankruptcy proceeding should be commenced; generally, venue is where the debtor resides or where the debtor business's primary business address or assets are located

---

13. 11 U.S.C. §301; Bankruptcy Rule 1002; Official Form No. B101 for individuals and B201 for
    nonindividuals. See Forms Disk, Form 4.1 and 4.2.
14. See chapters 6 and 8 infra.
15. 28 U.S.C. §1408, 11 U.S.C. §109(a).
16. 28 U.S.C. §1412.

Practice Pointer

It is also important to not lose sight of the impact that the debtor's length of domicile will independently have on his/her ability to claim certain exemptions under Section 522. See chapter 10 infra.

Venue may be changed if a party in interest moves before the court to have the case transferred because the proceeding was initiated in an improper district or if the transfer is for the convenience of the parties and witnesses and in the interest of justice. Alternatively, the court may dismiss a case that has been filed in an improper venue.[17] For instance, it may be more convenient for a business debtor's proceeding to take place in the district where the principal assets are located when this is different from the principal (or headquarters) business address. On the other hand, it may be more convenient and logical for the proceeding to take place in the district where the corporate headquarters is located when the debtor has multiple locations, such as the parent entity of a franchise business, or a chain of retail stores. Because most proceedings are initiated by consumers, venue is infrequently a problematic issue.

The Federal Rules of Bankruptcy Procedure require a number of documents be filed along with the petition at the commencement of a voluntary proceeding or within certain limited time periods thereafter. Some of the required documents will vary depending upon the type of Chapter proceeding filed. Some of the documents may further vary according to the local rules of the district where the proceeding is filed.

In addition to the petition, a debtor must file certain other documents when a Chapter 7 petition is filed or the petition may not be accepted for filing by the court.

FACT PATTERN

Jimmy Bond's advice that all of the schedules were not needed unless specifically requested by the court is incorrect and could (and did) cause the Cashes' first petition to be dismissed.

In a situation where the debtor is filing to avoid an imminent foreclosure, repossession, or levy, a failure to file the minimum documents necessary for the clerk to accept the petition may be tantamount to

---

17. 28 U.S.C. §1412; Bankruptcy Rule 1014.

legal malpractice. First, the filing fee must be paid when the case is filed. Debtors may also seek approval of the Bankruptcy Court to pay the filing fee in installments or to have the filing fee waived.[18]

> ***Jimmy Bond's statement that pro se debtors do not have to pay a filing fee is at best inaccurate. To avoid paying the filing fee, Owen would have had to first file an application to have the fee waived and have it approved by the court.***

FACT PATTERN

Second, every individual debtor must file a statement under penalty of perjury setting forth his/her Social Security number or a statement that the debtor has no Social Security number. This is because Federal Rule of Bankruptcy Procedure 1005 requires that all petitions contain only the last four digits of a debtor's Social Security number to protect privacy.[19] Third, a list containing the name and address of each creditor must be filed with the petition unless the Schedules of Assets and Liabilities are filed at the same time.[20] Fourth, the debtor's attorney must also file a declaration that there has been a disclosure to the debtor of the various types of Chapter proceedings available.[21] This last item has been incorporated in the petition in Official Form B101. Finally, 11 U.S.C. §521(b) requires a consumer debtor to file a prepetition credit counseling certificate showing compliance with Bankruptcy Code Section 109(h) as discussed in Section A, supra, or a certification explaining the "exigent circumstances" necessary to request 30 additional days to comply with the requirement.

A "bankruptcy petition preparer" shall provide the debtor with a declaration under penalty of perjury disclosing any fee received from or on behalf of the debtor within 12 months preceding the filing, and any unpaid fee charged to the debtor pursuant to Section 110 (see chapter 8 infra). An unsupervised paralegal may be a bankruptcy petition preparer as defined in the Code.[22]

---

18. Bankruptcy Rule 1006. 28 U.S.C. §1930(f) permits qualified indigent debtors to apply for a waiver of filing fees. This permits *in forma pauperis* petitions in appropriate circumstances. A qualified debtor is a debtor whose income is less than 150% of the official federal poverty line.
19. Bankruptcy Rule 1005; Bankruptcy Rule 1007(f). See Official Form B121, included in the Forms Disk.
20. Bankruptcy Rule 1007(a)(1).
21. 11 U.S.C. §342(b); Pub. L. No. 98-353 §322; 11 U.S.C. §521(a)(1); 11 U.S.C. §527; Bankruptcy Rule 2016(b). See Section A, supra.
22. Bankruptcy Rule 2016(c). A bankruptcy petition preparer must file a declaration with the petition. This declaration is Official Form B119 and is included in the Forms Disk.

Was Jimmy Bond in violation of the Code when he assisted Owen in preparing his petition since his involvement was not disclosed to the court?

These minimum requirements will generally be used by regular bankruptcy practitioners only in an emergency, such as avoiding an immediate foreclosure, repossession, or attachment. Otherwise, it is recommended to file all of the documents described in this chapter required to be filed in connection with the proceeding at the time of filing. A filing that complies with only the minimum requirements is sometimes colloquially referred to as a "quickie" or "short form" filing.

Statements and Schedules: common name of the Statement of Financial Affairs and Schedules of Assets and Liabilities filed by any debtor within the bankruptcy system; these pleadings will be the most important initial pleadings in any bankruptcy proceeding

All debtors who file short or otherwise incomplete petitions have 14 days from the date of filing to file the missing Schedules of Assets and Liabilities and a Statement of Financial Affairs.[23]

Individual debtors must also file copies of any evidence of payments received from any employer of the debtor within 60 days of filing, a Statement of Current Monthly Income, and if required, the form appropriate to the Chapter filed providing the calculations necessary to determine compliance with Needs Based Bankruptcy (see chapter 6F and 6G infra).[24] Failure to file a required document by the 45th day from the filing of the petition will result in automatic dismissal on day 46, although an extension of up to 45 days may be sought for "justification." The court may also decline to dismiss the case for failure to comply if the debtor has made a good faith effort to comply and the court finds that administration of the case would be in the best interests of the creditors.[25]

> ### Practice Pointer
> Always make it a habit to check the applicability of the court's local rules. For example, some courts want the copies of the pay statements filed with the trustee and not with the court.

---

23. 11 U.S.C. §521(a)(1); Bankruptcy Rule 1007(b)(1). In individual cases, Official Forms B106-B106J-2 are the Schedules and Official Form B107 is the Statement of Financial Affairs. In nonindividual cases, Official Forms B206-B206H are the Schedules and Official Form B207 is the Statement of Financial Affairs. These forms are included in the Forms Disk.
24. The Chapter 7 Statement of Current Monthly Income is Official Form B122-A. Debtors are required to complete the applicable means testing form corresponding to the chapter filed under. These forms are Official Forms B122A-1 through B122C-2 and are included in the Forms Disk.
25. 11 U.S.C. §521(a)(1); 11 U.S.C. §521(f); 11 U.S.C. §521(i).

Not later than seven days prior to the meeting of creditors, individual debtors must provide to the trustee a copy of the debtor's federal income tax return for the tax year ending immediately prior to the filing of the petition.

This will be an issue that the Cashes will have to address if they refile a bankruptcy petition since Les failed to file Owen's last tax return.

FACT PATTERN

Failure to do so may result in dismissal of the case. Failure by a debtor to file any postpetition tax return or to provide copies of any returns requested can also result in dismissal of the case.[26]

The **Statement of Financial Affairs** is a questionnaire designed to elicit sufficient information to determine whether the debtor should receive a discharge or to reveal the existence of preferences or other avoidable transactions. The **Schedules** are an extended form of an accrual-based financial statement disclosing all liabilities and all assets of the debtor. The Schedule of Current Income and Expenditures discloses the existence or lack of surplus income after the payment of basic monthly expenses. It is relevant in Chapter 7 and Chapter 13 proceedings.[27] Chapters 30 and 31 infra are devoted to an analysis of these documents. These documents comprise the core materials from which the trustee or the creditors may examine a debtor's financial affairs in any proceeding. They are the central "pleadings" of any bankruptcy. Whether the debtor is John Smith or a major corporation, the requirements are identical. The existence of nonexempt assets from which a distribution to creditors may occur is initially determined by analyzing the Statements and Schedules. The basic distributive rights of creditors to the assets can also be determined from a review of these documents.

Within 30 days of the filing, a consumer debtor must also file a statement of intention regarding disposition of secured collateral.[28] At the behest of consumer credit organizations, this provision was added to the Code in 1984 to expedite notification to secured creditors regarding a debtor's intent to retain and pay for, or to surrender, the collateral securing a secured debt. This requirement has helped to reduce relief

Statement of Financial Affairs: a fundamental bankruptcy pleading consisting of a questionnaire concerning a debtor's financial affairs

Schedules of Assets and Liabilities: a fundamental bankruptcy pleading consisting of a prioritized and itemized list of a debtor's assets (property) and liabilities (debt)

---

26. 11 U.S.C. §521(e).
27. 11 U.S.C. §521(a)(1); Bankruptcy Rule 1007(b). See chapter 24 infra.
28. 11 U.S.C. §521(a)(2). See Forms Disk, Form 22.3.

from stay motions described in chapter 13 infra while assisting debtors
and creditors alike in reducing the expenses and frustrations sometimes
encountered in resolving a consumer's secured claim within the bankruptcy system. Chapters 13 and 22 of this text describe in more detail
the automatic stay, the rights of a secured creditor, and the statement
of intention.

Debtor's counsel must file Official Form B2030 disclosing the compensation paid or to be paid in connection with the proceeding.[29] The
Forms Disk contains a copy. This document must be filed within 15 days of
the petition's filing.[30]

In a Chapter 13 proceeding, a debtor must also file his/her proposed
Chapter 13 plan within 15 days of the petition's filing.[31] A number of
additional documents must be filed in connection with a Chapter 11 or
12 proceeding. These materials are described in greater detail in chapters
25 and 28 infra.

Although it is permissible to file all of the required documents at
various times, as noted above, it is generally more efficient and prudent
to file them all together when the petition is filed. This will ensure that all
necessary actions have been taken to protect the debtor's rights from the
start of the proceeding. This will also eliminate any need to remember
what must be done next and within what time limit. These documents,
although numerous, are not generally so extensive or complex that they
cannot all be filed with the petition except in an emergency. Many districts, particularly those in urban areas, have approved forms available for
use, which helps make this task even easier to perform. Samples of all of
these forms appear on the Forms Disk accompanying this text.

In appropriate circumstances, such as a proceeding with numerous
creditors, or a debtor with complex financial transactions to be described
in the Statement of Financial Affairs, the court has discretion to grant an
extension of time for the filing of the Statements and Schedules.[32] Not
filing the documents in a timely manner, however, can result in a dismissal
of the proceeding because the failure evidences a lack of prosecution.[33]

Joint case: a bankruptcy pro- ceeding involving an individual and the individual's spouse

Section 302 of the Code permits the filing of **joint cases**. A joint case is
filed by an individual and the individual's spouse. No other related entities

---

29. 11 U.S.C. §329.
30. Bankruptcy Rule 2016(b).
31. 11 U.S.C. §1321; Bankruptcy Rule 3015. See chapter 24 infra.
32. Bankruptcy Rule 1007(c).
33. 11 U.S.C. §707(a); Bankruptcy Rule 1017; 11 U.S.C. §521(1).

may file a joint case.[34] However, there are provisions allowing the consolidation of two or more pending and related cases.[35]

For instance, if one spouse files a proceeding and then the other spouse files (assume they are separated so they each file a separate case), it is possible to obtain a court order consolidating the cases into one proceeding.

If Owen and Robin decide to separate, what impact would this have on their prospective bankruptcy filing?

FACT PATTERN

As another example, assume that a corporation files a bankruptcy proceeding and the owner of the corporation has guaranteed all of the corporation's debts and is subsequently forced to file an individual bankruptcy proceeding. Because many of the debts are identical (due to the guarantees), it is possible under the Bankruptcy Rules of Procedure to seek consolidation of the two proceedings into one.

Would Owen's individual bankruptcy filing protect any of the assets in The Lawn Cuttery business?

FACT PATTERN

As a third example, assume that a corporation and an individual file two separate and superficially distinct proceedings. Investigation discloses a distinct relationship between the two debtors. Consolidation may also be appropriate in this instance.

Finally, assume that a group of related partnerships or corporations file proceedings. The partnerships may have a common general partner or partners. The corporations may be subsidiaries or affiliates of one another. (Subsidiaries and affiliates are described in more detail in chapter

---

34. 11 U.S.C. §302(a). Although rarely tested, at least one court has determined that the spouses have to be of opposite sexes. See In re Kandu, 315 B.R. 123 (Bankr. W.D. Wash. 2004). In another case, the court allowed a same-sex couple to claim a joint homestead exemption under state law. See In re Rabin, 359 B.R. 242 (9th Cir. BAP 2007). In a recent case, the bankruptcy court declined to dismiss a joint case filed by a same-sex couple legally married in Vermont. See In re Somers, 448 B.R. 677 (Bankr. S.D.N.Y. 2011). The Defense of Marriage Act ("DOMA"), which defines a marriage as a legal union between one man and one woman, has been cited as the grounds to prevent same-sex joint filings. In United States v. Windsor 133 S. Ct. 2675 (2013), the Supreme Court ruled that DOMA is unconstitutional. Post-Windsor, at least one court has allowed a same sex couple to file a joint bankruptcy petition. See In re Matson, 509 B.R. 860 (Bankr. E.D.Wis. 2014) (same sex couple legally married in another state could file a joint petition in a state that did not recognize same sex marriages). See also In re Villaverde and Hight, 540 B.R. 431 (Bankr. C.D.Cal. 2015) (same sex domestic partners who chose not to marry after legalization of same sex marriage in California were not eligible to file a joint Chapter 13 petition).

35. 11 U.S.C. §302(b); Bankruptcy Rule 1015.

6 infra.) Investigation may disclose substantial interrelationships between the various debtors that would make all proceedings more efficient and result in a more equitable distribution to all creditors if consolidation took place.

In each of the above examples, consolidation may be appropriate, although only spouses may initiate a joint case. (A joint case could be commenced in the first example.) There are two standard forms of consolidation. The court may consolidate two or more proceedings for all purposes. This is known as **substantive consolidation**. Substantively consolidated proceedings are treated as one case. Alternatively, the court may consolidate two or more proceedings for less than all purposes. This lesser form of consolidation is sometimes known as **administrative consolidation**.[36] Administrative consolidation may often save substantial time and expense in the administration of multiple related estates, even though their assets and liabilities will remain segregated. It is a common occurrence in large corporate cases commonly filed in New York or Delaware that all the filing entities are administratively consolidated at the beginning of the case as a **first-day order**. See chapter 25 infra.

Substantive consolidation: when the court consolidates two or more proceedings for all purposes

Administrative consolidation: when the court consolidates two or more proceedings for less than all purposes

First-day order: common name of critical orders entered within the first day or two of a large corporate Chapter 11 filing

C.   INVOLUNTARY PETITIONS

An entity is placed into bankruptcy against its will by the filing of an involuntary petition. There are different instances in which creditors, shareholders, or partners may force an entity into bankruptcy. A petition filed by an entity other than the debtor is called an involuntary petition. Section 303 of the Code contains the rules governing involuntary proceedings.[37] Section 303 is designed to equitably resolve the rights of an entity and its creditors while the issue of the involuntary bankruptcy is pending.

As discussed in chapter 1 supra, until the Bankruptcy Act of 1898, most bankruptcies were initiated as involuntary proceedings initiated by creditors against an alleged debtor. Until the twentieth century, involuntary bankruptcy was the traditional method of placing an entity debtor into bankruptcy. This is no longer the case in the United States. Almost all proceedings now filed today are voluntary; involuntary proceedings are rare.

Under the Bankruptcy Act and its many predecessors, a debtor became legally bankrupt only when the court entered an order adjudicating the

---

36. Bankruptcy Rule 1015.
37. 11 U.S.C. §303.

debtor bankrupt.[38] The Code has adopted the phrase "order for relief" to replace the prior language of "adjudicated as a bankrupt." Under the Bankruptcy Code, an order for relief arises automatically when a voluntary petition is filed.[39] In an involuntary proceeding, an order for relief will only issue upon a default by the debtor or upon the court's finding that cause exists to enter an order for relief in a contested proceeding.

The best way to consider the practical effect of an involuntary proceeding is to think of it in terms of a traditional lawsuit. The creditors who file the petition are the equivalent of plaintiffs, although they are generally referred to as **petitioning creditors**. Until an order for relief is entered, the debtor is usually referred to as an alleged debtor. The alleged debtor is the equivalent of a defendant. The specific relief or judgment sought by the petitioning creditors is the entry of an **order for relief**.

An involuntary petition is filed and served in a manner identical to a summons and complaint in a traditional lawsuit. A debtor may or may not choose to contest the petition. If there is no opposition, the debtor will have an order for relief entered against it by default. If an alleged debtor contests the petition, the court will hold a trial to determine whether an order for relief should be entered. Discovery techniques and pretrial procedures may take place prior to the trial. The initiation of an involuntary petition thus constitutes the commencement of a lawsuit where the "plaintiffs" seek the entry of an "order for relief" as the judgment.[40] The time period between the filing of an involuntary petition and the entry of an order for relief can perhaps best be described as the period of time during which the creditors believe an alleged debtor is bankrupt while the alleged debtor believes it is not bankrupt. This period of time is often referred to as the "gap" or "limbo" period. Other provisions of the Bankruptcy Code help to establish the distributive rights of any creditors whose claims arise during this period.[41] These provisions are described in detail in chapter 21 infra.

Creditors may initiate involuntary proceedings for a number of reasons. First, a proceeding may be filed to prevent a debtor from continuing to commit known fraudulent transfers by wrongful dissipation of assets, thus improperly removing those assets from the reach of creditors.

Second, there might be a potential debtor who needs to file bankruptcy but who refuses. Perhaps the debtor owns a piece of property with enough equity to pay all creditors in full, but the property is about to be foreclosed upon. The potential debtor insists that no bankruptcy will

Petitioning creditors: creditors initiating an involuntary petition against a debtor

order for relief: a statutory term of art, which signifies that a debtor has filed for bankruptcy relief

---

38. 11 U.S.C. §41(f). This, of course, is a reference to 11 U.S.C. as it existed prior to October 1, 1978.
39. 11 U.S.C. §301.
40. 11 U.S.C. §303(h); Bankruptcy Rule 1018.
41. 11 U.S.C. §502(f); 11 U.S.C. §507(a)(2). See chapter 22 infra.

be filed. Creditors in this instance might initiate an involuntary bankruptcy to gain the benefits of the automatic stay thereby preventing the immediate foreclosure. This will protect any equity in the property for the payment of the creditor claims.[42]

A third common reason for filing an involuntary proceeding involves partnerships. As discussed above, a voluntary partnership filing must normally be accompanied by an authorization showing consent to the filing by all of the general partners or evidencing appropriate authority to file on behalf of all general partners.[43] Simply put, all general partners to a voluntary filing must sign the petition or the court must be provided with evidence that all general partners consent, such as a general management clause in favor of a managing partner or some other form of acceptable proxy. If one or more general partners refuse to consent to a voluntary filing, or if a debtor has a number of general partners and within the time limits for action it is not physically possible to obtain their written consent, the Code permits one general partner to file an involuntary proceeding.[44] Thus, one general partner may force a bankruptcy of the partnership over the objection of the remaining general partners.

An involuntary petition may only seek to place a debtor into Chapter 7 or Chapter 11 proceedings. An involuntary Chapter 12 or 13 proceeding cannot be initiated. Further, an involuntary proceeding may only be initiated against an entity that would also in the normal course qualify to be a debtor under Chapter 7 or Chapter 11.[45]

Three specific types of entities may not have involuntary proceedings initiated against them: certain charitable and nonprofit organizations (such as churches, schools, or charitable foundations), and family farmers. Farmers are exempt from involuntary proceedings because Congress has determined that one lean year should not permit a farmer to be forced into bankruptcy by its creditors. It is for this same reason that involuntary Chapter 12 proceedings may not be initiated, as they are proceedings for family farmers. Finally, because Chapter 13 is an effort by a consumer to repay debt, Congress has found that to permit involuntary Chapter 13 filings would be akin to creating a form of involuntary servitude, because it would force a debtor to repay debt.[46] Involuntary servitude is of course unconstitutional under the Thirteenth Amendment.[47]

---

42. 11 U.S.C. §362. See chapter 13 infra.
43. Bankruptcy Rule 1004(a).
44. 11 U.S.C. §303(b)(3).
45. 11 U.S.C. §303(a). See also chapter 5 infra.
46. 11 U.S.C. §303(a). See also Historical and Revision Notes to Section 303.
47. U.S. Const. amend. XIII. In re Clemente, 409 B.R. 288 (Bankr. N.J. 2009).

The format of an involuntary petition is contained in Official Form B105 for individuals and Official Form B205 for nonindividuals.[48] Because the filing of an involuntary petition initiates a lawsuit or assumes the status of a lawsuit, a summons must be issued and served on the alleged debtor. Once served with the summons, the alleged debtor has 20 days to respond to the petition.[49] If the alleged debtor does nothing, the creditors can have an order for relief entered by default. This activity is equivalent to obtaining a default judgment in traditional nonbankruptcy litigation.[50]

Section 303(b) identifies the creditors who may file an involuntary proceeding. If the debtor has 12 or more creditors, three unsecured creditors with undisputed aggregate claims of at least $15,775 are required to file a proceeding.[51] The three creditors join together and file the involuntary petition. If an alleged debtor has 11 or fewer undisputed unsecured creditors, then any one such creditor may file the petition as long as the petitioning creditor is owed at least $15,775.[52] For example, if a potential debtor has 11 unsecured creditors owed in the aggregate less than $15,775, it will be impossible for the creditors to file an involuntary proceeding against the debtor because there is less than $15,775 in total debt and no single creditor is owed at least $15,775.

Is it possible that creditors could get together and file an involuntary petition against The Lawn Cuttery?

If the alleged debtor is a partnership, an involuntary petition may be filed by one or more of the general partners. This allows a partnership, where there is disagreement between the partners, to file a proceeding without the consent of all general partners. If a general partner has filed a bankruptcy proceeding, the partner's bankruptcy trustee has the authority to initiate the involuntary proceeding against the partnership.[53] For instance, assume a general partnership composed of three general partners, Moe, Curly, and Larry. The partnership owns a valuable piece of property that is about to be foreclosed upon. Moe and Larry want the partnership to file a bankruptcy immediately to gain the protections of

---

48. See Forms Disk, Form 3.6.
49. Bankruptcy Rule 1010; Bankruptcy Rule 1011(b). Official Form B2500E is a summons in an involuntary case.
50. 11 U.S.C. §303(b).
51. 11 U.S.C. §303(b)(1). The 1994 Amendments added Section 104(b) to the Code. This provision acts to triennially adjust a number of the amounts set forth in various provisions of the Bankruptcy Code, such as Section 303(b)(1). The first adjustment took place on April 1, 1998. The text reflects the April 1, 2016, adjustments.
52. 11 U.S.C. §303(b)(2).
53. 11 U.S.C. §303(b)(3).

the automatic stay. Curly opposes this. Moe and Larry file an involuntary petition against the partnership seeking the entry of an order for relief over the objection of Curly. If either Moe or Larry were themselves debtors in a bankruptcy proceeding, their bankruptcy trustee would also have a right to file the involuntary petition. Once an involuntary petition is filed, additional qualified creditors may join in the filing of the petition simply by filing a one-page pleading with the court joining in the petition. This has the same effect as if the creditor had originally joined in the petition.[54] Significantly more than three creditors may therefore ultimately join in an involuntary petition.

There are benefits to be gained by the petitioning creditors in seeking the joinder of as many creditors as possible to an involuntary proceeding. For instance, a debtor may be able to show that one or more of the three originally petitioning creditors does not really have a proper claim, or that the total of the three claims is less than $15,775, or that one or more of the claims is actually in dispute. In each of these circumstances, a debtor may defeat an otherwise proper petition on this sort of technicality. The joinder of additional creditors provides for creditor unity and prevents a debtor from successfully contesting a petition on a procedural technicality. Joinder helps strengthen the case for the petitioning creditors.

The Code provides the alleged debtor an opportunity to contest the allegations of the petition.[55] The ability of an alleged debtor to do this makes the alleged debtor the functional equivalent of a defendant. If the allegations are contested, then the court will hold a trial to determine whether an order for relief should be entered. Due to the unique financial status that the involuntary filing creates for an alleged debtor, the Federal Rules of Bankruptcy Procedure direct the court to give preference to the matter on its calendar.[56] The Federal Rules of Bankruptcy Procedure applicable to adversary proceedings, which are essentially the Federal Rules of Civil Procedure, apply in contested involuntary proceedings.[57]

The petitioning creditors must prove the existence of one of two circumstances to obtain an order for relief. The first circumstance is that the debtor is generally not paying its debts as they become due.[58] This is not the same as being insolvent. Ironically, the debtor's solvency is technically irrelevant to the determination of whether to enter an order for relief in an involuntary proceeding. A debtor who is not paying its bills on time may or may not be insolvent.

---

54. 11 U.S.C. §303(c).
55. Bankruptcy Rule 1011(a).
56. Bankruptcy Rule 1013(a).
57. Bankruptcy Rule 1018. See Part VII of the Federal Rules of Bankruptcy Procedure. See also chapter 13 infra describing adversary proceedings.
58. 11 U.S.C. §303(h)(1).

> ### *Practice Pointer*
> Under the Code, "insolvent" means a
> financial situation in which the debtor's
> debts are greater than the fair valuation of all of his/
> her assets, exclusive of any exempt property or
> property improperly transferred or concealed. See
> 11 U.S.C. §101(32).

For example, a senior citizen with Alzheimer's disease may simply forget to pay bills or may throw them in the wastebasket. The person may be fabulously rich, but the person is not generally paying debts as they become due. An order for relief could be entered against this potential debtor. It is therefore important to recognize that the solvency of a debtor is not a conclusive issue to determine in connection with an involuntary proceeding except as insolvency may or may not relate to the debtor not generally paying its debts as they become due. Of course, presenting evidence of insolvency may be a relevant fact for the court to consider as evidence to assist it in making its determination.

The second circumstance that can result in the entry of an order for relief in an involuntary proceeding is that within 120 days prior to the filing of the petition, a custodian took possession of some portion of the estate's assets. For instance, the appointment of a receiver or an assignment for the benefit of creditors will cause this situation to arise.[59] This situation rarely arises in individual bankruptcy proceedings.

If the court can find that one of the two circumstances described above exists, then an order for relief will be entered. Once an order for relief is entered, the petition will then proceed exactly as if it had been initiated by the filing of a voluntary petition. All the documents previously described in this chapter will have to be filed, but the time limits will be counted from the date of the entry of the order for relief.[60] When the debtor is not available or does not file the required documents after the entry of an order for relief in an involuntary proceeding, it becomes the responsibility of the petitioning creditors to file the required documents to the best of their ability.[61]

---

59. 11 U.S.C. §303(h)(2).
60. Bankruptcy Rule 1007(c).
61. Bankruptcy Rule 1007(k).

The filing of an involuntary petition is a rather extreme creditor remedy. It has obvious and immediate adverse effects on an alleged debtor. For instance, a business may suffer immediate loss of business merely due to the announcement of the filing. Although the creditors require ample protection in appropriate cases, a debtor who may not be found bankrupt requires protection to preserve the estate without the burden or stigma of a pending Title 11 proceeding. An improperly filed petition or a contested petition that takes too long to resolve can sometimes be fatal to what may have previously been a successful individual or business and become a self-fulfilling prophecy. Because of the diametrically opposed concerns of the creditors and the alleged debtor in these circumstances, certain provisions contained in Section 303 protect an alleged debtor while the issue of the petition is pending. Other provisions are designed to protect the creditors during the "gap" or "limbo" period. Once again, this is the period of time between the initiation of the petition and either the entry of an order for relief or a dismissal of the petition. This limbo period can also be described as that period of time during which creditors consider the entity bankrupt, but the alleged debtor considers itself as not bankrupt.

Where a debtor may be attempting to dissipate assets of an estate to the detriment of his/her creditors while contesting a petition, the creditors can seek the immediate appointment of an interim trustee prior to the entry of an order for relief. The court has further discretion to enter any appropriate order necessary to preserve the estate.[62] This provision affords the creditors protection in an appropriate case.

On the other hand, the court also has discretion to enter appropriate orders that protect the debtor. Under Section 303(e), the court can require petitioning creditors to post a bond to satisfy any damages that may be sustained by the debtor in the event the debtor is successful in contesting the petition.[63] The imposition of a significant bond acts as a deterrent to abusive creditors and a protection for debtors who do not properly belong in the bankruptcy system.

An alleged debtor may conduct business as usual. Consistent with the foregoing, however, the court may enter any appropriate order to protect the creditors or the alleged debtor.[64] This may sometimes result in the imposition of some controls and disclosure to the creditors regarding an alleged debtor's financial affairs while the involuntary petition remains pending.

---

62. 11 U.S.C. §303(g).
63. 11 U.S.C. §303(e).
64. 11 U.S.C. §303(f).

If the court dismisses an involuntary petition, other than on agreement of the parties, the court has effectively rendered a judgment in favor of the alleged debtor. In this event, the court may order the petitioning creditors to pay the debtor's expenses, costs, attorneys' fees, and any actual damages caused by the petition. If the court further finds that the petitioners acted in bad faith, the court can also award the debtor punitive damages.[65] The bond referred to above should be based on an estimate of damages an alleged debtor may incur.[66] These burdens act as a deterrent to prevent creditors from abusing the system by wrongfully forcing entities into bankruptcy. If the court dismisses an involuntary petition against an individual and it determines that the petition was false or contained materially false statements, the court will seal all of the court records.[67] It may also enter an order preventing all consumer reporting agencies from reporting the bankruptcy and adversely affecting the debtor's credit.

Summary

A bankruptcy proceeding is initiated by the filing of a petition. The petition may be filed voluntarily or involuntarily: When a debtor files the petition, it is called a voluntary petition; when creditors file the petition, it is called an involuntary petition. The voluntary petition is the most frequently used method of initiating a bankruptcy proceeding. Consumer debtors must obtain a credit counseling certificate from an approved credit counseling service within 180 days prior to filing, absent exigent circumstances. A debt relief agency must provide disclosures to debtors and obtain written retainer agreements.

A debtor is not legally bankrupt until the court enters an order for relief. This order is automatic when a voluntary petition is filed, and it is the judgment that the petitioning creditors seek in an involuntary petition.

A debtor and his/her spouse may initiate a joint proceeding. No other combination of multiple debtors may initiate a proceeding together. However, two or more debtors may have their proceedings consolidated by motion for either substantive or administrative purposes.

---

65. 11 U.S.C. §303(i).
66. 11 U.S.C. §303(e).
67. 11 U.S.C. §303(l).

The procedure of an involuntary petition can be compared to a non-bankruptcy lawsuit. The petitioning creditors are essentially plaintiffs who seek the entry of an order for relief against an alleged debtor who is essentially a defendant. An order for relief is entered upon either the debtor's default or after the court holds a trial upon a contested petition.

When an involuntary petition is contested, the court must be able to make one of two findings to enter an order for relief. The first of these is that the debtor is not generally paying its debts as they become due. The second is that within 120 days prior to the filing, a custodian has been appointed to administer assets of the debtor. A custodian could be an assignee for the benefit of creditors or a state court receiver.

The period of time between the filing of an involuntary petition and the entry of an order for relief or dismissal of the petition is known as the "limbo" or "gap" period. During this period, the court may enter appropriate equitable orders to protect the rights of either the creditors or debtor. If the petition is dismissed, other than on agreement of the parties, the court may award the debtor costs, attorneys' fees, and actual damages. In an appropriate case, the court is empowered to award punitive damages.

When an order for relief is entered in an involuntary petition, the proceeding will thereafter continue as if it were a voluntary proceeding.

KEY TERMS

administrative
   consolidation
alleged debtor
assisted person
bankruptcy assistance
debt relief agency
first-day order
involuntary petition
joint case
order for relief
petitioning creditors

prepetition credit
   counseling
Schedules
Statement of Financial
   Affairs
Statements and
   Schedules
substantive
   consolidation
venue
voluntary petition

CHAPTER 4 CHECKLIST

4.1 VOLUNTARY PETITION DOCUMENT *Authority*
CHECKLIST

   4.1.1 To Be Filed with Petition:

       1. Petition   Official Form B101 or
                                            B201

       2. Filing fee   Bankruptcy Rule 1006
           Filing fees effective
           November 18, 2016
              Chapter 7 — $335
              Chapter 11 — $1,717
              Chapter 12 — $275
              Chapter 13 — $310
           Filing fees may be paid in
           installments or waived for
           indigent debtors

       3. Statement of Social Security Bankruptcy Rule
           number   1007(f)
                                       Official Form
                                       B121

       4. Corporate resolution or   Local rule
           partnership consent

       5. List of creditors   Bankruptcy Rule
                                        1007(a)(1)

       6. Prepetition credit   §109(h)
           counseling certificate

   4.1.2 To Be Filed With the Petition — §110(h) (2);
         Bankruptcy Petition Preparer   Bankruptcy Rule
         Statement of Compensation   2016(c)
                                       Official Form B119

   4.1.3 To Be Filed Within 14 Days of
         Petition — Statements and
         Schedules:

       1. Schedules of Assets and   11 U.S.C.
           Liabilities   §521(a)(1)(B)(i);
                                       Bankruptcy Rule
                                       1007(b); Official
                                       Form B106-B106J-2
                                       Or
                                       B206-206H

2.	Schedule of Current Income and Expenditures; Schedule of Executory Contracts and Unexpired Leases	11 U.S.C. §521(a)(1)(B)(ii); Bankruptcy Rule 1007(b); Official Form B122A-1-B122C-2, as applicable
3.	Statement of Financial Affairs	11 U.S.C. §521(a)(1)(B)(iii); Bankruptcy Rule 1007(b); Official Form B107 or B207
4.	Claims of exemptions	11 U.S.C. §522(1); Bankruptcy Rule 4003(a); Official Form B-106C
5.	Attorney statement of compensation paid or promised	11 U.S.C. §329; Bankruptcy Rule 2016(b); Official Form B2030

4.1.4	To Be Filed Within 30 Days of Petition: Statement of Intent re Secured Collateral	11 U.S.C. §521(a)(2); Official Form B108
4.1.5	To Be Filed Within 45 Days of Petition[68]	
	1. Attorney compliance with §342(b)	11 U.S.C. §521(a)(1)(B)(iii)
	2. Evidence of wages paid within 60 days of filing	11 U.S.C. §521(a)(1)(B)(iv)
	3. Calculation of current monthly income	11 U.S.C. §521(a)(1)(B)(v)
	4. Disclosure of any increases in income or expenses anticipated over the next 12 months	11 U.S.C. §521(a)(1)(B)(vi)
4.1.6	Within 7 Days of Creditor Meeting Provide Trustee Tax Return for Year Preceding the Filing	11 U.S.C. §521(e)(2)(A)(i)

---

68. BAPCPA imposes these new requirements but does not state their deadline for filing except as set forth in 11 U.S.C. §521(i) requiring automatic dismissal on the 46th day if the required documents are not filed. The Bankruptcy Rules will undoubtedly be revised to account for these new requirements and should be consulted.

4.1.7   Failure to File Any Required   11 U.S.C. §521(i)
        Document Within 45 Days of
        Filing Results in Automatic
        Dismissal on 46th Day. One 45-
        Day Extension May Be Obtained.

4.2   SPECIAL CHAPTER 13 REQUIREMENTS
      4.2.1   Chapter 13 Plan (Within 15   11 U.S.C. §1321;
              Days)   Bankruptcy Rule
                                               3015; Official Form
                                               B113

4.3   INVOLUNTARY PETITION CHECKLIST
      4.3.1   Summons and Involuntary   11 U.S.C. §303; Official
              Petition Official   Form B2500E
                                               (summons) and
                                               Official Forms B105
                                               or B205, as
                                               applicable

      4.3.2   Qualifying Creditors
              1.   Three undisputed   11 U.S.C. §303(b)(1)
                   unsecured creditors owed at
                   least $15,775 in aggregate
              2.   One undisputed unsecured   11 U.S.C. §303(b)(2)
                   creditor owed at least
                   $15,775 where there are 11
                   creditors or fewer
              3.   One or more general   11 U.S.C. §303(b)(3)
                   partners where less than all
                   consent to filing

      4.3.3   Obtaining an Order for Relief
              1.   Default   11 U.S.C. §303(b)
              2.   Grounds for entering order
                   in contested petition
                   a.   debtor is not generally 11 U.S.C. §303(h)(1)
                        paying debts as they
                        become due
                   b.   appointment of   11 U.S.C. §303(h)(2)
                        custodian within
                        120 days of filing

DISCUSSION QUESTIONS

1. How is a voluntary bankruptcy proceeding commenced?

2. What is a joint case?

3. How can multiple bankruptcy proceedings be consolidated? What is the difference between administrative and substantive consolidation?

4. Describe the basic documents required to be filed by any debtor in a bankruptcy proceeding.

5. What are some of the reasons for initiating an involuntary bankruptcy against a debtor?

6. What are the grounds that petitioning creditors must prove to obtain an order for relief in an involuntary bankruptcy proceeding?

7. What provisions of the Bankruptcy Code protect the rights of creditors or the alleged debtor while an involuntary bankruptcy petition is pending?

8. What purposes might the prepetition credit counseling requirement serve? What drawbacks, if any, might the requirement have?

PRACTICE EXERCISES

Exercise 4.1
Draft a letter for your firm's prospective clients, the Cashes, explaining to them what information they should bring to a first meeting with your supervising attorney to discuss their financial affairs.

Exercise 4.2
Draft a letter to the Cashes, explaining to them the prepetition credit counseling requirement, including what they can expect, when the counseling must be completed, and where the services may be obtained.

Exercise 4.3
Draft a letter to the Cashes, satisfying the Section 527 Debt Relief Agency notice requirements.

Exercise 4.4
Prepare a list of the first ten questions that you would ask the Cashes if you were conducting their initial client interview.

5

Chapter 1 — General Provisions

Learning Objectives

- Describe the basic motion procedures used in Bankruptcy Courts
- List the essential qualifications to qualify as a debtor under each Chapter of the Code
- Identify the remaining provisions of Code Chapter 1

Chapter 1 of the Code, 11 U.S.C. §101 et seq., contains a number of definitions and other general provisions. The provisions of Chapter 1 apply in all bankruptcy proceedings.[1] Many of the provisions of Chapter 1 are so broad and basic that their location and existence are sometimes forgotten when conducting bankruptcy research. Chapter 1 should not be overlooked. Substantial research time can be saved by seeking the meaning of a term or phrase within Chapter 1 rather than trying to find the answer by implication through use of another code section or case law. Many items that are implicit in other Code sections or are not discussed in the case law are in fact explicitly set forth in Chapter 1.[2]

---

1. 11 U.S.C. §103(a). See chapter 2 supra.
2. See, e.g., 11 U.S.C. §101 Definitions.

Practice Pointer

Key definitions found in Section 101
include: "claim," "current monthly
income," "debt relief agency," "domestic support
obligation," "insider," "person," "security," and
"transfer."

Section 102 contains several basic rules of construction. The phrases
defined in Section 102 will always have the same meaning whenever used
in another section of the Bankruptcy Code unless a specific provision
states otherwise.

A.   NOTICE AND A HEARING

The first provision of Section 102 describes the phrase "*after notice and a
hearing*." This phrase, wherever used, signifies that due process must be
given to the various parties involved in the proceeding before a court
order authorizing the action that is sought to be performed can be
obtained. In the context of the Bankruptcy Code, **due process** often
means that the affected parties must merely be given notice and an *opportunity* to be heard. A hearing may not always be required.

Due process:
notice and an
opportunity to be
heard

*Note that the Cashes were given notice of a hearing to dismiss
their case for failing to timely file all of their required statements and schedules in their first bankruptcy case.*

FACT PATTERN

Noticed motion:
a motion brought
by a party in
interest seeking a
ruling from the
Bankruptcy Court
with notice
provided to all
interested parties

Ex parte: an
application made
to the court
without notice or
with limited notice
to limited parties;
ex parte applica-
tions are specifi-
cally permitted for
various ministerial
functions

When the phrase "after notice and a hearing" is used in a specific Code
section, there are two basic ways to proceed: a **noticed motion** or an **ex
parte** application. Many routine matters can be determined with a
minimum of time and expense to all parties and prevent court calendars
from becoming impossibly congested.

The motion procedure set forth in Federal Rules of Bankruptcy Procedure (FRBP) Rule 9013 is the most common way of filing motions in the
Bankruptcy Courts. Most matters coming through the Bankruptcy Court
for decision will come before the court through this process.[3] The motion
should state with particularity the relief sought, contain a proof of service,

---

3. FRBP 9013.

a notice of hearing, a proposed order for the relief requested, and be accompanied by one or more supporting affidavits unless the debtor is an individual consumer debtor.[4] When the value of an asset is in issue, as will commonly be the case in a **motion for relief from the automatic stay** (see chapter 13 infra), a valuation report must be filed with the motion.[5]

> **Motion for relief from the automatic stay**: a motion made by a creditor, pursuant to 11 U.S.C. §362(d), to be freed from the effect of the automatic stay

> ### *Practice Pointer*
> Additional motion practice requirements may also be imposed by local court rule. Local court rules frequently specify the time and place of filing as well as rules regarding schedules, use of briefs, and certifications of service.

A motion typically must be served at least 21 days prior to the hearing date, although local rules may vary this period in some situations.[6] Since FRBP 9006(f) requires that three additional days be added to any required notice period when the notice is given by mail, and since most notices are mailed in everyday practice, three days should be added to all notice periods. Notice periods, as described throughout the text, do not include this additional three-day period. Notice of the motion must be given to any entity against whom relief is sought, including the debtor, the debtor's attorney, the trustee, any creditor committee in the case (see chapter 11 infra), any entity having a lien on any property that may be affected by the motion's outcome, and any other entity that may be entitled to notice, such as the United States Trustee.

Any response to a motion should be filed and served within any time periods set by the court's local rules. Any party or entity served with the original motion must be served with any response filed by any party responding to the motion. It is possible that there may be multiple responses.[7] For example, where a trustee seeks to sell a piece of real property subject to two mortgages, a tax lien, a judgment lien, and the

---

4. See FRBP 9006(d); FRBP 9013.
5. The local bankruptcy rules for your district will often include specific requirements for motions such as these.
6. FRBP 2002(a). There are some exceptions to this general rule. For example, FRBP 2002(b) requires 28 days' notice of a Chapter 11 disclosure statement hearing (see chapter 27 infra). The exceptions are noted in the text and are summarized in the Appendix.
7. FRBP 9014.

debtor's claim of exemption, all five of these parties could conceivably file a response to the motion.

Unless the debtor is an individual consumer debtor, any response must be accompanied by a proof of service, a proposed order for the relief requested, one or more supporting affidavits if there is a factual dispute, and a report of value if the value of a property is an issue in the motion, such as in a motion for relief from the automatic stay (see chapter 13 infra).[8]

Section 342(c) provides that any notice to a creditor contain the last four digits of the debtor's taxpayer identification number. Notices are to be sent to the address specified by the creditor, which the creditor may designate in at least two notices sent to the debtor within 90 days prior to the filing pursuant to new Section 342(c)(2) (as a practical matter, this information will likely be found in monthly statements). Creditors will also be able to file notices with the Bankruptcy Court designating an address to which bankruptcy notices are to be sent in Chapter 7 and 13 cases. Notices sent to a different address will not be effective until brought to the creditor's attention, pursuant to new Section 342(g).[9]

Sometimes a matter coming before the Bankruptcy Court by way of a motion may contain disputed issues of fact that require further hearing by the court before a ruling can be made. In these instances, the court may conduct one or more preliminary hearings, often known as status conferences; may permit the parties to conduct discovery as in a traditional lawsuit; and may ultimately conduct the equivalent of a trial, commonly known as an **evidentiary hearing**, when the trial arises from a motion.

Evidentiary hearing: a hearing held to take sworn testimony to permit a Bankruptcy Court to make a decision in a contested matter that is not a separate adversary proceeding

For example, consider that after your firm successfully files a second bankruptcy proceeding for the Cashes, Looks Like Jewelry, the jewelry store where Owen bought Robin's new engagement ring, files a proof of claim for the remaining amount due. Owen Cash now objects to the store's claim, insisting that the creditor store defrauded him into believing that the cubic zirconia he bought was really a big diamond. To resolve the matter, the court would permit the parties to conduct discovery and ultimately hold an evidentiary hearing to rule on the objection. If Owen were suing Looks Like Jewelry in a traditional lawsuit, the evidentiary hearing would be the trial.

Some matters may be applied for without a noticed motion, on an ex parte basis (without notice in certain limited circumstances). A matter that comes before the court in this manner is generally called an ex parte application. Some examples of matters that may be brought before the

8. FRBP 9014.
9. If the creditor violates the automatic stay as a result of not receiving such notice of the debtor's filing, monetary sanctions may not be imposed per Section 342(g)(2).

court on an ex parte application include conversion of a case (see chapter 9 infra), dismissal of a Chapter 13 case (see chapter 24 infra), and requests for Rule 2004 examinations (see chapter 8 infra).[10]

An ex parte application should set forth with particularity the relief sought and be accompanied by a proof of service and a proposed order.[11] All ex parte applications must be served on the debtor's attorney, the trustee, and the creditors' committee in a case where there is a creditors' committee and any other entity required by federal law or by the FRBP, including the United States Trustee. No response is required, and the court will generally enter the order requested if there is no response. The FRBPs do not set forth a response time. Typically, local rules require any response to be filed five to seven days prior to the hearing.[12]

Sometimes emergencies arise that may require court orders in less time than the rules permit. For example, a trustee is appointed the interim trustee of a restaurant or store that sells perishable goods. The trustee cannot wait 21 days or more to obtain court approval to sell the inventory. The tomatoes will get soft. The milk and eggs will spoil. The rules contemplate this sort of emergency and permit an order to be entered on less than 21 days' notice. In local procedure, such a practice may also be known as an *order shortening time*. Section 102(1)(B)(ii) specifically permits this sort of relief in appropriate circumstances.

The appendix summarizes matters that may be filed as noticed motions and matters that may be filed as ex parte applications, along with a summary of the parties to be served in each instance.

In understanding the due process provisions of the Code described in Section 102, it is helpful to identify the types of activities requiring some form of due process. It is also helpful to explore the practical implications of the imposition of due process upon both the courts and parties involved with the bankruptcy system. Affording parties due process is one of the most important and overriding features of the Bankruptcy Code.

Because virtually all of a debtor's financial affairs are placed under the jurisdiction of the court in a bankruptcy proceeding, many of a debtor's financial activities will require prior court approval. For instance, in a Chapter 11 case, a debtor will require court approval to liquidate assets, to assume or reject existing leases, and even to approve the officers'

---

10. FRBP 9013. See appendix 1 for a list of matters that may be the subject of an application for an order.
11. FRBP 9013.
12. See, e.g., Local Rule 9014-3(i) of the Eastern District of Pennsylvania (answer due 14 days after service of motion) and Local Rule 9013-(2)(a) of the District of New Jersey (answer due seven days prior to hearing). Each of these rules permits the court to enter an order if no response is filed within the response period.

salaries.[13] The trustee in a Chapter 7 case will require court approval to liquidate or abandon assets, among other things.[14]

Most matters affecting the administration of an estate will require notice to all creditors by the party seeking permission to take a specific action. Matters affecting the rights of particular parties or assets, such as a motion for relief from the automatic stay, will require notice only to affected parties. Court orders in some ex parte matters may limit the notice period and may limit the number of parties who will actually receive the notice.[15]

Court action takes time. This "legal time" is often not consistent with the logic or pace of the business world. The time involved in making business decisions is often shorter than the bankruptcy system's decision-making process. Knowing how to use the system effectively can help to synchronize these two disparate and inconsistent decision-making processes as much as possible without requiring substantial compromise. Besides, the minimum legal notice requirements cannot be compromised; they must be complied with.

B.   RULES OF GRAMMATICAL CONSTRUCTION

The remainder of Section 102 deals with various statements of grammatical or semantic construction. For example, use of the singular includes the plural.[16] This is self-explanatory. The word "or" is not exclusive.[17] This means that when the word "or" appears, its use means that any listed choice available in the affected section may apply. Proof of one given alternative will normally result in the application of the appropriate Code section in issue. Often more than one alternative may apply. For example, Section 363(f) provides five alternative means of selling a property "free and clear of liens." The existence of at least one alternative must be found to exist with regard to each lien upon the property.[18]

The words "include" and "including" are deemed to not be limiting.[19] This means that if a given Code section makes use of the words "includes" or "including," any following list provides examples of actions that may be

---

13. 11 U.S.C. §363; 11 U.S.C. §365; 11 U.S.C. §327; 11 U.S.C. §1107(b); Bankruptcy Rule 2014. See chapters 19 and 25 infra.
14. 11 U.S.C. §363; 11 U.S.C. §554. See chapters 19 and 21 infra.
15. Bankruptcy Rule 2002.
16. 11 U.S.C. §102(7).
17. 11 U.S.C. §102(5).
18. See chapter 19 infra.
19. 11 U.S.C. §102(3).

taken or proven to allow application of a particular section. If, however, actions or facts not within the given list are shown to be within the intent of the Code section involved, the additional action or facts may be considered by the court.[20]

Conspicuously absent from Section 102 is a provision stating that the masculine includes the feminine. This is because the Bankruptcy Code has been written in a gender-neutral format.

C. POWERS OF THE COURT

Section 105 concerns the court's powers. The Bankruptcy Courts have traditionally been considered courts of equity. Recall from chapter 1 of the text that composition agreements in seventeenth-century England were within the jurisdiction of the Chancery, or equity, courts. Courts of equity have always had much discretion to formulate rulings and orders to give practical effect to the matters before them. Section 105 specifically gives the Bankruptcy Court equitable authority to enact any orders that are necessary to carry out the provisions of the Bankruptcy Code.[21] Some would suggest that an argument to the court based upon Section 105 is weak, signifying no authority elsewhere in the Code to support a proposed action. In fact, a Section 105 issue may involve a request for the court to rule against a specific provision in the Code where it may not make logical sense to apply, such application not being in the best interests of the estate or creditors in a unique situation. This section is specifically designed to deal with those unique circumstances that may arise from time to time where no Code provision governs the conduct of the parties in a particular transaction, or where the court's equitable powers are necessary to enable the bankruptcy system to properly perform its intended purpose as a debt collection device to maximize creditor recoveries.[22] Thus, when formulating an argument under Section 105, the most practical method of analysis is to apply the traditional nonbankruptcy

---

20. For example, Section 1307(c) provides a list of situations that justify conversion of a Chapter 13 reorganization to a Chapter 7 liquidation. 11 U.S.C. §1307(a)(1). See chapter 24 infra.
21. 11 U.S.C. §105.
22. Section 105 represents "the broad authority granted to bankruptcy judges to take any action that is necessary or appropriate 'to prevent an abuse of process.'" Marrama v. Citizens Bank of Mass., 549 U.S. 365, 375 (2007). However, in Law v. Siegel, 134 S.Ct. 1188, 1194 (2014), the Court stressed that it was "hornbook law that §105(a) 'does not allow the bankruptcy court to override explicit mandates of other sections of the Bankruptcy Code.'" Quoting 2 Collier on Bankruptcy ¶105.01[2], p. 105–6 (16th ed. 2013).

concepts of equity balancing to the problem at hand. Reaching out to the court's inherent equitable powers is the essence of Section 105.

Practice Pointer

It is important to remember that Section 105 supplements powers already provided for under the Code. It does not create new substantive rights otherwise unavailable under the Code.[23]

Section 105(d) authorizes the court, on its own motion or at the request of a party in interest, and after notice to the parties in interest, to hold a status conference in any case and to issue any order deemed appropriate to ensure the expeditious and economic handling of a case. This provision was added to the Code in 1994 and simply codifies what had been the existing practice of many Bankruptcy Courts. Under this provision, for example, the court may monitor the status of an adversary proceeding.

D.   STATUTES OF LIMITATIONS

Section 108 concerns the effect of a bankruptcy proceeding upon non-bankruptcy statutes of limitation for any rights exercisable by the debtor or the bankruptcy estate. Section 108(a) effectively extends nonbankruptcy statutes of limitation for the protection of creditors and trustee. The reason for this is that the assets of a bankruptcy estate may include claims that a debtor has against third parties, such as personal injury claims or breach of contract claims. Sometimes, when a trustee is appointed in a proceeding, the debtor has not exercised its rights or a trustee does not immediately learn of the claim's existence. Section 108(a) therefore serves to extend any underlying nonbankruptcy statutes of limitation.

A trustee may select one of two defined limitations periods within which to proceed. The longer of the two periods may be utilized by the

---

23. Section 105 also does not serve as "an independent source of subject matter jurisdiction." In re W.R. Grace & Co., 591 F.3d 164, 170 (3d Cir. 2009).

trustee to commence an action. Under Section 108(a), the limitations period will be the later of the original expiration date of the underlying statute of limitations, or two years after the entry of the order for relief.

For example, in California the statute of limitations to commence an action for breach of a written contract is four years.[24] Assume that a bankruptcy is filed three years after a claim arises. The trustee would actually have a total of five years from the date the claim arose to bring an action on behalf of the estate, because the two-year extension provided for under Section 108(a) is later than the four-year period provided for under California law. If three years and 364 days had expired prior to the filing of the bankruptcy proceeding, the trustee would have two years and one day to bring the claim. On the other hand, if only one year has elapsed prior to the bankruptcy filing, the original four-year limitation period of nonbankruptcy law will apply because it is longer than two years after the entry of the order for relief. Finally, if the statute of limitations has expired prior to the bankruptcy filing, Section 108(a) does not revive the claim for the trustee.

In some cases, an order may have already been entered prepetition in a nonbankruptcy proceeding fixing the period to file a response, cure a default, or take some other specified action. If the period within which to take action has not already expired at the time of the debtor's bankruptcy filing, the trustee will be given until the end of that period within which to respond, or 60 days from the date of the petition, whichever is later.[25]

Practice Pointer

For example, Section 108(b) is frequently used to extend the state law period of redemption.

E.   WHO MAY BE A DEBTOR

Section 109 defines the entities that may be debtors in the various types of bankruptcy proceedings. Only *persons* may be debtors.[26] An individual is a

---

24. Cal. Code Civ. Proc. §337.
25. 11 U.S.C. §108(b).
26. 11 U.S.C. §109(a). See chapter 7 infra.

person. A corporation can be a person. A partnership can also be a person.[27] A person has to reside or be domiciled in the United States or have a place of business or property in the United States. United States citizenship, however, is not required for a person to be a debtor in bankruptcy proceedings.[28]

Practice Pointer

A "person" is defined under the Code to include individuals, corporations, and partnerships, but not governmental units.

Any person may file a bankruptcy proceeding under Chapter 7 except for railroads, insurance companies, banks, or savings and loan institutions.[29] The insurance company prohibition does not bar insurance agents from filing—only the companies actually writing the insurance policies. There are separate regulatory agencies that deal with insolvent insurance companies because there are myriad issues arising that are too complex and unusual to be considered within the purview of the bankruptcy system. For example, there are the rights of the policy holders, the rights of the claim holders, and the rights of the shareholders and other general creditors. Separate regulation pays more careful attention to these precise relationships. Similarly, banks and savings and loans are regulated when they become insolvent either by state agencies or, in the case of federally insured financial institutions, by either the Federal Savings and Loan Insurance Corporation (FSLIC), the Federal Deposit Insurance Corporation (FDIC), or their successor, the Resolution Trust Corporation (RTC). When a financial institution is taken over by a regulatory agency, it means that the institution is effectively bankrupt.

FACT PATTERN

The Cashes, as individuals, would qualify to file a Chapter 7 petition.

---

27. 11 U.S.C. §101(41). See chapter 7 infra.
28. 11 U.S.C. §109(a).
29. 11 U.S.C. §109(b).

Only municipalities may file under Chapter 9, if and only if state law permits the municipality to file a Chapter 9 bankruptcy case. States may bar municipalities from seeking Chapter 9 relief.[30]

Anyone who may be a debtor under Chapter 7 may also be a debtor under Chapter 11 except for stock brokers or commodity brokers.[31] A separate subchapter of Chapter 7 deals specifically with the issues arising when stock or commodity brokers file bankruptcy proceedings.[32] Filings of this type are most likely to occur only in those districts that are national financial centers, such as the Southern District of New York (New York City) and the District of Delaware. As a result, they are beyond the scope of this work. Railroads may file Chapter 11s. This is the only type of proceeding that railroads may file.[33]

In 1991, in Toibb v. Radloff, the U.S. Supreme Court examined whether or not an individual could qualify for Chapter 11 relief. In that case, an individual debtor not engaged in business sought Chapter 11 relief. The lower courts held that a nonbusiness debtor did not qualify for Chapter 11 relief. The Supreme Court disagreed, applying the literal language of the Code and concluding that individuals may seek Chapter 11 relief, because: "Under certain circumstances a consumer debtor's estate will be worth more if reorganized under Chapter 11 than if liquidated under Chapter 7."[34]

FACT PATTERN

The Cashes also qualify for Chapter 11 relief, but this Chapter is probably not the best choice for them. The 2005 BAPCPA legislation added Section 109(h) to the Code. This provision requires individual debtors to obtain a credit counseling certificate within the 180-day period prior to the petition filing as a prerequisite to filing, or to obtain a certificate within 30 days of filing when exigent circumstances are present. See chapter 4A supra.

The definition of who may be a debtor under Chapter 12 is described in chapter 28 infra.

There are four requirements that must be met to qualify for Chapter 13 relief. First the debtor must be an individual. *Individual* means a human

---

30. 11 U.S.C. §109(c).
31. 11 U.S.C. §109(d).
32. 11 U.S.C. §§741-766.
33. 11 U.S.C. §109(d).
34. Toibb v. Radloff, 501 U.S. 157 (1991).

being, not a partnership or corporation. Second, the debtor must have regular income. Under the Bankruptcy Act, a debtor had to be a wage earner to qualify for Chapter XIII. Under the Bankruptcy Code, a debtor need only be an individual with regular income. The following sorts of individuals can qualify to be Chapter 13 debtors: wage earners, individuals whose regular income sources are Social Security, disability, or other sorts of pensions, and individuals whose source of regular income may be dividends from trusts or stocks. Regular income can be many things. Sooner or later there is certain to be a reported proceeding where a state lottery jackpot winner will file a Chapter 13. If the jackpot to the debtor is paid over a period of time, the payments should meet the regular income requirements of Section 109.

Regular income: income sufficient and stable enough to support performance of a Chapter 13 plan by an individual; regular income is not limited to wages or salary

Regular income does not mean that the income must be the same amount whenever received. It means that the income should be received at regular intervals: once a week, once a month, once in a while. A real estate agent receiving sporadic commissions will qualify as long as the amounts earned from the commissions can be predicted with some regularity.

Third, a Chapter 13 debtor must have unsecured debts of less than $394,725. Fourth, and finally, a Chapter 13 debtor must have secured debts of less than $1,184,200. If a Chapter 13 debtor has unsecured debts of $394,725 or more or secured debts of $1,184,200 or more, the individual may not file a Chapter 13 but instead will be required to file a Chapter 11 if repayment to creditors over time is desired.

FACT PATTERN

The Cashes potentially also qualify to file for protection under Chapter 13. An analysis of the debtors' liabilities would be necessary to confirm this.

Further, Section 104(b) triennially adjusts the dollar limits contained in specified Code sections, including Section 109(e), to account for the effects of inflation. The limits stated in the text reflect the adjustment period for the three-year period beginning in 2016, which raised the respective limits from $$383,175 to $394,725 and from $1,149,525 to $1,184,200 effective on April 1, 2016.[35]

---

35. 11 U.S.C. §109(e); 11 U.S.C. §101(30); 11 U.S.C. §104(b). See n.33 supra.

Practice Pointer

To recap:

Chapter 7 debtors can be individuals, corporations, or partnerships, but not railroads, banks, or insurance companies.

Chapter 9 debtors are municipalities.

Chapter 11 debtors include anyone who could have filed under Chapter 7 plus railroads and certain banks.

Chapter 12 debtors are family farmers or family fishermen.

Chapter 13 debtors can only be individuals with regular income with less than a certain specified debt.

Section 109(g), added to the Code in 1984, exists to prevent an abuse to the system most commonly known as serial filing. A **serial filing** exists when a debtor files a bankruptcy and has it dismissed by the court (usually when the real estate is about to be foreclosed or when the repossession is about to occur after the automatic stay has been relieved). The same debtor immediately files another bankruptcy proceeding, requiring the creditor to return to court and seek relief from the automatic stay a second time. In this instance, the debtor may be attempting to abuse the system. Under Section 109(g), if the court dismisses a case because a debtor has willfully failed to abide by court orders or if a debtor dismisses a case voluntarily after a creditor obtains relief from the automatic stay, then the debtor will not qualify to file a new proceeding for 180 days.[36] In some situations, a Chapter 13 filed after receiving a Chapter 7 discharge will be permissible. (See chapter 24 infra.)

Serial filing or serial bankruptcy: a debtor who files a second (or third) bankruptcy proceeding after dismissal of one or more prior proceedings

If the Cashes file a second time, it could be considered a serial filing. Consider whether a second filing by the Cashes would have to wait 180 days since their first case was dismissed for failure to file required schedules by the court.

FACT PATTERN

---

36. 11 U.S.C. §109(g). Serial filing concerns are also addressed by Section 362(c)(3) and (c)(4) where automatic stay limitations are imposed. See chapter 11 infra.

Summary

Chapter 1 of the Bankruptcy Code sets forth basic rules of construction and definitions that apply throughout the Code.

The most important provision of Chapter 1 pertains to the due process requirements in Code practice. Most actions that require court approval will require notice to creditors and an opportunity for them to be heard either by way of a notice of intent or a formal properly noticed motion. As a result of Bankruptcy Rule 9006, the effective notice period by mail is 24 days. In exceptional circumstances, the court may approve an action without notice of a hearing or upon limited notice. An order obtained in such a manner is known as an ex parte order.

Section 105 provides Bankruptcy Courts with broad equitable powers to implement the purposes of the Bankruptcy Code.

Section 108 describes the effect of a bankruptcy proceeding on state statutes of limitation where the debtor is or may be a plaintiff.

Section 109 describes the entities that may be debtors in the various Chapter proceedings.

KEY TERMS

due process	**noticed motion**
evidentiary hearing	**regular income**
ex parte	**serial filing**
motion for relief from the	
automatic stay	

CHAPTER 5 CHECKLIST

	Authority
5.1 MOTIONS	
5.1.1 Notice and an Opportunity to Be Heard	11 U.S.C. §102(1)
5.1.2 Twenty-Four-Day Notice Requirement	Bankruptcy Rules 2002(a), 9006(f)
5.1.2.1 Include debtor's name, address, and taxpayer identification number in any notice given	§342(c)

5.1.3   Noticed Motions   FRBP 9013

         5.1.3.1   State relief sought includes   FRBP 9013
proof of service, proposed
order, affidavits

         5.1.3.2   Notice of hearing   Consult local rule

         5.1.3.3   Valuation report if value in   Consult local rule
issue

         5.1.3.4   Serve any entity against   FRBP 9013
whom relief sought or with
interest in property,
trustee, debtor, and U.S.
Trustee where required

         5.1.3.5   Response due no later than   Consult local rule
five days prior to hearing
date and served on parties
serving or served with
motion

         5.1.3.6   Response to include   Consult local rule
proposed order, report of
value if in issue, affidavits

         5.1.3.7   Court may enter order if   Consult local rule
no response filed

5.1.4   Application for an Order   FRBP 9013

         5.1.4.1   Set forth relief, proof of   FRBP 9013
service, and proposed
order

         5.1.4.2   Order may be entered if no   Consult local rule
response filed

5.2   WHO MAY BE A DEBTOR

Chapter		*Permitted Debtor*	*Exceptions*	*Authority*
5.2.1	7	Any person[37]	Railroads, insurance companies, federally insured financial institutions	11 U.S.C. §109(b)
5.2.2	9	Municipality		11 U.S.C. §109(c)

---

37. A debtor must always be a person. Persons are individuals, partnerships, or corporations. 11 U.S.C. §§101(41), 109(a).

5.2.3	11	Any person qualified to be a Chapter 7 debtor	Stockbrokers, commodity brokers, railroads[38]	11 U.S.C. §109(d)
5.2.4	12	Family farmer with regular income		11 U.S.C. §101(18), §109(f)
5.2.5	13	Individual with regular income	Unsecured debts >$394,725; secured debts >$1,184,200	11 U.S.C. §101(30), §109(e)

DISCUSSION QUESTIONS

1. Describe who may be a debtor in:

    (a) Chapter 7,

    (b) Chapter 11,

    (c) Chapter 13.

2. Why are certain industries (banking, insurance, and railroads) not permitted to file Chapter 7 proceedings?

3. What are the procedures for filing or opposing a motion?

4. What distinguishes a noticed motion from an ex parte application?

5. When may a notice period be shortened?

6. Under which Chapters could the Cashes file a bankruptcy proceeding?

---

38. Stockbroker and commodity broker liquidations have special subchapters in Chapter 7. Subchapter III of Chapter 7 (§§741-752) applies to the former. Subchapter IV of Chapter 7 (§§761-766) applies to the latter. Subchapter IV of Chapter 11 (§§1161-1174) applies to railroad proceedings.

6

Needs Based Bankruptcy or "Means Testing"

Learning Objectives

- Analyze means testing

- Describe the significant role paralegals play in the means testing process, by compiling and organizing data and assisting in performing the required calculations

- Describe the various formulas used in making the means testing calculation by discussion of the statute, form, and text examples

- Understand the need to maintain and organize the data used to perform the means testing calculations for a particular debtor

A. INTRODUCTION

Needs based bankruptcy or **means testing** is the centerpiece of the 2005 BAPCPA legislation. Means testing has fundamentally altered practice in consumer bankruptcy cases. The essence of means testing is that if an individual debtor can repay at least 25 percent of general unsecured debt over a 60-month period with minimum monthly payments of $128.33 ($7,700), or if a debtor can pay $12,850 or more over 60 months without regard to the percentage repaid, then a Chapter 7 petition is subject to dismissal for abuse unless the debtor consents to or voluntarily

Needs based bankruptcy/ Means testing: title given to formula contained in 11 U.S.C. §707(b)(2) to determine whether or not a consumer debtor is presumed to be abusing the bankruptcy system by filing a Chapter 7

converts the case to a Chapter 13.[1] Means testing may only apply if the debtor's current monthly income is greater than the applicable state median income for a household of the debtor's size.[2] However, in such an event, the court and United States Trustee may nonetheless seek dismissal of a case for abuse under 11 U.S.C. §707(b)(1), which is procedurally identical to the law as it existed prior to the 2005 legislation.[3]

Because debtors and their attorneys are subject to penalties for improperly filing a Chapter 7 that should have been filed as a Chapter 13, means testing is a threshold issue. Its nuances will determine a debtor's decision whether to file Chapter 7 or Chapter 13, and will greatly affect recommendations as to a client's options in seeking bankruptcy relief.

Means testing is a formula that determines a debtor's ability to repay a portion of unsecured debt under Chapter 13. If application of the formula determines that a debtor can repay the requisite amount of unsecured debt, it is presumed that the debtor's Chapter 7 filing is an abuse of Chapter 7, and a motion will be brought before the court to dismiss the petition. If application of the formula determines that the requisite amount of unsecured debt cannot be paid, then no presumption of abuse arises, but the court or United States Trustee may still seek dismissal for abuse without the benefit of the presumption.[4] Prior to the enactment of means testing, a Chapter 7 petition was subject to dismissal pursuant to 11 U.S.C. §707(b) only for a "substantial abuse" of Chapter 7. BAPCPA eliminated the word "substantial" from the statute in what is now 11 U.S.C. §707(b)(1). The existence of the means testing formula makes this determinant of abuse a brightline test.

B.   CURRENT MONTHLY INCOME

Current monthly income: the monthly income of a consumer debtor generally determined by the average of income received from all sources in the six months preceding the filing of a bankruptcy petition, as described in 11 U.S.C. §101(10A)

11 U.S.C. §707(b)(2)(A) contains the formula that determines when a Chapter 7 debtor's filing will be presumed an abuse of Chapter 7. The first element in the formula is the debtor's **current monthly income** as defined by Section 101(10A). This provision generally defines current

1. 11 U.S.C. §707(b)(2)(A). The amounts are subject to adjustment for inflation as per 11 U.S.C. §104(b). The amounts used in the text are those that became effective on April 1, 2016.
2. 11 U.S.C. §707(b)(7).
3. See chapter 8 infra. Perlin v. Hitachi Capital America Corp, 497 F.3d 264 (3d Cir. 2007); In re Paret, 347 B.R. 12 (Bankr. D. Del. 2007).
4. Ibid. A statutory presumption functions as a rule of evidence. When a statute creates a presumption, this generally means that if facts giving rise to the presumption exist, then the burden of proof shifts to the opposition. See, for example, Federal Rule of Evidence 301.

monthly income as a debtor's average monthly income received from all sources in the 180 days prior to filing, without regard to whether or not the income is taxable. Current monthly income also includes amounts regularly paid by an entity other than the debtor for the household expenses of the debtor or a dependent of the debtor, but does not include Social Security benefits or payments to victims of terrorism.[5]

For example, consider that Robert Banner earned $6,750 per month before being laid off three months prior to filing. He currently receives $1,400 every month in unemployment compensation and has received $4,200 since his layoff. He generally relies on receiving approximately $800 per month from piecemeal general construction work, but has only received $2,400 in the past six months, and nothing in the past three months. His father, who lives in the household, regularly contributes his $1,000 per month of Social Security benefits and his pension paycheck of $800 toward payment of the monthly household expenses. Robert's current monthly income is $5,275, consisting of a monthly average of $3,375 in compensation ($6,750 × 3 ÷ 6), $700 in unemployment ($1,400 × 3 ÷ 6), $400 in construction work ($800 × 3 ÷ 6), and $800 from his father's paycheck. Remember that Social Security benefits are excluded from the definition of current monthly income. However, his actual monthly income is only $3,200, consisting of his $1,400 unemployment compensation, his father's Social Security benefit of $1,000, and his father's $800 paycheck. The fact that Robert does not actually receive some of his "current monthly income" may or may not constitute "special circumstances" described below. Under means testing, "current monthly income" and actual income are often not identical.

> *For the Cashes, it would depend on when they file and whether Owen earned income during the winter months immediately prior to filing from his snow removal work, from the sale of collectibles, and/or if Robin earned income during this same period.*

FACT PATTERN

Robert's current monthly income multiplied by 12 is $63,300. This monthly income is disclosed on Official Form 122A-1. If this amount exceeds the median income of his state for a household of two, then in a Chapter 7 Robert must complete Official Form 122A-2, which contains the other necessary means testing calculations. If his current monthly income is equal to or less than the median income for his state, then

---

5. 11 U.S.C. §101(10A).

his Chapter 7 is not subject to dismissal for abuse under means testing.[6] Chapter 31 below is a means testing tutorial.

FACT PATTERN

Owen's household size may be an unknown variable that would need to be addressed. At the time of filing, Owen's dad is in a nursing home and Owen is more or less separated from his wife Robin.

Median family income: the most current figures provided by the Bureau of the Census as set forth in 11 U.S.C. §101(39A)

Median family income is defined as income calculated and reported by the Census Bureau for a family of similar size for the most recent year available, adjusted by the Consumer Price Index.[7] These amounts are adjusted frequently. The amounts currently applicable may be found on the United States Trustee Program Internet website: www.justice.gov/ust. Links may also be found on many local bankruptcy court websites.

Practice Pointer

Information important to means testing which changes on a regular basis, such as household median income and allowable expenses as calculated by various IRS collection standards, can be found on the United States Trustee Program website: www.justice.gov/ust.

C.   DEDUCTIONS

The second step in the formula is to deduct three groups of expenses from the current monthly income. The first group of deductions is the debtor's monthly expenses as calculated according to Internal Revenue Service collection guidelines, excluding payments for debts. Some of these standards are national, and some are local. There are national standards for day-to-day expenses, health care expenses, local expenses for housing and utilities, local expenses for transportation ownership and operation, and other necessary expenses.[8] Currently applicable amounts may be found

---

6. 11 U.S.C. §707(b)(7).
7. 11 U.S.C. §101(39A).
8. 11 U.S.C. §707(b)(2)(A)(ii)(I).

on the United States Trustee Program website. Links may also be found on many local bankruptcy court websites. The Forms Disk includes links.

In Ransom v. FIA Card Services, 562 U.S. 61 (2011), the Supreme Court held that an expense deduction may not be taken as part of the debtor's means test if the debtor has no such costs: "Expenses that are wholly fictional are not easily thought of as reasonably necessary." When he filed Chapter 13, Ransom owned his car free and clear. He claimed a vehicle ownership expense deduction even though the IRS collection guidelines only permit one if the debtor is making a loan or lease payment. Resolving a conflict in the circuits, the Court explained: "Because Congress intended the means test to approximate the debtor's reasonable expenditures on essential items, a debtor should be required to qualify for a deduction by actually incurring an expense in the relevant category."

The following additional amounts are also included in this group of expenses: an additional utility allowance if in excess of IRS allowances and documentation is provided; actual expenses paid for the care and support of an elderly or disabled household member or immediate family member; the actual expense of a dependent child, up to $1,925 per year for private school tuition; and the amount of expense incurred to pay a Chapter 13 trustee in a Chapter 13, up to 10 percent of Plan payments (depending on the judicial district).[9]

Would Owen be able to claim any of the expenses associated with his father under this section?

FACT PATTERN

The second group of deductions is the debtor's average monthly payments contractually due to secured creditors during the 60-month period following the petition. The payments to be made are totaled and then divided by 60. Thus, even if a car loan will be paid off in 24 months, the formula treats the total being paid over 60 months. For example, if the monthly payment is $300 and 24 payments remain when the bankruptcy is filed, then the formula treats the monthly payment as $120 ($300 × 24 ÷ 60 = $120). Additionally, cure payments for arrearages that would be made in a Chapter 13 for loans secured by the debtor's primary residence, and secured loans necessary for the support of a debtor or dependent are aggregated and divided by 60.[10]

The third group of deductions is the debtor's expenses for payment of priority claims (claims payable pursuant to 11 U.S.C. §507(a)), such as

---

9. 11 U.S.C. §707(b)(2)(A)(ii)(II)-(V).
10. 11 U.S.C. §707(b)(2)(A)(iii).

priority taxes or unpaid support or alimony. These expenses are totaled and divided by 60. The quotient is deducted from current monthly income.[11]

FACT PATTERN

Recall that Owen owes $125 a week in child support and he was six months behind at the time that he filed his first petition. This number would need to be updated.

Surplus monthly income: amount of monthly income available to repay unsecured creditors pursuant to means testing

If the amount of **surplus monthly income** available to a debtor after subtracting allowable deductions, multiplied by 60, would permit general unsecured creditors to be paid at least 25 percent of their claims or $7,700, or $12,850 or more over a 60-month period, without regard to the percentage repaid, then the Chapter 7 filing is presumed an abuse of Chapter 7. Stated another way, if a debtor can repay at least 25 percent over a 60-month period with minimum monthly payments of $128.33 ($7,700), or if a debtor can pay $12,850 or more over 60 months without regard to the percentage repaid, then abuse is presumed.[12] This means that if a motion is brought to dismiss the case as an abuse and the formula triggers the presumption of abuse, then the burden of proof shifts to the debtor to show that the filing is not an abuse.

For example, assume in the above example that Robert Banner is a family of two (himself and his 66-year-old father) living in New Castle County, Delaware. Since his annualized current monthly income of $63,300 exceeds the allowable median income of $62,567 for two people living in Delaware, Robert must fully complete Form 122A-2. He owes his unsecured creditors $20,000. His monthly mortgage including property taxes is $1,200. He is two payments behind. He has a $250 per month truck payment. The loan has 36 payments remaining. He is two payments behind. Based upon the IRS standards in effect as of April 1, 2016, Robert is allowed a National Standards allowance of $1,083, health care expenses of $184, a non-mortgage allowance of $577 and a housing allowance of $1,260, a transportation allowance of $270, and an ownership allowance of $471, for a total of $3,845. His monthly mortgage payment is $1,200. He will use the National Standard allowance amount instead of his actual mortgage because it is the higher of the two amounts, and he may not deduct the same expense twice. The mortgage cure amount of $2,400 is

---

11. 11 U.S.C. §707(b)(2)(A)(iv).
12. 11 U.S.C. §707(b)(2)(A)(i). The amounts are subject to adjustment for inflation as per 11 U.S.C. §104(b). The amounts in the text are the amounts that became effective on April 1, 2016.

divided by 60 and is $40 per month. Similarly, the car ownership expense of $471 is greater than his average monthly payment of $150, so the higher of the two expenses is used. The car payment cure amount of $500 is divided by 60 and is $8.33. This increases his allowable monthly expenses to $3,893.33. Subtracting this amount from his current monthly income of $5,275 results in monthly disposable income of $1,381.67. To this amount would be added an additional nominal deduction represented to be a hypothetical payment to a Chapter 13 trustee. According to the formula, Robert must either dismiss his case or convert it to a Chapter 13.

D. SPECIAL CIRCUMSTANCES

A debtor may rebut the presumption that a case is an abuse of Chapter 7 only by demonstrating the existence of "special circumstances" requiring an adjustment to current monthly income. To establish "special circumstances," a debtor must itemize each additional expense, provide documentation for each expense, and provide a detailed explanation of the special circumstances making the expense reasonable. The standard set forth in the statute is that the special circumstance must be like ". . . a serious medical condition or call to active duty military service." In the example, for instance, if Robert's unemployment runs out and he does not have a job, he will not have sufficient income to fund a plan. Deciding whether or not actually being broke is a special circumstance will be up to the courts. The debtor must attest to the accuracy of the information provided. The presumption of abuse is only rebutted if, after explaining and accounting for all the special circumstances, the debtor is unable to make the minimum payment required by the means testing formula. If he can still make the minimum payment the presumption is not rebutted.[13]

E. "TOTALITY OF CIRCUMSTANCES"

Even if a debtor successfully rebuts the presumption created by the means testing formula, the statute still permits dismissal as an abuse of Chapter 7

---

13. 11 U.S.C. §707(b)(2)(B).

if, for example, the debtor has filed the petition in bad faith or, if under the totality of circumstances, the filing is an abuse of Chapter 7. In practice, if the debtor's actual monthly income less the debtor's actual monthly expenses leaves disposable monthly income that would permit repayment of a substantial portion of unsecured debt over a 60-month period, under the "totality of the circumstances," abuse is more likely to be found. A below-median-income debtor's case is subject to dismissal for abuse under this provision.[14]

F. PROCEDURE

The court, the United States Trustee, the trustee, or any party in interest may bring a motion to dismiss a case as an abuse of Chapter 7, if the debtor's current monthly income exceeds the applicable state median income for a particular debtor. If the debtor's income is less than the applicable state median, then no party in interest or the court may bring a motion to dismiss under means testing.[15] The United States Trustee is to review the debtor's schedules and file a statement within ten days after the meeting of creditors indicating whether the case should be presumed an abuse of Chapter 7. Typically, this notification is entered into the court docket electronically. If the notification indicates that the case is presumed to be an abuse of Chapter 7, then the United States Trustee must either file an appropriate motion within 30 days or a further report indicating the reasons why such a motion would not be appropriate.[16]

    If a motion to dismiss for abuse of Chapter 7 is granted, and the court finds that the debtor was not substantially justified in filing Chapter 7, then the court may award the trustee attorneys' fees and costs. The debtor's attorney is subject to FRBP 9011 and sanctions for failing to properly investigate a debtor's financial affairs and in not assessing the case as an abuse of Chapter 7.[17] Alternatively, the court may also award a debtor attorneys' fees and costs if the court finds that a motion brought by a

---

14. 11 U.S.C. §707(b)(3). See Perlin v. Hitachi Capital America Corp., 497 F.3d 264 (3d Cir. 2007); In re Lanza, 450 B.R. 81 (Bankr. M.D. Pa 2011).
15. 11 U.S.C. §707(b)(6)(7). The case still remains subject to dismissal under the totality of circumstances as discussed above.
16. 11 U.S.C. §704(b). FRBP 1017(e) requires the motion to be filed within 60 days of the date first set for the meeting of creditors.
17. 11 U.S.C. §707(b)(4).

party in interest other than the United States Trustee or trustee was not substantially justified or that the motion was brought solely to coerce a debtor into waiving a right guaranteed by the Bankruptcy Code. This latter provision, however, will not apply to small businesses (businesses with 25 or fewer employees) with claims of less than $1,300.[18]

Practice Pointer

Practitioners should carefully maintain all the source material used to compute the various means testing calculations, so they can quickly corroborate how a particular item was calculated.

Means testing can be a difficult concept and raises many issues. The scope of the inquiry that counsel must conduct to avoid sanctions is problematic. To the extent that means testing requires bankruptcy practitioners to resort, on a regular basis, to materials outside of the bankruptcy system (IRS regulations and Census Bureau data), the bankruptcy system is no longer entirely self-contained.

G.   NEEDS BASED BANKRUPTCY EXAMPLES

Practice Pointer

The reader should locate the applicable median income and IRS expense allowance deductions on the United States Trustee website, www.justice.gov/ust, and refer to them when reading the examples below.

Example 1

Anthony Starke, of Montgomery County, Pennsylvania, lost his $132,000 per year job at an engineering firm two months ago. He has since been collecting $2,000 per month in unemployment. The

---

18. 11 U.S.C. §707(b)(5).

unemployment runs out in two months. His spouse does not work. They have two children, Bill and Ted, ages 10 and 12. Since Starke was laid off, the Starkes have missed one $2,000 payment on their mortgage in favor of the Shield Mortgage Co. Shield is threatening foreclosure of their home. They own a 2014 Chevrolet Blazer for which they make monthly payments of $500 to Justice Acceptance Corporation. They are current on their car payments. They have 20 more payments to make. They owe the Internal Revenue Service $1,500 for unpaid 2015 taxes, which they could not pay after Anthony was laid off. They have $20,000 in credit card debt.

The first step is to determine Starke's current monthly income. Starke worked for four of the past six months receiving $11,000 per month, earning $44,000. He has collected two months of unemployment benefits at $2,000 per month, receiving $4,000. Since current monthly income is the average of income from all sources during the six-month period preceding the petition, both figures need to be added together and divided by six, resulting in current monthly income of $8,000. Assuming a median income of $86,112 for a household of four in Pennsylvania, since Starke's annual income of $96,000 exceeds the median allowable income, then Starke must fully complete the version of Official Form 122 applicable to the Chapter filed.[19]

The next step is to deduct allowable expenses from Starke's current monthly income. Looking up the IRS national standards for living expenses permits Starke to deduct $1,509, health care expenses of $216, non-mortgage housing and utility expenses of $770, mortgage expenses of $1,914, $270 in motor vehicle operating expenses for one car, and $471 for an ownership expense, equaling deductions of $5,150 per month. However, since the statute excludes payments for debts, Starke may not use the IRS mortgage/rent expense allowances because his mortgage payment is higher; and to allow two deductions otherwise would create duplication.[20] Similarly, from the $471 ownership allowance, deduct the average monthly payment of $166.67. The total allowable expenses in this group are now $4,983.33. Starke may also deduct other necessary expenses, which minimally includes all of the

---

19. In Chapter 7 cases, Official Forms 122A-1 and 122A-2 apply; in Chapter 11, Form 122B applies; and in Chapter 13 Forms 122C-1 and 122C-2 apply. All consumer debtors must complete the applicable form to the extent applicable. Since most debtors are under median, they will only need to complete those portions applicable to determining current monthly income. The income and expense figures used in the text are those in effect for the period commencing April 1, 2016.

20. In re Hardacre, 338 B.R. 718 (Bankr. N.D. Tex. 2006).

taxes that were withheld from his paycheck. For purposes of this example, assume that this amount is $2,500 per month.

Pursuant to 11 U.S.C. §707(b)(2)(A)(iii), the Starkes must average their secured debt repayments for the next 60 months. Their average mortgage payment is $2,000.00. Twenty payments of $500 remaining on the car total $10,000. Dividing this by 60 results in an average car payment of $166.67. The payments necessary to cure the mortgage default may also be accounted for, resulting in an additional monthly expense of $33.33 ($2,000/60 = $33.33).

Payments on any priority debt that Starke would have to repay in a Chapter 13 represent a final allowable deduction from current monthly income pursuant to 11 U.S.C. §707(b)(2)(A)(iv). The tax liability for 2015 fits in this category. $1,500 divided by 60 is $25.

To summarize:

Current monthly income	$8,000.00
Deduct:	
National and Local Standards	$4,983.33
Taxes	$2,500.00
Car payment over 60 months	$166.67
Cure of defaults	$58.33
Surplus monthly income	$291.67

According to the formula, the Starkes have a surplus monthly income of $291.67. From this amount, the Starkes would be able to deduct an administrative expense multiplier representing fees that would be paid to a hypothetical Chapter 13 trustee, based on a monthly payment of $291.67. The administrative expense multiplier for the Eastern District of Pennsylvania is 8.6 percent, or $25.08, lowering the Starkes' surplus monthly income to $266.59.

Since the Starkes can pay their general unsecured creditors at least $266.59 per month for 60 months ($266.59 × 60 = $15,995.40), and since the total of $15,995.40 that can be paid exceeds $7,700 and would pay the Starkes' unsecured creditors at least 25 percent, the presumption of abuse exists pursuant to the means testing formula. The court, the United States Trustee, panel trustee, or any party in interest may bring a motion to dismiss for abuse because Starke's current monthly income exceeds the state median for a household of four. Starke may attempt to rebut the presumption of abuse by explaining to the court the special circumstances that his unemployment of $2,000 per month runs out in two months and his actual income will then be zero. If the court does not consider this a special circumstance, Starke must either dismiss his case or convert it to a Chapter 13.

Example 2

Steve Rogers earns $80,000 per year at Catch-22 Software in Santa Clara County, California. He recently had a personal injury judgment entered against him for $100,000. The judgment is not covered by any insurance. Rogers owes $50,000 in credit cards and $20,000 in unpaid child support for a child who does not live with him. He has a spouse and one child, Bucky. His mortgage payments of $4,000 per month are current. His car payment of $700 per month is current. There are 60 payments left. Rogers wants to file Chapter 7 to discharge the judgment and credit card debt.

First, calculate Rogers' current monthly income. $80,000 divided by 12 is $6,666.67. Since $80,000 exceeds the median California income for a household of three of $70,816, Rogers must complete Form 122A-2.

Second, deduct the Monthly National Standards for a family of three of $1,249, health care expenses of $162, a non-mortgage rent expense of $563, plus a vehicle operating expense allowance of $276. Since Rogers' monthly mortgage payment of $4,000 is greater than the allowable housing expense deduction of $2,830, Rogers will deduct the greater of the two. Similarly, he will not be entitled to an ownership expense deduction for his car payment, because the average payment of $700 exceeds the ownership allowance of $471, for a total living expense deduction of $2,250.

Assume that $2,000 per month is deducted from his paycheck for various taxes and other mandatory deductions. The average monthly payments for 60 months to secured creditors are $4,700 ($4,000 + $700). The child support claim would be a priority claim in Chapter 13. $20,000 divided by 60 is $333.33.

To summarize:

Current Monthly Income	$6,667.67
Deduct	
National and Local Standards	$2,250.00
Taxes	$2,000.00
Mortgage/Car payment over 60 mos.	$4,700.00
Child support claim over 60 mos.	$333.33
Surplus monthly income	($2,615.66)

Rogers' allowable deductions total $9,283.33, substantially exceeding his current monthly income of $6,666.67. Thus, no presumption of abuse will arise if Rogers seeks Chapter 7 relief. Keep in mind also that there are additional deductions from current monthly income that have not been included in these examples.

Summary

Means testing places limitations on the choice of Chapter under which individual consumer debtors may file by essentially requiring conversion to a Chapter 13 or dismissal of the case if application of the means testing formula creates a presumption of abuse by the filing of a Chapter 7. The essence of means testing is that if an individual debtor can repay at least 25 percent of general unsecured debt over a 60-month period with minimum monthly payments of $128.33 ($7,700) or if a debtor can pay $12,850 or more over 60 months without regard to the percentage repaid, then a Chapter 7 petition is subject to dismissal for abuse unless the debtor consents to or voluntarily converts the case to a Chapter 13.

The complete means testing formula must be completed if a debtor's current monthly income exceeds the state median family income for a household of similar size. Deductions are made from current monthly income for basic monthly living expenses according to the Internal Revenue standards for collecting taxes from delinquent taxpayers. Additional deductions for the payment of secured debts and for various other expenses permitted by the statute will determine if a debtor has sufficient surplus monthly income to trigger the presumption of abuse. A debtor may attempt to rebut the presumption of abuse upon a showing of "special circumstances."

Even if a debtor "passes" the means test, the case may remain subject to dismissal for abuse under the "totality of circumstances," or if the petition is filed in "bad faith."

A motion to dismiss for abuse, whether presumed abuse or the totality of the circumstances, must be brought within 60 days from the date first set for the meeting of creditors. Debtor's counsel is subject to potential sanctions if a motion is brought and granted, and counsel did not adequately confirm the debtor's representations. Alternatively, a moving party in interest that is a creditor is subject to sanctions for bringing an unsuccessful motion to dismiss or convert that is not well founded.

KEY TERMS

current monthly income	needs based bankruptcy
means testing	surplus monthly income
median family income	

CHAPTER 6 CHECKLIST

		Authority
6.1	NEEDS BASED BANKRUPTCY	11 U.S.C. §707(b)(2)
6.1.1	Calculate debtor's current monthly income	§707(b)(2)(A)(i)
6.1.2	Deduct IRS expense allowance	§707(b)(2)(A)(ii)
6.1.3	Deduct average 60-month debt service	§707(b)(2)(A)(iii)
6.1.4	Deduct priority claims paid over 60 months	§707(b)(2)(A)(iv)
6.1.5	Subtract the sum of 6.1.2–6.1.4 from 6.1.1	
6.1.6	Abuse is presumed if surplus monthly income permits repayment of 25 percent over 60 months with minimum payments of $128.33, or if debtor can repay $12,850 or more without regard to percent repaid	§707(b)(2)(A)(i)
6.1.7	Special circumstances may permit deviation	§707(b)(2)(B)

DISCUSSION QUESTIONS

1. What is meant by the phrase "needs based bankruptcy" or "means testing?"

2. What is "current monthly income?"

3. What purpose or purposes does the concept of means testing serve?

4. Does means testing foster debtor relief or debt collection?

5. What is dismissal for abuse based on the totality of circumstances?

6. What are the risks to a practitioner who fails to adequately investigate a debtor's financial affairs before filing a case? What, in your opinion, would constitute an adequate investigation?

PRACTICE EXERCISES

Exercise 6.1
Complete the Form B122A-2 Chapter 7 Means Test Calculations for the
Cashes.

Exercise 6.2
Complete Schedules B106I & J for the Cashes.

7

Useful Definitions — Section 101

Learning Objectives

- Define a number of important terms as they are used throughout the Bankruptcy Code

- Contrast and compare a *debt* with a *claim*

- Identify the different usages of the term *lien* as it is used in the Bankruptcy Code

Section 101 is often overlooked when conducting bankruptcy research. This is probably because many practitioners do not normally use Section 101 on a regular basis since it does not contain familiar substantive rules of bankruptcy law. Nevertheless, Section 101 is critical because it contains definitions of many terms that are used frequently throughout the Code. Reference to a Section 101 definition will sometimes save substantial research time and will help to explicitly resolve questions only answered implicitly by other Code provisions. This chapter is an analysis of the definitions used most frequently in all aspects of bankruptcy practice. This knowledge also helps in acquiring a basic understanding of the Bankruptcy Code and system.

A.   AFFILIATES

Section 101(2) defines *affiliates*. Affiliates are (1) nondebtor entities that own or control a 20 percent or more interest in a debtor, (2) nondebtor entities in which a debtor owns or controls 20 percent or more of the ownership interest, and (3) nondebtor entities that control or operate substantially all of a debtor's assets.[1] Affiliates may or may not be debtors. Affiliates may or may not also be insiders of a debtor. The distinction between affiliates and insiders acquires significance in the area of a trustee's avoiding powers and in the Code's distributive provisions.[2]

For example, Engulf and Devour, Inc., is the owner of more than 20 percent each of ten smaller entities. If Engulf and Devour files a Chapter 11, all of the smaller entities are affiliates. If one of the smaller entities files a proceeding by itself, Engulf and Devour would be a nondebtor affiliate.

B.   CLAIM

Section 101(5) defines *claim*. Because a primary function of the bankruptcy system is to determine and pay dividends upon claims, it is germane to know when a transaction is considered to be a claim. Although the Code definition appears lengthy and complex, it may be translated into two simple sentences. First, a claim is a right to payment of any kind, whether or not the amount has been previously determined or liquidated.[3] Second, a claim may also be a right to performance if the debtor's breach can be compensated by monetary damages, whether or not the amount has been previously determined.[4] A claim is considered liquidated when it has been reduced to a fixed sum.

FACT PATTERN

For example, the individuals who had property damage as a result of Owen Cash's drunk driving would hold unliquidated claims even if the matters had not yet gone to trial or had been otherwise resolved.

---

1. 11 U.S.C. §101(2).
2. See chapters 16-18 and 22 infra.
3. Most courts consider as a prerequisite that the claimant's "exposure" to the product or incident occur prepetition to qualify as a claim for bankruptcy purposes. See In re Grossman's Inc., 607 F.3d 114, 125 (3d Cir. 2010).
4. 11 U.S.C. §101(5).

> ### *Practice Pointer*
> Courts commonly turn to state law to
> determine the point at which an under-
> lying cause of action accrues.

C. COMMUNITY CLAIM

Section 101(7) defines *community claim* to mean: a claim against the debtor that would be enforceable against community property under non-bankruptcy law.[5] This is of importance in those states utilizing community property law.[6] A debtor's discharge will normally effectuate a discharge on all of the debtor's community property, even if one member of the community has not filed a proceeding.[7]

D. CORPORATION

Section 101(9) defines *corporation*. A corporation is a business organized and registered according to nonbankruptcy or state law. The definition also includes associations that have all the powers of corporations under state law but are not incorporated under state law, such as unincorporated associations or business trusts.[8] For example, an unincorporated labor union is considered a corporation under the Bankruptcy Code.

E. CREDITOR

Section 101(10) defines *creditor*. The definition of *creditor* is a corollary to the definition of *claim*. A creditor is normally an entity with a claim that

---

5. 11 U.S.C. §101(7).
6. California, Arizona, New Mexico, Texas, Louisiana, Idaho, Nevada, Washington, and Wisconsin. Puerto Rico also has community property laws, and Alaska is an opt-in community property state.
7. See chapter 8 infra.
8. 11 U.S.C. §101(9).

arises before the petition is filed.[9] This is known, more simply, as a pre-petition claim. Entities whose claims arise after filing are not generally considered creditors for purposes of payment through the bankruptcy estate and are not affected by the bankruptcy proceeding except in several specific instances described elsewhere in this text.[10] A creditor not affected by a filing generally does not have its claim discharged and is generally not entitled to participate in any distribution of dividends.

F.   CURRENT MONTHLY INCOME

An individual debtor's *current monthly income* is defined to include the debtor's average monthly income, from all sources, received in the six months preceding the filing of a bankruptcy petition as set forth in 11 U.S.C. §101(10A). This includes any amount received on a regular basis from any household member for payment of household expenses, excluding Social Security payments and payments to war crimes victims. Current monthly income is utilized to determine the applicability of means testing for an individual debtor. See chapter 6 supra.

For example, Henry Pimm lives with his spouse and three children. Two of the children are his wife's children from a former marriage. Henry receives $700 per month in SSI income. His wife, Janet, receives $3,000 wages that started three months ago. The family received food stamp assistance in the amount of $300 per month, but this ended two months ago. Janet is also entitled to receive $250 per month in child support, but she hasn't received any payments in three months. To determine Henry's current monthly income, each of the above amounts must be averaged for six months. Multiply each amount by the number of months actually received, divide by six, and then total the results. In the example, the Pimms' current monthly income is $1,825, calculated as follows: (($3,000 × 3) + (300 × 4) + ($250 × 3) = $10,950) ÷ 6 = $1,825. Note that Henry's SSI income is not included.

---

9. 11 U.S.C. §101(10).
10. See chapters 9 and 22 infra. See also 11 U.S.C. §348(d); 11 U.S.C. §502(f), (g), (h), (i); 11 U.S.C. §503.

G.   CUSTODIAN

Section 101(11) defines *custodian*: a third party appointed to administer assets of a debtor outside of the bankruptcy system. *Custodian* is a term of art used in the Bankruptcy Code to distinguish state court receivers, and others similarly situated, from bankruptcy trustees. A state court receiver appointed before the filing or an assignee for the benefit of creditors are the most common custodians encountered in bankruptcy practice. The trustees of a business trust are also custodians.[11]

H.   DEBT

Section 101(12) defines *debt* as a liability on a claim.[12] That is, a debt is the legal obligation to pay a certain amount owed to the holder of a claim. A claim is what a creditor says it is owed; a debt is simply the existence of the obligation to pay. Ultimately, the two definitions are no more than two perspectives regarding an identical transaction or event. Debts that are discharged in bankruptcy are no longer owed to the creditor by the debtor, regardless of the amount of the claim that was asserted with respect to that debt.

I.   DEBT RELIEF AGENCY

A *debt relief agency*, as defined under 11 U.S.C. §101(12A), is essentially an individual consumer debtor's bankruptcy attorney or bankruptcy petition preparer (see chapter 8 infra).[13] Debt relief agencies are required to provide individual consumer debtors with written retainer agreements and the various prepetition notices described at chapter 4A supra.

---

11. 11 U.S.C. §101(11).
12. 11 U.S.C. §101(12).
13. Additionally, §101(3A) defines most individual consumer debtors as "assisted persons." An assisted person is an individual consumer debtor with less than $192,450 in nonexempt assets. This definition includes most consumer debtors. The amount is subject to triannual adjustment pursuant to 11 U.S.C. §104(b). Section 101(4A) defines "bankruptcy assistance" as goods or services provided to an assisted person for the purpose of providing advice or representation with respect to a bankruptcy case.

FACT PATTERN

Would Jimmy Bond qualify as a debt relief agency notwithstanding his attempts to distance himself from disclosure in the Cashes' first bankruptcy filing?

 Practice Pointer

In 2010, the Supreme Court in Milavetz, Gallop & Milavetz, P.A. v. U.S., 130 S. Ct. 1324, 1333 (2010), resolved a circuit split by holding that "attorneys who provide bankruptcy assistance to assisted persons are debt relief agencies within the meaning of the BAPCPA."

J.   DOMESTIC SUPPORT OBLIGATIONS

A *domestic support obligation* is defined in Section §101(14A) as an obligation owed for the payment of spousal support, child support, or maintenance, whether or not the unpaid amount accrued before or after the filing of the bankruptcy petition.

FACT PATTERN

Considering that Owen was never married to Helen, would Owen's court ordered child support for Lottie still qualify as a DSO?

K.   EQUITY SECURITY HOLDER

Section 101(17) defines *equity security holder*: an entity owning an interest in a debtor.[14] The shareholders of a corporation are its equity security holders. The partners of a partnership are its equity security holders. Equity security holders normally receive dividends from a bankruptcy estate only after all other creditors are paid in full.[15]

---

14. 11 U.S.C. §101(16), (17).
15. See chapter 23 infra.

L.   INDIVIDUAL WITH REGULAR INCOME

Section 101(30) defines *individual with regular income*. The meaning of this phrase has been previously described in chapter 5 supra. It includes individuals who have "regular" income that is "sufficiently stable" to make monthly payments to the trustee under a Chapter 13 plan.

> ***In light of the fact that Owen's work is seasonal, would he still be considered an individual with regular income?***

FACT PATTERN

M.   INSIDERS

Section 101(31) defines *insiders*. Insiders are generally those entities in control of a debtor, or the debtor's relatives. The exact definition of an *insider* varies depending upon whether the debtor is an individual, a corporation, or a partnership. However, the basic principle is the same throughout. Those who are in control of, or who are related to, a debtor (in a family or business sense) are normally considered insiders.[16] Thus, the officers and directors of a bankrupt corporation are insiders of the corporation. The corporation is also an insider of any officer or director who files a proceeding. Partners are insiders of one another. For example, Alicia Florik and Will Gardner are insiders to one another because they are partners of Lockhart and Gardner. If they were married they would also be insiders because they would then be relatives.

An insider relationship between a debtor and creditor can affect the priority of dividend distribution to the insider creditor.[17] Insider status will also affect the time limits for certain transactions that may be avoidable by a trustee.[18] It is erroneous to believe that insiders and equity security holders are synonymous. They are not. An insider may or may not be an equity security holder. An equity security holder may or may not be an insider. For example, Lester Cash owns one share of IBM. He is therefore an equity security holder of IBM but not an insider. On the other hand, if IBM's president, Ginni Rometty, owns no IBM stock, she is considered an insider of IBM but not an equity security holder.

---

16. 11 U.S.C. §101(31).
17. See chapter 23 infra.
18. See chapters 16-18 infra.

N.   INSOLVENT

Section 101(32) defines *insolvent*. An entity is normally insolvent when the entity's liabilities (debts) exceed the value of its assets (property). This is a common accountancy definition of *insolvent* and is also commonly known as "balance sheet insolvency." This definition will suffice for most bankruptcy purposes. However, for purposes of the Code, the value of exempt and fraudulently transferred property is specifically excluded when performing this calculation.[19]

A partnership is insolvent if its debts are greater than the value of the partnership assets, excluding any fraudulently transferred assets, plus the net worth of each general partner, determined independently of the partnership in issue.[20] This method of calculation is consistent with the common law principle that a general partner is personally liable for partnership debts. For example, the Huey, Dewey, and Louie partnership has assets with a value of 25. The partnership has liabilities of 20. It is solvent. The partners fraudulently transfer assets with a value of 15 to Uncle Scrooge. The partnership is now insolvent, without considering the partners' net worth. Each partner, exclusive of the partnership, has a net worth of 1. The total asset value is now 13 (the total value of the partnership assets and each partner's net worth). The value of the fraudulently transferred asset is not included in the computation. Because the debt owed is still 20, the partnership's liabilities (20) exceed its assets (13), and the partnership is deemed insolvent under the Code.

Historically, a debtor had to be insolvent to be bankrupt. However, the Code does not require that a debtor be insolvent to file a petition.[21] Insolvency is absent from the Section 109 requirements of who may be a debtor.[22] Nor is insolvency an element of proof required to obtain the entry of an order for relief against a debtor in an involuntary proceeding. Proving that a debtor is not generally paying its debts as they become due does not necessarily imply that a debtor is insolvent. As described in chapter 4 supra, situations may arise where a solvent entity can have an order for relief entered against it in an involuntary proceeding. It is therefore erroneous to believe that a debtor must be insolvent to be bankrupt. Under the Code, the insolvency of a debtor is normally only a specific

---

19. 11 U.S.C. §101(32)(A).
20. 11 U.S.C. §101(32)(B).
21. The exception to this rule is in the context of municipalities filing for bankruptcy under Chapter 9. 11 U.S.C. §109(c).
22. See chapter 4 supra.

issue to determine in connection with the application of certain of the trustee's avoiding powers.[23]

O.   JUDICIAL LIEN

Section 101(36) defines a *judicial lien*: a lien obtained by virtue of a court order or judgment. It can be a judgment, a prejudgment writ of attachment, or a postjudgment writ of execution.[24]

> ***Assuming there is a delay in filing the second bankruptcy petition for the Cashes, which creditors would be likely to seek a judgment and/or judicial lien against them?***

FACT PATTERN

P.   LIEN

Section 101(37) defines a *lien* to mean: a charge against or a right to property to secure repayment of a debt or the performance of an obligation.[25] A lien in this sense may be either a judicial, consensual, or statutory lien. A trust deed or mortgage on real estate or a bank's security interest in a vehicle is a consensual lien. A mechanic's or landlord's lien is a statutory lien. A judicial lien has just been described above. The common factor of these various rights is that they all create liens, legally enforceable interests in property to secure repayment or performance of an obligation. The Code also contains some fine distinctions between the various types of liens.

> ***Assuming they are properly recorded, the mortgage held by Second American Trust & Loan Co. and the line of credit by Third American Trust & Loan Co. would constitute consensual liens against the Cash home.***

FACT PATTERN

---

23. See chapters 16-18 infra.
24. 11 U.S.C. §101(36).
25. 11 U.S.C. §101(37).

Q.   MEDIAN FAMILY INCOME

Section 101(39A) defines *median family income* as the median income most recently calculated and reported by the Bureau of the Census, or if not currently calculated and reported, the most recently calculated and reported amount, adjusted upward by the Consumer Price Index.

R.   PERSON

Section 101(41) defines a *person* to include: any kind of entity, individual, partnership, or corporation, except a governmental unit.[26] However, a governmental unit is considered a person when it has acquired rights in connection with a loan guaranty agreement and seeks placement on a Chapter 11 creditors' committee.[27] This definition, however, should not be construed to mean that governmental units are unaffected by operation of the Bankruptcy Code. Governmental units that are creditors are affected as much by the Bankruptcy Code as private creditors. Section 106 specifically waives any sovereign immunity of a governmental unit when the governmental unit is a claimant.[28]

 Practice Pointer

Note that there is a distinction between a "person" and an "individual." An "individual" can only be a "person," but a "person" encompasses more than just an "individual."

---

26. 11 U.S.C. §101(41).
27. 11 U.S.C. §101(41); 11 U.S.C. §1102.
28. 11 U.S.C. §106. In United States v. Nordic Village, Inc., 503 U.S. 30 (1992), the Supreme Court held that 11 U.S.C. §106 does not act to waive the sovereign immunity of the federal government to permit the recovery of money claims. A similar ruling was applied to the states in Hoffman v. Connecticut Dept. of Income Maint., 492 U.S. 96 (1989). Section 106 was completely rewritten in 1994 to overrule these holdings. The revised Section 106 constitutes, for all practical purposes, an effective waiver of sovereign immunity in bankruptcy cases. Pub. L. No. 103-394 §113 (1994). However, as a result of the Supreme Court's ruling in Seminole Tribe of Florida v. Florida, 517 U.S. 44 (1996) (a nonbankruptcy case), numerous courts have held that Section 106, even as rewritten, remains in violation of the Eleventh Amendment. See, e.g., Sacred Heart Hospital of Norristown v. Commonwealth of Pa. Dept. of Pub. Welfare, 133 F.3d 237 (1998). In Central Virginia Community College v. Katz, 546 U.S. 356 (2006), the Supreme Court held that 11 U.S.C. §106 is constitutional.

S.   SECURITY

Section 101(49) defines *security*. Several definitions within the Bankruptcy Code use the term *security*. Each definition is separate. The definition of the word *security* in Section 101(49) includes the various commercial documents commonly used to evidence an ownership interest in an entity or in certain sorts of financial assets, such as bonds or certificates of deposit.[29] Use of the word *includes* in the definition means that the court has discretion to interpret a document not included on the list as also being a security.[30] For purposes of a basic understanding, any document that evidences an intangible financial right will generally be considered a security under the Code. However, currency, checks, and certain specialized options or commodities are specifically not considered security.[31] Although these items may evidence the existence of an asset or claim, they do not constitute security within the Code.

T.   SECURITY AGREEMENT

Section 101(50) defines *security agreement*: an agreement that creates or provides for a security interest.[32] A security interest is an agreement that creates a lien.[33] A bank loan to finance a new car purchase usually creates a security interest in the car. A home loan is an agreement that usually creates a security interest in the real property by way of a mortgage or deed of trust. A security interest is generally considered perfected when the trust deed or mortgage is properly recorded or when a "UCC-1" is properly filed in a secured commercial transaction.

U.   SINGLE ASSET REAL ESTATE

Section 101(51B) defines *single asset real estate*. Single asset real estate is real property that generates substantially all the gross income of a debtor

---

29. 11 U.S.C. §101(49).
30. See chapter 5 supra.
31. 11 U.S.C. §101(49)(B).
32. 11 U.S.C. §101(50).
33. 11 U.S.C. §101(51).

who is not a family farmer and on which no substantial business is con-ducted other than the operation of the property and activities incidental thereto. Residential real property with three or fewer units is excluded from the definition. The purpose of this definition was to codify, for the sake of consistency, the many disparate conceptions of single asset real estate that had arisen in the case law.

For example, an apartment building with five units and secured debt of $500,000 (and whose only income is rental receipts) is single asset real estate. A golf course, restaurant, and subdivision project with secured debt of $20 million may or may not be a single asset real estate case. An office building with secured debt of $100 million is typically a single asset real estate case. Undeveloped land generating no income but with secured debt is single asset real estate.[34] This provision is most relevant in con-nection with the automatic stay (see chapter 13 infra).

V.   STATUTORY LIEN

Section 101(53) defines *statutory lien* as: a lien created by operation of law and not by court order (a judicial lien) or agreement (consensual lien). A statutory lien does not include a judicial or consensual lien even if it is created by statute. In this event, the lien would either be a judicial or consensual lien but not a statutory lien.[35] Mechanic's liens or landlord's liens are common examples of liens that are created by statute or statutory liens.

W.   TRANSFER

Section 101(54) defines a *transfer*. The definition is intentionally broad. A transfer is any type of means that human beings might devise to dispose of property or interests in property. Additionally, the creation of a lien, the creation of a security interest, and the foreclosure of a debtor's equity of

---

34. 11 U.S.C. §101 (51B). See In re Oceanside Mission Assocs., 192 Bankr. 232, 234 (S.D. Cal. 1996), where the court stated: "If the debtor has no income, then substantially all of its income could be said to be generated by the property; i.e., substantially all of nothing is nothing."
35. 11 U.S.C. §101(53).

redemption of property are all expressly noted as transfers.[36] This is an intentionally broad definition, because as technology develops there become more and more ways of creating means of transferring property or an interest in property.

> ***The unsigned Assignment of Interest discovered by Owen in his father's papers would comprise a transfer if it were signed and recorded.***

FACT PATTERN

Identifying precisely when a transaction takes place will determine the application of many substantive provisions of the Code, including determining when a preference or fraudulent transfer has occurred. Many of the following chapters will have occasion to discuss the effect of a transfer upon the operation of the Code section in issue.

Summary

Section 101 of the Code specifically defines many terms that are frequently used in other Code sections. This Section should not be overlooked when conducting bankruptcy research.

A claim is generally a right to payment or performance. A debt is the legal obligation to pay.

Insiders are given special treatment in various Code sections. Whether the debtor is an individual, partnership, or corporation will determine who is an insider in relation to the debtor. Generally, family members or persons in control of a debtor's financial affairs will be insiders within the bankruptcy system.

The word *security* is contained within four different Section 101 definitions. Each of these definitions is different. This chart may assist in distinguishing between them:

Definition	Description	Authority
equity security holder	holder of an ownership interest in debtor (e.g., stock)	11 U.S.C. §101(17)
security	evidence of ownership (e.g., stock certificate)	11 U.S.C. §101(49)

---

36. 11 U.S.C. §101(54).

security agreement	agreement creating a security interest	11 U.S.C. §101(50)
security interest	a consensual lien	11 U.S.C. §101(51)

Similarly, Section 101 contains four definitions of liens. These definitions are summarized as follows:

Definition	*Description*	*Authority*
lien	an interest in property to secure repayment or performance	11 U.S.C. §101(37)
judicial lien	a lien created by court order (e.g., writ of execution)	11 U.S.C. §101(36)
statutory lien	a lien created by statute	11 U.S.C. §101(53)
consensual lien	a lien created by a security agreement	11 U.S.C. §101(50), (51)

DISCUSSION QUESTIONS

1. What is the relationship between a claim and a debt?

2. What is an insider? Identify some possible reasons why the Bankruptcy Code may want to distinguish insiders from other parties to the proceeding?

3. What is a lien?

4. Identify the types of liens defined by the Bankruptcy Code.

5. What is the difference between *security* and *security agreement* as the Bankruptcy Code defines these terms?

6. Why is an equity security holder not defined as an insider by the Bankruptcy Code?

PART II

Debtor Relief

8

Overview of Chapter 7

Learning Objectives

- List the three general elements of bankruptcy relief
- Describe the basic events that occur in all bankruptcy proceedings
- Explain the rules relating to professional retention and compensation in bankruptcy proceedings
- Define the concept of discharge
- Define the concept of reaffirmation and describe the procedures utilized to reaffirm a debt

A **consumer no asset bankruptcy** Chapter 7 case is a proceeding filed by an individual debtor or joint debtors in which there will normally be no assets available for the trustee to administer to distribute dividends to unsecured creditors. Any assets owned by the debtor will be either secured or exempt. Consumer no asset proceedings comprise a majority of all of the proceedings that are filed. The basic outline of a consumer no asset Chapter 7 proceeding is equally applicable to all other types of bankruptcy proceedings. This is because the practical process of a consumer no asset proceeding, including documents to be filed and appearances to make, forms the core of all activity occurring in any bankruptcy proceeding.

Consumer no asset bankruptcy: a Chapter 7 bankruptcy proceeding for an individual in which there are normally no assets available for distribution to creditors

 Practice Pointer

Note that a "no asset" case does not mean that the debtor has no assets at all, but rather that the debtor's assets are all exempt or they do not hold recoverable equity.

Exempt: free
from the reach of
creditors or the
trustee

Discharge: legal
relief from debt
provided for by
Section 524 of the
Bankruptcy Code

Automatic stay:
a statutory bar to
the conducting of
any collection ac-
tivity by creditors
after a bankruptcy
petition has been
filed

Fresh start: the
phrase most fre-
quently used col-
loquially to
describe the basic
elements of
debtor relief: dis-
charge, exemp-
tions, and the
automatic stay

FACT PATTERN

A no asset Chapter 7 proceeding is filed by one person or by joint debtors. The Bankruptcy Code describes "joint debtors" as an individual debtor "and such individual's spouse." The Code recognizes married couples but no other joint filings.[1]

In a consumer no asset Chapter 7, all debtors seek the three basic goals of debtor relief. One goal is to be able to claim all, or substantially all, of the debtor's assets as **exempt** and therefore free from the reach of the creditors or the trustee.[2] In plain English, the debtor gets to keep exempt property. Second, debtors seek to obtain a discharge of their debt and the creditors' claims subject to the bankruptcy proceeding. A **discharge** is the term used to describe the release from personal debt that a debtor receives after satisfying the requirements of the particular bankruptcy chapter filed.[3] The protection afforded by the **automatic stay** comprises the final element of debtor relief. These elements of debtor relief permit debtors to obtain a fresh start in managing their financial affairs.

The so-called **fresh start** afforded by these three major components is the primary reason for a consumer debtor to seek bankruptcy relief. Describing how to accomplish this objective is the subject of the next three chapters of this text. The initiation of a proceeding, the entry of an order for relief, and the documents that must be filed in connection with a Chapter 7 proceeding have already been identified in chapter 5 supra. This chapter concerns the basic activities that occur after the filing of a petition in a typical proceeding. Focusing on a consumer no asset proceeding will provide us with the basic model of the essential activities that occur in all bankruptcies.

The relief from creditor contact and collection activities is often cited as a major benefit of filing for bankruptcy. How do you think this relief would specifically help the Cashes?

A.   EMPLOYMENT AND COMPENSATION OF PROFESSIONALS

The Bankruptcy Code regulates the employment and compensation of professionals rendering services in any bankruptcy proceeding. Attorneys,

---

1. 11 U.S.C. §§301, 302. See chapter 4 supra.
2. See chapter 10 infra.
3. 11 U.S.C. §524.

accountants, appraisers, brokers, and the trustee are the most common such professionals. The provisions regulating professional employment and compensation are contained in Sections 326-331 of the Code.

Prior to filing a petition for an individual debtor, a debt relief agency, bankruptcy attorney, or petition preparer (see chapters 4 and 7 supra) must provide the disclosures required by Section 527. These notices must be given within three business days of first rendering services to a debtor. Additionally, a bankruptcy attorney or petition preparer must enter into a written retainer agreement within five business days of first rendering services to a debtor pursuant to Section 528. Section 526 provides penalties for noncompliance with these provisions. See chapter 4A supra.

Did Jimmy Bond comply with these provisions? Is ignorance of the law a valid excuse in this particular situation?

FACT PATTERN

In addition, all attorneys representing debtors must file a Statement of Compensation with the Bankruptcy Court. This Statement describes the fee that an attorney has received or is going to receive in connection with the proceeding. This requirement is mandated by Section 329(a) and is implemented by Bankruptcy Rule 2016(b). All fees paid to attorneys by the debtor within the one year period prior to the filing of the petition are also subject to disclosure.[4] Section 110 imposes a similar requirement on non-attorneys who are considered bankruptcy petition preparers (paralegals, see chapter 8B infra).

> ### *Practice Pointer*
> A standardized form for the disclosure of attorney compensation can be found on the forms disk at Form 4.5.

Generally, a debtor or trustee may employ professionals. Attorneys, accountants, appraisers, and auctioneers are all professionals. A professional must be disinterested. The phrase **disinterested person** is defined in Bankruptcy Code Section 101(14). Most commonly, creditors, equity security holders, insiders, and persons who have an interest materially adverse to an estate are not disinterested. That is, the professional cannot normally

Disinterested person: a person who is not a creditor, equity security holder, or insider, or who does not have an interest materially adverse to an estate

---

4. 11 U.S.C. §329(a); Bankruptcy Rule 2016(b). See chapter 4 supra.

have a potential or actual conflict of interest with the estate.[5] An attorney who is representing the debtor in a case therefore cannot represent the trustee in the same proceeding. Their interests are generally adverse to one another. Note, however, that the statute does not bar a nondisinterested person from representing a Chapter 7 debtor.[6] This is the one exception to the general rule. Thus, in-house counsel for a corporate debtor may represent the debtor in the corporation's Chapter 7 proceeding even if counsel is a creditor in the proceeding.

FACT PATTERN

What professionals do you envision may be necessary to assist with the Cashes' case?

Practice Pointer

Note also that it is not a conflict of interest for an attorney to serve as both the Chapter 7 trustee and as counsel for the trustee (i.e., as counsel for him or herself).

A professional is not disqualified from employment solely due to representation of a creditor, unless another creditor objects and the court finds an actual conflict of interest.[7] This provision permits counsel for a single creditor to be approved as counsel for a creditors' committee in a Chapter 11 case.[8] In such cases, counsel will normally be required to cease representing other parties in interest in connection with the bankruptcy proceeding.

A nondisinterested professional may also be employed for a special purpose provided that the professional is not adverse to the estate on the subject matter of the retention.[9] For instance, an attorney's knowledge and background of a debtor's activities may be so important that time and expense can be saved if the attorney/creditor continues to represent the debtor or trustee for limited purposes in the bankruptcy proceeding. Similarly, a debtor may have a personal injury claim as an asset and the trustee may wish to hire the debtor's personal injury attorney as special counsel for the estate to continue to prosecute the personal injury claim.

---

5. 11 U.S.C. §§101(14), 327(a).
6. 11 U.S.C. §327(a).
7. 11 U.S.C. §327(c).
8. 11 U.S.C. §327(c); 11 U.S.C. §1103(b).
9. 11 U.S.C. §327(e).

The court will normally approve such applications to be retained for a special purpose.

To become properly retained by the estate or trustee, other than in a no asset proceeding, which merely involves the filing of the Statement of Compensation referred to above, a professional must file an application with the court and have the court approve the professional's retention by the estate or by the trustee.[10] This is the most important rule in connection with professional retention, namely that there be disclosure and prior court approval. If the professional does not obtain court approval for the retention, the court may deny the award of any compensation to the unapproved professional, regardless of the quality or quantity of the services.[11] A law firm performing services in a bankruptcy estate must therefore be certain to obtain prompt court approval of its retention, or counsel risks not being paid for the services rendered prior to approval of the retention.

A professional becomes approved to render services to a trustee, debtor-in-possession, or Official Creditors' Committee by filing a motion for an order authorizing employment.[12] The motion must include facts showing the necessity of employment, the name of the person to be employed, and reasons for the selection. The motion must describe the services to be rendered, disclose compensation arrangements, state that the professional is qualified to be retained within the meaning of Section 327, and disclose any interest that may be adverse to the estate. The motion must also be accompanied by a statement of the professional that the professional is a disinterested person. Any issue reflecting upon disinterestedness must be disclosed, and this remains a continuing duty throughout the course of employment. The court may also approve the professional on an interim basis, for the period of time prior to the hearing, as an ex parte matter. Failure to proceed promptly to become properly retained can result in a denial of payment, as described above.[13]

Section 328 provides that professional fees are to be reasonable. This Section also provides for the payment of contingent fees in appropriate matters. Although contingent fee arrangements were not permitted in practice under the Bankruptcy Act, the Bankruptcy Code specifically

---

10. 11 U.S.C. §327(a); Bankruptcy Rule 2014.
11. See, e.g., Palmer v. Statewide Group, 134 F.3d 378 (9th Cir. 1998) (nunc pro tunc retention is only approved in "exceptional circumstances").
12. 11 U.S.C. §327(a); 11 U.S.C. §1103(b); 11 U.S.C. §1107(b).
13. Bankruptcy Rule 2014; Bankruptcy Rule 2002; 11 U.S.C. §102. Representative forms are included on the forms disk accompanying this text. As to the duty of full disclosure and the risks of nondisclosure, see In re Leslie Fay Co., 175 B.R. 525 (Bankr. S.D.N.Y. 1993). Additional disclosures are required in cases with $50 million or more of assets and liabilities pursuant to Appendix B Guidelines for Reviewing Applications for Compensation and Reimbursement of Expenses Filed Under United States Code by Attorneys in Larger Chapter 11 Cases, 78 Fed. Reg. 116 at 36248 (2013).

allows them in appropriate instances.[14] A contingent fee agreement will not be used in representing a debtor for general purposes of the proceeding itself. A contingent fee arrangement might, however, be acceptable to collect accounts receivable or to continue to prosecute personal injury claims. These are areas of legal practice in which contingent fees are ordinary and customary.

In Chapter 7, 12, and 13 proceedings, prefiling retainers paid to counsel are acceptable although the reasonableness of the retainer may be examined by the court. Local custom should be ascertained to determine the generally accepted fees permitted for Chapter 7 or 13 proceedings in a given district. Although prefiling retainers are permitted in Chapter 9 and Chapter 11 proceedings, local rule or practice may require compliance with the fee application process described below before any fees may be paid. Whether a retainer may be applied to the payment of fees prior to compliance with the fee application process is a matter of debate in the reported cases.[15]

Practice Pointer

The debtor's obligation to pay for prepetition bankruptcy services is generally not dischargeable and the retainer paid is not considered to be a preference.

Interim fee application: a fee application brought during the pendency of a proceeding

Professionals approved to render services to a bankruptcy estate or trustee are not paid for their services every month. Most law firms and other businesses customarily send bills to clients or customers every month and there is an expectation of prompt payment. In bankruptcy practice this is not the case. The Bankruptcy Code does not allow professionals to apply for compensation more than once every 120 days. A fee application brought during the pendency of a proceeding is commonly known as an **interim fee application**. In an exceptionally large proceeding the court may approve more frequent periods for the bringing of interim fee applications, but this is a rare practice.[16] Frequently, a period of time significantly longer than 120 days will pass before an application for compensation is brought, for the simple reason that to pay compensation the estate has to have funds available. If there are no available

---

14. 11 U.S.C. §328(a).
15. See In re Printcrafters, Inc., 208 B.R. 968 (Bankr. D. Colo. 1997) for a representative example.
16. 11 U.S.C. §331.

means for paying, it will be pointless to bring an application for compensation. Applications for interim compensation should be brought only upon giving due consideration to the needs of the estate and the ability of the professional to render competent services with or without receiving compensation until the close of the case. An application to approve compensation is always required at either the close of the proceeding or when all services to be rendered are complete. Such an application is known as a **final fee application**.

Interim and final fee applications are brought before the bankruptcy court as noticed motions pursuant to FRBP 2016 and 9013. (See chapter 4 supra.) FRBP 2016(a) requires a fee application to detail all time and charges and describe the services rendered and expenses incurred. Any payments previously made must be disclosed. A description in summary form of all services rendered, broken down by amounts and percentage of time spent, should also be included and is required in many local rules.[17] A sample application is included on the forms disk accompanying this text.

Final fee application: an application to approve compensation; required at either the close of the proceeding or when all services to be rendered are complete

---

Practice Pointer

Remember to always check local court rules and forms for the appropriate procedures to follow in seeking compensation. Courts frequently have rules governing the allowability of certain expenses and the manner in which application may be sought. Some courts have also adopted short form or standard order fee applications for certain routine services such as relief from stay motions and appearances in court.

In Lamie v. United States Trustee, 540 U.S. 526 (2004), the Supreme Court held that the precise wording of Bankruptcy Code Section 330(a)(1) does not permit a professional not employed by the estate to seek compensation therefrom. Thus, debtor's counsel in a case converted from Chapter 11 to Chapter 7 and in a Chapter 7 may not seek compensation from the bankruptcy estate.

The court will hold a hearing on an interim or final application for compensation. While a proceeding remains pending, the court will typically

---

17. 11 U.S.C. §§330, 331; Bankruptcy Rule 2016(a). Additional disclosures are required in cases with $50 million or more of assets and liabilities pursuant to Appendix B Guidelines for Reviewing Applications for Compensation and Reimbursement of Expenses Filed Under United States Code by Attorneys in Larger Chapter 11 Cases, 78 Fed. Reg. 116 at 36248 (2013).

award only a percentage of the current charges for which compensation is sought. A typical award is 70-80 percent of the current charges. This percentage may vary from district to district in accordance with local practice. At the end of the proceeding, there will be a final hearing to approve all compensation earned in the proceeding. At this time, any withheld portions of prior applications may or may not be approved for payment.

The bankruptcy system makes a serious effort to control and limit the compensation paid to professionals. If counsel performs less than competently, the court has the discretion to "reward" such behavior when an application for compensation is brought. The "reward" may be a denial or reduction in the amount of compensation actually approved for payment. The Bankruptcy Courts scrutinize fee applications carefully. The United States Trustees have been specifically directed to review and comment upon applications for compensation brought in bankruptcy proceedings. The guidelines of the local United States Trustee will also need to be complied with. The Bankruptcy Court may, on its own motion, award less compensation than is requested. Among the factors the court will consider are the time spent, whether the services were necessary or beneficial to the estate, the complexity of the services, and the rates charged. In Baker Botts v. Asarco, the Supreme Court held that fees incurred in defending objections to fee applications are not themselves compensable because they are not a service rendered to the estate but, rather, to the affected professional.[18]

A trustee's compensation is governed solely by Section 326. The trustee's maximum compensation is determined by a mathematical formula based upon the percentage of an estate's assets that a trustee actually administers. The maximum compensation permitted a trustee is 3 percent of the value of the assets administered where the value of the assets administered is greater than $1 million. The percentage is higher for estates with a value of less than $1 million, but the maximum dollar compensation permitted at this level is $53,250.[19] This maximum compensation to a trustee is subject to review based on the same factors applicable to other professionals. Typically, a Bankruptcy Court will base a trustee's compensation on an equivalent hourly rate for legal or accounting services multiplied by the time a trustee has spent on a case, up to the maximum compensation permitted. In addition, a trustee is entitled to receive $60 from the debtor's initial filing fee.[20] Sometimes a trustee may put in ten minutes of work for the $60. Sometimes a trustee will work for

---

18. 11 U.S.C. §330, 28 U.S.C. §586(a)(3)(A). See chapter 11 infra. Baker Botts v. Asarco, U.S., 135 S. Ct. 2158 (2015).

19. 11 U.S.C. §326(a). 11 U.S.C. §330(a)(7) provides that a trustee's compensation awarded pursuant to Section 326 be treated as a commission.

20. 11 U.S.C. §330(b).

many hours on a proceeding and still earn only the same $60. Further, a trustee does not receive compensation immediately, but normally receives the statutory percentage compensation at the close of a proceeding. The fee from the debtor's filing fee is usually received some time after a proceeding is closed. In a large case with many assets and a lot of work, a trustee may apply for interim compensation, although the maximum compensation sought must remain within the limits permitted by Section 326.[21] A trustee's application for interim or final compensation is brought before the court as a noticed motion pursuant to FRBP 2016 and 9013. (See chapter 5 supra.)

All professional compensation is considered an expense of administration and does not normally create a claim as described in this chapter supra. Administrative expenses are further described in chapter 22 infra.

B.   BANKRUPTCY PETITION PREPARERS

Section 110 of the Bankruptcy Code applies to bankruptcy petition preparers. Section 110(a) defines a **bankruptcy petition preparer** as a person other than the debtor's attorney or the attorney's employee under that attorney's direct supervision who prepares for compensation a document for filing with the Bankruptcy Court. An unsupervised paralegal may be a bankruptcy petition preparer. A *document for filing* is any document prepared for filing by a debtor in a bankruptcy case.

Section 110 is directed specifically at unsupervised paralegals preparing documents for filing by debtors with the Bankruptcy Court. This Section does not, however, authorize unsupervised paralegals to prepare or file documents with the Bankruptcy Court unless applicable state law permits such activities by paralegals. Thus, Section 110 does not affect state laws concerning the unlawful practice of law. Such laws remain expressly in effect (§110(k); see chapter 10C infra and the cases cited therein). A paralegal must therefore ascertain local law before acting independently to prepare bankruptcy documents for filing with the Bankruptcy Court.

Section 110 sets forth eight basic requirements for bankruptcy petition preparers to comply with. They are as follows:

1. The preparer must sign the document and include the preparer's name and address (§110(b)).

> **Bankruptcy petition preparer:** a person other than an attorney or an attorney's employee who prepares for compensation a document for filing with the Bankruptcy Court

---

21. 11 U.S.C. §331.

2. Provide a notice to the debtor, prior to the preparation of any document, stating that a petition preparer may not give legal advice (§110(b)(2)).
3. The preparer shall include the preparer's Social Security number on the document (§110 (c)).
4. The preparer shall furnish the debtor with a copy of the document not later than the time the document is presented to the debtor for signature (§110(d)).
5. The preparer shall not execute any document on behalf of a debtor nor provide legal advice to the debtor (§110 (e)).
6. The preparer shall not use the word *legal* or any other similar term in advertisements or advertise under any "legal" category (§110(f)).
7. The preparer may not receive or collect payment for court fees (§110(g)).
8. The preparer shall, at the filing of the petition, file a declaration under penalty of perjury disclosing any fees paid or promised by or on behalf of the debtor (§110(h); FRBP 2016(c)).

Violations of any of the foregoing requirements are subject to a discretionary fine of $500 (§110(1)(1)). Under §110(h), the court shall also disallow and order turned over to the trustee any fee found to be excessive. Acceptable fees will invariably vary from district to district; however, the 2005 legislation permits the adoption of rules that would set the fees bankruptcy petition preparers may charge.

Section 110(i) creates a civil remedy for damages against a bankruptcy petition preparer who violates Section 110 or commits any fraudulent, unfair, or deceptive act. The debtor, trustee, or the United States Trustee may move and seek recovery of the debtor's actual damages, the greater of $2,000 or twice the amount paid by the debtor to the preparer, plus reasonable costs and attorneys' fees for bringing the motion.

Section 110(j) provides yet a further check on a bankruptcy petition preparer's conduct by authorizing a party in interest, including the United States Trustee, to seek to enjoin a bankruptcy petition preparer from continuing to act as such where the preparer has engaged in fraudulent or deceptive conduct, has misrepresented the preparer's experience or education, or has violated Section 110 on a continuing basis. Like Section 110(i), Section 110(j) authorizes the court to award reasonable attorneys' fees and costs to the successful moving party.[22]

---

22. See In re Clarke, 426 B.R. 443 (Bankr. E.D.N.Y. 2009), aff'd in part, rev'd in part, 426 B.R. 457 (E.D.N.Y. 2010) (tailoring an injunction); In re Kangarloo, 250 B.R. 115 (Bankr. C.D. Cal. 2000) (calculating damages); In re Bernales, 345 B.R. 206 (Bankr. C.D. Cal. 2006) (permanently enjoining petition preparer). Section 110(l)(2), added by BAPCPA, permits the court to triple the fines assessed against a bankruptcy petition preparer who advises a debtor to

Focusing on Section 110(b), (i), (j) and (l), what is Jimmy Bond's potential liability if he is found to be in violation of Section 110?

A bankruptcy petition preparer also falls within the definition of a debt relief agency and is therefore also required to provide the notices set forth in Sections 342(b), 526, and 527 as described in chapters 5 and 8A supra.

The effect of Section 110 is to impose a heavy burden of compliance upon unsupervised paralegals who can prepare bankruptcy documents for debtors in a jurisdiction that has authorized such activities as not constituting the unlawful practice of law. However, although the requirements are numerous, any qualified and properly trained paralegal will not find compliance to be difficult.

C.   THE CHAPTER 7 PROCESS

Although the Chapter 7 process is not set in motion in business cases until the debtor files a petition, in consumer cases, BAPCPA created new requirements to be complied with before a petition is filed. Recall that a consumer debtor must obtain a prepetition credit counseling certificate as a prerequisite to filing a petition absent a showing of exigent circumstances. Even if exigent circumstances are shown, the certificate must be obtained within 30 days of filing, or the case is subject to dismissal on the forty-sixth day after filing. See chapter 5A supra. Also, recall that a debt relief agency must provide various notices to the debtor and enter into a written retainer agreement, within short intervals of time after first meeting a debtor. All of these provisions ought to be complied with at the initial conference with a client. See chapters 5A and 8A supra.

Once a debtor files a petition, a clear process is set in motion. The first event that occurs is the appointment of an interim trustee by the United States Trustee pursuant to Section 701. The **interim trustee** will serve as the trustee until the meeting of creditors.[23] In all judicial districts, there exist panels of private trustees. Private panel trustees are persons who act as trustees on a regular basis.

Interim trustee: the trustee appointed by the United States Trustee to administer a bankruptcy estate prior to the meeting of creditors called for by Section 341(a) of the Bankruptcy Code

---

exclude assets or use a false Social Security number, who fails to advise a debtor that the debtor is in fact filing a bankruptcy petition, or who files documents that do not disclose the bankruptcy petition preparer's identity.

23. 11 U.S.C. §701.

CHAPTER 7
Debtor's View Timeline

Document	Authority
Petition	Official Form 1
Filing Fee	FRBP 1006
List of Creditors	FRBP 1007(a)(1)
	§521(a)(1)(A)
Statement of SSN	Official Form 21; FRBP 1007(f)
Credit counseling certificate	521(b)
List of 20 Largest Unsecured Claims — Chapter 11	FRBP 1007(d)
Corporate Debtor — Exhibit A	Official Form IX
Bankruptcy Petition Preparer/	§110(h)
Statement of Compensation	

Document	Authority
Statement of Financial Affairs	§521(a)(1)(B), FRBP 1007(7)
Schedules of assets and liabilities	§521(a)(1)(B), FRBP 1007(b)
Schedule of current income and expenses	§707(b)(2)(c)
Certificate of debt relief disclosures and payments received within 60 days	§521(a) (1)
Statement of Compensation Plan Chapter 13	§329; FRBP 2016 FRBP 3015

Document	Authority
Statement of Intention	§521(a)(2)
1st Plan Payment — Ch. 13	§1326(a)
DIP Bank Accounts — Ch. 11	§345
Retain Professionals. Pay Insiders — Ch. 11	§327
Commence Operating Reports — Ch. 11	FRBP 2015(a)

Document	Authority
Prepetition credit counseling	§109(h)
Debt relief agency disclosures/ signed contract	§§526-528

Time (Days) (approx.)	0	10	14	30	40	70	90	100	150
	A	**B**	**C**		**D**	**E**		**F**	**G**
Event	Petition Filed	Interim Trustee	Notice to Creditors		Creditor Meeting	Objections to Exemptions		Objection to Discharge/ Dischargeability	Discharge/ Reaffirmation
Authority	11 U.S.C. §301	11 U.S.C. §701	11 U.S.C. §341 FRBP 2002, 2003		11 U.S.C. §341(a)	FRBP 4003 (30 days after "D")		FRBP 4004, 4007 (60 days after "D")	11 U.S.C. §524 FRBP 4004 Personal Financial Management Course 11 U.S.C. §727(a)(11)

Under the United States Trustee system, which went into effect nationwide in 1988, the United States Trustee has been given the responsibility to appoint interim trustees.[24]

Next, the United States Trustee will send a notice to the creditors, to the debtor, and to the interim trustee advising all parties of the entry of an order for relief (the filing) and the appointment of the interim trustee.[25] This notice is usually given about five days after a proceeding is filed. Next, the United States Trustee will provide notice to the creditors advising them of the time and place of the **creditors' meeting** to be held pursuant to Section 341.[26] The form of the notice shall be substantially in the manner of Official Form B309A-D, depending on whether or not the debtor is an individual or a corporation, and whether distributable assets are expected. A sample is included on the forms disk accompanying this text.

Section 342(c) of the Bankruptcy Code, added by BAPCPA, requires that a debtor include the last four digits of the debtor's Social Security number and provide notice to a creditor at the address specified by the

Creditors' meeting: a mandatory hearing, held within 40 days after the entry of an order for relief in any Chapter proceeding

---

24. 11 U.S.C. §701(a); 28 U.S.C. §586(a)(1). See chapter 11 infra.
25. 11 U.S.C. §342(a); Bankruptcy Rule 2002(a); Bankruptcy Rule 2008.
26. 11 U.S.C. §§341, 342(a); Bankruptcy Rule 2002(a); Bankruptcy Rule 2003.

creditor in either communications to the debtor or in a registry main-tained by the court. Creditors are given an opportunity to advise the Bankruptcy Court of the address to send notices in Chapter 7 and 13 cases. Notices to creditors not given in compliance with this provision are not effective until brought to the creditor's attention.[27]

The creditors' meeting is often erroneously called a "first meeting of creditors," even though under the Code there is only one required meet-ing of creditors. This misnomer has arisen because under the Bankruptcy Act there was a first meeting of creditors and a last meeting of creditors. The word "first" is now superfluous. Federal Rule of Bankruptcy Proce-dure 2003 requires that the meeting of creditors take place not less than 21 (because 21 days' notice is required under Bankruptcy Rule 2002(a)) and not more than 40 days after the order for relief is entered.[28] Because this timing is based upon the entry of an order for relief, the same time limit applies in both voluntary and involuntary proceedings. Remember, once an order for relief is entered in an involuntary proceeding, the matter proceeds in a manner identical to a voluntary proceeding.[29]

The meeting of creditors is the most visible aspect of many bankruptcy proceedings. In a no asset proceeding, it is normally the only appearance a debtor is required to make.[30] There is no judge present at the meeting of creditors, only a representative of the United States Trustee.[31] The representative administers the oath to the debtor and recites the debtor's duties under the Code as well as the discharge and reaffirmation process. The United States Trustee has been given the responsibility of conducting creditors' meetings under the United States Trustee program.[32]

At the meeting of creditors, the creditors are given an opportunity to elect a trustee. Elections for a specific trustee are infrequent. Section 702 contains the procedure for conducting such an election. The interim trustee will become the permanent trustee unless the creditors elect another trustee.[33]

The trustee and creditors may examine the debtor or debtors at the creditors' meeting. The trustee will ask questions based upon the trustee's review of the Statements and Schedules. In the typical no asset consumer

---

27. 11 U.S.C. §342(c); 11 U.S.C. §342(g). The consequences of noncompliance for debtors and creditors alike will have to evolve in the case law. For example, the automatic stay is generally effective without notice (see chapter 13 infra). For a detailed analysis of the operation of Section 342(g), see In re Harvey, 388 B.R. 440 (Bankr. D. Me. 2008).

28. 11 U.S.C. §342(a); Bankruptcy Rule 2003. In a Chapter 13 case, the meeting of creditors may take place within 50 days of filing.

29. See chapter 4 supra.

30. 11 U.S.C. §343; Bankruptcy Rule 4002.

31. 11 U.S.C. §341(c); Bankruptcy Rule 2003(b).

32. 11 U.S.C. §341(a); 28 U.S.C. §586(a)(5); Bankruptcy Rule 2003.

33. 11 U.S.C. §702(d).

proceeding, a trustee will normally ask ten basic questions. These questions are:

1. State your name, Social Security number, and current address for the record. The Trustee will also request proof of the same, such as a Social Security card and a driver's license or other similar document.[34]

2. Have you provided payment advices to confirm your Current Monthly Income?[35]

3. Did you sign the petition, schedules, statements, and related documents you filed with the court?

4. Did you read the petition, schedules, statements, and related documents before you signed them?

5. Are you personally familiar with the information contained in the petition, schedules, statements, and related documents?

6. To the best of your knowledge, is the information contained in the petition, schedules, statements, and related documents true and correct?

7. Are there any errors or omissions to bring to my, or the court's, attention at this time?

8. Are all of your assets identified on the schedules?

9. Have you listed all of your creditors on the schedules?

10. Have you filed bankruptcy before? (If so, the trustee must obtain the case number and the discharge information to determine the discharge eligibility of the debtor(s).)[36]

Many trustees will also ask the debtor: "What caused your financial difficulties?" The reason for this question is to comply with one of the requirements for a discharge—namely, that a debtor be able to describe satisfactorily a lack of assets to satisfy liabilities. See chapter 14E infra.

Section 341(d) to the Code requires the trustee to examine the debtor further to make sure the debtor is aware of:

1. the consequences of seeking a discharge, including the effects on credit history;

2. the debtor's right to file a petition under a different Chapter of the Code;

---

34. 11 U.S.C. §521(h).
35. Many trustees will have reviewed payment advices prior to the meeting but will nonetheless put the information on the record. See chapter 6 supra.
36. A debtor may only receive a discharge once every eight years. 11 U.S.C. §727(a)(8). See chapter 14 infra.

3. the effect of receiving a discharge of debts; and
4. the effect of reaffirmation (see section E infra).

If there are specific assets in the estate or issues involving the estate that the trustee is concerned about, additional questions will likely be asked. For example, if the debtor owns a home, the trustee will probably ask a series of questions to determine whether there may be any equity in the home that may be used to pay a dividend to unsecured creditors. If the debtor owns a vehicle, the trustee may ask similar questions pertaining to it. If the debtor is a plaintiff in any lawsuit or if the debtor has previously been involved in a business, the trustee will ask questions about each of these activities.

In light of what you already know about the Cashes, what additional matters can you anticipate that the trustee will ask about?

FACT PATTERN

However, in a typical no asset consumer proceeding, the average debtor may not own real estate, and there is little or no realizable equity in vehicles in most instances. So the basic questions will be asked and no others. Because creditors' meetings are usually scheduled in groups of ten or more, all to take place within an hour, there is not much time for extended examination. However, if the Statements and Schedules are complete and understandable and if the trustee is prepared, it is possible to successfully complete a series of examinations within a relatively short period of time.

After the trustee completes the examination, creditors are given an opportunity to further examine the debtor. A nonattorney may appear on behalf of creditors in consumer bankruptcy cases. For example, a paralegal working in the collection department of a department store could appear and question debtors.[37] Sometimes creditors or their counsel will advise the trustee and demonstrate that a debtor may not be disclosing all pertinent information. Sometimes creditors or their counsel waste everybody's time asking irrelevant questions unrelated to a debtor's financial affairs. Sometimes a representative of a bank or finance company simply wants to know where a secured asset is and if it is currently insured. Creditors do have a right to come to the creditors' meeting and make inquiry of the debtor's assets and liabilities, but in actual practice, creditors rarely appear at these hearings.

---

37. 11 U.S.C. §341(c). This provision was added by the 2005 legislation.

D.   RULE 2004 EXAMINATIONS

Rule 2004 Examination: an extended examination of any person pursuant to Federal Rule of Bankruptcy Procedure 2004 regarding one or more aspects of a debtor's financial affairs

Sometimes, creditors or a trustee will want to examine a debtor for more time than is available at the creditors meeting. Alternatively, a trustee or creditor may desire to examine a third party, not the debtor, regarding the debtor's financial affairs. The Federal Rules of Bankruptcy Procedure provide a method that allows any party in interest to take the examination of any person concerning a debtor's financial affairs. This method is called a **Rule 2004 Examination**.[38] Under the Bankruptcy Act, this was known as a Rule 205 Examination. The prior and present rules are virtually identical. It has been stated of Rule 205, the predecessor to Rule 2004, that it is "in the nature of an inquisition."[39] Objections on grounds of relevancy are not normally acceptable during one of these examinations. In fact, most objections will not be appropriate in a Rule 2004 Examination and any matter relevant to the proceeding is fair game.[40] Rule 2004 exists for the benefit of creditors or for the benefit of the trustee who desires to conduct an extensive examination of the debtor or a third party beyond the time limitations of the creditors' meeting.

 Practice Pointer

A Rule 2004 Examination is simply another form of a "deposition."

An order for a Rule 2004 Examination is obtained when the party seeking to conduct the examination files an application for an order with the court.[41] The order must be served personally, in a manner identical to service of a subpoena.[42] Nondebtor examinees and debtors, when required to travel more than 100 miles, one way, are entitled to compensation for mileage in reaching the place of examination.[43]

A Rule 2004 Examination, when appropriate, has several benefits in addition to the time factors described above. It is a form of discovery that permits a trustee or party in interest to determine the existence of assets or claims and the rights of the parties without incurring the additional

---

38. Bankruptcy Rule 2004.
39. 12 Collier on Bankruptcy §705.15 at 2-93 (14th ed. 1973).
40. Bankruptcy Rule 2004(b).
41. Bankruptcy Rule 2004(a).
42. Bankruptcy Rule 2004(c).
43. Bankruptcy Rule 2004(e).

expenses of commencing an adversary proceeding. In short, the Rule 2004 Examination is a method for conducting what are essentially depositions without having to file a lawsuit first. Rule 2004 Examinations are used extensively in motion practice under the Code. For example, a party may wish to take an appraiser's Rule 2004 Examination in connection with a motion for relief from the automatic stay. A creditors' committee may take Rule 2004 Examinations in connection with a motion to appoint a trustee in a Chapter 11 proceeding.

E.   DISCHARGE AND REAFFIRMATION

After the creditors' meeting, the next and final event that occurs in a typical no asset consumer proceeding is that an individual debtor or joint debtors will receive a discharge.[44] Up until 1986, debtors were also required to appear in court, before a judge, to receive their discharge.[45] The discharge hearing was typically held between 60 and 90 days after the meeting of creditors. The 1986 amendments to the Code made the requirement of discharge hearings discretionary with the court unless there is a **reaffirmation agreement** to approve.[46] Under the 2005 amendments, there will be a hearing if the debtor does not have an attorney or if the reaffirmation agreement is presumed an undue hardship within the meaning of 11 U.S.C. §524(m)(1). Receipt of a discharge will be automatic unless an objection to the discharge itself is filed. Pursuant to the 2005 legislation, a debtor will not receive a Chapter 7 discharge unless the debtor also completes a course in personal financial management approved by the United States Trustee.[47]

Reaffirmation agreement: a debtor's agreement to remain legally liable for repayment of a debt otherwise dischargeable in a bankruptcy proceeding

A discharge pursuant to Section 524 legally relieves a debtor of all personal dischargeable obligations.[48] Generally, a discharge voids any existing judgment and permanently enjoins the collection of any debt subject to the discharge. Certain debts are specifically not dischargeable. These debts are analyzed in chapter 14 infra. Secured debts are effectively not dischargeable if the debtor wants to keep the collateral.[49] The right to

---

44. 11 U.S.C. §524; 11 U.S.C. §727. See chapter 14 infra.
45. See 11 U.S.C. §521(5) as it existed prior to November 1986.
46. 11 U.S.C. §524(d).
47. See chapter 14 infra; Bankruptcy Rule 4004. 11 U.S.C. §707(a)(11); 11 U.S.C. §111. See chapter 14 infra; Bankruptcy Rule 4004. A personal financial management course is also required to receive a Chapter 13 discharge. 11 U.S.C. §1328(g). See chapter 24 infra.
48. 11 U.S.C. §524.
49. See chapter 22 infra.

receive a discharge may not be waived.[50] In community property states, the community property of a nonfiling spouse is entitled to a discharge unless the nonfiling spouse would not be entitled to receive a discharge in a proceeding under the Code.[51] This would be the case if the nonfiling spouse would be unable to receive a discharge for any of the reasons enumerated in Section 727 as described in chapter 14 infra.

Only a debtor's legal obligation to repay a discharged debt is relieved by a bankruptcy discharge; the underlying moral obligation to repay one's just debts is not affected by a bankruptcy discharge. Section 524(f) specifically states: "Nothing contained in . . . this section prevents a debtor from voluntarily repaying any debt."[52] So if a discharged debtor wants to voluntarily repay the neighborhood doctor, the law permits performance of the moral obligation. The reason for specific inclusion of this principle into the Code is historical.

FACT PATTERN

Absent any consideration of fraud, would Owen's $40,000 obligation to his father be dischargeable? Assuming that it was, could Owen still agree to repay it?

 ## *Practice Pointer*

Remember that a discharge in bankruptcy relieves the debtor's personal obligation to repay a debt, *but* it does not (without some further action taken) remove the creditor's "in rem" remedies. In other words, the debtor's personal obligation to continue to make his car payments may be discharged, but if he/she stops making postpetition payments, the creditor may still get relief from the automatic stay to repossess the car.

FACT PATTERN

Which of the Cash liabilities are likely subject to in rem remedies?

---

50. 11 U.S.C. §524(a).
51. 11 U.S.C. §524(a)(3), (b).
52. 11 U.S.C. §524(f).

Before the enactment of the Bankruptcy Code, the common law of many states held that a bankrupt debtor retained the moral obligation to repay debts after receiving a bankruptcy discharge. If a debtor performed any part of the moral obligation by voluntarily repaying a portion of the debt, common law held that a new legal obligation to pay had been created by reaffirmation. Under this pre-Code law, creditors would try to convince a debtor who had received a bankruptcy discharge to "Come on, be a good guy and send in a payment." Many people who receive persistent phone calls like this tire of receiving them. Often, a payment will be made simply to stop the phone from ringing. This one act could constitute reaffirmation under existing pre-Code state law and restore the previously discharged debtor's liability. The creditor could thus negate the effects of the bankruptcy and obtain a judgment for the balance of the "reaffirmed" debt.[53] While some reaffirmations were indeed proper, all were suspect under the Act because of the abuses committed by some creditors.

The various reaffirmation provisions contained in Section 524 are intended to curb creditor abuse. Thus, Section 524(f) is essential to explain the intent of Congress in enacting the specific reaffirmation provisions into the Code. The practical effect of this provision is that a debtor may voluntarily repay a discharged debt without creating a new legal obligation. The moral obligation is free to be performed by a debtor without risk. If the discharged debtor stops paying, the creditor has no enforceable claim. A new legal obligation is created only when the Code's reaffirmation provisions are complied with. A further practical effect of Section 524(f) is that a basic principle of contract law has been altered by enactment of the Bankruptcy Code.[54]

For example, Sam Wilson receives a discharge. Under Bankruptcy Act practice, if Jarvis could convince Sam to repay any part of the discharged debt, and Sam performed, a new legal obligation had been created free of the effects of the prior bankruptcy discharge. Sam would again be legally obligated to pay his debt to Jarvis. Under the Bankruptcy Code, no new legal obligation is created if Sam voluntarily makes a payment to Jarvis unless the court has properly approved a reaffirmation agreement.

No discharged debt is considered to be legally reaffirmed unless the provisions of Sections 524(c), (d), and (k) are strictly complied with. Although the provisions are lengthy, their basic elements are not difficult to comprehend. First, there must be a written reaffirmation agreement

---

53. A. Corbin, Corbin on Contracts, Chapter 9, §§222-230 (student ed. 1952), contains an excellent description of the moral obligation/reaffirmation law under common law.
54. 11 U.S.C. §524(c).

entered into prior to entry of the debtor's discharge.[55] The agreement
must contain a statement that it may be rescinded by the debtor at any
time prior to receiving a discharge or 60 days from when the agreement is
filed with the court, whichever comes later. The agreement must comply
with the provisions of Section 524(k).[56] A debtor's attorney must file a
declaration or affidavit representing that the agreement is fully informed
and voluntary, that the agreement does not impose an undue hardship on
the debtor, and that the attorney has fully advised the debtor of the effect
and consequences of the reaffirmation and any default made under it.[57] If
the debtor is not represented by an attorney, the court must also find that
the agreement will not impose an undue hardship on and be in the best
interests of the debtor.[58]

Section 524(k) specifies the documentation, contents of the documentation, and the procedures to follow to obtain approval of a reaffirmation agreement. The Amount Reaffirmed and Annual Percentage Rate
must be the most conspicuously displayed terms, along with any intro-
ductory instructions to review the documents carefully.[59] A five-part document comprises the reaffirmation agreement. Part A contains numerous
preliminary disclosures, primarily with respect to credit terms, repayment
terms, whether or not there is any collateral, instructions about the
approval procedure, and that the debtor has 60 days from the filing of
the reaffirmation with the bankruptcy court to rescind the agreement.[60]
Part B is the actual reaffirmation agreement and contains signature lines
for the parties.[61] Part C is a certification of the debtor's attorney, if the
debtor has an attorney, that the reaffirmation agreement is voluntary and
will not create an undue hardship for the debtor.[62] Part D is the Debtor's
Statement in Support of Reaffirmation Agreement, which acknowledges
that the agreement is voluntary, that it will not impose an undue hardship,
and that entering into the agreement is in the debtor's financial interest.[63]
Part E is the Motion for Court Approval. This is used if the debtor is not
represented by an attorney.[64]

55. 11 U.S.C. §524(c)(1).
56. 11 U.S.C. §524(c)(2)(3).
57. 11 U.S.C. §524(c)(3).
58. 11 U.S.C. §524(c)(6).
59. 11 U.S.C. §524(k)(2). Annual Percentage Rate has the same meaning given it in the Federal
    Truth in Lending Act (TILA), 15 U.S.C. §1601 et seq.
60. 11 U.S.C. §524(k)(3); 11 U.S.C. §524(c)(4).
61. 11 U.S.C. §524(k)(4).
62. 11 U.S.C. §524(k)(5). In re Vargas, 257 B.R. 157 (Bankr. N.J. 2001), discusses counsel's
    obligations to clients with respect to reaffirmation agreements.
63. 11 U.S.C. §524(k)(6).
64. 11 U.S.C. §524(k)(7). If the agreement creates a presumption of undue hardship by the
    debtor's expenses exceeding income, in the disclosures made in Part D, then the court
    must hold a hearing to determine if the debtor can make the proposed payments or disap-
    prove the reaffirmation agreement. 11 U.S.C. §524(m).

> ### *Practice Pointer*
> See Form 8.8 on the forms disk for a
> sample reaffirmation agreement.

The court may then hold a discharge and reaffirmation hearing that, if held, the debtor is required to attend.[65] The court must find that the elements of Section 524(c) have been strictly complied with and must further instruct the debtor that a reaffirmation agreement is not required for the debtor to voluntarily repay the debt, that approval of the agreement will create a new legally enforceable obligation of the debtor.[66] To reiterate, if a debtor decides to pay $20 to Dr. Jones on a discharged debt because the debtor feels like she wants to pay the doctor, and the next month the debtor does not make a payment, Dr. Jones has no legal right to sue the debtor for any balance. There is no balance due because it has been discharged unless a reaffirmation agreement has been entered into and approved by the court. The courts are very strict about approving reaffirmation agreements and are reluctant to approve any except those concerning secured debts for the necessaries of life, such as car loans or certain purchase money security agreements. Very rarely will the court approve a reaffirmation agreement for an unsecured debt.

The case of In re Latanowich, 207 B.R. 326 (Bankr. D. Mass. 1997), illustrates the proposition that the reaffirmation requirements must be strictly complied with to be enforceable. In this case, Sears Roebuck and Co. solicited a reaffirmation agreement from a debtor. Although the debtor entered into the agreement, Sears did not file the agreement with the court, rendering it unenforceable. The court not only found the agreement to be invalid, but sanctioned Sears for attempting to enforce it and enjoined Sears from seeking to enforce any reaffirmation agreement not filed with the court in compliance with the statute. The outcome in this case contributed to the substantial changes in reaffirmation agreements enacted in Section 524(k) in the 2005 legislation.

Section 524(i) provides that creditors who willfully misapply payments received under a confirmed plan are in violation of the discharge injunction provided for by Section 524. This requires, for example, mortgage lenders to properly credit payments made to them in Chapter 13 cases. Section 524(j), on the other hand, permits creditors to communicate with debtors about postpetition payments on home mortgages

---

65. 11 U.S.C. §524(d); 11 U.S.C. §524(k)(7); 11 U.S.C. §521(a)(5).
66. 11 U.S.C. §524(d)(1), (2), §524(k)(7), (m).

without the communications constituting a violation of the discharge injunction.

The above has been a synopsis of what takes place in a typical no asset consumer Chapter 7 proceeding. Objections to a debtor's discharge and the nondischargeability of specific debts are described in greater detail in chapter 14 infra.

Summary

The process that occurs in a no asset consumer Chapter 7 bankruptcy forms a basic model of the essential core activities that occur in all bankruptcy proceedings. Initiating the proceeding and identifying the documents required to be filed have been described in detail in chapter 4 supra.

All professionals rendering services to a bankruptcy estate, such as attorneys, accountants, and appraisers, must have their employment approved by the court at the commencement of the representation. In a Chapter 7, 12, or 13, this task is normally accomplished by filing the Statement of Compensation required by Bankruptcy Rule 2016(b). In Chapter 9 or 11 proceedings, an application to be retained must be filed with and approved by the court. Additionally, a debt relief agency must also provide the various disclosures and enter into a written contract to provide services in a consumer bankruptcy case pursuant to Sections 526-528 as described in chapter 4 supra.

The fees of approved professionals rendering services to a bankruptcy estate may not be paid until the fees have been approved by the court. Court approval is obtained by filing an application for compensation, which is noticed to the creditors. A fee application brought while a case is pending is called an interim application. Generally, interim fee applications may not be brought in less than 120-day intervals. A fee application brought at the close of a proceeding or when all services have been rendered is called a *final application*.

Section 110 of the Code imposes eight requirements on bankruptcy petition preparers who prepare documents for filing by a debtor in the Bankruptcy Court. Paralegals not in the employ of an attorney are subject to this Section. Fines, damages, and injunctive relief can be sought and obtained against a bankruptcy petition preparer found violating Section 110. However, while the Section regulates the conduct of bankruptcy petition preparers, it expressly does not permit a bankruptcy petition preparer to perform services in a jurisdiction where the performance of such services will constitute the unauthorized practice of law.

When a Chapter 7 is filed, the United States Trustee will appoint an interim trustee. The interim trustee will normally become the permanent trustee, although creditors may elect a trustee. A creditors' meeting will be held within 21-40 days of the filing. In a typical consumer no asset proceeding this will usually be the only appearance required by the debtor. At the meeting of creditors, the trustee and creditors may ask questions of the debtor concerning the debtor's financial affairs. If an extended examination is required, a party in interest (such as the trustee or a creditor) may take the equivalent of a deposition of the debtor pursuant to Bankruptcy Rule 2004.

Approximately 60 to 90 days after the meeting of creditors, a debtor will normally receive a discharge. Individual debtors are required to complete a course in personal financial management as a prerequisite to receiving their discharge. The discharge relieves a debtor of all dischargeable legal obligations. Most debts are dischargeable. The discharge is the primary element of debtor relief provided for by the Bankruptcy Code. Exemptions (chapter 10 infra) and the automatic stay (chapter 13 infra) comprise the remaining elements of debtor relief.

Debtors may desire to reaffirm debts. When a debtor agrees to reaffirm a debt, the debt will not be subject to the discharge. The legal obligation to pay the debt will remain. To prevent abuse, a specific statutory procedure must be complied with for a debt to be considered legally reaffirmed.

KEY TERMS

automatic stay
bankruptcy petition
    preparer
consumer no asset
    bankruptcy
creditors' meeting
discharge
disinterested person

exempt
final fee application
fresh start
interim fee application
interim trustee
reaffirmation agreement
Rule 2004 Examination

CHAPTER 8 CHECKLIST

8.1 COMPENSATION OF PROFESSIONALS
    8.1.1 Retention of Counsel (Sections 327, 328, 329)
        1. Chapter 7, 12, or 13 debtor counsel — compliance with Bankruptcy Rule 2016(b) statement

  2. In all other situations, court approval required. File:
   a. noticed motion for approval of retention,
   b. declaration of disinterest,
   c. order approving retention.
 8.1.2 Applications for Compensation (Sections 327, 330, 331; Bankruptcy Rule 2016)
  1. Not more than once every 120 days
  2. Noticed motion
  3. Application should include
   a. summary of services
   b. itemization of time and charges

8.2 REAFFIRMATION AGREEMENTS (Section 524(c)(k))

 8.2.1 Elements
  1. Written agreement prior to discharge (Section 524(c)(1))
  2. Compliance with Section 524(k)
  3. Affidavit of counsel that agreement is voluntary and informed (Section 524(c)(3))
  4. Statement in agreement that debtor has 60 days to rescind (Section 524(c)(2))
 8.2.2 Section 524(k) Requirements

	Document	*Authority*
1.	PART "A" — Preliminary Disclosures	11 U.S.C. §524(k)(3)
2.	PART "B" — Reaffirmation Agreement	11 U.S.C. §524(k)(4)
3.	PART "C" — Debtor's Attorney Certification	11 U.S.C. §524(k)(5)
4.	PART "D" — Debtor's Statement in Support of Reaffirmation Agreement	11 U.S.C. §524(k)(6)(A)
5.	Debtor Statement if attorney	11 U.S.C. §524(k)(6)(B)

6. PART "E" — 11 U.S.C. §524(k)(7)
   Motion for
   Court Approval
   (No attorney)
7. Court Order 11 U.S.C. §524(k)(8)

8.2.3 Hearings
1. If debtor has no attorney in connection with reaffirmation agreement 11 U.S.C. §524(d);
2. With or without an attorney if undue hardship is presumed, except where the debt is owed to a credit union pursuant to 11 U.S.C. §524(m).

8.3 BANKRUPTCY PETITION PREPARERS (Section 110)
8.3.1 Requirements
1. Must sign document including name and address of preparer (Section 110(b));
2. Provide notice that preparer may not give legal advice (Section 110(b)(2));
3. Must include preparer's Social Security number on document (Section 110(c));
4. Must furnish debtor a copy of the document on or before its being presented to debtor for signature (Section 110(d));
5. May not execute a document on behalf of a debtor or provide legal advice to a debtor (Section 110(e));
6. May not use the word *legal* or similar term in advertising and may not advertise under a "legal" category (Section 110(f));
7. May not receive or collect payment for court fees (Section 110(g));
8. Shall, at the filing of the petition, file a statement of compensation paid or promised (Section 110(h)).

8.3.2 Penalties
1. Discretionary fine of $500 (11 U.S.C. §110(k));
2. Disallowance of excessive fees (11 U.S.C. §110(h));
3. Actual damages of $2,000 or twice amount paid by debtor (11 U.S.C. §110(i));
4. Triple damages for disclosure failures (11 U.S.C. §110(k));
5. Injunction against repeated conduct (11 U.S.C. §110(j));
6. Attorneys' fees and costs (11 U.S.C. §110(i)(j)).

DISCUSSION QUESTIONS

1. When must the employment of a professional be approved by the court?

2. What is a fee application? Why might it be important to monitor professional fees in a bankruptcy proceeding?

3. Describe the basic Chapter 7 process.

4. What occurs at the creditors' meeting?

5. What is a Rule 2004 Examination and when is such an examination commonly conducted?

6. What is the effect of a discharge?

7. What is reaffirmation? What are the legal requirements of a reaffirmation agreement?

8. May a paralegal receive fees from clients for the preparation of bankruptcy petitions and schedules if not authorized by state law? What are the potential consequences of preparing bankruptcy petitions for compensation without supervision when not authorized by state law?

PRACTICE EXERCISES

Exercise 8.1
Prepare a draft Rule 2016(b) attorney compensation disclosure statement.

Exercise 8.2
Draft a letter to the Cashes, explaining what they can expect to occur at the 341(a) meeting of creditors, including questions that the trustee may ask.

Exercise 8.3
Draft a reaffirmation agreement on behalf of your client, A to Z Motors, to be presented to the debtors.

9

Conversion and Dismissal

Learning Objectives

- List which conversion requests require a motion before the court

- Describe when a bankruptcy proceeding may be dismissed

- Describe the procedure to convert or dismiss a proceeding and discuss the effect of the conversion or dismissal of a bankruptcy proceeding upon the debtor's financial affairs

A party in interest, such as the debtor, may seek to have a case converted from one Chapter to another, or dismissed. **Conversion** means, for example, that a debtor's Chapter 7 liquidation case is changed to a Chapter 11 or a Chapter 13 reorganization case or vice versa. The most common occurrence is converting a failed effort at reorganization to a liquidation, i.e., converting a Chapter 13 case to a Chapter 7 case, or a Chapter 11 case to a Chapter 7 case. A case may be converted more than once in the course of a single bankruptcy filing.[1]

Conversion: the act of converting a bankruptcy proceeding from one Chapter to another

A proceeding may also be dismissed upon a motion by a party in interest under appropriate circumstances such as presumed abuse of the Chapter 7 process under the needs based bankruptcy formula (see chapter 6 supra). A **dismissal** will terminate a bankruptcy proceeding and render the proceeding ineffective.

Dismissal: the act of terminating a bankruptcy proceeding, the general effect of which is to restore the parties to their rights and liabilities as they existed prior to the bankruptcy filing

---

1. See Fed. R. Bankr. P. 1019.

141

Practice Pointer

It is important to understand the distinction between a "discharge," which relieves the debtor of his/her personal liability, and a "dismissal," which returns the debtor back to his/her prepetition position and reinstates all of his/her prepetition debts and obligations.

Sections 348 and 349 of the Bankruptcy Code contain provisions that apply to the conversion or dismissal of a proceeding. In addition, each separate Chapter proceeding has a specific conversion or dismissal provision applicable only to that particular Chapter.[2] All of these provisions, however, are somewhat similar. The basic principles contained in them are identical, particularly where the issue is conversion rather than dismissal. In this chapter, we will focus on the generic conversion procedure applicable to all proceedings, the general effects of conversion in all proceedings, the effect of a dismissal in all proceedings, and the grounds for dismissal or conversion in Chapter 7 proceedings. The specific grounds for dismissal or conversion of Chapter 11, 12, and 13 reorganization proceedings are described in greater detail elsewhere in this text.[3]

A.   CONVERSION

Generally speaking, a debtor has one opportunity to freely convert a proceeding from one Chapter to another. For example, a debtor may convert a Chapter 7 case to a case under another Chapter, unless the proceeding has been previously converted.[4] The legislative history characterizes this as a "one[-time] absolute right of conversion."[5] A debtor may convert from a Chapter 11 case to a Chapter 7 case, unless a trustee has already been appointed, the proceeding was commenced as an involuntary proceeding, or the proceeding has been previously converted from another Chapter without the debtor's request.[6] A debtor may also convert from

---

2. 11 U.S.C. §§706, 707, 1112, 1208, 1307.
3. See chapters 24, 25, and 28 infra.
4. 11 U.S.C. §706(a).
5. H.R. Rep. No. 595, 95th Cong., 1st Sess. 380 (1977); S. Rep. No. 989, 95th Cong., 2d Sess. 94 (1978).
6. 11 U.S.C. §1112(a). See chapter 24 infra.

Chapter 12 to Chapter 7,[7] or from Chapter 13 to Chapter 7.[8] A waiver of the right to convert is unenforceable.[9] As noted, the most common situation is to convert a failed reorganization to a liquidation proceeding under Chapter 7.

For example, Jed Clampett files a Chapter 7. One week later he discovers oil on his property. He may freely convert his Chapter 7 case to a Chapter 11 or 13 proceeding. Alternatively, Ponzi, Inc., files a Chapter 11 case. A trustee is appointed. Ponzi, Inc., now may no longer freely convert the proceeding to a Chapter 7.

For a debtor to convert from one Chapter proceeding to another, the debtor must also be able to be a debtor under the particular Chapter to which conversion is desired. This is consistent with Section 109.[10]

The Supreme Court has held that the right to convert from a Chapter 7 to another Chapter under the Bankruptcy Code is not entirely absolute. First, the debtor must be qualified to be a debtor under the new Chapter (see chapter 5 supra), and second, the debtor must not be acting in bad faith.[11] In the Marrama case, the debtor fraudulently transferred property to protect it from his creditors, and then he attempted to mislead the court and his creditors. When the trustee attempted to administer the asset, the debtor sought conversion of his case to a Chapter 13 to avoid having a trustee administer the fraudulently transferred property. The Court denied the debtor's right to convert.

To exercise the option to convert, a debtor typically files an ex parte application simply stating that the debtor desires to convert to a specified Chapter and that the debtor is qualified to be a debtor under the Chapter proceeding to which conversion is sought. Theoretically, a statement as simple as, "I am a Chapter 13 debtor and desire to convert to Chapter 7. I am qualified to be a debtor under Chapter 7," will suffice in most instances. A sample form is included on the forms disk that accompanies this text. Although conversion is often effectuated by the filing of an ex parte application as noted above, technically, FRBP 1017(f) requires a noticed motion. Local rules should be consulted for the acceptable procedure in a given court.

Other than the debtor's one opportunity to freely convert from one Chapter proceeding to another, a proceeding may only be converted by obtaining court approval after proper notice to all parties in interest.

---

7. 11 U.S.C. §1208(a). See chapter 28 infra.

8. 11 U.S.C. §1307(a). See chapter 24 infra.

9. 11 U.S.C. §706(a); 11 U.S.C. §1208(a); 11 U.S.C. §1307(a).

10. See chapter 5 supra. See also 11 U.S.C. §706(d); 11 U.S.C. §1112(f); 11 U.S.C. §1208(e); 11 U.S.C. §1307(f). The trend in the case law is that the debtor must seek conversion in good faith. See, e.g., In re Copper, 314 B.R. 628 (6th Cir. BAP 2004).

11. Marrama v. Citizens Bank of Massachusetts, 549 U.S. 365 (2007).

Thus, a debtor desiring to convert from Chapter 7 to Chapter 11, when the proceeding has been previously converted, must first obtain court approval. Any other party in interest, the trustee, or any of the creditors may also move before the court to convert a Chapter 7 to a Chapter 11.[12] Any party in interest may move before the court to convert a proceeding from Chapter 11 to Chapter 7,[13] or to convert a proceeding from Chapter 13 to Chapter 7, and may move to convert a Chapter 13 to a Chapter 11 or 12 prior to confirmation of a Chapter 13 plan.[14] FRBP 1017(f) implements the various applicable provisions.

A nondebtor may not seek conversion of a proceeding from Chapter 7 to a Chapter 12 or 13 unless the debtor consents,[15] nor may a nondebtor seek conversion of a Chapter 11 to a Chapter 12 or 13.[16] A nondebtor may not seek conversion from Chapter 12 to Chapter 7 or 13.[17] A nondebtor may also not seek conversion from Chapter 11 to Chapter 7 for those debtors who may not have an involuntary proceeding filed against them (charitable institutions, for instance),[18] nor may a nondebtor seek conversion of a Chapter 13 to another Chapter 7 if the debtor is a farmer, unless the debtor requests conversion.[19] The rationale of these various prohibitions on the ability of nondebtors to seek conversion of a proceeding from one Chapter to another is identical to the rationale described in chapter 5 supra regarding the exclusion of certain types of debtors from involuntary proceedings, and the prohibition against filing an involuntary Chapter 13.[20]

Section 348 describes the effects of conversion. For most purposes, the basic premise of Section 348 is that if a case is converted from one Chapter to another, the proceeding is generally considered to have been filed under the converted-to Chapter as of the original petition date.[21] Although there are some exceptions, their normal effect is slight.[22] All claims, except the administrative claims that arose in the converted proceeding, are considered to have arisen before the original filing date.[23] For example, consider a Chapter 7 case that is filed on May 28 and then converted to a Chapter 11 case on May 29. Under Section 348, the May 28 order for relief will generally be the effective date of the Chapter 11 filing. The major reason for this rule is that any other date would hopelessly

---

12. 11 U.S.C. §706(b).
13. 11 U.S.C. §1112(b).
14. 11 U.S.C. §1307(c); 11 U.S.C. §1307(d).
15. 11 U.S.C. §706(c).
16. 11 U.S.C. §1112(d).
17. 11 U.S.C. §§1208, 1307.
18. 11 U.S.C. §1112(c). See chapter 4 supra.
19. 11 U.S.C. §1307(f).
20. See chapter 4 supra.
21. 11 U.S.C. §348(a).
22. 11 U.S.C. §348(b), (c).
23. 11 U.S.C. §348(d).

complicate and confuse the many accounting features contained in the bankruptcy system. Because one function of the bankruptcy system is to reconcile the financial affairs of a debtor as of a date certain, only one date should be used, not two or more.

When a Chapter 11 or 13 is converted to a Chapter 7, the debtor or superseded trustee is responsible for filing a final report and accounting with the court. Additionally, any necessary updating that may be required to conform the Statements and Schedules to reflect changes in the debtor's financial condition occurring between the original filing date and the conversion date should also be prepared.[24]

When a Chapter 13 is converted to a Chapter 7, the Supreme Court has ruled that undistributed Chapter 13 plan payments made from a debtor's wages and held by the trustee when the case is converted are to be returned to the debtor. In *Harris v Viegelahn,* U.S., 135 S. Ct. 1829 (2015), the Chapter 13 trustee was holding over $5,000 of plan payments made from the debtor's postpetition wages and wanted to distribute the proceeds to creditors. Because a debtor's postpetition wages are not considered property of the bankruptcy estate in a Chapter 7, and because the effect of conversion is to treat a case as if it had originally been filed under the converted to chapter, the debtor, and not her creditors, was entitled to a return of the undistributed funds. The Supreme Court stated: "By excluding postpetition wages from the converted Chapter 7 estate, §348(f)(1)(A) removes those earnings from the pool of assets that may be liquidated and distributed to creditors. Allowing a terminated Chapter 13 trustee to disburse the very same earnings to the very same creditors is incompatible with that statutory design."[25]

To summarize the rules on conversion:

Type of Application	Applicant	Motion Required	Notice Required	Code Section
Convert 7 to 11, 12, or 13	Debtor	Yes, FRBP 1017(f)(2); 9013	Service by debtor; conversion order served by clerk FRBP 2002(f)	706(a)
Convert 7 to 11	Any party in interest	Yes, FRBP 9014	21 days' notice by clerk FRBP 2002(a)(4)	706(b)
Convert 11 to 7	Debtor	Yes, FRBP 1017(f)(2); 9013	21 days' notice by clerk FRBP 2002(a)(4)	1112(a)

---

24. Bankruptcy Rule 1019.
25. As to property of the estate, see Chapter 15 infra.

Type of Application	Applicant	Motion Required	Notice Required	Code Section
Convert 11 to 7	Any party in interest	Yes, FRBP 9014	21 days' notice by clerk FRBP 2002(a)(4)	1112(b)
Convert 11 to 7	UST	Yes, FRBP 9014	21 days' notice by clerk FRBP 2002(a)(4)	1112(e)
Convert 11 to 12 or 13	Debtor	Yes, FRBP 9014	21 days' notice by clerk FRBP 2002(a)(4)	1112(d)
Convert 13 to 7	Debtor	No, FRBP 1017(f)(3)	Conversion notice served by clerk on UST FRBP 1017(f)(3)	1307(a)
Convert 13 to 7	Any party in interest or UST	Yes, FRBP 9014	No; conversion notice served by clerk on UST FRBP 1017(f)(3)	1307(c) or 1307(e) for failure to file tax returns
Convert 13 to 11 or 12	Any party in interest or UST	Yes, FRBP 9014	21 days' notice by clerk FRBP 2002(a)(4)	1307(d)

B. DISMISSAL

A Chapter 7 case may be dismissed upon order of the court. Unlike conversion, dismissal always requires a noticed motion, except that a Chapter 13 debtor may voluntarily dismiss a Chapter 13 case by filing an ex parte application if the case has not previously been converted.[26] Additionally, Section 521(i) requires automatic dismissal of a case on the forty-sixth day after filing if a debtor has not filed all documents required by Section 521(a)(1).[27] A debtor's case may also be dismissed if he/she fails to file any tax returns that come due, or to seek an extension of the time frame, postpetition.[28] Creditors, the trustee, or the United States Trustee may seek dismissal of a Chapter 7 for cause, including unreasonable delay or failure to pay filing fees.[29] The United States Trustee may seek dismissal if a debtor fails to file Statements and Schedules in a timely manner.[30]

---

26. 11 U.S.C. §1307(b).
27. 11 U.S.C. §521(a)(1). See chapter 4B supra. The provision does permit a debtor to seek one 45-day extension.
28. 11 U.S.C. §521(j).
29. 11 U.S.C. §707(a)(1)(2).
30. 11 U.S.C. §707(a)(3).

The court, the United States Trustee, the Chapter 7 trustee, or any party in interest may also seek a dismissal of a consumer proceeding pursuant to Section 707(b)(1) if allowing the proceeding to continue would constitute an abuse of Chapter 7. This ground for dismissal creates a mechanism that, in appropriate circumstances, effectively forces a debtor to file a Chapter 11 or 13 if bankruptcy relief is to be obtained. Under means testing, Section 707(b)(2) requires dismissal of a case where abuse is presumed pursuant to the formula described in chapter 6 supra. A motion brought pursuant to this provision must be brought within 60 days of the creditors' meeting unless this deadline is extended by the court.[31]

A proceeding may also be dismissed upon a noticed motion if the court finds that dismissal is in the best interests of creditors.[32] For example, if a sale of the debtor's assets produces sufficient revenue to pay all creditors in full and provide a dividend to the debtor, dismissal may be a cost-effective remedy, as long as the order protects the creditors' rights to ensure prompt payment of the claims. Dismissal in such a manner may save substantial time and expense, result in payment to all creditors, and remove the bankruptcy as a stigma upon the debtor. The court's ruling on a motion to dismiss on this basis is not reviewable by appeal or otherwise.[33]

Section 349 describes the effects of a dismissal. Generally, a dismissal returns all parties to their rights and liabilities as they existed prior to the filing, as if nothing had ever happened.[34]

To summarize the rules on dismissals:

Type of Application	Applicant	Motion Required	Notice Required	Code Section
Dismiss 7	Any party in interest	Yes, FRBP 9014	21 days' notice by clerk FRBP 2002(a)(4); expect for failure to pay filing fee or file schedules or for substantial abuse	707(a)

---

31. 11 U.S.C. §707(b)(1); FRBP 1017(e). See, e.g., In re Kornfeld, 164 F.3d 778 (2d Cir. 1999).
32. 11 U.S.C. §305(a).
33. 11 U.S.C. §305(c).
34. 11 U.S.C. §349.

Type of Application	Applicant	Motion Required	Notice Required	Code Section
Dismiss 7 for abuse	UST or court	Yes, FRBP 9014 Within 60 days of 341 meeting FRBP 1017(e)(1)	Service by UST or court on debtor, trustee & UST FRBP 1017(e); dismissal notice served by clerk FRBP 2002(f)	707(b)
Dismiss 11	Any party in interest	Yes, FRBP 9014	21 days' notice by clerk FRBP 2002(a)(4)	1112(b)
Dismiss 13 if no prior conversion	Debtor	Yes, FRBP 1017(f)(2); 9013	Service by debtor; dismissal notice served by clerk FRBP 2002(f)	1307(b)
Dismiss 13 for failure to file tax return	Any party in interest or UST	Yes, FRBP 9014	21 days' notice by clerk FRBP 2002(a)(4)	1307(e)
Dismiss for failure to file schedules (all Chapters)	UST or court	Yes, FRBP 9014	UST to serve debtor & trustee in Ch. 7 & 13 FRBP 1017(c); 21 days' notice by clerk for Ch. 11 FRBP 2002(a)(4)	707(a)(3) 1112(e) 1307(c)(9)
Dismiss for nonpayment of fees	Court for filing fees/ clerk's fees	No for court Yes for party in interest FRBP 9014	Court fees — notice goes to trustee & debtor FRBP 1017(b)	707(a)(2) 1112(b)(4) 1307(c)(2)
	Party in interest or UST for Ch. 11 & 13		Ch. 11 UST quarterly fees — 21 days' notice by clerk FRBP 2002(a)(4)	

Summary

A bankruptcy proceeding may be converted or dismissed. A conversion will switch a bankruptcy proceeding from one Chapter to another (such as from Chapter 11 to Chapter 7). A dismissal will terminate a bankruptcy proceeding and restore the parties to their prepetition status.

Normally, a debtor is given one opportunity to convert a proceeding from one Chapter to another. This act is accomplished by filing an Application to Convert with the court. Provided that the debtor is qualified to be a debtor in the Chapter for which conversion is sought, and that the debtor is acting in good faith, then the right to convert is absolute.

Other than the debtor's one opportunity to convert, conversion may only otherwise occur upon court order after a noticed motion. Thus, a creditor or the United States Trustee seeking to convert a case must always do so by way of a noticed motion. If the proceeding has been previously converted (such as a debtor desiring to convert a second time) or if a trustee has been appointed in a Chapter 11 proceeding, without regard to any prior conversion, even the debtor must convert by way of a noticed motion.

The general effect of a conversion is that the proceeding is considered to have been filed under the converted-to Chapter as of the petition's original filing date. When a proceeding is converted, some additional reports will also be required to be filed with the court, primarily to update changes from the original filing.

Any Chapter proceeding may be dismissed for one of two reasons: for cause or when it is in the best interest of creditors. Each Chapter proceeding contains specific provisions defining the grounds for a dismissal for cause. Unreasonable delay that prejudices creditors or a failure to pay filing fees are two common reasons for dismissal for cause. A case may also be dismissed if the court finds that dismissal will be in the best interest of creditors. A consumer Chapter 7 case is subject to dismissal if allowing the proceeding would constitute an abuse of Chapter 7. The general effect of a dismissal is to essentially render the bankruptcy proceeding ineffective, and restore all parties to their prepetition status to the greatest extent possible.

KEY TERMS

conversion   dismissal

DISCUSSION QUESTIONS

1. What does it mean to convert a bankruptcy proceeding?

2. When may a debtor convert a case from one Chapter to another without a noticed motion?

3. When must a motion to convert be made?

4. What is the difference between conversion of a bankruptcy proceeding and a dismissal of a bankruptcy proceeding?

5. What sorts of conduct may be an abuse of Chapter 7 in addition to the presumption of abuse that may exist pursuant to "needs based bankruptcy"?

PRACTICE EXERCISE

Exercise 9.1
Draft a motion to convert the Cashes' Chapter 7 to a Chapter 13.

10
Exemptions

Learning Objectives

- Define exemptions
- Demonstrate the concept of exemptions and their importance to individual debtors in bankruptcy proceedings
- Describe the Code concept of the "opt out" provision
- Analyze which exemptions to select, when a choice is available
- Identify how exemptions are claimed by individual debtors
- Identify specific exemptions
- Describe the homestead exemption and how a homestead is claimed in many jurisdictions
- Describe how a claim of exemption is opposed by the trustee or a creditor

A. BACKGROUND

Individual debtors seek two primary goals in obtaining bankruptcy debtor relief: a discharge and the exemption of property. The achievement of these goals provides a debtor with a **fresh start** in the debtor's financial affairs. The fresh start concept is the basic foundation of congressional intent in permitting individual debtors to seek bankruptcy relief.[1]

Fresh start: the phrase most frequently used colloquially to describe the basic elements of debtor relief: discharge, exemptions, and the automatic stay

---

1. H.R. Rep. No. 595, 95th Cong., 1st Sess., 366-367 (1977); S. Rep. No. 989, 95th Cong., 2d Sess., 81 (1978).

Only individual debtors may claim **exemptions**.[2] Exemptions allow a debtor to protect property from the reach of creditors or the trustee in a bankruptcy proceeding. Property for which an exemption is claimed and allowed is not subject to administration by a trustee and is not available for liquidation to pay a dividend to creditors.[3] A debtor may keep exempt property.

The concept of exemptions for individual debtors is a relatively recent one.[4] The Bankruptcy Act did not contain independent exemptions. Exemptions existed only as provided for under the state law of the debt-or's domicile or residence. This led to the development of 50 bodies of law regarding exemptions in bankruptcy proceedings.

State exemption statutes have traditionally offered more protection to owners of real property (referring to homes and other real estate) than to owners of nonreal property (sometimes referred to as personalty). The most common form of such protection is called the **homestead exemption**. This exemption exists in spite of the practical reality that many individual debtors do not own real property. The rise of this exemption is a historical anachronism most likely rooted in sixteenth- and seven-teenth-century English bankruptcy law, which gave substantial protection to real property owners by preventing bankruptcy proceedings from being initiated against them.[5]

When Congress enacted the Bankruptcy Code, it decided to create a uniform set of federal exemptions. The **federal exemptions**, when properly utilized, eliminate the inherent economic discrimination that has existed between real property owners and those people who do not own real property but who hold other forms of property, so that these personal property owners may now have an opportunity to exempt property of a value equal to that of real property owners.[6] The federal exemption scheme also seeks to bring some national consistency to the concept of exempt property. In some states, exemption statutes reflect the style of early twenty-first century living, while other states have not significantly revised their exemption statutes in the past 100 years. There are still states in which church pews may be claimed exempt.[7] There are some states in which specific types of obsolete nineteenth-century farm-ing implements may be claimed exempt.[8] And there are still other states

---

2. 11 U.S.C. §522(b).
3. 11 U.S.C. §522(c).
4. See chapter 1 supra.
5. Leventhal, The Early History of English Bankruptcy, 67 U. Pa. L. Rev. 1 (1919).
6. See discussion concerning 11 U.S.C. §522(d)(5) infra.
7. Ala. Code §6-10-5.
8. See 32 L.P.R.A. §1130(3) permitting "one cart or wagon" to be exempt.

with even more obscure exemptions that relate only to the nineteenth-century lifestyle.[9]

Section 522(b) provides that a debtor or joint debtors may elect to exempt property from one of two allowable sets of exemptions. A debtor may elect to utilize the exemptions that exist under the state or local law where the debtor has been domiciled for at least 730 days (two years) immediately prior to the filing of the petition, or the place where the debtor resided for a majority of the 180 days preceding the 730-day period, as well as any other nonbankruptcy exemptions permitted by federal law, plus any interest in property held by the debtor immediately preceding the filing as a tenant by the entirety or joint tenant to the extent that it is exempt under nonbankruptcy law, and various individual retirement accounts and retirement funds that are exempt from federal income taxation.[10] Or the debtor may elect to utilize the exemptions provided for under the federal exemption scheme contained in 11 U.S.C. §522(d). If the time limits prevent a debtor from claiming any exemptions, then a debtor may select the federal exemptions. BAPCPA also limits the debtor's ability to claim a homestead exemption under state law to $160,375, even if the state law provides for a greater exemption, unless the property involved was acquired more than 1,215 days prior to the filing of the petition, except for property acquired during the same period from a transfer of the debtor's principal residence in the same state.[11]

For example, Tom Braidy resides in Massachusetts. His employer, Inflation Engineering, transfers Tom to California. If Tom files bankruptcy in California within 730 days of moving, his allowable state exemptions would be those of Massachusetts, and his homestead exemption would be limited to $160,375. On the other hand, if Tom lived in California in the first place and is transferred from northern to southern California, then his homestead exemption would be determined solely by California law since he has only moved within the state.

Although each individual debtor may choose which set of exemptions they wish to utilize, joint debtors must each select the same set of exemptions.[12] That is, joint debtors must each elect to utilize either the

---

9. See N.H. Rev. Stat. Ann. §511:2(VII) permitting exemption of "the uniform, arms and equipments of every officer and private in the militia."

10. In Clark v. Rameker, 573 U.S., (2014), the Supreme Court held that an inherited IRA account is not a retirement fund within the meaning of the Bankruptcy Code.

11. 11 U.S.C. §522(b); 11 U.S.C. §522(p). The extended time periods and limitations on homestead amounts were added to the Bankruptcy Code by BAPCPA. Their intent is to discourage persons from moving to a state with high exemption limits and then declaring bankruptcy. These revisions will require the Bankruptcy Courts to become familiar with the exemption law of all jurisdictions.

12. 11 U.S.C. §522(b)(1); 11 U.S.C. §522(m).

> **Practice Pointer**
>
> If the debtor elects to use the so-called "state exemptions" available under 522(b)(3), they are entitled to:
>
> 1. state and local law exemptions;
> 2. all federal law exemptions, except those provided in 11 U.S.C. §522(d);
> 3. property interests held as a tenant by the entirety or joint tenant IF it is exempt under nonbankruptcy law; and
> 4. retirement funds to the extent they are exempt from federal taxation.

applicable state exemptions or the federal exemptions provided for in Section 522(d). They are not permitted to have one spouse claim the state exemptions while the other spouse attempts to claim the federal exemptions. If joint debtors cannot agree on which set to claim, or where none are claimed, the debtors are deemed to have selected the federal exemption scheme.[13] The now-prohibited practice of one debtor claiming exemptions under state law and one debtor claiming federal exemptions was known as **stacking**. However, if each debtor holds an interest in a given item of property, they may each claim an exemption in that property, effectively doubling their marital exemption.[14]

Stacking: individual joint debtors claiming state and federal exemptions

For example, let's assume that Owen and Robin Cash wish to file a Chapter 7 proceeding. Each may select the allowable exemptions under the state law of their domicile (residence) or each may select the federal exemptions provided in 11 U.S.C. §522(d).[15] Both Owen and Robin will be able to claim a full set of exemptions under this election. If Owen and Robin forget to claim exemptions, or if they cannot agree on which set to claim, they will be deemed to have selected the federal exemptions. Owen, however, cannot claim exemptions under state law while Robin claims the federal exemptions.

There is, however, one provision of 11 U.S.C. §522(b) that complicates a debtor's election to claim exemptions. Section 522(b)(2) provides that debtors can claim property exempt under subsection (d) unless the state law applicable to the debtor does not so authorize. This means that

---

13. 11 U.S.C. §522(b).
14. 11 U.S.C. §522(m).
15. The exemptions allowed under 11 U.S.C. §522(d) shall hereafter be referred to as the *federal exemptions*.

Congress has provided the states an opportunity to withdraw from the federal exemption scheme of 11 U.S.C. §522(d). That is, state law may properly prevent a debtor or joint debtors from electing the federal exemptions. Thus, although the Bankruptcy Code gives a debtor an election to use state or federal exemptions, Congress has also given individual states the opportunity to "opt out" of the federal exemption scheme. In any state that has chosen to opt out of the federal exemptions, debtors are not given a choice of exemptions to elect. Debtors residing in such a state may only claim the exemptions provided for under the law of that particular state. In the above example, if Jane and John Smith resided in a state that has successfully opted out of the federal exemptions, they would not be permitted an election. They could claim the exemptions of their state of domicile or they could claim no exemptions. Thirty-two states had successfully opted out of the federal exemption scheme as of November 2016.[16] In those remaining states that have not opted out of the federal exemptions, a debtor will be able to elect state or federal exemptions pursuant to 11 U.S.C. §522(b).

B.   SELECTING EXEMPTIONS

Other than the initial decision to file a bankruptcy petition in the first place, the decision to select appropriate exemptions is the most important decision to be made in the scope of a consumer no asset Chapter 7 proceeding, and it is also one of the most important decisions to make in any Chapter 12, 13, or individual Chapter 11 proceeding. Advice to a debtor concerning the proper exemptions to select is a legal decision and may only be made by a licensed attorney. Counseling a potential debtor regarding the choice of exemptions constitutes the practice of law. A nonattorney rendering this advice to a potential debtor may be guilty of the unauthorized practice of law, which is a criminal violation in many states.[17] In a state that has authorized paralegals to prepare bankruptcy

---

16. As of November 2016, they are: Alabama, Arizona, California, Colorado, Delaware, Florida, Georgia, Idaho, Illinois, Indiana, Iowa, Kansas, Louisiana, Maine, Maryland, Mississippi, Missouri, Montana, Nebraska, Nevada, North Carolina, North Dakota, Ohio, Oklahoma, Oregon, South Carolina, South Dakota, Tennessee, Utah, Virginia, West Virginia, and Wyoming. William H. Brown, Lawrence R. Ahern, III & Nancy F. MacLean, Bankruptcy Exemption Manual, §4.02 (2010).
17. In re Anderson, 79 B.R. 482 (Bankr. S.D. Cal. 1987). This case has been widely followed. See, e.g., In re Reynoso, 477 F.3d 1117 (9th Cir. 2007) (concluding the use of web-based software to complete schedules constituted unauthorized practice of law); Wynns v. Adams, 426 B.R. 457 (E.D.N.Y. 2010).

petitions, the provisions of Code Section 110 will apply (see section 8B supra). This principle applies regardless of the apparent simplicity involved in counseling many potential debtors regarding the proper exemptions to select. This is not a study on the exemption law of individual states. Readers are left to their own devices to ascertain the specific exemption statutes of individual states. However, many of the items permitted to be claimed exempt under federal law are commonly permitted as exemptions under relevant state law.

Generally, a debtor should elect the exemptions that will allow the most property to be claimed exempt. Occasions may arise, however, in which a debtor, for noneconomic reasons, will not want to elect the exemptions that will exempt the most property. In these situations, a professional must always remember that the client always makes the ultimate choice when alternatives are available. But, as a general rule, one should always recommend selection of the exemptions that will exempt the most possible property from administration by a trustee.

The debtor's ownership of real property subject to a homestead exemption under state law will normally determine which set of exemptions will be most appropriate for a debtor to select. In this instance, counsel must make certain that the proper procedure to declare a homestead has been followed under the applicable state law or the exemption may be lost and the property subject to administration by the trustee. Generally, a homestead declaration must be recorded prior to filing any bankruptcy petition or the exemption will be subject to invalidity under the trustee's avoiding powers.[18] However, where equity in the subject real property is limited or nonexistent, a debtor owning real property subject to a potential homestead exemption may, as a practical matter, gain greater ultimate benefits by claiming the federal rather than state exemptions.

Equity: the value in an asset over and above that of any liens or encumbrances, such as equity in a home or motor vehicle

A homestead exemption will normally allow an individual debtor to claim as exempt a defined amount of **equity** in the debtor's residence. Equity is the value of an asset over and above that of any liens or encumbrances. Of course, the equity must exist for the exemption to acquire any real value. Popular misconception to the contrary, a homestead exemption is not a guarantee to the property owner. For example, the Simpsons own a home with a value of $100,000. A mortgage in the amount of $80,000 encumbers the property. The Simpsons' equity in the home is thus $20,000. In a state with a homestead exemption of $20,000 or more, all of the equity may be claimed exempt. In a state with a homestead exemption of less than $20,000, only the maximum statutory amount would be subject to the exemption. BAPCPA limits a homestead exemption to

---

18. See chapter 16 infra.

$160,375 where a debtor has moved from one state to another in the 730 days preceding the filing of the petition, as discussed at chapter 10A supra.

C.   FEDERAL EXEMPTIONS

Section 522(d) contains the substantive federal exemptions. When reference is made to the federal exemptions, the reference is normally to the exemptions contained within Section 522(d). Consumer no asset Chapter 7 debtors not owning real estate with any significant equity will usually be able to exempt more property under these provisions than under any applicable state law, where the federal exemptions are available.

Bankruptcy Code Section 104(b), enacted in 1994, is designed to account for the effects of inflation on the Section 522(d) exemption amounts. Section 104(c) provides that the adjustments do not apply to cases filed before the date of a particular adjustment. For example, the previous exemption of $3,675 applicable to motor vehicles under Section 522(d)(2) applies only to cases filed before April 1, 2016, and after April 1, 2013. The new value of $3,775 applies to cases filed on or after April 1, 2016.

Every third April, commencing in 1998, the exemption amounts are increased to reflect changes in the published Department of Labor Consumer Price Index for all urban consumers for the most recent three-year period. The amounts are published in the Federal Register one month before they become effective. For example, if the total inflation for the period January 1, 1995, to December 31, 1997, was 10 percent, then all of the Section 522(d) amounts would be raised accordingly, rounding off to the nearest $25. For example, a $15,000 limit in Section 522(d)(1) would become $16,500. For our purposes here, the text reflects the changes effective as of April 1, 2016.

Section 522(d)(1) allows a debtor to exempt equity in the residence of the debtor, or in real property owned by the debtor and resided in by a dependent, or in a burial plot owned by the debtor, up to $23,675. Joint debtors selecting the exemptions under 522(d) can conceivably exempt up to $47,350 of equity in real property of these types.[19] To claim this exemption under federal law, it is not necessary to record a homestead or to take any action other than the procedures described below in this

---

19. 11 U.S.C. §522(d)(1); §522(m).

chapter. When claiming the federal exemptions, this exemption is automatically available.

Under Section 522(d)(2) each debtor may claim exempt $3,775 of equity in one motor vehicle.[20] Joint debtors may therefore each claim a $3,775 exemption in equity in two separate vehicles if each debtor claims one vehicle exempt. However, a debtor owning more than one vehicle may only claim one exemption because the statute limits the exemption to only one vehicle.

Section 522(d)(3) permits a debtor to exempt household goods, household furniture, wearing apparel, books, animals, musical instruments, or crops held primarily for personal or household use. In other words, this exemption permits a debtor to exempt the so-called necessities of life. The Code eliminates the image of paupers wearing barrels with suspenders. The exemption is limited to an aggregate value of $12,625, while each item claimed exempt must have a value not exceeding $600.[21]

Market value: the value of an asset, real or personal, sold in the ordinary course of business according to commercially reasonable terms

Value is determined by looking at the realistic **market value** of the particular asset claimed exempt. This applies to all exemptions. BAPCPA requires that assets be valued in the Statements and Schedules at their **replacement value**, defined as "the price a retail merchant would charge for property of that kind considering the age and condition of the property at the time value is determined."[22]

Replacement value: the price a retail merchant would charge for property of that kind considering the age and condition of the property at the time value is determined

As a practical matter, the realistic market value of an asset is normally the asset's **liquidation value**, except in the case of real property. While personal property often has a depressed value in a bankruptcy, the fair market value of real property is usually affected less in the eyes of potential buyers. Liquidation value is normally the value that one would obtain in the context of a forced sale, such as a garage liquidation sale, public auction, or "going out of business" sale. This is a realistic perception, because if the same assets are liquidated by a bankruptcy trustee they will most likely be sold at a public auction to the highest bidders.[23]

Liquidation value: the value to be obtained from a forced sale of assets

The dollar limitations contained in 11 U.S.C. §522(d)(3) apply to each individual item of personal property claimed exempt. This proviso means exactly what it says: "any particular item." For example, if a debtor has an imported Chinese rosewood dining room table and eight accompanying rosewood chairs, the whole set together may be very valuable. However, "any particular item" means each individual chair and the table are all

---

20. 11 U.S.C. §522(d)(2).
21. 11 U.S.C. §522(d)(3).
22. 11 U.S.C. §506(a)(2); 11 U.S.C. §522(a)(2); 11 U.S.C. §527(a)(2)(B).
23. See chapters 11 and 19 infra. In the reorganization proceedings of Chapter 11 or 13, the retail value may need to be applied. See Associated Commercial Corp. v. Rash, 520 U.S. 953 (1997), discussed in chapter 22 infra. Case law will determine how *Rash* may be affected by BAPCPA and how "replacement value" is interpreted relative to liquidation value.

considered as separate items. A living room set meets with the identical approach: Each end table is an individual item, each chair is an individual item, and so forth. The same applies to a bedroom set. The same analysis can apply to a home entertainment system: The television monitor is an individual item, the DVD or Blu-ray is an individual item, the video game hardware is an individual item, each computer monitor is an individual item, each hard drive, each sound system attached to each computer, and so forth and so on are all individual items. So long as the aggregate value is not greater than $12,625, and an individual item has a value not exceeding $600, all of the debtor's personal property may be properly claimed exempt under 11 U.S.C. §522(d)(3).

As a practical matter, it is not necessary to have a potential individual debtor provide a line-by-line itemization of all personal assets. Although there are occasions when a trustee will desire such data, it is generally not a necessity. A potential individual debtor need not normally provide an itemized list of wearing apparel, such as "twelve t-shirts, six Fruit-of-the-Looms" and so forth. Local practice may vary, however, and inquiry should always be made as to local custom, local rule, or any applicable guidelines of the United States Trustee.

For particular items that may have a value of more than $600, the exemption provided for under Section 522(d)(5), described below, may be an effective remedy for claiming such assets exempt. It is, however, prudent to itemize any items that may exceed the $600 per item limit.

Any unique collections should be itemized. If a debtor has potentially valuable furnishings or wardrobe, such as the rosewood dining room set mentioned above or a fur, or a unique collection such as a collection of Happy Meal toys, or autographs of all of the original Star Trek actors, obtaining a written appraisal prior to filing is helpful in preparing the debtor's schedules and in claiming exemptions. The appraisal will also be helpful in answering any questions of the trustee or creditors in connection with the asset's value. This one act can save time and expense, in the form of attorneys' fees, should the trustee wish to object to the exemption simply because no prior appraisal has been obtained. Debtors in this possible situation should reasonably be able to afford the nominal appraisal costs. Case law may very well determine that the duties imposed upon counsel under BAPCPA, to make "reasonable inquiry" to establish an asset's value, require written appraisals of unique assets. See Bankruptcy Code §527(a)(2)(B).

What unique or potentially valuable items will the Cashes have to list or be potentially concerned about exempting?

FACT PATTERN

Section 522(d)(4) permits the exemption of $1,600 in jewelry held for personal use of the debtor or a dependent.[24] Most wedding rings can be safely exempted under this provision. Potentially valuable items of jewelry should be appraised beforehand as described above.

FACT PATTERN

How should Owen Cash handle disclosing and attempting to exempt the engagement ring that he recently purchased but did not yet give to his wife Robin?

Catch-all exemption: consists of any unused portion of the federal homestead exemption, up to the amount of $11,850, plus $1,250, for a total of $13,100 in any property of any kind

Section 522(d)(5) is perhaps the most important of the federal exemptions. It is the exemption that sets the federal exemptions apart from traditional state exemptions. In common parlance, Section 522(d)(5) is called the "omnibus," "catch-all," or "wildcard" exemption. The **catch-all exemption** consists of any unused portion of the federal homestead exemption (11 U.S.C. §522(d)(1) supra), up to the amount of $11,850, plus $1,250, for a total of $13,100 in any property of any kind.[25] "Any property" means all property, with one limited exception described below. Individual items of household goods worth more than $600 a piece may be claimed exempt under this provision. Jewelry not exempt under Section 522(d)(4) may be claimed exempt under this provision. Equity in a vehicle greater than $3,775 may be claimed exempt here. An otherwise nonexempt tax refund may be claimed exempt under this provision. Cash in the bank may be claimed exempt. A second vehicle owned by one debtor or a third vehicle owned by joint debtors may be claimed exempt under this provision. Anything — absolutely, positively anything — may be claimed exempt under this provision.

Property recovered for the estate by the trustee's avoiding powers may conceivably be claimed exempt under Section 522(d)(5) as long as the transfer avoided by the trustee has been involuntary on the part of the debtor. Thus, property subject to an avoidable lien may be claimed exempt. However, if the debtor voluntarily made the avoidable transfer such as a preference or a fraudulent transfer to a relative, intending to conceal the property from creditors, or if the debtor fails to disclose the transfer in the Statements and Schedules, the transaction may not be claimed exempt under Section 522(d)(5). This is the one exception to the broad meaning of the phrase "any property." For example, creditor Sheldon Cooper obtains a judicial attachment on Debtor Penny's assets immediately prior to Penny filing her Chapter 7. Because the trustee can avoid this transaction, Penny may claim the assets exempt under Section

---

24. 11 U.S.C. §522(d)(4).
25. 11 U.S.C. §522(d)(5).

522(d)(5) or any other allowable exemption. If the trustee does not seek to set aside the avoidable transaction, Penny may take action herself to do so. However, if Penny proffered voluntary payment to Sheldon as a preference, she likely could not claim the assets so transferred as exempt.[26]

The catch-all provision of Section 522(d)(5) attempts to eliminate the economic discrimination that existed prior to enactment of the Bankruptcy Code, when the existing exemptions available under state law favored homeowners substantially more than nonhomeowners. For individuals who did not own their homes, there generally existed no exemptions in state law beyond vehicle equity and the bare necessities of life. In enacting the Bankruptcy Code, Congress has concluded that it would be fair to create an exemption for nonhomeowners to afford them the same opportunities for a fresh start in their financial affairs that exists for homeowners able to take advantage of homestead exemptions. Hence, the catch-all exemption, which allows a debtor or debtors to claim exempt any property in existence up to the limits of the catch-all in lieu of a homestead exemption.

A debtor claiming real property exempt under the federal homestead provision (11 U.S.C. §522(d)(1)) may claim additional property exempt under the catch-all provision if there is an available balance after accounting for the real property equity. For example, Joe Debtor owns a house with $15,000 of equity. There is an unused balance of the Section 522(d)(1) exemption available for use under Section 522(d)(5) of $8,675 plus $1,250, for a total of $9,925. This amount may be used by Joe to claim any property in existence exempt.

Section 522(d)(6) allows a debtor to exempt $2,375 of value in tools of the trade or professional implements. For example, a data entry technician working as an independent contractor might be able to exempt a personal computer under this provision.[27]

Unmatured life insurance contracts are exempt under Section 522(d)(7).[28] Term insurance or policies with no cash value may also be claimed exempt under this provision.

---

26. See the Legislative Notes to 11 U.S.C. §522(d). See also chapters 15-18 for a discussion of the trustee's avoiding powers. Although it may have been thought that voluntary preferences and even voluntary fraudulent transfers could be claimed exempt under §522(d)(5), recent case law has begun to disfavor use of §522(d)(5) to claim these transactions exempt. See, e.g., In re Kaba, 2007 WL 1556842 (Bankr. N.D. Tex. 2007) (preference found not to be property of the estate and thus not subject to exemption); In re Terry, 279 B.R. 240 (Bankr. W.D. Ark. 2002) (fraudulently concealed property not subject to exemption). See also 11 U.S.C. §522(g), (h), (j), which supports this view. 11 U.S.C. §522(o), added by BAPCPA, reduces the value of property by any amount attributable to fraudulent transfers.
27. 11 U.S.C. §522(d)(6).
28. 11 U.S.C. §522(d)(7).

Section 522(d)(8) allows a debtor to claim as exempt cash value in an insurance policy up to $12,625.[29] A whole life insurance policy bearing a cash value may therefore be fully or partially claimed exempt under this provision. Loans or other debts owed against the policy's cash value are specifically excluded from the total cash value claimed exempt when the insurance company has a right to set off the debt owed it against the policy's cash value.[30]

Professionally prescribed health aids of a debtor or a debtor's dependent such as glasses, contact lenses, or orthopedic shoes are exempt under Section 522(d)(9). There is no dollar limitation on this exemption.[31] Social Security benefits, welfare benefits, veterans' benefits, alimony, qualified pension and profit sharing plans, and disability and unemployment benefits may all be claimed exempt under Section 522(d)(10).[32] In Rousey v. Jacoway, 544 U.S. 320 (2005), the Supreme Court held that IRA accounts may be claimed exempt within the meaning of Section 522(d)(10), resolving a conflict among the circuits. Section 522(d)(12), enacted by BAPCPA, codifies this result. See below.

Under Section 522(d)(11) certain aspects of personal injury compensation may be claimed exempt. A right to receive compensation or property under a crime victim's reparation law may be claimed exempt without regard to amount.[33] Wrongful death recoveries for an individual of whom the debtor was a dependent, payment from a life insurance policy insuring the life of an individual of whom the debtor was a dependent, and compensation for lost future earnings of the debtor or of an individual of whom the debtor was or is a dependent may be claimed exempt "to the extent reasonably necessary for the support of the debtor or a dependent of the debtor."[34] The amount reasonably necessary for the support of a debtor or dependent of the debtor will be a question of fact in each individual case. Personal injury compensation may be claimed exempt up to $23,675. However, pain and suffering and actual damages are specifically not included in calculating the exemption amount.[35] For example, a debtor with a million-dollar personal injury claim may conceivably claim all the recovery exempt depending on how the recovery is based. However, as a practical matter, since this debtor may be able to pay all creditors in full and leave a substantial balance for the debtor, if there is

---

29. 11 U.S.C. §522(d)(8).
30. 11 U.S.C. §542(d).
31. 11 U.S.C. §522(d)(9).
32. 11 U.S.C. §522(d)(10).
33. 11 U.S.C. §522(d)(11)(A).
34. 11 U.S.C. §522(d)(11)(B), (C), (E).
35. 11 U.S.C. §522(d)(11)(D). As to the pain and suffering calculation, see In re Scotti, 245 B.R. 17 (Bankr. D. N.J. 2000).

a recovery, a debtor in this situation might seek a dismissal of the bankruptcy proceeding under Section 305(a).[36]

11 U.S.C. §522(d)(12) expressly permits retirement funds exempt from taxation pursuant to the Internal Revenue Code to be claimed exempt. This includes 401 employer plans and IRA accounts. This exemption, added by BAPCPA and intended to resolve the case law debate upon whether or not IRA accounts could be claimed exempt, is consistent with the identical exemption also permitted to debtors not claiming the federal exemptions. See chapter 10A supra.

D. UNAFFECTED CLAIMS

Exemptions, contrary to popular opinion, do not protect a debtor's exempt property from the reach of all creditors. Exemptions do not protect otherwise exempt property from properly secured liens or properly filed tax liens. Nor do exemptions protect a debtor's otherwise exempt property from nondischargeable taxes, nondischargeable domestic support obligations, or debts incurred by fraud in obtaining school financial aid.[37] For example, Arthur Curry has a mortgage debt and a tax lien recorded upon his home. His divorced spouse, Mera, is owed support payments. Arthur's homestead will not protect a foreclosure by the mortgage holder, a sale to the state for the nondischarged taxes, or a judicial seizure by Mera for collection of the unpaid support.

It is not improper for a debtor to convert nonexempt to exempt property at any time prior to filing. The Legislative Notes to Section 522 specifically state that "the debtor will be permitted to convert nonexempt property into exempt property before filing a bankruptcy petition. However, the excessive conversion of nonexempt to exempt property on the eve of a bankruptcy filing can result in the denial of a debtor's discharge."[38] Thus, Midas Touch could sell a piece of nonexempt antique jewelry prior to filing, buy a new refrigerator with the proceeds, and then claim the refrigerator exempt under Section

---

36. See chapter 9 supra.
37. 11 U.S.C. §522(c).
38. See Historical and Revision Notes to 11 U.S.C. §522. See also In re Grand Jury Proceedings, G.S., F.S., 609 F.3d 909 (8th Cir. 2010) (transfer of hundreds of thousands of dollars in nonexempt assets prepetition suggested fraudulent intent); In re Jennings, 533 F.3d 1333 (11th Cir. 2008) (a large premature, prepetition payment on home improvements paid to take advantage of homestead exemption was held to be fraudulent and the debtor's discharge was denied); In re Stern, 345 F.3d 1036 (9th Cir. 2003) (conversion of nonexempt to exempt on eve of bankruptcy is not per se fraudulent).

522(d)(3) or 522(d)(5). How the 2005 legislation may affect these practices will clarify itself in the case law.

E.   LIEN AVOIDANCE TO PRESERVE EXEMPTION

An *unsecured* creditor cannot ask a debtor to agree to waive exemptions or any of a debtor's rights under Section 522. Any such waiver is unenforceable.[39] A debtor may avoid a judicial lien or a nonpossessory, **nonpurchase money security interest** in consumer, personal, or household goods, tools of the trade, or professionally prescribed health aids to the extent that any such lien impairs an otherwise allowable exemption. Judicial liens attributable to domestic support obligations are not avoidable.[40] Generally, a secured creditor has a nonpurchase money security interest if the debt that created the security interest was not obtained for the purpose of purchasing the collateral subject to the security interest. Otherwise, the security interest is generally a **purchase money security interest**. For example, a debtor purchases a new living room set and obtains credit to do so. If the seller retains a security interest in the goods, it will likely be a purchase money security interest. However, if a debtor obtains a loan from the friendly neighborhood finance company for the purpose of going on vacation, any security interest the debtor grants the finance company in household furniture will be a nonpurchase money security interest. In this instance, if the debtor then files a bankruptcy petition, the latter security interest may be avoided if it impairs the debtor's ability to claim household furniture exempt.

Nonpurchase money security interest: a security interest in collateral where the purpose of the loan is other than to purchase the collateral

Purchase money security interest: a security interest in collateral when the purpose of the loan is to purchase the collateral

FACT PATTERN

Focusing on Robin's credit card debt, how would you characterize the security interest, if any, that her creditors hold?

Section 522(f)(1)(B) allows a debtor to avoid a nonpurchase money security interest to the extent that the collateral can be claimed exempt. So if all of the furniture given as collateral can be claimed exempt, the debtor can avoid the lien. Section 522(f)(4), added by BAPCPA, defines "household goods," solely for purposes of lien avoidance, as generally one TV, one VCR, plus other specifically enumerated household goods. The same provision also excludes various items, such as works of art

---

39. 11 U.S.C. §522(e).
40. 11 U.S.C. §522(f)(1)(A).

except by relatives, from the definition of "household goods." Once the debtor's personal obligation is discharged under Section 524, the finance company may not thereafter seek payment. Because the security interest is avoided, the debtor need not worry about the finance company repossessing the furniture. Section 522(f)(3) further limits the ability to avoid a nonpurchase money security interest in tools of the trade, farm animals, or crops if the value of the collateral exceeds $6,425.

A debtor must file a noticed motion to successfully avoid a lien subject to avoidance under Section 522(f). See chapter 6A supra.[41]

F.   CLAIMING AND OBJECTING TO EXEMPTIONS

To properly claim exemptions, a debtor must file a list of exemptions with the court. If a debtor fails to do so, a dependent of the debtor may file the list.[42] A debtor's claim of exemptions is to be filed at the same time as the Statements and Schedules, within 14 days of the date of filing.[43] The exemption schedule may be amended at any time prior to the close of the proceeding.[44]

Practice Pointer

Remember to check your local bankruptcy court rules for the fee for amending your exemption or other bankruptcy schedules.

The trustee or any creditor may object to a claim of exemption. An objection must be filed within 30 days of the conclusion of the Section 341(a) creditors' meeting or within 30 days after any amendment is filed unless the court orders otherwise. Unless an objection is made, the property claimed exempt is exempt. The party raising an objection to a claim of exemption has the burden of proving the impropriety of the exemption at any hearing held to resolve the objection.[45] An objection to a claim of

---

41. Bankruptcy Rule 4003(d); Bankruptcy Rule 9013.
42. 11 U.S.C. §522(l).
43. Bankruptcy Rules 1007(c), 4003(a). See chapter 4 supra and chapter 30 infra.
44. Bankruptcy Rule 1009(a).
45. 11 U.S.C. §522(l); Bankruptcy Rule 4003(b)(c).

exemption is filed as a noticed motion (see chapter 5A supra). A sample notice of objection is contained on the forms disk.

In Taylor v. Freeland & Kronz, the Supreme Court held that the 30-day deadline to object to a debtor's claim of exemption is to be strictly construed. In this case, a debtor claimed an exemption in the potential proceeds of an employment discrimination lawsuit against her former employer. She disclosed to the trustee at the creditors' meeting that the suit might be worth $90,000. The trustee, however, did not object to the exemption because he did not believe the claim had any value. After the debtor obtained a $110,000 settlement, the trustee sought to recover the proceeds for the estate. The Supreme Court found a fatal flaw in the trustee's failure to object to the exemption in a timely manner. "Deadlines may lead to unwelcome results, but they prompt parties to act and they produce finality."[46]

In Schwab v. Reilly, the debtor listed a value for certain assets in Schedule B and claimed the full amount exempt in Schedule C.[47] When an appraisal indicated that the value of the assets could be in excess of the debtor's claimed exemption, the trustee sought permission to auction the assets, even though the trustee did not object to the debtor's claimed exemptions. The lower courts denied the trustee's relief and the Supreme Court reversed. The Court concluded that the trustee had no duty to object to the exemption where the value of the property exceeded the limits of the exemption under the Code.

In *Taylor*, the debtor scheduled a litigation asset with an unknown value. She sought to claim the entire asset exempt. The trustee did not object to the exemption in a timely manner, although the exemption claim was objectionable because it exceeded the allowable dollar amount. The Court held, in this instance, that the trustee's failure to have objected to the inappropriate exemption in a timely manner allowed the debtor to retain the asset. In *Schwab*, on the other hand, the amounts claimed exempt ". . . are facially within the limits the Code prescribes and raise no warning flags that warranted an objection."

Finally, if a debtor claims an exemption in property successfully recovered by the trustee's avoiding powers, the debtor's interest can be assessed its fair share of the costs incurred in recovering the asset.[48] For example, a trustee successfully avoids the transfer of an asset worth $10,000. The amount claimed exempt is $5,000. The cost of recovery is $2,000. One thousand dollars of the costs can be charged against the

---

46. Taylor v. Freeland & Kronz, 503 U.S. 638 (1992).
47. 130 S. Ct. 2652 (2010).
48. 11 U.S.C. §522(k).

exemption (the debtor's fair share). The debtor will effectively realize $4,000 through use of the exemption in this example.

However, a debtor's exemption may not be surcharged due to inequitable conduct. In *Law v. Siegel*, the trustee successfully avoided the debtor's fraudulent transfer of property and then sought to surcharge the debtor's exemption as a result of the debtor's inequitable conduct. The Supreme Court held that the Code does not provide authority to deny an exemption on a ground not specified in the Code.[49]

Summary

Exemptions are property that an individual debtor may protect from administration by a bankruptcy estate. Exempt property is not available for liquidation to pay a dividend to creditors. A debtor may keep exempt property. Exemptions are a primary element of debtor relief.

Section 522(b) of the Code permits individuals to claim exemptions either under applicable state law, generally where the debtor has been domiciled for the 730 days preceding the filing of the petition, or under Section 522(d) of the Code. These latter exemptions are commonly known as the federal exemptions. However, states have been afforded an opportunity to withdraw from the federal exemption scheme. Approximately 33 states have done so. Pursuant to 11 U.S.C. §522(p), homestead exemptions under state law are limited to $160,375 in certain circumstances.

The decision as to which set of or specific exemptions to select is one of the more important decisions to be made in any individual bankruptcy proceeding. The federal exemption list contains common exemptions, many of which are also normally permitted under state law.

Several specific types of debt are immune from a debtor's claim of exemptions. These types of debt include consensual liens and tax liens upon the property sought to be claimed exempt, as well as domestic support obligations, and student financial aid obligations that were fraudulently obtained.

A debtor may, however, successfully avoid certain liens that may impair an allowable exemption. Judicial liens and nonpurchase money consensual liens are subject to this potential lien avoidance. A motion is normally required to avoid such a lien.

Exemptions are claimed by filing a list of exemptions with the court. This list comprises Official Form B106C.

---

49. U.S., 134 S. Ct. 1188 (2014).

A party in interest, such as a creditor or the trustee, wishing to object to a claim of exemption, must do so by way of a noticed motion. The motion must be brought within 30 days of the creditors' meeting. If an amendment to a claim of exemption is filed, any objection to the amendment must be brought within 30 days of the amendment's being filed.

KEY TERMS

catch-all exemption
equity
exemptions
federal exemptions
fresh start
homestead exemption
liquidation value
market value

nonpurchase money
   security interest
purchase money security
   interest
replacement value
stacking

CHAPTER 10 CHECKLIST

10.1 SUMMARY OF FEDERAL EXEMPTIONS

Item	Exemption Amount	Authority
10.1.1 residence of debtor or dependent	$23,675	11 U.S.C. §522(d)(1)
10.1.2 motor vehicle	$775	11 U.S.C. §522(d)(2)
10.1.3 household goods, furniture, and wearing apparel	$600 per item up to $12,625 in aggregate	11 U.S.C. §522(d)(3)
10.1.4 personal jewelry	$1,600	11 U.S.C. §522(d)(4)
10.1.5 any property catch-all	any unused portion of (d)(1) up to $11,850 plus $1,250 ($13,100 total)	11 U.S.C. §522(d)(5)
10.1.6 tools of trade	$2,375	11 U.S.C. §522(d)(6)

DISCUSSION QUESTIONS

1. What are exemptions?

2. What is the purpose of exemptions?

3. What factors should be considered in selecting federal or state exemptions? Specific exemptions?

4. What is a homestead?

---

50. This is a general procedure. Further reference to specifically applicable state law is recommended.

5. How does an individual debtor claim exemptions in a bankruptcy proceeding?

6. How are exemptions objected to in a bankruptcy proceeding?

7. How can a debtor avoid a lien that impairs an exemption?

PRACTICE EXERCISES

Exercise 10.1
Complete Official Form B106 C for your clients, the Cashes.

Exercise 10.2
Draft a motion on behalf of the Cashes to avoid the lien held by A to Z Motors.

11

Trustees, Examiners, and Creditors' Committees

Learning Objectives

- Describe the role and basic duties of the bankruptcy trustee
- Define the role of the debtor-in-possession in Chapter 11 proceedings
- Identify the United States Trustee
- Describe the Official Creditors' Committee
- Recognize the role of examiner

Chapter 7 supra described the general procedure for selecting and compensating trustees. This chapter focuses on the trustee's qualifications and duties. The related concepts of Chapter 11 Examiners and Official Creditors' Committees are also discussed briefly, as they exist almost exclusively in Chapter 11 cases. The role and function of the **United States Trustee** is discussed. The 2005 BAPCPA legislation added ombudsmen to the mix in selected situations. These various entities collectively comprise the various fiduciaries peculiar to the bankruptcy system.

Trustees, examiners, creditors' committees, ombudsmen, and the United States Trustee are unique players in the bankruptcy system, and these entities are of equal or greater importance than the debtor and individual creditors. Without these additional players, the bankruptcy system would simply not function because there would be no effective control or oversight over a debtor or the debtor's assets. There would also be no effective personnel to effectuate a proper distribution of dividends to creditors.

United States Trustee: division of the Department of Justice responsible for monitoring the administration of bankruptcy estates

171

A.   TRUSTEES

Trustee: fiduciary appointed by the United States Trustee to administer a bankruptcy estate

Code Sections 321 to 325 address the issues of who may be a **trustee**, how a trustee qualifies, and how a trustee is removed. The trustee may be either an individual or a corporation authorized to serve as a trustee. Section 321 provides that a competent individual who has an office or resides in the district or in an adjacent district where the proceeding is pending may be a trustee in a Chapter 7, 12, or 13 case. A competent individual is normally a disinterested person who has not previously served as examiner in the proceeding.[1]

 Practice Pointer

Remember, a "disinterested person" is a defined term under the Bankruptcy Code. It includes a person who is not a creditor, an insider, or someone who holds "an interest materially adverse to the interest of the estate." 11 U.S.C. §101(14).

A corporation that is authorized by its charter or bylaws to be a trustee and has an office in the district where the proceeding is pending may also serve as a trustee.[2] Alternatively, the United States Trustee for that judicial district may also serve as trustee in a proceeding if necessary.[3]

In the normal course of a Chapter 7 proceeding, after the debtor files the petition, the United States trustee will appoint an interim trustee from a panel of private trustees already selected by the United States Trustee's office. Once selected, the trustee "qualifies" by posting a bond. In the case of private panel trustees, described in chapter 7 supra, the trustee need take no action if the court or United States Trustee has authorized a blanket bond that the trustee has previously obtained. This bond inures to the benefit of the creditors in all Chapter 7 estates in which the particular trustee has been appointed. A nonpanel trustee or a trustee serving in a district that has not authorized a blanket bond for trustees

---

1. 11 U.S.C. §321(a)(1), (b); 11 U.S.C. §701(a)(1).
2. 11 U.S.C. §321(a)(2).
3. 11 U.S.C. §321(c).

will be required to post a bond with the court in each case that the trustee is appointed. The bond has to be posted with the court within seven days of the trustee's appointment.[4] These rules apply to trustees appointed in all proceedings, voluntary and involuntary.[5]

Practice Pointer

In some jurisdictions, the United States Trustee will appoint one or more standing Chapter 13 trustees to handle all of the Chapter 13 cases filed within a particular district.

Prior to the enactment and implementation of the United States Trustee system on a national basis in 1988, the bankruptcy court had the duty to set the amount of the trustee's bond.[6] Under the United States Trustee system, the United States Trustee has now been given this responsibility.[7]

The amount of the trustee's bond is generally based upon a percentage of the estimated value of the assets subject to administration in a particular proceeding. The amount of a blanket bond is generally based on a percentage of the value of all funds on deposit by a panel trustee in all cases subject to the blanket bond. Local rule may require the bond amount to exceed 100 percent of all funds on hand to ensure maximum protection to the creditors of estates being administered by the trustee. Local rules will generally require a trustee to file a quarterly report of funds on deposit with the court or the United States Trustee. The report may result in the bond being increased or decreased.[8]

The trustee is the official legal representative for the bankruptcy estate and in such capacity may sue as a plaintiff on behalf of the estate or be sued as a defendant, representing the estate.[9]

---

4. 11 U.S.C. §322(a); Bankruptcy Rule 2010.
5. 11 U.S.C. §701; 11 U.S.C. §1104(d); 11 U.S.C. §1202(a); 11 U.S.C. §1302(a); Bankruptcy Rule 2001.
6. See 11 U.S.C. §322(b) as it existed prior to October 27, 1986.
7. 11 U.S.C. §322(b).
8. Bankruptcy Rule 2015.
9. 11 U.S.C. §323.

> ### *Practice Pointer*
>
> Remember, once the debtor files for
> bankruptcy, all legal interests or actions
> that the debtor could have maintained prepetition
> now belong to the bankruptcy estate. Once
> appointed, the trustee represents the estate and may
> pursue those actions on behalf of the estate.

Sections 324 and 325 concern the removal of a trustee and the appointment of a successor. A trustee may always be removed for cause. For example, cause will exist to remove a trustee who absconds with estate funds. However, it is unlikely that a trustee would be removed for exercising business judgment that creditors disagree with, unless such judgment is tantamount to gross negligence or gross incompetence. The procedure for removing a trustee requires that a motion be made before the court. If a trustee dies or resigns during the administration of a proceeding, a successor will have to be appointed.[10]

A trustee will always be appointed in Chapter 7, 12, and 13 proceedings.[11] A trustee may or may not be appointed in a Chapter 11 case.[12] Although the United States Trustee has separate duties to perform in all proceedings, the United States Trustee does not generally serve as the individual trustee in a specific proceeding, unless the United States Trustee has been directed to do so by the court. The United States Trustee is, however, considered to be a party in interest for all purposes and "may appear and be heard on any issue in any case."[13]

B.   THE UNITED STATES TRUSTEE

The United States Trustee program started as an experiment in selected districts when the Bankruptcy Code first became effective in 1979. In 1986, Congress decided to implement the program nationally. The 1986 Code amendments were entitled in part as the "United States Trustees . . . Act of 1986."[14]

---

10. 11 U.S.C. §324, 325, 703; 11 U.S.C. §1105; Bankruptcy Rule 2012.
11. 11 U.S.C. §§701-703; 11 U.S.C. §1202; 11 U.S.C. §1302.
12. 11 U.S.C. §1104. See infra this chapter.
13. 11 U.S.C. §307; 28 U.S.C. §586(a)(1), (2).
14. Pub. L. No. 99-554, Title II §257(c), 100 Stat. 3114 (Oct. 27, 1986) (28 U.S.C. §§581-586).

The United States Trustee system operates as a division of the Department of Justice. The Office of the United States Trustee serves primarily an administrative function. Prior to enactment of the Code, Bankruptcy Judges performed many of the administrative acts that have been delegated to the United States Trustee. This change was initiated in an effort to redefine the Bankruptcy Judge in a more traditional judicial role. Under the Bankruptcy Act, Bankruptcy Judges were known as Referees until 1974. In practice under the Bankruptcy Act, as referees the judges played an active role in the administration of the estate while simultaneously determining the rights of all other parties in the proceeding. This created an inherent conflict within the system. Divesting the Bankruptcy Judges of their administrative duties and delegating those duties to the United States Trustee system was intended to resolve this conflict. Now, Bankruptcy Judges remain integral to, but independent from, the day-to-day administration of individual bankruptcy proceedings.

The Office of the United States Trustee is charged with monitoring the progress of all cases, regardless of Chapter, and to act appropriately to "prevent undue delay."[15] The United States Trustee should be served with all notices required under the Code, as described in chapter 5 supra. The United States Trustee is statutorily required to ensure that all debtors pay all of the fees and file all of the required documents in connection with all proceedings filed with the Bankruptcy Court.[16] The United States Trustee also monitors applications for the retention of professionals and applications for professional compensation and is permitted to comment thereon to the Bankruptcy Court.[17] The local United States Trustee may have published guidelines to assist in this process. See a representative sample on the forms disk. The United States Trustee may also refer any matters for investigation to the United States Attorney that may constitute a bankruptcy crime.[18]

In Chapter 7 proceedings, the United States Trustee maintains and supervises a panel of trustees.[19] In everyday practice, the United States Trustee's performance of this duty includes appointing private panel Chapter 7 trustees and supervising and monitoring the private trustee's prompt administration of asset estates (see chapter 22 infra).

---

15. 25 U.S.C. §586(a)(3)(G).
16. 28 U.S.C. §586(a)(3)(D).
17. 28 U.S.C. §586(a)(3)(A), (H). See chapter 8 supra.
18. 28 U.S.C. §586(a)(3)(F). Bankruptcy crimes are defined in 18 U.S.C. §§151-157. Generally, bankruptcy crimes include the fraudulent concealment of assets in connection with a pending proceeding or the commission of perjury or the taking of a false oath. These crimes include penalties of fines and/or imprisonment for not more than five years. Altering, destroying, or concealing records with the intent to obstruct proper administration of the estate could also lead to additional fines and/or imprisonment of up to 20 years. 18 U.S.C. §1519.
19. 28 U.S.C. §586(a).

The 2005 BAPCPA legislation created new responsibilities for the United States Trustee. First, Bankruptcy Code Section 704(b) charges the United States Trustee to review the debtor's materials filed pursuant to Section 521 (see chapters 4 and 7 supra), and to file a statement within ten days of the meeting of creditors indicating whether or not the filing creates a presumed abuse of Chapter 7 under "needs based bankruptcy" (see chapter 5 supra).

 Practice Pointer

It is always important to confirm when the tolling period is triggered. Frequently, the statutory period begins counting from the date of the "first" scheduled meeting of creditors.

If abuse is presumed, then within 30 days of filing the statement, the United States trustee must file a motion to dismiss or convert or a statement setting forth the reasons why no motion is to be filed if abuse is presumed pursuant to "needs based bankruptcy." Second, Section 603 of BAPCPA requires random audits of one out of 250 cases. Under BAPCPA, the United States Trustee is directed to retain auditors and to file the audit reports with the Bankruptcy Court.[20]

Third, the United States Trustee is charged with the approval and oversight monitoring of the various nonprofit budget and credit counseling agencies providing both the prepetition credit counseling required by Section 109(h) and the postpetition personal financial management courses mandated by Sections 727(a)(11) and 1328(g) (see chapters 4 and 8 supra).

In Chapter 11 proceedings, the United States Trustee will function to a large degree as the "eyes and ears" of the court. The United States Trustee is directed to appoint and monitor Chapter 11 creditors' committees.[21] The United States Trustee has also been charged with monitoring Chapter 11 Reorganization Plans and Disclosure Statements and is given the authority to comment upon them.[22] This authority is also granted to the United States Trustee in connection with Chapter 12

---

20. 28 U.S.C. §586(f).
21. 11 U.S.C. §1102; 28 U.S.C. §586(a)(3)(E). See infra this chapter.
22. 28 U.S.C. §586(a)(3)(B).

and 13 proceedings.[23] In a Chapter 11 case, the United States Trustee provides the necessary oversight when no committee has been appointed. In everyday practice the United States Trustee's involvement in a Chapter 11 proceeding can be extensive, particularly during the first 60 days of a Chapter 11. During this period, the United States Trustee will interact with a **debtor-in-possession** in several areas.

Debtor-in-possession: the fiduciary entity created by a debtor filing a Chapter 11 reorganization proceeding

First, the United States Trustee will conduct an initial debtor interview with the estate's representatives approximately two weeks after filing. At the initial debtor interview, the United States Trustee will generally interview the debtor to obtain an overview of the case and to instruct counsel and the parties as to any local United States Trustee guidelines and as to the various administrative duties and responsibilities of a debtor-in-possession. In a small business Chapter 11 (see chapter 24 infra), 28 U.S.C. §586(a)(7) requires the United States Trustee to conduct an initial debtor interview. (See chapter 24 infra for a description of these duties.) The forms disk contains representative samples. The United States Trustee will follow up to monitor the debtor-in-possession's compliance with the rules and guidelines.

Second, the United States Trustee will preside at the meeting of the creditors held pursuant to 11 U.S.C. §341(a) and 11 U.S.C. §343.

Third, the United States Trustee will act to facilitate the organizing of an Official Creditors' Committee. See infra this chapter.

The United States Trustee will collect quarterly fees from a debtor-in-possession pursuant to 28 U.S.C. §586(a)(3)(D) and 28 U.S.C. §1930(a)(6) (see chapter 24 infra).

Finally, the United States Trustee may bring motions to dismiss or convert Chapter 11 proceedings pursuant to 11 U.S.C. §586(a)(8) (see chapter 23 infra).

C.   THE TRUSTEE'S DUTIES

Although there are separate provisions in each Chapter that specify the duties of a trustee appointed under that particular Chapter, the essential duties are the same throughout the Code. Section 704(a) contains a list of 12 items that specify the duties of a Chapter 7 trustee. Section 1302 contains a list of items that specify the duties of a Chapter 13 trustee. A number of the duties described in Section 704(a) have been incorporated into this

---

23. 28 U.S.C. §586(a)(3)(C).

provision. Section 1106 specifies the duties of a Chapter 11 trustee. This Section also incorporates many of the elements from Section 704(a). A similar situation pertains to the duties of a Chapter 12 trustee contained in Section 1202.[24] The essential duties of a trustee may be synthesized into four duties that can best be remembered by use of a mnemonic device that we shall refer to as the four "ATEs." That is, the essential duties of a trustee can be described as follows: investig*ate*, liquid*ate*, litig*ate*, and administr*ate*.

Investigation is the initial duty performed by any trustee. A trustee must initially determine whether or not there are assets in an estate that can be liquidated to pay a dividend to creditors of the estate. In a consumer no asset or a small business proceeding, performance of this duty may involve little more than reviewing the Statements and Schedules and questioning the debtor at the meeting of creditors. In a larger proceeding, investigation may involve a review of significant records and documents and the taking of one or more Rule 2004 Examinations (see chapter 8 supra) before the trustee can logically proceed further in the administration of an estate.[25]

FACT PATTERN

We know that the Cash household is full of "stuff" and that Owen has sold items online. Absent disclosure by the Cashes, how could the trustee learn about this potential stockpile and Owen's past and/or current online sales?

The liquidation duty is the most visible of the trustee's duties. Liquidation involves the trustee converting nonexempt assets into cash. This is always the trustee's goal in a Chapter 7 case. Liquidation can be as simple as having a private sale or a public auction of the inventory and equipment of a bankrupt business or can be as complex as selling the assets of a major business to one or more buyers in what may be complex and unrelated transactions. BAPCPA imposes the additional requirement for a trustee to make his/her best efforts to transfer the patients of a health care business to another appropriate health care business.[26]

FACT PATTERN

Assuming the Cashes are not able to protect/exempt all of the items that Owen has accumulated over the years, will the trustee have the necessary expertise to properly liquidate

---

24. 11 U.S.C. §1302(b); 11 U.S.C. §704(a); 11 U.S.C. §1106(a); 11 U.S.C. §1202(b).
25. 11 U.S.C. §704(a)(4); 11 U.S.C. §1106(a)(3); 11 U.S.C. §1202(b)(2); 11 U.S.C. §1302(b)(1).
26. 11 U.S.C. §704(a)(1), (12).

Owen's collection? What options are available to the Cashes and to the trustee?

> ### *Practice Pointer*
> The source for the funding for the bankruptcy estate depends upon the Chapter of the case. In a Chapter 7 proceeding, the liquidation of assets is the major source of the payment tendered to the estate's creditors. In a Chapter 13 proceeding, the money usually comes from monthly payments made by the debtor.

Fully liquidating an estate may require a trustee to sue third parties. Litigation is the third of the four ATEs. As the official representative of an estate, a trustee may pursue claims against third parties that would exist even if there had been no bankruptcy. For example, collecting accounts receivable that are due a debtor may require a trustee to initiate litigation. The trustee may also be able to exercise one or more of the avoiding powers to recover assets of the estate for the benefit of creditors.[27] Presumably, when a trustee sues, the litigation will result in the obtaining of additional cash to pay the creditors of the estate. Thus, to a certain extent, litigation is also a part of liquidation.

Would the trustee be interested in pursuing the accounts receivable from Owen's business, The Lawn Cuttery? Why or why not?

FACT PATTERN

Finally, a trustee is required to administer the assets that have been reduced to cash by liquidation or litigation. The trustee follows additional rules and procedures for distributing the cash to creditors in the form of dividends. The accomplishment of this process is the major goal of unsecured creditors affected by the bankruptcy system and forms the essence of the debt collection aspects of the Bankruptcy Code. The entire process of maintaining and distributing the cash to creditors is known as the "administration of the estate." The specific details of this administrative process are described in chapter 23 infra.

---

27. See chapters 16-18 infra.

BAPCPA imposed an additional administrative duty upon trustees, requiring them to provide notice to the holders of claims for domestic support obligations, informing them that they may seek support assistance from a state agency, and requiring the trustee to provide notice of the debtor's discharge and contact information to the claim holder and the state support agency when the discharge is granted.[28]

In a Chapter 12 or 13 proceeding, a trustee is not specifically directed to liquidate assets. A Chapter 12 trustee is required to ensure that the debtor commences to make timely payments under the debtor's plan.[29] A Chapter 13 trustee actually collects payments made under a Chapter 13 plan and distributes them to the creditors on a regular basis.[30]

D.   DEBTOR-IN-POSSESSION

In Chapter 11 proceedings, there may or may not be an active trustee. In the reorganization process that Chapter 11 represents, there is normally no trustee. Instead, the debtor functions as a "debtor-in-possession."[31] The essence of this concept is that the debtor acts as its own trustee. Section 1107 describes the rights, powers, and duties of the Chapter 11 debtor-in-possession. These rights, powers, and duties are essentially the four ATE*s* described above. However, because the purpose of a Chapter 11 is to reorganize rather than to liquidate, it is more accurate to substitute the term *reorganize* in place of the term *liquidate*. How a debtor properly fulfills the duty to reorganize is described in chapters 24-26 infra.

E.   OFFICIAL CREDITORS' COMMITTEES

A number of mechanisms have been created to provide the creditors in a Chapter 11 proceeding with the ability to oversee and monitor the performance by a debtor-in-possession of its statutory duties. These various mechanisms include providing the creditors an opportunity to seek the

---

28. 11 U.S.C. §704(c); 11 U.S.C. §1106(c); 11 U.S.C. §1202(c); 11 U.S.C. §1302(d).
29. 11 U.S.C. §1202(b)(4). See chapter 27 infra.
30. 11 U.S.C. §1302(b)(3)(5). See chapter 23 infra.
31. 11 U.S.C. §1101(1); 11 U.S.C. §1107.

appointment of a trustee or examiner and/or the formation of an **Official Creditors' Committee**.[32]

The Official Creditors' Committee will help monitor and oversee a debtor-in-possession's Chapter 11 financial affairs.[33] Keep in mind that a debtor experiencing financial difficulty will generally remain in full control of its activities. To the extent that a debtor can isolate one or more of its creditors and attempt to deal with each creditor independently, this is merely an application of the ancient Roman principle of "divide and conquer." The remedy to a debtor's use of this principle is another equally ancient principle: "In unity there is strength." The Official Creditors' Committee is simply a mechanism that puts the latter principle into practice. The major purpose of the committee is to unite the unsecured creditors so they can deal with the debtor-in-possession collectively and not as individual isolated creditors. The Official Creditors' Committee is appointed by the United States Trustee from among the 20 largest unsecured creditors of a debtor-in-possession. At the initiation of a Chapter 11 proceeding, the debtor-in-possession files a list of its 20 largest unsecured creditors with the court along with all of the other documents required to be filed by a debtor upon initiating a proceeding. This list is to be filed with the Chapter 11 petition.[34] From this list the United States Trustee will solicit creditors to serve on the committee.[35] When a sufficient number, in the United States Trustee's discretion, consent to appointment, the committee is officially appointed. The Official Creditors' Committee is a **party in interest** to the proceeding. This means that the committee may file pleadings, initiate motions, or file plans of reorganization.[36]

Section 1102(a)(3), added to the Code in 1994, permits a small business Chapter 11 debtor to request the court not to appoint an Official Creditors' Committee. (A **small business debtor** is defined in Chapter 11 as a debtor with less than $2,566,050 of debt who elects treatment as a small business.) Upon a showing of cause, the request shall be granted. Since the concept of the creditors' committee is important to the Chapter 11 process, the case law will probably impose strict requirements on the granting of such motions.

Official Creditors' Committee: entity created in a Chapter 11 proceeding to act on the collective behalf of unsecured creditors

Party in interest: a party with a stake in the outcome of a bankruptcy proceeding. The debtor, creditors, trustee, United States Trustee, and equity security holders are all parties in interest

Small business debtor: a Chapter 11 debtor with liquidated debts not in excess of $2,566,050 who elects treatment as a small business debtor, excluding a debtor whose primary activity is owning and operating real estate; small business debtors are defined in Bankruptcy Code Section 101(51D)

---

32. The 2005 legislation also created ombudsmen to deal with privacy issues in the sale of customer lists, and the best interests of patients in health care bankruptcies. 11 U.S.C. §332; 11 U.S.C. §333; 11 U.S.C. §§1102-1103; 11 U.S.C. §1104. See below this chapter and chapter 24 infra.
33. 11 U.S.C. §§1102-1103.
34. Bankruptcy Rule 1007(d).
35. 11 U.S.C. §1102(a)(1).
36. 11 U.S.C. §1103.

Administrative expenses: generally, all expenses incurred by a bankruptcy estate after a bankruptcy filing: Trustee's fees, auctioneer fees, attorneys' fees, and postpetition rent are common Chapter 7 administrative expenses

The Official Creditors' Committee has authority under the Code to hire its own professionals, such as counsel and accountants.[37] The expenses of the professionals employed by the Official Creditors' Committee are the **administrative expenses** of the estate. This means that any fees incurred are payable by the estate. Because many unsecured creditors do not necessarily have a right to recover attorneys' fees from a debtor when attempting to collect debts that are due, this is a powerful tool. The committee's professionals are retained and paid in the manner described in chapter 7 supra. Their employment must be approved by the court, and the committee's professionals are subject to the same fee application requirements discussed in chapter 7 supra. The membership of an Official Creditors' Committee may also receive reimbursement of expenses incurred in the performance of duties for the estate, pursuant to Section 503(b)(3)(F).

Historically, creditors' committees fail to become active in many Chapter 11 proceedings, usually to the ultimate detriment of the creditors. This failure may be directly attributed to the appointed committee members simply having no one explain to them the meaning and significance of the committee and membership upon it. This has been unfortunate because in many cases where the creditors' committee organizes itself and retains professional assistance, the chances for a successful reorganization can improve immeasurably. The committee can seek the prompt conversion of a Chapter 11 to a Chapter 7 if it appears reorganization will not succeed, thereby preserving any possible equity in the assets to pay dividends to the creditors. The committee can also cooperate with the debtor in negotiating a feasible and confirmable plan of reorganization.[38] In an effort to increase the number of active committees, the Code has directed the United States Trustee to meet with the appointed committee promptly after its appointment so the committee can be educated as to its rights and purposes.[39] In an appropriate proceeding it may also be helpful for the debtor-in-possession to meet with a committee promptly after its appointment. This is not as incongruous as may appear at first glance to those used to thinking solely in adversarial terms. Because a successful Chapter 11 will result in payments to creditors and survival of the debtor, the best results are often achieved when the debtor and creditors find ways to work together to resolve the situation through a confirmable plan of reorganization. Input from the committee into the internal

---

37. 11 U.S.C. §1103(a).
38. 11 U.S.C. §1103(c)(3)(5).
39. 11 U.S.C. §1103(d).

reorganization of a Chapter 11 debtor's affairs can also often provide an invaluable and essential service to an estate.[40]

An Official Creditors' Committee has the right to investigate the debtor's financial affairs, consult with the debtor or trustee (if one is appointed), request the appointment of a trustee or examiner, and perhaps most important, assist in the formulation of a plan of reorganization on behalf of all unsecured creditors.[41] In the absence of the appointment of a trustee in a Chapter 11 proceeding, the court will often look to input from the committee to assist the court in making decisions that affect the estate. This is especially so where the committee has been organized and has independently investigated the debtor's financial affairs in a manner similar to that which would be conducted by a trustee.[42] In an exceptionally large proceeding, the court may approve the appointment of multiple creditors' committees. For example, there may be a committee of trade creditors and a committee of unsecured lenders.[43] On rare occasions, a creditors' committee may be appointed in a Chapter 7.[44] If a committee investigates a debtor and reasonably believes that the debtor or its insiders have committed fraud or are incompetent, the committee may seek the appointment of a trustee or examiner. Additionally, if a debtor-in-possession fails to follow the appropriate Chapter 11 operating rules (described in chapter 24 of this text), a committee, any creditor, or the United States Trustee may seek through motion a court order appointing a trustee or examiner in a Chapter 11 proceeding.[45]

F.   CHAPTER 11 TRUSTEES AND EXAMINERS

Section 1104(a) provides three grounds for the appointment of a trustee or examiner in a Chapter 11 proceeding. The first ground is for cause, including fraud, dishonesty, incompetence, or gross mismanagement. For instance, the owner of a restaurant who is found to be misreporting sales while concealing cash is committing fraud against the creditors. Or, the insiders of a business may simply be incapable of managing it properly. They may have no concept of budget, cash flow, or overhead costs, the

---

40. 11 U.S.C. §1103(c)(1). In large Chapter 11 cases, the debtor and official creditors' committee frequently cooperate with one another from the moment the committee is appointed.
41. 11 U.S.C. §1103(c).
42. 11 U.S.C. §1103(c)(2).
43. 11 U.S.C. §1102(a)(2).
44. 11 U.S.C. §705.
45. 11 U.S.C. §1104(a). As to the operating rules of a Chapter 11 debtor-in-possession, see chapter 24 infra.

inevitable results of which may be to operate the business unprofitably. Simple incompetence may be the greatest single cause of a majority of all Chapter 11 proceedings filed by operating businesses.

A second ground for granting a motion to appoint a trustee or examiner is if the appointment is found to be in the best interests of the creditors.[46] This can be a rather nebulous concept. It usually comes into play when the creditors' committee or a single creditor or the United States Trustee moves for the appointment of a trustee or examiner, alleging any of the factual scenarios described above, but with insufficient proof to justify the appointment of a trustee or examiner for cause. Nevertheless, if it is clear to the court that the creditors have lost confidence in the debtor's management and that the appointment of an independent third party, a trustee, may help to restore confidence, then the appointment of a trustee or examiner may be found to be in the best interests of creditors. This situation can arise in partnership proceedings where the general partners are in constant dispute and can agree on no course of action in any matter. The impossibility of general partners' agreeing is a classic situation that justifies the appointment of a trustee in the best interests of creditors.

Third, if grounds exist to dismiss or convert the case from a Chapter 11, the court may instead appoint a trustee in the best interests of creditors.[47]

A Chapter 11 trustee is in a powerful position. For example, a corporate debtor not in a bankruptcy proceeding is controlled by its board of directors and officers under applicable state law. However, a Chapter 11 trustee is superior to the officers and board in the chain of command, becoming, in a word, the boss. A Chapter 11 trustee is functionally a dictator. A Chapter 11 trustee has full power and authority under the Code to retain any insider in a management position or to relieve any or all insiders of their duties. To this extent, the appointment of a Chapter 11 trustee acts to supersede the charter or bylaws of a debtor corporation. Because the debtor has submitted itself to the court's jurisdiction, the appointment of a trustee is a burden it must accept.

A Chapter 11 trustee has the duties to investigate, litigate, and administrate as described above. Administration here includes following all Chapter 11 operating rules. A Chapter 11 trustee also has a duty to file a plan of reorganization or seek conversion of the proceeding to a Chapter 7.[48] In many cases, a trustee will retain current management. The decision to retain or relieve current management is, as a practical matter, the most important decision a Chapter 11 trustee makes. For instance, in a relatively small business the only people who really care

---

46. 11 U.S.C. §1104(a)(2).
47. 11 U.S.C. §1104(a)(3).
48. 11 U.S.C. §1106(a). See Chapters 24-26 infra.

enough about the business's survival and reorganization to operate it on a daily basis are the owners who are also insiders. If such individuals are replaced by third parties, the new operators may not necessarily be concerned about the business's ultimate survival. The owners/insiders are usually the persons with the greatest incentive to save the business despite their actions possibly being a cause of the filing.

A decision to change current management should not be made unless it is obvious that current management is either utterly incompetent, will not follow the trustee's instructions, or is demonstrably committing fraud. A Chapter 11 trustee best fulfills the role in a Chapter 11 by finding and implementing a path to an effective reorganization or by seeking conversion of the proceeding to a Chapter 7 if reorganization is not feasible.

Examiners are unique to Chapter 11 proceedings. Simply put, an **examiner** is someone who examines the debtor's affairs.[49] An examiner is usually appointed when a party has moved for the appointment of a trustee and the court determines that further independent investigation is required before a final decision can be made on the issue. An examiner may also be appointed to investigate a specific issue and to act as the "eyes and ears" of the court in a fact-finding capacity. An examiner is an independent third party who is usually given specific instructions by the court to investigate certain aspects of a debtor's financial affairs. An examiner may be required to investigate all matters or simply a limited aspect of a debtor's financial affairs. The examiner will prepare a report for the benefit of the court and creditors, providing a frank and objective opinion upon the subject matter of the examination. A Chapter 11 trustee also has a duty to prepare such a report regarding the debtor's financial affairs for the benefit of the court and creditors.[50] An examiner's report may support the debtor or it may recommend the appointment of a trustee or conversion of the proceeding to a Chapter 7. Persons who serve as examiners are often the same individuals who are on a panel of trustees in a given district. The only qualification to serve as an examiner, however, is to be a disinterested person.

The court has discretion to expand the powers of the examiner without appointing a trustee, effectively making the examiner with expanded powers a quasi-trustee.[51] This may actually help to reduce expenses and expedite the administration of a large and complex case. However, a person who has served as examiner in a proceeding may not serve as trustee in the same proceeding.[52]

Examiner: an individual appointed in a Chapter 11 proceeding to conduct an independent investigation of some or all of a debtor's financial affairs

---

49. 11 U.S.C. §1106(b).
50. 11 U.S.C. §1106(a)(3)(4).
51. 11 U.S.C. §1106(b).
52. 11 U.S.C. §321(b).

Ombudsman: an independent person who may be appointed to serve the best interests of patients in the bankruptcy of a health care business; an ombudsman may also be appointed to report to the court on the protection of personally identifiable information in the sale of customer lists

Personally identifiable information: information that may generally be used to contact or locate an individual, such as name and address, Social Security number, date of birth, and other similar information; Section 101(41A) of the Bankruptcy Code defines personally identifiable information

Health care business: a business that provides health care services: Special rules apply for a trustee's disposition of health care business records and for the placement of patients in alternative facilities; the court will appoint an ombudsman to speak for the best interests of the patients unless the court can find that such an appointment is not necessary; Section 101(27A) of the Bankruptcy Code defines health care business

G.   OMBUDSMAN

The 2005 legislation added **ombudsman** to the list of specialized entities that may perform services for a bankruptcy estate. An ombudsman may be appointed in two discrete situations. First, where an asset sale (see chapter 18) involves the sale of **personally identifiable information** (such as a customer list), then the court shall order the appointment of an ombudsman to review the seller's privacy policy and report on the potential losses or gains to consumers and the estate by the proposed sale.[53] Second, in a **health care business** bankruptcy, the court shall order an ombudsman to represent the interests of the patients where necessary and to regularly report to the court on the quality of patient care.[54]

Summary

The Bankruptcy Code has created several unique types of fiduciaries without which the bankruptcy system could not function. These fiduciaries are the trustee, United States Trustee, debtor-in-possession, Official Creditors' Committee, examiners, and ombudsmen.

The trustee is appointed by the United States Trustee. The trustee administers the bankruptcy estate. Chapter 7, 12, and 13 proceedings will always have a trustee appointed. In a Chapter 11 proceeding, a trustee may only be appointed by way of a noticed motion. The grounds for granting such a motion are cause, such as fraud or gross incompetence, or because appointment of a trustee would be in the best interest of the creditors.

The United States Trustee program is a division of the Department of Justice responsible for monitoring the administration of bankruptcy estates. The United States Trustee also appoints private trustees in separate proceedings.

The debtor-in-possession is the entity created by a debtor filing a Chapter 11 reorganization proceeding. A debtor-in-possession is essentially a debtor acting as its own trustee.

The Official Creditors' Committee is an entity created in a Chapter 11 to act on the collective behalf of unsecured creditors. The committee may retain professionals, appear as a party in interest, and propose a plan of reorganization.

---

53. 11 U.S.C. §332. "Personally identifiable information" is defined at 11 U.S.C. §101 (41A) and is generally a person's private information typically maintained in a customer list.
54. 11 U.S.C. §333. "Health care business" is defined at 11 U.S.C. §101 (27A) and generally includes hospitals, hospices, long-term care facilities, and home health agencies.

An examiner is an individual appointed in a Chapter 11 proceeding to conduct an independent investigation of some or all of a debtor's financial affairs.

An ombudsman is appointed in connection with the sale of customer lists and in health care business bankruptcies to speak for the interests of the patients.

A trustee's duties can be summarized: investigate, liquidate, litigate, and administrate. A trustee's investigation may lead to the discovery of assets. The assets are then reduced to cash by either liquidation or litigation. The process of collecting, maintaining, and distributing the cash to creditors is referred to as the administration of the estate.

KEY TERMS

administrative expenses
debtor-in-possession
examiner
health care business
Official Creditors'
    Committee
ombudsman

party in interest
personally identifiable
    information
small business debtor
trustee
United States Trustee

DISCUSSION QUESTIONS

1. What is the basic role of a bankruptcy trustee?

2. What are a bankruptcy trustee's basic duties? What is the difference between the duties of a Chapter 7 trustee and a trustee in a reorganization proceeding (Chapter 11, 12, or 13)?

3. What is the United States Trustee? What is its function?

4. What is a debtor-in-possession? What are a debtor-in-possession's duties?

5. What is an Official Creditors' Committee? What is the committee's role? May a committee retain its own professionals?

6. What are the grounds for the appointment of a trustee in a Chapter 11 proceeding?

7.   What is an examiner?

8.   What is an ombudsman? When is an ombudsman appointed?

PRACTICE EXERCISE

Exercise 11.1
Draft a letter on behalf of the trustee, identifying what documents you wish the Cashes to bring with them to the meeting of creditors.

12

Preparing a Proceeding for a Trustee

Learning Objectives

- Describe a number of simple actions that can be taken to greatly ease the handling of any bankruptcy proceeding

- Provide a specific checklist of acts that can be taken in an asset proceeding to enhance the likelihood of creditor dividends

- List questions commonly posed by individual consumer debtors

Private panel Chapter 7 trustees are busy people. In some districts a private panel trustee may be assigned 45 or more proceedings per month. Perhaps 10 to 15 percent of these proceedings will require the trustee to do more than review the file and ask the questions at the creditors' meeting described in chapter 8 supra. If the trustee has been on a private panel for an extended period of time, the trustee will have an enormous case load. As a result, private panel trustees can be difficult to communicate with. However, there are some effective methods that can be used to promote effective communication with a trustee. Use of these methods will help to expedite efficient and prompt administration in consumer no asset proceedings and will also aid in the efficient and proper administration of small asset proceedings. In the latter type of proceeding, these methods will also increase, sometimes significantly, the recovery obtained for the payment of creditor dividends. This benefits a debtor as well as the creditors.

A.   PREFILING ACTIONS

The primary rule for properly preparing a proceeding for filing is to make
the Chapter 7 trustee's job as easy as possible in order to achieve the
greatest recovery and, hence, distribution. In a typical consumer no
asset proceeding this will be relatively simple. In this instance all that is
usually necessary is to prepare the Statements and Schedules thoroughly
and clearly so that all the relevant data is easily analyzed. Chapter 30 of this
text is a tutorial regarding the preparation of these documents in a clear
and efficient manner. The general rule of preparation applies in all proceedings, but in a consumer no asset case the Statements and Schedules
will constitute a majority of the effort involved. Their clarity will expedite
administration and minimize the questioning that occurs at the creditors'
meeting under Section 341. For debtors that have little or no contact with
the legal system, adequate preparation will help to minimize any trauma
associated with the bankruptcy filing.

In all consumer cases, BAPCPA imposes new requirements upon debtors, their counsel, and trustees, requiring more preparation. Counsel will
need to prove that the prepetition disclosures required by Sections 527
and 528 have been given and that there is a prepetition retainer agreement
as described in chapter 4 supra. The statement of current income will
need to comply with the needs based bankruptcy formula described in
chapter 6 supra; counsel will need to obtain all evidence of payments
received by the debtor within 60 days of the filing date; and counsel
will also need to obtain from the debtor the debtor's most recent tax
return and for the three years preceding the filing if requested, as
described in chapter 4 supra.

BAPCPA imposes the further requirement upon counsel to make "reasonable inquiry" as to the disclosures made by debtors in their Statements
and Schedules, or risk the prospect of sanctions.[1] Case law will clarify the
meaning of "reasonable inquiry," but at a minimum it is likely to include
all the information otherwise required to be filed, credit reports, values of
vehicles obtained from credible Internet sources, and copies of documents of title, among other things. All documents relied upon by the
practitioner in making the calculations appearing on the Statement of
Current Monthly Income should be retained in case they are requested
by the United States Trustee.

Even in consumer no asset proceedings a situation may be present
where it is likely the trustee will want to ask questions in addition to those

---

1. 11 U.S.C. §527(a)(2)(B); 11 U.S.C. §707(b)(4). See chapters 5 and 6 supra.

described in chapter 8 supra. Perhaps there may be some form of inheritance as a potential asset, or a homestead. In these instances, the best thing to do is to obtain copies of any relevant documents from the debtor prior to filing. In any proceeding where it can be reasonably anticipated beforehand that the trustee will want to review documents in addition to the Statements and Schedules, it is always a good idea to have any such documents available so they can be delivered to the trustee promptly upon request.

In a small asset Chapter 7 business proceeding (and in all larger proceedings), effective preparation of the proceeding for the Chapter 7 trustee will require more effort. Although a larger proceeding will require more effort still, the type of effort will not vary. A typical small asset Chapter 7 liquidation, such as a small retail store or restaurant, will normally involve an inventory valued from a nominal amount to $50,000 or more and equipment of similar value. There may also be accounts receivable to collect. In small asset business proceedings, one of the most common problems of debtors or their principals (whether the debtor is an individual, a corporation, or a partnership) is payroll or other non-dischargeable taxes.[2] In proceedings of this sort, the debtor's or its insiders' primary concern will be to raise sufficient cash from the estate's liquidation to be able to satisfy a maximum amount of the nondischargeable obligations.

It is important to note that when a trustee is appointed, the trustee generally learns of the appointment only by receiving a copy of the bankruptcy petition and schedules in the mail, along with a stack of perhaps 15 or 20 other proceedings. If an estate contains assets that require prompt liquidation, unless the trustee reviews the files immediately (even if just to ascertain the existence of assets), the trustee may not know that any such assets exist until the meeting of creditors.

Recall that the creditors' meeting may not occur until 40 days after the initial filing.[3] If nothing is done during this period, assets may be at a business's premises without any type of security protection. Theft and burglary are a risk. Rent will continue to accrue. This rent will be an administrative expense payable before any tax creditors receive dividends. Gas and electric bills may continue to accrue and they will also receive administrative priority.[4] The longer assets go unattended the greater the likelihood they will dissipate to the detriment of all. As illustrated, this dissipation can occur by improper means or simply by the accrual of administrative expenses in the normal course of business. Both methods

---

2. See chapter 14 infra.
3. See chapter 8 supra.
4. See chapter 22 infra.

of dissipation can be substantially avoided by recognizing the practical difficulties encountered by trustees and by taking appropriate and simple commonsense actions that will effectively minimize any unintentional dissipation of assets.

Prior to a filing, there are at least nine things that a debtor or counsel can do to properly prepare a proceeding for the trustee. The accomplishment of these tasks will expedite the liquidation at a minimum of time and expense. Because most of these tasks can be performed by the debtor, any additional time required to be spent by counsel is minimal. Generally, a debtor and counsel should take any action reasonably designed to achieve the mutually desirable goals of expediting liquidation at a minimum of expense. A paralegal will often participate in much of this activity. Every possible penny that can reasonably be saved or earned will only serve to increase the ultimate funds available for distribution to prepetition creditors.

First, the debtor should obtain valuations, estimates, or appraisals of any property owned by the debtor. In a typical no asset consumer case, this is usually not as much an issue. Where there is equity in the property and/or there is the existence of other unencumbered property, accurate valuations are a must.

 Practice Pointer

The debtor's property tax appraisal is generally not accepted as evidence of the fair market value for the debtor's property.

Second, all documents of title pertaining to the debtor's assets should be assembled. You should be able to provide copies of the debtor's mortgage or lease as well as ownership documents of any vehicles owned by the debtor. The debtor should also seek to obtain payoff values for any mortgages or automobile loans. Having them in hand will save the trustee time and expense if issues arise later.

Third, obtain the name, address, and telephone number of the debtor's mortgage company and/or any landlords so the trustee will be able to make prompt arrangements to sell the property or to vacate the premises if necessary.

Fourth, the debtor should always be prepared to provide as detailed an itemization as possible of all personal belongings and household goods. If a valuation of these items is also included, this data will be invaluable to the trustee. This detailed information will not always be possible to have, but when it is, it should be provided to the trustee.

Fifth, the debtor should turn over to counsel the most recent copies of all records and checks of all bank accounts. Evidence of these accounts should be promptly disclosed to the trustee if it differs in any way from the debtor's schedules. Personal accounts should not be turned over unless requested by the trustee. Providing unrequested information only clutters the trustee and distracts attention from the prompt liquidation of those assets requiring it.

Sixth, the debtor should provide the trustee with any documentation of any prepetition lawsuits or claims, pursued or otherwise. If the debtor has already obtained prepetition counsel with respect to these claims, contact information should also be provided to the trustee.

What lawsuits or claims for damages were the Cashes aware of before they came to your office?

FACT PATTERN

Practice Pointer

Frequently, the trustee will seek to retain debtor's prepetition counsel to continue to pursue a particular state law claim, such as in a personal injury matter, only this time on behalf of the bankruptcy estate.

Seventh, the debtor should have available any documentation relating to any leased equipment or vehicles.

Eighth, the debtor will need to provide proof of insurance, both homeowners and automobile insurance, in order to provide adequate assurance that the property is insured and protected.

Finally, the debtor needs to provide his/her last three state and federal tax returns. The trustee will need this data to properly administer the estate. Any tax benefits contained in the prior returns will aid in reducing any taxes that may be incurred by a bankruptcy estate.

B.   POSTFILING ACTIONS

Once a proceeding is filed, it is necessary to promptly communicate with the trustee to ensure that liquidation of the physical assets will proceed promptly. Trustees, like anyone else, cannot act if they do not know that something needs to be acted upon. There are four things that can be done promptly on filing to ensure rapid communication with a trustee. These items will help the liquidation process proceed without delay.

First, and most obvious, is for counsel to learn who the trustee will be. You cannot communicate with the trustee unless you know who the trustee is. Because the United States Trustee must promptly appoint an interim trustee, the United States Trustee's office will generally know who the interim trustee will be within 24 hours of filing.[5] Thus, if counsel contacts the United States Trustee and asks to know who the interim trustee is, prompt contact becomes possible. Under the prevailing Electronic Filing System in use by the courts (see chapter 32 infra), the interim trustee is appointed immediately and the trustee's name, address, and telephone number will appear on the court docket.

The second obvious action is to pick up the telephone and call the trustee. Because trustees do not necessarily return all phone calls, it is necessary to leave a message that will alert the trustee about the existence of the asset proceeding. The basic word to leave in the message is "assets." Use of the word *assets* will normally result in the trustee responding within 24 hours. If more than 24 hours elapse without a reply from the trustee, then written correspondence is required. In a pressing matter, such as a restaurant or other debtor with perishable goods, the correspondence should be hand-delivered immediately. It is a good idea to enclose a copy of the Statements and Schedules in the correspondence. Once the trustee has been reached, the trustee will normally move into action and commence the liquidation process.

The third action is for the debtor to close all bank accounts for turnover to the trustee and either write a check to the trustee for the balance or obtain a cashier's check from the bank for the amount of the account balance. This will eliminate any further charges by the bank for maintenance of the account. Section 521(a)(2) of the Bankruptcy Code requires turnover of all records to the trustee.

Finally, the debtor or its insiders should cooperate fully with the trustee in the liquidation process. The trustee, or the trustee's representative, may want to meet the debtor at the business premises, for example. The trustee may need assistance in properly assembling accounts receivable data for collection purposes. The liquidation process will be easier and less expensive the greater the level of cooperation given the trustee by the debtor or its insiders. Section 521(a)(3) of the Bankruptcy Code requires cooperation of the debtor with the trustee.

---

5. 11 U.S.C. §701. See chapter 8 supra.

All of the practical and commonsense actions just described, both pre- and postfiling, will be useful in expediting the physical aspects of liquidation at a minimum of expense. This will ensure that a maximum amount of cash will be raised to distribute to the creditors as dividends. Where this results in payment in full of nondischargeable taxes, the debtor or its principals will be grateful.

Summary

It is important to make the trustee's job as simple as possible. Properly preparing a case before it is filed will often be sufficient to accomplish this task.

In all proceedings, proper preparation of the Statements and Schedules is critical. Chapter 30 of this text is a tutorial on this subject. Further, whenever it can be anticipated that the trustee may request additional documentation (such as a declaration of homestead, an escrow closing statement, or bank records), the documents should be obtained from the client before the filing. Counsel must also maintain all documents required by BAPCPA together with any materials relied upon to satisfy the "reasonable inquiry" standard.

In business proceedings, there are nine simple steps that can be taken before a filing and four additional steps that can be taken immediately after a filing to rapidly commence the liquidation process, all of which will help to economize expenses while helping to maximize returns. Generally, a debtor and counsel should take any action reasonably designed to achieve the mutually desirable goals of expediting liquidation at a minimum of expense.

CHAPTER 12 CHECKLIST

12.1   PREFILING — ASSET CASE
      12.1.1   Value Assets
      12.1.2   Obtain Documents of Title (Such as Vehicle Ownership Documents) and Keys to All Vehicles
      12.1.3   Obtain Name and Address of Landlord(s)
      12.1.4   Obtain Itemized Inventory and Equipment List, with Values, If Possible
      12.1.5   Obtain Bank Records
      12.1.6   Compile Accounts Receivable Data
      12.1.7   Return Leased Equipment to Lessors

DISCUSSION QUESTIONS

1. What are the most important concerns of a debtor in a consumer no asset Chapter 7 proceeding?

2. What is a common primary concern in an asset proceeding?

3. What actions, before and after the filing of an asset case, should be taken by the debtor or counsel that can assist the trustee in maximizing a liquidation at a minimum of expense?

PRACTICE EXERCISES

Exercise 12.1

Prepare a list of documents for the Cashes to provide to your firm for their case file and for possible turnover to a trustee.

Exercise 12.2

The Cashes have a copy of their local tax bill and property assessment and do not understand why an appraisal is necessary. Draft a letter to the Cashes explaining the different types of property appraisals and identifying the type of appraisal that may be required by the trustee.

PART III

Bankruptcy Litigation

13

The Automatic Stay—
11 U.S.C. §362

Learning Objectives

- Explain the concept of the automatic stay as an element of debtor relief

- Describe creditor activities subject to the automatic stay

- Describe creditor activities not subject to the automatic stay

- Discuss the procedures utilized by creditors to obtain relief from the stay

- List the serial filing provisions enacted by BAPCPA

- Identify when the stay is no longer automatic and must be imposed by the court

A.   THE AUTOMATIC STAY

The final element of debtor relief is contained in Section 362 and is known as the **automatic stay**. (The other elements of debtor relief, discharge and exemptions, have been discussed in chapters 8 and 10 supra.) It is now commonplace to see commercials on television or to read advertisements online or in newspapers that may advertise bankruptcy as follows: "Stop creditor harassment. Stop foreclosure. Stop repossession." It is the automatic stay that allows these advertisements to make such bold and brazen claims. As shall be shown, these claims are not entirely accurate.

Automatic stay: a statutory bar to any collection activity by creditors after a bankruptcy petition has been filed

The essence of the automatic stay is that as of the moment a bankruptcy proceeding is filed, voluntarily or involuntarily, and with or without notice of the bankruptcy filing, all creditor activity to collect debts, obtain judgments, or obtain property of a debtor to satisfy a debt must be completely stopped. The automatic stay is effective the moment a petition is filed. The debtor does not have to do anything special to initiate the automatic stay; it does not require the filing of a particular form or order. The effectiveness or applicability of the automatic stay is also not related to actual notice or the entry of an order for relief.[1] It is simply triggered by the filing of the debtor's petition.

Once a proceeding has been commenced, creditors can take no further action that affects the assets or rights of the estate or debtor except in compliance with Section 362. Relief is also available in this section where creditors can attempt to be relieved of the stay's effect and may often be successful. The stay is automatic but it is not permanent. Any implication to the contrary in any legal advertising is simply untrue.

FACT PATTERN

What actions in the Cashes' case would the automatic stay operate against?

A petition does not have to be filed within any particular time before an act is to occur to permit the automatic stay to become effective. For example, if a foreclosure sale is scheduled for 10:00 A.M. and a petition is filed at 9:59 A.M., the automatic stay prevents the foreclosure sale from occurring or from being valid if it does still go forward.

 Practice Pointer

In some jurisdictions, a distinction is made between actions taken in violation of the automatic stay that are considered to be "void" as opposed to merely "voidable."

However, if the bankruptcy filing occurs at 10:01 A.M., after the foreclosure sale, the automatic stay will not affect the foreclosure because it was not in effect when the foreclosure occurred.[2]

---

1. 11 U.S.C. §362(a). See chapter 4 supra.
2. In re Sands, 328 B.R. 614 (Bankr. N.D.N.Y. 2005) illustrates the point. Debtor's counsel began filing the case electronically at 10:49 A.M. The foreclosure sale took place at 11:00 A.M. The bankruptcy filing was not completed until 12:05 P.M. Since the filing did not take place until after the foreclosure sale, the foreclosure sale was valid.

> ### *Practice Pointer*
> The bankruptcy filing may, however, still
> have an impact upon the debtor's state
> law redemption remedies.

The automatic stay is, as its name suggests, "automatically" effective
with or without notice the moment the bankruptcy petition has been
filed.[3] Nevertheless, it is certainly better practice to provide a creditor
with notice that a petition has been filed, even if only by telephone.
The best approach is to transmit by facsimile or electronic means (e.g.,
e-mail) a file stamped copy of the first two pages of the petition to any
specific creditor, or the creditor's attorney, to whom you want to provide
immediate notice of the filing. This includes, for example, a creditor
threatening to repossess a car, a creditor conducting an imminent foreclosure, or a utility company attempting to terminate the debtor's service
for nonpayment.

> ***Which creditors in the Cashes' case would you consider***
> ***providing independent actual notice of their second bank-***
> ***ruptcy filing?***

FACT PATTERN

B. ACTIVITY SUBJECT TO THE AUTOMATIC STAY

Section 362(a) itemizes the types of creditor activity that are affected by
imposition of the automatic stay. Section 362(a)(1) prohibits the commencement or continuation of any judicial, administrative, or other proceeding against the debtor that was or could have been commenced
before the filing of the petition to recover a prepetition claim.[4] In practical
terms, this means, for example, that the ABC Collection Company cannot
file a lawsuit against the debtor once a petition has been filed, and the XYZ
Collection Agency cannot execute on the judgment that it obtained before
the petition was filed. Nor can the LMN Collection Company proceed with

---

3. There is no requirement anywhere in the Code or Rules that requires prior notice of a filing to
   make the automatic stay effective. However, sanctions against a creditor without notice who
   violates the stay are likely to be minimal.
4. 11 U.S.C. §362(a)(1).

its motion for summary judgment in a case that was pending when the petition was filed, and the QRS Collection Agency cannot obtain a default judgment on its prepetition claim. All legal actions initiated against the debtor are stopped.

Section 362(a)(2) prohibits the enforcement of any prepetition judgment against the debtor or property of the estate.[5] Thus a collection agency cannot execute upon its judgment or take a postjudgment debtor examination to ascertain the existence of assets. Recall, however, that all of this information will be disclosed in the bankruptcy, since it is contained in the Statements and Schedules.

Practice Pointer

Remember, however, the creditor may still make use of a 2004 examination.

Section 362(a)(3) stays any act to obtain possession of property of the estate or any act to exercise control over property of the estate.[6] This means that either by judicial process or otherwise, creditors cannot show up at the debtor's home or business and start repossessing unpaid-for merchandise. Thus, the automatic stay suspends any future attachments against the debtor or the estate. This also means that creditors cannot proceed outside of the bankruptcy system to seek the appointment of a receiver or other custodian to take control of a debtor's business or property.

FACT PATTERN

What property held or used by the Cashes will or will not be protected from repossession or foreclosure by Section 362(a)(3)?

Section 362(a)(4) stays any act to create, perfect, or enforce a lien against property of the estate.[7] This means that a creditor that has not perfected a security interest in collateral before the petition is filed can no longer do so; a creditor with an unperfected lien can no longer perfect it. There is one limited exception to this, which will be discussed in connection with Section 362(b)(3) below. A secured creditor is also stayed, under

5. 11 U.S.C. §362(a)(2). As to property of the estate, see chapter 14 infra.
6. 11 U.S.C. §362(a)(3).
7. 11 U.S.C. §362(a)(4).

this subsection, from repossessing or foreclosing upon a perfected security interest, absent any other provision in Section 362.

Section 362(a)(5) stays any act to create, perfect, or enforce against property of the debtor any lien that secures a claim that arose before commencement of the case. This subsection extends the protections of Section 362(a)(4) to property of the debtor as opposed to property of the estate.[8] Thus, the exempt property of a debtor is also subject to the protections of the automatic stay.

Section 362(a)(6) stays any act to collect, assess, or recover a claim that arose before the filing of the petition.[9] This subsection includes within it the judicial activity referred to in Section 362(a)(1) and Section 362(a)(2) but also broadly extends the stay to any other form of creditor collection activity. Phone calls from a creditor seeking payment are stayed pursuant to this provision. A collection agency or other creditor also cannot continue to send the debtor collection notices in the mail. In short, this subsection prevents creditor harassment.

Section 362(a)(7) stays the making of setoffs without first obtaining relief from the automatic stay.[10] A setoff is the common law right of a creditor to balance mutual debts with a debtor. For example, Murat owes Ney $10 while Ney owes Murat $5. Ney can set off his debt to Murat and thus only have to collect $5 from Murat for both debts to be satisfied. Or Murat can offer Ney $5, set off the $5 Ney owes Murat, and both debts are extinguished.

Section 362(a)(8) stays the commencement or continuation of a proceeding before the United States Tax Court concerning the debtor.[11] This Section is unusual because it does not stay an act against the debtor, but a proceeding concerning the debtor. This means that if the debtor has initiated an action in the Tax Court, the action will still be stayed. The reason for this is that Section 505 of the Bankruptcy Code permits the Bankruptcy Court to determine tax issues in a bankruptcy proceeding.[12]

As is apparent from a review of the foregoing, only actions against the debtor or property of the estate or debtor are stayed. Actions by the debtor to collect debts or property from third parties are not. Creditors are not normally stayed from enforcing a debt against a nonbankruptcy debtor, guarantor, cosigner, or statutorily liable party (such as principal liability for payroll taxes).

---

8. 11 U.S.C. §362(a)(5).
9. 11 U.S.C. §362(a)(6).
10. 11 U.S.C. §362(a)(7).
11. 11 U.S.C. §362(a)(8).
12. 11 U.S.C. §505. See chapter 22 infra.

> ### *Practice Pointer*
>
> To determine whether an action was initiated by the debtor (usually in the context of an appeal), courts will often look to see who commenced the first action, not the current appeal. In other words, the debtor's appeal of an action originally filed against him will still be stayed, but not the debtor's appeal of an action that he originally commenced.

C.   ACTIVITY NOT SUBJECT TO THE AUTOMATIC STAY

Even though the automatic stay is a basic debtor relief protection of the bankruptcy system and even though it unquestionably applies to a very broad range of activities, there are also a number of actions that are not subject to the automatic stay. Actions that are not subject to the stay can proceed or continue without regard to the existence of the bankruptcy. These actions are the subject of Section 362(b). Many of these actions do not typically arise in consumer bankruptcy cases. The text focuses on the exceptions most likely to arise in a consumer bankruptcy practice.

The commencement or continuation of a criminal action or proceeding against the debtor is not stayed.[13] A debtor cannot avoid a murder trial by filing a bankruptcy petition. The reason for this exception to the automatic stay is obvious.

> ### *Practice Pointer*
>
> Courts often resort to state law to address the question of what is considered to be a "criminal" action. For example, certain traffic violations may be considered to be quasi-criminal and Section 362(b)(1) may or may not apply.

---

13. 11 U.S.C. §362(b)(1).

After the enactment of the Bankruptcy Code, an issue arose in those states where creditors could instigate criminal prosecutions against bad check writers. The question became, was the prosecution an act to collect a debt and subject to the stay pursuant to 11 U.S.C. §362(a)(6) or was it a criminal prosecution and therefore not subject to the stay pursuant to 11 U.S.C. §362(b)(1)? The reported cases went both ways. Some Bankruptcy Courts held such prosecutions to be mere collection devices and therefore stayed, while other courts found them to be excepted criminal prosecutions.

In Kelly v. Robinson, the Supreme Court ruled that a criminal sentence to make restitution to creditors whose debts are subject to discharge in a bankruptcy proceeding is enforceable and therefore collection does not violate the automatic stay. The facts in this case were that in November 1980, Carolyn Robinson pleaded guilty to larceny based on her wrongful receipt of $9,932.95 in welfare benefits from the State of Connecticut. She was placed on probation, one condition of which was the payment of $100 per month in restitution. In February 1981, Robinson filed a Chapter 7 bankruptcy. She listed the creditor in her schedules. The creditor did not oppose the dischargeability of the debt and Robinson received her discharge in May 1981. Subsequently, when the creditor sought to collect the debt, Robinson sought an order from the Bankruptcy Court that the debt, and hence the restitution order, had been discharged. The Supreme Court disagreed. Because criminal sentences and restitution orders were not dischargeable under either the Bankruptcy Act or the Bankruptcy Code, the Court reasoned, collection of the restitution order is not subject to the automatic stay. In addition, a further rationale to support this position is that society's interest in the criminal justice system outweighs its interest in the bankruptcy system.[14]

What creditor actions, if any, may fall within the exception provided by Section 362(b)(1) in the Cash case?

FACT PATTERN

Section 362(b)(2) excepts from operation of the automatic stay the collection of "domestic support obligations" from property that is not property of the estate. The commencement or continuation of a paternity suit or the commencement or continuation of an action for domestic support obligations is also excepted from the automatic stay. Custody

14. Kelly v. Robinson, 479 U.S. 36 (1986). This holding was excluded from Chapter 13 proceedings in Pennsylvania Dept. of Public Welfare v. Davenport, 495 U.S. 552 (1990). However, this ruling was overruled by Congress in 1991 when it enacted 11 U.S.C. §1328(a)(3), which makes criminal restitution orders not dischargeable in Chapter 13 proceedings.

disputes, domestic violence matters and the divorce case itself, except to the extent it affects property of the estate (see chapter 14 infra) are not subject to the automatic stay.[15] As described in chapter 14 infra, domestic support obligations are not normally dischargeable.

Does a DSO require the parties to have been married at some point to one another? Will Helen be able to file an action for past due child support on behalf of Lotta, or will the action be stayed by Owen's bankruptcy filing?

The collection of these nondischargeable debts other than from property of the estate does not violate the automatic stay. Property of the estate is described in greater detail in chapter 15 infra, but in a Chapter 7 case, property of the estate does not include a debtor's postpetition wages.[16] One practical effect of Section 362(b)(2) is that a creditor with a prepetition claim for domestic support obligations is not barred from proceeding in the proper forum to obtain any necessary orders to permit collection of domestic support obligations from a Chapter 7 or 11 debtor's wages. Because exemptions are also ineffective against these claims, Chapter 7 or 11 is essentially ineffective against them.[17] Thus, unless Mr. Smith files a Chapter 13, Mrs. Smith will retain many of her rights to collect alimony, support, or maintenance due, without regard to Mr. Smith's Chapter 7 petition.

Practice Pointer

Note that domestic support obligations are nondischargeable in Chapter 7, 11, and 13 proceedings.

Section 362(b)(3) is a limited exception to the effect of the automatic stay regarding acts to perfect or to maintain or continue the perfection of an interest in property described in connection with Section 362(a)(4) above. Essentially, a secured creditor that has a nonbankruptcy law right to perfect an interest in property (such as by recording a Uniform

---

15. 11 U.S.C. §362(b)(2).
16. 11 U.S.C. §541(a)(6). See chapter 15 infra. This is not the case in a Chapter 11 or 13 proceeding, where a debtor's postpetition earnings are considered property of the estate. 11 U.S.C. §1115; 11 U.S.C. §1306(a)(2). See chapters 15, 24, and 25 infra.
17. 11 U.S.C. §522(c). See chapter 10 supra.

Commercial Code (UCC) security interest in personal property by recording a mortgage or deed of trust upon real estate) within a statutory period
of time may do so within the allowed time period or within 30 days of the
underlying transaction otherwise subject to the automatic stay.[18] This
situation will arise most commonly in secured transactions subject to
the UCC. Generally, the UCC permits creditors in certain secured transactions grace periods to perfect security interests by properly filing any
required documents with a County Recorder or Secretary of State for a
particular state.[19] Thus, if a debtor files a bankruptcy proceeding within
this time period, this exception to the automatic stay provides that it will
not be violated if the creditor perfects its security interest within the nonbankruptcy statutory period or 30 days from the date of the bankruptcy
filing. For example, if Paul Walker buys a new car on Thursday and files a
Chapter 7 on Friday, as long as the bank perfects its lien upon the vehicle
within any underlying statutory period, the act of perfection will not be a
violation of the automatic stay under Section 362(b)(3). This provision
may also permit the perfection of a state law mechanic's lien without such
perfection being considered a violation of the automatic stay.

There is substantial case law in existence on this latter point. It is
beyond the scope or purpose of this basic text to analyze this case law
in detail. A creditor in this situation should carefully review the status of
the case law on this point before proceeding so that no unintended violation of the stay is committed.

Section 362(b)(4) excepts from the stay the commencement or continuation of an action or proceeding by a governmental unit to enforce its
police or regulatory power.[20] The rationale for this exception is identical
to the exception for criminal actions or proceedings. For example, the EPA
may still enjoin Polluters Inc. from violating the Environmental Protection
Act. A zoning commission may still find a debtor in violation of zoning laws
for having a restaurant in the middle of a residential neighborhood. These
actions are not subject to the automatic stay.

Section 362(b)(4) also permits enforcement of any orders resulting
from the enforcement of a governmental unit's police or regulatory
powers other than the collection of a money judgment.[21] For instance,
if the EPA issues an order against Polluters Inc. to pay a fine and clean up
the mess, the monetary portion of the order is subject to the automatic
stay, but the cleanup order is not.[22]

---

18. 11 U.S.C. §362(b)(3).
19. The time period for perfection may vary from state to state pursuant to UCC §9-301(1).
20. 11 U.S.C. §362(b)(4).
21. 11 U.S.C. §362(b)(4). The enforcement aspect of Section 362(b)(4) was contained in Section
    362(b)(5) prior to 1994. In 1994, the two provisions were merged into the present form.
22. Midlantic Natl. Bank v. New Jersey Dept. of Envtl. Protection, 474 U.S. 494 (1986).

Section 362(b)(9) provides that the issuance to the debtor of a notice of tax deficiency will not violate the automatic stay.[23] Although the Historical and Revision Notes explain that this provision is associated with a debtor's right to have the Bankruptcy Court or Tax Court determine the amount of the tax, a practical reason for this exception to the automatic stay is that the IRS computers are not designed to factor in the bankruptcy filing of a taxpayer. Despite the law and even manual adjustments to the program, the IRS computers often still function incorrectly and send out notices. So Congress simply made the issuance of a tax deficiency an exception to the automatic stay to preclude taxing entities' being accused of violating the stay by issuing notices of deficiency. Section 362(b)(9) includes audits, demands for returns, and the assessment and issuance of a demand to pay a tax as additional exceptions to the automatic stay.

FACT PATTERN

What impact will the automatic stay have on the IRS audit sent to Owen Cash? Will Owen's failure to timely file last year's tax return have a negative impact on his bankruptcy case?

Practice Pointer

Note that a debtor's failure to file both pre- and postpetition tax returns may lead to dismissal of the bankruptcy case.

Section 362(b)(19) permits the withholding of payment from a debtor's postpetition wages for the repayment of loans from retirement plans that are qualified as such pursuant to the Internal Revenue Code, such as 401(k) plans or loans from IRA accounts.

A number of provisions designed to curb the abuse of serial bankruptcy filings were added to the Code by BAPCPA. A **serial bankruptcy** filing takes place when a debtor files successive bankruptcies in an effort to delay creditor action, typically foreclosure of a home, eviction, or repossession. The expectation is that each time a debtor files, the automatic stay will stop the creditor and force the creditor to seek relief from the stay. The debtor will then usually allow the case to be dismissed and then refile again just prior to the next scheduled foreclosure sale. In actual practice, it

Serial bankruptcy: a debtor who files a second (or third) bankruptcy proceeding after dismissal of one or more prior proceedings

---

23. 11 U.S.C. §362(b)(9).

has not been uncommon to see debtors filing three or more consecutive bankruptcies and potentially delay a foreclosure for over a year.

Section 362(b)(20) is the first provision affecting serial bankruptcy filings. This provision excepts from the automatic stay actions to enforce liens against property for two years after the entry of an order by the court in a prior bankruptcy case that the prior filing was part of a scheme to delay, hinder, and defraud creditors involving multiple bankruptcy filings or a transfer of an interest in the property not consented to by the secured creditor. This sort of scheme is also now a separate and independent ground for seeking relief from the automatic stay pursuant to 11 U.S.C. §362(d)(4). A debtor can seek to have the stay imposed in the subsequent case by filing a motion showing changed circumstances or good cause.[24]

Section 362(b)(21) excepts from the stay the enforcement of liens or security interests against real property if the debtor is not eligible to file because the new bankruptcy has been filed within 180 days of dismissal of a prior case in violation of §109(g) (see chapter 5 supra), or if the bankruptcy court entered an order in a prior bankruptcy case prohibiting the debtor from being a debtor in another bankruptcy case.

Section 362(b)(22) permits an eviction to proceed if the landlord obtained a judgment for possession of residential property prior to the filing of the bankruptcy. Section 362(l) defers this for 30 days to provide the debtor an opportunity to cure and deposit all past due rent. To trigger this relief, the debtor must deposit with the bankruptcy court any rent that accrued during the 30-day period and also certify that nonbankruptcy law (usually meaning state law) allows for such a cure. Section 362(b)(23) permits evictions based upon endangerment to property or person or upon the use of illegal drugs, provided that the procedures of Section 362(m) are complied with.

Section 362(b)(26) permits the setoff of prepetition tax refunds against prepetition tax claims. For example, if a debtor is owed a tax refund for 2015, owes taxes for 2014, and files Chapter 7 in 2016, the Internal Revenue Service may use the 2015 refund and apply it to the 2014 tax liability without violating the automatic stay pursuant to this provision.

---

24. 11 U.S.C. §362(b)(20); 11 U.S.C. §362(d)(4). See chapter 13E infra. As to the transfer of an interest in property to defraud creditors, this is designed to prevent a person from transferring a partial interest in real property to a third person for the primary purpose of having the third person file bankruptcy to gain the benefits of the automatic stay for the property.

D.   DURATION OF THE AUTOMATIC STAY

The automatic stay, despite popular opinion and legal advertisements to the contrary, is not perpetual. The automatic stay may terminate by operation of law, it may be relieved on a motion by a creditor, it may effectively merge into the permanent injunction created by a debtor's discharge, or it may not exist at all in serial filing cases.[25] Section 362(c) concerns the duration of the automatic stay. Generally, the automatic stay remains in effect with regard to property of the estate until such time as the property is no longer property of the estate.[26] One way in which property might no longer be property of the estate would be if the trustee "abandons" it as burdensome.[27] Another way in which property will no longer be property of the estate is when the trustee files a Report of No Distribution in a no asset proceeding. This report effectively acts to abandon previously unadministered assets.

Practice Pointer

When a trustee "abandons" property, the property is not lost in the traditional sense. Rather, the estate relinquishes its interest and the property returns to the debtor, along with any prepetition interests (i.e., mortgages) attached to it.

Any other acts affected by the automatic stay continue until the earliest of the time a proceeding is closed, the time a proceeding is dismissed, or, if a proceeding is an individual Chapter 7 or any Chapter 9, 11, 12, or 13, the time a discharge is granted or denied.[28] In practice, the earliest of these various dates in a Chapter 7 is usually when the discharge is granted or denied, which, as described in chapter 8 supra, normally occurs about 90 days after the proceeding is filed. In a Chapter 11, a discharge is not received until a plan of reorganization is confirmed, except when the debtor is an individual.[29] In Chapters 12 and 13, and in an individual Chapter 11, a discharge is not granted until the debtor's plan has been

---

25. 11 U.S.C. §362(c), (d); 11 U.S.C. §524(a). See chapter 8 supra.
26. 11 U.S.C. §362(c)(1).
27. 11 U.S.C. §554. See chapter 21 infra.
28. 11 U.S.C. §362(c)(2).
29. 11 U.S.C. §1141(d). See chapter 27 infra.

fully performed, which in a Chapter 13 is three to five years.[30] Thus, in non-Chapter 7 proceedings, events other than receipt of a discharge will often be the earlier of the possible dates upon which the automatic stay terminates.

BAPCPA added two additional situations in which the stay is terminated by operation of law. Each situation is designed to curb serial filings, except when a debtor can demonstrate that the debtor is proceeding in good faith. Section 362(c)(3) terminates the stay 30 days after a filing in an individual debtor case where the debtor had a case pending within the preceding year that was dismissed, except for a case refiled under a reorganization chapter if the dismissal was under Section 707(b), discussed in chapter 6 supra.[31] A party in interest, presumably the debtor in this situation, may file a motion to extend the stay if it can be demonstrated that the current petition has been filed in good faith. There is a presumption that the case is not in good faith if there have been two or more cases filed by the debtor within one year; or a prior case within one year was dismissed for failure to file required documents; or the debtor failed to make adequate protection payments; or the debtor defaulted in performing a confirmed plan; or the debtor's financial or personal affairs are unchanged from the most recent previous case; or the previous case was dismissed after a creditor moved for or obtained relief from the automatic stay (see infra this chapter).

What information regarding the application of the automatic stay will need to be given to the Cashes if they do file a second bankruptcy case using your firm?

FACT PATTERN

Section 362(c)(4) provides that the stay does not go into effect at all, despite the debtor's bankruptcy filing, for an individual debtor who has filed two or more cases within the preceding year that were dismissed, except for a case refiled under a reorganization chapter if the dismissal was under Section 707(b), discussed in chapter 5 supra. A party in interest (presumably an affected creditor) can seek an application for an order that no stay is in effect, often referred to as a "comfort order." A party in interest, presumably the debtor, may file a motion seeking to impose the stay in a manner identical to that set forth in Section 362(c)(3).

---

30. 11 U.S.C. §1141(d); 11 U.S.C. §1228(a); 11 U.S.C. §1328(a). See chapters 24, 27, and 28 infra.
31. There is some question in the case law regarding the extent to which the automatic stay is terminated. Section 362(c)(3) states that the stay terminates "with respect to the debtor." The question arises whether this also extends to property of the estate.

For example, Homer and Marge Simpson file Chapter 7. They fail to file schedules, and their case is dismissed. One month later they file a second Chapter 7. Pursuant to Section 362(c)(3), the automatic stay will terminate as to their secured and leasehold creditors 30 days after the second filing unless the Simpsons successfully move before the bankruptcy court to extend the stay. If their second case is dismissed and they want to file a third, pursuant to Section 362(c)(4), the stay will not go into effect at all unless the Simpsons successfully move before the court to impose the stay. In this latter situation, the creditors may obtain an ex parte order stating that there is no stay in effect.

Although the automatic stay terminates when a debtor receives a discharge, creditors are not suddenly free to once again collect prepetition debts. Recall that the discharge is a permanent injunction with respect to all debts that are discharged.[32] In addition, exempt property is not liable for prepetition debts.[33] Technically, therefore, the automatic stay merges into the permanent injunction that results from the discharge order. Many people have an erroneous perception that the automatic stay is eternal. It is not. Rather, the automatic stay merges into a debtor's discharge. The discharge acts as an injunction against the collection of all discharged debts. This is a more accurate representation of what occurs as a result of the discharge.

BAPCPA also added an additional situation in which the automatic stay is terminated by operation of law. Pursuant to Section 362(h), if a debtor fails to timely file a Statement of Intention and begins performance with respect to secured or leased personal property (see chapter 5 supra and chapter 22 infra), the property ceases to be property of the estate (see chapter 15 infra), which effectively terminates the stay.

E.   OBTAINING RELIEF FROM THE AUTOMATIC STAY

Motion for relief from the automatic stay: a motion made by a creditor, pursuant to 11 U.S.C. §362(d), to be freed from the effect of the automatic stay

A creditor may seek a court order, in appropriate circumstances, granting it "relief" from the automatic stay. In other words, the creditor is allowed to pursue its nonbankruptcy (state law) remedies notwithstanding the debtor's bankruptcy filing. This procedure is a noticed motion commonly known as a **motion for relief from the automatic stay**. A majority of bankruptcy litigation involves such motions. Relief from the automatic

---

32. 11 U.S.C. §524(a). See chapter 8 supra.
33. 11 U.S.C. §522(c). See chapter 10 supra.

stay may take the form of annulling, conditioning, terminating, or modifying the stay.[34] The Code describes four grounds for a party to seek relief from the automatic stay. They include: (1) "for cause," including a lack of adequate protection regarding the creditor's interest in the debtor's property; (2) with regard to acts against property of the estate (such as repossessions or foreclosures), if the debtor does not have any equity in the property and the property is not necessary for an effective reorganization; (3) with respect to a single asset real estate case, where the debtor fails within 90 days after the order for relief to file a plan that has a reasonable possibility of being confirmed within a reasonable time, or the debtor commences monthly payments to all consensual secured lenders at the contract rate of interest; or (4) real property that is part of a scheme to delay, hinder and defraud creditors involving multiple bankruptcy filings or a transfer of an interest in the property not consented to by the secured creditors.[35]

Which of the Cashes' creditors, if any, would be likely to file a motion for relief from the automatic stay?

FACT PATTERN

Attempting to obtain relief from the automatic stay for cause introduces the concept of **adequate protection**. This concept is utilized frequently throughout the Bankruptcy Code. Adequate protection is defined in Section 361. In its essence, adequate protection simply means maintaining the status quo for an affected creditor during the pendency of the stay, to prevent the erosion of the creditor's interest in the property. Generally, only secured creditors will benefit from this provision. The most common form of adequate protection is requiring the trustee or debtor to continue to make periodic postpetition payments on a debt subject to a secured claim.[36] Because the payments will act to minimize any increase in the creditor's claim occasioned by the stay, the payments will inhibit the erosion of the creditor's interest in the property. Providing additional or replacement collateral is also an acceptable method of providing adequate protection.[37] Finally, any other method that will serve the underlying purpose of preserving the value of the creditor's claim will also constitute adequate protection, except that a secured

Adequate protection: methods of protecting a creditor's interest in property of the estate during pendency of the automatic stay

---

34. 11 U.S.C. §362(d). Bankruptcy Rule 4001(a)(1).
35. 11 U.S.C. §362(d)(1), (2), (3), (4).
36. 11 U.S.C. §361(1). These payments can be limited to interest on the secured portion of a debtor's debt. See United Savings Assn. of Texas v. Timbers of Inwood Forest Assocs., 484 U.S. 365 (1988). See also chapter 22 infra.
37. 11 U.S.C. §361(2). Also see chapter 22 infra.

creditor cannot be given an administrative claim.[38] To do so would violate the distributive scheme of the Bankruptcy Code.[39]

For instance, if Chapter 7 debtors Jack and Jill Smith want to keep their home or vehicle, adequate protection simply means continuing to make their normal scheduled payments to the secured creditor. If the Smiths are already in default (a common occurrence), adequate protection will also require the ultimate curing of the default. Although Chapter 13 may provide a better remedy for the Smiths than Chapter 7 if they wish to save their home or car from foreclosure or repossession, any default will ultimately have to be cured. Typically, the ability to make current payments will permit the court to grant the Smiths some additional time to sell or refinance their home or car, thereby at least attempting to preserve any equity the Smiths may have in the home or car through any exemptions they have claimed.

FACT PATTERN

Which debts in the Cash case may require adequate protection payments?

Cause for obtaining relief from the automatic stay is not limited to lack of adequate protection. Recall that a Code section's use of the term "including" does not limit the statute's applicability to only those items specifically mentioned.[40] A common cause for relief from the stay, other than lack of adequate protection, arises in the case of a personal injury claimant where the debtor is a defendant. Many personal injury defendants have insurance coverage. The insurance company will normally pay the claim up to the policy limits. It is traditional to grant relief from the stay to a creditor who can look to an insurance policy for recovery. The claimant may then proceed with litigation of the claim as long as the creditor agrees that it will not seek to enforce any judgment beyond the limits of the debtor's insurance coverage. Other creditors are not prejudiced because they have no right to payment of the claim covered by insurance. The trustee does not have any rights to collect the creditor's claim. The claim will only be paid to the one affected creditor, not to all of the estate's creditors.

---

38. 11 U.S.C. §361(3).
39. See chapters 22 and 23 infra.
40. 11 U.S.C. §102(3). See chapter 4 supra.

MOTIONS FOR RELIEF FROM STAY
(11 U.S.C. §362)

Creditor files motions
and pleadings as per
Checklist 12.3

Prior notice (Consult local rules)

```
OPPOSITION —
TRUSTEE, DEBTORS,
PARTY IN INTEREST
```

Court Options (11 U.S.C. §362(d))
  1. Grant motion:
      a) for cause, including lack of
          adequate protection;
      b) no equity;
      c) property not necessary for
          an effective reorganization
      d) single asset real estate
      e) multiple bankruptcy scheme
  2. Deny motion
  3. Schedule a final hearing within
      30 days (11 U.S.C. §362(e)(1)).
  4. Stay terminates 30 days after
      motion filed in individual case
      unless parties agree or court
      orders otherwise
      (11 U.S.C. §362(e)(2)).

```
PRELIMINARY
HEARING
11 U.S.C. §362(c)
```

```
FINAL HEARING
11 U.S.C. §362(c)
```

> ### *Practice Pointer*
>
> The money provided by the insurance coverage in this context is not "property of the estate," and therefore is not subject to administration by the trustee and is not part of the pool of funds gathered for the estate's general unsecured creditors.

The second ground for obtaining relief from the automatic stay, lack of equity in property, is the most frequent ground utilized by creditors seeking relief from the automatic stay. Simply put, a secured creditor will be entitled to some form of relief from the automatic stay if the debtor has no equity in the property. The example of a debtor with real estate subject to foreclosure illustrates the most common scenario. The methodology of the example, however, applies to any motion for relief from the automatic stay based on lack of equity.

Assume that debtor V. Diesel owns a home worth $100,000. Assume that a first trust deed or mortgage debt exists encumbering the home in the amount of $75,000. Assume further that there are past due payments owed on the trust deed or to the mortgage holder of $10,000. This means that the lender is actually owed $85,000 (including principal, interest, and relevant late fees and charges). This suggests a possible equity recovery of $15,000. However, the estimated costs of selling the property should be taken into account. This includes an estimate of commissions and closing costs, usually 8 to 10 percent of the selling price for a parcel of residential real property. In the example, then, 10 percent of the sales price would be $10,000. The amount of any equity in the property is determined simply by subtracting the value of all liens, encumbrances, and the estimated costs of sale from the gross value of the property. Any remainder represents equity in the property. In the example, there would thus be $5,000 of realizable equity in V Diesel's home. If the debtor has claimed this equity as exempt pursuant to Section 522(d), there are no grounds for relief from the automatic stay because the debtor has protected equity in the property. So even if a sale of the property would provide no dividend to the unsecured creditors, if there is some equity available for the debtor to realize, the debtor may be able to maintain the automatic stay in effect.[41]

---

41. 11 U.S.C. §362(d)(2).

Assuming for the moment that Owen's loan from his father was never recorded or is otherwise found to be invalid, what recoverable equity would be available in the Cash home?

Generally, where the debtor's equity is less than 10 percent of the property's value, the courts are normally hesitant to maintain the stay for any length of time without requiring the debtor to provide some additional form of adequate protection as described above. The reason for this is that the value given is really only an estimate. If the actual sales price turns out to be lower than the estimate, the secured creditor's interest in the property may be impaired. Remember the concept of adequate protection exists for the benefit of the creditor with an interest in the property, not for the benefit of the debtor.

Thus, in the situation where the equity is marginal, the court may not be inclined to grant relief from the stay, but will likely require the making of adequate protection payments as a condition of the automatic stay remaining in effect. The court will also probably set a deadline for the debtor to obtain a sale or refinancing of the property that will result in the cure of any prefiling arrearages. This deadline may be two months, three months, or six months, or as otherwise set by the court. The court has discretion in structuring relief from automatic stay orders to try to do equity to the rights of both the creditor and the debtor.

Generally, if there is no equity in the property, the stay will be terminated. If the equity is marginal, as in the example, the stay may be maintained for a limited period of time conditioned upon the making of adequate protection payments. As the equity cushion increases above 10 percent of the property's estimated value, the court will become less inclined to require adequate protection payments or to set a deadline for the sale or refinance of the asset. Where there may be substantial equity for the unsecured creditors beyond any homestead exemption for the debtor, the court may decline to grant any relief, limited or otherwise, from the automatic stay. Such a denial of relief in this latter instance will normally be without prejudice to the creditor to renew its motion at a later date.

In a Chapter 7 case, because the proceeding is a liquidation, the property will never be necessary for an effective reorganization and this will not normally be an issue in a motion for relief from the automatic stay. The necessity of the property to an effective reorganization does, however, become a critical issue in reorganization proceedings under Chapter 11, 12, or 13.[42] The principles illustrated above will also apply in these

---

42. 11 U.S.C. §362(d)(2)(B).

situations, but the intrinsic value of the asset to the debtor's business must also be taken into account. For instance, a print shop cannot do business without a printing press. Even if there is no equity in the press itself, because it is essential to the ability of the business to reorganize, relief from the stay may not necessarily be granted except after a period of time, so that all interested parties can ascertain whether the debtor has any realistic ability to reorganize. The courts must be creative in framing appropriate orders to protect the interests of all parties in these circumstances. On the one hand, the printing business in the example must effectively liquidate if the stay is terminated. On the other hand, the secured creditor is entitled to adequate protection of its interest in the property while the stay remains in effect.

Section 362(d)(4) permits relief from the stay to be granted if the court finds that the bankruptcy filing was part of a scheme to delay, hinder, or defraud creditors involving a transfer of an interest in real estate not consented to by a secured creditor or without court approval, or multiple bankruptcy filings affecting the real property. For example, Harry Potter files an individual Chapter 7 case to stop the foreclosure of his home by Gringotts Bank. The Bank obtains relief from the stay in Harry's case, and just prior to the next scheduled foreclosure date, Harry's wife Ginny files Chapter 7 for the sole purpose of gaining the benefit of the automatic stay. The Bank may obtain relief from the stay on the ground that Ginny's filing was part of a scheme to defraud the Bank involving multiple filings affecting Harry and Ginny's home. If Harry, alternatively, transfers a 10 percent interest in the real property to his best friend Ron, who then files bankruptcy to help prevent the home's foreclosure, the Bank may seek relief from the stay on the ground that Harry's transfer to Ron was for the sole purpose of delaying the Bank's foreclosure on the home.

In consumer cases, preparation of the motion documents, either in support of or in opposition to the motion, is relatively simple. Sample forms are contained on the forms disk accompanying this text. This is a form of litigation and should be approached in a manner identical to any other litigation in the legal system.[43]

Section 362(e) deals with the length of time that the stay remains in effect once a motion for relief from the automatic stay is filed. This subsection effectively requires that a motion for relief from the automatic stay be resolved on an expedited basis.

First, the automatic stay terminates 30 days after a motion for relief is filed unless the court orders otherwise during the 30-day period.[44]

---

43. Bankruptcy Rule 4001(a)(1).
44. 11 U.S.C. §362(e)(1).

If a hearing is requested, the court will hold it within this 30-day period. This hearing is known as a preliminary hearing, but it may be considered a final hearing if the court so determines. The court will usually not accept oral testimony at a preliminary hearing. It will review any declarations submitted by the parties instead. If the court determines that it needs to hear further evidence, a final hearing will be scheduled. The final hearing must take place within 30 days of the preliminary hearing.[45]

Even if there is a preliminary hearing, the automatic stay will still terminate 30 days after the motion is filed unless the court maintains the automatic stay in effect pending the final hearing.[46] Often the court cannot schedule a final hearing within 30 days of the preliminary hearing, and the final hearing will take place more than 30 days after the motion is filed. When a debtor or trustee is in this situation, it is imperative to obtain an order from the court unequivocally maintaining the automatic stay in effect until the date of the final hearing. Unless this is done, the stay will be terminated pursuant to Section 362(e). The three different time periods explicit or implicit within Section 362(e) are sometimes referred to as the "30/30/30 rule."

Practice Pointer

The "30/30/30 Rule":

- Thirty days after a request for relief the stay will terminate;
- a preliminary hearing must be held within 30 days of the motion;
- a final hearing, if necessary, must be held within 30 days of the preliminary hearing.

Section 362(e)(2) applies in individual cases and terminates the stay 60 days after a motion for relief from stay is filed unless the court renders a final decision within the 60-day period, the parties agree otherwise, or the court orders otherwise. For example, if the court denies the motion, the stay will remain in effect because the court has reached a final decision. If the parties reach an agreement to keep the stay in effect and reduce the

---

45. 11 U.S.C. §362(e)(1).
46. 11 U.S.C. §362(e)(1).

agreement to an order approved by the court, the statutory requirement will have been satisfied. In an emergency, where irreparable harm may occur, it is possible to obtain ex parte relief from the automatic stay without a formal hearing.[47] This is extraordinary relief and as a result should not be taken lightly.

In any motion for relief from the automatic stay, the party bringing the motion bears the burden of proof on the issue of equity, while a party opposing the motion bears the burden of proof on all other issues.[48] Finally, a party willfully violating the automatic stay can be sanctioned by the court. Sanctions may include actual damages, costs including attorneys' fees, and, in appropriate circumstances, punitive damages.[49]

Summary

The automatic stay is one of the three fundamental features of the debtor relief provided for by the Bankruptcy Code, the other two being the discharge and the debtor's exemptions, discussed respectively in chapters 8 and 10 supra. The automatic stay is the subject of Section 362 of the Bankruptcy Code. The automatic stay is a statutory bar to collection activity by creditors after a bankruptcy petition has been filed. A summary of the most common actions subject or not subject to the automatic stay are contained in the checklist following this summary.

The automatic stay is not permanent. Pursuant to 11 U.S.C. §362(c), the stay will terminate upon the earlier of the time that the case is closed or dismissed, or, in an individual proceeding, when the debtor has received a discharge and the property is no longer property of the estate, or when the debtor has engaged in serial filings. In individual proceedings, the latter circumstances will normally trigger termination of the automatic stay. However, the effects of the automatic stay will merge into the permanent injunction contained in the debtor's discharge.

A creditor may bring a motion for relief from the automatic stay pursuant to 11 U.S.C. §362(d). Normally, secured creditors are the greatest beneficiaries of this provision. A sample motion is included on the forms disk accompanying this text. Relief from the automatic stay may be brought on one of four basic grounds: cause, including lack of adequate protection; lack of equity in the property; a single asset real estate case that

---

47. 11 U.S.C. §362(f); Bankruptcy Rule 4001(a)(3).
48. 11 U.S.C. §362(g).
49. 11 U.S.C. §362(k).

fails to file a potentially confirmable plan or commence adequate protection payments within 90 days from the entry of the order for relief; or when the property has been subject to serial filings. A Bankruptcy Court may maintain the automatic stay in effect if the debtor or trustee can provide adequate protection. If adequate protection cannot be provided or if there is no equity in the property for the debtor or estate, the automatic stay will likely be relieved.

Adequate protection is described in Section 361 of the Code. Adequate protection involves various methods of protecting a secured creditor's interest in property of the debtor or estate during pendency of the automatic stay. The making of periodic payments and the providing of additional or replacement collateral are all methods of adequate protection.

A motion for relief from the automatic stay is to be given expedited treatment by the Bankruptcy Court as described in 11 U.S.C. §362(e). The automatic stay will terminate 30 days after it is filed unless the motion is opposed. If the motion is opposed, the court must hold a preliminary hearing within 30 days of the motion's filing. The automatic stay will also terminate 30 days after the motion is filed unless the court continues it in effect or unless the court requests or requires a final hearing. The final hearing must take place within 30 days of the preliminary hearing. The automatic stay will terminate 30 days after the preliminary hearing unless the court orders otherwise. In any scenario where any of these time limits will be exceeded, the party opposing the motion (debtor or trustee) must obtain a court order maintaining the automatic stay in effect until the later date. In individual cases, the stay will automatically terminate 60 days after the motion has been filed unless the parties agree or the court orders otherwise.

In any motion for relief from the automatic stay, the party bringing the motion bears the burden of proof on the issue of equity, while a party opposing the motion bears the burden of proof on all other issues.

KEY TERMS

adequate protection   serial bankruptcy
automatic stay
motion for relief from the
   automatic stay

CHAPTER 13 CHECKLIST

		Authority
13.1	ACTIONS SUBJECT TO AUTOMATIC STAY	
	13.1.1 Civil Actions or Administrative Legal Proceedings	11 U.S.C. §362(a)(1)
	13.1.2 Enforcement of Judgments	11 U.S.C. §362(a)(2)
	13.1.3 Acts to Obtain Possession or Control of Property of the Estate	11 U.S.C. §362(a)(3)
	13.1.4 Acts to Perfect Liens upon Property of the Estate	11 U.S.C. §362(a)(4)
	13.1.5 Acts to Perfect Liens upon Property of the Debtor	11 U.S.C. §362(a)(5)
	13.1.6 Any Act to Collect a Prepetition Claim	11 U.S.C. §362(a)(6)
	13.1.7 The Making of Setoffs	11 U.S.C. §362(a)(7)
	13.1.8 Proceedings Before the United States Tax Court	11 U.S.C. §362(a)(8)
13.2	COMMON ACTIONS EXCEPTED FROM THE AUTOMATIC STAY	
	13.2.1 Criminal Prosecutions	11 U.S.C. §362(b)(1)
	13.2.2 Collection of Domestic Support Obligations	11 U.S.C. §362(b)(2)
	13.2.3 Lien Perfection Within Statutory Grace Period	11 U.S.C. §362(b)(3)
	13.2.4 Governmental Proceedings to Enforce Police or Regulatory Powers Other Than Enforcement of Money Judgments	11 U.S.C. §362(b)(4)
	13.2.6 Issuance of a Notice of Tax Deficiency, Audit, Demand for Returns or Assessment	11 U.S.C. §362(b)(9)
	13.2.7 Retirement Loan Repayments	11 U.S.C. §362(b)(19)
	13.2.8 Residential Evictions	11 U.S.C. §362(b)(22)
13.3	MOTION FOR RELIEF FROM AUTOMATIC STAY[50]	
	13.3.1 Moving Party	

---

50. See chapter 5A supra.

        1. Notice of motion
        2. Motion
        3. Declaration in support
        4. Exhibits
           a. promissory note
           b. document evidencing security interest (UCC-1, mortgage, or trust deed)
           c. appraisal
        5. Any other document required by local rule including compliance with any local rules requiring itemization of the amount due

13.3.2 Opposing Party
        1. Request for hearing
        2. Declaration or affidavits in opposition
        3. Memorandum of law
        4. Exhibit: appraisals
        5. Any other document required by local rule

13.3.3 Motion to Impose Stay for Cause Shown
        1. Serial filings   11 U.S.C. §362(c)(3), (4)
        2. Statement of Intention   11 U.S.C. §362(h)
        3. Small Business Cases   11 U.S.C. §362(n)
        4. Residential evictions   11 U.S.C. §362(b)(22), (l)

13.4 MOTION TIME LIMITS (11 U.S.C. §362(e))
13.4.1 Hearing Dates
        1. Preliminary hearing within 30 days of filing motion
        2. Final hearing within 30 days of preliminary hearing
13.4.2 Length of Stay (30/30/30 Rule)
        1. Terminates 30 days after motion filed, if unopposed
        2. Terminates 30 days after preliminary hearing, unless court orders otherwise
        3. Terminates 30 days after final hearing, unless court orders otherwise
        4. Terminates 60 days from filing of motion in individual cases unless the parties or court orders otherwise

DISCUSSION QUESTIONS

1. What is the purpose of the automatic stay?

2. What activities are subject to the automatic stay?

3. What activities are not subject to the automatic stay?

4. How long does the automatic stay remain in effect? What is the effect of a discharge on the automatic stay?

5. Describe the procedure used for obtaining relief from the automatic stay.

6. What is adequate protection? Why is a secured creditor entitled to adequate protection?

7. Describe the situations in which a debtor may want to file a motion to impose the automatic stay. Why would a debtor want to do so?

PRACTICE EXERCISE

Exercise 13.1
Draft a relief from stay motion on behalf of A to Z Motors, to repossess Owen Cash's Ford F150. In lieu of exhibits, prepare a list of the exhibits you believe you would need to support the motion.

14

Objections to Discharge and the Dischargeability of Individual Debts

Learning Objectives

- Distinguish that a discharge may not relieve a debtor from all debts and that, in certain circumstances, a debtor may be denied a discharge altogether

- Describe which debts are automatically not dischargeable

- Describe which debts are not dischargeable only if a creditor obtains a judgment that the affected debt is not dischargeable

- List those acts that can prevent a debtor's discharge altogether

- Describe the procedure for filing a complaint to determine the dischargeability of a debt or the debtor's discharge

A. DISTINGUISHING A DISCHARGE FROM THE DISCHARGEABILITY OF INDIVIDUAL DEBTS

The debtor's personal liability on most debts is relieved when the debtor receives a discharge. However, some debts are not dischargeable. These **nondischargeable debts** are described in Section 523 of the Code. Within Section 523, specific types of debts are excepted from the debtor's discharge. That is, even if the debtor receives a discharge, the bankruptcy will not relieve the debtor of personal liability on such a claim. The

Nondischargeable debts: a debt not subject to a debtor's discharge; a debtor is not relieved from legal liability for the affected debt

225

creditor's right to collect the debt will remain unaffected by the bankruptcy. This nondischargeability status extends only to that particular claim. In addition, a debtor's exempt property will not be exempt from some nondischargeable debts.[1]

An analogous provision to Section 523 is the objection to discharge described in Section 727 (applicable only in Chapter 7 proceedings).[2] Under Section 727, a debtor may be denied a discharge completely. That is, notwithstanding the bankruptcy filing, a denial of discharge will prevent a debtor from obtaining relief from personal liability for *any* and all debts. This is the critical distinction between Sections 523 and 727. Section 523 concerns the dischargeability of specific individual debts while Section 727 is concerned with the discharge of all of the debtor's debts in their entirety. If the debtor's discharge is denied, the debtor will remain legally obligated to pay all prepetition debt.

 Practice Pointer

Even if the creditor takes no action, the debtor will normally not be discharged of most debts relating to taxes, money obtained through fraud, domestic support obligations, governmental fines or penalties, and death or personal injury caused by drunk driving.

Section 523 contains 19 specific types of debt that are not dischargeable. Three of these debts require the affected creditor to initiate an adversary proceeding, commonly known as a "Complaint to Determine the Dischargeability of Debt," and to thereafter obtain a judgment that the debt is nondischargeable.[3] For any such affected debts, the creditor must file a complaint within a specific deadline or the debt will be automatically discharged when the debtor receives his/her discharge.[4]

---

1. 11 U.S.C. §522(c). See chapter 10 supra.
2. 11 U.S.C. §103. See chapter 2 supra.
3. 11 U.S.C. §523(c); Bankruptcy Rules 4004 and 4007. See section D infra.
4. Bankruptcy Rule 4007. See section D infra.

Practice Pointer

To be considered nondischargeable, the burden is on the creditor to file an adversary complaint when the debt was obtained through a fraudulent representation, through fraud while the debtor was serving in a fiduciary capacity, through embezzlement or larceny, or as the result of willful and malicious injury.

All of the other 16 types of debts described by Section 523(a) will automatically not be dischargeable, unless successfully challenged by the debtor in an **adversary proceeding**. In these latter instances, an affected creditor will not be required to take any action for the debt to be deemed not dischargeable by operation of law. We will focus first on nondischargeable debts, which do not require a judgment of nondischargeability. Then we will analyze nondischargeable debts that require a judgment of nondischargeability by the filing of a complaint.

Adversary proceeding: a separate lawsuit filed in connection with a bankruptcy proceeding

B. DEBTS NONDISCHARGEABLE WITHOUT CREDITOR ACTION

Section 523(a)(1) provides that obligations accorded priority status under Section 507(a)(8) or gap claims incurred during the pendency of an involuntary proceeding will not be discharged.[5] These types of debts comprise most tax obligations. As a practical matter, this will commonly mean that all payroll taxes, sales taxes, and most income taxes are not dischargeable. The exceptions to this general rule are extremely limited and their analysis is beyond the scope of this basic text. The tax claims that most frequently appear in bankruptcy proceedings will be of the variety that more likely than not will be nondischargeable. As well, the debtor's right to specific exemptions will not protect otherwise exempt property from a nondischargeable tax claim.[6]

---

5. 11 U.S.C. §523(a)(1). See chapter 5 supra and chapter 22 infra.
6. 11 U.S.C. §522(c). See chapter 10 supra.

Practice Pointer

As a general rule, "exempt" property cannot be reached by any of the debtor's prepetition creditors. An exception exists, however, for most tax liens and domestic support obligations.

FACT PATTERN

Unlisted debt: a debt not included in a debtor's schedules

If the IRS files an estimated tax liability for Owen Cash, will this claim be nondischargeable? Will it require any action on the part of the IRS to obtain this protection?

The second type of debt that is automatically nondischargeable is the so-called **unlisted debt**, the subject of Section 523(a)(3). Under this provision, if a debtor fails to list a creditor in the schedules so that the creditor does not receive notice of the filing, then the claim will be non-dischargeable if the creditor is prevented from filing a timely proof of claim or otherwise object to dischargeability where there would have been grounds to do so. Thus, if no claims bar date is set, such as in a no asset proceeding, the claim will still be discharged because there has been no deadline set for creditors to file claims.[7]

Actual knowledge of the bankruptcy by a creditor, despite lack of notice, will also cause an unlisted debt to be discharged.[8] The rationale behind this provision is that if a creditor is prevented from receiving a dividend due to a lack of notice to permit filing of a claim, then the claim should not be discharged. On the other hand, if there has been no prejudice to the creditor, the discharge should be unaffected. For example, Robert Goodwin files a Chapter 7 and fails to list the Williamsburg Diner as a creditor because he is embarrassed and doesn't want to lose his job. If the proceeding has a claims bar date set and the Diner has no actual knowledge of the case so that a timely claim can be filed, the debt will be nondischargeable. In addition, if the Diner has a claim against Robert for fraud, the unlisted claim might also be nondischargeable. Otherwise, the debt will be discharged.

As a practical matter, it may occasionally become necessary for a creditor to initiate an adversary proceeding to seek a judgment from the

---

7. See In re Egleston, 448 F.3d 803, 914 n.12 (5th Cir. 2006); In re Nielsen, 383 F.3d 922, 926 (9th Cir. 2004). But see Colonial Sur. Co. v. Weizman, 564 F.3d 526 (1st Cir. 2009) (an unlisted debt is not discharged).

8. 11 U.S.C. §523(a)(3)(A), (B). See Judd v. Wolfe, 78 F.3d 110 (3d Cir. 1996).

Bankruptcy Court that an unlisted debt is nondischargeable so that a state court judge will then believe the creditor in any subsequent action initiated to collect the debt. Conversely, the debtor may seek to initiate a complaint to determine that the debt has indeed been discharged so as to convince a state court that the debt may not be collected. A debtor may always initiate a complaint to determine the dischargeability of a debt.[9]

 Practice Pointer

Moreover, there is no fee to reopen a case to determine the dischargeability of a particular debt. Fed. R. Bankr. P. 4007(b).

Similarly, if a creditor's claim is one that would be nondischargeable only if a timely complaint is filed as described above, and the creditor cannot do so due to lack of actual knowledge of the proceeding, the debt will also be nondischargeable.[10] A creditor in this position has been prejudiced because it has been deprived of the ability to file a timely complaint to determine the dischargeability of the debt.

Section 523(a)(5) addresses a third type of debt that is nondischargeable without requiring affirmative action by a creditor, and that is a debt for a domestic support obligation, unless the debt has been assigned to another entity except for collection purposes. Domestic support obligations are also accorded a priority status in the payment of claims.[11] For example, suppose a spouse who is meant to receive child support does not receive it and is required to go on temporary aid to needy families (TANF, formerly AFDC) so the children can eat. When the spouse obtains TANF, the spouse is normally required to assign any child support rights to the TANF agency for purposes of seeking collection from the nonpaying spouse. Once the obligation has been assigned, it becomes generally dischargeable. If the support right has not been assigned to a third entity, then the obligation remains nondischargeable and the unpaid spouse may still collect any arrears. Exemptions will not protect otherwise exempt property from a nondischargeable support obligation.[12] Debts incurred in connection with a divorce or a separation made in accordance with nonbankruptcy law or approved by a governmental unit, that are not

---

9. Bankruptcy Rule 4007(a).
10. 11 U.S.C. §523(a)(3)(B).
11. 11 U.S.C. §523(a)(5); 11 U.S.C. §507(a)(1). See chapter 22 infra.
12. 11 U.S.C. §522(c). See chapter 10 supra.

domestic support obligations, are also nondischargeable pursuant to Section 523(a)(15). This means that separation agreements, property settlements, and decrees of equitable distribution are all automatically nondischargeable. This provision, added by BAPCPA, radically alters the former law, which held, through case law and the predecessor provision of Section 523(a)(15), that property settlement agreements and similar documents were only nondischargeable if found to be in the nature of support or, for cases filed from October 22, 1994, through the effective date of BAPCPA, October 17, 2005, if the nonfiling debtor challenged the discharge of the debt as a hardship. The ensuing discussion retains its vitality because the prior law is often used to interpret the new provisions.

Prior to October 22, 1994, property settlements were fully dischargeable, although whether or not an obligation was alimony, support, or otherwise was left to the sole discretion of the bankruptcy courts.[13] The courts looked to a number of factors to determine whether a domestic obligation was nondischargeable support or otherwise, including the length of the marriage, interpretation of the document, whether or not the payments were intended for dependents, and so forth.[14]

Under the Bankruptcy Reform Act of 1994, Section 523(a)(15) was added to the Code, rendering obligations for other than alimony or support nondischargeable unless the debtor could show sufficient hardship such that discharge of the debt would result in a benefit to the debtor that outweighs the detrimental consequences to a former spouse or child of the debtor. Further, debts subject to this provision were not automatically nondischargeable, but required the nonfiling spouse to affirmatively challenge the discharge. The 2005 amendment to this Code section makes the debt automatically nondischargeable.

FACT PATTERN

Does Owen's court-ordered child support obligation for Lotta fall under Section 523(a)(5) or (a)(15)? Is it nondischargeable?

For example, Tom and Kitty Katt enter into a dissolution agreement that provides that Kitty gets the house, Tom gets the car, and Tom is to pay all family bills and is to pay Kitty a monthly support allowance equal to the monthly mortgage payment on the home. If Tom had filed a Chapter 7 case under BAPCPA, all of these debts would likely have been nondischargeable domestic support obligations. Under the prior law, in Tom's Chapter 7, the obligation to pay the family bills is probably

---

13. 11 U.S.C. §523(a)(5)(B) as it existed prior to October 17, 2005.
14. In re Nero, 323 B.R. 33, 36 (Bankr. D. Conn. 2005) (identifying eight factors); In re Herbert, 304 B.R. 67, 77 (Bankr. E.D.N.Y. 2004).

dischargeable while the obligation to pay the monthly support allowance is not. Under pre-BAPCPA Section 523(a)(15), Kitty may object to the dischargeability of Tom's obligation to pay the family bills and the mortgage. If Tom is discharged from the family bills, Kitty may remain liable to the creditors without recourse against Tom, which may also result in a bankruptcy filing by Kitty as well. Also remember that if Tom is in arrears on his support payments when he files his petition, Kitty is unaffected by the automatic stay in her ability to collect the arrears from Tom's postpetition wages.[15] Nor will Tom's claimed exemptions protect his property from Kitty's efforts to collect any arrears.[16]

> ### Practice Pointer
>
> All obligations related to a divorce or separation agreement need to be viewed in the context of both Sections 523(a)(5) and (a)(15).

The next type of debt that is automatically nondischargeable, under Section 523(a)(7), is a fine or penalty owed to a governmental unit, other than compensation for actual pecuniary loss. A penalty relating to a non-dischargeable tax will remain nondischargeable. A fine or penalty assessed more than three years before a bankruptcy filing will be dischargeable.[17] For example, Tom Toxic is fined $50,000 for the cost of a toxic waste cleanup and is penalized another $25,000 for the violation. Toxic then files a Chapter 7 proceeding. The $50,000 fine is dischargeable because it represents a fine for actual pecuniary loss. The $25,000 penalty fine is not dischargeable.

Student loans are automatically nondischargeable under Section 523(a)(8). However, for a student loan to be nondischargeable, the student loan must be made, insured, or guaranteed by a governmental unit or made under a program funded by a governmental unit or a nonprofit institution. The loan will only be dischargeable if the debtor can show that the loan's nondischargeability would impose an undue hardship upon the debtor and the debtor's dependents.[18] As a practical matter, it is the debtor who will normally file the complaint to determine the dischargeability of a student loan obligation because, as has been noted, the

---

15. 11 U.S.C. §362(b)(2). See chapter 13 supra.
16. 11 U.S.C. §522(c); 11 U.S.C. §522(f). See chapter 10 supra.
17. 11 U.S.C. §523(a)(7). The pendency of a prior bankruptcy proceeding during this period may act to extend it. Young v. United States, 535 U.S. 43 (2002). See chapter 22 infra.
18. 11 U.S.C. §523(a)(8). Failure to pay an invoice for unpaid tuition may be dischargeable because no loan has been made. See, e.g., In re Mehta, 310 F.3d 308 (3d Cir. 2002).

debtor would be seeking a determination that an otherwise nondischarge-able debt is indeed dischargeable.[19]

The judicial test that has gained the widest acceptance in determining when a student loan is dischargeable on the grounds of undue hardship is known as the *Brunner* test (for Brunner v. New York State Higher Education Services Corp., 831 F.2d 395 (2d Cir. 1987)). Under this approach, a student loan may be discharged if the debtor can pass a three-part test: (1) Based on current income and expenses, the debtor cannot maintain a "minimal" standard of living for the debtor and dependents, if the educational loan is repaid as scheduled; (2) the debtor's present situation is likely to continue for a significant portion of the repayment period; and (3) the debtor has made good faith efforts to repay the educational loans.

The *Brunner* test has been adopted by the Third (In re Coco, 335 Fed. Appx. 224, 226 (2009)); Fourth (In re Spence, 541 F.3d 538, 544 (2008)); Fifth (In re Ostrom, 283 Fed. Appx. 283, 285-286 (2008)); Sixth (In re Barrett, 487 F.3d 353 (2007)); Seventh (Goulet v. Educational Credit Mgmt. Corp., 284 F.3d 773 (2002)); Ninth (In re Hedlund, 368 Fed. Appx. 819, 821 (2010)); Tenth (In re Roe, 295 Fed. Appx. 927, 929 (2008)); and Eleventh (In re Mosley, 494 F.3d 1320 (2007)) Circuits. The Eighth Circuit follows a "totality of the circumstances approach" using similar factors with an emphasis upon "fairness" and "equity" (In re Long, 322 F.3d 549 (2003)). In Tennessee Student Assistance Corp. v. Hood, 541 U.S. 440 (2004), the Supreme Court held that the sovereign immunity provided for by the Eleventh Amendment does not prevent debtors from bringing complaints to determine the dischargeability of student loan debts (see chapter 7P supra).

For example, Justin Long obtains a guaranteed student loan to attend South Harmon Institute of Technology, graduates, and then defaults in the loan repayment. Justin majored in physical education with a specialty in surf instruction. Justin files a Chapter 7 to discharge the loan. Justin initiates a complaint to determine the debt's dischargeability on the grounds of undue hardship, citing an inability to earn sufficient income as a surf instructor to repay the debt. Unfortunately for Justin, this will probably not act to discharge the debt. The inability to earn sufficient income from one's education will not render a student loan discharge-able. On the other hand, if Justin were involved in an accident and thereby rendered physically incapable of being a surf instructor, under the *Brunner* test, the debt might be held dischargeable only if the court could find that the injury would render him incapable of repaying the loan for a significant portion of the repayment period. The court has broad

---

19. Bankruptcy Rule 4007(a).

discretion in this area, but it is generally very difficult for a debtor to obtain discharge of a guaranteed student loan on the grounds of undue hardship.

Robin Cash agreed to file bankruptcy because Owen convinced her that her student loans would be discharged. Is that result likely under the Code?

A mere bank loan obtained by a student for educational purposes, but not subject to a governmental student loan insurance or guarantee program, will be discharged. For instance, Amy Wilson obtains a loan from the XYZ bank and uses it to go to the Pitch Perfect School of Composition. Because the loan is not insured or guaranteed, if Amy subsequently commences a Chapter 7 proceeding, the debt will be discharged.

Section 523(a)(9) makes debts arising as a result of the debtor driving or operating a vessel or aircraft while intoxicated or under the influence of other substances nondischargeable.[20] Prior to enactment of this provision into the Code, it was a common practice for uninsured drivers who had caused damages while driving under the influence to simply file a bankruptcy to discharge any liability to the damaged or injured party. Some case law prior to 1984 held that damages caused while driving while intoxicated were willful and malicious and denied a discharge of the debt on this ground.[21] This, however, required the damaged party to initiate a complaint objecting to the debt's dischargeability. The enactment of Section 523(a)(9) obviates a party damaged in such circumstances from having to file a separate action to determine the debt's dischargeability.

Several complaints have been filed and/or are likely to be filed against Owen Cash. Which actions, if any, do you think could fall within the scope of Section 523(a)(9)?

 Practice Pointer

Remember, the exception to discharge under Section 523(a)(9) relates to debts incurred for "death or personal injury." It does not extend to property damage.

---

20. 11 U.S.C. §523(a)(9).
21. See the discussion concerning §523(a)(6) infra in this chapter.

Section 523(a)(10) provides that any debt or debts that were or could have been listed in a prior bankruptcy proceeding where the debtor waived discharge or was denied a discharge under Section 727(a)(2)-(7) will be nondischargeable in the new proceeding.[22] Section 523(b) further provides that any debt not discharged in a proceeding under the former Bankruptcy Act will remain automatically not discharged in a proceeding filed by the same debtor under the Bankruptcy Code.[23]

Sections 523(a)(11) and (12) make automatically nondischargeable debts due to a federal depository institution where the debtor was in a fiduciary relationship with the financial institution.

Section 523(a)(13) makes nondischargeable restitution awards in criminal cases.

Section 523(a)(14) excepts from discharge debts incurred to pay federal taxes that would otherwise be nondischargeable. For example, Willie Nelson owes $1,000 in federal income taxes. He gets a cash advance on a credit card, pays the taxes, and files Chapter 7 four months later. Under Section 523(a)(14), because the taxes were not dischargeable, the cash advance becomes nondischargeable. One problem that creditors may have with this provision is the level of proof necessary to show that the loan was obtained to pay a nondischargeable tax claim. Section 523(14A), added in 2005, extends this approach to all other taxing authorities.[24]

Section 523(a)(16) makes nondischargeable any postpetition condominium or cooperative housing assessments that are incurred while the debtor or the trustee has an interest in the unit.

FACT PATTERN

Since Robin effectively abandoned her condominium after she got married, will she have to worry about the application of Section 523(a)(16)?

Section 523(a)(17) makes nondischargeable debts incurred by prisoners for court fees. Section 523(a)(18) makes nondischargeable debts owed to pension or retirement plans, such as a loan from a 401(k) plan.

Section 523(a)(19) makes nondischargeable debts arising under violations of federal or state securities laws or regulations. This provision was added to the Code by the Sarbanes-Oxley Act of 2002 (Pub. L. No. 107-204, 116 Stat. 745) in the wake of accounting scandals that occurred in well-publicized bankruptcies such as Enron Corporation and Global Crossing.

---

22. 11 U.S.C. §523(a)(10).
23. 11 U.S.C. §523(b).
24. Section 523(a)(14B) extends nondischargeability to fines and penalties imposed under federal election laws.

C.   DEBTS NONDISCHARGEABLE WITH CREDITOR ACTION

The three remaining types of debt that are nondischargeable under Section 523(a) all require the creditor to first initiate an adversary proceeding and obtain a judgment denying dischargeability of the debt in question. If no complaint is filed in a timely manner or the debtor obtains a judgment in its favor, the debt involved will be discharged.[25]

The first and most frequently utilized of these provisions is Section 523(a)(2), which concerns various forms of fraud. Under this provision, there are three forms of fraud that may not be dischargeable. The simplest of these is the form of fraud that makes nondischargeable any debt obtained by the use of a materially false written financial statement concerning the debtor or its insider upon which the creditor relies in extending credit and that the debtor has made with the intent to deceive.[26] Simply put, a debt may be held nondischargeable if the debt was incurred by use of an intentionally false written financial statement.

For example, Fred and Wilma go visit the Pre-Cambrian Finance Company to obtain a vacation loan. In completing their financial statement, they omit a $10,000 debt owed to Wilma's parents. Subsequently, Fred and Wilma file a Chapter 7 listing the debt owed to Wilma's parents. Pre-Cambrian may seek to have the vacation loan debt ruled nondischargeable based on the omission of the $10,000 debt to Wilma's parents in the original loan application.

> **Which of the Cashes' debts, if any, raise the spectre of a Section 523(a)(2) determination?**

FACT PATTERN

In situations where a debtor obtains a renewal of credit or borrows additional funds from a creditor, if a new financial statement is obtained that is materially false, then it is possible that both the portion of the debt representing the new funds borrowed in reliance upon the false written financial statement, as well as the renewed previous extension of credit, will be subject to nondischargeability.[27] Previous case law had focused only on the existence of any new credit that was extended. This was known as the **fresh cash rule**.[28] Using the above example, Fred and

Fresh cash rule: portion of a debt incurred by use of a false written financial statement

25. 11 U.S.C. §523(c).
26. 11 U.S.C. §523(a)(2)(B).
27. In re Campbell, 159 F.3d 963 (6th Cir. 1998); In re McFarland, 84 F.3d 943 (7th Cir. 1996).
28. In re Duncan, 123 B.R. 383 (C.D. Cal. 1991).

Wilma are already indebted to the finance company when they seek the vacation loan. The finance company rewrites the loan, adding in the new funds borrowed. Because the financial statement obtained in connection with the rewritten loan is false, the original debt, as well as the additional funds borrowed, will probably be nondischargeable if the creditor timely objects. The creditor's damages from the fraud in that case are beyond the additional monies borrowed.

A second form of fraud that may be nondischargeable exists where the debtor obtained money through actual fraud, false pretenses, or a false representation, other than a statement concerning the debtor's or an insider's financial condition.[29] Note that false statements concerning a debtor's financial condition are excluded from this definition. This means that any oral misrepresentation regarding the debtor's financial condition will not by itself constitute grounds for an objection to the discharge of a debt based on fraud. A false written financial statement is covered as described above.

In practice, the sort of actual fraud that often is held to be non-dischargeable is fraud so egregious that it would be an injustice to permit a debtor to be relieved from the liability. The necessary elements to prove this form of fraud nondischargeable are the traditional tort elements of fraud: that the debtor has made a knowingly false representation with intent to deceive the creditor; that the creditor has relied on the misrepresentation; and, has sustained damages as a result.[30] For example, debtor Peter Quill visits Mr. Yondu, a custom tailor recently emigrated from Italy to the United States. Mr. Yondu makes Quill a couple of custom suits, and Quill pays for them. In the process, he convinces Mr. Yondu that he is part owner of a trucking company. However, in reality and unknown to Yondu, Quill is actually a minister. After paying for the first two suits, Mr. Yondu gives debtor Quill a charge account. In the space of the next six months, Quill incurs a debt to Mr. Yondu in excess of $30,000. Meanwhile, Reverend Quill is continually complimented by his congregants about his beautiful new suits. He tells his congregants that he has met a new tailor who is a real nice guy and that he is being provided the suits for free. Because he is up on the pulpit where many people see him, it is a good promotion for the tailor. Reverend Quill then files bankruptcy, and Yondu objects to the

---

29. 11 U.S.C. §523(a)(2)(A). Recently in Husky Intern. Electronics, Inc. v. Ritz, 136 S. Ct. 1581 (2016), the U.S. Supreme Court ruled that actual fraud included fraudulent conveyance schemes even where there was no actual false representation between the debtor and the creditor.
30. In re Britton, 950 F.2d 602 (9th Cir. 1991).

discharge of the debt due him. The debt would be found to be nondischargeable.[31]

In Field v. Mans, 516 U.S. 59 (1995), the U.S. Supreme Court examined the form of reliance that a plaintiff must prove in a nondischargeability fraud claim brought under 11 U.S.C. §523(a)(2). The Court ruled that a creditor need only prove that reliance was justifiable as opposed to reasonable, although "[t]he subjectiveness of justifiability cuts both ways, and reasonableness goes to the probability of actual reliance." In *Field*, Mans transferred property in violation of a due-upon transfer clause and then sought the lender's consent, which was not given. At a later date, the debtor filed for bankruptcy. Only then did the lender learn that the property had been improperly transferred, wiping out the lender's position in the collateral. The lender had never reviewed the relevant real estate records to determine whether the unconsented-to transfer had taken place. In reversing the lower courts, which had ruled in Mans' favor, and in ruling that Field's reliance upon the debtor's representations need only be justifiable, the Supreme Court rejected the notion that a lender must always investigate the veracity of a debtor's representations.

In Cohen v. De La Cruz, 523 U.S. 213 (1998), the Supreme Court extended the finding of nondischargeability to all damages resulting from the debtor's fraud. In *Cohen*, a debtor landlord had been found liable for willfully and intentionally violating a rent control ordinance. The damages awarded by the trial court included treble damages for violation of the New Jersey Consumer Fraud Act. The Supreme Court held that once it is established that specific money or property has been obtained by fraud, "any debt" arising therefrom is excepted from discharge.

In Archer v. Warner, 538 U.S. 314 (2003), the Supreme Court considered whether a settlement agreement superseded the underlying fraudulent activity. In that case, the Archers had sued the Warners for fraud in connection with the sale of a business. The parties entered into a settlement and release agreement. After performing most of the settlement agreement, the Warners filed bankruptcy. The Archers, as creditors, contended that the remaining claim was nondischargeable as a result of fraud. The Warners, as debtors, contended that the settlement agreement created an entirely new debt that was not obtained fraudulently. The Supreme Court held that the prebankruptcy settlement did not prevent the creditor from seeking a determination of dischargeability in the debtor's subsequent bankruptcy since the settlement debt "arose" from "false pretenses, a false representation or actual fraud."

---

31. See In re Burklow, 60 B.R. 728 (Bankr. S.D. Cal. 1986). Note that although this case was decided under the earlier "reasonable reliance" standard, the same result would still be reached under the "justifiable reliance" standard under Field v. Mans.

The third form of fraud concerns debtors who have a problem sometimes colloquially referred to as "credit carditis." This problem is also known as the prepetition "shopping spree." The essence of the problem pertains to debtors who, on the eve of bankruptcy, purchase luxury goods on credit or make credit purchases up to maximum credit limits and then file a Chapter 7 petition, seeking to discharge their liability on the credit cards while claiming all of the goods purchased as exempt. A similar situation arises where a debtor obtains cash advances on credit cards immediately prior to filing, spends the money, and then files a Chapter 7 proceeding. In each instance, either the goods are exempt or the money is gone but the debt has been discharged.

Section 523(a)(2)(C) was enacted in an effort to help resolve this perceived abuse of the bankruptcy system by debtors. Under this provision, consumer debts owed to a single creditor totaling more than $675 for luxury goods or services incurred within 90 days prior to the filing are presumed nondischargeable. This means that if a creditor can show transactions that fall within this description, the objection to dischargeability is considered to have been proven and the burden of proof will then shift to the debtor to prove that the debt should be dischargeable. Likewise, cash advances totaling more than $950 and incurred within 70 days prior to filing are also presumed nondischargeable.[32] Thus, a debt incurred by obtaining a large cash advance in excess of this limit from an automatic teller immediately prior to filing a bankruptcy may be presumed to be nondischargeable.

FACT PATTERN

Will Owen Cash be able to discharge his credit card debt, including the cash advances that he took shortly before his trip? What factors do you need to consider?

This subsection defines *luxury goods or services* as goods or services not reasonably necessary to support or maintain the debtor or a dependent of the debtor. Thus, a cash advance obtained by the debtor at the racetrack is probably nondischargeable, but if the debtor can show that the money has been used to purchase food, medicine, or other necessaries, the debt may be dischargeable. Alternatively, if $675 or more is spent on a 60-inch flat screen television, the debt is probably nondischargeable, but if the money is used for summer clothes for

---

32. The current text reflects amounts provided for by BAPCPA, including the adjustments that became effective on April 1, 2016.

the kids, for blue jeans and shorts and socks, the debt may be dischargeable.[33]

The second type of debt that is nondischargeable only upon the obtaining of a judgment of nondischargeability is for fraud or defalcation while acting in a fiduciary capacity, or through embezzlement or larceny. For instance, a trustee who takes trust money, goes to Tahiti, and then files a bankruptcy will find that the trust fund debt thus created is nondischargeable. A state court receiver who absconds to another state with receivership property and then files a bankruptcy will find the debt created to be nondischargeable. An employee who falsifies business records while embezzling funds from the business and who then goes bankrupt will also find that this debt is nondischargeable.[34]

Practice Pointer

There is a lot of litigation regarding the definitions used for "defalcation" and "fiduciary capacity." There are varying levels of culpability required by the courts for defalcation, although most agree that it must occur in the context of an express or a technical trust.

Finally, willful and malicious injury by the debtor to another or another's property may also be nondischargeable, but the creditor must first file a complaint in order to determine the issue.[35] In Kawaauhau v. Geiger, 523 U.S. 57 (1998), the Supreme Court held that "willful and malicious" means that the actor must act with the intent to cause injury, and "not merely [perform] a deliberate or intentional act that leads to injury," to become nondischargeable. In this case, Geiger had been found liable for medical malpractice and reckless conduct, but not for a malicious act. The Court found that gross negligence or recklessness does not satisfy the statutory standard.

Many intentional torts will not be dischargeable. However, just as in the instance of actual fraud discussed above, the willful and malicious injury has to be such that it would be an injustice to permit the debtor

---

33. 11 U.S.C. §523(a)(2)(C). Section 104(b), added in 1994, accounts for the effects of inflation on these amounts at three-year intervals. The first adjustment took place in April 1998.
34. 11 U.S.C. §523(a)(4). In *Bullock v. Bankchampaign*, 113 S. Ct. 1754 (2013), the Supreme Court held that for defalcation to be nondischargeable, there must be a culpable state of mind or reckless conduct of the kind the criminal law often treats as the equivalent.
35. 11 U.S.C. §523(a)(6).

to be freely relieved of liability for the wrong committed. Keep in mind that issues of nondischargeability are not as concerned with the underlying issue of liability so much as they are concerned with whether, despite the bankruptcy filing, the debt created should be relieved through the bankruptcy system. Certainly though, if there is no underlying liability, then there is no debt for which to determine the dischargeability.

D.   COMPLAINTS TO DETERMINE DISCHARGEABILITY OF A DEBT

Virtually all the issues previously discussed in this text that require a court decision are brought before the court through the various motion procedures described in chapter 6 supra. A second way in which issues are brought before the court for a decision is known as the adversary proceeding. Many of the subjects discussed in the next several chapters are commenced by the filing of an adversary proceeding in connection with the bankruptcy proceeding (case in chief). When an issue is brought before the court in the form of a motion and is opposed, it is considered a **contested matter**. A contested matter is treated as an adversary proceeding pursuant to Federal Rule of Bankruptcy Procedure 9014.

Contested matter: an opposed motion: A contested matter is treated as an adversary proceeding pursuant to Federal Rule of Bankruptcy Procedure 9014

An adversary proceeding, except for its title, assumes the form of traditional nonbankruptcy litigation. That is, an adversary proceeding is an independent lawsuit taking place in the bankruptcy proceeding. Part VII of the Federal Rules of Bankruptcy Procedure contains the pertinent procedural rules applicable to adversary proceedings. With minor variations, these rules are essentially the Federal Rules of Civil Procedure, with which all practitioners should be familiar. The discovery and trial aspects of these rules may also apply in noticed motions.[36] The practical equivalent of a trial in a contested matter is commonly known as an evidentiary hearing.

In remarking at how similar bankruptcy litigation is to other federal court litigation, at least one judge has commented: "In a routinized area, such as bankruptcy motion practice, one easily loses sight of some of such basics as the need to make out a prima facie case by competent evidence. Bankruptcy litigation is no different than any other federal litigation practice in this respect." (In re Roberts, 210 Bankr. 325 (Bankr. D. Iowa 1997)).

---

36. Bankruptcy Rule 9014.

Federal Rule of Bankruptcy Procedure 4007 contains rules regarding who may file and the time limits for initiating a **complaint to determine dischargeability of a debt**. As already noted, the debtor or any affected creditor may initiate such a complaint.[37] A debtor may desire to file a complaint to seek a judgment that a debt that would normally be considered automatically nondischargeable should in fact be discharged. For example, a debtor may file an adversary proceeding to seek a judgment that a student loan is dischargeable on the grounds of undue hardship. A complaint to determine the dischargeability of a debt that is normally considered automatically nondischargeable may be filed at any time, and a bankruptcy proceeding may be reopened to allow for this determination to be made.[38]

Complaint to determine dischargeability of a debt: an adversary proceeding initiated by a creditor or debtor to determine the dischargeability of a specific debt pursuant to Bankruptcy Code Section 523

On the other hand, where the determination involves the type of debt that requires the creditor to initiate a complaint, the rules contain strict time limits on the initiation of such complaints. If no complaint is timely initiated, the debt will be discharged.[39] In a Chapter 7, 11, or 13, the complaint must be filed within 60 days of the date first set for the meeting of creditors held pursuant to Section 341.[40] In a Chapter 13, there is also a special carve-out for actions under Section 523(a)(6) where the deadline is set when the debtor applies for a discharge upon completion of a Chapter 13 plan.[41] In either situation, the time period may be extended by motion or voluntary agreement, provided that the motion or agreement is made before the expiration of the deadline set for the filing of the complaint.[42]

If a creditor objects to the discharge of a consumer debt on the grounds of fraud and if the debt is found dischargeable, the court may award costs and attorneys' fees to the debtor if the court finds that the creditor's position was not substantially justified.[43] The purpose of this provision is to deter creditors from initiating unfounded objections to dischargeability solely in order to gain an undue economic advantage over a debtor.

In Grogan v. Garner, 498 U.S. 279 (1991), the Supreme Court ruled that in complaints objecting to the dischargeability of debts, the burden of proof is by a preponderance of the evidence. This ruling reversed the law of many circuits that had required a plaintiff to prove its case by clear and convincing evidence to prevail.

---

37. Bankruptcy Rule 4007(a).
38. 11 U.S.C. §350; Bankruptcy Rule 4007(b).
39. 11 U.S.C. §523(c).
40. Bankruptcy Rule 4007(c).
41. Bankruptcy Rule 4007(d).
42. Bankruptcy Rules 4007(c) and (d).
43. 11 U.S.C. §523(d).

In *Grogan*, the creditor had obtained a jury verdict for fraud, which was affirmed on appeal. After the debtor filed Chapter 11, the creditor filed a timely complaint objecting to the debt's dischargeability pursuant to 11 U.S.C. §523(a)(2)(A), actual fraud. The Bankruptcy Court, relying on the jury verdict, held the debt to be nondischargeable. The Eighth Circuit Court of Appeals reversed, but the Supreme Court reinstated the trial court's holding. The Court noted that the Code does not specify a burden of proof standard in dischargeability complaints. The Court also rejected the argument that the higher level of proof required by a "clear and convincing" standard is necessary to aid in a debtor's fresh start.

E.   OBJECTING TO DISCHARGE

While Section 523 affects only the dischargeability of certain specific debts, under Section 727, a debtor's discharge can be denied in its entirety. A debtor whose discharge is denied under Section 727(a) will not receive legal release from any debt. Although Section 727 appears only in Chapter 7, it is also applicable in Chapter 11 proceedings, but not in Chapter 12 or 13 proceedings.[44]

Only individual debtors receive Chapter 7 discharges. Corporations and partnerships do not.[45] A Chapter 7 discharge may be obtained only once every eight years, and may not be obtained within six years of receiving a Chapter 12 or Chapter 13 discharge unless the Plan provided for payment of at least 70 percent of unsecured claims.[46]

So, if a debtor has filed a bankruptcy petition within the past eight years and has received a Chapter 7 discharge, the debtor is not entitled to a discharge in the second proceeding. A debtor may also waive a discharge if the waiver is in writing executed after the bankruptcy filing and is approved by the court.[47]

Most of the remaining provisions of Section 727(a) deny debtors a discharge due to activities that can be most succinctly described as inequitable conduct. That is, these provisions will deny a discharge if the debtor's conduct is such that it would be unjust to grant the debtor a discharge. A discharge may be denied if the debtor has concealed, transferred, or

---

44. 11 U.S.C. §103; 11 U.S.C. §1141(d)(3)(c). See chapter 2 supra and chapter 27 infra.
45. 11 U.S.C. §727(a)(1).
46. 11 U.S.C. §727(a)(8); 11 U.S.C. §727(a)(9). FRBP 4004(d) requires objections to discharge based upon these provisions to be raised by way of motion and not by way of an adversary proceeding.
47. 11 U.S.C. §727(a)(10).

destroyed records or property of the estate with the intent to hinder, delay, or defraud creditors within one year prior to filing.[48]

A discharge may be denied if the debtor knowingly and fraudulently makes a false oath or withholds records relating to the debtor's financial condition from the trustee.[49] A discharge may be denied if the debtor refuses to obey court orders in connection with the case or fails to testify unless immunity has been granted.[50] The denial of a discharge on the grounds set forth in this paragraph may also result in criminal violations under federal law.[51]

A discharge may be denied if the debtor fails to satisfactorily explain any loss or deficiency of assets to meet the debtor's liabilities.[52] For instance, Mack MacSheath files a set of Statements and Schedules describing no assets and no prior businesses but listing claims of $10 million, and he fails to explain how he acquired $10 million of debt while retaining no assets and not being engaged in business. Someone does not normally acquire substantial debt without being engaged in business or retaining any assets without explanation. In this circumstance, the discharge may be denied.

A discharge may be denied to a debtor who destroys, conceals, mutilates, falsifies, or fails to keep books and records from which the debtor's financial condition may be ascertained, unless such acts are justified under the circumstances of the case.[53] For instance, most individual consumer debtors do not keep many financial records. There is no law requiring individuals to maintain checkbooks. Low-income debtors may not have earned sufficient income to require the filing of income tax returns. But most individual debtors do have some files at home with perhaps some bills, checkbook registers, and prior-year income tax returns. An individual ordinary consumer debtor cannot be expected or required to have many more records than this. Many individuals do have substantially more personal financial records in their possession, but, at a minimum, recent bills, checkbook registers, and tax returns are all that can or should be expected.

The general rule is that a debtor should be able to produce the minimum amount of records necessary or required by nonbankruptcy law to support the type of financial activity in which the debtor has

---

48. 11 U.S.C. §727(a)(2).
49. 11 U.S.C. §727(a)(4).
50. 11 U.S.C. §727(a)(6).
51. 18 U.S.C. §152.
52. 11 U.S.C. §727(a)(5).
53. 11 U.S.C. §727(a)(3).

been engaged prior to the bankruptcy filing.[54] Thus, octogenarian Miss Daisy, who subsists solely on Social Security and pays all of her expenses by cash or money order, should not be denied a discharge because she does not keep books and records. She is keeping the books and records necessary to support the activities in which she is engaged, which in this case is virtually none. However, if Miss Daisy has $10 million of debts and makes the same representations, her discharge may be denied.

On the other hand, if a debtor is engaged in business, there are certain minimum records that the debtor will be required to maintain under nonbankruptcy law. Payroll wage and tax records are required by both federal and local law. Sales tax records and sales records will be required to be maintained where there are local sales taxes to pay. If the debtor has not maintained these records or cannot adequately justify their lack of existence, the discharge may be denied.

A discharge may be denied a debtor who has committed any of the above described acts within a year prior to filing, during the pendency of the debtor's bankruptcy proceeding, or in connection with another bankruptcy proceeding concerning an insider.[55] For example, Mack MacSheath files a Chapter 7 for his corporation, Mack's Knives, Inc. The corporation has no records whatsoever. MacSheath then files his own personal Chapter 7. His personal discharge may be denied due to his failure to have kept records for his bankrupt insider corporation.

BAPCPA added Section 727(a)(11), which requires individual debtors to complete a postpetition financial management course in order to receive a discharge. Thus, coupled with the requirement to undergo credit counseling as a prerequisite to filing a petition (see chapter 4 supra), individual bankruptcy debtors must now undergo both pre- and postpetition financial counseling, the former as a prerequisite to filing, and the latter as a prerequisite to receiving a discharge.

---

54. This test has also been restated as whatever is reasonable based on the particular circumstances. See, e.g., In re French, 499 F.3d 345, 355 (4th Cir. 2007); In re Cacioli, 463 F.2d 229, 235 (2d Cir. 2006); In re Schifano, 378 F.3d 60 (1st Cir. 2004) and whatever is necessary to ascertain the debtor's financial condition, see, e.g., In re Juzwiak, 89 F.3d 424 (7th Cir. 1996). See also In re Costello, 299 B.R. 882 (Bankr. N.D. Ill. 2003) (where the debtor's discharge was denied because his only explanation as to the unavailability of records was that mice ate them).

55. 11 U.S.C. §727(a)(7).

F. COMPLAINTS OBJECTING TO DISCHARGE

Any creditor, the trustee, or the United States Trustee may file a **complaint to determine discharge** under Section 727(a).[56] The objection is made by filing an adversary proceeding objecting to the discharge within 60 days of the date first set for the creditors' meeting under Section 341(a) in a Chapter 7, or no later than the date first set for the confirmation hearing on the debtor's plan of reorganization in a Chapter 11 proceeding.[57] An extension of this time period can be obtained for cause if a motion for the extension is made before expiration of the time periods permitted by the rules.[58] Unless a timely complaint is filed, the debtor will receive a discharge.[59]

Complaint to determine discharge: an adversary proceeding initiated to entirely avoid a debtor's discharge

In Kontrick v. Ryan, 540 U.S. 443 (2004), the Supreme Court examined whether the 60-day time limit was jurisdictional or subject to waiver if not raised until after a trial on the merits. In this case, Ryan obtained a judgment against Kontrick. Kontrick intentionally concealed his assets from Ryan and admitted as much. Although Ryan filed his complaint objecting to discharge in a timely manner, he amended the complaint to add an additional claim after expiration of the 60-day time limit. After losing at trial, Kontrick moved the court to dismiss the added claim because it had not been filed in a timely manner. Ryan contended that Kontrick's earlier failure to have raised the issue acted to waive the defense. The Supreme Court held that the 60-day time limit to file the complaint objecting to discharge is not jurisdictional and is waived if not raised until after the matter has been litigated. Although involving an objection to discharge, the scope of this holding will likely apply to complaints objecting to the dischargeability of debts subject to FRBP 4007, since the operative language in the applicable rules is identical.

A discharge may be revoked if fraudulently obtained and the fraud is not known until after the discharge has been granted, if the debtor fails to turn over property of the estate subsequent to receiving a discharge, or if the debtor fails to cooperate in a random audit (see chapter 8 supra). The trustee, a creditor, or the United States Trustee may file a complaint to revoke the discharge within one year of the original discharge date where the ground of revocation is fraud. Where the ground for revocation is a failure to turn over estate property, the same parties may initiate a complaint before the later of one year after the discharge is received or one

---

56. 11 U.S.C. §727(c).
57. Bankruptcy Rule 4004(a).
58. Bankruptcy Rule 4004(b).
59. Bankruptcy Rule 4004(c).

year after the proceeding is closed.[60] Normally, the later date will be one year after the proceeding is closed.

Summary

Certain debts will not be affected by a debtor's discharge. These debts are known as nondischargeable debts. Occasionally, a debtor may be denied a discharge. When a debt is nondischargeable or a debtor is denied a discharge, the bankruptcy will not provide the debtor with legal relief from a specific debt in the former instance and from all debt in the latter.

The following debts are nondischargeable without an affected creditor being required to take any affirmative action.

Debt	Code Section
Priority tax claims	523(a)(1)
unlisted debts	523(a)(3)
domestic support obligations	523(a)(5), (15)
certain fines and penalties	523(a)(7)
guaranteed student loans	523(a)(8)
damages from DWI conviction	523(a)(9)
debt nondischarged in prior bankruptcy	523(a)(10)
financial institution fraud	523(a)(11), (12)
restitution award	523(a)(13)
debts obtained to pay nondischargeable taxes, or other fines under election laws	523(a)(14), (14A), (14B)
postpetition homeowner's assessments	523(a)(16)
prisoner court costs	523(a)(17)
pension plan loans	523(a)(18)
debts arising from federal or state securities law violations	523(a)(19)

A creditor may object to the discharge of the following debts:

Debt	Code Section
fraud	523(a)(2)
intentional fraud	523(a)(2)(A)
false written financial statement	523(a)(2)(B)
limited prepetition credit transactions	523(a)(2)(C)
defalcation, larceny, embezzlement	523(a)(4)
willful and malicious injury	523(a)(6)

---

60. 11 U.S.C. §727(d)(e).

A creditor objects to the dischargeability of a debt by filing a complaint to determine the dischargeability of the debt. The creditor's goal is to obtain a judgment that the debt is not dischargeable. The complaint must be filed within 60 days of the date first set for the meeting of creditors pursuant to Section 341(a) or the debt will be discharged.

A debtor may also initiate a complaint to determine dischargeability of a debt and may do so at any time. A debtor might want to initiate such a complaint to obtain a judgment that an automatically nondischargeable debt is, in fact, dischargeable.

Only individuals are entitled to a Chapter 7 discharge; corporations and partnerships are not. A Chapter 7 discharge may only be obtained once every eight years. A discharge can be denied if a debtor has engaged in various sorts of inequitable conduct, including a failure to maintain proper books and records or for concealing assets. Individual debtors will be denied a discharge if they fail to complete a postpetition financial management course.

KEY TERMS

adversary proceeding
complaint to determine
    discharge
complaint to determine
    dischargeability of a
    debt

contested matter
fresh cash rule
nondischargeable debts
unlisted debt

DISCUSSION QUESTIONS

1. What is the difference between an objection to a debtor's discharge and an objection to the dischargeability of a debt?

2. Why are certain debts nondischargeable without an affected creditor being required to initiate an adversary proceeding? Identify these debts.

3. What debts become nondischargeable only by a creditor commencing a complaint objecting to dischargeability of the debt?

4. What are the deadlines for initiating a complaint to determine dischargeability of a debt or an objection to the debtor's discharge?

5. Why would a debtor desire to initiate a complaint to determine dis-chargeability of a debt?

6. Under what circumstances can a debtor be denied a discharge?

PRACTICE EXERCISES

Exercise 14.1
Prepare a draft adversary complaint on behalf of the Cashes challenging the nondischargeability of Robin's student loan obligation.

Exercise 14.2
Prepare an objection to the debtors' discharge on behalf of Beca Mitchell, who is one of Owen's unsatisfied online creditors who is asserting that Owen destroyed all of his internet sales records to avoid liability.

15

Property of the Estate and Turnover Complaints

Learning Objectives

- Define "property of the estate"
- Identify those assets that are not property of the estate and therefore not subject to the trustee's administration
- Describe the trustee's various rights to recover estate property, the turnover rights, and the avoiding powers

A.   PROPERTY OF THE ESTATE

The concept of **property of the estate** has been mentioned frequently but has not been previously explained in detail. Just as exemptions and discharge are fundamental to debtor relief, the concept of property of the estate is fundamental to a trustee's administration of an estate and is fundamental to the rights of creditors affected by a bankruptcy filing. Property of the estate not claimed exempt is subject to administration by a trustee by way of liquidation or abandonment of the property. With regard to secured creditors, the automatic stay protects property of the estate from foreclosure or repossession. With regard to unsecured creditors, the proceeds obtained from any liquidation of estate property by the trustee represent the funds that will ultimately be available for a distribution of dividends to the creditors. The basic mechanism for a trustee to recover property of the estate is known as a turnover complaint.

Property of the estate: property subject to administration by a bankruptcy trustee for the distribution of dividends to creditors

249

Avoiding powers: the right of a trustee to set aside certain pre- or postfiling transactions that might otherwise be valid under nonbankruptcy law; preferences, fraudulent transfers, and the ability to set aside unauthorized postpetition transfers are the most common avoiding powers

Additional rights, commonly known as **avoiding powers**, have been provided to the trustee to permit the further recovery of property of the estate.[1]

Section 541 defines and describes *property of the estate*. The commencement of a proceeding creates an estate. This occurs whether the proceeding is voluntary or involuntary and irrespective of the Chapter proceeding filed.[2] The basic concept is that all property in which the debtor has an interest, wherever located and by whomever held, constitutes property of the estate once the debtor files for bankruptcy relief.[3] In short, property previously considered to be assets of the debtor soon becomes synonymous with property of the estate. Even exempt property constitutes property of the estate, although such property is not available for the payment of creditor dividends.[4] The balance of Section 541 makes an effort to clarify and create specific exclusions to the rather broad definition of *estate property* provided for by the Bankruptcy Code.

Practice Pointer

Property of the estate includes any potential causes of action that the debtor may have.

In a community property jurisdiction, all interests of the debtor and the debtor's spouse in community property as of the commencement of the proceeding that is under the sole, equal, or joint management and control of the debtor or that is liable for an allowable claim against the debtor or both the debtor and the debtor's spouse constitutes property of the estate.[5] More simply put, property of the estate generally includes the community property interests of a nonfiling debtor spouse. For example, if a debtor in a community property jurisdiction files a bankruptcy proceeding but the debtor's spouse does not, all community property is still normally considered to be property of the estate.

---

1. See chapters 16-18 infra with regard to the trustee's avoiding powers.
2. 11 U.S.C. §541(a).
3. 11 U.S.C. §541(a)(1). See, e.g., In re Koonce, 262 B.R. 850 (Bankr. D. Nev. 2001) (lottery prize payments payable postpetition constitute property of the estate); In re Neto, 215 B.R. 939 (Bankr. D. N.J. 1997) (same).
4. See Historical and Revision Note to Section 541. See also 11 U.S.C. §522(b) and chapter 10 supra.
5. 11 U.S.C. §541(a)(2).

The above rule as to community property is consistent with the treatment of community debt and the debtor's discharge. It should be recalled that community debts will normally be discharged as to the community property of both spouses.[6] It is possible to file a Chapter 7 proceeding for one spouse in a community property jurisdiction and effectively gain a discharge for both spouses as to all community debts for which any community property may be liable. However, the separate property of the nonfiling spouse will remain liable for the otherwise discharged community debts and the automatic stay will be ineffective as to the nonfiling spouse, who may still potentially be the subject of creditor action to collect the debts. Nevertheless, any judgment obtained against the nonfiling spouse will not be enforceable against community property that has been property of the bankruptcy estate.

PROPERTY OF THE ESTATE

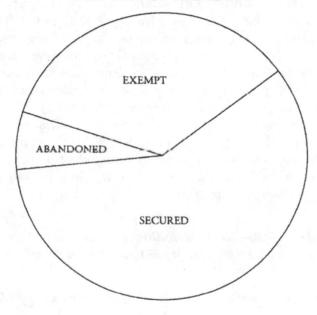

All property in which the debtor has a legal or equitable interest at the commencement of a case is property of the estate (11 U.S.C. §541(a)). During the course of the case, the trustee must "administer" all the property. The figure illustrates a typical consumer no asset Chapter 7 where all property is either collateral for one or more secured creditors (see chapter 21 infra), exempt (see chapter 10 supra), or abandoned by the trustee as

---

6. 11 U.S.C. §524(a)(3). See chapter 8 supra.

burdensome or of inconsequential value to the estate (see chapter 21 infra).

Property of the estate also includes any property recovered by the trustee through use of the avoiding powers or by operation of any other Code section.[7] For instance, if the court finds that counsel has received excessive compensation under Section 329(b), any portion of the fee ordered to be refunded by counsel becomes property of the estate.

Section 541(a)(5) concerns certain limited interests in property acquired by a debtor within 180 days after filing a bankruptcy so long as the property in question would have been property of the estate had the interest existed on the date of filing. These limited interests are property a debtor becomes entitled to receive by bequest, devise, or inheritance; property that a debtor becomes entitled to receive by way of a property settlement, agreement, or interlocutory or final divorce decree with the debtor's spouse; and property that the debtor becomes entitled to receive as a beneficiary of a life insurance policy or a death benefit plan.[8] By virtue of this subsection, Congress has expressed a policy that potential windfalls to the debtor received within 180 days of filing shall be made available to pay a dividend to the creditors. Note, however, the irony that true windfalls, such as a lottery jackpot, are not subject to this provision. Thus, a lottery jackpot won by the debtor ten days after a bankruptcy filing from a lottery ticket purchased postpetition will not be available to satisfy the claims of prepetition creditors unless the debtor desires it. Of course, if the debtor purchased the winning lottery ticket prepetition, the winnings would be property of the estate.[9] On the other hand, if the debtor's grandmother dies 175 days after the bankruptcy filing, any inheritance will be property of the bankruptcy estate.

FACT PATTERN

With Owen's father in poor health, what impact will that have on the filing advice that you provide to the Cashes?

FACT PATTERN

What other potential "windfalls" should the Cashes be counseled about?

---

7. 11 U.S.C. §541(a)(3)(4).
8. 11 U.S.C. §541(a)(5).
9. See note 3 supra.

> ### Practice Pointer
> At least one court has determined that postpetition spousal maintenance payments received by the debtor during the 180-day period are not property of the estate. In re Wise, 346 F.3d 1239 (10th Cir. 2003).

An important clarification to the concept of property of the estate is that items that may best be called "the fruit of the tree" are also property of the estate. Proceeds, product, offspring, or rent from property of the estate will also be property of the estate.[10] More simply put, property generated from property of the estate will itself be property of the estate. For example, the proceeds earned by an operating business after a Chapter 11 filing are property of the estate. If a fruit orchard is part of an estate, the fruit growing on the trees is part of the estate. If the debtor owns a sheep ranch, the lambs born after the filing are property of the estate. Property produced from estate property will itself be estate property.

Earnings from personal services performed by an individual debtor after the bankruptcy filing are not included as part of the property of the estate in a Chapter 7 case. Simply put, an individual debtor's postpetition wages are not property of the estate.[11] This rule applies to self-employment earnings for personal services as well as to a wage earner's paycheck. For example, a doctor's postpetition fees earned for providing services to patients are not property of the estate in the doctor's Chapter 7 case. If the debtor is a real estate agent, a commission earned postfiling is not property of the estate. If the debtor is a movie star or professional athlete bound to a prefiling long-term contract, the fee earned for personal services rendered after the bankruptcy filing is not property of the estate.[12]

Because Owen in essence can control when he works or not works, can he postpone some work originally scheduled to occur prepetition and instead complete it after his petition is filed?

FACT PATTERN

---

10. 11 U.S.C. §541(a)(6).
11. 11 U.S.C. §541(a)(6).
12. In re Tia Carrere, 64 B.R. 156 (Bankr. C.D. Cal. 1986); In re Clark, 100 B.R. 317 (E.D. La. 1989) (professional football player's postpetition salary was not property of estate).

There is one major exception to the rule that postpetition earnings for personal services are not property of the estate. This exception applies in individual Chapter 11, 12, and 13 proceedings. In these Chapters, post-petition earnings *are* considered to be property of the estate.[13] The reason for this rule is that the debtor's postfiling earnings generally comprise the source of the funding behind the distributions made to the creditors in individual reorganization cases. It is logical that the source of creditor repayment itself be considered estate property. However, when a Chapter 13 case is converted to Chapter 7, the Supreme Court has ruled that undistributed Chapter 13 plan payments made from a debtor's wages and held by the trustee when the case is converted are to be returned to the debtor.[14]

Property of the estate does *not* include any power that the debtor may exercise solely for the benefit of another entity.[15] For example, if a debtor possesses a power of attorney exercisable for a third party, the power of attorney is not property of the estate.

FACT PATTERN

In this case, the power of attorney that Owen held for his father would not constitute property of the estate.

Practice Pointer

When potential property of the estate is alleged to be held instead in trust, the burden is on the claimant to establish the trust relationship.

Any interest that a debtor may claim to have in a nonresidential lease of real property, the term of which has expired prior to filing or during the proceeding, is not property of the estate or ceases to be property of the estate in the latter event.[16] Thus, the landlord of an expired nonresidential lease need not seek relief from the automatic stay to be able to remove the lessee from the premises subject to the expired lease. In the first place, the landlord's action is excepted from the automatic stay. In the second place, the automatic stay is terminated as to an act against property when

---

13. 11 U.S.C. §1115; 11 U.S.C. §1207(a)(2); 11 U.S.C. §1306(a)(2). See chapters 24, 26, and 28 infra.
14. Harris v. Viegelahn, U.S., 135 S. Ct. 1829 (2015). See Chapter 9 supra.
15. 11 U.S.C. §541(b)(1).
16. 11 U.S.C. §541(b)(2).

the property ceases to be property of the estate.[17] A nonresidential lease would normally be considered a commercial lease in a nonbankruptcy environment. BAPCPA provides additional exclusions from property of the estate, including certain educational IRA or TAP funds, some retirement funds, and property that has been pledged as collateral for a loan. This latter category comprises pawned property.[18]

Sometimes a trust or other transactional document contains **ipso facto clauses** that restrict a transfer of or purport to forfeit an interest in property upon the holder of the interest becoming insolvent or commencing a bankruptcy proceeding. These ipso facto clauses are not enforceable in a bankruptcy proceeding to defeat the holder's property interest. A debtor's interest in such a transaction will remain property of the estate.[19] For example, Thurston Howell III gives his nephew Gilligan title to an island. The deed contains language that renders Gilligan's title to the island forfeited if Gilligan becomes insolvent or files a bankruptcy proceeding. If Gilligan then files a bankruptcy, the forfeiture clause will be unenforceable. Gilligan's trustee may be able to sell the island to pay a dividend to Gilligan's creditors.

> **Ipso facto clause:** a clause in a contract defining insolvency or a bankruptcy filing as an act of default: These clauses generally are not enforceable in bankruptcy proceedings

On the other hand, **spendthrift trusts** are enforceable in bankruptcy proceedings, and the principal property of a valid spendthrift trust will not be considered property of a bankruptcy estate.[20] A spendthrift trust exists when the trust instrument contains provisions restricting the transfer of a beneficial interest in the trust. Spendthrift trusts are trusts that are created to prevent creditors of the trust beneficiaries from seizing the trust's principal assets to pay the beneficiaries' debts. One form of spendthrift trust is created to preserve a family fortune from the financial indiscretions of the family members who are its beneficiaries. For example, Richie Rich has a very bad day in Las Vegas and is left with no choice but to file a Chapter 7 to attempt to discharge the legal gambling debts owed to his casino creditors. He is the beneficiary of a valid spendthrift trust. Neither the trustee nor the creditors can invade the trust principal to satisfy Richie's debts. However, the income that Richie receives from the trust for at least 180 days after filing may become property of the estate because the income is not earnings from personal services and is likely an interest from bequest, devise, or inheritance.[21]

> **Spendthrift trust:** a trust containing a clause precluding invasion of the trust assets to satisfy the debts of a beneficiary

A second form of spendthrift trust may come into existence through a qualified pension plan containing so-called spendthrift provisions. In 1992, in Patterson v. Shumate, 504 U.S. 753, the Supreme Court held

---

17. 11 U.S.C. §362(b)(10); 11 U.S.C. §362(c). See chapter 13 supra.
18. 11 U.S.C. §541(b)(5), (6), (7), (8).
19. 11 U.S.C. §541(c)(1).
20. 11 U.S.C. §541(c)(2).
21. 11 U.S.C. §541(a)(5). See above discussion.

that a debtor's beneficial interest in an Employment Retirement Income Security Act (ERISA) qualified pension plan is excluded from property of the estate.

Mr. Shumate was one of 400 participants in the Coleman Furniture Corporation pension plan. The plan qualified as an ERISA plan and contained spendthrift provisions. In 1984, Shumate became a Chapter 7 debtor. Shumate's trustee attempted to recover Shumate's interest in the pension plan as estate property. The district court ruled in the trustee's favor. Its decision was based on its interpretation that the phrase "applicable nonbankruptcy law" used in Section 541(c)(2) meant only state law, not federal law. The Supreme Court reversed the district court, holding that the phrase "applicable nonbankruptcy law" includes federal non-bankruptcy law such as ERISA. Accordingly, a valid spendthrift provision in an ERISA plan will exclude the debtor's beneficial interest from being considered property of the estate.

Finally, property in which the debtor holds bare legal title only is property of the estate only to the extent of the debtor's interest in it.[22] For example, if the debtor is a real estate trust deed or mortgage company servicing loans for third parties, the debtor's interest will extend only to any fees the debtor may be entitled to receive in connection with the loan servicing agreements. Any interest in the proceeds of the notes payable to nondebtor third parties would not be property of the estate.

B.   TURNOVER COMPLAINTS

Having defined *property of the estate*, the next task is to describe how a trustee or debtor-in-possession acquires the property for purposes of liquidation or other administration. Recall that recovery of estate property for purposes of liquidation and administration is an important aspect of the trustee's duties.[23] When a bankruptcy is filed, estate property will be in one of two places: either in the possession or control of the debtor or in the possession or control of third parties. The Code provides the trustee with various rights that allow the trustee to recover all estate property for purposes of administration. Property of the estate is recoverable by a trustee through the use of a **turnover complaint** or through exercise of the trustee's various avoiding powers.

Turnover complaint: the right of a bankruptcy trustee under 11 U.S.C. §542 to recover property of an estate in the possession of the debtor or other third party: A trustee generally obtains a turnover by filing a turnover complaint

22. 11 U.S.C. §541(d).
23. See chapter 11 supra.

What about the vehicles and equipment that have been repossessed from Owen and The Lawn Cuttery? Will Owen be able to recover any of those items pursuant to this concept of turnover?

The concept of turnover is straightforward. Someone has property of the estate: It may be the debtor, it may be a third party, it could be anyone. If the third party refuses to voluntarily turn the property over to the trustee, the court can order the third party to turn it over. The concept is that simple. The trustee has an almost absolute right, with few exceptions, to recover property of the estate for the benefit of creditors.[24]

Practice Pointer

Courts have even required a creditor to turn over a vehicle that was lawfully repossessed prepetition.

The exceptions to this rule are quite limited. An entity without actual knowledge or notice of the bankruptcy that transfers property of the estate to an entity other than the trustee does not later have to turn the property over to the trustee.[25] For instance, XYZ, Inc., files a Chapter 7 proceeding. XYZ's customers continue to send in their payments to XYZ instead of to the trustee. Whether or not the trustee ultimately receives the payments as property of the estate, the payments are considered to have been made. An insurance company with automatic premium payment requirements may pay itself from property of the estate to the extent the payment is required to pay a premium or carry out a nonforfeiture option.[26] Any applicable setoff right may also limit a trustee's turnover rights.[27]

Attorneys or accountants in possession of the books or records of an estate can be directed to turn over such records to the trustee. Although, in limited instances, traditional privileges may be utilized to protect the materials from turnover, in cases involving entities other than individuals, the trustee normally becomes the holder of any applicable privilege.[28]

---

24. 11 U.S.C. §542(a).
25. 11 U.S.C. §542(c).
26. 11 U.S.C. §542(d).
27. 11 U.S.C. §542(b). See chapter 17 infra.
28. 11 U.S.C. §542(e); 11 U.S.C. §521(4); Commodity Futures Trading Commn. v. Weintraub, 471 U.S. 343 (1985).

Custodian: a third party appointed to administer a debtor's assets under non-bankruptcy law; a court-appointed receiver or assignee for the benefit of creditors are examples of custodians: This term distinguishes bankruptcy trustees from non-bankruptcy fiduciaries

Special rules govern the turnover of estate property in the hands of a **custodian**.[29] In this instance, the custodian is a third party with custody of the property prior to the bankruptcy filing, such as an assignee for the benefit of creditors, or a state court receiver, or a nonbankruptcy trustee.[30] Although a custodian with knowledge of the commencement of a bankruptcy proceeding is supposed to turn over property of the estate to the bankruptcy trustee, Section 543 gives consideration to the custodian's rights.[31] The custodian may file an accounting of the custodian's activities, seek payment of any compensation that may be due, and generally be permitted to take all actions that would be required to fulfill and relieve the custodian's duties under nonbankruptcy law.[32] In an exceptional instance, the court, notwithstanding the appointment of a bankruptcy trustee, may permit the custodian to remain in possession of the property if the estate is solvent and if the custodian's continued presence would be in the best interest of the owners of the debtor.[33] For instance, perhaps the debtor owns a large apartment project and the custodian is better suited than the trustee to continue management of the property on behalf of the estate. The custodian ought to stay put. This is an instance where logic and common sense should prevail.

A turnover order is normally sought by filing an adversary proceeding known as a turnover complaint and joining as defendants those parties against whom the turnover is sought. However, a turnover proceeding may be brought before the court by way of a noticed motion rather than a complaint when the sole purpose of the motion is to seek a turnover of property held only by the debtor.[34]

Summary

The filing of a bankruptcy proceeding creates an estate. All property in which the debtor has a legal or equitable interest becomes property of the estate. Property of the estate is subject to administration by the bankruptcy trustee for the distribution of dividends to the creditors. Property of the estate is the subject of Code Section 541.

There are a number of clarifications contained in Section 541 including or excluding certain interests as property of the estate. The following list identifies these special inclusions or exclusions:

---

29. 11 U.S.C. §543.
30. 11 U.S.C. §101(11). See chapter 6 supra.
31. 11 U.S.C. §543(b).
32. 11 U.S.C. §543(b)(2), (c)(2); Bankruptcy Rule 6002.
33. 11 U.S.C. §543(d).
34. Bankruptcy Rule 7001(1).

1. Included as Property of the Estate:

	Item	Statute
a.	Community property	11 U.S.C. §541(a)(2)
b.	Property recovered by the trustee	11 U.S.C. §541(a)(3)(4)
c.	Property acquired within 180 days of filing by bequest, inheritance, or devise, domestic property settlement, life insurance proceeds	11 U.S.C. §541(a)(5)
d.	Proceeds, product, or offspring from property of the estate	11 U.S.C. §541(a)(6)
e.	Postpetition property acquired by the bankruptcy estate	11 U.S.C. §541(a)(7)
f.	Property subject to an ipso facto clause	11 U.S.C. §541(c)(1)

2. Excluded as Property of the Estate:

	Item	Statute
a.	Personal postfiling earnings of an individual Chapter 7 debtor	11 U.S.C. §541(a)(6)
b.	Powers exercisable for the benefit of another (e.g., power of attorney)	11 U.S.C. §541(b)(1)
c.	Interest in an expired nonresidential lease	11 U.S.C. §541(b)(2)
d.	Principal assets of a spendthrift trust	11 U.S.C. §541(c)(2)
e.	Property in which the debtor holds bare legal title	11 U.S.C. §541(d)

The trustee may recover property of the estate by initiating an adversary proceeding known as a turnover complaint. This right is provided the trustee by Section 542 of the Code. Where the turnover is sought from the debtor, the trustee may proceed by way of a noticed motion.

KEY TERMS

avoiding powers   property of the estate
custodian   spendthrift trust
ipso facto clause   turnover complaint

DISCUSSION QUESTIONS

1. What is meant by the phrase "property of the estate"?

2. Why is the general definition of estate property contained in 11 U.S.C. §541(a) intentionally broad?

3. What is a trustee supposed to do with property of the estate?

4. Why are postpetition wages of a debtor not considered property of the estate in Chapter 7? Why are postpetition wages of an individual debtor included as property of the estate in Chapters 11, 12, and 13?

5. Why is the product or proceeds of estate property also considered estate property?

6. What is an ipso facto clause?

7. What is a turnover complaint?

16

Avoiding Powers — Introduction

Learning Objectives

- Describe the concept and purpose of the trustee's avoiding powers
- List the general limitations upon the trustee's avoiding powers

A. FUNCTION OF THE TRUSTEE'S AVOIDING POWERS

In addition to the turnover right, the Bankruptcy Code has provided the trustee rights to recover for the estate property previously held by the debtor, but transferred to other parties prepetition, including property fraudulently transferred or property distributed inequitably to the creditors during certain defined periods prior to a bankruptcy filing. Unauthorized postpetition transfers may also be recoverable. Collectively, these rights are commonly known as the trustee's avoiding powers. An **avoiding power** is the ability of a trustee to avoid certain pre- or post-petition transactions that would otherwise be valid under nonbankruptcy law. The purpose of the avoiding powers is to effectuate the Bankruptcy Code's function as a debt collection tool. This purpose is often described as the orderly and consistent liquidation of a debtor's assets and their distribution to creditors. The successful use by a trustee of an avoiding power will recover as estate property assets that would no longer be considered property of the debtor in a nonbankruptcy environment.

Avoiding power: the right of a trustee to set aside certain pre- or postfiling transactions that might otherwise be valid under nonbankruptcy law: Preferences, fraudulent transfers, and the ability to set aside unauthorized postpetition transfers are the most common avoiding powers

261

FACT PATTERN

What, if any, potentially avoidable transfers exist in the Cash case?

The avoiding powers are designed to provide consistency and uniformity to the liquidation of bankruptcy estates and the distribution of dividends to creditors. The existence of the trustee's avoiding powers acts to prevent creditors from racing to the courthouse on the eve of a debtor's bankruptcy filing to seek unfair advantage relative to the overall creditor body. The avoiding powers also act to prohibit the enactment of conflicting nonbankruptcy nonfederal laws that might otherwise tend to defeat operation of the bankruptcy system.

The avoiding powers are contained in multiple sections of the Bankruptcy Code. The most commonly used avoiding powers are the strong arm clause, preferences, fraudulent transfers, and unauthorized postpetition transfers. The following two text chapters focus on the avoiding powers.

B.   STRONG ARM CLAUSE

Strong arm clause: the trustee's rights as a super-creditor, which are contained in the Bankruptcy Code Section 544

Section 544 gives the trustee various powers collectively and commonly known as the strong arm powers, or the **strong arm clause**. These are the first, most basic, of the avoiding powers. This provision existed under the Bankruptcy Act as Section 70(c).[1] Because much prior case law concerning this provision remains effective under the Code, it is a useful reference for those requiring additional research. In its essence, Section 544 transforms a trustee into a "super-creditor" as of the commencement of a bankruptcy proceeding.[2]

First, the trustee is given the power of a creditor who at the time of filing obtains a judicial lien on all of the debtor's property subject to a judicial lien, whether or not such a creditor actually exists.[3] Thus, the trustee acquires the status of a perfected and secured judgment creditor. This power gives the trustee priority over all other creditors who do not possess any superior lien rights upon property of the estate. This provision gives the trustee a superior right to all assets of the estate for the protection of all creditors.

---

1. See Historical and Revision Notes to 11 U.S.C. §544.
2. It is generally accepted that a Chapter 13 debtor may utilize the trustee's strong arm powers provided for in 11 U.S.C. §§544, 545, 547, 548, and 549 to the extent provided for in 11 U.S.C. §522 (g) and (h).
3. 11 U.S.C. §544(a)(1).

Which of the Cash creditors may be affected by this provision?

> ### *Practice Pointer*
> The rights of this hypothetical lien cred-
> itor are still determined by the relevant
> state law.

Second, Section 544 gives the trustee the power of a creditor who at the time of filing has an execution of judgment returned unsatisfied, whether or not such a creditor actually exists.[4] This provision, in conjunction with the first, provides a trustee with blanket protection to avoid any other creditor's efforts to gain a superior right in estate property subsequent to the commencement of the bankruptcy proceeding.

Third, the trustee is given the status of a bona fide purchaser of real property from the debtor, whether or not such a purchaser actually exists.[5] Thus, no entity can obtain an interest superior to the trustee's in a debtor's real estate subsequent to the bankruptcy filing. For example, a debtor's transfer of real estate one day after a petition is filed is in violation of the trustee's strong arm rights.

The strong arm rights collectively place the trustee in full command of all of a debtor's assets affected by the bankruptcy proceeding. It is the trustee, through proper use of the Bankruptcy Code, who initially determines the rights of the creditors to the various assets and the proper order of distribution of any funds received from a liquidation of the assets. The trustee can of course be aided by the court in making these determinations.

C.   LIMITATIONS ON AVOIDING POWERS

Section 546 contains several limitations on the exercise of the trustee's avoiding powers. Actions on the avoiding powers must be commenced within one year of the trustee's appointment or two years after the entry of the order for relief, whichever is later, but any action must be commenced

---

4. 11 U.S.C. §544(a)(2).
5. 11 U.S.C. §544(a)(3).

before the close or dismissal of the case.[6] This provision is essentially a statute of limitations upon the exercise of the trustee's avoiding powers.

Please note that this limitations period is measured from the entry of the order for relief or the date of the trustee's appointment, whichever is later. For example, a Chapter 11 may have been pending for 23 months prior to the trustee's appointment. Nonetheless, the trustee has one year from the date of appointment to exercise the avoiding powers. The logic of this rule is to prevent Chapter 11 debtors from filing a proceeding and then refraining from exercising an avoiding power to the detriment of all creditors. For example, John Smith fraudulently transfers real estate to his children on the eve of a Chapter 11 filing. He then files a Chapter 11 and plans to delay action for two years to be unable to avoid the fraudulent transfer because of the Section 546 time limits. Twenty-three months later, a trustee is appointed. Unfortunately for John Smith, the trustee will have one year to commence action rather than one month.

A second limitation on the exercise of the trustee's avoiding powers concerns the limited rights of certain creditors to perfect or to continue the perfection of a security interest in property notwithstanding the commencement of a bankruptcy proceeding.[7] This is a corollary to and is consistent with the identical exception to the automatic stay.[8] The limitation is that if nonbankruptcy law permits the perfection of an interest in property to relate back to a time prior to actual perfection, the fortuitous intervention of a bankruptcy filing will not defeat the creditor's nonbankruptcy rights to perfect the interest in accordance with nonbankruptcy law. The most common scenario that arises is the perfection of a security interest under the Uniform Commercial Code. Under the UCC a creditor normally has a ten-day statutory grace period to perfect a security interest.[9] If a bankruptcy intervenes during any applicable time period, Section 546(b) permits the creditor to complete perfection of its security interest within the statutory time period. In this event the validity and priority of the security interest will be honored in the bankruptcy proceeding. Similarly, if a state mechanic's lien law permits perfection of the lien to relate back to a prior date, then a mechanic's lien may be perfected by an affected creditor subsequent to a bankruptcy filing.

One purpose that this provision serves is to prevent a debtor from buying an asset on credit and then filing a bankruptcy before the creditor can perfect its security interest. If this could be done, then a debtor could claim the asset exempt, and the creditor would be unsecured. Such a rule

---

6. 11 U.S.C. §546(a).
7. 11 U.S.C. §546(b).
8. 11 U.S.C. §362(b)(3). See chapter 12 supra.
9. UCC §9-301(1).

would undoubtedly increase the cost of consumer credit and decrease its availability. Giving the creditor the benefit of any statutory grace period is simply fair. The Historical and Revision Notes to Section 546(b) state:

> The purpose of the subsection is to protect, in spite of the surprise intervention of a bankruptcy petition, those whom State law protects by allowing them to perfect their liens or interests as of an effective date that is earlier than the date of perfection.[10]

Assuming that Owen never recorded the loan he received from his father, could he still do so now? Does it matter if he files it before or after his bankruptcy filing?

FACT PATTERN

A third limitation on exercise of the trustee's avoiding powers concerns the rights of creditors to reclaim goods under either common law or the Uniform Commercial Code.[11] A right of reclamation is a creditor's right, in certain defined circumstances, to repossess goods previously sold to the debtor on an unsecured basis. Under this provision, a seller with a reclamation right may actually reacquire the merchandise from the buyer/debtor despite the filing of the bankruptcy if the debtor has received the goods in the ordinary course of business while insolvent within 45 days before the bankruptcy filing, and if the seller makes written demand to reclaim the goods not later than 45 days after the debtor receives the goods or 20 days after the case is filed if the 45 days expires after commencement of the case. For example, the owner of an insolvent store buys $10,000 of inventory on Thursday and files a bankruptcy on the following Monday. If the creditor gives a written reclamation notice to the debtor within 45 days after delivery, the seller may be able to recover the goods despite the intervening bankruptcy filing. The Bankruptcy Court may deny the reclamation demand, but only if the court gives the seller an administrative claim.[12] These issues arise infrequently in consumer bankruptcy cases but are common at the beginning of many Chapter 11 proceedings.

Section 546(d) was added to the Bankruptcy Code in 1984 in reaction to a then well-publicized matter that put bankruptcy law on the nightly national news. A grain elevator cooperative in Arkansas filed bankruptcy. The Bankruptcy Court held that the grain stored in the bankrupt grain elevator by the farmers was no longer their property but was property of

---

10. Historical and Revision Notes to Section 546.
11. 11 U.S.C. §546(c).
12. 11 U.S.C. §546(c)(2). As to administrative claims, see chapter 22 infra.

the estate. The farmers were mere unsecured creditors. The farmers who had stored their grain in the grain elevator then showed up with shotguns to reclaim their grain, and federal marshals were required to prevent the vigilante repossession.[13] Congress thought that this was an unfair predicament to put farmers in, so Section 546(d) was enacted to deal with the rights of farmers or fishermen who sell their products to a grain storage facility or fish-processing plant. Under Section 546(d), a farmer or fisherman is given the right to reclaim products from an insolvent grain storage facility or fish-processing plant if a written demand for reclamation is made within ten days after the product is delivered. The court may deny the reclamation request but must give the farmer or fisherman, like the seller of goods, an administrative claim or a lien on other assets of the estate.[14]

In stockbroker Chapter 7 proceedings, margin payments are normally not avoidable.[15] Section 546(h) of the Code allows a trustee to return to a seller of goods any goods sold to the debtor prepetition, if such return is in the best interests of the estate. Warehouseman's liens are not avoidable by a trustee pursuant to 11 U.S.C. §546(i).

D. STATUTORY LIEN AVOIDANCE

Statutory lien: a lien created by operation of law other than a court order; a state law mechanic's lien is a statutory lien; Section 101(53) of the Bankruptcy Code defines statutory lien

Section 545 allows a trustee to avoid certain types of statutory liens. Recall that a **statutory lien** is a lien created by operation of law, not by court order (a judicial lien) or agreement (a consensual lien).[16] The first type of statutory lien that is avoidable is a lien that purports to become effective only upon the debtor's insolvency, the filing of a bankruptcy proceeding, or having a financial condition that fails to meet a defined standard.[17] Such statutes are the legislative equivalent of ipso facto clauses, which are disfavored by the Code.[18] The purpose of this provision is to prevent states from enacting liens that would give certain creditors priority only in the event of a debtor's bankruptcy filing.

Second, a statutory lien may be avoided if it cannot be enforced against a bona fide purchaser of the debtor's property at the commencement of the bankruptcy proceeding, whether or not such a purchaser

---

13. Missouri v. United States Bankr. Ct. for E.D. of Ark., 647 F.2d 768 (8th Cir. 1981).
14. 11 U.S.C. §546(d).
15. 11 U.S.C. §546(e), (f), (g).
16. 11 U.S.C. §101(53). See chapter 7 supra.
17. 11 U.S.C. §545(1).
18. See chapter 15 supra.

exists except for a purchaser at a government tax lien sale.[19] For example, if a state mechanic's lien law requires recordation of the lien prior to the lien being deemed perfected, a lien recorded subsequent to a bankruptcy filing may be avoidable. Finally, statutory rent liens or liens for distress of rent are avoidable.[20]

Summary

The abilities given a trustee to avoid certain pre- or postfiling transactions that would otherwise be valid under nonbankruptcy law are known as the avoiding powers. Preferences, fraudulent transfers, and the ability to set aside unauthorized postpetition transfers are the most common avoiding powers.

The underlying purpose of the avoiding powers is often described as the orderly and consistent liquidation of a debtor's assets and their distribution to creditors. This philosophy is the foundation of the debt collection features of the bankruptcy system. The avoiding powers attempt to eliminate the effects of creditors racing to the courthouse to improve their position on the eve of a bankruptcy filing.

The initial avoiding power provides a trustee rights that make the trustee a "super-creditor" with priority to estate assets over the claims of most creditors. This permits the trustee to properly collect the assets for liquidation. This provision is known as the strong arm clause. Statutory liens, liens created by statute, will be avoidable in some situations, most notably where the lien comes into existence only if a debtor files a bankruptcy proceeding.

A trustee is given a period two years from the date of appointment to initiate an adversary proceeding to exercise an avoiding power.

Not all transactions or creditors will be subject to the avoiding powers. Limited creditors may be permitted to perfect liens in property for a limited period of time after a bankruptcy is filed. Limited unsecured creditors may also possess a right of reclamation, the right to repossess goods or crops.

KEY TERMS

avoiding power	strong arm clause
statutory lien	

---

19. 11 U.S.C. §545(2).
20. 11 U.S.C. §545(3), (4).

DISCUSSION QUESTIONS

1. What is the concept underlying the trustee's avoiding powers?

2. Why is a trustee considered a "super-creditor"?

3. When may a secured creditor perfect a claim after a bankruptcy filing?

4. How long does a trustee have to exercise the avoiding powers?

5. How are a trustee's avoiding powers exercised?

17

Avoidable Preferences — 11 U.S.C. §547

Learning Objectives

- Explain the concept of avoidable preferences under the Bankruptcy Code
- Describe the elements of an avoidable preference
- List the affirmative defenses that a creditor may assert to defeat a trustee's claim of an avoidable preference
- Describe the basic procedures of a preference complaint

A. INTRODUCTION AND DEFINITIONS

The two most common of the trustee's avoiding powers are known as **preferences** and fraudulent transfers. Preferences permit a trustee to recover assets transferred to a creditor on the eve of the bankruptcy filing so that the assets may be distributed fairly to all creditors. The thrust of the preferential transfer provisions is to avoid payments or other prepetition transfers made to a creditor that increase the creditor's recovery at the expense of other similarly situated creditors. A secondary function of preference avoidability is to stop creditors from racing to the courthouse on the eve of bankruptcy to unfairly improve their chances of receiving payment.

A preference generally occurs when a debtor, on the eve of bankruptcy, transfers property or an interest in property to one or more creditors in full or partial satisfaction of their debt to the exclusion of all other

Preference: a transfer of property or an interest in property to a creditor, on the eve of bankruptcy, in full or partial satisfaction of debt to the exclusion of other creditors: A preference meeting certain defined conditions will be avoidable by a bankruptcy trustee

269

creditors. The avoidable transfer may be voluntary or involuntary. Creditors receiving a preference have their claims wholly or partially satisfied while the remaining creditors receive nothing. Permitting a trustee to avoid these transactions and to recover property transferred for the estate so that it may be liquidated and the proceeds distributed fairly to all creditors is the goal of this avoiding power.

To illustrate, U.S. Grant owns an insolvent dry goods store. One month before filing a Chapter 7, Grant voluntarily pays in full the claims of creditors Sherman, Sheridan, and Meade. Creditors Lee, Jackson, and Longstreet receive no payments. Utilizing preference powers, Grant's Chapter 7 trustee, Lincoln, may recover the payments made to the first group of creditors so that equal dividends may ultimately be paid to all of Grant's creditors. If Lee, Jackson, and Longstreet obtain a writ of attachment, outflanking Grant with this involuntary transfer, Lincoln would also be able to avoid this transaction as a preference.

The concept of avoidable preferences does not exist outside of the bankruptcy system. When a consumer or business pays its debts in a non-bankruptcy environment, the debts may be paid in any desired order. For instance, in a month where cash flow is insufficient to pay all debts on a current basis, a consumer decides to postpone payment of the dentist's bill until next month. Other creditors have been "preferred" over the dentist. A debtor that is not bankrupt may normally "prefer" or pay creditors in any order desired.

Culpability or the intent of the entity receiving or giving the preference is not an issue in determining whether a preference is avoidable. The only concern is the overriding philosophy of the bankruptcy system that all creditors with the same distributive priority under the Bankruptcy Code should be treated equally in the receipt of dividends. Intent or culpability is irrelevant to this consideration.

Keep in mind that the avoiding powers are also possessed by a Chapter 11 debtor-in-possession.[1] So even though a debtor-in-possession may in fact be the very entity that committed the preference in the first place, the debtor-in-possession still has an opportunity to avoid the preference for the benefit of all creditors. Section 547 of the Bankruptcy Code regulates the avoidance of preferences. The most practical way to gain a basic understanding of this Section and its various subdivisions is to conceive of an avoidable preference as a cause of action or claim upon which relief may be granted. In this sense, the determination of the existence of or defenses to an avoidable preference can most easily be described in the format of a traditional lawsuit. That is, to successfully avoid a preference,

---

1. 11 U.S.C. §1107. See chapter 10 supra.

there are various elements that the trustee must prove. Similarly, the party or parties against whom a preference is sought to be avoided may raise issues that in traditional litigation would be considered affirmative defenses. Actions to avoid preferences are always commenced as adversary proceedings when the trustee seeks affirmative relief.[2] The trustee is the plaintiff; the party or parties who received the preference are the defendants.

Section 547 is one of the few Bankruptcy Code sections containing definitions that are unique to it. These definitions are contained in Section 547(a). The first of these is **inventory:** any form of personal property that a debtor uses to produce revenue. Thus, inventory for preference purposes may be raw material, finished product, merchandise on shelves, or cars available for rental.[3]

The second unique definition that is relevant primarily in business bankruptcy proceedings, and the most critical, is **new value**. *New value*, in simple and practical terms, means new consideration for the debt. **Consideration** is normally the element of exchange in any contract. New value is not created when a new obligation is substituted for an existing obligation.[4] A preference may arise by the payment of money, a transfer of property, or the granting of a security interest in property of the debtor. For example, George owes Brad $10,000. George offers Brad a lien on his pearl-handled revolver to secure repayment of the debt. To the extent that Brad is not loaning more money to George in exchange for the lien, there is no new value. The lien on the revolver will be an avoidable preference. A preference is therefore any transaction that places one creditor in a preferred position over other otherwise similar creditors, such as an unsecured creditor's becoming secured on the eve of a bankruptcy filing. Much of the preference litigation taking place before the Bankruptcy Court does not usually involve a creditor that has been paid money but rather a creditor that has received a security interest in property on the eve of bankruptcy. The definition of *new value* helps in determining whether the granting of such a security interest is or is not a transfer that may be deemed an avoidable preference.

Receivable is a third unique definition in Section 547. A *receivable* is a right to payment, whether or not such right has been earned by performance.[5] A fourth and final definition is not a definition at all but a necessary rule that helps create a consistent national scheme regarding tax preferences, because the Internal Revenue Code and each individual

---

Inventory: any form of personal property that a debtor uses to produce revenue

New value: the providing of new consideration in a transaction between a debtor and creditor; an avoidable preference will generally not exist where a transaction occurs for new value: This definition is unique to avoidable preferences

Consideration: the element of exchange in any contract

Receivable: a right to payment, whether or not such right has been earned by performance

---

2. Bankruptcy Rule 7001.
3. 11 U.S.C. §547(a)(1).
4. 11 U.S.C. §547(a)(2).
5. 11 U.S.C. §547(a)(3).

state have their own independent definitions concerning when a tax debt is incurred. Section 547(a)(4) provides that a tax debt is incurred on the date it is last payable without penalty, including any extensions.[6] This means that for purposes of income taxes, for example, a tax debt is incurred on April 15 for a prior year's taxes.

B. ELEMENTS OF A PREFERENCE

A trustee must prove six elements to successfully avoid a preference. Each element must be proven for the trustee to prevail. Failure to prove any element will result in a failure to avoid the preference. These six elements constitute the cause of action or claim for relief.

The first element is that there must be a "transfer of an interest of the debtor in property."[7] Any sort of **transfer** of a debtor's interest in an asset may be avoidable. Recall that the Code defines *transfer* as any method that human beings may devise to convey property or an interest in it.[8] This definition of *transfer* is intentionally broad. Thus, outright payment of cash or the transfer of a physical asset, such as real estate or personal property, to a creditor by a debtor will constitute a transfer. The grant or attempted granting of a security interest in real or personal property to a creditor by a debtor will also constitute a transfer.

> **Transfer:** any means that may be devised to dispose of property or an interest in property; this is an intentionally broad definition; Section 101(54) of the Bankruptcy Code defines transfer

Practice Pointer

The Code defines a "transfer" to mean:
(1) the creation of a lien; (2) retention of title; (3) foreclosure of the debtor's equity of redemption; or (4) any mode, "direct or indirect, absolute or conditional, voluntary or involuntary, of disposing of or parting with property or an interest in property."

The second element of an avoidable preference is that the transfer be "to or for the benefit of a creditor."[9] The "to a creditor" portion is fairly

---

6. 11 U.S.C. §547(a)(4).
7. 11 U.S.C. §547(b).
8. 11 U.S.C. §101(54). See chapter 6 supra.
9. 11 U.S.C. §547(b)(1).

simple: The money, property, or security interest is transferred directly to the creditor by the debtor.

A transfer is made "for the benefit of a creditor" if it is to a creditor of a creditor. In this instance, even though the original creditor has received no direct transfer, the transfer has still been made for that creditor's benefit. For example, Huey owes Louie, and Louie owes Dewey. Louie tells Huey that if Huey pays Dewey for Louie, then Huey will no longer owe Louie, and Louie will no longer owe Dewey. Huey's payment of Louie's debt to Dewey is a transfer for the benefit of a creditor, namely Louie. Huey's financial books may not show that the payment to Dewey is for Louie, but Louie's claim against Huey has still been satisfied.

The third element is that the transfer be "for or on account of an antecedent debt owed by the debtor before the transfer was made."[10] **Antecedent debt** means that the debt was incurred or existed before the transfer was made. The most common form of antecedent debt is a past-due bill. In the George and Brad example, supra, the $10,000 debt due Brad is an antecedent debt when the lien is offered by George.

Antecedent debt: a debt incurred or existing before the making of a transfer

 ### *Practice Pointer*

To qualify as an antecedent debt, there must be some delay between when the debt arises and when payment is made. In other words, the debt must have been incurred prior to the alleged preferential transfer, although it need not have been past due.

The fourth element of an avoidable preference is that the transfer be made "while the debtor was insolvent."[11] As noted earlier in this chapter, if the debtor is not insolvent, the order of debt repayment is of no concern to anyone. A debtor is generally **insolvent** when the debtor's liabilities exceed the debtor's assets.[12]

Insolvent: an entity is generally insolvent when its liabilities exceed its assets; Section 101(32) of the Bankruptcy Code defines insolvency

The fifth element is time. One of two time periods is considered in determining the existence of an avoidable preference. The first of these is the period 90 days prior to filing of a bankruptcy. An otherwise preferential transfer occurring before this time period will not constitute an avoidable preference.[13] However, when insiders are the subject of a preference

---

10. 11 U.S.C. §547(b)(2).
11. 11 U.S.C. §547(b)(3).
12. 11 U.S.C. §101(32). See chapter 6 supra.
13. 11 U.S.C. §547(b)(4)(A).

action, the relevant time period is extended to one year prior to the filing of the bankruptcy petition.[14] For example, Elle Woods owes $10,000 to a grandparent for money loaned to attend law school. The grandparent is repaid from Woods's first paycheck. Woods files a bankruptcy proceeding six months later. The payment will be an avoidable preference since it was made to an insider within one year prior to filing of the petition.

The sixth and final element of an avoidable preference is that the creditor must "receive more than such creditor would receive" in a Chapter 7 if the transfer had not been made.[15] Simply put, the transfer must result in the creditor having a greater percentage of its debt repaid by the transfer than the creditor would have received through a Chapter 7 dividend if the transfer had not been made. For example, a creditor receiving payment in full, when a Chapter 7 dividend would have only paid 50 percent, has received a preference payment equal to 50 percent of the debt. Similarly, a creditor that improves its position from unsecured to secured by the transfer of a security interest in property receives more than it would otherwise receive as a Chapter 7 dividend because it receives the collateral rather than a speculative right to a portion of the proceeds from a sale of the collateral.

Carefully focusing on the final element of an avoidable preference may aid in facilitating the settlement of preference disputes. In any situation where the parties can reasonably estimate the potential dividend to an affected class of creditor in a Chapter 7 proceeding, it is necessary only to calculate any excess received by the creditor and to then have the creditor return this excess to the estate and waive any further claim against the estate. The creditor will have received its dividend while the remaining creditors will have had their "fair share" returned at a minimum of expense in attorneys' fees or litigation expenses, not to mention a substantial savings in time. All this will further increase the total ultimate return to the estate's creditors, of whom the creditor receiving the preference is one.

The trustee bears the initial burden of proving the existence of each element in order for the preference to be avoided. If one element remains unproven, a preference may exist, but it will not be an avoidable preference.[16]

Under Section 547(f) a debtor is presumed insolvent during the 90 days immediately prior to the filing of the bankruptcy petition.[17] This means that the trustee does not have to affirmatively prove the debtor's

---

14. 11 U.S.C. §547(b)(4)(B).
15. 11 U.S.C. §547(b)(5).
16. 11 U.S.C. §547(g).
17. 11 U.S.C. §547(f).

insolvency when the preferential transfer occurs within 90 days prior to a bankruptcy filing. In this instance, the entity against whom the claim is brought will bear the burden of proving that the debtor was solvent during the 90-day period. As a corollary, this also means that if the subject of the avoidable preference is an insider transaction occurring more than 90 days prior to filing but within one year of the bankruptcy filing, the trustee will now have the burden of proving the debtor's insolvency during the period of time more than 90 days prior to the bankruptcy filing.

Robin Cash pays $4,000 to release the judgment for possession of her condominium so she can move back into the property. The Cash joint bankruptcy is filed 40 days later. Is it likely that the trustee will consider the payment to be a preference and pursue it?

FACT PATTERN

In the most common preference cases, many of the elements are generally not difficult to prove. For instance, payment of a long-overdue loan owed to a relative or payment of a long-overdue bank loan is easily identified as a transfer to a creditor on account of an antecedent debt. If the payment was made within 90 days of filing, the debtor is presumed insolvent. Because most proceedings have no assets, most avoidable preferences should generally be fully recoverable. Documents evidencing the debt, the transfer, and the transfer's timing should generally be sufficient to prove all the basic elements of an avoidable preference.

The final element of a preference, that the creditor has received more than the creditor would otherwise receive in a Chapter 7 proceeding, is also often easy to prove, as noted above. Full analysis of the ultimate effect on the creditor body can result in settlement of many preference claims asserted by a trustee. This usually requires some educated guesswork but is not overly difficult. Because the most common proceeding is a no asset Chapter 7, any creditor receiving a preference is receiving more than it otherwise would in a Chapter 7 proceeding. If a creditor owed $1,000 receives a preference of $1,000, does the creditor receive more than it otherwise would in the Chapter 7? Obviously, yes. But, the more difficult question is, how much more? For example, assume that the creditor receiving $1,000 is one of ten creditors. Assume also that the aggregate total of debts is $10,000. If $1,000 is available to distribute to creditors, the amount of dividend that each of these creditors will receive is 10 percent, because 1,000 is 10 percent of 10,000. The creditor in the example therefore received $900 more than it would in the Chapter 7. Thus, $900 is the actual amount of the avoidable preference. The creditor should be permitted to settle the dispute by returning $900 to the estate and waiving further claims against the estate.

In a large proceeding, these calculations can become complex and uncertain. Nevertheless, agreement as to an estimated amount of dividend often may lead to swift and economical settlement of avoidable preference disputes. This approach is more practical than incurring significant attorneys' fees in avoiding the preference, because the fees act to erode the ultimate dividend payable to all creditors. The suggested approach should result in greater overall distributions to the creditor body, primarily due to the reduced attorneys' fee burden.

C.   AFFIRMATIVE DEFENSES

The elements of an avoidable preference thus constitute a cause of action or claim upon which relief may be granted that is unique to a bankruptcy proceeding. To complement the cause of action or claim, there also exists the functional equivalent of affirmative defenses to an avoidable preference claim. These "affirmative defenses" are described in Section 547(c) and (i) and can be easily grasped if conceived of as affirmative defenses to the avoidable preference claim. Most of these defenses exist to legitimize transactions occurring in the normal course of business, transactions that the fortuity of a bankruptcy filing should not invalidate.

Contemporaneous exchange: the presence of consideration in the transfer of property from a debtor to a creditor; a contemporaneous exchange for new value is a defense to a *preference* claim by the trustee

The first affirmative defense is that the transfer is intended to be a **contemporaneous transfer for new value** and is in fact a substantially contemporaneous exchange.[18] That is, if there is new consideration present from both parties, the transfer will not be an avoidable preference. For example, in the typical preference transaction, a debtor in default to a creditor pays the creditor all or a portion of the debt due. The debtor receives nothing in return for the payment. Recall the example earlier in this chapter of the debt owed by George to Brad. There is no new value between the parties in the example, and the payment therefore is an avoidable preference. New value generally involves an exchange of present or new consideration between the debtor and creditor. For instance, when Opie Taylor goes to the Ziffle Finance Company to refinance an existing loan and borrows an additional $500, the $500 is new value. It was not owed by or previously loaned to Opie. Conversely, the preexisting loan amount would be an antecedent debt.

---

18. 11 U.S.C. §547(c)(1).

Practice Pointer

Some courts view "contemporaneous" as occurring within ten days of each other, while other courts look at the question on a case-by-case basis.

Substantially contemporaneous generally means an exchange taking place in the normal course of business. If a transfer is perfected within any nonbankruptcy grace periods, as described in chapter 14 supra, the transfer will normally be considered substantially contemporaneous. For example, if the bank loans a debtor money to purchase a new car but the bank fails to perfect its lien in the vehicle for one week, the transaction will still be considered substantially contemporaneous because the lien date will likely fall within any applicable nonbankruptcy grace period. The reason for this flexibility is that if such a rule did not exist, it would be possible for trustees or debtors to avoid recently obtained valid liens on a debtor's assets by successfully claiming that the security interest is a preference. If this were the case, the credit industry would be in chaos and the availability of credit would be reduced significantly. The statute therefore tries to reconcile this necessary fact of economic existence with the orderly distribution of assets to all creditors in the event of financial failure.

Substantially contemporaneous: an exchange taking place in the normal course of business

If the deed from Lester to Owen is recorded and the mortgage in favor of Second American Trust & Loan Co. is recorded at the same time, the transaction is a substantially contemporaneous exchange for new value.

FACT PATTERN

The second affirmative defense to a preference action involves the payment of debts in the ordinary course of business. Some businesses pay them once every 30 days, or once every 40 days, or perhaps only once every 90 days, but they pay them on a regular basis. Consumers who make regular monthly payments to their creditors are making payments in the ordinary course of business. If a creditor can show that the debt was incurred and paid in the ordinary course of the debtor's and creditor's financial affairs or according to ordinary business terms, then the transfer will not constitute an avoidable preference.[19] This provision attempts to accept the reality of the marketplace and does not attempt to alter it due to the happenstance of a bankruptcy filing.

---

19. 11 U.S.C. §547(c)(2).

A difficult situation arises when a debtor makes a customary monthly payment on a long-term unsecured obligation, such as the outstanding balance owed on a line of credit or unsecured promissory note obligation. Does the antecedent nature of the debt render payments made within any applicable preference period avoidable, or, because the payments are made in the ordinary course of business, are they defensible? The Supreme Court faced this issue in Union Bank v. Wolas, 502 U.S. 151 (1991).

On December 17, 1986, the debtor ZZZZ Best Co., Inc., borrowed $7 million from Union Bank. On July 8, 1987, the debtor filed a Chapter 7 petition. In the 90 days preceding the bankruptcy, the debtor paid Union Bank $100,000 in interest payments and a $2,500 loan commitment fee. The Bankruptcy Court and district courts found for the bank creditor. The Ninth Circuit reversed. Because of a conflicting ruling from the Sixth Circuit, the Supreme Court granted certiorari to review the matter.[20]

The Supreme Court held that a payment in the ordinary course will qualify for the preference exception irrespective of whether the underlying nature of the debt is long-term or short-term. Thus, the payments to the bank fell within the ordinary course of business exception.

The third affirmative defense to an avoidable preference is that, so long as the security interest secures new value, perfection of a security interest within 30 days of a debtor acquiring the property will not be an avoidable preference.[21] For example, Alfred Newman borrows $10,000 from the Last National Bank and gives the bank a security interest in an obsolete stereo system. If the bank perfects its security interest within 30 days, the perfection will not constitute an avoidable preference. Recall that even if Newman files a bankruptcy proceeding within the 30-day period, under Section 546 the bank might still be able to perfect its interest within the 30-day period.[22]

FACT PATTERN

Assume Owen records the deed to the home one day before his bankruptcy filing and the mortgage in favor of Second American Trust & Loan Co. is filed on the same day. Is the recordaton of the mortgage a preference? What if the deed is recorded two months before the bankruptcy but the mortgage is not recorded until the day before the bankruptcy? What if the mortgage is not recorded until the day after the bankruptcy?

---

20. The conflicting Sixth Circuit ruling was In re Finn, 909 F.2d 968 (1990).
21. 11 U.S.C. §547(c)(3).
22. 11 U.S.C. §546(b). See chapter 16 supra. Recall also that the bank may perfect its interest within any applicable postfiling period as an exception to the automatic stay. 11 U.S.C. §362(b)(3). See chapter 13 supra.

> **Practice Pointer**
> Perfection of the security interest in this context is governed by federal bankruptcy law and not by the individual state laws.

The fourth affirmative defense will normally arise only in proceedings involving business debtors. Essentially, a transfer will not be avoidable as a preference if, after the transfer, the creditor gives new value to the debtor that is unsecured.[23] For example, a payment in advance will not generally be an avoidable preference.

The fifth affirmative defense concerns a business financing arrangement commonly known as a **floating lien**. A floating lien is typically a line of credit from a bank or other financial institution secured by the inventory, equipment, or proceeds of the debtor's business. In the normal course of business, a debtor constantly sells existing inventory and replaces it with more inventory. Because the security interest attaches to the new inventory that the debtor purchases in place of the sold merchandise, the lien is said to "float." The test of this defense to avoidable preferences is identical to the test described in Section 553 involving setoffs.[24] This test is commonly referred to as the "improvement of position" test. Generally, a floating lien will not constitute a preference to the extent that the creditor does not "improve its position" in the 90 days prior to a bankruptcy filing.[25] To determine whether a creditor has improved its position, the amount of the debt and the value of the collateral as of a date 90 days prior to the bankruptcy filing are compared with the amount of the debt and the value of the collateral on the date of the bankruptcy filing. To the extent that the creditor improves its secured position during the 90-day period, the improvement will be an avoidable preference, but maintenance of the creditor's position at the level held 90 days prior to the bankruptcy filing will not be.

Floating lien: a line of credit from a bank, financial institution, or other lender secured by the existing and after-acquired inventory, equipment, and proceeds of a debtor's business

For example, 90 days prior to filing a Chapter 11, Total Roto, Inc., owes the Bank of Plunger $200,000 secured by $100,000 in collateral. At this time, $100,000 of the debt is unsecured. On the date of filing, the debt has been decreased to $100,000 and remains secured by $100,000 of collateral. There is no longer an unsecured portion of the debt. The $100,000 in payments will be considered a preference because they have reduced the amount by which the debt exceeded the value of the

---

23. 11 U.S.C. §547(c)(4).
24. See chapter 21 infra.
25. 11 U.S.C. §547(c)(5).

security interest from $100,000 to zero. Stated another way, payments made to an undercollateralized secured creditor within 90 days of a bankruptcy filing (one year if the creditor is an insider) are preferential to the extent that the unsecured portion of the debt is decreased. The reduction of the unsecured portion of a secured claim is the portion of the debt measured. In the example, this decrease is $100,000. On the other hand, if payments of $100,000 are made during the preference period but the amount of debt and value of the collateral remain respectively at $200,000 and $100,000 on the date of filing, then the $100,000 in payments would not constitute an avoidable preference because the unsecured portion of the debt has not been reduced.

The example may be illustrated by the following diagram and formula:

	d	si	(d − si)	
1. 90 days prior*	$200,000	$100,000	$100,000	or $(d_1 - si_1)$
2. filing date	$100,000	$100,000	-0-	$> (d_2 - si_2)$

d = amount of debt; si = value at collateral; $(d - si)$ = unsecured portion of claim

*One year if insider.

To the extent that the unsecured portion of the debt is greater on the earlier date than on the later date, the difference will constitute an avoidable preference. To the extent there is no change or an increase in the undersecured portion of the debt, there is no avoidable preference. In the example, the creditor has eliminated all of its unsecured debt during the preference period: The entire amount may be preferential. The same statement can be stated mathematically: If $(d_1 - si_1) > (d_2 - si_2)$, then the difference is an improvement in position and thus preferential. The first sum is a computation as of the commencement of the preference period, 90 days or one year prior to the filing, respectively. The second sum is computed as of the filing date.

This formula can be described in a third and perhaps even simpler way: A secured creditor is only considered secured up to the value of its collateral.[26] Any additional amount due the creditor is considered an unsecured debt. Thus, determine the amount of the unsecured debt due the creditor at the beginning of the preference period and compare it to the amount of the unsecured debt due the creditor on the filing. To the extent that the amount of the unsecured debt has decreased, the decrease may be an avoidable preference. On the other hand,

---

26. See chapter 21 infra. 11 U.S.C. §506.

unfortunately for the creditor, to the extent that the amount of unsecured debt increases, the creditor bears the consequences.

The fixing of a statutory lien that the trustee cannot avoid under Section 545 is also not avoidable as a preference.[27] In this context, the term "fixing" is not defined. A distinction should be drawn between a statutory lien already fixed or established and one in which the alleged transfer sets the statutory lien.[28]

Transfers made in the payment of domestic support obligations are also not avoidable as preferences.[29]

One affirmative defense to an avoidable preference applies only to consumer debtors. An individual consumer debtor may make aggregate transfers of less than $600 and the transfers will not constitute avoidable preferences.[30] This defense reflects a common occurrence in consumer situations. A potential no asset consumer debtor may have two or three creditors whom the debtor really wants to pay and not include as creditors in the bankruptcy filing. The creditors might be a credit card or medical bill, a phone bill, or perhaps a gas and electric bill. Without this defense to the trustee's avoidable preference powers, payment of all of these small debts would be avoidable. However, because an individual consumer debtor is permitted to make preferences of less than $600 in aggregate, a consumer debtor may pay small debts that they prefer to not include in the bankruptcy filing. The only limitation is that the grand total not exceed $600.

BAPCPA added a final affirmative defense available in business bankruptcies. If the value of the transfer is less than $6,425, the transfer is not avoidable as a preference. As a practical matter, this will eliminate many transactions that would otherwise be avoidable preferences.[31]

D.   MISCELLANEOUS PROVISIONS

Section 547(d) permits a trustee to avoid a transfer to a surety furnishing a bond to dissolve a judicial lien if the underlying lien is also avoidable by the trustee.[32] For example, Snidely Whiplash attaches Nell's assets by a court order. Nell obtains a bond, giving the bond company a lien on her

27. 11 U.S.C. §547(c)(6). See also chapter 16 supra.
28. See In re Ramba, Inc., 416 F.3d 394 (5th Cir. 2005).
29. 11 U.S.C. §547(c)(7).
30. 11 U.S.C. §547(c)(8).
31. 11 U.S.C. §547(c)(9). The amount reflects the 2016 adjustments required by Section 104. See chapter 4 supra.
32. 11 U.S.C. §547(d).

home to release the attachment. In Nell's subsequent Chapter 7 filing, the trustee may avoid the bonding company's lien if Snidely's judicial lien can also be avoided.

Section 547(e) clarifies the timing of when a transfer occurs for purposes of determining whether the transfer is an avoidable preference. A transfer of real property is completed when the trust deed or grant deed or other deed is recorded or when the transferee acquires an interest in property that is superior to that of a bona fide purchaser.[33] Similarly, the transfer of an interest in personal property is considered perfected when the creditor files its UCC documents, or when the creditor cannot acquire a judicial lien superior to the rights of the transferee.[34] In Barnhill v. Johnson, 503 U.S. 393 (1992), the Supreme Court ruled that a transfer by check is not complete until the check has cleared the payor's bank. In this case, the debtor delivered a check to Barnhill on November 18. The check was dated November 19 and was honored by the bank on November 20. After the debtor filed Chapter 11, it was agreed that November 20 was the ninetieth day prior to the bankruptcy filing.

In holding that the check's date of honor by the debtor's bank is the relevant date of transfer, the Supreme Court reasoned that because under the Uniform Commercial Code the debtor could dishonor the check until it cleared, the debtor therefore retained rights in the funds and that the transfer was not complete within the meaning of 11 U.S.C. §547(e)(1)(B).

This decision may lead to some uncertainty in practice on the part of creditors because the date that a check is honored by debtor's bank will generally be known only to the debtor because this date will appear only on the canceled check. This information will not be readily available to a creditor unless the debtor discloses it.

A second portion of Section 547(e) makes it unequivocal that creditors have at least 30 days to perfect security interests before a transfer will be considered a preference. Thus, a creditor will usually have at least 30 days to perfect a security interest, even if a bankruptcy intervenes during the 30-day period.[35]

Section 547(g) allocates the burden of proof in preference actions. The trustee bears the burden of proving the elements of an avoidable preference itemized in Section 547(b). Conversely, the creditor or other defendant has the burden of proof regarding the defenses provided for in Section 547(c).[36] This rule is consistent with the prior observation that the elements of a preference constitute a traditional cause of action or claim peculiar to the bankruptcy system, while the defenses are the

---

33. 11 U.S.C. §547(e)(1)(A).
34. 11 U.S.C. §547(e)(1)(B).
35. 11 U.S.C. §547(e)(2). See chapters 13 and 16 supra.
36. 11 U.S.C. §547(g).

equivalent of affirmative defenses available to defendants in traditional nonbankruptcy litigation.

Section 547(h) exempts from preference liability any payments made to creditors pursuant to a repayment plan created for an individual debtor by a prepetition repayment plan. This provision encourages composition agreements in individual cases. See chapter 2 supra. Section 547(i) creates the equivalent of another affirmative defense in preference actions. This provision provides that when the trustee can avoid a security interest preference because the transfer benefited an insider, the trustee may only recover against the insider to the extent that the transfer took place between 90 days and one year prior to the bankruptcy. For example, DePrizio guarantees the debt of DePrizio, Inc. Six months prior to filing bankruptcy, DePrizio, Inc., gives creditor Crystal a security interest in business assets to secure repayment of an overdue loan. After DePrizio, Inc., files bankruptcy, its trustee may avoid the preference only as to DePrizio, but not as to Crystal.

Summary

A transfer of property or an interest in property to a creditor, on the eve of bankruptcy, in full or partial satisfaction of debt to the exclusion of other creditors, is a preference. A preference meeting the elements of Code Section 547 will be avoidable by a trustee. When a preference is avoided, a trustee will recover the property transferred so that it may be liquidated and the proceeds distributed fairly to all creditors. An avoidable preference is determined by the trustee initiating an adversary proceeding.

A trustee must prove six elements to prove the existence of an avoidable preference. The defendant in the adversary proceeding may be able to show the existence of one or more of several available defenses to defeat the trustee's preference claim. The elements of the claim and the potential defenses are summarized in the checklist below.

KEY TERMS

antecedent debt
consideration
contemporaneous
    transfer for new value
floating lien
insolvent
inventory

new value
preference
receivable
substantially
    contemporaneous
transfer

CHAPTER 17 CHECKLIST

17.1	ELEMENTS OF A PREFERENCE (ALL MUST BE PROVEN)	*Authority*
	17.1.1 Transfer of Property or an Interest in Property	11 U.S.C. §547(b)
	17.1.2 To or for the Benefit of a Creditor	11 U.S.C. §547(b)(1)
	17.1.3 On or for Account of an Antecedent or Preexisting Debt	11 U.S.C. §547(b)(2)
	17.1.4 Made While the Debtor Is Insolvent	11 U.S.C. §547(b)(3)
	(Insolvency Is Presumed Within 90 Days of Filing)	11 U.S.C. §547(f)
	17.1.5 Made	
	1. Within 90 days of filing, or	11 U.S.C. §547(b)(4)(A)
	2. Within one year if the transferee is an insider	11 U.S.C. §547(b)(4)(B)
	17.1.6 That Enables the Creditor to Receive a Greater Chapter 7 Dividend Than It Would Otherwise Receive	11 U.S.C. §547(b)(5)
17.2	PREFERENCE DEFENSES (ONE MUST BE SHOWN)	
	17.2.1 A Contemporaneous Exchange for New Value	11 U.S.C. §547(c)(1)
	17.2.2 A Debt Incurred and Paid in the Ordinary Course of Business	11 U.S.C. §547(c)(2)
	17.2.3 Within Any Nonbankruptcy Perfection Periods or Within 30 Days of Debtor Receiving Possession	11 U.S.C. §547(c)(3)
	17.2.4 Unsecured Debt Incurred for New Value	11 U.S.C. §547(c)(4)
	17.2.5 Floating Liens, Except for Improvement of Position	11 U.S.C. §547(c)(5)
	17.2.6 Unavoidable Statutory Liens	11 U.S.C. §547(c)(6)
	17.2.7 Domestic Support Obligations	11 U.S.C. §547(c)(7)

DISCUSSION QUESTIONS

1. What is the concept underlying avoidable preferences in the bankruptcy system?

2. What are the elements of an avoidable preference?

3. What affirmative defenses exist to defeat an otherwise avoidable preference?

4. What presumption exists to assist a trustee in proving the existence of an avoidable preference?

5. When is a transfer considered complete for purposes of an avoidable preference?

PRACTICE EXERCISE

Exercise 17.1

The trustee has learned that one month prior to the bankruptcy filing, Robin Cash repaid a $3,000 personal loan from her sister, Amanda Banks. Prepare a draft adversary complaint on behalf of the trustee to recover this money from Amanda for the bankruptcy estate.

18

Fraudulent and Postpetition Transfers

Learning Objectives

- Describe fraudulent transfers as they exist in the bankruptcy code

- Describe the avoidability of unauthorized postbankruptcy filing (postpetition) transactions

- List the damages recoverable by a trustee who successfully exercises the avoiding powers

- Explain the bankruptcy code's treatment of a creditor's common law right of setoff

A. FRAUDULENT TRANSFERS

Section 548 permits a trustee to avoid a **fraudulent transfer**. In addition, many states have adopted the Uniform Fraudulent Transfer Act. This Act creates independent rights, under state law, for creditors to attempt to set aside fraudulent transfers.[1] The concept of fraudulent transfers is relatively simple. Generally, fraudulent transfers are transfers made by a debtor with actual intent to hinder, delay, or defraud creditors. A transfer without reasonable or fair consideration may also be a fraudulent transfer. A common example of a fraudulent transfer is when a debtor transfers money or property to a close friend or relative to "hold on to this for me

Fraudulent transfer: a transfer made by a debtor with an intent to hinder, delay, or defraud creditors; a transfer without reasonable or fair consideration made while a debtor is insolvent or that renders a debtor insolvent will also be fraudulent: Fraudulent transfers are the subject of Bankruptcy Code Section 548 and are one of the trustee's avoiding powers

---

1. Uniform Fraudulent Transfer Act, 7A U.L.A. §7 (West Supp. 2012).

until things get a little better." The debtor then files bankruptcy expecting to "reclaim" the asset transferred when the bankruptcy is over. Similarly, when the debtor conveys a quitclaim deed to a close friend or relative for the same reason, it is also a fraudulent transfer. In each instance the critical action is that the debtor has attempted to conceal property from creditors. These sorts of transactions have traditionally been disfavored in the law. The earliest forms of "insolvency" debt collection laws and those prevalent in the Middle Ages involved the avoidance of fraudulent transfers described in chapter 1 supra.

FACT PATTERN

Would Owen's deposit of money into his father's safety deposit box constitute a fraudulent transfer?

There are two basic ways to prove a fraudulent transfer under the Bankruptcy Code. The first is to prove that the transfer was made with an actual intent to hinder, delay, or defraud creditors.[2] Each of the above examples likely satisfies this standard.

A second way to prove a fraudulent transfer is to show that the transfer has been made for less than a reasonably equivalent value in exchange and that the debtor was insolvent either prior to or as a result of the transfer.[3] For instance, if Dr. Smith sells Will Robinson a robot for $10 when the robot has been appraised for $1 million, the transfer is likely to be deemed transferred for less than a reasonably equivalent value in exchange. Similarly, if a debtor transfers a $30,000 boat to the debtor's best friend for $500, this transfer is likely to be deemed for less than a reasonably equivalent value in exchange. However, the "less than reasonably equivalent exchange" standard should not be interpreted necessarily to imply that the consideration should or must be at the fair market value of the asset that is subject to transfer. For example, a liquidation sale may be a "reasonably equivalent exchange."[4]

In BFP v. RTC, 511 U.S. 531 (1994), BFP contended that the price obtained at a regularly conducted foreclosure sale constituted a fraudulent transfer because the property was sold at the foreclosure sale for $433,000, whereas the alleged fair market value of the property was $725,000 at the time of foreclosure. In holding that the price obtained in a noncollusive real estate mortgage foreclosure sale, held in compliance with applicable state law, does not constitute a fraudulent transfer,

---

2. 11 U.S.C. §548(a)(1)(A).
3. 11 U.S.C. §548(a)(1)(B).
4. In re BFP, 974 F.2d 1144 (9th Cir. 1992); *affirmed*, BFP v. RTC 511 U.S. 531 (1994).

Justice Scalia wrote that: ". . . the only legitimate evidence of the property's value at the time it is sold is the foreclosure sale price itself."

   In addition to the transfer being for less than a reasonably equivalent
value in exchange, either the transfer must have been made while the
debtor is insolvent or as a result of the transfer the debtor must have
been rendered insolvent or undercapitalized (without sufficient remaining assets to conduct ordinary business).[5] Thus, a transfer for less than a
reasonably equivalent exchange made while a debtor is solvent or that
does not render the debtor insolvent will not be considered fraudulent on
this basis. A solvent multi-millionaire may transfer assets to charity on a
regular basis without fear of reprisal from creditors. On the other hand, if
the multi-millionaire is rendered insolvent as a result of the charitable
giving, the gift may become an avoidable fraudulent transfer. BAPCPA
modified Section 548(a) to expressly render transfers made to insiders
under employment contracts and not in the ordinary course of business to
be fraudulent transfers where the debtor is insolvent or rendered
insolvent as a result of the transfer, or if the purpose of the transfer is
to hinder, delay, or defraud creditors. A primary purpose of this provision
is to eliminate large bonuses given to corporate executives shortly prior to
the corporations they manage filing for bankruptcy relief.

   Section 548(a)(2) limits the recovery by a trustee of charitable contributions considered fraudulent transfers. A charitable contribution can
be a fraudulent transfer because it is a gift and is therefore made without
consideration. Section 548(a)(2) provides that charitable contributions of
up to 15 percent of a debtor's gross annual income for the year in which
the contribution is made, or whatever is consistent with the debtor's
practices in making the contribution, shall not be avoidable by the trustee.
For example, a debtor earns $40,000 per year. Payment of a church tithe by
the debtor of up to $6,000, 15 percent of the debtor's income, will not be
avoidable as a fraudulent transfer by the debtor's bankruptcy trustee.

Practice Pointer

This safe harbor provision is not applied
on a transfer-by-transfer basis but rather
on the aggregate annual contribution basis.

---

5. 11 U.S.C. §548(a)(1)(B)(ii).

Section 548(b) concerns a special problem relating to partnership debtors. Any transfer of partnership property or an interest therein to a general partner within one year prior to a bankruptcy filing by the partnership is avoidable by a trustee if the transfer is made when the partnership is insolvent or if the partnership has been rendered insolvent as a result of the transfer.[6] The rationale behind this provision is that a general partner is an insider of the partnership. The general partner cannot "take the money and run."

Section 548(c) contains some protection for the transferee, the entity receiving the fraudulent transfer. If the transferee obtained the transferred property for value and in good faith and if the transfer is not avoidable as a preference or other avoiding power, then the transferee is granted a lien on the transfer to the extent of any value given by the transferee.[7] For instance, a purchaser of real estate who has a purchase set aside as a fraudulent transfer obtains a lien upon the property to the extent of the purchase price paid as long as the purchase was in good faith and not avoidable under any other avoiding power of the trustee. Thus, if the transfer is also a preference, Section 548(c) will not apply.

A transfer is deemed complete for the purpose of determining the existence of a fraudulent transfer when the transfer is perfected so that a good-faith purchaser cannot acquire an interest in the property superior to that of the transferee.[8] That is, a transfer is complete when the deed is recorded or the transferee acquires rights to the property that would be superior to those of third parties under nonbankruptcy law.

The major difference between Bankruptcy Code Section 548 and nonbankruptcy fraudulent transfer law is that under nonbankruptcy law the statute of limitations is typically longer than that provided for by Section 548.

Recall that pursuant to Section 546(a) a trustee has only two years from the date of appointment to assert the claim. Further, Section 548 limits bankruptcy fraudulent transfers to those transfers occurring within two years prior to the bankruptcy filing.[9] Nonbankruptcy fraudulent transfer statutes under state law may provide longer time periods both for commencing the action and for determining what transfers are subject to challenge. Recall further that under Section 108 a trustee may have as long as two years added to a nonbankruptcy statute of limitations.[10] Thus, a trustee may seek to avoid as a fraudulent transfer under nonbankruptcy

---

6. 11 U.S.C. §548(b).
7. 11 U.S.C. §548(c).
8. 11 U.S.C. §548(d)(1).
9. 11 U.S.C. §548(a).
10. See chapter 5 supra.

law a transfer that would not necessarily be avoidable under the Bankruptcy Code.

An action to avoid a fraudulent transfer is always initiated by filing an adversary complaint. When initiating such a complaint, it is always a recommended practice to allege the trustee's rights under both the Bankruptcy Code and any applicable nonbankruptcy law for the reasons described in the preceding paragraph.

B.   POSTPETITION TRANSFERS

The trustee's final avoiding power permits the avoidance of certain **postpetition transfers**. Transfers of estate property taking place after the bankruptcy is filed may be avoidable by the trustee. For instance, in an involuntary proceeding, a debtor may transfer property of the estate before an order for relief is entered. Whether or not a subsequently appointed trustee may set aside this transfer is the subject matter of Section 549. Stated another way, a debtor files a bankruptcy and transfers property of the estate to a third party after the filing but before the trustee can acquire custody of the property. Or a Chapter 11 debtor pays prepetition debt postpetition without court approval. Although these various transactions may have been avoidable as fraudulent transfers or preferences had they occurred before the bankruptcy filing, when they occur after a filing they are avoidable as improper postpetition transactions.

A trustee may avoid any postpetition transaction that has not been authorized by the Bankruptcy Court or otherwise permitted by the Bankruptcy Code.[11] Section 549(a) acts to assist the trustee in performing the duty to liquidate the property of the estate. Many sales, uses, or leases of property of an estate require prior court approval.[12] A sale of property of the estate without obtaining prior court approval is avoidable.

> *Upon his return from Cancun, Owen starts selling off collectibles at flea markets. He testifies at his meeting of creditors that he made $5,000 in the first month after filing. What are Owen's trustee's rights?*

Postpetition transfer: a transfer of estate property after a bankruptcy filing that is made without court approval or is not otherwise authorized by the Bankruptcy Code; an unauthorized postpetition transaction may be avoided by a bankruptcy trustee: Postpetition transactions are the subject of Bankruptcy Code Section 549

FACT PATTERN

---

11. 11 U.S.C. §549(a). Postpetition transactions occurring in the normal course of business in a Chapter 11 proceeding will not necessarily require prior court approval. See chapter 19 infra.
12. See chapter 19 infra.

Transactions, for present consideration, that take place during the gap period in an involuntary proceeding are not normally avoidable.[13] This is consistent with Section 303(f), which allows the alleged debtor in an involuntary proceeding to conduct business as usual prior to the entry of an order for relief unless the court orders otherwise.[14]

Under Section 549(c), a trustee cannot avoid a postpetition transfer of real property to a bona fide purchaser unless a copy of the petition has been filed in the place where the transfer of property may be perfected to complete the transaction.[15] This provides notice to all that the property is subject to the jurisdiction of the Bankruptcy Court. As long as the property remains property of the estate, it cannot be sold without court approval. This is similar to the concept of the lis pendens in nonbankruptcy proceedings affecting title to real estate. The effect of the recording is to prevent an unauthorized transfer of the real property.

A complaint to avoid a postpetition transaction may only be commenced within the earlier of two years after the transfer or the time the bankruptcy proceeding is closed or dismissed.[16] An action to avoid a postpetition transaction is always commenced as an adversary proceeding.

C.   LIABILITY OF TRANSFEREES

Section 550 concerns the liability of the transferee of an avoided transfer: what the recipient of the avoidable preference must return or pay to the estate, what the transferee of a fraudulent transfer must return or pay to the estate, or what the transferee of an improper postpetition transaction must return or pay to the estate. This Section also concerns any rights retained by the transferees of avoided transactions.

A trustee may recover from a transferee the property transferred or the value of the property transferred.[17] The recovery may be obtained not only from the actual transferee but from a transferee of the transferee who does not acquire the property in good faith.[18] Thus, in successfully avoiding a fraudulent transfer, the trustee may recover either the real estate or payment for it from the transferee or from a transferee of the transferee who

---

13. 11 U.S.C. §549(b).
14. 11 U.S.C. §303(f). See chapter 4 supra.
15. 11 U.S.C. §549(c).
16. 11 U.S.C. §549(d).
17. 11 U.S.C. §550(a).
18. 11 U.S.C. §550(a)(2), (b).

has knowledge that the transaction is fraudulent. For example, if Jethro Clampett fraudulently transfers real estate to his Granny and she then transfers the property to Miss Hathaway, the trustee can recover the value of the property from Granny or may recover the property from Miss Hathaway if Miss Hathaway had knowledge that the transfer was fraudulent. On the other hand, if Miss Hathaway has acted in good faith, the trustee may not recover from her.

Similarly, if a trustee is avoiding a preference, the recovery is limited to the property transferred or the value of the property. Thus, if a security interest in property of the estate is successfully avoided, invalidating the security interest will be the trustee's recovery. If the successfully avoided preference is a cash payment or other outright transfer of property, the trustee is entitled to a recovery of the property to the extent the transfer exceeds the Chapter 7 dividend that the transferee would otherwise receive. For example, a creditor receiving full payment where the total dividend might be 50 percent should only have to return 50 percent of the property transferred.

Regardless of how many potential entities a trustee may be entitled to recover from in a successful avoidance action (such as a transferee and then a transferee of the transferee), the trustee is only entitled to one satisfaction.[19] Thus, in the first of the above examples, the trustee could recover either the value of the property from Granny or the property itself from Miss Hathaway, but not both.

If a trustee recovers property from a good-faith transferee, then the good-faith transferee is given a right to reimbursement from the estate for any improvements made to the property. Improvements are considered to be physical additions to the property, or repair or maintenance costs expended in preserving the asset, or the cost of servicing any debt existing on the property. This right to reimbursement assumes the status of a lien upon the property.[20] This rule is equitable in nature. An estate should not receive a windfall in recovering property subject to a successful avoidance action. For instance, a debtor makes an unauthorized postpetition transfer of a motor home to a prepetition creditor in repayment of a prepetition debt. The creditor is unaware of the bankruptcy filing at the time of the transfer. While the creditor has possession of the motor home, the creditor makes payments on a loan secured by the motor home, replaces the tires, insures and maintains the vehicle. Then a trustee learns of the transfer and commences an avoiding action. Because the creditor was unaware of the bankruptcy filing and has therefore presumably acted in good faith, the creditor is entitled to reimbursement for the costs of maintaining the

---

19. 11 U.S.C. §550(d).
20. 11 U.S.C. §550(e).

vehicle, the new tires, insurance payments, and any payments made on the underlying loan.

Section 551 preserves for the benefit of the estate any avoided transfer. That is, any right obtained by an estate from the avoidance of a transfer is a right of the estate, not of any other creditor.[21] The practical effect of this Section is that if, for example, a trustee avoids a second priority security interest in an asset, the estate becomes, in essence, the second priority holder of an interest in the asset. Any junior lienholders of the asset do not benefit from the avoidance by improving their position in the property. Their position is unaffected. Stated another way, the estate steps into the shoes of the transferee of an avoided transfer. This is similar to an insurance company's right of subrogation in tort law.

Section 552 concerns the postpetition effect of a security interest. The applicability of this Section will normally arise only in business Chapter 11 proceedings. Recall that the **floating lien** is a common financing arrangement of a retail or manufacturing business;[22] a financing entity has given the debtor a line of credit secured by all of the debtor's existing or after-acquired physical assets. This is why the lien is called a floating lien: because it "floats" upon the proceeds and products acquired by the debtor from the original collateral. If the debtor defaults upon a loan subject to a floating lien, the financing entity may repossess all the assets subject to the lien.

Floating lien: a line of credit from a bank, financial institution, or other lender secured by the existing and after-acquired inventory, equipment, and proceeds of a debtor's business

Under Section 552, any property that a debtor acquires after the filing of a bankruptcy proceeding is not subject to a prepetition lien resulting from a security agreement.[23] That is, after-acquired property is not generally subject to a prepetition consensual lien, except for floating liens. Floating liens do retain their hold on postpetition property, to the extent that the afteracquired property is traceable to the collateral subject to the lien, unless the court orders otherwise. A perfected security interest in the rents and revenues of a hotel, motel, or public facility therein also extends to the postpetition rents and revenues unless the court orders otherwise.[24] For example, Chat 'N Chew Restaurant files Chapter 11 owing its secured creditor bank $100,000. Among the bank's collateral are inventory and the cash generated from sale of the inventory. As long as Chat 'N Chew uses the cash subject to the bank's lien to purchase more inventory, the bank's lien will remain intact subject to Section 552(b). On the other hand, if Chat 'N Chew sequesters the proceeds received from the sale of the inventory and uses other cash to make new purchases, the

---

21. 11 U.S.C. §551.
22. See chapter 17 supra in connection with 11 U.S.C. §547(c)(5).
23. 11 U.S.C. §552(a).
24. 11 U.S.C. §552(b).

bank's lien will not extend to this new inventory not purchased from the bank's cash collateral.[25]

Section 552 should not be construed to imply that a secured creditor loses its rights upon the filing by a debtor of a bankruptcy proceeding. Quite the contrary is true. Remember that a secured creditor is entitled to adequate protection of its security interest, and a secured creditor may seek relief from the automatic stay to enforce its rights as a secured creditor.[26] Other provisions restrict a debtor's right to utilize a secured creditor's cash collateral.[27] Section 552 concerns only the effect of a prepetition security agreement on property acquired by a debtor or the estate after filing, not the validity of the security agreement itself.

D.   SETOFFS

Section 553 concerns the treatment of setoffs under the Bankruptcy Code. A **setoff** is the common law right of a creditor to balance mutual debts with a debtor.[28] In bookkeeping terms setoffs are also known as reconciliations. To determine a setoff, simply subtract the smaller debt from the larger. Any balance remaining due either of the parties is still owed, but the remainder of the mutual debts has been set off. For example, Harold owes Kumar $10 and Kumar owes Harold $5. To set off these debts, the debt owed from Kumar to Harold is deemed satisfied ($5) and Harold now owes Kumar $5 instead of $10.

Setoff: the common law right of a creditor to balance mutual debts with a debtor

Section 553 permits the setoff of mutual prepetition debts.[29] Court approval is theoretically required because the automatic stay applies to the making of setoffs.[30] A creditor may not use a disallowed claim to make a setoff.[31] A creditor may not utilize as a setoff a claim assigned to it by another entity within 90 days of the bankruptcy filing.[32] Nor may a creditor utilize, for purposes of setoff, a debt owed to the debtor and incurred within 90 days prior to filing for the purpose of obtaining a setoff right.[33] As is the case with preferences, the debtor is presumed insolvent 90 days

---

25. As to a secured creditor's rights in cash collateral, see chapter 19 infra.
26. See chapter 13 supra.
27. See chapter 19 infra.
28. See chapter 12 supra.
29. 11 U.S.C. §553(a).
30. 11 U.S.C. §362(a)(7). See chapter 13 supra.
31. 11 U.S.C. §553(a)(1). See chapter 22 infra.
32. 11 U.S.C. §553(a)(2).
33. 11 U.S.C. §553(a)(3).

prior to the bankruptcy filing.[34] These provisions effectively preclude the obtaining of a preference by setoff.

Section 553(b) is a repetition of the improvement of position test described previously in connection with avoidable preferences.[35] Essentially, the trustee may recover from a creditor who has made a setoff within 90 days prior to the bankruptcy filing the amount of the setoff to the extent that the setoff constitutes an improvement of the creditor's position in relation to other creditors. Or, more plainly, the trustee may avoid a setoff to the extent that it constitutes an avoidable preference. In this context, the setoff is the equivalent of a transfer. To the extent the transfer creates a preference, the setoff is avoidable. Simply consider a creditor's ability to make a setoff as identical to having a security interest in one of the debtor's assets, namely the debt owed to the debtor by the creditor. In this context, the same formula described in chapter 16 supra can be applied with no actual change: $(d_1 - si_1) > (d_2 - si_2)$, where d is the debt due the creditor by the debtor and si is the debt due by the creditor to the debtor. The numerals 1 and 2 pertain respectively to the dates 90 days prior to the bankruptcy filing (1) and the filing date (2). To the extent that the sum on date 2 is less than the sum on date 1, the creditor cannot make the setoff. This difference is the extent of the "improved position." As a practical matter, most creditors do not bring relief from stay motions to obtain permission to make setoffs. Most debtors and trustees do not seek sanctions against creditors for doing so. Setoff issues will most commonly arise by way of noticed motions. The issue may arise in connection with relief from stay motions or in the context of claims objections, to name but two instances.

Summary

A transfer made by a debtor with intent to hinder, delay, or defraud creditors is a fraudulent transfer. A transfer without fair or reasonable consideration made while a debtor is insolvent or that renders a debtor insolvent is also fraudulent. Transfers to corporate executives not in the ordinary course of business, such as the payment of large bonuses on the eve of bankruptcy, may also be avoidable as a fraudulent transfer.

Section 548 of the Bankruptcy Code permits a trustee to avoid fraudulent transfers occurring within two years prior to the bankruptcy filing. Nonbankruptcy or state law may also permit creditors to avoid fraudulent transfers. A trustee may also be able to utilize the state law of fraudulent transfers. This may permit a trustee to avoid fraudulent transfers occurring

---

34. 11 U.S.C. §553(c).
35. See chapter 17 supra.

more than two years before the bankruptcy filing. An action to avoid a fraudulent transfer is commenced by filing an adversary proceeding.

A transfer of estate property after a bankruptcy filing that is made without court approval or is not otherwise authorized by the Bankruptcy Code is an unauthorized postpetition transaction that may be avoided by the trustee. Actions to avoid postpetition transactions are initiated by filing an adversary proceeding. Avoidable postpetition transactions are the subject of Bankruptcy Code Section 549.

Section 550 determines the liability of a transferee of an avoided transfer. Conversely, Section 550 also defines the recovery that each party may receive. Generally, the trustee is entitled to either a recovery of the property or the value of the property. A good-faith transferee will be allowed a claim for reimbursement from the estate for any improvements or repairs made to the asset or maintenance costs expended in preserving the asset. This claim will assume the status of a lien upon the property.

Section 551 provides a right of subrogation to a trustee successfully avoiding an avoidable transfer. That is, the trustee takes the place of the former transferee. This preserves the status of the transferred assets in relation to the rights of all other creditors.

Section 552 defines the postpetition effect of a security interest. Normally, a prepetition lien will not attach to property acquired by an estate after filing except for floating liens.

Section 553 retains for creditors the common law right of a creditor to set off mutual debts with a debtor. However, in certain defined circumstances, a setoff will be avoidable to the extent that it constitutes the equivalent of a preference. Properly, the making of a setoff by a creditor requires obtaining relief from the automatic stay. Setoff issues will normally arise within the context of a motion.

KEY TERMS

floating lien   postpetition transfer
fraudulent transfer   setoff

DISCUSSION QUESTIONS

1. What is a fraudulent transfer?

2. How is applicable state law concerning fraudulent transfers useful to a trustee seeking to set aside a fraudulent transfer?

3. What is an improper postpetition transfer?

4. What may a trustee recover in the successful exercise of an avoiding power?

5. What is a setoff?

PRACTICE EXERCISE

Exercise 18.1
Prepare a draft adversary complaint on behalf of the trustee to recover the Civil War relics from Owen's father.

PART IV

Liquidation and Claims

19

Use, Sale, or Lease of Property

Learning Objectives

- Identify the common methodologies of the liquidation process: private sales and public auctions

- Define the concept of cash collateral and the limits upon its use

- Introduce the sale "free and clear of liens"

- Describe the special rules concerning the sale of joint tenancy or tenancy in common property

A.   LIQUIDATING ESTATE ASSETS

The next five chapters describe the basic concepts regarding the liquidation and distribution of estate assets or, in the case of reorganization proceedings, the preservation of assets for the benefit of creditors. The process of liquidation, allowance and classification of claims, and ultimate distribution of dividends to creditors is the core of the Code's debt collection features.

The first aspect of this process concerns the use, sale, or lease of property of the estate. Related to this subject are the issues of an estate incurring credit or exercising or terminating the benefits or burdens of a lease or franchise type agreement.[1] Preservation of an estate's cash after its

---

[1]. 11 U.S.C. §364; 11 U.S.C. §365. See chapters 20 and 21 infra.

physical assets have been liquidated and how property may be abandoned by a trustee complete the liquidation provisions of the Code.[2] Collectively, these matters comprise the methods by which the property of an estate is liquidated and cash preserved for the payment of dividends to creditors through the bankruptcy system.

Section 363 concerns the use, sale, or lease of estate property. The liquidation of any asset in a bankruptcy estate is subject to this section.

B.   GENERAL RULES

The basic rule is that a trustee may use, sell, or lease property of the estate, other than in the ordinary course of business, only after notice and a hearing.[3] This means that in a Chapter 7 liquidation, *any* use, sale, or lease of estate property will require notice and a hearing because a liquidation is *not* conducted in the ordinary course of business. On the other hand, in a Chapter 11, 12, or 13 proceeding, only transactions *not* in the ordinary course of business will require prior court approval.[4] Recall that the phrase "notice and a hearing" is specifically defined in Section 102.[5] Bankruptcy Rule 6004 sets forth the procedure used to obtain court approval for a sale of estate property. The rule requires at least 21 days' prior notice of the sale and notice of a hearing date if a party objects. Only if a party objects to the sale within five days of any deadline set forth in the notice does the matter then receive treatment as a noticed motion.[6] The rule is structured in this way so that a sale or auction can go forward with certainty in most cases. In actual practice, objections to sales are rare except in the largest cases. A sale may take place by private sale or public auction. A private sale is a sale to a single buyer at an agreed-upon price. A public auction may be conducted by either a professional auctioneer or in open court where, essentially, a private sale is held subject to overbid in a court-supervised bidding procedure.[7]

---

2. See chapter 21 infra.
3. 11 U.S.C. §363(b)(1). When the asset for sale is a customer list with private data, the trustee must comply with the privacy policy of the seller. The court will order the United States Trustee to appoint an ombudsman pursuant to 11 U.S.C. §332. The ombudsman's purpose is to ensure that the privacy policy is followed. See chapter 11 supra.
4. 11 U.S.C. §363(c)(1). See infra this chapter.
5. 11 U.S.C. §102(1). See chapter 5 supra.
6. Bankruptcy Rule 6004(a). A sale of property with a value of $2,500 or less requires objection within 14 days of notice, or the sale may proceed. Bankruptcy Rule 6004(d).
7. Bankruptcy Rule 6004(f)(1).

The phrase **ordinary course of business** generally means normal, everyday business transactions. If a trustee is authorized to conduct the business of the debtor or if the debtor is a debtor-in-possession, ordinary course, everyday business transactions do not require prior court approval. Transactions that are not part of the ordinary course of the debtor's financial affairs do require prior court approval. A practical test is to determine if the assets to be sold are capital or not. A sale involving capital assets must always have prior court approval before proceeding. If the transaction does not involve the sale of a capital asset, prior court approval will probably not be required. A **capital asset** is one that is used to operate the business, such as equipment or fixtures. A **noncapital asset** is, for example, the inventory of an operating business.

If Owen filed bankruptcy for his company, The Lawn Cuttery, which assets would be capital assets and which would be noncapital assets?

For instance, Rick Blaine's Belle Aurora Restaurant, Inc. is a debtor-in-possession. It is not necessary for Rick to get a court order every time the restaurant needs supplies or inventory so the restaurant can operate. It is also unnecessary to get a court order before serving a meal to a customer. (It is doubtful that customers would be patient enough to wait for such an order.) However, if Rick wants to sell the restaurant, court approval will be required; a sale of the restaurant is not in the ordinary course of the restaurant's business.

Conducting normal business operations in a Chapter 11 does not require prior court approval. In a Chapter 7, however, because the business is being liquidated, nothing that a trustee does is in the ordinary course of business. Any sale of assets that a Chapter 7 trustee undertakes requires prior notice to creditors.

Section 721 gives a Chapter 7 trustee the opportunity to operate a business for a limited time with court approval.[8] When such approval is obtained, the Chapter 7 trustee will be able to conduct normal business operations of the debtor for the order's duration.[9] A Chapter 7 trustee may seek such approval when it is in the best interests of creditors. For instance, if the debtor's primary asset is a bakery, keeping the facility open to sell all produced inventory at full value may be a good idea. If a sale of the business is pending when the Chapter 7 is filed, the buyer may want the business to continue operations prior to court approval of the

Ordinary course of business: generally, normal everyday business transactions

Capital asset: an asset used to operate a business, such as equipment or fixtures

FACT PATTERN

Noncapital asset: an asset not used to operate a business, e.g., inventory is generally a noncapital asset

---

8. 11 U.S.C. §721.
9. 11 U.S.C. §363(c)(1).

sale. In these instances, the best interest of creditors will involve a prudent business judgment by the trustee — namely, taking the course of action that will provide the maximum value to the estate.

Since Owen was actively involved in selling items online, can the trustee step in his shoes and sell some of Owen's "collection" online without court approval as a normal operation? Could it be done with court approval?

Normally, a Chapter 7 trustee will hold a public auction of an estate's assets. A trustee may seek ex parte approval to liquidate estate assets where the liquidation must be conducted immediately if the assets are to retain any value. For example, if the estate's primary asset is a restaurant and there is unused inventory, the trustee might obtain an ex parte order to sell the inventory without delay because a 21-day notice will only result in stale eggs, lettuce, tomatoes, and milk that are not likely to fetch a worthwhile price.

Practice Pointer

In the individual debtor context, common Section 363(b) sales include the sale or auction of personalty, the sale of automobiles, and even the sale of the debtor's personal residence.

Section 363(c)(1) is the converse of Section 363(b)(1). If the debtor is authorized to operate a business, ordinary business operations may be conducted without prior court approval.[10] The difference between the two sections is that Section 363(b)(1) requires a trustee to give notice if property is being used, sold, or leased other than in the ordinary course of business, while Section 363(c)(1) affirmatively states that a trustee or debtor-in-possession does not need to obtain prior court approval to conduct ordinary business transactions of the estate. Section 363(c)(1) makes explicit what Section 363(b)(1) only implies.

The forms materials contain a number of sample forms used in conducting bankruptcy sales. Generally, any notice should contain enough description so a creditor or party in interest can determine whether to

---

10. 11 U.S.C. §363(c)(1).

oppose the sale. Identification of the asset or assets being sold, the buyer, and the purchase price should be adequate in a private sale. The treatment to be afforded any claim secured by the property being sold should be disclosed. In the case of a public auction or sale subject to overbid in court, the notice should additionally disclose the location of the auction or sale and any requirements to qualify as a bidder. In the larger cases typical of the Southern District of New York or the District of Delaware, a debtor-in-possession will often file a motion to obtain approval of the procedures that will be used to conduct a sale. These motions are commonly referred to as bidding procedure motions.

C.   USE OF CASH COLLATERAL

Section 363(c)(2) restricts a trustee's use of a secured creditor's **cash collateral**. *Cash collateral* is defined, for purposes of this provision, as cash or cash equivalents in which an entity other than the estate may have an interest. Cash collateral also includes hotel or motel revenues.[11] For example, a secured creditor with a security interest in accounts receivable, the proceeds of sales, or a floating lien as described in chapter 17 supra, has a security interest in cash collateral. Cash collateral issues generally do not arise in a consumer bankruptcy case.

> **Cash collateral:** cash, or its equivalent, in which a secured creditor may have an interest: Section 363(c) of the Bankruptcy Code restricts the use of cash collateral absent court approval

Section 363(c)(2) prohibits a debtor from using a creditor's cash collateral unless one of two conditions can be satisfied. The first condition that permits a debtor to use cash collateral is the secured creditor's consent.[12] This is the easiest way to proceed. If consent is not obtained, prior court approval is required by filing a motion.[13] To obtain court approval, a debtor or trustee will be required to provide adequate protection to any affected secured creditor.[14] In practice, this typically involves negotiations between the debtor and creditor that result in an agreed-upon cash collateral order.

Obtaining the use of cash collateral is a critical issue in the early stages of a Chapter 11 proceeding. If a secured creditor does not consent to the debtor's use of the cash collateral, it can become impossible to conduct business operations because a debtor is selling products and the secured creditor is receiving the proceeds, but the day-to-day expenses have no

---

11. 11 U.S.C. §363(a).
12. 11 U.S.C. §363(c)(2)(A).
13. 11 U.S.C. §363(c)(2)(B). Bankruptcy Rule 4001(b).
14. 11 U.S.C. §363(c)(3); 11 U.S.C. §363(e). See chapter 13 for a discussion of adequate protection.

source of repayment. It becomes difficult to meet payroll and other basic expenses in this situation. As a result, the Code directs the court to give calendar priority to a motion to use cash collateral. The motion is to be scheduled "in accordance with the needs of the debtor" and the court is to act promptly on any request to use cash collateral.[15]

It is improper to use a secured creditor's cash collateral without the secured creditor's consent or prior court order. A secured creditor whose cash collateral is used without consent will obtain a first priority administrative claim upon the assets of the estate up to the amount of any improperly used cash collateral.[16] In Chapter 11 cases involving large corporations such as U.S. Air or Borders Books, consensual cash collateral orders generally containing these priority protections are typically approved by the court as a *first-day order*.

A motion to use cash collateral bears many similarities to a motion for relief from the automatic stay. Adequate protection for a creditor in these circumstances may require more than a monthly cash payment. A debtor may have to show the court that a creditor's equity in the collateral will not be impaired. This may very well require additional or replacement collateral. The court may also be required to make a preliminary determination as to the debtor's prospects of achieving a successful reorganization. Like a motion for relief from the automatic stay, there may also be both a preliminary and final hearing in connection with a motion to use cash collateral.[17]

A debtor-in-possession or trustee is required to keep cash collateral sequestered in a separate identified bank account.[18] This means that a debtor cannot commingle a creditor's cash collateral with other estate funds that are not cash collateral, unless the use of such funds has been permitted. Presumably, the segregation requirement acts as a further form of adequate protection to a secured creditor.

D.   EFFECT OF THE AUTOMATIC STAY

Subsection 363(d) concerns the interaction between Section 363 and Section 362, the automatic stay. If the court has entered any order modifying or relieving the stay, then any sale, use, or lease of estate property

---

15. 11 U.S.C. §363(c)(3); Bankruptcy Rule 4001(b).
16. 11 U.S.C. §507(b).
17. 11 U.S.C. §363(c)(3).
18. 11 U.S.C. §363(c)(4).

has to be consistent with any order modifying or granting relief from the stay that has already been entered.[19] This means, in practical terms, that if the court grants a creditor relief from the automatic stay to foreclose upon estate property, any sale by the trustee must occur before the foreclosure sale unless the court orders otherwise. The property must also be sold in accordance with applicable nonbankruptcy law. For example, if there is a local law requirement that there be title insurance, then the requirement must be followed.

E.   SALES FREE AND CLEAR OF LIENS

While the above provisions pay careful heed to the rights of secured creditors, Section 363(f) acts to protect an estate's rights to sell estate property over the objection of a recalcitrant or hostile secured creditor. For example, Rick Carver obtains a second deed of trust or mortgage on Lynn Nash's home as security for a loan. Lynn defaults and then files a Chapter 7 proceeding to prevent the foreclosure sale.[20] Lynn's trustee, Dennis Spors, obtains a buyer for the property that will pay all secured claims in full, Lynn's homestead, and a dividend to unsecured creditors. Rick plans to object because if he can foreclose and resell, he will receive a big profit for himself instead of Lynn and her other creditors. Rick would prefer to obtain relief from the automatic stay and foreclose. Preventing this tactic by a secured creditor is one function of Section 363(f). Section 363(f) is a frequently litigated provision of Section 363. It allows a trustee to sell property free and clear of liens or interests.[21] The essence of this provision is that the bankruptcy court may order a sale of property over the objection and free of the interest of a recalcitrant or hostile secured creditor. Use of this procedure will be effective to pass clear title to the property over the objection of any lienholders. Use of this provision requires a noticed motion. A motion to sell property free and clear of liens must be brought as a noticed motion, not by way of the abbreviated notice procedures discussed earlier in this chapter.[22]

A property may be sold free and clear of liens or interests if one of five described conditions is satisfied as to each lienholder. Each condition is exclusive. Only one condition need be found applicable to each lien for

---

19. 11 U.S.C. §363(d).
20. See chapter 13 supra.
21. 11 U.S.C. §363(f).
22. Bankruptcy Rule 6004(c). See also chapter 5 supra.

the section to be effective, although compliance with more than one condition will often be possible.

First, the sale may occur if nonbankruptcy law will permit a sale of the property free and clear of the interests or liens.[23] For instance, a property may be sold free and clear of a trust deed or mortgage interest but not sold free and clear of a public utility easement or a government lien for real property taxes. Although nonbankruptcy law will permit a sale free of the interest in the first instance, nonbankruptcy law will not generally permit a sale free of the interest in the latter two instances.

Second, if an affected creditor consents to the sale, the property may be sold free of the consenting creditor's interest.[24] If an affected creditor agrees to allow an act that it might otherwise prohibit or object to, the Bankruptcy Code will normally recognize such consent. This is simply common sense. Undisputed secured creditors who are going to be paid in full from the sale's proceeds will normally consent. Conversely, seriously undersecured creditors who may receive only a partial or no payment from the sale will often consent or not object to the proposed sale, as a practical matter.

Third, if the property is being sold for an amount greater than the value of all liens owed upon it, then the sale will be permitted.[25] For example, if a house is worth $100,000 while the bank is owed $50,000 and the Whiplash Finance Company another $15,000, a sale for $100,000 will be for more than the two creditors are owed and the sale will be permitted to take place over the objection of either creditor. Because the two creditors will receive what they are entitled to — namely, payment in full of their claims — they will not be permitted to prevent the sale. It is this specific provision that most frequently prevents a recalcitrant or hostile lien creditor from wrongfully preventing liquidation of estate property. The creditor is paid its claim from the sale proceeds. In the event of a dispute, the lien will attach to the proceeds, and their distribution will occur only upon further court order. Permitting the lien to attach to the proceeds is a form of adequate protection for the affected lienholder.[26]

Fourth, the sale will be permitted if the interest is in bona fide dispute.[27] This is unrelated to the issue of whether the property is being sold for more than the amount of the liens upon it. In this instance, the sale price might even be for less than the amount of the liens upon the property. For example, property encumbered by $65,000 of liens is being sold

---

23. 11 U.S.C. §363(f)(1).
24. 11 U.S.C. §363(f)(2).
25. 11 U.S.C. §363(f)(3).
26. See legislative history to 11 U.S.C. §363(f)(3).
27. 11 U.S.C. §363(f)(4).

for $60,000. However, the trustee asserts that one lien is a preference, and the court believes that this assertion may be meritorious. Because the creditor's interest is in bona fide dispute, the sale may be permitted to take place free of the creditor's disputed interest. This provision permits a sale free of the alleged interest of a creditor who may be ultimately found to have no interest in the property. Normally, however, the court will allow the interest to attach to any available proceeds and require the funds to be sequestered pending resolution of the dispute. The creditor is entitled to this protection.

Finally, the entity, usually the secured creditor, could be compelled to accept money rather than an interest in the property.[28] That is, if the lien-holder could be ordered to receive payment in a nonbankruptcy legal proceeding in exchange for a release of the lien, the sale may be permitted.

If Lester files Chapter 7 still owning the home, his trustee could sell the home and sequester the proceeds until any disputes with the mortgage holders are resolved. Any alleged lien would attach to the proceeds in their order of priority.

FACT PATTERN

As noted above, if at least one of the above five circumstances exists as to each lien or interest, a property may be sold free and clear of the liens or interests. Often, especially when dealing with a piece of property that may have multiple lien or interest holders upon it (such as three trust deeds or mortgages), one or more of the conditions will have to be satisfied to allow the sale to proceed. For example, a tax lien for real property taxes will require full payment (Section 363(f)(1)). A secured creditor may consent to the sale (Section 363(f)(2)). A junior disputed lien may not be paid in full (Section 363(f)(4)). In this latter instance, the lien may attach to the proceeds of sale. Many situations will arise in which compliance with multiple provisions of Section 363(f) will be necessary to permit a sale of property free and clear of all liens and interests.

F. OTHER PROPERTY INTERESTS

Section 363(g) permits a trustee to sell property of an estate free and clear of any right of dower or curtesy. This provision applies only in those states where dower and curtesy exist. Hence, this provision has no applicability

---

28. 11 U.S.C. §363(f)(5).

in a community property jurisdiction. Sections 363(i) and (j) act to protect the rights of a co-owner with a dower or curtesy right by either permitting the interest holder to match the sale price of the property or requiring the trustee to pay to the interest holder any share of the proceeds to which the interest holder may be entitled.[29]

In a community property jurisdiction, a nondebtor community property interest holder in estate property may match the purchase bid of a proposed sale and thus preserve the property for the nondebtor. However, a nondebtor community property interest holder is not entitled to a separate distribution of the sale proceeds when a sale does occur. This is because all community property of a debtor constitutes property of the estate and all community debt is discharged to the extent of the community property.[30]

Section 363(h) concerns the sale of property that is subject to joint ownership interests such as joint tenancy, tenancy in common, or tenancy by the entirety. For example, a husband and wife own a home in joint tenancy. One spouse files bankruptcy and the other does not. The couple is also involved in a divorce. A property settlement agreement has been entered into, which provides that each spouse retains a joint tenancy interest in the home while one spouse retains rights to reside in the home until the children reach the age of 18. When the children reach 18, the home will be sold and the spouses will realize the value of their respective interests. The spouse not residing in the home then files a bankruptcy proceeding. The trustee determines that there is equity in the home to pay unsecured creditors a dividend and the trustee decides to sell the house. The spouse residing in the house opposes the sale. Section 363(h) allows the trustee to sell the property over the objection of the nondebtor joint or co-tenant only if four conditions can be complied with. Bankruptcy Rule 7001(3) requires the filing of an adversary proceeding to obtain approval of a sale subject to Section 363(h). In this instance, the motion procedures will be inappropriate.

The first condition that the trustee must show is that it would not be practicable to partition the property.[31] For example, it is not likely that a single family residence can be legally partitioned, such as splitting the lot in two and giving half to the filing spouse and half to the nonfiling spouse.

Second, the trustee must show that a sale of only the estate's interest in the property will realize significantly less for the estate than a sale of the whole.[32] For instance, it is not likely that someone would want to

---

29. 11 U.S.C. §363(g), (i), (j).
30. 11 U.S.C. §363(i); 11 U.S.C. §541(a)(2); 11 U.S.C. §524(a)(3). See also chapters 8 and 15 supra.
31. 11 U.S.C. §363(h)(1).
32. 11 U.S.C. §363(h)(2).

purchase a half-interest in a home as a tenant in common or joint tenant with an unknown third party, particularly when the buyer might not be able to reside in the premises. A sale of the whole property is therefore likely to generate more proceeds than a sale of the debtor's interest alone.

Third, the trustee must show that the benefit to the estate of a sale of the property outweighs any detriment to the co-owners.[33] Generally, this comparison is based solely on economic factors. If the sale will provide an economic benefit to an estate's creditors and the co-owner is paid the value of the co-owner's interest in the property, there will usually be no detriment found to the nondebtor co-owner. Frankly, in the case of a nondebtor spouse with a right of occupancy, a check for the net equity in the property may have substantially less ultimate monetary value than the right to live in the premises for a fixed period of time, not to mention the potential adverse effects on a family's quality of life from being dispossessed from one residence to another.

If Owen and Robin owned real property and only one of them files bankruptcy, the trustee of the bankrupt spouse would make use of this provision if the property is sold.

FACT PATTERN

Fourth, the trustee must show that the property is not used in the production, transmission, distribution, or sale of electric energy, natural or synthetic gas, or light and power.[34] If the trustee demonstrates all four of the above conditions, the court may approve a sale of the property including the interest of the nondebtor co-owner. The nondebtor has a right to match the proposed purchase price and thus purchase the estate's interest in the asset.[35] If the property is sold, the trustee must distribute the net proceeds to the estate and co-owners according to their respective interests.[36] That is, the nonfiling spouse will receive payment of his or her interest in the property. For example, if a sale generates $30,000 in net proceeds to two equal co-owners, the estate will receive $15,000 for distribution to the creditors and the nondebtor co-owner will receive the remaining $15,000.

Thus, the best remedy for a nonfiling spouse who lives in a property and wants to continue to live there is to find a way to purchase the bankrupt spouse's interest in the property and pay the trustee pursuant to 11 U.S.C. §363(i). This right exists in both community property and noncommunity property jurisdictions. Although this may not be a feasible approach in some cases, it is usually the path of least resistance.

---

33. 11 U.S.C. §363(h)(3).
34. 11 U.S.C. §363(h)(4).
35. 11 U.S.C. §363(i).
36. 11 U.S.C. §363(j).

G.   MISCELLANEOUS PROVISIONS

A secured creditor, like a co-owner, may bid on a sale of the property subject to the secured claim and, if the successful bidder, may offset against the bid price the amount of the secured claim.[37] This right is commonly known as a **credit bid**. In Radlax Gateway Hotel, LLC v. Amalgamated Bank, 132 S. Ct. 2065 (2012), a Chapter 11 debtor proposed a plan to sell its property but deprive the bank of its right to bid the amount of the lien to purchase the property. The Supreme Court held that the debtor could not propose a sale process which deprived the bank of its credit bid right.

Credit bid: the right of a secured creditor to use the debt to bid on the purchase of property

Section 363(l) concerns ipso facto clauses.[38] Recall that a bankruptcy **ipso facto clause** is a clause in a contract or deed or other document that makes insolvency, financial condition, or a bankruptcy filing an act of default. Such clauses are generally disfavored by the Bankruptcy Code and are unenforceable.

Ipso facto clause: a clause in a contract defining insolvency or a bankruptcy filing as an act of default: These clauses generally are not enforceable in bankruptcy proceedings

Section 363(n) prevents collusive bidding in a bankruptcy sale.[39] For example, a group of potential bidders at a bankruptcy auction conspire together beforehand by agreeing to not bid against one another for certain assets. Each conspirator is thus assured of purchasing certain assets at a predetermined price. If the trustee discovers that this sort of activity has occurred, the trustee may avoid the sale and recover either the property or the difference between the actual price and the fair value price of the assets, including costs and attorneys' fees. Section 363(o) protects consumers to the extent that the sale of commercial paper in consumer credit transactions retains all of the protections provided for by consumer law, such as the Federal Truth in Lending Act (15 U.S.C. §1601 et seq.).

It is difficult to successfully appeal a Bankruptcy Court order approving a sale, lease, or use of property under Section 363. The primary reason for this is that unless the transaction is stayed pending appeal, the reversal or modification upon appeal will not affect the validity of the sale to a good-faith purchaser. Knowledge of the appeal's existence will not deprive the purchaser of good faith.[40] In short, unless the sale is stayed pending appeal, any appeal will likely be moot once the transaction closes. This is a strict and arbitrary provision. It exists to protect estates from frivolous appeals designed solely to delay or frustrate the effective administration of the bankruptcy system.

---

37. 11 U.S.C. §363(k).
38. 11 U.S.C. §363(l). See chapter 15 supra.
39. 11 U.S.C. §363(n).
40. 11 U.S.C. §363(m).

Federal Rule of Bankruptcy Procedure 6003(b) prohibits the sale of estate assets during the first 20 days of a case except to the extent necessary to avoid immediate and irreparable harm. For example, the sale of the perishable assets of a store would likely satisfy this standard. In any hearing under Section 363, the trustee has the burden of proof on any issue of adequate protection. A party asserting an interest in estate property bears the burden of proof on any issue regarding the validity, priority, or extent of the interest in the property.[41]

Summary

Section 363 of the Bankruptcy Code is the basic Code provision regulating the liquidation of estate assets by the use, sale, or lease of estate property. This section, along with the material in chapters 20 through 23 infra, comprises the core of the Code's debt-collection features.

Many sales, leases, or uses of estate property will require prior Bankruptcy Court approval. Some will not. The checklist categorizes the general types of activities that will require prior court approval and those that will not. When prior court approval is necessary, notice and a hearing will also be required. Bankruptcy Rule 6004 requires prior notice of a sale. If an objection is filed, the matter is then treated as a noticed motion.

A sale requiring court approval may take place by way of either a private sale or public auction. A private sale is a sale to a specific buyer identified in advance (such as a buyer of real estate). A public auction is a sale to the highest bidder bidding at the auction. Sometimes a private sale will be subject to overbid in open court. This is a form of auction.

Where an estate's cash is part of a secured creditor's lien, the cash collateral may not be used by the estate unless the creditor consents or the court approves use of the cash collateral. A creditor with cash collateral rights is entitled to adequate protection to permit use of the cash collateral by the estate. The Code requires the Bankruptcy Court to give expedited treatment to a motion for the use of cash collateral.

Any use, sale, or lease of estate property must be consistent with any existing orders relieving or modifying the automatic stay pursuant to 11 U.S.C. §363(d).

Section 363(f) permits property of an estate to be sold free and clear of liens or interests. This provision permits the court to approve a sale over the objection or recalcitrance of lienholders. The provision contains five conditions, at least one of which must be found applicable to each lien or

---

41. 11 U.S.C. §363(p).

interest holder for the sale to be approved. The checklist summarizes these conditions.

Sections 363(g) and (i) account for the marital property interests of dower, curtesy, and community property.

Section 363(h) permits a sale of property subject to co-ownership by a nondebtor only if four conditions can be shown. The three most relevant conditions are that a partition of the property is impracticable, that a sale of only the estate's interest would realize significantly less than a sale of the whole, and that any benefit to the estate outweighs any detriment to the co-owner.

KEY TERMS

capital asset	**noncapital asset**
cash collateral	**ordinary course of**
credit bid	**business**
ipso facto clause	

CHAPTER 19 CHECKLIST

19.1	SALES REQUIRING PRIOR COURT APPROVAL	*Authority*
	19.1.1 Prior Court Approval Required	11 U.S.C. §363(b)(1)
	1. All Chapter 7 sales, except as in 19.1.2 ¶2	11 U.S.C. §363(b)(1)
	2. Sales not in the ordinary course of business	11 U.S.C. §363(b)(1)
	19.1.2 Court Approval Not Required	
	1. Chapter 9, 11, 12, or 13 sales in the ordinary course of business	11 U.S.C. §363(b)(1), (c)(1)
	2. Chapter 7 sales in the ordinary course of business when a Chapter 7 trustee is authorized to operate	11 U.S.C. §363(c)(1)
19.2	SALES FREE AND CLEAR OF LIENS— CONDITIONS	
	19.2.1 Nonbankruptcy Law Permits	11 U.S.C. §363(f)(1)
	19.2.2 Lienholders Consent	11 U.S.C. §363(f)(2)
	19.2.3 All Liens Will Be Paid in Full	11 U.S.C. §363(f)(3)

		Authority
19.2.4	Lien Is in Good-Faith Dispute	11 U.S.C. §363(f)(4)
19.2.5	Lienholder Could Be Legally Compelled to Accept Money Satisfaction	11 U.S.C. §363(f)(5)

DISCUSSION QUESTIONS

1. Describe the common methods by which a bankruptcy trustee liquidates an estate's assets. When does a sale of estate property require court approval?

2. What is cash collateral? What actions must a trustee take to be authorized to use cash collateral?

3. How can property be sold over the objection of a lienholder?

4. Under what conditions may a trustee sell a nondebtor's interest in property owned as a co-tenant or joint tenant with the debtor?

5. Why is it necessary to protect private information in the sale of customer lists?

PRACTICE EXERCISE

Exercise 19.1
Prepare a motion to sell the real property that would comply with applicable procedures in your local bankruptcy court.

20

Executory Contracts and Leases

Learning Objectives

- Define the term "executory contract" as a specialized form of asset

- Define the term "adequate assurance"

- Describe the procedure that is taken by a party seeking to assume or reject an executory contract or unexpired lease

- List the deadlines contained in the Code to assume an executory contract or unexpired lease

- Describe the conditions when assumption of an executory contract or unexpired lease may not be assumed

A.   EXECUTORY CONTRACTS

Executory contracts are contracts for which performance remains due to some extent by both parties.[1] This is the most widely accepted definition. For example, an unexpired lease is an executory contract. The landlord has a continuing obligation to provide the premises to the tenant while the tenant has a continuing obligation to pay rent to the landlord and

Executory contract: contracts for which performance remains due to some extent on both sides: Franchise or license agreements are common executory contracts

---

1. See Historical and Revision Notes to 11 U.S.C. §365. This is also known as the "Countryman" definition in honor of Professor Vernon Countryman, who described it in two articles titled Executory Contracts in Bankruptcy, 57 Minn. L. Rev. 439 (1973); 58 Minn. L. Rev. 479 (1974).

abide by the remaining lease provisions. Performance remains due to some extent on both sides.

Many business activities take place through executory contracts. These contracts can at times constitute the most important asset of a bankruptcy estate. A franchise agreement to operate a business is usually an executory contract. **License** agreements to operate a business or to market a product line are executory contracts. Thus, a golf shop's license to use a specific name, such as "MacDuffer," in exchange for royalty payments, is an executory contract. The entity issuing the license, the **licensor** (the owner of the name "MacDuffer"), has a continuing obligation to allow the license holder to use the name and sell products with the "MacDuffer" name. The holder of the license, the **licensee**, has a continuing obligation to provide accountings to the licensor and to pay regular royalties, called license fees, to the licensor. Substantial performance remains due on both sides, and hence the transaction is an executory contract. Without the license, the golf shop's value or ability to succeed may be seriously or fatally impaired. A Burger King restaurant franchise is an executory contract. Certainly the value of the franchise is lower if the franchisee loses the right to operate the hamburger stand as a Burger King restaurant.[2] An uncompleted contract to manufacture products or to construct a building is an executory contract.

In each of the above instances, if a trustee or debtor-in-possession is the holder of the franchise or the manufacturer of the product, the value of the franchise or value of the contract may be critical to the ability of the debtor to successfully reorganize or to provide creditors with a dividend in the event of a Chapter 7 proceeding. In this situation, the executory contract is a benefit. Assigning the executory contract to a third party or retaining the contract and continuing to perform according to its terms is a right a debtor or trustee may seek to preserve. On the other hand, if the contract is burdensome and is itself a major cause of the bankruptcy filing, the debtor or trustee may desire to abandon or reject the contract.[3]

Conversely, in each of the above instances, the nondebtor party to the contract is a creditor. This should be obvious in instances where the debtor owes payments to the nondebtor party when the bankruptcy is filed, but this is also true where payments may be current when the bankruptcy is filed but where future performance remains due. If monies are due or performance is not forthcoming, the creditor may seek to preserve its right to collect payment or terminate the contract. Yet recall that the automatic stay prevents collection or termination of the contract

License: an agreement to operate a business or market a product

Licensor: entity issuing a license

Licensee: entity to whom a license is issued; the holder of the license

---

2. In re Rovine Corp., 6 Bankr. 661 (W.D. Tenn. 1980).
3. As to abandonment, see chapter 20 infra.

unless there is no equity in the property or the property is not necessary to an effective reorganization (not likely where the nondebtor claims are not secured by collateral).

Section 365 of the Bankruptcy Code addresses executory contracts and unexpired leases. Were it not for this provision, executory contracts and unexpired leases would be treated in a manner identical to all other property of the estate and be subject to the same rules. The reason for this special treatment is that an executory contract or unexpired lease is a specialized interest in property, which often may be sold, used, or leased. Under the executory contract or lease, the parties may have rights or interests to protect that are different from or something more than a simple right to receive payment or performance. Section 365 was created to account for the special conditions existing between the parties to an executory contract or unexpired lease.

Section 365 attempts to reconcile the competing desires of a debtor or creditor to retain or terminate an executory contract. In its essence, Section 365 treats a nondebtor party to an executory contract as the functional equivalent of a secured creditor with the contract rights constituting the creditor's security for the debtor's performance of the contract. Because the court must approve a decision to assume or reject the contract when called upon to do so, the matter also bears similarities to a motion for relief from the automatic stay.

Owen's lease with Pathway Equipment Company is subject to Section 365.

FACT PATTERN

One of two actions may be taken with respect to an executory contract in a bankruptcy: a trustee or debtor-in-possession may assume or reject an executory contract or unexpired lease. In individual Chapter 7 cases, the debtor may assume a lease of personal property if it is not assumed by the trustee.[4] This is accomplished either by way of a noticed motion procedure to assume or reject the contract or by operation of the various time periods contained in Section 365.[5] The remainder of Section 365 describes the conditions and time periods under which an executory contract or unexpired lease may be assumed or rejected.

---

4. 11 U.S.C. §365(a), (p). The phrase *executory contract* will also mean *unexpired lease* for the duration of this chapter except where otherwise stated.
5. Bankruptcy Rule 6006. See chapter 5 supra and part C of this chapter infra.

B.   ASSUMING A CONTRACT

Adequate assurance: providing the equivalent of *adequate protection* to the non-debtor party of an executory contract subject to Bankruptcy Code Section 365

A trustee must meet three conditions to assume an executory contract. Section 365(b) requires that every condition be complied with to permit assumption. The first condition requires the trustee to cure or provide **adequate assurance** that any existing default will be promptly cured. Nonmonetary defaults that are impossible for a trustee to cure need not be cured at the time of assumption.[6] As a practical matter, the term *adequate assurance* has essentially the same meaning as adequate protection.[7] Thus, either six months of past-due rent must be paid, an agreement must be made with the landlord to cure the arrearage over a period of time, or the trustee must prove to the court that the default can be cured within a prompt period of time. A trustee or debtor-in-possession who wants the benefits of an executory contract must also accept the burdens and perform under the contract.[8]

Second, the trustee must provide compensation or adequate assurance that the nondebtor party will be compensated for any actual damages arising from any default. This compensation may include attorneys' fees and any costs incurred.[9]

Third, and perhaps most important, a trustee or debtor-in-possession must provide adequate assurance of future performance under the contract.[10] This may be as simple as the court's reviewing a future financial projection and concluding that the trustee will likely be able to pay the rent on time or as complex as a debtor-in-possession's being required to convince the court and the creditor that the debtor-in-possession has sufficient financial and physical resources to provide adequate assurance that performance will be rendered and the contract completed. In the case of a sale, this will generally mean that the buyer has the financial ability to perform the contract.

All of these conditions are consistent with the discussion in chapter 13 supra about adequate protection in connection with the automatic stay. Recall that adequate protection requires making payments or providing additional or replacement collateral. Curing a default and providing assurances of future performance under the term "adequate assurances" are virtually identical.[11] Further, although Section 365(b) is phrased so as to apply only to defaulted executory contracts, the Bankruptcy Courts

---

6. 11 U.S.C. §365(b)(1)(A).
7. 11 U.S.C. §361. See chapter 13 supra.
8. 11 U.S.C. §365(b)(1).
9. 11 U.S.C. §365(b)(1)(B).
10. 11 U.S.C. §365(b)(1)(C).
11. See chapter 12 supra.

generally require compliance with Section 365(b)(1) by a trustee or debtor-in-possession in any motion to assume an executory contract.[12]

Section 365(p) of the Bankruptcy Code permits an individual Chapter 7 debtor to assume a personal property lease if the trustee does not do so. In this event, the creditor may condition the assumption on cure of any outstanding default set by the contract. Further, a creditor contacting an individual debtor to assume a personal property lease will not violate the automatic stay. Unless the trustee assumes the lease or the debtor seeks to reaffirm the lease (see chapter 22 infra), rejection of the lease terminates the automatic stay as to the leased property. This means that the creditor may then seek repossession of its property without having to formally seek relief from the stay pursuant to the procedures described in chapter 13 supra.

A default created by an alleged *ipso facto clause* is not enforceable by the nondebtor party. Any clause in a contract placing a debtor in default solely because a bankruptcy proceeding has been filed or because the debtor may be insolvent is not enforceable. A debtor is not required to provide adequate assurances that it will not be bankrupt. Additionally, penalty rates imposed by virtue of nonmonetary defaults cannot be enforced by the nondebtor party.[13]

Subsection 365(b)(3) concerns shopping center leases and the meaning of adequate assurance of performance of a shopping center lease. A unique concern in shopping center leases is provisions regarding the tenant mix and the necessary fact that a shopping center contains multiple leases often with interrelated provisions. In these instances, adequate assurance of future performance will mean that the lease will be used for its intended purpose only and will not violate any other lease agreement concerning the shopping center.[14] A lease provision limiting a premise's use to a boutique or a provision barring other boutique tenants are examples of tenant mix provisions.

Finally, where a lease requires a lessor to provide services or amenities to a debtor, the lessor may refuse to provide the services or amenities prior to assumption unless the trustee can pay for the services.[15]

Section 365(c) further limits a trustee's ability to assume an executory contract, even if adequate assurance can be provided and a cure of any defaults cured. First, if nonbankruptcy law excuses a party from accepting performance from an assignee of the trustee, then nonbankruptcy law will be honored unless the nondebtor party to the contract consents to the assignment.[16] That is, if a nonbankruptcy statute permits a party to a

---

12. See also 11 U.S.C. §365(f)(2).
13. 11 U.S.C. §365(b)(2). See discussion of ipso facto clauses generally in chapter 15 supra.
14. 11 U.S.C. §365(b)(3).
15. 11 U.S.C. §365(b)(4).
16. 11 U.S.C. §365(c)(1).

contract to prohibit assignment of an executory contract, then this statute will be honored. For example, federal law generally prohibits the assignment of a government contract unless the federal government consents. This is known as the **Anti-Assignment Act**.[17] If a trustee proposes to assume and assign a government contract to a third party, the Anti-Assignment Act will be given effect and the executory contract may not be assigned unless the federal government consents. On the other hand, an anti-assignment clause in a contract may not be an effective bar to a Section 365 assignment because the contract clause is not a statute.

Anti-Assignment Act: a federal statute, 41 U.S.C. §15, that prohibits the assignment of a federal government contract except upon the government's consent

If a nonresidential lease of real property has been terminated prior to the entry of an order for relief, the lease may not be assumed.[18] This is a rational rule because in this event there is nothing for a trustee to assume. The lease has expired.

As a practical matter, from the debtor's perspective, if there is a risk that an executory contract will be terminated prior to a bankruptcy filing, the filing should take place beforehand. The automatic stay will prevent the contract's termination. This rule of thumb applies to all executory contracts. In most situations, if a nondebtor party properly terminates an executory contract prior to commencement of the bankruptcy proceeding, then there is no executory contract in existence to assume. Whether or not the contract exists to assume can sometimes mean the difference between a successful or unsuccessful result for the estate and its creditors.

If an executory contract is to make a loan or other financial commitment, then the contract may not be assumed. A debtor or trustee cannot force a lender to perform a loan commitment if the borrower files a bankruptcy.[19] This does not imply that a bankruptcy estate may not obtain credit. The question of an estate obtaining credit is governed solely by Section 364, not Section 365.[20] Thus, a debtor with a prepetition loan commitment will have to proceed by Section 364 if postpetition approval of the loan is sought. This is described in chapter 20 infra.

C.   TIME LIMITS FOR ASSUMPTION

Section 365(d) provides the time limits within which executory contracts may or must be assumed. Different rules will apply depending on the type

---

17. 41 U.S.C. §15.
18. 11 U.S.C. §365(c)(3).
19. 11 U.S.C. §365(c)(2).
20. See chapter 21 infra.

of Chapter proceeding involved and whether the subject matter of assumption is a lease of real or personal property or of other executory contracts. Real property is further distinguished by its characterization as residential or nonresidential real property. A lease of **residential** real property most commonly exists when the debtor resides in the premises subject to the lease. A lease is **nonresidential** in virtually all other situations. This chapter's checklist summarizes the time limits.

In a Chapter 7 proceeding, if a trustee does not affirmatively act to assume or reject an executory contract or lease of real or personal property within 60 days after the order for relief is entered, then the contract or lease is deemed rejected. No court action is required to effectuate the rejection.[21] Stated another way, a Chapter 7 trustee has 60 days to assume or reject an executory contract or unexpired lease of real property or personal property. If the trustee takes no action within the 60-day period, then the contract or lease is deemed to be automatically rejected and terminated. The burden is therefore on the Chapter 7 trustee to obtain a court order if assumption is desired. A trustee who has a buyer will proceed by Section 365 to assume and assign the contract. In Chapter 11 proceedings, a motion to assume and assign executory contracts will almost always be combined with a motion to sell the assets of business as discussed in chapter 18.

> **Residential real property:** real property in which a debtor resides: A real property lease is a lease in which the debtor resides in the premises
>
> **Nonresidential lease:** any real property lease that is not a *residential* lease: A store rental is a common nonresidential real property lease

Practice Pointer

Generally, the debtor or the trustee may not assume a personal service contract, a contract to loan money, or a nonresidential lease that terminated prepetition.

As a practical matter, in consumer Chapter 7 proceedings, trustees do not usually act to assume residential real property leases, nor do debtors proceed to obtain court approval to assume them. Also, as a practical matter, lessors do not proceed to court on day 61 seeking to evict the debtor tenant. A lessor is generally satisfied if a tenant is continuing to pay rent. On the other hand, if the rent is in default upon the entry of an order for relief, the automatic stay may bar an eviction of the tenant debtor from the premises in some circumstances (see chapter 13 supra). A lessor may move before the court for rejection of the lease or relief from the stay to terminate the lease. Alternatively, if the lessor waits until the sixty-first day

---

21. 11 U.S.C. §365(d)(1); §365(d)(4).

after the entry of an order for relief, the lease will be deemed rejected and the lessor may be able to obtain a writ of possession directly from the Bankruptcy Court.

In an individual Chapter 7 case, if a trustee does not assume a lease of personal property, the debtor may assume the lease by notifying the creditor and curing the lease pursuant to the terms of the contract as set forth in Section 365(p), discussed above. This may or may not mean that an individual debtor may assume the lease more than 60 days after a filing, because the provision also provides that the automatic stay is automatically terminated if the lease is not assumed. Since Section 362(h) (see chapter 13 supra) relieves the stay with respect to personal property leases if the lease is not assumed within the "Statement of Intention" period (see chapter 22 infra), this may mean that a debtor must effectively act to assume a lease of personal property within the first 30 days of the case irrespective of the Section 365 time limits. Compliance with the Statement of Intention procedure should act to satisfy this provision.

In proceedings other than a Chapter 7, such as a Chapter 11 reorganization, a trustee or debtor-in-possession may assume or reject an executory contract or lease of personal property or an unexpired residential lease at any time prior to court confirmation of a plan proposed under the particular Chapter.[22] Thus, a franchise does not terminate 60 days after filing if a debtor-in-possession does not assume the franchise prior to this date. Conversely, because there is no definite time limit to assume an executory contract in a non-Chapter 7 proceeding, any party may bring the matter before the court and request that a date certain be set for the debtor to assume or reject the contract.

A motion to assume or reject may or may not be combined with a motion for relief from the automatic stay. The latter is not necessary in this instance. In the case of a personal property lease, a motion may take the form of a motion for relief from stay, as opposed to a motion to assume or reject.

FACT PATTERN

If Owen were to file a Chapter 11 for The Lawn Cuttery, he could bring a motion to cure the lease defaults and assume the lease with Pathway Equipment Company. Pathway could bring a motion for relief from the stay or a motion to compel assumption or rejection of the equipment lease.

In the case of a real estate lease, a lessor will bring a motion to assume or reject the lease before the court, so that any defaults can be ordered

---

22. 11 U.S.C. §365(d)(2). However, in Chapter 13, personal property lease payments must be paid current during pendency of the case. 11 U.S.C. §1326(a)(1). See chapter 24 infra.

promptly cured or the lease rejected without undue delay. A nonresidential real estate lessor may take this approach when the lessor desires to act promptly after the lessee's bankruptcy filing rather than wait 120 days (see infra this chapter). Any motion will also ask the court to order appropriate adequate protection in the form of adequate assurances of future performance.

Recall that a lessor of residential real property may continue prosecution of an unlawful detainer or eviction proceeding as an exception to the automatic stay if the debtor does not pay postpetition rent on a timely basis, if the lease has already been terminated pursuant to the lease or State law, or if the debtor has filed a bankruptcy petition within the past year and failed to pay postpetition rent. See chapter 13 supra. The effect of all these provisions is to minimize the effect of bankruptcy upon landlords of residential real estate.

In the case of other forms of executory contracts, such as a manufacturing contract, a trustee or debtor-in-possession may want to bring a motion to assume the contract if the nondebtor party refuses to perform after the debtor's bankruptcy filing. This will force the nondebtor to abide by the contract's terms. A nondebtor party may wish to bring a motion to have the contract rejected if there are prepetition defaults that require cure before the contract's performance can be completed.

If a trustee or debtor-in-possession does choose to assume an executory contract, the contract's terms must be abided by, although the court may defer performance for up to 60 days.[23] A trustee or debtor-in-possession must accept the burdens as well as the benefits in assuming an executory contract.[24]

In any Chapter proceeding, a lease of nonresidential real property must be assumed within 120 days after an order for relief is entered or the lease will be deemed rejected. A nonresidential lease that is rejected requires the trustee or debtor-in-possession to surrender the premises to the lessor and thus, conversely, entitles the lessor to obtain immediate court approval for an eviction order. The court may extend this 120-day period only upon a motion of the lessor or trustee for cause and only for 90 days, unless the lessor consents to further extensions.[25] This 120-day time limit is strictly enforced by most Bankruptcy Courts.

The 120-day rule is of critical importance where the debtor is a party to a nonresidential real property lease. If the debtor is a restaurant or retail store, a failure to properly act to assume the lease in a timely manner can result in the debtor's liquidation. When the debtor is a chain of retail

---

23. 11 U.S.C. §365(d)(3).
24. 11 U.S.C. §365(f)(2).
25. 11 U.S.C. §365(d)(4).

stores, there can be hundreds of leases to assume or reject. The liquidation of large national retailers like Borders Books and Radio Shack are good examples.

D.   MISCELLANEOUS PROVISIONS

Section 365(e) concerns *ipso facto* clauses where a trustee wants to assume an executory contract that is not otherwise in default at the time of assumption. Ipso facto clauses are unenforceable. However, if nonbankruptcy law permits termination upon bankruptcy or insolvency unless the nondebtor party consents, such nonbankruptcy law will be honored. Further, a contract to extend credit may not be enforceable postpetition. The rationale for this is the same as described in connection with Section 365(c) supra.[26]

Often when a trustee or debtor-in-possession wants to assume an executory contract, it is for the primary purpose of assigning the contract to a third party. For example, the debtor who owns the Burger King franchise desires to sell it. Section 365(f) concerns the issues that arise in the effort to assign the contract.

Section 365(f) generally permits the assignment of an executory contract.[27] However, the assignment will only be permitted if any defaults are cured, and only if the nondebtor party is provided with adequate assurance of future performance.[28] In other words, a contract must be assumed in order to be assigned. The general policy of the Bankruptcy Code is to permit the assignment of executory contracts.[29]

If an executory contract is rejected, a determination must be made as to the type of claim against the estate the nondebtor party will have. The claim can become either a prepetition unsecured claim or an administrative claim. The status of the claim will have a dramatic effect upon the distributive priority accorded to it.[30] Generally, the rejection of an executory contract is considered a breach of the contract.[31] Where a contract is rejected without ever having been assumed, rejection is considered to have occurred immediately prior to the bankruptcy filing.[32] This means

---

26. 11 U.S.C. §365(e).
27. 11 U.S.C. §365(f)(1).
28. 11 U.S.C. §365(f)(2).
29. See Historical and Revision Notes to Section 365(f).
30. See chapter 22 infra.
31. 11 U.S.C. §365(g); 11 U.S.C. §365(h)(1).
32. 11 U.S.C. §365(g)(1).

that the nondebtor party will normally obtain the status of a prepetition unsecured creditor.

Practice Pointer

In the case of rejection, the nondebtor party may have rejection damages under state law. The damages for rejection of real property leases are limited under Section 502(b)(6). See chapter 22 infra.

On the other hand, if a trustee does assume an executory contract but then later rejects it, or if the executory contract is assumed and the proceeding is then converted to a Chapter 7, the breach is considered to have occurred at the time of rejection or, if the proceeding has been converted, immediately prior to conversion.[33] Thus, the assumption of an executory contract will have the practical effect of making any subsequent claim of the nondebtor party an administrative claim. Administrative claims have a higher distributive priority than general unsecured claims.[34]

Section 365(h)(2) concerns the rights of a nondebtor lessee where the trustee or debtor-in-possession is the lessor or seller of timeshare interests and rejects, rather than assumes, the executory contract.[35] The lessee or timeshare purchaser may elect either to treat the contract as terminated or to remain in possession for the term of the lease or timeshare interest.[36] In the former situation, the nondebtor's rights are limited to a claim for damages, which will likely be a general unsecured claim. In the latter instance, the nondebtor's claim is limited to a setoff against the lease or timeshare price to the extent of any actual damages sustained as a result of the trustee's rejection of the contract.[37]

E.   REAL ESTATE CONTRACTS

A contract for a sale of real estate that is pending when a bankruptcy proceeding commences is an executory contract. Because the seller still

---

33. 11 U.S.C. §365(g)(2).
34. See chapter 22 infra.
35. The timeshare provision was added to the Code in 1984.
36. 11 U.S.C. §365(h)(1).
37. 11 U.S.C. §365(h)(2).

has an obligation to convey title to the property and the purchaser still has an obligation to pay the price, performance remains due to some extent on both sides. Sections 365(i) and (j) concern the issues raised by this scenario. If a trustee rejects an executory contract in which the debtor is the seller, the purchaser's rights will vary depending upon whether the buyer is in possession of the real property. If the purchaser is not in possession, the purchaser is unaffected by Section 365(i) and its rights will be determined elsewhere in the Code. If the purchaser is in possession, the purchaser may elect to treat the contract as terminated or may remain in possession of the property. If the purchaser remains in possession of the property, the purchaser may complete the purchase and force the debtor or trustee to convey title. The purchase price may be offset by the amount of the purchaser's damages but the purchaser acquires no further claim.[38] To summarize, a purchaser in possession may elect either to terminate the transaction or to enforce the contract.

If the purchaser of real estate in a rejected sale of real estate treats the contract as terminated, the purchaser acquires a lien on the debtor's interest in the property to recover any part of the purchase price paid prior to rejection. A purchaser not in possession of real estate that is the subject of a rejected executory contract has a similar lien right.[39] This lien right will make the rejected purchaser the equivalent of a secured creditor.

The assignment of an executory contract under Section 365 relieves the trustee and estate of any liability arising after the assignment.[40]

F.   INTELLECTUAL PROPERTY

Intellectual property: patents, copyrights, and trademarks.

The provisions of Section 365(n) give special treatment to executory contracts involving **intellectual property**. Patents, copyrights, and trademarks are common forms of intellectual property. Prior to enactment of these provisions, an executory contract involving intellectual property was governed by the rules described above.

The most common form of intellectual property contract is known as a license. The owner of the patent or copyright is known as the licensor. The manufacturer or publisher is known as the licensee.

If a trustee rejects an intellectual property executory contract and the debtor is the licensor, the licensee has an option to either retain its rights

---

38. 11 U.S.C. §365(i).
39. 11 U.S.C. §365(j).
40. 11 U.S.C. §365(k).

and keep the contract in effect, or to terminate the contract. If the licensee keeps the contract in effect, performance proceeds. The only effect of the bankruptcy is that the trustee is directed to cooperate with the licensee.[41] Of course, to the extent that royalties are not exempt, they will normally constitute property of the estate.

Summary

Executory contracts are contracts for which performance remains due to some extent on both sides. Franchise or license agreements are common executory contracts. Real estate leases, whether of residential or nonresidential property, are specialized types of executory contracts. The effect of bankruptcy upon executory contracts and unexpired leases is the subject of Bankruptcy Code Section 365.

An executory contract may either be assumed or rejected by a bankruptcy estate. In an individual Chapter 7, if the trustee does not assume a lease of personal property, the debtor may do so. At some point in time in any bankruptcy proceeding, all executory contracts will have to be assumed or rejected. In many situations, assumption will have to occur within a fixed time period, normally 60 days after the bankruptcy filing, or the contract will be deemed rejected. The checklist accompanying this chapter describes the time limits involved in the assumption of executory contracts. Assumption of an executory contract will always require a court order or be contained within the provisions of a confirmed reorganization plan.

When an estate wants to assume an executory contract, the estate must promptly cure any existing monetary defaults, compensate the non-debtor party for any actual damages, and provide adequate assurance of future performance. This latter requirement is very similar to the concept of adequate protection that has been previously discussed in connection with automatic stay and cash collateral issues in chapters 12 and 18 supra.

A trustee may not assume or assign an executory contract if a non-bankruptcy statute prohibits assignment absent the consent of the non-debtor party to the contract. Executory contracts to extend credit or make loans to a debtor may not be assumed or assigned. These transactions are more properly characterized as loans to the estate. These transactions are described in chapter 20 infra.

The effect given to a rejected executory contract differs depending upon whether the contract has been previously assumed. Claims arising from a contract rejected by operation of the time limits set forth in the

---

41. 11 U.S.C. §365(n).

Code or that are never assumed are treated as prepetition unsecured claims. When an executory contract is assumed, however, claims arising from it will thereafter receive treatment as an administrative expense and be entitled to a higher distributive priority in the event of liquidation. That is, an executory contract assumed in a Chapter 11 proceeding is treated as an administrative claim of the Chapter 11 in the event the proceeding is converted to a Chapter 7.

Section 365 contains several other features pertaining to specific types of contracts. Contracts for timeshare ownership are given special treatment in Section 365(h). Sections 365(i) and (j) regard contracts for the sale of real estate. Generally, a nondebtor buyer in possession will have greater rights to force assumption of the contract than a nondebtor buyer not in possession. Section 365(n), added to the Code in 1988, clarifies the effect of bankruptcy upon an executory contract involving intellectual property, such as patents or copyrights.

KEY TERMS

adequate assurance
Anti-Assignment Act
executory contracts
intellectual property
license

licensee
licensor
nonresidential
residential

CHAPTER 20 CHECKLIST

20.1 TIME LIMITS FOR ASSUMPTION OR REJECTION OF EXECUTORY CONTRACTS OR UNEXPIRED LEASES

	Chapter	Nonresidential Leases	Executory Contracts/ Residential Leases	Statute
20.1.1	7	120 days	60 days	11 U.S.C. §365(d)(1), (4)
20.1.2	9	120 days	before confirmation or prior court order after motion	11 U.S.C. §365(d)(2), (4)

20.1.3	11	120 days	before confirmation or prior court order after motion	11 U.S.C. §365(d)(2), (4)
20.1.4	12	120 days	before confirmation or prior court order after motion	11 U.S.C. §365(d)(2), (4)
20.1.5	13	120 days	before confirmation or prior court order after motion	11 U.S.C. §365(d)(2), (4)

DISCUSSION QUESTIONS

1. What is an executory contract? Can the following be executory contracts: license agreement? royalty contract? franchise agreement? unexpired lease? pending contract for the sale of real estate? installment loan contract? employment agreement?

2. What is adequate assurance of performance?

3. What must a trustee or debtor-in-possession do to assume an unexpired lease or executory contract?

4. What are the time limits within which an executory contract must or may be assumed in a Chapter 7 or 13 proceeding? Residential lease?

5. What is the difference between assumption and assignment?

6. What is the effect of assumption or rejection of an executory contract or lease upon any claims of the nondebtor party to the contract?

7. What are the rights of a purchaser of an executory contract for the purchase of real estate?

21

Miscellaneous Provisions Regarding Property of the Estate

Learning Objectives

- List the restrictions placed upon a trustee's use of an estate's cash assets

- Describe the disposition of burdensome or valueless property through the abandonment procedure

- Describe when and how a bankruptcy estate obtains a loan

A. PRESERVATION OF CASH

The ultimate asset that a trustee will administer in any estate is cash. This is implicit in the trustee's primary duty to liquidate the assets of an estate and distribute dividends to creditors and shareholders.[1] Cash in the possession of a Chapter 11 debtor-in-possession is an estate asset. Section 345 regulates the preservation and use of cash assets in bankruptcy estates.

Section 345 illustrates the major difference between a bankruptcy and a nonbankruptcy trustee. Under nonbankruptcy law, nonbankruptcy trustees are generally permitted to invest trust funds in any prudent business manner. For example, a nonbankruptcy trustee may invest trust funds in

---

1. See chapter 11 supra.

making secured loans (secured by adequate collateral), stocks, bonds, or other investments designed to yield the greatest return at a minimum of risk. In fact, a nonbankruptcy trustee who invests trust funds only in savings accounts could possibly be held in violation of the trustee's duties to prudently maximize returns on the assets.

On the other hand, a bankruptcy trustee is not given broad discretion to invest estate assets. A bankruptcy trustee is quite restricted in the uses that may be made of an estate's cash. One fear is that because the bankruptcy system is designed to protect the assets of an estate for its creditors, no risks should be taken to cause further losses to the pool of money collected for ultimate distribution to creditors. Further, giving bankruptcy trustees the discretion to invest estate funds would likely result in substantial litigation by debtors and creditors alike, constantly challenging a trustee's business judgment. Under these circumstances, no reasonable person would want to serve as a bankruptcy trustee. Thus, rather than creating a complex set of rules about what might or might not be a prudent investment of estate funds and permitting second guessing or Monday morning quarterbacking, the Bankruptcy Code limits a bankruptcy trustee's use of funds to deposits in a federally insured bank or savings and loan institution unless the court orders otherwise.[2]

A trustee may do one of two things with estate funds. They may be placed on deposit in an interest bearing account or they may be placed into insured certificates of deposit.[3]

In addition to being limited to investing estate funds as described, a trustee must also keep the money in approved depositories. An approved Bankruptcy Court depository is a federally insured bank or savings and loan that is willing to guarantee payment of estate funds in excess of $250,000 on deposit.[4] At all federally insured banks or savings and loan institutions, individual accounts are normally guaranteed only up to $250,000. This means that if the institution is itself declared insolvent, the insurance will only pay up to $250,000 per account. As a result, a financial institution wanting to act as a depository for bankruptcy funds must guarantee payment of deposits in excess of $250,000 per account.[5] This is a great irony of the Bankruptcy Code.

Local bankruptcy rules will often further amplify the above rules and relate them to the amount of the trustee's bond, as discussed in chapter 11

---

2. 11 U.S.C. §345(a).
3. 11 U.S.C. §345(a). See also the Historical and Revision Notes to Section 345(a). The notes imply that government bonds may also be appropriate investments. However, as a practical matter, the administration of most bankruptcy estates can be completed in substantially less time than the longevity rates of most government bonds. This makes them impractical as useful investments by a bankruptcy trustee.
4. 11 U.S.C. §345(b).
5. 11 U.S.C. §345(b).

of this text. Many Bankruptcy Courts or United States Trustees will maintain lists of approved depositories for bankruptcy funds in a given area. An approved depository is one that has posted at the requisite guaranty of funds on deposit of more than $250,000.[6]

Many financial institutions are willing to comply with these provisions of the Bankruptcy Code or Rules. A major reason is that the funds are likely to be on deposit with the bank for a significantly longer time than ordinary nonbankruptcy accounts. The financial institution will thereby have use of the funds for exceptional periods of time at relatively low rates of interest. As a result, the handling of bankruptcy deposits is profitable for many financial institutions, despite the above rules.

B. UTILITY SERVICE/DISCRIMINATION

Section 366 concerns the rights of public utility companies to discontinue or to provide service to debtors or bankruptcy estates. This provision eliminates a practice that existed under the former Bankruptcy Act. Under the Bankruptcy Act, if a debtor listed a public utility company as a creditor, the public utility could promptly cut off the debtor's service. To restore service, the utility would charge the debtor an excessive deposit, the practical effect of which was to make utility debts nondischargeable. Section 366 was enacted into the Code to give a debtor protection from discrimination by a public utility.[7] Generally, a public utility may not refuse or discontinue service because a debtor initiates a bankruptcy proceeding and lists the utility as a creditor.

The public utility may, however, request a reasonable deposit or security from the debtor or trustee to serve as adequate assurance of future performance. This phrase generally means the same as "adequate protection" in other than Chapter 11 cases. If the deposit is not made, then the utility can discontinue service. The method of determining the reasonableness of the deposit may vary from district to district. This is an area where local custom and practice should be ascertained. If either a debtor, a trustee, or a debtor-in-possession believes that the deposit request is unreasonable, the Bankruptcy Court has the authority to rule on the question of the reasonableness of the request. In Chapter 11 cases, "adequate assurance" means a cash deposit or other similar security. In larger Chapter 11 cases, a typical first-day order may limit the deposit to one

---

6. 11 U.S.C. §345(b).
7. 11 U.S.C. §366(a).

month's service or a fraction thereof, while giving the utility the opportunity to object or request more. In reviewing the reasonableness of a security deposit request the court may not consider the lack of security prepetition or the fact that the debtor may be current to a particular utility. Additionally, as an exception to the rule that setoffs are subject to the automatic stay (see chapter 13 supra), a utility company of a Chapter 11 debtor may set off a prepetition security deposit against a prepetition debt without a court order.[8]

FACT PATTERN

Does this mean that the Cashes' various utilities companies may be compelled to turn services back on if they file for bankruptcy?

Similar to Section 366, Section 525 prevents governmental and private discrimination against debtors under the Bankruptcy Code. In addition, a government entity or business that makes government-insured or guaranteed student loans may not deny such a loan to a person who is or has been a debtor in a bankruptcy case.[9]

In FCC v. Nextwave Personal Communications, Inc., 537 U.S. 293 (2003), the Supreme Court examined Section 525(a), which prevents governmental discrimination or action against an entity that files bankruptcy owing dischargeable debts to the government. In this case, Nextwave owned a number of valuable licenses that had been issued by the FCC. When Nextwave sought Chapter 11 relief, it owed the government substantial unpaid obligations for the purchase of the licenses. When Nextwave attempted to treat the licenses as estate property, the FCC asserted that the licenses had been revoked due to the defaulted payments. The Supreme Court affirmed the ruling of the Court of Appeals, finding that by revoking the licenses for nonpayment, the FCC had violated Section 525(a): "We think that Congress meant what it said: The government is not to revoke a bankruptcy debtor's license solely because of a failure to pay his debts."

C.   ABANDONMENT

Sometimes an asset subject to administration is of no value or is burdensome to an estate. The asset may be an unfavorable executory contract, a

---

8. 11 U.S.C. §366(b)(c).
9. 11 U.S.C. §525.

worthless piece of equipment, or a parcel of real property with no equity. Section 554 allows a trustee to **abandon** property of the estate that is burdensome or of inconsequential value. A creditor or party in interest may move the court to compel the trustee to abandon an asset.[10] Federal Rule of Bankruptcy Procedure 6007 requires notice of the trustee's intention and contains the technical procedure for the formal abandonment of an asset. If the notice is opposed, the matter is treated as a noticed motion.[11] Local rules may add further details. An abandonment procedure is initiated by way of the notice procedures described in chapter 6 supra. Form 21.1 on the Forms Disk is a sample report of abandonment.

Abandon: to remove from property of an estate assets that are burdensome or of inconsequential value to the estate

Practice Pointer

Abandonment simply returns the asset to its prepetition status and removes it from the bankruptcy process and the protection of the automatic stay.

The term *burdensome* generally means that the trustee cannot afford to maintain the property. The term *inconsequential value to the estate* generally means either that the property has no equity or the property has no realizable value for the creditors.

The question of what will be burdensome will vary from case to case. Burdensome may mean that a trustee will incur substantial expenses to maintain the property and has no source of money to accomplish the task. A common example is a parcel of real property with no equity. It is a waste of estate assets to incur maintenance expenses on such property. The asset will therefore be abandoned so the trustee can avoid the expense.

Practice Pointer

If the debtor's house has no equity above the mortgages on the property and the debtor's exemption, the trustee will often abandon it.

---

10. 11 U.S.C. §554(a), (b).
11. 11 U.S.C. §554(c), (d); Bankruptcy Rule 5009. See chapter 23 infra.

Another common example of burdensome property is the uncollected accounts receivable of a business. On paper, the amount of uncollected accounts receivable may be substantial, but after investigation, the trustee may determine that the costs of collection will exceed any likely recovery. The trustee can then abandon the assets. Perhaps a debtor lists a tort claim as an asset in the Schedules and the trustee determines, after investigation, that the claim is meritless. The trustee abandons the claim because it is burdensome or of no value to the estate. Because all property of the estate must be administered, the trustee must make this decision of whether or not to abandon certain property.

A secured creditor may sometimes be able to make use of abandonment as a potentially less expensive alternative to a motion for relief from stay since any party in interest may seek an abandonment order.[12] Recall that the automatic stay is terminated as to certain acts against property when a debtor has been discharged and the property is no longer property of the estate.[13] Thus, when a debtor is discharged, if a secured creditor obtains an abandonment of its collateral by the trustee, the automatic stay is then relieved without further action since the property is no longer property of the estate.

However, a trustee may not necessarily abandon an asset as burdensome simply because the asset is subject to an environmental cleanup order of a governmental unit. In this instance, the Supreme Court has placed the public policy of environmental concerns above that of the Bankruptcy Code.[14]

D.   OBTAINING CREDIT

Section 364 of the Bankruptcy Code concerns the subject of an estate obtaining credit during a bankruptcy proceeding. This is not as ludicrous as it may appear at first glance. To the uninitiated, the question is certain to arise as to why a debtor would want to obtain credit in a bankruptcy proceeding, or, perhaps more importantly or practically, why anyone would give credit to a trustee or a debtor-in-possession in a bankruptcy proceeding. Obtaining credit does not usually occur in a Chapter 7 proceeding except in very extraordinary circumstances. For instance, a trustee with permission to operate the debtor's business for a limited

---

12. 11 U.S.C. §554(b). A motion to compel abandonment requires a $176 filing fee.
13. 11 U.S.C. §362(c). See chapter 13 supra.
14. Midlantic Natl. Bank v. New Jersey Dept. of Envtl. Protection, 474 U.S. 494 (1986).

period of time under Section 721 while a business is in the process of being sold might require credit to do so.

In a Chapter 11 proceeding, obtaining postpetition credit is often critical to a successful outcome to the case. Sometimes, obtaining new credit is the only way in which a Chapter 11 debtor-in-possession can acquire a realistic opportunity to survive and rehabilitate. Remember that a Chapter 11 debtor can be a very large entity. Whether the debtor-in-possession is an airline, a chain of retail stores, a chain of restaurants, or a manufacturer, the debtor will usually require some form of credit to function efficiently. Larger debtors generally have large credit lines from banks or other financial institutions. Whether or not the loans are in default at the time of filing, the debtor-in-possession will require the consent of the lender banks or financial institutions to continue a credit relationship, or the debtor will probably not survive for very long in the Chapter 11. Many times in Chapter 11 proceedings, the debtor finds, and the creditors will concur, that if the debtor receives an infusion of cash in the form of credit or otherwise, the debtor will gain the opportunity needed to restore viability, which may result in a successful plan of reorganization and repayment to creditors.

Sometimes credit will come from entities that are already creditors of the estate who merely extend additional credit to the debtor in exchange for additional collateral and adequate protection. A lender may also improve its priority position by extending postpetition credit, as shall be described below. In this event, a motion to incur postpetition credit may be combined with a motion to use cash collateral under Section 363(c).[15] Sometimes the lender is an entirely new third party. Some investment banks have insolvency departments, which specialize in financing Chapter 11 or other distressed debtors.[16]

There are different forms of credit that may be incurred by a trustee or debtor-in-possession. The simplest is unsecured credit. If a trustee or debtor-in-possession is operating a business under any Chapter proceeding, the estate will incur debt in the ordinary course of business. When office supplies are ordered and billed, this is unsecured credit. Any other ordinary trade payable is unsecured debt. A debtor-in-possession or trustee operating a business may obtain unsecured credit in the ordinary course of business without prior court approval.[17] Thus, every time a restaurant in a Chapter 11 buys 100 pounds of hamburger on a 30-day

---

15. See chapter 19 supra.
16. For example, Deutsche Bank. Most major banks also have specialized departments for the type of debtor-in-possession financing seen in larger cases of the variety that are frequently filed in the Southern District of New York or the District of Delaware.
17. 11 U.S.C. §364(a).

Ordinary course of business: generally, normal everyday business transactions

invoice, a court order is not required to permit the purchase. This is a transaction in the **ordinary course of business**.

On the other hand, if an estate requires unsecured credit not in the ordinary course of business, then the estate must obtain prior court approval by a noticed motion.[18] A loan is not in the ordinary course of business when it is obtained for other than the day-to-day operations of the estate. An unsecured loan for purposes of meeting payroll is not in the ordinary course of business.[19] If prior court approval is obtained, then the debt will be accorded administrative priority for purposes of repayment.[20] If prior court approval is not obtained, then the creditor may find itself subordinated to the status of a general unsecured prepetition creditor.[21] This may seem a harsh result, but the purpose of the rule is to attempt to protect the prepetition creditor body from any further erosion or impairment of their ultimate ability to receive a dividend. Any creditor with administrative priority will get paid before prepetition creditors. Thus, the Code requires prior court approval so a determination can be made that the incurring of new debt not in the ordinary course of business will be in the ultimate best interests of the prepetition creditors.

If a trustee or debtor-in-possession cannot obtain unsecured credit outside the ordinary course of business, it may be able to obtain the credit on a secured basis. This always requires court approval by a noticed motion.[22] The reasons for this are identical to the reasons just given for obtaining unsecured credit outside the ordinary course of business. The loan will become an administrative expense and be payable before any dividends to the prepetition creditors. Because approval of the loan may decrease the prepetition creditors' likelihood of receiving a dividend, the court has to weigh this risk against the positive effects the loan may have upon the estate's ultimate ability to successfully reorganize.

Under Subsection 364(c), the court has a number of choices to exercise in granting secured priority administrative credit. The court may give the loan priority over all other expenses of the bankruptcy, including all other administrative expenses. That is, the loan may be given priority over even the professional fees incurred in the bankruptcy. Or the court may permit the lender to obtain a security interest in any assets of the debtor not already subject to a secured interest. Or the court

---

18. 11 U.S.C. §364(b). Bankruptcy Rule 4001(c).
19. See In re Lockwood Enters., Inc., 52 Bankr. 871 (S.D.N.Y. 1985). But see In re Gloria Mfg. Corp., 65 Bankr. 341 (E.D. Va. 1985).
20. See chapter 21 infra.
21. In re Lockwood Enters., Inc., 52 Bankr. 871 (S.D.N.Y. 1985); In re Ockerlund Const. Co., 308 Bankr. 325 (N.D. IL 2004).
22. 11 U.S.C. §364(c). Bankruptcy Rule 4001(c).

may give the creditor a junior lien on property that is already secured, such as a second deed of trust or mortgage upon a parcel of real estate.[23]

Sometimes when a Chapter 11 debtor-in-possession seeks to obtain approval of a secured administrative debt, all of the estate property is already subject to liens by prepetition secured creditors. In this situation, the court may still permit the incurring of secured administrative debt, but the court must find that the credit is not otherwise obtainable and any existing secured creditor whose position may be affected by the new debt must be given adequate protection. The trustee has the burden of proving that such adequate protection exists.[24] A proposed administrative loan that seeks priority over existing prepetition secured debt is known as a **priming loan**.

Priming loan: administrative loan with priority over existing prepetition secured debt

As in the case of the sale of estate property, the approval of a postpetition loan transaction is unaffected by any appeal unless the order has been stayed pending appeal.[25]

The approval of postpetition credit under Section 364 is governed by the motion procedures described in chapter 5 supra. Notice of the hearing is limited to the Official Creditors' Committee or the 20 largest unsecured creditors of the estate and any other parties the court directs. This permits a debtor to act promptly in the early stages of a proceeding.[26]

E.   HEALTH CARE BANKRUPTCIES

BAPCPA added provisions designed to account for the disposition of patient records in all situations and the transfer of patients to another facility in a **health care business** bankruptcy when the business is closing. The primary purpose of these provisions is to protect the privacy of the records and the safety of the patients. A health care business is generally any business that provides services to patients.[27] The court will appoint an ombudsman to represent the interests of patients unless the court finds that the appointment is not necessary.[28] If a trustee has insufficient funds to preserve and store patient records, Section 351 specifies the procedure to follow to make the records available to patients or to abandon the records. Section 704(12) imposes upon a Chapter 7 trustee

Health care business: a business that provides health care services; special rules apply for a trustee's disposition of health care business records and for the placement of patients in alternative facilities

---

23. 11 U.S.C. §364(c)(1), (2), (3).
24. 11 U.S.C. §364(d).
25. 11 U.S.C. §364(e).
26. Bankruptcy Rule 4001(c).
27. 11 U.S.C. §101(27A).
28. 11 U.S.C. §333. See chapter 11 supra.

the obligation to transfer patients to other appropriate facilities. Sections 1106 and 1107 impose a similar obligation upon a Chapter 11 debtor-in-possession.

F.   SYSTEM EXAMPLE

A major premise of the Bankruptcy Code is that it is designed to function as a self-contained system.[29] An example utilizing many of the issues raised in this and the preceding two chapters illustrates this theory. Gizmos Inc. manufactures gizmos and whatchamacallits for Engulf & Devour. Gizmos has a credit line with the Yours Is Ours Bank. All assets of Gizmos are secured in favor of the bank. Gizmos falls behind in its payments to its suppliers, who cease shipping parts needed for Gizmos to produce its products. Gizmos falls behind in its production schedule. Engulf & Devour want to terminate the contract. The bank wants to call the credit line due. Gizmos files a Chapter 11 to prevent the contract from being terminated and to prevent the bank from seizing assets by virtue of the automatic stay (Section 362). An investor, Alex Keaton, comes forward. He agrees to loan monies to Gizmos on a superpriority secured basis and further agrees that the loan will be converted from debt to equity if Gizmos can reorganize. Gizmos then files a motion to incur superpriority secured debt under Section 364(d), a motion to assume the Engulf & Devour contract under Section 365(a), and a motion to use the bank's cash collateral under Section 363(c). Both Engulf & Devour and the bank are entitled to adequate protection as defined in Section 361. All of these provisions working together will be required to accomplish the goals sought by Gizmos and to properly protect the rights of all creditors.

Summary

Section 345 of the Bankruptcy Code restricts the investment of an estate's cash assets. Generally, cash assets must be placed on deposit in interest bearing accounts or certificates of deposit in federally insured financial institutions. An estate's funds may also be invested in government bonds, but, as a practical matter, the longevity of the bonds exceeds the effective length of most bankruptcy proceedings. A financial institution accepting

---

29. See chapter 2 supra.

the deposit of bankruptcy funds must guarantee the amount on deposit greater than the normal government limits of $250,000.

A utility may not refuse to continue or to provide service to a bank-ruptcy estate or debtor simply because of a bankruptcy filing. A utility may, however, request a reasonable deposit as a condition of providing future service.

A government or private entity may not discriminate against a debtor solely as a result of a bankruptcy filing.

A trustee may abandon assets that are burdensome to or of inconse-quential value to the estate. All assets must be administered by the trustee before the bankruptcy proceeding may be closed. An asset is generally burdensome if the trustee cannot afford to maintain it. An asset is gener-ally of inconsequential value to an estate if it is valueless or if the likely costs of collection would exceed any likely recovery. A secured creditor may sometimes be able to make effective use of the abandonment proce-dure as an alternative to a motion for relief from the automatic stay.

Section 364 regulates the obtaining of credit by a bankruptcy estate. A Chapter 7 estate will only make use of this provision if a trustee is autho-rized to operate a business or in extraordinary circumstances. A reorga-nization debtor will frequently make reference to or use of this provision.

Obtaining unsecured credit in the ordinary course of business does not require court approval. Any postpetition secured loan or loan not incurred in the ordinary course of business will always require court approval. If court approval is obtained, the loan will have priority as an administrative expense. On the other hand, if the loan is obtained without court approval, it may be relegated to the status of a prepetition unse-cured claim.

An administrative secured loan may be given priority over all other expenses of the estate, including other administrative expenses. However, the court will not permit a secured loan or priority secured loan unless it can be shown that there is no other form of loan available to the debtor. In health care business bankruptcies, special provisions protect the privacy and disposition of patient records, and facilitate the safe transfer of patients from a closing facility. The court will appoint an ombudsman to represent the interests of the patients.

KEY TERMS

abandon	ordinary course of business
health care business	priming loan

DISCUSSION QUESTIONS

1. Why does the Bankruptcy Code restrict the use of an estate's cash by a trustee?

2. How must a trustee maintain a bankruptcy estate's cash assets?

3. What are the purposes of abandonment?

4. How does a trustee abandon estate property?

5. When may a secured creditor benefit from the abandonment procedure?

6. Under what circumstances may an estate incur unsecured credit without court approval?

7. Under what circumstances must an estate obtain court approval to incur credit?

8. Identify reasons why special provisions exist to protect patients and their records in health care bankruptcies.

PRACTICE EXERCISE

Exercise 21.1

The Cashes receive a notice from the Bankruptcy Court that the trustee has abandoned their collectibles and wants to know what they are supposed to do with them. Prepare a draft of a letter to the Cashes explaining the impact of the trustee's abandonment of the collectibles.

22

Claims

Learning Objectives

- Explain the procedures and forms used in filing creditor claims in bankruptcy proceedings

- List the various basic objections that a trustee may make to a creditor's claim

- Define the various classifications given to creditor claims in bankruptcy estates: secured, administrative, priority, unsecured, and subordinated

- Describe the Statement of Intention procedure applicable in consumer proceedings

A. CLAIM DETERMINATION

Three of the trustee's four basic duties have been described elsewhere in this text: investigation (chapters 8, 11, 12, 14, 16), liquidation (chapters 19-21), and litigation (chapters 11, 13-19). The process of completing these duties and distributing dividends to the creditors comprises the fourth basic trustee duty: administration. This process is the least discussed and least visible of the trustee's duties unless it is being performed inefficiently, usually in terms of undue delay. Once all of the estate's assets have been liquidated, the prompt determination of "who gets what and in what order" is the goal of efficient bankruptcy administration. This chapter shall describe the general rules and procedures for determining claims — their priority. The next chapter describes the process of dividend distribution.

An easy way to comprehend the claim determination process is to compare it to a nonbankruptcy action to collect a debt. Picture the creditor as a plaintiff who wants its bill paid. The debtor is the defendant. The debtor may or may not have defenses to the claim. These same defenses may be raised in bankruptcy.[1]

Allowed claim: a claim entitled to receive a dividend from a bankruptcy estate

A claim that is determined to be entitled to receive a dividend from the bankruptcy estate is referred to as an **allowed claim**.[2] Whether a claim is allowed or disallowed and the order in which the claim is paid should not be confused with the concept of dischargeability. These two concepts are often confused by practitioners who do not properly perceive the difference between them. Whether a claim is dischargeable has no effect on its allowability. A claim that is nondischargeable may be allowable, in which case the creditor will receive a dividend from the bankruptcy estate if a dividend becomes payable. This means that if a debt is nondischargeable, the creditor's receipt of a dividend will reduce the debtor's remaining nondischargeable liability. The creditor with a nondischargeable allowable claim will therefore retain two sources of recovery, the estate and the debtor. The fact that a debt is not dischargeable does not normally affect the creditor's right to receive a dividend from the estate.

> ### *Practice Pointer*
> Remember that a "claim" is defined as a "right to payment, whether or not such right is reduced to judgment, liquidated, unliquidated, fixed, contingent, matured, unmatured, disputed, undisputed, legal, equitable, secured, or unsecured." 11 U.S.C. 101(5).

Sections 501 through 510 concern the filing and allowance of claims. Recall that all debtors, regardless of chapter, are required to file a list of creditors with their Schedules and also to state whether the claim is disputed, contingent, or unliquidated.[3] These labels place the creditors and trustee on notice as to the debtor's position regarding each claim.

1. 11 U.S.C. §§502(b)(1), 558.
2. 11 U.S.C. §§502(a), 507, 724, 726, 1111, 1123, 1222, 1322.
3. See chapter 8 supra; 11 U.S.C. §521(a)(1); Bankruptcy Rule 1007. See also chapter 30 infra.

B.   FILING A PROOF OF CLAIM

For a claim to be allowed and entitled to a dividend, a **proof of claim** must always be filed in a Chapter 7 case.[4] In Chapter 11, a creditor whose claim is listed as undisputed by the debtor is not required to file a claim in order for the claim to be deemed allowed. A claim scheduled as undisputed in a Chapter 11 is deemed allowed without a proof of claim having to be filed.[5] It is always wise to file a proof of claim. Even when a notice from the court or the United States Trustee recommends against filing a claim until further notice, a proof of claim should always be filed as promptly as possible if it is known that there will most likely be a distribution of dividends. There is one very good reason for following this approach.

> **Proof of claim:** the filing of a formal written claim by a creditor in a bankruptcy proceeding

The original notice to creditors from the United States Trustee requesting that claims not be filed is the standard procedure in most districts. See the sample notice in the forms materials. Note how the form requests creditors not to file claims. The customary no asset notice is disseminated without regard to whether there will in fact be funds available to distribute as dividends. If a subsequent notice is distributed six or twelve months later requesting creditors to file claims, the creditors may forget to do so or may have to locate closed records before the amount of the claim can be properly calculated. On the other hand, if a claim is promptly filed at the inception of the bankruptcy, it usually takes little time to complete the proof of claim form, attaching any relevant documents as exhibits. Once this is done, the creditor's right to receive a dividend from the estate is fully protected and there is nothing else to be done except to wait and see if any dividend is produced by the estate.

A creditor or a codebtor of the debtor may file their own proof of claim. The debtor or trustee may file a proof of claim for a particular creditor. This rarely happens in actual practice. An equity security holder may file a proof of interest.[6] Because definite deadlines are set for the filing of proofs of claim, codebtors, the debtor, or the trustee may file a claim to preserve a creditor's rights to receive a dividend. For example, if a debtor owes substantial tax liabilities, the debtor may want to file a proof of claim on behalf of any tax creditors to ensure that the tax claims will be entitled to receive any dividend that may become payable by the estate.

Once a claim is filed, if a creditor later changes its address, the creditor must advise the court of the address change. If this is not done, the trustee

---

4. 11 U.S.C. §502(a); Bankruptcy Rules 3002, 3003(c).
5. 11 U.S.C. §1111(a).
6. 11 U.S.C. §501; Bankruptcy Rule 3001.

will not know where to send a dividend check, and the check may be returned and the dividend possibly forfeited.[7]

In a Chapter 7 proceeding, the deadline for filing a proof of claim is 90 days after the date first set for the Section 341 creditors' meeting, except for governmental creditors, who receive a bar date of 180 days after the entry of the order for relief (normally the filing of the bankruptcy petition). This deadline is known as the **claims bar date** in all bankruptcy proceedings. There are several important exceptions to this general rule. Two of them affect most proceedings. The first important exception is if the United States Trustee initially notifies creditors not to file claims, as noted in the sample notice included on the Forms Disk. If a bar date is set at a later date, the creditors are then given 90 days' notice from the time of the later notice to file proofs of claim. The second exception permits a nondebtor party to a rejected executory contract to file a proof of claim within such time as the court may direct.[8] In a Chapter 11 proceeding, as noted above, claims listed as undisputed are deemed allowed. Other claimants must file a proof of claim within any deadline that is set by the court upon application by the debtor-in-possession and providing notice to creditors of the claims bar date.[9]

> **Claims bar date:** a deadline set in a bankruptcy proceeding for creditors to file claims; a claim filed after the expiration of a claims bar date is subordinated to all timely filed claims

A proof of claim may be filed by using a standard form that replicates Official Bankruptcy Form B410. A sample form is included in the forms materials. The form will be self-explanatory once the reader has completed this chapter. In addition to the form, evidence of the claim should be attached to the form, such as a promissory note, the invoice, and so forth. Evidence of a security interest, such as a recorded mortgage or UCC Financing Statement, should also be attached. This data is summarized in checklist 22.1 accompanying this chapter. The proof of claim should be served on the trustee.[10]

When the debtor is an individual, there are additional requirements. All charges are to be itemized, including principal, interest, and any other fee or expense for which compensation is sought. Where the creditor claims a security interest, documentary proof is required, along with a statement of the amount necessary to cure any default as of the petition date. When the collateral is the individual debtor's principal residence, the proof of claim must also include a current escrow statement when there is an escrow account. Failure to comply may subject the claimant to penalties.[11] When a claim is secured by a security interest in a debtor's personal

---

7. 11 U.S.C. §347; Bankruptcy Rule 3009. In a Chapter 7, this forfeiture is to the United States (28 U.S.C. Chapter 129). In other proceedings the forfeiture is to the debtor or entity acquiring the debtor's assets under the plan.
8. Bankruptcy Rule 3002(c).
9. Bankruptcy Rule 3003(c).
10. Bankruptcy Rule 3001.
11. Bankruptcy Rule 3001(c)(2).

residence, such as a mortgage or deed of trust, Bankruptcy Rule 3002.1 imposes additional requirements. The creditor must file and serve notice of any changes in payments or addition of postpetition fees and expenses. At the end of the case, a Notice of Final Cure Payment will be made by the trustee. This latter notice has the practical effect of discharging the cured default through the bankruptcy proceeding. See chapter 24, infra.

C.   CLAIM OBJECTIONS — PROCEDURE

Section 502 contains the basic rules for determining the allowance or disallowance of a claim. Administratively, once the claims bar date expires, the trustee will review the claims and may or may not object to them. A claim is deemed allowed unless a party in interest objects.[12] An allowed claim is entitled to receive a dividend if a distribution is made.

A claim is objected to by a party in interest, typically the trustee or debtor, when a formal written objection is filed and noticed to all interested parties. A sample notice of claim objection for use by a Chapter 7 trustee is included on the Forms Disk accompanying this text. A hearing on an objection to a claim requires 30 days' notice to the creditor. An opposed objection will assume the status of a contested matter that will treat the objection as an adversary proceeding as described in chapter 13 supra.[13]

Practice Pointer

Although there is a deadline within which to file proofs of claim, there is no statutory deadline in the Code within which the trustee or the debtor must file an objection.

A trustee may object to a claim on either procedural or substantive grounds. There are three common procedural grounds for objecting to claims. First, the trustee may assert that the claim was filed untimely, such as after expiration of the claims bar date. The Supreme Court has ruled that a standard of excusable neglect may, in appropriate circumstances, obviate the harsh effects on a late-filed claim. In Pioneer Investment

---

12. 11 U.S.C. §502(a).
13. Bankruptcy Rule 3007.

Services Co. v. Brunswick Associates, L.P., 507 U.S. 380 (1993), the creditors received the customary Notice to Creditors. However, the notice actually contained a claims bar date. Experienced bankruptcy counsel, assuming that the notice did not contain a claims bar date, advised the creditor that it would not be necessary to file a claim until a bar date was set. The Supreme Court set aside the rulings of the lower courts, which disallowed the creditor's late-filed claim, stating:

> We do, however, consider significant that the notice of the bar date provided by the Bankruptcy Court in this case was outside the ordinary course in bankruptcy cases. . . . [W]e conclude that the unusual form of notice employed in this case requires a finding that the neglect of respondents' counsel was, under all the circumstances, "excusable." 507 U.S. 398-399.

Section 502(b)(9) of the Bankruptcy Code provides that a late-filed claim is not allowed except for priority claims (see Section 22K infra), which, pursuant to 11 U.S.C. §726(a)(1), may now be filed up to the date the trustee commences final distribution of the estate.

A second procedural claims objection is that the claim is a duplicate of a claim previously filed. It is only necessary to file a proof of claim once. The trustee must object to a duplicate claim since each claim filed must be reconciled before any distribution can occur. A third common procedural objection to a proof of claim is that the claim lacks adequate supporting documentation. Generally, a claim should contain documentation that would be sufficient to support a default judgment in a nonbankruptcy debt collection case. Nevertheless, a proof of claim properly signed and filed constitutes prima facie evidence of the claim's allowability. That is, a properly filed claim creates a presumption of the claim's validity.[14] It is then up to the trustee and the debtor to object.

D.   CLAIMS OBJECTIONS — SUBSTANCE

Substantive claims objections are more complex than procedural objections. There are two groups of substantive objections. The first is any defense the debtor would have had to the claim outside of the bankruptcy system. Any such defense is also a defense to the claim in a bankruptcy proceeding.[15] This is common sense. If a debt would be defensible

---

14. Bankruptcy Rule 3001(f).
15. 11 U.S.C. §502(b)(1); 11 U.S.C. §558.

outside the bankruptcy system, the fortuity of the bankruptcy should not eliminate the defense. For example, Frank Gallagher owes Fiona Gallagher $10,000. However, the statute of limitations has expired. If Frank files a bankruptcy, Fiona's claim is not revived. The expiration of the statute of limitations will remain a defense to the claim in the bankruptcy.

The second group of substantive claim objections exists because of, rather than in spite of, the bankruptcy. These objections exist to a large degree because of the accounting peculiarities of the bankruptcy system, which attempts to account for the collective rights of all creditors. Secondarily, these objections limit certain types of claims from receiving potential windfalls as a result of the bankruptcy. These various objections are contained in Section 502(b).

A claim for unmatured interest is not allowable. That is, an unsecured creditor may only claim interest accrued up to the date of the bankruptcy filing. Postpetition interest on an unsecured claim is generally not allowable. An unsecured creditor cannot file a claim six months after a filing, adding any finance charges that have accrued between the date of the bankruptcy filing and the date the proof of claim is filed.[16] Postpetition interest on unsecured claims only becomes payable if all unsecured claims are paid in full and assets still remain available for distribution, as described in chapter 23 infra.

A claim for a property tax that exceeds the value of the estate's interest in the property is disallowed to the extent of the excess.[17] Do not confuse this limitation on allowability of the claim with the claim's dischargeability. The objection to a property tax claim is not related to the claim's dischargeability. A claim objection concerns the amount of a debt that will be entitled to receive a dividend from the bankruptcy estate. If the debt is also nondischargeable, the debtor will remain liable for any portion of the debt not paid by the bankruptcy estate.

Next, if the claimant is an insider or an attorney of the debtor, the claim will be disallowable to the extent it exceeds the reasonable value of the attorney's or insider's services. This provision also aids a trustee in fully investigating the financial relationships between a debtor, its insiders, and attorneys.[18]

An unmatured and nondischargeable claim for a domestic support obligation is not allowable.[19] For example, Mrs. Kramer is owed $1,000 in child support when Mr. Kramer files a Chapter 7. A proof of claim may be filed for the past due amount, even though the debt is

---

16. 11 U.S.C. §502(b)(2).
17. 11 U.S.C. §502(b)(3).
18. 11 U.S.C. §502(b)(4).
19. 11 U.S.C. §502(b)(5).

nondischargeable. Any dividend will reduce the unpaid portion of the nondischargeable claim as described above. However, if Mr. Kramer continues to not pay the support after the bankruptcy filing, Mrs. Kramer may not file a claim for the additional support because it had not matured when the Chapter 7 petition was filed.

Remember that the collection of a domestic support obligation from property that is not property of the estate is excepted from the automatic stay.[20] As a result, a creditor spouse may continue to exercise all available nonbankruptcy remedies to collect nondischargeable or newly accruing domestic support obligations as long as the source of payment is not property of the estate.

FACT PATTERN

Assume that Owen files bankruptcy owing past due child support to Helen for Lotta. Also assume he continues to not pay after filing. Can Helen can file a claim for the unpaid prepetition support? Can she also collect directly from Owen irrespective of the automatic stay or Owen's exemptions? How is the postpetition support affected by Owen's Chapter 7 filing?

Section 502(b)(6) limits a landlord's claim for future rent caused by the rejection of an unexpired real property lease. In many states, a landlord may obtain judgment against a tenant for the entire amount of rent remaining due under the term of a lease. In a multi-year commercial lease, this amount can be substantial. The Bankruptcy Code places limitations upon the future rent that a landlord may seek in determining the amount of an allowed claim. A claim based upon a real property lease is limited to the amount of unpaid rent due on the earlier of the date prior to filing of the petition or the amount of unpaid rent due on the date the landlord regains possession of the premises. The landlord's claim for future rent is limited to the greater of one year's rent reserved under the lease or 15 percent of the total rent remaining under the lease, not to exceed three years. It is thus necessary to calculate the total rent under the lease for one year and then 15 percent of the total rent for three years. The greater of these two amounts is the maximum amount of a real property lessor's future rent claim.[21]

For example, assume that Hagrid's Magic Shoppe has a five-year lease. The first year's rent is $1,000 per month. The lease provides that the

---

20. 11 U.S.C. §362(b)(2). See chapter 12 supra.
21. 11 U.S.C. §502(b)(6).

monthly rent will rise $500 in each subsequent year. Thus, the rent in year five will be $3,000 per month. Hagrid stops paying rent at the end of ten months and files a Chapter 7 proceeding at the end of year one of the lease. Under Section 502(b)(6), the landlord's claim will be $20,000. The claim for unpaid rent on the date of filing is $2,000, and the second year's rent is $18,000 ($1,500 × 12). Fifteen percent of three years' rent is $10,800. (The total rent for year two is $18,000, year three, $24,000, and year four, $30,000. Fifteen percent of this total is $10,800.) One year's rent is therefore greater than 15 percent of three years' rent.

A future rent claim is determined without regard to acceleration. This means that any clause in a lease that accelerates the rent due upon termination of the lease will not serve to increase the amount of allowable claim.[22] A claim for a terminated employment contract is limited to one year's compensation dated from the earlier of the date of the petition's filing or the date when the contract is terminated, plus any compensation actually unpaid at the time of the bankruptcy filing.[23] For example, a professional track team, The Snails, files Chapter 7. Athletes with multi-year contracts will have their claims limited to one year's compensation and any compensation unpaid at the time of filing.

Sometimes, claims are filed that cannot be readily computed. For instance, a personal injury claim filed against an estate, which has not proceeded to judgment, may have an unknown value. Section 502(c) allows a trustee to have the court estimate the claim. This procedure is an expedient that allows a trustee to administer a bankruptcy estate in a reasonable period of time. Sometimes estimation is the only practical solution, and the Code permits it.[24]

Section 502(d) permits a trustee to utilize the avoiding powers as the basis for an objection to a claim. In this context, the avoiding power is used defensively as opposed to offensively. Here, the trustee does not seek an affirmative judgment but defeats a claim filed by a creditor that is the transferee of an avoidable transfer or other unreturned property of the estate.[25]

Section 502(e) concerns a creditor that files a claim for contribution or for reimbursement in some form from the debtor. For example, one of two general partners pays all the partnership debt while the other general partner files a Chapter 7. The general partner who has paid all the

---

22. 11 U.S.C. §502(b)(6)(B).
23. 11 U.S.C. §502(b)(7).
24. 11 U.S.C. §502(c).
25. 11 U.S.C. §502(d).

partnership debt files a proof of claim for contribution in the bankrupt partner's bankruptcy proceeding. The claim for contribution will be allowable only if there is no nonbankruptcy defense to the bankrupt partner's contribution.[26] Claims arising in the ordinary course of business in an involuntary proceeding are deemed prepetition claims for the purpose of allowance to the extent they arise between the filing of the involuntary petition and the earlier of the appointment of a trustee or the entry of an order for relief.[27] A claim arising from the rejection of an executory contract is considered to have arisen immediately prior to the date of filing of the petition.[28] A claim arising from the disallowance of a setoff, of a returned avoided transfer, or avoidance of a lien under Section 522 will also be considered to have arisen immediately prior to the filing of the original petition.[29] In each of these instances, this means that the amount of the claim that will be allowed will be determined as if the claim had been incurred prepetition. However, the distributive priority accorded the claim may vary, as described infra this chapter.

A priority tax claim that does not arise or is not assessed until after the filing, but that is for a prefiling tax period, is considered to arise immediately before the bankruptcy filing. This makes the claim a prepetition priority claim as opposed to a potential administrative expense claim.[30]

Section 502(j) permits the court to reconsider for cause any claim that has been disallowed. An affected creditor may bring a motion before the court to reconsider an order disallowing the claim.[31]

Section 502(k) permits a debtor to bring a motion to reduce a consumer claim by up to 20 percent if the debtor can prove by clear and convincing evidence that the creditor unreasonably refused to negotiate, within 60 days of the bankruptcy filing, an alternative repayment schedule to repay at least 60 percent of the debt within a reasonable period. Any payment made pursuant to such a proposal is also protected from the trustee's preference powers. The purpose of these provisions is to encourage composition agreements in consumer cases (see chapter 2 supra).

---

26. 11 U.S.C. §502(e).
27. 11 U.S.C. §502(f). See chapter 4 supra.
28. 11 U.S.C. §502(g). See chapter 20 supra.
29. 11 U.S.C. §502(h). See chapter 10 supra.
30. 11 U.S.C. §502(i).
31. 11 U.S.C. §502(j); Bankruptcy Rule 3008.

E. ADMINISTRATIVE EXPENSES

Section 503 describes **administrative expenses**. Generally, administrative expenses are all claims incurred by an estate after an order for relief has been entered as well as any approved professional expenses incurred after the bankruptcy filing. Administrative expenses are normally accorded the highest distributive priority under the Bankruptcy Code except perhaps for superpriority secured claims approved by the court under Sections 364 or 507(b).[32] In a Chapter 7 proceeding, administrative expenses will normally include the trustee's fees pursuant to Section 326 and all costs the trustee incurs in administering and liquidating the estate, such as auctioneer's fees, postpetition rent, and the trustee's attorneys' fees. In a Chapter 11, all expenses incurred in operating the estate's business will be administrative expenses, including postpetition taxes, rent, payroll, and accounts payable. Generally, any expense incurred by an estate after the commencement of a bankruptcy will be an administrative expense.[33] Regardless of the type of claim incurred as an administrative expense, administrative expenses are all considered to be one class of claim for purposes of ultimate distribution. If an estate cannot pay all of its administrative expenses in full, all of the administrative claims will be placed into one class and will share the estate proceeds on a pro rata basis. In this instance, administrative tax claims would share an estate's proceeds pro rata with other administrative claims.[34]

Administrative expenses also include attorneys' or professionals' fees approved by the court after notice and hearing.[35] These fees are subject to the notice and hearing requirements of Sections 330 and 331 prior to payment being made.[36] The expenses incurred by a creditor in successfully prosecuting an involuntary petition, the recovery of property of the estate or the rendition of a substantial contribution to a proceeding, including attorneys' and accountants' fees, are also given administrative priority. Expenses incurred by members of Official Creditors' Committees in the performance of their duties are payable as an administrative expense after court approval.[37] The theory is that a creditor rendering a substantial benefit to an estate and to all its creditors should be rewarded by receiving reimbursement for any reasonable expenses incurred.

Administrative expenses: generally, all expenses incurred by a bankruptcy estate after a bankruptcy filing; trustee's fees, auctioneer fees, attorneys' fees, and postpetition rent are common Chapter 7 administrative expenses

---

32. See chapters 19 and 21 supra, and infra this chapter. In individual bankruptcies, domestic support obligations may have priority over most administrative expenses. See infra this chapter.
33. 11 U.S.C. §503(b)(1).
34. 11 U.S.C. §507(a)(1); 11 U.S.C. §726(b). See chapter 23 infra.
35. 11 U.S.C. §503(b)(2).
36. See chapter 8 supra.
37. 11 U.S.C. §503(b)(3), (4), (5).

Section 503(c) of the Bankruptcy Code provides the court with rules and standards to guide the court regarding the payment of bonuses to corporate executives in Chapter 11 cases.

If a lease is assumed during the course of a case, presumably a Chapter 11, and is later rejected, the landlord is entitled to an administrative claim equal to any unpaid postpetition obligations and two years of unpaid rent under the lease. The balance of any claim is computed as per Section 502(b)(6) discussed in Section 22D above.[38]

The costs of closing a health care facility and disposing of patient records are allowed administrative expenses.[39] Finally, the value of goods sold within 20 days prior to the filing in the ordinary course of business are given administrative priority.[40]

F.   FEE SHARING PROHIBITION

Section 504 prohibits fee sharing, a practice that is common in some areas of the legal profession outside of the bankruptcy system. Section 504 prohibits referral fees in bankruptcy proceedings. A professional performing services in a bankruptcy proceeding may not share a fee or agree to share a fee except with members of that person's own firm or a public service attorney referral program.[41] For example, if Denny Crain refers a bankruptcy to Lockhart & Gardner, and requests a one-third referral fee, he may not receive the referral fee. If a fee sharing agreement is made and it is discovered by the trustee, Denny Crain will be required to reimburse the estate with the amount of the fee paid to him as the referral fee.

G.   TAX CLAIMS DETERMINATION

Section 505 permits the Bankruptcy Court to determine previously undetermined tax claims.[42] This provision specifically provides that the

---

38. 11 U.S.C. §503(b)(7).
39. 11 U.S.C. §503(b)(8). See chapter 21 supra.
40. 11 U.S.C. §503(b)(9). See chapter 16 supra.
41. 11 U.S.C. §504.
42. 11 U.S.C. §505(a)(1).

Bankruptcy Court has jurisdiction to rule on the validity of tax claims affecting an estate.

One activity trustees must complete in virtually all asset estates before an estate may be closed is filing a final tax return for the estate and paying any taxes owed by the estate. However, just because a return has been filed and any taxes paid does not mean that the trustee is released from potential liability. Any prudent trustee will therefore not close an estate until the tax return filed is no longer subject to audit or redetermination. Section 505(b) attempts to solve this problem; without this provision, no prudent bankruptcy trustee would ever close an estate.

Under Section 505(b), a trustee may submit a tax return to a taxing entity, complying with any applicable regulation for the filing of tax returns by bankruptcy estates, paying any taxes that are due, and requesting that the taxing entity determine within 60 days whether it wants to examine the tax return. If the taxing entity does not request an examination or other review within 60 days, the taxing entity can no longer object to the trustee's return, and both the estate and the trustee are released from further liability. If the taxing entity does request a review or audit, the review or audit must be completed within 180 days after the return is filed or the estate and the trustee are relieved from any further liability.[43] The trustee may then conclude administration of the estate without the risk of incurring further liability for any additional or unknown taxes by the estate.

H.   SECURED CLAIMS

The problem of determining the extent of a secured creditor's secured claim is the subject of Section 506. A **secured creditor** is a creditor with a lien upon property in which the estate has an interest. The lien may be consensual, judicial, or statutory.[44] A creditor with a right of setoff is also considered a secured creditor for purposes of this provision. The significance of the value of a secured creditor's collateral has been previously described in connection with Sections 362 and 361, relief from the automatic stay and adequate protection.[45]

Secured creditor: a creditor with collateral that may satisfy part or all of the creditor's allowed claim

---

43. 11 U.S.C. §505(a)(1).
44. See chapter 6 supra.
45. See chapter 12 supra.

FACT PATTERN

Which of the Cash creditors will be considered secured creditors?

The focal point of Section 506 lies in determining the value of the collateral securing a secured claim. A secured creditor will often argue that its collateral is worth less than the amount of its claim. A debtor or trustee, on the other hand, will often argue that the collateral is worth more than the amount of the secured claim upon it. A creditor who successfully argues that the value of its collateral is less than the amount of its claim may have grounds for relief from the automatic stay due to lack of equity in the property securing the claim. This may also affect the amount of any adequate protection payments ordered by the court. For example, in United Savings Association of Texas v. Timbers of Inwood Forest Associates, Ltd., 484 U.S. 365 (1988), the Supreme Court held that an **undersecured creditor**, a creditor whose collateral is worth less than the amount of its claim, is not entitled to adequate protection payments on the undersecured portion of its claim. In Timbers, the debtor owed the creditor over $4.3 million, while the value of the collateral was not more than $4.25 million. Because the value of the collateral was worth less than the amount of the debt, the creditor was undersecured. Because Section 506(b) of the Code limits the allowance of postpetition interest only up to the value of the collateral, the Supreme Court reasoned that the undersecured creditor was not entitled to interest as adequate protection.[46]

Undersecured creditor: a secured creditor whose collateral is worth less than the total amount of its allowed claim

FACT PATTERN

Which of the Cash creditors will likely be determined to be an undersecured creditor? What will that determination depend upon?

Conversely, a debtor or trustee will want to show that the value of a secured creditor's collateral is more than that suggested by the creditor, because then there may be equity in the property that may result in the automatic stay remaining in effect. If the debtor or trustee can show that the collateral has significant equity, then it is possible the court will not order interim adequate protection payments. This can happen in consumer Chapter 7 cases involving residences. If the court feels that there is a significant **equity cushion** in the debtor's residence, the difference between the amount of the claim and the actual value of the collateral, the court may leave the automatic stay in effect indefinitely and not require

Equity cushion: the value in an asset over and above that of any liens or encumbrances, such as equity in a home or motor vehicle

---

46. United Savings Assn. of Texas v. Timbers of Inwood Forest Assocs., Ltd., 484 U.S. 365 (1988). 11 U.S.C. §506(b).

any adequate protection payments. Recall the more extensive discussion of this issue in chapter 13 supra.

In Associates Commercial Corporation v. Rash, 520 U.S. 953 (1997), the Supreme Court confronted the valuation issue head on. In this case, a Chapter 13 debtor attempted to have a tractor truck valued at its wholesale value of $28,500, while the secured lender argued that the value should be the vehicle's retail value of $41,000. The creditor argued that the higher retail value should be used because the debtor was intending to retain and use the vehicle. In agreeing with the creditor, the Supreme Court adopted a replacement value approach, stating:

> The "disposition or use" of the collateral thus turns on the alternative the debtor chooses — in one case the collateral will be surrendered to the creditor, and in the other, the collateral will be retained and used by the debtor. Applying a foreclosure-value standard when the cram down option is invoked attributes no significance to the different consequences of the debtor's choice to surrender the property or retain it. A replacement-value standard, on the other hand, distinguishes retention from surrender and renders meaningful the key words "disposition or use." 520 U.S. 953, 962 (1997).

BAPCPA codifies the result in *Rash* at 11 U.S.C. §506(a)(2), applicable in individual Chapter 7 and 13 cases.

Assuming that Owen is current on his payments and he purchased his 2013 Ford F150, regular cab XLT with 4WD with $1,000 down and his payments were $500 a month for seven years, would A to Z Motors be considered to be over or undersecured?

FACT PATTERN

Regardless of the type of lien involved, a claim is secured only to the extent of the value of the creditor's interest in the property. To this extent, the creditor must look to the collateral for satisfaction of its claim. A creditor who is undersecured, whose collateral is not worth the amount of its claim, becomes an unsecured creditor for any deficiency and is entitled to receive a dividend as an unsecured creditor for the unsecured portion of the claim. However, if the property is not disposed of in the bankruptcy, the lien "passes through bankruptcy unaffected." This was the ruling of the Supreme Court in Dewsnup v. Timm, a case in which the debtor owed the creditor $120,000, while the value of the collateral was only $39,000.[47] The debtor

---

47. 502 U.S. 410 (1992). In Bank of America v. Caulkett, 135 S. Ct. 1995 (2015), the Supreme Court declined to allow a wholly undersecured junior lien to be stripped off. See chapter 24 infra.

contended that the amount of debt that exceeded the value of the collateral should be considered discharged as an unsecured claim, thus reducing the creditor's secured obligation to $39,000. Relying on precedent established in the case law under the Bankruptcy Act, the Court disagreed with the debtor's position, stating: "[W]e are not convinced that Congress intended to depart from the pre-Code rule that liens pass through bankruptcy unaffected."[48] The secured creditor will thus bear the burden of any postbankruptcy depreciation or, conversely, gain the benefit of any postbankruptcy appreciation in the value of the collateral, up to the amount of the claim.

Practice Pointer

Note that secured creditors are not required to file proofs of claim but may have incentive to do so to participate in any distributions from the estate toward their unsecured deficiencies.

To the extent that the value of the collateral is greater than the amount of a secured claim, the lienholder is entitled to payment of interest, attorneys' fees, and other reasonable charges provided for under any agreement that is the source of the claim.[49] A trustee incurring expenses in preserving the collateral of a secured creditor may seek to have such costs surcharged against the secured claim.[50] A secured creditor is not required to file a proof of claim for the secured portion of its claim to be allowed.[51] The reason for this latter provision is that a secured creditor's interest in collateral is proprietary in nature.

Strip down: ability to avoid the unsecured portion of an otherwise secured debt in some circumstances in Chapter 13 cases

In Chapter 13 cases, when personal property collateral is worth less than the amount of the claim, debtors have sought to **strip down** the loan and to pay the creditor the value of the collateral only. The stripped-down portion is treated an unsecured claim. For example, Doug Frasier owns a 2010 pickup truck worth $5,000. The Bank of Ours is owed $7,000 and has the truck as collateral. In a Chapter 13 case, Doug can strip down the $2,000 unsecured portion of the debt by proposing to pay the Bank $5,000, the value of the collateral.

---

48. Id. at 417.
49. 11 U.S.C. §506(b).
50. 11 U.S.C. §506(c). Only the trustee may assert this right. Individual creditors may not. See Hartford Underwriters Ins. Co. v. Union Planters Bank, N.A., 530 U.S. 1 (2000).
51. 11 U.S.C. §506(d)(2).

BAPCPA places limits on the practice of stripping down purchase money loans on motor vehicles in Chapter 13 cases. Recall that a purchase money loan is the loan obtained for the purpose of purchasing the car. Section 1325(a) effectively provides that strip-down may not take place where the debt was incurred to purchase a motor vehicle within 910 days preceding the bankruptcy filing, or one year preceding the bankruptcy filing for any other personal property. If the debtor files a second case within two years of the first case, then the value of the security in the second case is treated the same as in the first case. In the above example, if Doug bought the car within 910 days of his filing, Bank's secured claim would be the entire $7,000 debt. However, if Doug did not give the car as collateral to finance its purchase, then he may still be permitted to strip down the loan under BAPCPA. However, if Doug surrenders a vehicle purchased within 910 days of filing, the circuit courts have uniformly held that the secured creditor may assert any deficiency as an unsecured claim.[52]

A noticed motion to determine the value of a secured creditor's collateral will be heard by the court in a **valuation hearing**. It begins as a noticed motion and will become a contested matter if it is opposed. A valuation hearing may be sought by any party in interest and will most commonly arise in connection with a relief from stay motion or a reorganization proceeding confirmation hearing.[53]

Valuation hearing: a hearing held, pursuant to 11 U.S.C. §506, to determine the value of a secured creditor's collateral

If Owen's truck becomes the subject of a valuation hearing, what factors do you think would favor a lower valuation estimate for the vehicle?

FACT PATTERN

I.   STATEMENT OF INTENTION

A debtor with consumer debt secured by estate property is required to advise secured creditors as to the debtor's intention regarding the disposition of the creditor's collateral during the bankruptcy proceeding. See 521(a)(2). This notice must be given within 30 days of filing and is known as a **Statement of Intention**. A sample form is included in the forms materials accompanying this text. Essentially, the debtor must advise each secured creditor that the debtor intends either to return the

Statement of Intention: a notice to be given, within 30 days after a filing, to the holders of collateral security during the repayment of consumer debt

---

52. See In re Wright, 492 F.3d 829 (7th Cir. 2007); In re Long, 519 F.3d 288 (6th Cir. 2008).
53. Bankruptcy Rule 3012. See chapter 13 supra and chapters 24, 27, and 28 infra.

collateral, to reaffirm the obligation, or to redeem the collateral. The debtor must perform the intention within 30 days of the date first set for the meeting of creditors. If the debtor fails to reaffirm or redeem within the time period, the automatic stay is terminated by operation of law, and the property is no longer considered to be property of the estate, unless the trustee brings a motion that the property will benefit the estate.[54] The rationale behind this provision is that the notice will allow a secured creditor to determine whether a motion for relief from the automatic stay or other such relief is necessary, and allow a creditor to determine when the automatic stay is terminated by operation of law pursuant to Section 362(h).

Many secured creditors are satisfied if a debtor's intent is merely to continue making payments, and the debtor may advise the creditor of this intention in the statement.[55] Debtors should welcome the apathy of secured creditors who will accept the simple continuation of payments. The reason for this is that if a debtor continues making payments but does not formally reaffirm the debt, the creditor's only remedy upon a subsequent default would be repossession of the collateral. Any deficiency will have been discharged in the bankruptcy proceeding as an unsecured claim. Secured creditors should always insist on reaffirmation agreements as a condition of allowing a debtor to retain collateral where the creditor would have no recourse to a deficiency after a repossession. An approved reaffirmation agreement will preserve the creditor's deficiency rights in the event of a subsequent default.[56]

Section 521(a)(6) limits a debtor's choice to surrender of the collateral, reaffirmation of the debt, or redemption of the collateral. However, the "fourth option" or "ride through" may still exist if a debtor otherwise complies with the statement of intention provisions but the court refuses to approve the proposed reaffirmation agreement.[57] This is a logical approach because the debtor has done everything required of the debtor. If the debtor is current and continues to make payments in this instance, the debtor should not be treated any differently than the debtor would be outside the bankruptcy system because the creditor has not been harmed.

---

54. 11 U.S.C. §362(h); 11 U.S.C. §521(a)(2), (6).
55. Continuing to make installment payments as they become due is also known as the "fourth option," or "ride through," the other three options being redemption, surrender, or reaffirmation, as discussed in the text. There was a dispute among the courts on whether or not this option still exists. Compare In re Dumont, 581 F.3d 1104 (9th Cir. 2009) (no) with In re Hart, 402 B.R. 78 (Bankr. D. Del. 2009) (yes).
56. See chapter 8 supra.
57. See, e.g., In re Chim 381 B.R. 191 (Bankr. D. Md. 2008), collecting citations.

J. REDEMPTION

Redemption involves the right of a Chapter 7 consumer debtor to pay a secured creditor the fair market value of the collateral, thereby obtaining a release of the lien. If consumer property is exempt or abandoned, a debtor may pay to the secured creditor, in a lump sum, the amount of its secured claim. This means, in essence, paying to the secured creditor the collateral's value.[58] For example, the Simpsons are Chapter 7 consumer debtors. They owe $2,000 to Crazy Vaclav's Used Cars, which has a lien in a 2007 Saturn as collateral. The vehicle is worth $500. If the Simpsons pay Crazy Vaclav a lump sum of $500 and claim the vehicle exempt, the lien will be released from the vehicle and the balance of Crazy Vaclav's claim will be discharged as an unsecured debt. A valuation hearing may be held to determine the amount necessary for the debtor to pay to redeem the collateral.

> **Redemption:** a right given a Chapter 7 consumer debtor to pay a lump sum to a secured creditor in an amount equal to the value of any collateral

K. PRIORITY CLAIMS

Certain claims are categorized as unsecured priority claims. **Priority claims** are required to be satisfied prior to other general unsecured claims in all proceedings unless an affected creditor agrees to a lesser treatment. Priority claims are themselves prioritized in the order described in Section 507(a). Each higher-numbered class of claims described in Section 507(a) has priority over each of the lower-numbered claims. Thus, all claims under Section 507(a)(1) will be paid in full before any claims under Section 507(a)(2) and so forth. Contrary to popular belief, there are actually a number of claims that take priority over tax claims.

> **Priority claim:** a claim given priority over other unsecured claims. Section 507(a) of the Bankruptcy Code describes priority claims

The first category of priority claims are claims for domestic support obligations. However, the expenses of the Chapter 7 trustee, including professional fees, shall be paid ahead of the domestic support obligations. This ensures that the trustee and the trustee's professionals will be compensated for collecting the funds that pay the domestic support obligation.[59]

The second category of priority claims includes administrative expenses under Section 503, including any filing fees incurred in

---

58. 11 U.S.C. §722.
59. 11 U.S.C. §507(a)(1)(C). See chapter 14 supra.

connection with the bankruptcy.[60] The third category of priority claims is unsecured gap claims incurred under Section 502. Note, however, that although the claim is allowed as if it were incurred prepetition, as described supra in this chapter, the claim has a distribution priority over virtually all other unsecured claims. A **gap period claim** is a claim incurred during that period of time between the filing of an involuntary petition and prior to the entry of an order for relief.[61]

Gap period claim: a claim arising during the period of time between the filing of an involuntary petition and the entry of an order for relief.

The fourth category of priority claims concerns unpaid wages. Wage claims, including vacation, severance, or sick leave pay, are accorded a priority of up to $12,850 per individual for wages earned within 180 days prior to the commencement of the proceeding or the date on which the debtor's business ceased operating, whichever occurs first. Priority wage claimants include independent contractors who earned at least 75 percent of their independent contractor income from the debtor in the 12 months prior to the bankruptcy filing or cessation of the business.[62] These alternative dates account for the close of a business several months or more prior to an actual bankruptcy filing. A wage claim of greater than $12,850 becomes a general unsecured claim to the extent of any excess. For example, Wimpy is owed $13,000 from Brutus Burgers. The wages were all incurred within 180 days prior to Brutus Burgers' bankruptcy filing. The $12,850 of the claim will be a priority claim under Section 507(a)(4). The remaining $150 will be a general unsecured claim.

Section 507(a)(5) is for unpaid contributions to an employee benefit plan, up to $12,850 per employee for unpaid contributions earned within 180 days prior to the date of the bankruptcy filing or the close of the debtor's business, whichever occurs first.[63] Any excess is treated as a general unsecured claim as described above in connection with priority wage claims.[64] The sixth priority claim concerns the unsecured claims of grain producers or fishermen for their produce or catch in the possession of a storage facility as previously described in the context of Section 546.[65] Recall that under Section 546(d) farmers or fishermen have a right to reclaim their products within ten days after delivery to an insolvent storage facility. These same creditors are also granted a priority claim of up to $6,325 per claimant.[66] Once again, similar to wage claims, to the extent the claim exceeds $6,325, the excess becomes a general unsecured claim.

---

60. 11 U.S.C. §507(a)(2).
61. 11 U.S.C. §507(a)(3). See chapter 4 supra.
62. 11 U.S.C. §507(a)(4).
63. 11 U.S.C. §507(a)(5).
64. In Howard Delivery Service, Inc. v. Zurich American Insurance Co., 547 U.S. 651 (2006), the Supreme Court held that unpaid worker's compensation premiums are not entitled to priority under this provision.
65. See chapter 16 supra.
66. 11 U.S.C. §507(a)(6).

The seventh category of priority claims deals with a situation that frequently arises when a retail business files a bankruptcy proceeding. This situation involves consumers who have made deposits for consumer goods or services, such as furniture or appliances. The business files a bankruptcy before the furniture or appliance is delivered. In this case, the individual consumer is given a priority claim of up to $2,850 for the goods or services not provided.[67] Once again, any excess amount of the claim will become a general unsecured claim. The eighth priority claim covers priority tax claims. Congress has determined, in enacting the Bankruptcy Code, that all of the preceding categories of priority claims will be paid in full *before* satisfaction of unsecured prepetition tax claims. Suffice it to say that the most common (income, sales, and payroll taxes) are all given priority status. Priority tax claims include income taxes incurred within three years prior to the bankruptcy filing, withholding taxes of any kind (this will include all payroll and most sales taxes), any employer taxes due on any priority wage claims, excise taxes, customs duties, and any penalties on any of the above where the penalty is compensation for actual loss.[68] Priority tax claims are those taxes that are deemed nondischargeable.[69] This is the only claim provision in the Code that relates directly to the issue of the claim's dischargeability. Section 507(a)(9) makes a commitment by a financial institution to meet minimum capital requirements to an appropriate regulatory agency as a ninth priority unsecured claim.

Section 507(a)(10) grants priority status to claims for death or personal injury resulting from the operation of a motor vehicle or vessel because the debtor was intoxicated on alcohol or drugs.

Section 507(b) provides a secured creditor a priority claim superior to all other administrative expenses where the creditor's collateral has been sold, used, or leased without consent or court approval.[70]

L.   PARTNERSHIP CLAIMS

Section 508 requires that a creditor of a partnership who receives a dividend from a nondebtor general partner may not receive further dividends

---

67. 11 U.S.C. §507(a)(7).
68. 11 U.S.C. §507(a)(8). The three-year period is tolled during any period in which a prior bankruptcy is pending. Thus, where the debtor filed Chapter 7 during the three-year period, received a discharge, and then filed Chapter 13, the Supreme Court has held that the three-year period would be extended to include the time period of the first bankruptcy. Young v. U.S., 535 U.S. 43 (2002).
69. See chapter 14 supra.
70. 11 U.S.C. §507(b). See the discussion of cash collateral in chapter 19 supra.

from the partnership's bankruptcy proceeding in which the identical claim has been filed until all other creditors have received a distribution equal to that received from the general partner.[71] For example, a creditor of The Three Musketeers receives a payment from Porthos, a general partner, equal to 50 percent of the claim. The creditor, Richelieu, may not receive a dividend from the bankruptcy estate until all the other Musketeer creditors have received payment of 50 percent of their claims. This provision is intended to facilitate the fundamental debt collection concept of bankruptcy proceedings that creditors in an equal class should share the assets of the debtor estate on an equal basis.

M.   CODEBTOR CLAIMS

Section 509 is about the claims of a codebtor of a debtor. The cosigner of a loan is a codebtor. A general partner of a partnership personally liable for the partnership debts is a codebtor. A junior lienholder that satisfies a senior lienholder is considered a codebtor for these purposes.

Generally, if a codebtor pays the debts of a debtor, then the codebtor acquires the rights of the satisfied creditor.[72] For example, if a general partner pays a partnership debt, the general partner will acquire the claim of the satisfied creditor and will essentially become that creditor. A codebtor asserting a claim in such circumstances should provide proof of payment of the claim in any proof of claim filed by the codebtor in the debtor's bankruptcy proceeding.[73] However, the codebtor will not acquire the rights of the paid creditor to the extent that the claim is disallowed or subordinated under Section 510.[74]

N.   SUBORDINATION

Subordination:
The relegation of a claim to a lesser status than it is otherwise entitled to under the Bankruptcy Code.

The final concept to be dealt with in the area of claims is that of **subordination**. A claim that is subordinated is given a lesser priority than it is

---

71. 11 U.S.C. §508.
72. 11 U.S.C. §509(a).
73. Bankruptcy Rule 3001(e).
74. 11 U.S.C. §509(b).

otherwise entitled to under the Bankruptcy Code. A creditor may be subordinated for two reasons.

The first and most logical reason is if a creditor consents to subordinate itself to a lesser priority claim.[75] Frequently, in Chapter 11 proceedings, for example, creditors may request insiders to subordinate any claims to those of the noninsiders as a condition to the noninsiders' approval of a reorganization plan. In large reorganizations where there may be multiple issues of bonds, each issue typically contains consensual provisions that rank a particular bond issue in order of priority with any predecessor issues. A creditor may agree to subordination. It is a guiding principle of the distributive aspects of the Bankruptcy Code that a creditor may always agree to accept lesser treatment than the law may otherwise entitle it to.

A second common manner in which a creditor may be subordinated is under the doctrine of *equitable subordination*. A claim may be equitably subordinated by motion.[76] There are logical and equitable reasons why the claim of a creditor might be equitably subordinated. The most common reason for subordination of a claim under this theory is because the creditor has engaged in bad faith conduct. The creditor has taken actions that in all fairness requires the creditor to be paid after other creditors instead of along with them.

For instance, insiders receive excessive salaries from a debtor corporation and then loan a portion of the salary back to the company, becoming among the company's largest creditors in the process. If the excessive salaries have damaged the company at the expense of the company's creditors, perhaps the insider claims should be subordinated and paid after other claims. Perhaps one factor for the company's predicament is the excessive insider payroll.

Summary

The determination of claims and the distribution of dividends to allowed claimholders is a basic function of the trustee's duty to administrate a bankruptcy estate. This and the next chapter describe this process. Sections 501 to 510 of the Bankruptcy Code govern the determination of claims against a bankruptcy estate.

A creditor, other than a secured creditor not entitled to a deficiency, must always file a proof of claim to be entitled to receive a dividend from a Chapter 7 estate. A proof of claim must be filed before the expiration of any claims bar date set by the United States Trustee or court to receive

---

75. 11 U.S.C. §510(a).
76. 11 U.S.C. §510(c).

proper treatment. A late claim, other than a priority claim, is subordinated to all other claims. As a practical matter this means no dividend in most cases. A Chapter 11 claim scheduled as undisputed by the debtor-in-possession need not file a proof of claim.

It is recommended that a creditor should always file a proof of claim. A sample proof of claim is included in the forms materials accompanying this text. A proof of claim should always attach documentary evidence verifying the claim. When the debtor is an individual, or where the claim is secured by a mortgage in the debtor's principal residence, the claim must be itemized and there must be proof the claim is secured or the claimant may be subject to penalties.

A trustee or the debtor may object to a claim. A hearing on an objection to a claim requires 30-day notice. A claims objection is a noticed motion, and it is treated as a contested matter, as described in chapter 13 supra, if it is opposed. A sample notice of objection for use by a Chapter 7 trustee is included in the forms materials.

Objections to a claim may be procedural or substantive in nature. Examples of procedural objections include duplicate claims, claims not containing supporting evidence, and late-filed claims.

Substantive objections to a claim fall into two groups and are primarily the subject of Code Section 502(b). The first group includes any defense existing to the claim under nonbankruptcy law. A defense based upon expiration of an appropriate statute of limitations is an example. The second group consists of a number of objections to specific types of claims specifically provided for in the Bankruptcy Code. These various objections are outlined in the checklist accompanying this chapter.

Administrative expenses are claims incurred by a bankruptcy estate. In a typical Chapter 7, administrative expenses will consist primarily of the costs of liquidation. In a Chapter 11, all expenses incurred in operating the debtor-in-possession are administrative expenses. The professional fees of trustees, attorneys, or other professionals and the expenses of Official Creditors' Committee members are also administrative expenses.

Bankruptcy Code Section 504 prohibits referral fees in bankruptcy proceedings except to public service attorney referral programs. The recipient of a referral fee must reimburse the referral fee to the estate.

Section 505 provides the Bankruptcy Court with jurisdiction to hear and determine tax claims affecting an estate. The provision also contains a procedure providing for expedited release of a bankruptcy estate and trustee from liability for taxes due by a bankruptcy estate for which returns have been filed and all taxes paid.

Section 506 contains provisions relating to the determination of a secured claim. The provisions will also have relevance in relief from stay and adequate protection matters. A claim is generally secured only to the value of any collateral. In Chapter 13 proceedings, the value of the collateral will be the amount of the debt due for purchase money loans on motor vehicles acquired within 910 days of the bankruptcy filing, or one year prior to the filing in the case of personal property contracts. To the extent that the collateral is worth less than the claim, the deficiency is an unsecured claim. To the extent that the collateral is worth more than the claim, a secured creditor is entitled to have postpetition interest and all charges allowed under the security agreement added to the claim. The value of collateral is determined by a valuation hearing. A secured claim may also be charged with the costs incurred by the estate in maintaining or preserving the collateral. If the collateral is not disposed of in the bankruptcy, the lien will survive the bankruptcy unaffected.

A debtor is required to advise a secured creditor of consumer debt of the debtor's intent as to disposition of the creditor's collateral after the bankruptcy filing. A debtor may reaffirm the debt or return or redeem the collateral. Redemption permits an individual consumer debtor to pay a lump sum to a secured creditor equal to the value of the collateral. A valuation hearing may be necessary to determine the adequacy of the redemption amount. A valuation hearing is a noticed motion. If a debtor fails to file a Statement of Intention, or fails to perform a stated intention, within 45 days after the meeting of creditors, the automatic stay will be terminated by operation of law pursuant to Section 362(h).

Section 507 identifies priority claims. The listed claims are given priority over all other claims in the specific order set forth by Section 507(a). Priority claims are summarized in the checklist to this chapter.

Section 508 concerns the effect on partnership cases of distributions by nondebtor partners. Section 509 permits a codebtor of a debtor to acquire the claims of any claim paid by the codebtor. A payment by a nondebtor guarantor to a creditor is an example.

Section 510 allows a claim to be subordinated. When a claim is subordinated, it is accorded a lesser status than the claim is otherwise entitled to by the Bankruptcy Code. For example, an insider may subordinate its claims to that of noninsiders. A claim may be subordinated by agreement or by court order.

KEY TERMS

administrative expenses	redemption
allowed claim	secured creditor
claims bar date	Statement of Intention
equity cushion	strip down
gap period claim	subordination
priority claim	undersecured creditor
proof of claim	valuation hearing

CHAPTER 22 CHECKLIST

22.1   FILING A PROOF OF CLAIM   *Authority*

    22.1.1   Deadline: By Claims Bar Date Set   Bankruptcy Rule
               by Court or United States Trustee   3002(c)

    22.1.2   Documents
          1.   Proof of claim—   Bankruptcy Rule
              Official Form B410   3001(a)
          2.   Evidence of claim (such as   Bankruptcy Rule
              promissory note; invoice)   3001(c)
          3.   Evidence of perfection of   Bankruptcy Rule
              security interest (such as   3001(d)
              recorded mortgage or UCC   Rule 3001(c)
              financing statement)
              Escrow statement when
              there is an escrow account

22.2   OBJECTION TO PROOF OF CLAIM

    22.2.1   Objection Documents
          1.   Notice of objection—30-day   Bankruptcy Rule
              notice required   3007
          2.   Declarations, where necessary
          3.   Points and authorities, where
              necessary

22.3   PROCEDURAL CLAIMS OBJECTIONS

    22.3.1   Late-Filed Claims   11 U.S.C.
                                    §502(b)(9)
                                    Bankruptcy Rules
                                    3002, 3003

    22.3.2   Duplicate Claims

    22.3.3   Claim Lacks Adequate Supporting   Bankruptcy Rule
               Documentation   3001(c), (d), (f)

22.4   SUBSTANTIVE CLAIM OBJECTIONS

    22.4.1   A Defense to the Claim Applicable   11 U.S.C.
               Under Nonbankruptcy Law (Such as   §502(b)(1)
               Statute of Limitations)

---

77. The expenses incurred by the trustee in administering assets resulting in payment of the domestic support obligations are paid first. 11 U.S.C. §507(a)(1)(C).

Authority

22.5.5   Pension Plan Contributions Incurred   11 U.S.C.
         Within 180 days up to $12,850 per   §507(a)(5)
         Employee

22.5.6   Farmers or Fishermen with Crops or   11 U.S.C.
         Catch in Storage Facility up to $6,325   §507(a)(6)

22.5.7   Deposits for Consumer Goods or   11 U.S.C.
         Services of Up to $2,850   §507(a)(7)

22.5.8   Most Tax Claims   11 U.S.C.
                                                  §507(a)(8)

22.5.9   Financial Institution Minimum   11 U.S.C.
         Capital   §507(a)(9)

                          22.5.10   Death or
                                                  Personal Injury
                                                  Caused by
                                                  Substance Abuse

11   U.S.C.   §507(a)(10)

                          22.5.11   Secured
                                                  Administrative
                                                  Claim Where
                                                  Collateral Used
                                                  Without Consent
                                                  or Prior Court
                                                  Order

11   U.S.C.   §507(b)

22.6   STATEMENT OF INTENTION (11 U.S.C. §521(2))

22.6.1   Contents
         1.   Notice required to be given
              secured creditors of consumer
              debt, advising of intended
              disposition of collateral after a
              Chapter 7 filing
         2.   Methods of disposition
              a.   reaffirm
              b.   return collateral
              c.   redeem collateral

22.6.2   Time Limits
         1.   Notice must be given within 30
              days of filing

2. Intention must be performed within 30 days of date first set for meeting of creditors
3. Stay relieved by operation of law at end of time period (11 U.S.C. §362(h)).

DISCUSSION QUESTIONS

1. How and when should a creditor file a proof of claim in a bankruptcy proceeding?

2. How does the trustee object to a proof of claim? What are the various grounds for objection to a proof of claim that the trustee may raise?

3. What is an administrative claim?

4. How is the amount of a secured claim determined? Does a secured claim survive the bankruptcy?

5. What is the Statement of Intention procedure? What are its purposes? Should a debtor be permitted to continue payments unless the creditor objects?

6. What are the various priority unsecured claims?

7. What does it mean to subordinate a creditor's claim? How may a creditor's claim be subordinated in a bankruptcy proceeding?

PRACTICE EXERCISES

Exercise 22.1
Prepare the Cashes' Statement of Intention. Assume that they are going to reaffirm the debt to A to Z Motors.

Exercise 22.2
Prepare a proof of claim on behalf of any listed Cash creditor.

23

Administration

Learning Objectives

- List the order of distribution to classes of creditors
- Outline the bankruptcy administrative process, in terms of both steps and time

A. ORDER OF DISTRIBUTION

When the assets of an estate have been fully liquidated and all allowable claims have been determined as to priority and amount, the proceeds will be distributed to the creditors. This is the ultimate goal of creditors in any bankruptcy proceeding: the receipt of a dividend. Success in any bankruptcy proceeding is based not upon the traditional adversary notions of winning or losing but upon the percentage of dividend that the unsecured creditors ultimately receive. This simple concept is the forest; everything else becomes the trees. This very basic and fundamental goal can often be overlooked or forgotten by the parties when they get mired in the seemingly infinite details of bankruptcy litigation and administration. Unlike many other areas of the law, a bankruptcy proceeding has no winners or losers in the conventional sense of these terms. A bankruptcy proceeding is considered to be most successful when all of the creditors are paid in full and the debtor still retains assets. This can happen in reorganization proceedings and even, on rare occasions, in Chapter 7 proceedings. Certainly when all of the parties receive precisely what they are entitled to, no one is a loser.

The order of distribution for nonsecured creditors is specifically outlined in Section 726. Although described only in Chapter 7, these distributive provisions apply by implication in all other Chapter proceedings.

This is because all reorganization plans must be consistent with the provisions of Chapter 7 and must provide unsecured creditors with at least the same treatment that they would have received in a Chapter 7 proceeding.[1]

Under Section 726, the first category of claims that receives payment are timely filed Section 507 claims, so long as the priority claims are filed before the distribution is made.[2] The first priority claim allowed under Section 507 involves domestic support obligations. Next, allowed administrative expenses are paid. If a Chapter 11, 12, or 13 case is converted to a Chapter 7, the Chapter 7 administrative expenses will have priority over the prior Chapter's administrative expenses and the administrative expenses of the superseded Chapter will drop into a second priority.[3] For example, if a Chapter 11 case is converted to a Chapter 7, the administrative expenses of the Chapter 7 case will have priority over the administrative expenses of the Chapter 11. Collectively, the administrative expenses will have priority over other nonsecured claims.

Each subclass of priority claim described in Section 507 must be satisfied in full before the next subclass may receive a dividend.[4]

Although not entirely accurate, the next category of claims to logically place on a list of payment priorities would be secured claims. This is not entirely accurate because a secured creditor, by virtue of its security interest, is entitled to receive its collateral or the value thereof. This may be done by the creditor obtaining relief from the automatic stay and a subsequent foreclosure or repossession of the collateral, abandonment, or return of the collateral by the debtor. Alternatively, if the trustee sells the collateral, a secured creditor is entitled to payment from the sales proceeds up to the amount of the secured claim.[5] If the secured creditor's collateral has a value of less than the amount of the allowed claim, then any deficiency becomes an unsecured claim and it is treated like any other unsecured claim.

General unsecured creditors comprise the next group entitled to receive dividends from a bankruptcy estate. Unsecured creditors who file their claims in a timely manner will receive dividends first. A claim is filed in a timely manner if it is filed before the expiration of the claims bar date, as described in chapter 22 supra.[6] Unsecured creditors filing proofs of claim after expiration of a claims bar date will have their dividends subordinated to timely-filed unsecured claims.[7] Penalties that are

---

1. 11 U.S.C. §§1129(a)(7), 1225(a)(4), 1325(a)(4). See chapters 24, 27, and 28 infra.
2. 11 U.S.C. §726(a)(1); 11 U.S.C. §507. See chapter 22 supra.
3. 11 U.S.C. §726(b).
4. 11 U.S.C. §726(b). See chapter 22 supra.
5. 11 U.S.C. §506. See chapters 19 and 22 supra.
6. 11 U.S.C. §726(a)(2); 11 U.S.C. §501; Bankruptcy Rules 3001-3003. See chapter 21 supra.
7. 11 U.S.C. §726(a)(3).

not compensation for actual damages or claims for punitive or exemplary damages are payable only after payment in full is provided to all other unsecured creditors.[8]

After all unsecured creditors are paid in full, any creditors subordinated under Section 510(c) will then receive dividends.

If all creditors are paid in full and there are still assets available for distribution, then the creditors are entitled to payment of postpetition interest on their claims.[9] If interest is paid and there are still assets remaining, any remainder is distributed to the debtor.[10] In the latter instance, it is said that the estate is *solvent* because its assets exceed its liabilities. The chart below sets forth the general order of distribution in the bankruptcy system. The checklist accompanying this chapter is a more complete list.

GENERAL PRIORITY OF CLAIMS
1. Priority (507)
2. Administrative (503)
3. Secured (506)
4. Unsecured (726)
5. Subordinated (510(c))
6. Interest (726)

Solvent Estate 7. Debtor (726)

When a Chapter 7 trustee knows that there will be a distribution to the creditors, the trustee will request the court or the United States Trustee to set a claims bar date. This is because, as a practical matter, a claims bar date is generally only set in a Chapter 7 case after a trustee determines that there are assets to distribute.[11] When a claims bar date is set, all creditors will receive a notice advising them to file claims prior to the claims bar date.

Assuming a distribution is made, when would Lotta's child support claim be paid?

FACT PATTERN

8. 11 U.S.C. §726(a)(4).
9. 11 U.S.C. §726(a)(5).
10. 11 U.S.C. §726(a)(6).
11. Bankruptcy Rule 3002(c)(5). See chapter 22 supra.

B.   METHOD OF DISTRIBUTION

Pro rata: a distribution to creditors within a given class on a proportional basis

When assets are distributed, they are distributed on a **pro rata** basis to each claimant in a class of claims until the class has been paid in full.[12] *Pro rata* means that if there are insufficient assets to pay the claims of a class in full, then the claimants within the class are paid an equal percentage of their claims. In essence, pro rata means share and share alike. This concept is the principle underlying the trustee's avoiding powers, that creditors of the same class shall share the assets available for distribution equally. For example, if there is only enough to pay half of the unsecured claims, each claim will receive a dividend of 50 percent. If a senior class of claims is paid in full, the immediately junior class of claims will receive a dividend, and so forth until a class is reached in which only a pro rata distribution can be made, or all classes are paid in full and the debtor gets the remainder. In a typical Chapter 7 small asset case, the administrative and priority claims are often paid in full, secured creditors will obtain their collateral, and there is a pro rata distribution to unsecured creditors. Of course, secured creditors are always paid according to their rights in their secured collateral. This is the one exception to the rule of pro rata distribution.

C.   BANKRUPTCY ADMINISTRATION TIMELINE

The schematic below illustrates the *minimum* period of time it should reasonably take to administer most small asset Chapter 7 proceedings through the bankruptcy system. This minimum period is in excess of one year. Typically, the length of time it takes to fully administer an estate is longer than the minimum shown. The actions identified attempt to itemize the most important events that take place during the process, from the petition's filing to the close of the case.

The act of filing is obvious. The Section 341(a) creditors' meeting is required to take place within 40 days of the date of filing.[13] A discharge is usually received about 90 days after the Section 341(a) meeting. The discharge is to be issued forthwith after expiration of the deadline to object to the discharge, 60 days after the date first set for the meeting of creditors.[14]

In consumer debtor no asset proceedings, virtually all involvement by the debtor and counsel with the proceeding will terminate when the

---

12. 11 U.S.C. §726(b).
13. Bankruptcy Rule 2003 requires a hearing no less than 21 days and no more than 40 days from the order for relief. See chapter 8 supra.
14. Bankruptcy Rule 4004.

discharge is received or about four months after the case is filed. As a practical matter, this is the end of the bankruptcy for the debtor. But note that if there are assets in the estate, the second phase of the proceeding has just begun. The trustee may be liquidating or litigating over the assets for an indefinite period of time. That is why liquidation and litigation are shown as indicated on the illustration. The length of time these functions take can vary considerably.

BANKRUPTCY ADMINISTRATION TIMELINE

Event	Approximate time between events	
Filing		
	40 days	
341(a) Meeting		
	90 days	
524 Discharge		
Request for claims bar date		
	90 days	LIQUIDATION OF ASSETS AND LITIGATION
Claims bar date		
	30-60 days	
Claims docket		
	Review 30-60 days	
Claims objections		
	30-60 days	TAX RETURNS AND CLEARANCE (60 DAYS)
Final report		
Notice of intent to distribute		
	30-60 days	
Order for distribution supplemental report		
Close of Case, Bankruptcy Rule 5009	**370 days minimum**	

The next items on the timeline are the actual steps that a trustee must take to fully administer a proceeding within the bankruptcy system. First, the trustee in an asset proceeding has to request a claims bar date unless such a date was set in the original notice to creditors, which, as noted in chapter 22 supra, rarely occurs. Creditors are required to be given 90 days' notice to file claims in a Chapter 7 or 13 proceeding, except that a governmental unit may file a claim within 180 days from the filing date.[15]

Claims docket: an itemized summary of creditor claims filed in a bankruptcy proceeding

When the bar date expires, the court will prepare a **claims docket** for the trustee. The *claims docket* is an itemized summary of the filed claims, including the name and address of the creditor, the general classification of the claim (secured, unsecured, priority), and the amount of the claim. This information is compiled from the proof of claims forms.

The trustee will then review the docket and inspect the filed claims where necessary. If a purpose would be served, the trustee must then object to any objectionable claims, and have them determined by the court.[16] A purpose is served if the objections will increase the ultimate dividends payable to creditors. A trustee is not required to bring objections that will provide no benefit to an estate. For example, let's assume that a trustee anticipates a 5 percent distribution to unsecured creditors in a proceeding. Several creditors have included postpetition interest in their claims. The amounts of included interest are less than $100. Although the postpetition interest claims are objectionable, the only result to be achieved is having $5 more to distribute (5 percent of $100), hardly worth the time and effort of a claim objection.

Creditors are given 30 days' notice of any hearing on an objection to a claim. If the objection is to the claim's substance, the court may treat the objection as a contested matter or adversary proceeding. The objection may then take an indefinite period of time to resolve because it has now entered the realm of litigation.[17]

Once all liquidation, litigation, and claims objections have been resolved, the trustee will finally know which creditors are entitled to receive a dividend. The trustee will also know what funds are available from which to pay a dividend. The trustee will then prepare and file a final report with the court and the United States Trustee.[18] When the final report is approved, the distribution will occur. The creditors will be given notice of the trustee's intent to distribute the estate and, of course, they may object to the proposed distribution. Any court hearing held to determine any such objection will result in further delay.

---

15. 11 U.S.C. §502(b)(9); Bankruptcy Rule 3002(c).
16. 11 U.S.C. §704(5).
17. Bankruptcy Rule 3007. See chapter 22 supra.
18. 11 U.S.C. §704(9); Bankruptcy Rule 2015.

Federal Rule of Bankruptcy Procedure 5009 provides that if a trustee has filed a final report and certified that the estate has been fully administered, then there is a presumption that an estate has been fully administered.[19] The case can then be closed.

If all of the above time limits are totaled, in the smallest and simplest type of asset proceeding, the fastest administration will be approximately 12 to 15 months. In a no asset proceeding, administration is usually completed in about six months. The trustee will file a report of no assets in the matter and the proceeding will then be closed by the court in the normal course of business.

Summary

The ultimate goal of creditors in any bankruptcy proceeding is to receive a dividend. The percentage of dividend returned to the creditor body determines the success of any proceeding. Adversarial notions of winning or losing are not part of this final equation. Often, cooperation of the creditor body toward the ultimate common goal will achieve a greater return to all classes of creditors.

Dividends are distributed to claims by classes. Each class must be paid in full before the next immediate junior class receives a dividend. When there are insufficient assets to pay a class in full, the creditors within the class receive a pro rata or percentage distribution of their claims. No lesser classes will receive a dividend. When all classes are paid in full and assets remain available to return to the debtor, an estate is considered solvent. The general order of classification is: priority, administrative, secured, unsecured, subordinated, interest, and finally debtor. The checklist accompanying this chapter is a more thorough list.

It takes approximately 12 to 15 months to administer even the simplest asset estate. Estates with substantial assets or litigation, or both, can take years to fully administer. A no asset proceeding will take about six months to fully administer. The administration timeline contained in this chapter itemizes the steps taken to fully administer an estate.

KEY TERMS

claims docket   pro rata

---

19. Bankruptcy Rule 5009. See also 11 U.S.C. §350(a).

CHAPTER 23 CHECKLIST

			Authority
23.1	ORDER OF CLAIMS DISTRIBUTION		
	23.1.1	Priority Secured Administrative Claims	11 U.S.C. §§503, 507(a)(1), 507(b), 726(a)(1)
	23.1.2	Administrative Claims	11 U.S.C. §§503, 507(a)(1), 726(a)(1)
	23.1.3	Priority Claims Authority	11 U.S.C. §§507(a)(2)-(10), 726(a)(2)
	23.1.4	Secured Claims[20]	11 U.S.C. §506
	23.1.5	Timely-Filed Unsecured Claims	11 U.S.C. §726(a)(2)
	23.1.6	Late-Filed Unsecured Claims	11 U.S.C. §726(a)(3)
	23.1.7	Fines or Penalties Not Compensation for Actual Damages; Punitive Damages	11 U.S.C. §726(a)(4)
	23.1.8	Subordinated Claims	11 U.S.C. §510(c)
	23.1.9	Postpetition Interest	11 U.S.C. §726(a)(5)
	23.1.10	Debtor — Solvent Estate	11 U.S.C. §726(a)(6)

DISCUSSION QUESTIONS

1. What is the order of claims distribution in a bankruptcy proceeding? How does a class of claims receive a distribution when the trustee has insufficient funds to pay the class members in full?

2. What basic events must occur before a Chapter 7 bankruptcy asset estate may be closed?

---

20. This is the logical placement for secured claims in a table of this nature. However, as the text indicates, this placement is not entirely accurate, because the secured creditor has a property interest in its collateral.

PART V

Reorganization Proceedings

24

Chapter 13: Reorganization Proceedings

Learning Objectives

- Define reorganization proceedings

- Understand the rationale of Chapter 13

- List the grounds for conversion, dismissal, or reorganization proceedings

- Know the necessary documents and their filing deadlines in Chapter 13 proceedings

- Understand the elements of a Chapter 13 plan

- Describe the procedures for confirming and performing a Chapter 13 plan

- Compare and contrast Chapter 13 and Chapter 7 discharges

Liquidations: the sale of an estate's assets to repay creditors; a Chapter 7 bankruptcy is a liquidation proceeding

A. INTRODUCTION — REORGANIZATION PROCEEDINGS

There are two basic types of proceedings available to debtors in the bankruptcy system: **liquidations** and **reorganizations**.[1] Chapter 7 is a

Reorganizations: a bankruptcy proceeding where a debtor seeks confirmation of a plan that will repay creditors while permitting the debtor to retain assets or continue in business

---

1. See chapter 2 supra.

liquidation proceeding. In a liquidation case, nonexempt assets are liquidated, which may result in dividends distributed to creditors, and the
debtor is relieved of further personal liability by receiving a discharge.[2]
In a reorganization proceeding, on the other hand, creditors are paid over
time according to a "plan" wherein the debtor attempts to repay the debt
while retaining nonexempt assets and/or continuing to operate the business. Reorganization proceedings are, in their essence, no more or less
than judicially approved composition agreements, the approval of which
is binding upon all creditors of a debtor.[3]

The next five chapters of this text describe the most common reorganization proceedings, Chapters 13, 11, and 12. Chapter 9, applicable to
municipal corporations, is rarely filed. Chapter 13 is a reorganization
proceeding for individuals with regular income. Chapter 12 is a reorganization proceeding for family farmers or fishermen with regular income.
Chapter 11 is a reorganization proceeding for all other debtors.[4]

Chapter 13 is a program for individuals (and their spouses) with
regular income who have unsecured debts of less than $394,725 and
secured debts of less than $1,184,200.[5] A qualified individual may attempt
to repay his/her debts through a Chapter 13 plan over a period of time not
to exceed five years.[6] If the plan is successfully performed, the Chapter 13
debtor will be able to retain nonexempt assets and receive a discharge.[7]
Debtors typically file a Chapter 13 case to protect their homes from foreclosure or their cars from repossession because the Chapter 13 process
provides them with an opportunity to cure the defaults on their secured
debt in a manner that has a potentially less onerous effect on their ability
to obtain new credit.

B.   SPECIAL CHAPTER 13 PROVISIONS

Chapter 13 has its own trustee system. Under Section 1302 of the Code, a
judicial district may have a standing Chapter 13 trustee, one individual

---

2. See chapter 8 supra.
3. See chapter 2 supra.
4. See chapter 5 supra.
5. 11 U.S.C. §109(e). 11 U.S.C. §104(b). This provision triennially adjusts the dollar limits
contained in §109(e). The amounts shown reflect the amounts that became effective April
1, 2016. See chapter 5 supra.
6. 11 U.S.C. §1322(d).
7. 11 U.S.C. §1328(a).

who will serve as the trustee for all of the Chapter 13 proceedings filed within the district, or each case may have a Chapter 13 trustee appointed in a manner similar to Chapter 7 trustees. Most districts have one or more standing trustees. The United States Trustee appoints all of the Chapter 13 trustees.[8] The major difference between a Chapter 13 trustee and a Chapter 7 trustee is that the Chapter 13 trustee is responsible for administering monthly plan payments from Chapter 13 debtors and distributing the payments to the creditors on a regular basis.[9]

Chapter 13 has the added benefit of extending the automatic stay to a codebtor of a consumer debtor who has not filed a bankruptcy proceeding.[10] For example, if a debtor files a Chapter 13 case but the debtor's spouse does not, under Section 1301, the automatic stay will apply to the debtor and to the spouse of the nonfiling debtor. As a result, there will be instances in which only one spouse will need to file a Chapter 13 case because the other nonfiling spouse will still gain the benefit of the automatic stay while avoiding the burden of having filed a bankruptcy proceeding.

Would it make sense in the instant case for Owen Cash to file an individual Chapter 13 case, and for his wife Robin to simply rely on the codebtor stay?

FACT PATTERN

Chapter 13 debtors have rights and powers that are slightly different from those of Chapter 7 or Chapter 11 debtors. Unlike Chapter 7 or Chapter 11 trustees, generally, Chapter 13 trustees will not go out into the community and attempt to operate a small business owned by a Chapter 13 debtor. If a Chapter 13 debtor is engaged in business, the debtor is permitted to continue to operate the business and is given the right to use, sell, and lease property of the estate pursuant to Section 363 or to incur credit pursuant to Section 364.[11] Thus, a debtor who operates a sole proprietorship business and who satisfies the Chapter 13 filing requirements may be a Chapter 13 debtor and is permitted to continue operating the business after the filing. The income from operating the business will constitute the regular income required to perform the Chapter 13 plan.

---

8. 11 U.S.C. §1302(a).
9. 11 U.S.C. §1326(c).
10. 11 U.S.C. §1301.
11. 11 U.S.C. §§1303, 1304. See chapters 27 and 29 infra.

Practice Pointer

Remember, under Chapter 13, only "individuals," not corporations or other types of business entities, may seek relief.

Property of the estate: property subject to administration by a bankruptcy trustee for the distribution of dividends to creditors

Section 1306 concerns **property of the estate** in a Chapter 13 case. In Chapter 13, or Chapter 11 for an individual, unlike under Chapter 7, a debtor's postpetition earnings from services are considered to be property of the estate. The reason for this is that the regular income that is the source of the plan payments will come from the postpetition earnings received for services performed by the debtor. As a result, postpetition income is considered to be property of the estate. Because repayment is generated from the debtor's postpetition earnings, a Chapter 13 debtor will normally remain in possession of all its property. Nonexempt property will not normally be turned over to the trustee's custody for liquidation.[12]

Like all other individual debtors, a Chapter 13 debtor must also comply with the requirement to file a prepetition credit counseling certificate as a prerequisite to filing the case (see chapter 5 supra). Along with the regular requirements to file a Statement of Financial Affairs, bankruptcy schedules, a statement of current income and current expenditures (Schedules B106I and B106J), and a statement of current monthly income (Official Form B122C-1) for application of means testing to Chapter 13 (which must be filed within 14 days of filing the petition unless the court orders otherwise).[13] A Chapter 13 debtor must also file a "plan" within 14 days of filing the petition, unless the court orders otherwise. Official Form B113, to become effective December 1, 2017, is a national form Chapter 13 plan. The form will be used in any district that has not opted out of the national form, as many local districts have Chapter 13 form plans. The form is included in the forms materials and is representative of many local forms.[14]

Section 1326(a) requires Chapter 13 debtors to make adequate protection payments to creditors holding security interests in personal property, and to provide evidence of the payment to the trustee. A debtor must also provide proof of any required insurance coverage to the creditor within 60 days after filing the case. Section 1308 also requires that a debtor must have filed all tax returns for the four-year period prior to the filing.

---

12. 11 U.S.C. §1306. See chapter 15 supra. 11 U.S.C. §1115. See chapter 26 infra.
13. 11 U.S.C. §109(h) (see chapter 5 supra). Bankruptcy Rule 1007(b)(1)(6), (c).
14. Bankruptcy Rule 3015, 3015.1.

The meeting of creditors may be continued for up to 120 days to permit the debtor to file the returns. Failure to file the returns can be grounds for dismissal of the case or conversion to Chapter 7 (see section C infra).

C. DISMISSAL OR CONVERSION— REORGANIZATION PROVISIONS

Section 1307 concerns the **dismissal** of a Chapter 13 case or the **conversion** of a Chapter 13 case to another proceeding.[15] Section 1112, applicable in Chapter 11 proceedings, is very similar. Accordingly, this discussion summarizes both provisions. Each section provides the grounds for a proceeding to be dismissed or converted to another Chapter under the Code. The typical situation is conversion from a Chapter 13 or 11 to a Chapter 7 proceeding—that is, from a reorganization case to a liquidation proceeding.

Dismissal: the act of terminating a bankruptcy proceeding, the general effect of which is to restore the parties to their rights and liabilities as they existed prior to the bankruptcy filing

Consistent with the principles described in chapter 9 supra, Sections 1112 and 1307 permit a debtor one opportunity to convert a proceeding from one Chapter to another. In a Chapter 13, this right may not be waived. If a debtor wishes to convert from a Chapter 11 to a Chapter 13, the debtor must, however, meet the Chapter 13 filing qualifications. In a Chapter 11 proceeding, if the debtor is no longer a debtor-in-possession (for example, if a trustee has been appointed), or the proceeding has been commenced as an involuntary proceeding or has been previously converted, the debtor will not be able to freely convert the proceeding to another Chapter. In these circumstances, the debtor will have to obtain a court order to permit conversion. The ability to freely convert a proceeding from one Chapter to another takes place by filing a one-page application with the court stating that the Chapter 13 (or other reorganization) debtor is qualified to be a Chapter 7 debtor and wants to be a Chapter 7 debtor.[16]

Conversion: the act of converting a bankruptcy proceeding from one chapter to another

Conversely, if a debtor has previously converted from one Chapter to another and conversion is desired for a second time, court approval will be required. A motion procedure is required to accomplish this task. The court will not permit debtors to convert from Chapter to Chapter repeatedly.

Subsections 1112(b) and 1307(c) provide a number of grounds for obtaining the dismissal or conversion of a reorganization proceeding to

---

15. See chapter 9 supra.
16. 11 U.S.C. §1112(a); 11 U.S.C. §1307(a). See chapter 9 supra.

another Chapter for cause upon a noticed motion. Section 1112(b)(4) lists 16 examples and Section 1307(c) provides 11 examples. The common situation that arises is where a trustee or creditors seek conversion of a proceeding from a reorganization to a Chapter 7 liquidation because the reorganization has failed. Each provision uses the term *including* before listing the grounds that can result in dismissal or conversion. Recall that use of the term *including* means that the list is not exhaustive.[17] The court may find additional causes that may also constitute grounds for dismissal or conversion. However, the circumstances identified cover the most common causes for converting a Chapter 11 or 13 to a Chapter 7 or why the proceeding should be dismissed. In a Chapter 11 case, if it is shown that a plan may be confirmed within the exclusivity periods of Section 1121 (see chapter 26 infra) or a reasonable time or if there is reasonable justification for the debtor's actions or lack thereof, the court may deny a motion to convert or dismiss. Unless the moving parties agree, a motion to convert or dismiss a Chapter 11 must be decided within 45 days of its filing.[18]

For example, the first cause under 1112(b)(4) is a continuing *loss or diminution* of the estate and the absence of a reasonable likelihood of rehabilitation.[19] This means that when a Chapter 11 estate is continuing to lose substantial amounts of money in operating under Chapter 11, or when it becomes apparent to the court and creditors that the reorganization has failed, conversion or dismissal will be in the best interest of the creditors and should occur. For example, Grandma Takeda's Instant Kosher Chicken Soup, Inc., a Chapter 11 debtor-in-possession, files operating reports that show that over an extended period of time the debtor is profitable. However, no plan has been proposed and the debtor intends to operate for as long as possible without filing a plan. Some debtors will take this approach because they incorrectly believe that Chapter 11 is a comfortable security blanket and it may appear possible to remain a Chapter 11 debtor indefinitely. This perception is an illusion. If the debtor persists, such behavior will return to haunt the debtor because it will ultimately constitute cause for a conversion or dismissal of the proceeding. The United States Trustee regularly files motions to dismiss or convert based on a debtor's unreasonable delay. The purpose of this Subsection is to prevent debtors from abusing the system by indefinitely postponing a resolution of their financial difficulties. In Chapter 11 cases, failure to comply with the administrative rules of Chapter 11 (see chapter 25 infra), gross mismanagement of the estate, unauthorized use of

---

17. 11 U.S.C. §102(3). See chapter 5 supra.
18. 11 U.S.C. §1112(b)(3).
19. 11 U.S.C. §1112(b)(4)(A).

a secured claimant's cash collateral (see chapter 19 supra), failure to maintain insurance in force, failure to pay postpetition taxes or to file tax returns can all constitute cause for conversion or dismissal of the case.[20]

The first example under Section 1307(c) is an *unreasonable delay prejudicial* to the creditors of a Chapter 13 case.[21] Unreasonable delay takes place when a debtor fails to file a plan for no apparent purpose.

Both sections include a cause for conversion or dismissal of a reorganization proceeding where there is a *failure to propose a plan* within any deadline set by the court. This time period may be flexible in Chapter 11. However, as noted above, a Chapter 13 plan must be filed 14 days after a petition is filed.[22]

Another cause for dismissal or conversion of a reorganization proceeding is *failure to obtain confirmation* by the court of every plan proposed.[23] Usually, if the court denies confirmation of a first attempt at a plan, the debtor may make a second attempt to get a plan modified and/or confirmed. If the second plan cannot be confirmed, the debtor can theoretically try again and again and again. Ultimately, the creditors will tire of this. When they do, the repeated failure to obtain confirmation will constitute cause for conversion or dismissal of the reorganization proceeding.

In Bullard v. Blue Hills Bank, a Chapter 13 debtor appealed an order denying confirmation of his plan. The Bank contended that the order was not a final order because the debtor had a right to file another plan. The Supreme Court agreed, stating: "An order denying confirmation is not final, so long as it leaves the debtor free to propose another plan."[24]

A related cause for dismissal or conversion of a reorganization is if the *confirmation of a plan is revoked*.[25] In all reorganization proceedings, a confirmed plan may be revoked, primarily on the grounds of fraud. A confirmation's revocation may be grounds for conversion or dismissal of the proceeding.

The debtor's *inability to effectuate consummation* of a confirmed plan, or failure to commence making timely payments constitutes another cause for dismissal or conversion.[26] This means that if a plan is confirmed but performance does not commence, this failure may constitute cause for dismissal or conversion. This cause is to be distinguished from another listed cause, which permits dismissal or conversion due to a *material*

---

20. 11 U.S.C. §1112(b)(4)(B), (C), (D), (F), (H), (I).
21. 11 U.S.C. §1307(c)(1).
22. 11 U.S.C. §1112(b)(4)(J); 11 U.S.C. §1307(c)(3); 11 U.S.C. §1321; Bankruptcy Rule 3015.
23. 11 U.S.C. §1307(c)(5); 11 U.S.C. §1112(b)(4)(J).
24. 575 U.S. — (2015).
25. 11 U.S.C. §1112(b)(4)(L); 11 U.S.C. §1307(c)(7).
26. 11 U.S.C. §1112(b)(4)(M); 11 U.S.C. §1307(c)(4).

default with regard to a confirmed plan.[27] In this latter event, performance has begun, but then stops or defaults.

A plan-related cause for conversion or dismissal of a reorganization proceeding occurs when the plan terminates because of some condition specified in the plan other than the completion of payments.[28] For example, the plan provides that unless an escrow closes by a date certain, the proceeding will automatically be converted to a Chapter 7. If the condition occurs, the proceeding will be converted.

Failure to pay any required court fees will also constitute cause for dismissal or conversion.[29] In a Chapter 13, the United States Trustee may seek dismissal or conversion if the debtor *fails to timely file required pleadings*, such as the Statement of Financial Affairs, Schedules, Schedule of Current Income and Expenditures, or tax returns for the four years prior to the filing of the Chapter 13 petition. In a Chapter 11, failure to provide information reasonably requested by the United States Trustee will produce a similar result.[30]

Finally, under both Chapter 11 and Chapter 13, failure to pay a post-petition domestic support obligation is grounds for dismissal or conversion.[31] When a reorganization proceeding is converted to a Chapter 7, the debtor is required to file a final report and to update the Statement of Financial Affairs and Schedule of Assets and Liabilities to account for the estate's activities during the reorganization proceeding. When a Chapter 13 is converted to another Chapter under the Bankruptcy Code, the property of the estate consists of all the property under the possession or control of the debtor on the conversion date, and the value of any secured claim shall continue to be considered fully secured unless the claim has been paid in full prior to conversion of the case.[32]

D.   CHAPTER 13 PLAN PROVISIONS

Plan: a Chapter 13 plan or Chapter 11 Plan of Reorganization

The main component of a Chapter 13 proceeding is, of course, the **plan**. Sections 1321 through 1330 contain the provisions regarding the contents

---

27. 11 U.S.C. §1112(b)(4)(N); 11 U.S.C. §1307(c)(6).
28. 11 U.S.C. §1112(b)(4)(O); 11 U.S.C. §1307(c)(8).
29. 11 U.S.C. §1112(b)(4)(K); 11 U.S.C. §1307(c)(2).
30. 11 U.S.C. §1112(b)(4)(H); 11 U.S.C. §1307(c)(9)(10)(e); 11 U.S.C. §1308.
31. 11 U.S.C. §1112(b)(4)(P); 11 U.S.C. §1307(c)(11).
32. Bankruptcy Rule 1019; 11 U.S.C. §348(f). In Harris v Viegelahn, U.S., 135 S. Ct. 1829 (2015) the Supreme Court ruled that undisbursed Chapter 13 payments from the debtors' postpetition wages are to be returned to the debtor upon conversion because they are not property of the estate in Chapter 7. See chapter 9 supra.

of and the procedure for obtaining **confirmation** (approval), and performance of the plan. The plan is, in essence, a new contract between the debtor and all the creditors. A confirmed plan is nothing more than a composition agreement that has obtained court approval. The Forms Disk contains a sample Chapter 13 plan.

The filing of a Chapter 13 plan is not optional. It is a required part of the process.[33] The Federal Rules of Bankruptcy Procedure require that a Chapter 13 plan be filed within 14 days of the petition's filing. A failure to do so, as noted above, will constitute cause for dismissal or conversion.[34] A Chapter 13 debtor must file the plan promptly because the entire procedure is intended to be expeditious.

Section 1322 prescribes the contents of a Chapter 13 plan. There are **mandatory elements** that are required to be in any plan. There are also permissive provisions that may be included in a plan.

The mandatory elements of a Chapter 13 plan are described in Section 1322(a). These provisions must be included in a Chapter 13 plan. The first mandatory provision is that the debtor must pay all of his/her future earning or a sufficient sum into the plan so that it can be performed.[35]

The second requirement is that all priority claims must be paid in full unless the holder of any such claim agrees otherwise.[36] As has been noted elsewhere in this text, a creditor may always voluntarily agree to a lesser treatment than may be mandated by the Code. For example, a priority wage claimant may agree to accept repayment as a general unsecured creditor.

The third mandatory element of a Chapter 13 plan is that if the plan classifies claims, each claimholder within a given class must be treated identically, unless a creditor agrees to a lesser treatment.[37] In other words, a debtor cannot propose to pay some unsecured creditors a 20 percent dividend and other unsecured creditors a 50 percent dividend. All of the creditors in a given class must be treated equally unless a specific creditor consents to a lesser treatment. This is consistent with the repayment philosophy of the bankruptcy system described in chapter 23 supra.

Section 1322(a)(4) provides that if there is a domestic support obligation owed to a governmental entity, then the plan may provide for less than full payment of this claim if the debtor pays all of his/her disposable income into the plan for a five-year period.

Section 1322(b) describes the **permissive elements** that may be included in a Chapter 13 plan. A permissive element is a provision that may be included in the plan but is not required to be in the plan. A

Confirmation: the act of obtaining court approval of a reorganization plan in the reorganization proceedings of Chapters 9, 11, 12, or 13

Mandatory element: provisions that must be included in a Chapter 13 or Chapter 11 plan

Permissive element: provisions that may be included in a Chapter 13 or Chapter 11 plan.

---

33. 11 U.S.C. §1321.
34. Bankruptcy Rule 3015; 11 U.S.C. §1307(c)(3).
35. 11 U.S.C. §1322(a)(1).
36. 11 U.S.C. §1322(a)(2). As to priority claims, see chapter 22 supra.
37. 11 U.S.C. §1322(a)(3).

permissive plan provision may also involve facts that, if present, will make inclusion of the permissive plan provision mandatory. For example, if a Chapter 13 debtor has an executory contract, it must be assumed or rejected in the plan. Section 365(p), requires that an executory contract be assumed prior to confirmation of a Chapter 13 plan, or be deemed rejected and the automatic stay terminated by operation of law (see chapter 20 supra).

Section 1322(b) lists 11 permissive elements. First, a debtor may designate more than one class of unsecured claims, so long as there is no discrimination between creditors.[38] (Typically, there is not more than one class of unsecured claims in a Chapter 13 case, but multiple classes is a common occurrence in Chapter 11 proceedings.[39]) For example, a Chapter 13 debtor has several claims for which there is also a codebtor who is not a debtor in the bankruptcy proceeding. These creditors could theoretically be placed into a separate class to account for the codebtor's liability.

However, a debtor may not create two classes of unsecured claims and pay one class a 10 percent dividend and the other class a 50 percent dividend. This latter activity will constitute unfair discrimination against the affected creditors receiving the lesser dividend.

As noted in Section B supra, Official Form B113, effective December 1, 2017, is a national form Chapter 13 plan. The form will be used in any district that has not opted out of the national form, as many local districts have Chapter 13 form plans. The form is included in the forms materials. The form contains sections for mandatory and permissive provisions, as well as provisions that serve as a motion to avoid liens pursuant to Section 522(f) of the Code, discussed in chapter 10 supra, and provisions that act to strip down or strip off secured liens from undersecured or wholly unsecured collateral as discussed below in this section.

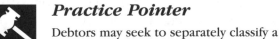

Practice Pointer

Debtors may seek to separately classify a nondischargeable debt so as to pay it in full to avoid postdischarge liability. The trend in the case law is to deny such separate classification, except in the context of public policy concerns, such as domestic support obligations.

---

38. 11 U.S.C. §1322(b)(1).
39. See chapter 26 infra.

Second, a Chapter 13 plan may modify the rights of secured creditors other than those creditors whose only security is real property that is the debtor's principal residence.[40] Stated another way, a Chapter 13 plan may seek to modify the rights of secured creditors whose collateral is other than the debtor's residence. For instance, a Chapter 13 plan may propose to reduce the amount of monthly payments and extend the loan repayment period on a secured car loan so the debtor will be able to afford to complete the contract and keep the car. However, the debtor cannot propose to modify the terms of secured home loans, except to cure any prepetition default, unless the affected secured creditors agree.

Practice Pointer

Note that this protection extends only to the debtor's "principal residence" and not to a second or vacation home.

In Nobelman v. American Savings Bank, 508 U.S. 324 (1993), the Supreme Court prohibited a practice that had been approved in some circuits, permitting the bifurcation of a secured claim into secured and unsecured portions. Under this practice, a claim secured by a lien upon a Chapter 13 debtor's residence was considered secured only up to the value of the collateral; the undersecured portion of the debt became an unsecured debt subject to a Chapter 13 discharge. For example, in *Nobelman*, supra, the debtor sought to value the creditor's residential collateral at $23,500, although the total amount of the debt was $71,335 at the time of the petition. The Supreme Court held that Section 1322(b)(2) prevents modification of the creditor's rights and thus precludes bifurcation. That is, the debtor would be required to account for the full amount of the creditor's claim ($71,335) rather than the lesser value ($23,500) of the collateral. In short, the statutory language of Section 1322(b)(2) means what it says.

BAPCPA placed limits on this practice of bifurcating or "stripping down" secured claims, at least where the collateral is personal property. First, if the debtor has purchased personal property collateral within one year from the filing date, or if the claim is for a purchase money security

---

40. 11 U.S.C. §1322(b)(2). The collapse of the home mortgage market has spawned a plethora of federal legislation aimed at protecting the homeowner. Recent legislation includes the HOPE NOW Alliance, the Housing and Economic Recovery Act of 2008, Hope for Homeowners Act of 2008, Foreclosure Prevention Act of 2008, and the Streamlined Mortgage Modification Plan introduced jointly by Fannie Mae and Freddie Mac.

interest in a motor vehicle purchased within 910 days (2.5 years) prior to the filing, Section 1325(a) effectively provides that the allowed amount of the secured claim will be the amount due under the contract. Second, Section 506(a) requires that the collateral be valued at the price a retail merchant would charge for similar collateral (see chapter 22 supra). The practical effect of these provisions is to effectively eliminate the ability to bifurcate or strip down a secured claim into secured and unsecured portions, since many purchase money contracts are of short duration.

When the collateral is the debtor's home, there is a debate in the case law as to whether a claim secured by real property or a combination of real and personal property may be "stripped off" or eliminated in a Chapter 13 case. The majority view holds that if there is no value at all in the real property for the benefit of the secured claimant, then the claim is fully unsecured. The minority view holds that any secured claim secured by an interest in the debtor's home must be paid. For example, Mr. Truman owns real estate worth $50,000. He owes Dome Mortgage Company a senior mortgage of $55,000 and the Control Finance Company a junior mortgage of $10,000. Under one view, the Control debt may be stripped off because there is no value in the property to support it. Under the contrary view, the debt may not be stripped off because the collateral is Truman's home. If the debt is stripped off, it is treated as an unsecured claim and is subject to Truman's Chapter 13 discharge. See chapter 21H, supra. BAPCPA may limit this practice to the extent that the debtor must either pay the claim or receive a Chapter 13 discharge for the secured claim subject to **strip-down** or **strip-off** to be so treated. If the case is dismissed or converted to a Chapter 7, the strip-off or strip-down will not apply.[41]

Strip-down/strip-off: ability to avoid the unsecured portion of an otherwise secured debt in some circumstances in Chapter 13 cases

A related issue concerns the debtor who seeks Chapter 13 relief to pay secured debt after receiving a Chapter 7 discharge. The Supreme Court examined this issue in Johnson v. Home State Bank, 501 U.S. 78 (1991). In this case, the Johnsons owed the bank $470,000 secured by a mortgage upon real estate. During the pendency of a state court judicial foreclosure action, the Johnsons filed a Chapter 7 case and received a discharge. The

41. "'Stripping off' a lien occurs when the entire lien is avoided, whereas 'stripping down' occurs when an undersecured lien is bifurcated and the unsecured portion is avoided." In re Yi, 219 B.R. 394 (E.D. Va. 1998). Every Circuit that has ruled on the debtor's ability to avoid a wholly undersecured lien has allowed it. See, e.g., In re Zimmer, 313 F.3d 1220 (9th Cir. 2002); In re Lane, 280 F.3d 663 (6th Cir. 2002); In re Pond, 252 F.3d 122 (2d Cir. 2001); In re Tanner, 217 F.3d 1357 (11th Cir. 2000); In re Bartee, 212 F.3d 277 (5th Cir. 2000); In re McDonald, 205 F.3d 606 (3d Cir. 2000). The minority view is represented by American General Finance, Inc. v. Dickerson, 229 B.R. 539 (M.D. Ga. 1999). See also In re Dickerson, 222 F.3d 924 (11th Cir. 2000) (following Tanner but stating that if it was not bound, would follow minority approach). Section 1325(a)(5)(B)(i) is the provision limiting the effect of a strip-off or strip-down in a dismissed or converted case.

bank's right to proceed against the collateral survived the bankruptcy.[42] After obtaining relief from the stay, the bank obtained a foreclosure judgment of $200,000. The Johnsons then filed a Chapter 13 and proposed to pay the claim in five annual payments. The Supreme Court held that notwithstanding the prior Chapter 7 discharge, the bank still possessed a claim against the property, so the Johnsons could file Chapter 13 to satisfy it.

Section 1322(c) of the Code limits a debtor's ability to cure a default on an obligation secured by the debtor's principal residence by requiring the cure to be made before a foreclosure sale can be properly conducted. The provision therefore overrules Johnson v. Home State Bank because the facts of the case involved a cure of the default after the foreclosure sale had been conducted. However, Section 1322(c) also permits a Chapter 13 debtor to modify, within the plan, an obligation secured by the debtor's principal residence that becomes due during performance of the plan so long as the obligation is paid in full by the completion of the plan.

The filing of a Chapter 13 after receiving a Chapter 7 discharge is colloquially known as a "Chapter 20" and is not uncommon. In *Johnson*, supra, for example, the Johnsons did not originally qualify for Chapter 13 because the secured debt owed the bank, $470,000, exceeded the then-Chapter 13 secured debt limit of $350,000. After they received their Chapter 7 discharge and the bank obtained its foreclosure judgment, the $200,000 secured claim fell within the Chapter 13 debt limit, permitting the Johnsons to seek Chapter 13 relief.

Practice Pointer

The case law is divided on whether or not the debtor may have two simultaneous filings that effectively serve as a Chapter 20.

Third, a Chapter 13 plan may provide for the cure or waiver of any default.[43] This is precisely what most Chapter 13 plans attempt. There are five different classes of creditors that are generally paid through a Chapter 13 plan. They are administrative claims, priority claims, defaults on car loans, defaults on home loans, and general unsecured creditors. A common Chapter 13 plan will cure the defaults on the home loan or the car loan or both and pay a dividend to the unsecured creditors. The

---

42. See discussion of Dewsnup v. Timm, 502 U.S. 410 (1992), chapter 22 supra. See also Bank of America v Caulkett, 135 S. Ct. 1995 (2015) (denying strip off of a wholly undersecured junior lien in Chapter 7).

43. 11 U.S.C. §1322(b)(3).

major purpose in filing a Chapter 13 is commonly to protect a home or car from foreclosure or repossession rather than to satisfy unsecured debt.

A fourth permissive element that a Chapter 13 plan may include is that payments to unsecured creditors may be made at the same time as payments to secured creditors.[44] In other words, a Chapter 13 plan is not required to provide that all payments will first go to satisfy secured creditor defaults and then unsecured creditors will receive dividends. A Chapter 13 plan may allocate its payments toward secured claim defaults and unsecured creditors at the same time.

Fifth, a Chapter 13 plan frequently may provide for a cure of defaults on any claim, priority, secured, or unsecured, even though the final payment on the claim is not due until after the plan is completed.[45] For example, John Smith is three payments behind on his car loan. He files a Chapter 13 to cure the default, thereby preventing repossession. The plan proposes to repay the three payments over 12 months. There are three years of payments left under the contract. This plan will cure the default on a secured claim for which the last payment is due after the plan is performed. This is permissible and is what many debtors are seeking with a Chapter 13, a mechanism to cure existing defaults.

This same provision also requires that any current payments coming due on any underlying long-term debts must be paid during pendency of the Chapter 13.[46] Some Chapter 13 debtors form an improper impression that if the Chapter 13 plan payments are made, other ongoing payments do not have to be made. This is absolutely untrue. All that the Chapter 13 payment will do is cure any default owed prior to the filing date. A debtor still has the obligation to continue to make current payments on home or car loans and any other secured debt that comes due in the normal course. The inevitable result of a failure to maintain current payments by the debtor will be a motion for relief from stay brought by a secured creditor or a motion for dismissal or conversion.

Practice Pointer

A Chapter 13 debtor must continue to make their regular postpetition payments "outside of the plan" on any long-term secured debt if the debtor wants to keep the collateral, such as a home or car.

---

44. 11 U.S.C. §1322(b)(4).
45. 11 U.S.C. §1322(b)(5).
46. 11 U.S.C. §1322(b)(5).

Next, a Chapter 13 plan may assume or reject executory contracts or unexpired leases. Section 365(p) relieves the automatic stay as to leased property if the lease is not assumed in the plan.[47] The plan may also provide for the payment of certain limited postpetition tax claims or consumer debts necessary for a debtor's performance of the plan.[48] The plan may provide for payment of a claim from property of the estate. For example, the debtor may propose to sell a nonexempt asset and to apply the proceeds toward performance of the plan.[49] The plan may provide that property of the estate will vest in the debtor upon confirmation.[50] If all claims are paid in full, and if there are nondischargeable claims, then postpetition interest becomes payable on the claims.[51] The plan may contain any other provision that is not inconsistent with the Bankruptcy Code.[52]

Section 1322(e) permits a lender to obtain interest on the cure of a default if the underlying agreement or nonbankruptcy law permits the same.

If the debtor's and the debtor's spouse's income are equal to or greater than the median national family income for a family of equal or lesser size, then the plan must be five years in duration. If the debtor's and the debtor's spouse's income are less than the median national family income for a family of equal or lesser size, then the plan must be a minimum of three years in duration, and the court may approve a plan of up to five years in length. National median family income is determined as last reported by the Census Bureau. For example, the Census Bureau provides that for a family of four filing after May 1, 2013, the median family income in California is $81,837. A family earning more than this would be required to have a five-year Chapter 13 plan. A family earning less than this would be required to have a minimum three-year Chapter 13 plan. The length of time that a Chapter 13 plan must be is known as the **applicable commitment period.** Recall that median family income is also a threshold amount of income for application of means testing in Chapter 7 cases (see chapter 6 supra).[53]

A Chapter 13 plan may be modified at any time before confirmation. Of course, any such modification must comply with Section 1322. A debtor might discover that the plan is in error and amend it. This is

Applicable commitment period: the required length of a Chapter 13 repayment plan, dependent upon whether or not the debtor's income is higher or lower than the state median family income; if equal to or higher, the period is five years, if lower, the period is three years

---

47. 11 U.S.C. §1322(b)(7); 11 U.S.C. §365(p)(3). See chapter 20 supra.
48. 11 U.S.C. §1322(b)(6); 11 U.S.C. §1305.
49. 11 U.S.C. §1322(b)(8).
50. 11 U.S.C. §1322(b)(9).
51. 11 U.S.C. §1322(b)(10).
52. 11 U.S.C. §1322(b)(11).
53. 11 U.S.C. §1322(d). Census Bureau national median family income data may be accessed at http://www.census.gov/hhes/www/income/statemedfaminc.html and www.justice.gov/ust.

analogous to amending a complaint before an answer is filed in traditional nonbankruptcy litigation.[54]

E.   CONFIRMATION HEARINGS

Unlike Chapter 11, which is far more complex, the procedures for obtaining confirmation of a Chapter 13 plan are expedited and somewhat summary.[55] A Chapter 13 plan is confirmed at a confirmation hearing. Creditors do not have an opportunity to vote on acceptance of a Chapter 13 plan, although they may object.[56] However, unlike the creditors' meeting, the confirmation hearing is held before a judge. This entire process is very expeditious. The confirmation hearing is required to be held within 45 days of the meeting of creditors. The debtor will have filed Statements and Schedules along with a plan. Notice of the creditors' meeting and confirmation hearing will have been given to all parties in interest. A sample Chapter 13 notice to creditors is included on the Forms Disk.

A debtor must commence making payments under the plan within 30 days of filing the plan. If the plan has not yet been confirmed, then the debtor is supposed to tender the first plan payment to the trustee, who will then tender the payment or payments to the creditors when the plan has been confirmed. Recall that adequate protection payments to personal property secured claimants or lessors must be made until distributions under the plan begin. This acts as additional incentive to expedite the payment and confirmation process.[57] The above procedures make it relatively inexpensive and speedy for a debtor to pursue a Chapter 13 alternative as a solution for financial distress. In addition, these rapid procedures prevent debtors from abusing Chapter 13 as a haven to avoid debt repayment.

 Practice Pointer

Plan payments must commence within 30 days of filing the plan. The trustee will hold the payments until the plan is confirmed.

---

54. 11 U.S.C. §1323.
55. As to the Chapter 11 confirmation procedures, see generally chapter 27 infra.
56. 11 U.S.C. §1324.
57. 11 U.S.C. §1326(a)(3). See chapter 24B supra.

F.   CONFIRMATION CONDITIONS

At the confirmation hearing, the court will confirm the plan, but only if the court finds that the plan meets all the conditions of Section 1325(a). Under Section 1325(a), the court must make nine findings to approve the plan. If any of the nine items is missing, the plan cannot be confirmed.

The first finding that the court must make is that the plan complies with the provisions of Chapter 13 and the Bankruptcy Code.[58] This will not generally be a problematic issue. Second, the court must find that any filing fees required to be paid for initiating the Chapter 13 have been paid.[59] Third, the court must find that the plan has been proposed in good faith and not for any means forbidden by law.[60] For example, if the debtor is seeking to utilize Chapter 13 to accomplish an improper motive or to commit an act that would otherwise be illegal, the plan will not be confirmable.[61]

Fourth, the court must find that unsecured creditors will receive a dividend not less than what they would have received if the proceeding were filed under Chapter 7.[62] This requirement is commonly known as the "best interests of creditors" test. For example, if there is $10,000 of nonexempt property in the debtor's Chapter 13 estate, the Chapter 13 priority and unsecured creditors must receive a total dividend of at least $10,000, because this is what they would receive in a Chapter 7. Because most Chapter 13 proceedings would be no asset Chapter 7 proceedings, this finding is rarely a problematic issue.

The fifth finding relates to secured claims. Three alternatives are provided. The existence of at least one alternative must be found as to each secured claim for the plan to be confirmed. These requirements, in their essence, comprise alternative methods of adequate protection and preservation of the secured creditor's rights during performance of the plan. First, a secured creditor may accept the plan. If a secured claimant accepts the plan, the acceptance will aid in obtaining confirmation. The remaining alternatives concern what happens if a secured claimant does not accept the plan. If the plan provides that the holder of the claim will retain its lien until the earliest of payment in full of the debt or receipt of a Chapter 13 discharge then confirmation may occur over the secured

---

58. 11 U.S.C. §1325(a)(1).
59. 11 U.S.C. §1325(a)(2).
60. 11 U.S.C. §1325(a)(3).
61. *In re McGinnis,* 453 Bankr. 770 (Bankr. D. Or. 2011). Proposal to fund plan with revenues from medical marijuana growing operation could not be confirmed because marijuana is illegal under federal law. This issue becomes cloudy in light of the recent adoption by at least 20 states of laws allowing medical or recreational use of marijuana.
62. 11 U.S.C. §1325(a)(4).

Cramdown: the act of obtaining confirmation of a reorganization plan over the objection of creditors

creditor's objection. The lien is also retained if the case is converted or dismissed. The concept of approving a plan under these circumstances over a creditor's objection is commonly known as a **cramdown**. A creditor will not be heard to object to confirmation if the creditor will receive all that it would have received in a nonbankruptcy environment. This is the underlying principle of the cramdown concept in reorganization proceedings. Finally, a debtor may propose to surrender the collateral to the secured creditor. To summarize, as to each secured claim, the court must find that each creditor either agrees to the plan, is paid the full amount of the secured claim, or will receive the return of its collateral.[63]

BAPCPA added three new confirmation requirements. First, that the petition has been filed in good faith. This provision will likely be used in reconciling means testing issues with Chapter 13, and in dealing with the continuing problems raised by serial bankruptcy filings (see chapter 12 supra); second, that all postpetition domestic support obligations have been paid; and third, that all postpetition tax returns have been timely filed pursuant to Section 1308.[64]

In Till v. SCS Credit Corp., 541 U.S. 465, the Supreme Court held that secured creditors, for cramdown purposes, are entitled to interest on their claims based upon the prime interest rate plus a premium for risk that can be proven by the creditor, and not on the underlying rate provided for by the contract. In this case, the debtors owed $4,894.89 to the creditor when they filed their Chapter 13. They proposed to pay the secured portion of the claim, $4,000, over installments at an interest rate of 9.5 percent, or the prime rate plus 1.5 percent. The creditor insisted upon receiving its contract rate of 21 percent. A likely effect of this ruling will make it easier for Chapter 13 creditors to reduce interest rates on collateral not secured solely by their primary residence.

G. FEASIBILITY ANALYSIS

The final finding that the court must make to permit confirmation of a Chapter 13 plan is that the debtor will be able to make all of the payments under and comply with the plan.[65] In other words, the court must find that the plan is feasible. This determination is the most critical and problematic in a Chapter 13 case. If a plan is not feasible, the debtor will likely need to

---

63. 11 U.S.C. §1325(a)(5).
64. 11 U.S.C. §1325(a)(7), (8), and (9).
65. 11 U.S.C. §1325(a)(6).

convert to Chapter 7 if the bankruptcy system is to be of use in resolving the debtor's financial problems. Determining whether a feasible plan can be proposed will most likely decide the type of proceeding filed by the debtor in the first place. The following analysis reflects the state of the law before BAPCPA. The text will attempt to point out some of BAPCPA's effects. To determine a plan's feasibility, some calculation is required. First, determine the amount necessary to pay in full all administrative expenses and priority claims and to cure any defaults on secured debts. Second, determine the minimum amount necessary to pay unsecured creditors at least as much as they would receive in a Chapter 7. This total will be the minimum amount necessary to pay through the plan over its proposed length. Nonetheless, some courts do not generally favor zero percent or nominal unsecured dividends over objection even if the debtor's Chapter 7 would be a no asset proceeding. This is an area where local practice and custom should be ascertained.[66]

The third step used in determining the feasibility of a Chapter 13 plan is to determine the debtor's monthly budget. Schedules B106I and J comprise an estimated monthly family budget. This budget shows the income the family receives every month and what it will cost this family to meet its basic expenses before making its Chapter 13 plan payments. The expenses are subtracted from the income. If there is a surplus left after meeting the monthly living expenses, the surplus represents the amount available to pay into the plan on a monthly basis. If there is no surplus or if there is a deficit, the plan is not feasible. The debtor should file a Chapter 7 if the debtor wants to use the bankruptcy system.

 Practice Pointer

An interesting question arises where the debtor's Section 707(b) calculation is negative but the debtor's Schedule I and J show surplus income. The courts are divided as to whether or not a dividend must be paid to unsecured creditors.

---

66. See discussion above regarding 11 U.S.C. §§1322(a), 1325(a)(5), and 1325(a)(4). Whether or not this amount must include a minimum calculated means testing payment under Section 707(b)(2), or whether or not means testing eliminates zero percent or nominal plans in Chapter 13 cases that would fall under means testing (see chapter 5 supra), are issues being explored by the courts. Compare In re Frederickson, 545 F.3d 652 (8th Cir. 2008) (commitment period is a temporal requirement even with negative disposable income) with In re Kagenveama, 541 F.3d 868 (9th Cir. 2008) (commitment period does not apply where there is no disposable income).

If the budget shows a surplus of available income with which to make plan payments, the fourth step of the feasibility calculation can be performed. Divide the total minimum amount that must be paid into the plan by the available monthly surplus.[67] The quotient will be the number of months it will take to perform the plan. If the quotient is equal to or less than 60, the plan is likely feasible. The smaller the available surplus or the closer the plan approaches to 60 months in duration, the more doubtful it will be that the plan will be found feasible by the court. Under BAPCPA, if the debtor's median family income is less than the national family median income for a family of similar size (see chapter 24D supra), then the plan may not exceed three years in duration unless the court orders otherwise, but in no event may the plan exceed five years in duration. If the debtor's median family income is equal to or greater than the national family median income for a family of similar size, then the plan must be five years in duration. If the minimum available payment would make a plan exceed five years, it is not feasible.[68] Checklist 24.2 infra summarizes the above in a formula format.

A greater understanding of the feasibility issue can be gained through use of an extended example. Robinson Crusoe files a Chapter 13. He owes $1,000 in income taxes and $600 as a priority wage claim to his servant Friday. Bank of Defoe holds a mortgage on Crusoe's island that is six payments in default, totaling $2,500. Crusoe's unsecured creditors are owed $5,000. All Crusoe's assets are exempt. Thus, Crusoe's unsecured creditors would receive no dividend in a Chapter 7. The minimum amount that Crusoe *must* pay back is therefore $4,100 (income tax, wage claim, and past-due mortgage payments).

Crusoe's Chapter 13 statement shows that he will have surplus income of $150 per month with which to make payments under the plan. Performing the final calculation, dividing $4,100 by $150, yields a result of 27.33. It will take approximately 28 months for Crusoe to pay the minimum possible Chapter 13 plan he might propose. This plan could be found feasible, but note that it does not provide any dividend to unsecured creditors. This can affect feasibility and will not permit a cramdown in the event of objections by unsecured creditors.

Under BAPCPA, Crusoe's current monthly income would need to be known. If Crusoe's income is less than the national family median income for a family of similar size, then he must propose at least a three-year (36-month) plan if he wants to effectuate a cramdown. This would pay his

---

67. In 2010, the U.S. Supreme Court held that in calculating a Chapter 13 debtor's projected disposable income, the court may take a forward-looking approach and account for changes to the debtor's income or expenses known or virtually certain as of the date of confirmation. Hamilton v. Lanning, 560 U.S. 505 (2010).

68. 11 U.S.C. §1322(d).

unsecured creditors a dividend of approximately 25 percent (36 − 27.33 = 8.67 × \$150 = \$1,300.50). If Crusoe's income is equal to or greater than the national family median income for a family of similar size, then he must propose a five-year (60-month) plan to effectuate a cramdown. This would pay his unsecured creditors substantially in full (60 − 27.33 = 32.67 × \$150 = \$4,900.50). Whether or not either of these scenarios would be confirmable and subject to cramdown over the objection of unsecured creditors is the subject of 11 U.S.C. §1325(b).

H.   CRAMDOWN

Secured or unsecured creditors may object to the plan. Unlike Chapter 11, there is no voting procedure in Chapter 13. Unless a creditor objects to the plan, the creditor's acceptance is presumed. If a creditor or creditors do object to the plan, confirmation can still be obtained through a procedure commonly known as cramdown. This procedure has already been identified with regard to the secured creditors of a Chapter 13 debtor. Section 1325(b) describes the cramdown procedure when unsecured creditors object to a Chapter 13 plan.

Under Section 1325(b), there are two methods by which the debtor may effectuate a Chapter 13 cramdown upon unsecured creditors. The first method is that if the creditors are going to be paid in full, then the plan will be confirmed over their objection.[69] Creditors who will be paid in full through the plan will not be heard to object. Payment in full is, after all, the ultimate creditor goal in a bankruptcy proceeding.

> ### Practice Pointer
> The primary effect of means testing in Chapter 13 cases is to determine whether a plan must be either three or five years long, unless creditors can be paid in full in a shorter period of time.

Most of the time, however, unsecured creditors will not be paid in full. In this instance, the second method of cramdown is necessary. If the

---

69. 11 U.S.C. §1325(b)(1)(A).

Disposable income: all income not necessary for the maintenance or support of the debtor or a dependent of the debtor

unsecured creditors cannot be paid in full, a cramdown may still occur if the debtor proposes to place all disposable income into the plan for the applicable commitment period.[70] **Disposable income** invokes application of means testing (see chapter 5 supra). The debtor's current monthly income and expenses are determined in a manner identical to Chapter 7, except for additional deductions allowed for postpetition domestic support obligations, charitable religious contributions of up to 15 percent of gross income, and business expenses if the debtor is engaged in the operation of a business. If the debtor's current monthly income is less than the state median income for the debtor's household size, then the plan must be no less than three years in duration to effectuate a cramdown. If the debtor's current monthly income is equal to or greater than the state median income for the debtor's household size, then the plan must be of five years duration to effectuate a cramdown. When the creditors are paid in full, the plan may be less than these time periods.[71]

Thus, if Robinson Crusoe's unsecured creditors in the above example object to the plan, Crusoe must either pay them in full or propose a three- or five-year plan, depending upon his current monthly income as illustrated above. If Crusoe proposes to pay all disposable income into the plan for the appropriate three- or five-year period, the plan can be confirmed over the objection of unsecured creditors.

I. EFFECT OF CONFIRMATION AND CHAPTER 13 DISCHARGE

A confirmed Chapter 13 plan is a judicially approved composition agreement. When a Chapter 13 plan is confirmed, it acts as a new contract between the debtor and all of the creditors. All creditors are bound by a confirmed Chapter 13 plan.[72] This is the big difference between a Chapter 13 and a nonbankruptcy composition agreement. In the latter case, any objecting creditors are not bound by the agreement.

Once performance of a Chapter 13 plan has been completed, and the debtor certifies that any postpetition domestic support obligations have been paid, a Chapter 13 debtor becomes entitled to a Chapter 13 discharge. A Chapter 13 discharge is similar to a Chapter 7 discharge.

---

70. 11 U.S.C. §1325(b)(1)(B).
71. 11 U.S.C. §1325(b)(2), (3), (4).
72. 11 U.S.C. §1327.

A Chapter 13 debtor must also complete a postpetition personal financial management course identical to Chapter 7.[73]

An obligation for which final payment is due after the plan is completed is not dischargeable in Chapter 13.[74] For example, in the fifth year of a 30-year mortgage the debtor files a Chapter 13. The Chapter 13 plan cures the default and the debtor receives a discharge. The mortgage itself is not discharged because the last payment is due after the last payment under the plan.[75] Taxes are not dischargeable to the same extent that they are not dischargeable in Chapter 7 cases (but since all priority taxes must be paid in full through the plan, this is a moot point). Domestic support obligations are not discharged by a Chapter 13. Next, student loans remain nondischargeable to the same extent that they are not dischargeable in Chapter 7 proceedings. Debts incurred fraudulently, unlisted debts, and fiduciary defalcations are not dischargeable in Chapter 13. Damages resulting from substance abuse are nondischargeable to the same extent that they are not dischargeable in Chapter 7 proceedings.[76] Criminal restitution orders or criminal fines are not dischargeable.[77] Finally, restitution orders or civil damage awards resulting from willful or malicious injury, or wrongful death, are not dischargeable.[78]

A Chapter 13 debtor who has not fully completed a plan may still apply for and receive a discharge if the court finds that a failure to complete the plan is due to circumstances for which the debtor should not justly be held accountable and if unsecured creditors have received at least the amount of dividend they would have received in a Chapter 7 proceeding.[79] A death of one of two joint debtors is such a circumstance. If the court can make such findings for a debtor that has not completed a Chapter 13 plan, the debtor will receive a discharge that is identical to a Chapter 7 discharge.[80]

Prior to the 2005 BAPCPA legislation, many debts that were not dischargeable in Chapter 7 were in fact dischargeable in Chapter 13. The theory was that since a debtor was making an effort to repay debt, the scope of the discharge should be broader. However, as the 2005 reforms evidence a strong swing of the pendulum in favor of debt collection as opposed to debtor relief, the net effect of the reforms makes Chapter 13 more significant as a debt collection tool as opposed to providing honest

---

73. 11 U.S.C. §1328(a)(g).
74. 11 U.S.C. §1328(a)(1).
75. Bankruptcy Rule 3002.1(f), (g), and (h) comprise a procedure entitled Notice of Final Cure Payment designed to result in a court order that any prepetition default has been cured, effectively discharging this amount.
76. 11 U.S.C. §1328(a)(2).
77. 11 U.S.C. §1328(a)(4).
78. See chapter 14 supra.
79. 11 U.S.C. §1328(b).
80. 11 U.S.C. §1328(c).

but unfortunate debtors with a fresh start in their financial affairs. If the debtor has received a discharge in a Chapter 7, 11, or 12 filed within four years preceding the Chapter 13 filing, then no debts are dischargeable. If the debtor received a Chapter 13 discharge within two years prior to the filing, then no debts are dischargeable. These provisions, added by BAPCPA, are an important departure from prior law and will seriously limit the concept of the Chapter 20 described above in chapter 24D supra.[81]

Practice Pointer

Note that the so-called "super discharge" historically provided under Chapter 13 has been greatly curtailed following the BAPCPA amendments.

A Chapter 13 discharge may be revoked if the court finds that the discharge was fraudulently obtained. Revocation must be sought within one year of the discharge's being granted.[82] Confirmation of a Chapter 13 plan that has been fraudulently obtained may also be revoked.[83]

One of three things can happen during the life of a confirmed plan. The debtor may perform and complete the plan in a timely manner. This is the goal of the system. Or the debtor may receive a windfall during the life of the plan and wish to accelerate performance. Under Section 1329, the debtor may ask the court for permission to modify the plan to accelerate its performance. Or, third, the debtor may become unable to make payments under a confirmed plan. In this instance, the debtor may ask the court to modify the plan to lower the payments or to extend the plan's duration. This is permissible as long as the modified plan still complies with the provisions of Chapter 13 and as long as final performance of the plan is still no longer than five years from the original commencement of the plan.[84] If the plan cannot be successfully modified, then conversion of the proceeding to a Chapter 7 may become necessary.

---

81. 11 U.S.C. §1328(f).
82. 11 U.S.C. §1328(e).
83. 11 U.S.C. §1330.
84. 11 U.S.C. §1329.

Summary

This and the next four text chapters describe the reorganization proceedings of Chapter 13, Chapter 11, and Chapter 12. In a reorganization proceeding, a debtor will attempt to repay debt and retain nonexempt assets or continue to operate a business. Reorganization proceedings are, in their essence, no more or less than judicially approved composition agreements.

Chapter 13 is a program for individuals with regular income who have unsecured debts of less than $394,725 and secured debts of less than $1,184,200. A qualified individual may attempt repayment of debt over a period not to exceed five years.

The Chapter 13 procedure is expedited. The checklist accompanying this chapter itemizes the important deadlines, documents to file, and the hearing dates involved in a Chapter 13 proceeding.

A trustee will always be appointed in a Chapter 13. The most important function of the Chapter 13 trustee is to collect the plan payments and distribute dividends to creditors.

A Chapter 13 plan must contain four mandatory elements. A Chapter 13 plan may contain various permissive elements. The mandatory requirements are that the plan provide for payments, that priority claims be paid in full, that all claims within a given class be treated equally, and that domestic support obligations owed to a governmental entity may only be paid less than in full if the debtor proposes a five-year plan.

The permissive elements of a Chapter 13 plan include the debtor's providing for more than one class of unsecured claims, modifying the rights of certain secured creditors, the cure or waiver of defaults, and simultaneous payments to secured and unsecured creditors.

A Chapter 13 plan is confirmed at a confirmation hearing. The court must make nine findings to confirm a plan. If one of the findings cannot be made, the plan may not be confirmed. The plan must comply with the provisions of the Bankruptcy Code. Any filing fees must be paid. The plan must be proposed in good faith. The creditors must receive a dividend not less than the dividend that they would receive in a Chapter 7 proceeding. These issues are not generally problematic. With regard to secured creditors, the court must find either that the creditor consents, the creditor will be paid the full value of its secured claim, or that any collateral will be returned to the creditor. The petition must have been filed in good faith. All postpetition domestic support obligations must be current. All postpetition tax returns must be filed.

Finally, the court must find that the plan is feasible. This requires a determination that the debtor can afford to make the plan payments. The checklist accompanying this chapter describes a simple formula to use in making this calculation.

If creditors object to a Chapter 13 plan, the plan may still be approved over their objections through use of a procedure commonly known as cramdown. A cramdown of unsecured creditors will occur in a Chapter 13 if the plan will pay the creditors in full or if all the debtor's disposable income is paid into the plan for a period of time from three to five years, depending upon whether or not the debtor's family income is less or more than the national median family income for a family of similar size. Disposable income is determined in accordance with needs based bankruptcy (see chapter 6 supra).

A Chapter 13 plan may be modified after confirmation to accelerate or reduce performance. The modified plan must still meet the confirmation requirements.

A debtor completing performance of a Chapter 13 plan, completing a financial management course, and remaining current on postpetition domestic support obligations receives a discharge. Under BAPCPA, a Chapter 13 discharge is virtually identical to a Chapter 7 discharge. Additionally, debts for which the last payment is due after performance of the plan (such as a 30-year home loan) are not dischargeable. In special circumstances, a debtor may receive a hardship discharge in Chapter 13, which has the same effect as a Chapter 7 discharge. A discharge will not issue if the debtor received a Chapter 7, 11, or 12 discharge within four years from the filing of the Chapter 13, or has received a Chapter 13 discharge in another case within two years of the filing.

Confirmation of a Chapter 13 plan may be revoked if the court finds that confirmation was fraudulently obtained.

A reorganization proceeding may be dismissed or converted to a Chapter 7 liquidation for cause. The causes identified by the Code are delineated in the checklist accompanying this chapter.

KEY TERMS

applicable commitment period	mandatory element
confirmation	permissive element
conversion	plan
cramdown	property of the estate
dismissal	reorganization
disposable income	strip down
liquidation	strip off

CHAPTER 24 CHECKLIST

24.1   DOCUMENTS AND DEADLINES IN CHAPTER 13

		Deadline	*Statute*
24.1.1	Petition	at filing	Bankruptcy Rule 1002
24.1.2	Credit Counseling Certificate at Filing		11 U.S.C. §109(h)
24.1.3	Statement of Financial Affairs, Schedules	14 days	Bankruptcy Rule 1007(b)(2), (c)
24.1.4	Statement of Current Monthly Income	14 days	Bankruptcy Rule 1007(b)(5), (c)
24.1.5	Chapter 13 Plan	14 days	Bankruptcy Rule 3015
24.1.6	Attorneys' Fee Statement	creditors' meeting	Bankruptcy Rule 2016
24.1.7	First Plan Payment	30 days	11 U.S.C. §1326
24.1.8	Adequate Protection Payments	30 days	11 U.S.C. §1326(a)
24.1.9	Plan Performance:		
	1. Family Income ➔ SMFI[85]	3 years	11 U.S.C. §1322(d)
	2. Family Income SMFI[86]	5 years	11 U.S.C. §1322(d)
24.1.10	File Tax Returns for Last Four Years	creditors' meeting	11 U.S.C. §1308

---

85. "SMFI" means state family median income for a family of similar size.
86. Ibid.

24.2   CHAPTER 13 FEASIBILITY FORMULA

       24.2.1   Add (A)dministrative Claims, (P)riority Claims, and (M)inimum Chapter 7 Dividend (A + P + M)

       24.2.2   Determine Existence of Surplus or Deficit in Monthly Budget (Deficit Means Plan Is Not (B) Feasible)

       24.2.3   Divide the Total Reached in 23.2.1 by Any Budget Surplus (A + P + M) ÷ B

       24.2.4   If Answer Obtained in 23.2.3 Is 36 or Less, the Plan Is Likely Feasible. If Answer Obtained in 23.2.3 Is 36-60, the Plan May Be Feasible. (A + P + M) ÷ (B) ≤ 60

       24.2.5   Plan Must Be 3-5 Years Duration Depending upon Current Monthly Income. Add Amounts Necessary to Comply with Mandatory Length to 23.2.4.

24.3   CAUSES FOR CONVERSION OR DISMISSAL

		Statute
24.3.1	Loss or Diminution — Reorganization Unlikely	11 U.S.C. §1112(b)(4)(A)
24.3.2	Failure to Follow Operating Rules	11 U.S.C. §1112 (b)(4)(B)(C) (C)(F)(H)(I)
24.3.3	Unreasonable Delay Prejudicial to Creditors	11 U.S.C. §1307(c)(1)
24.3.4	Failure to Propose a Plan Within Court Deadlines	11 U.S.C. §§1112 (b)(4)(J), 1307(c)(3)
24.3.5	Failure to Obtain Confirmation of Any Plan	11 U.S.C. §1307(c)(5)
24.3.6	Revocation of Confirmation	11 U.S.C. §§1112(b) (4)(L), 1307(c)(7)
24.3.7	Inability to Commence Plan	11 U.S.C. §§1112(b) (4)(M), 1307(c)(4)

24.3.8	Material Default in Plan	11 U.S.C. §§1112(b)(4)(N), 1307(c)(6) *Statute*
24.3.9	Occurrence of a Condition Stated in Plan	11 U.S.C. §§1112(b)(4)(Q), 1307(c)(2)
24.3.10	Failure to Pay Court Fees	11 U.S.C. §§1112(b)(4)(K), 1307(c)(2)
24.3.11	Failure to File Chapter 13 Statement	11 U.S.C. §1307(c)(9), (10)
24.3.12	Failure to Pay Postpetition Domestic Support Obligations	11 U.S.C. §1307(c)(11)
24.3.13	Failure to File Tax Returns	11 U.S.C. §1308

DISCUSSION QUESTIONS

1. What is the purpose of a reorganization proceeding?
2. What are the grounds for dismissal or conversion of a reorganization proceeding?
3. What documents must a Chapter 13 debtor file with the court? What are the deadlines for filing each document? What is the effect of a failure to file a required document?
4. What is the permissible length of a Chapter 13 plan?
5. What elements must be included in a Chapter 13 plan? What elements may be included?
6. What findings must the court make to confirm a Chapter 13 plan? How is a plan's feasibility determined?
7. How does a creditor object to confirmation of a Chapter 13 plan?
8. What is meant by the term *cramdown*? How can a Chapter 13 debtor cram down a plan over the objection of an unsecured creditor?
9. How and when may a Chapter 13 plan be modified?
10. What is the effect of a Chapter 13 discharge? How, if at all, does a Chapter 13 discharge differ from a Chapter 7 discharge? What is a "hardship" discharge?
11. What is a "Chapter 20"?

PRACTICE EXERCISE

Exercise 24.1

Assuming that the debtors' case is originally filed or converted to Chapter 13, prepare a proposed Chapter 13 plan for Robin and Owen that proposes to repay any missed mortgage or car payments, along with any other debt necessary to obtain confirmation of the plan.

25

Chapter 11: Introduction and Administration

Learning Objectives

- Gain a basic understanding of Chapter 11, the most complex type of bankruptcy proceeding

- Describe the basic documents filed in a Chapter 11 proceeding

- Identify the appropriate filing deadlines

- Understand the various activities that should or must be taken by a Chapter 11 debtor-in-possession within the first 60 days of filing

- Describe the operating report requirements of Chapter 11 proceedings

A. INTRODUCTION TO CHAPTER 11

Chapter 11 is the most complex, time-consuming, and expensive of all bankruptcy proceedings to prosecute. Chapter 11 cases comprise less than 1 percent of all bankruptcies filed, but they consume substantial amounts of the court's time.[1] The various topics described elsewhere in this text — relief from stay motions, the assumption or rejection of executory contracts, the use or sale of property including the use of cash

---

1. According to figures available from the United States Courts, Chapter 11 proceedings comprised .9 percent of all filings for the calendar year ending September 30, 2016, or 7,450 out of 805,580 total filings.

collateral, and the obtaining of credit by a bankruptcy estate — are all recurring issues in Chapter 11 proceedings. Each issue must be dealt with independently, but the resolution of each issue may involve one or more evidentiary hearings. Further, and most critically, the resolution of one or more of these issues can often be essential to the outcome of the case.

Chapter 11 is generally thought of as a business reorganization vehicle. It can, however, be used by individuals. An individual seeks Chapter 11 relief when the debtor owes debt in excess of the Chapter 13 limits described in the preceding chapter.

Often, a resolution of any or all of the above issues may be required at the inception of a Chapter 11 proceeding. For example, a manufacturing debtor-in-possession may need to obtain a cash collateral order, obtain postpetition secured credit, and assume existing manufacturing contracts within a relatively short period of time after the Chapter 11 filing. These activities will involve motions under Sections 363, 364, and 365, respectively.[2] Simultaneously, a debtor-in-possession may be required to defend motions to appoint a trustee or examiner under Section 1104 or motions for relief from stay or adequate protection under Sections 362 and 361.[3] All of these activities may occur and be determined before a debtor-in-possession can even begin to consider proposing a plan of reorganization. It is in Chapter 11 practice that the Bankruptcy Code most frequently and visibly operates as a complete system affecting all of a debtor's financial affairs. In large reorganizations typical of the Southern District of New York or the District of Delaware, any or all of those matters may be the subject of one or more **first-day orders** sought at the beginning of the case.

First-day order: common name of orders entered within the first day or two of a large corporate Chapter 11 filing

Like Chapter 13, the goal of a Chapter 11 proceeding is for a debtor to successfully reorganize its affairs so it may repay debt, retain assets, and remain in business. Like Chapter 13, this is accomplished by a debtor-in-possession proposing a plan of reorganization and obtaining its confirmation. Unlike Chapter 13, the Chapter 11 plan confirmation process is complex and lengthy. At least two significant court hearings are required to confirm a plan. A further important difference from Chapter 13 is that the creditors in a Chapter 11 case are given the opportunity to vote for or against the plan. It normally takes a minimum of four to six months to obtain confirmation of a typical Chapter 11 plan.[4] Like a Chapter 13, a confirmed Chapter 11 plan is nothing more or less than a judicially approved composition agreement.

A number of actions, many of which have been described elsewhere in this text, need to be taken by a Chapter 11 debtor within 120 days of filing to ensure that all provisions of the Bankruptcy Code and Federal Rules of

---

2. See chapters 19, 20, and 21 supra.
3. See chapters 11 and 13 supra.
4. See chapter 27 infra.

Bankruptcy Procedure are properly complied with in the prosecution of the Chapter 11 proceeding. In addition, because a Chapter 11 may remain pending for an indefinite period of time prior to confirmation of a plan and because the debtor acts as its own trustee as a debtor-in-possession, a number of operating rules have been created to monitor a debtor-in-possession's compliance with the Bankruptcy Code and Rules. These operating rules are generally implemented by guidelines published by the local United States Trustee. A sample set of guidelines is contained on the Forms Disk accompanying this text. This chapter concerns the initial actions and ongoing operating procedures that a debtor-in-possession must follow prior to confirmation of a plan. The following two chapters will describe the procedure and requirements for proposing and obtaining confirmation of a Chapter 11 plan.

Any entity that may file under Chapter 7 is also eligible to file a Chapter 11 case.[5] Chapter 11 is intentionally designed this way. A corporation as large as General Motors or an individual debtor owing just slightly in excess of the Chapter 13 debt limits is each eligible to file a Chapter 11 proceeding.[6] Chapter 11 is thus designed to work for small debtors as well as large debtors. When a large corporation files, the filing is undoubtedly reported in the media. For example, United Airlines, U.S. Air, General Motors, American Airlines, and Hostess Bakeries have all been involved in widely publicized Chapter 11 cases in recent years. In remarks before the American Bankruptcy Institute, Chief Justice William H. Rehnquist stated: "Chapter 11 has become a major tool for restructuring corporate America, with broad implications for employees, retirees, business competitors, and the economy as a whole."[7]

> **FACT PATTERN**
>
> *If Owen elects to file bankruptcy for The Lawn Cuttery, does it make sense to file a Chapter 7 or a Chapter 11 case?*

The Bankruptcy Reform Act of 1994 created a new subcategory of Chapter 11 debtor, the **small business debtor**. A small business debtor is defined as a debtor with liquidated debts not in excess of $2,566,050 who elects treatment as a small business. A small business, however, may not be a debtor whose primary activity is owning and operating real estate.[8] A small business may have no creditor committee if the court

Small business debtor: a Chapter 11 debtor with liquidated debts not in excess of $2,566,050 who elects treatment as a small business debtor, excluding a debtor whose primary activity is owning and operating real estate; small business debtors are defined in Bankruptcy Code Section 101(51D)

---

5. 11 U.S.C. §109. See chapter 5 supra.
6. Toibb v. Radloff, 501 U.S. 157 (1991), discussed in section 5E supra, held that individuals may file Chapter 11 proceedings.
7. Remarks of Chief Justice William H. Rehnquist, Annual Spring Meeting of the American Bankruptcy Institute, May 18, 1992.
8. 11 U.S.C. §101(51C). The amount is subject to adjustment as per 11 U.S.C. §104(b). See chapter 4 supra. The text reflects amounts in effect as of April 1, 2016.

so orders and must expedite the formulation of a reorganization plan (see chapter 11 supra and chapter 26 infra).

FACT PATTERN

The Lawn Cuttery would qualify as a small business debtor.

Chapter 11 is more than a legal program for the reorganization of a debtor. It is incorrect to think of Chapter 11 reorganization as solely a legal process. A debtor often may have one or more serious problems that may precipitate the Chapter 11 filing. Sometimes, as in the case of Texaco, the problem is related to one event, such as a large judgment that the debtor cannot satisfy without imposition of a repayment plan over the objection of the judgment creditor. Or, the event could be a sudden collapse in the market price of a commodity such as oil that recently took place in the oil market, triggering a wave of bankruptcy filings in the oil industry.

Sometimes a debtor's problems are related to fraud, mismanagement, or the gross incompetence of its insiders. Fraud was the precipitating factor in the bankruptcy of Madoff Securities and its owner Bernie Madoff. In these situations, more than a legal reorganization may be required to solve the debtor's problems. As a practical matter, a business may also need to be reorganized internally in addition to the external reorganization represented by the plan with creditors. Internal reorganization may be as simple as teaching a debtor how to count and manage a budget over an extended period of time. This single problem is a major cause of many Chapter 11 filings. Sometimes, internal reorganization can be quite complex and involve a change of insider management, plant closings, layoffs, and so forth. The ability to propose a confirmable plan requires financing and building consensus amongst the various groups of creditors so they will vote for the plan. Ultimately, Chapter 11 presents a unique confluence of law, economics, and politics.

Sometimes a Chapter 11 will involve a partnership with one piece of real property that is in foreclosure. This sort of proceeding has relatively few problematic issues because all the debtor seeks is to refinance or sell the property so as to avoid the foreclosure and realize a profit. Not much may happen in the proceeding until a secured creditor moves for relief from the stay or the debtor can propose a plan, typically through a sale or refinancing of the debtor.

Debtor-in-possession: the fiduciary entity created by a debtor filing a Chapter 11 reorganization proceeding

The filing of a Chapter 11 proceeding makes the petitioner a "**debtor-in-possession**."[9] A debtor-in-possession is the functional equivalent of a trustee.[10] As illustrated elsewhere, the debtor-in-possession is authorized

---

9. 11 U.S.C. §1101(1).
10. 11 U.S.C. §1107. See chapter 11 supra.

to conduct ordinary business affairs without court approva415l except as required by Sections 363, 364, or 365.[11]

The United States Trustee has been charged with monitoring a Chapter 11 debtor-in-possession's postpetition operations to ensure compliance with the provisions of the Bankruptcy Code and Rules.[12] Additionally, one role of the Official Creditors' Committee is to be active in monitoring the debtor's affairs during the proceeding.[13]

There are definite benefits that a debtor gains from a Chapter 11 filing. A business in serious financial condition may continue to operate without danger of immediate closure by any of its creditors. This breathing spell theoretically provides the debtor with an opportunity to attempt a successful reorganization of its financial affairs. Various Code provisions also exist to allow the debtor to restructure the repayment of its debt. However, there are also burdens that a debtor must accept along with the benefits of a Chapter 11 proceeding.

The largest burden is that the debtor will be required to comply with many new operating and/or reporting rules. The practical impact of these rules is that by filing a Chapter 11, the debtor-in-possession effectively becomes an involuntary partner with its creditors. The debtor's financial affairs are no longer private. They will be subject to constant monitoring and criticism by the creditors' committee, individual creditors, and/or the United States Trustee.[14] All of these entities have the opportunity to intrude into and attempt to control the debtor's financial affairs in manners not normally possible in a nonbankruptcy environment.

If a debtor-in-possession fails to comply with the operating rules, the Official Creditors' Committee or the United States Trustee or any other creditor may move before the court for the appointment of a trustee or an examiner, thus removing the debtor from possession.[15] Alternatively, if the proceeding fails as a Chapter 11 or if the debtor fails to comply with the operating rules, a Chapter 11 proceeding may be converted to a Chapter 7 or dismissed pursuant to Section 1112.[16]

Practice Pointer

Failure to file operating reports may qualify as "cause" for dismissal or conversion of the case.

---

11. See chapters 19, 20, and 21 supra.
12. 28 U.S.C. §586(a)(3). See chapter 11 supra.
13. 11 U.S.C. §1103. See chapter 11 supra.
14. See chapter 11 supra.
15. See chapter 11 supra.
16. 11 U.S.C. §1112. See chapter 24 supra for a more detailed description of §1112.

B.   ACTIONS TO TAKE WITHIN 120 DAYS OF FILING

At the moment of filing a Chapter 11, a debtor must file the following documents with the court:

1. petition, along with payment of an $1,717 filing fee;
2. a corporate resolution or partnership consent authorizing the filing;
3. a list containing the names and addresses of each creditor unless the Schedules are filed with the petition;
4. a list of the 20 largest unsecured claimants including the amount of the claims; and
5. a corporate debtor must file Official Form 201A.
6. an individual debtor must file a credit counseling certificate (11 U.S.C. §109(h); 11 U.S.C. §521(b). See chapter 4 supra).
7. a small business debtor must file, within three days, its most recent balance sheet, statement of operations, cash-flow statement, federal income tax return or a statement under penalty of perjury as to which of the items has not been prepared or filed (11 U.S.C. §1116(1)).

Some of these time periods may be extended upon application to the court or United States Trustee.[17]

FACT PATTERN

Focusing on these seven items, what hurdles do you see for Owen in filing a Chapter 11 case for the Lawn Cuttery?

Within 14 days of filing the petition, a Chapter 11 debtor must file the following additional documents with the court:

8. a list of all equity security holders of the debtor;
9. the Statement of Financial Affairs;
10. Schedules of Assets and Liabilities; and
11. a Statement of Executory Contracts.

These time periods may be extended upon application to the court or United States Trustee.[18] The United States Trustee will conduct an

---

17. 11 U.S.C. §302; Bankruptcy Rules 1002, 1004, 1006, 1007(a), (d). See chapter 5 supra.
18. Bankruptcy Rules 1007(a)(3)(4), 1007(b)(1).

informal conference known as an Initial Debtor Interview with representatives of the debtor to discuss the operating requirements and to implement compliance with the rules and guidelines applicable within a given
district. In a small business case, Section 1116(2) mandates an Initial
Debtor Interview. Form 10.1 is a sample of a local United States Trustee
guidelines.

Within 30 days of filing, the debtor must also file an inventory, if
ordered to do so by the United States Trustee, and commence to file
operating reports.[19] Local rules may also supplement these basic requirements. Any applications to retain professionals, such as attorneys or
accountants, must also be filed during the same initial 30-day period or
within 30 days of the professional's retention.

Finally, a debtor-in-possession must act within 120 days to assume any
lease of nonresidential real property or the lease is deemed rejected.[20]

C.   DEBTOR-IN-POSSESSION BANK ACCOUNTS

Local rules or United States Trustee guidelines may impose additional
requirements that a Chapter 11 debtor-in-possession must perform
promptly after the filing or on an ongoing basis. First, a debtor-in-possession will be required to deposit all funds in an approved depository pursuant to Section 345. Recall that an approved depository is a bank or
savings and loan that guarantees bankruptcy deposits greater than
$250,000.[21]

Next, local rules will require a debtor-in-possession to close its old
bank accounts and open new ones. Because part of the theory behind the
debtor-in-possession concept is that it is a new entity separate and distinct
from the prepetition debtor, the requirement of establishing new bank
accounts helps implement the theory. This requirement also serves as a
useful accounting mechanism for the debtor because it closes the prepetition books and opens new ones.

Local rules or United States Trustee guidelines may require that at
least three accounts be established. They are normally a general account,
a payroll account, and a tax account. These new accounts will be required
to identify the debtor as a debtor-in-possession. For example, it will not

---

19. Bankruptcy Rule 2015. As to small business debtors, 11 U.S.C. §1116 codifies these
    requirements.
20. 11 U.S.C. §365(d)(4). See chapter 20 supra.
21. 11 U.S.C. §345. See chapter 21 supra.

generally be acceptable for ABC Inc. to identify itself as such on its checks. The checks must now state "ABC Inc., Debtor-in-Possession," along with the case number. Local rules or United States Trustee guidelines should be consulted to identify the acceptable legend required in a given district.

FACT PATTERN

Because The Lawn Cuttery is a small business at this stage, will it be able to skip the requirement of multiple bank accounts and continue to manage its business through one account?

The requirement of multiple bank accounts is designed to assist debtors in efficiently managing their cash flow, ensuring to the greatest extent possible that payroll and tax obligations will be satisfied properly and promptly and that any party in interest who desires may easily trace a debtor's cash flow during the Chapter 11. All income that a debtor receives is to be deposited into the general account. From the general account all disbursements are made by the debtor. For example, there will be disbursements from the general account into the payroll account to meet payroll. There will be disbursements from the general account into the tax

D.I.P. Account/Cash Flow

ALL INCOME

Cash Collateral Account
(if required)

General Account

| Payroll Account | All Other Disbursements | Tax Account |

| Payroll Disbursements | | Tax Payments |

account as the taxes are incurred. All other postpetition debts of the estate will be paid from the general account.

A large debtor may actually have more than three bank accounts. For example, a debtor-in-possession accumulating cash surpluses should open a savings account so the surplus funds can earn interest. In addition, any secured creditor's cash collateral will be required to be deposited into a separate cash collateral account before disbursement into other accounts. If use of the cash collateral is allowed, disbursements from the cash collateral account will be directed as the parties and court agree. The accompanying diagram indicates the general flow of cash through debtor-in-possession accounts.

D. INSIDER COMPENSATION

Local rules may require that a debtor-in-possession obtain an order from the court approving any compensation to be paid the debtor's insiders. In districts utilizing a rule of this nature, a Chapter 11 debtor will subject the salary of its insiders to the scrutiny of creditors and approval by the court. Approval of insider salaries will generally require a noticed motion.[22] The court may approve compensation on an interim basis while this process is pending. The United States Trustee normally monitors applications for insider compensation and may challenge the amount sought.

It is in the court's discretion to decide what will constitute reasonable compensation to an insider. The practitioner should be prepared to demonstrate two sets of facts to the court. First, the court should be shown what duties the insider performs for the debtor, such as the number of hours per week worked, a job description, and, if available, a comparison of salaries for similar positions in the debtor's industry. Second, the court may require disclosure of the insider's basic monthly living expenses. A budget statement similar to those used in Chapter 7 and Chapter 13 proceedings should suffice in most situations. The insider employees of a debtor-in-possession will necessarily be entitled to salaries, because it will be difficult or impossible for the debtor to reorganize if its key employees are prohibited from receiving a paycheck at least sufficient to meet basic monthly living expenses, especially in small business debtor cases. This is common sense. Once all of the foregoing acts have been accomplished, the Chapter 11 proceeding has been properly organized to fulfill

---

22. See chapter 5 supra.

all but two initial operational requirements of the Bankruptcy Code and Federal Rules of Bankruptcy Procedure. A Chapter 11 debtor-in-possession has the continuing duty to file operating reports and the obligation to pay quarterly fees to the United States Trustee pursuant to 28 U.S.C. §1930(a)(6). The amount of this fee depends on the total disbursements made by the debtor-in-possession until dismissal or conversion of a case.[23] Checklist 24.3 infra is a table of United States Trustee quarterly fees.

FACT PATTERN

As an employee of The Lawn Cuttery, Owen should not have any difficulty getting approval for his salary. If he claims an additional salary or expenses as the corporate president for which he provides no additional duties, the court may take a closer look before granting approval.

E.   OPERATING REPORTS

The most important ongoing duty of a Chapter 11 debtor-in-possession is to file monthly operating reports. This is required by both the Code and the Rules.[24] Local rules or United States Trustee guidelines will generally require the reports to be filed on a monthly basis. Section 308 mandates the basic items to be included in operating reports in small business cases. A format approved by the United States Trustee is included on the Forms Disk accompanying this text.

Operating reports: a regular report of a Chapter 11 debtor-in-possession's postpetition financial activity; local rules will normally require the filing of monthly reports

   The **operating report** serves a number of critical functions in the administration of a Chapter 11 proceeding. It is a regular report of a debtor's ongoing postpetition business operations. It will advise the creditors, Official Creditors' Committee, and the United States Trustee if the debtor is generating profits or losses during the proceeding. If the debtor is incurring debts that it is not timely paying, if any improper disbursements are being made (avoidable postpetition transactions, for example), or if any transactions have taken place without the requisite prior court approval (such as administrative loans or unauthorized use of cash collateral), this information will be disclosed in the report.[25] Undue delay in the formulation of a plan to the creditors' prejudice can be ascertained from review of a series of operating reports. Examination of the

---

23. 28 U.S.C. §1930(a)(6).
24. 11 U.S.C. §308; 11 U.S.C. §1106(a)(1); 11 U.S.C. §704(8); 11 U.S.C. §1116(4); Bankruptcy Rule 2015(a)(3).
25. 11 U.S.C. §§364, 549, 363(c). See chapters 18, 19, and 21 supra.

report will allow a creditor, the Official Creditors' Committee, or the United States Trustee to determine whether a proceeding should continue, be converted or dismissed, or have a trustee appointed to oversee the debtor's operations even more closely. From the results contained in operating reports, the parties will be able to evaluate the feasibility of any proposed plan that relies on operating revenues for performance.

For example, if Linus's Security Blankets, Inc., has been in a Chapter 11 for four years while accumulating cash profits sufficient to pay all claims in full, the creditors might propose their own plan or seek dismissal or conversion of the proceeding. On the other hand, if a proceeding appears interminable and a series of reports indicates that adequate profits cannot be generated to repay creditors, then the creditors may use this data to seek conversion of the proceeding to a Chapter 7. In short, the operating reports comprise an official record of a debtor-in-possession's postpetition financial activities. This record will demonstrate whether a proceeding is destined for success or failure.

Ideally, an accurate operating report will contain elements of the two basic accounting methods, cash or accrual. Each accounting method will disclose certain aspects of the debtor's postpetition financial status that may be germane to a continuation of the proceeding as a Chapter 11.

The **cash method** of accounting is the accounting method that virtually all individuals use every day of their lives. The cash method of accounting accounts for cash at the time it is received or spent. The **accrual method** of accounting, on the other hand, identifies as income any right to receive payment for goods delivered or services performed. For example, an account receivable is considered income under the accrual method of accounting, while it would not be so considered in the cash method of accounting until the payment is actually received. In addition, the accrual method of accounting identifies as an expense any debt that has been incurred even though it has not yet been paid. Most businesses that have inventory are required, for tax purposes, to use the accrual method of accounting on a regular basis. Manufacturing entities are also required to use the accrual method of accounting. The Schedules of Assets and Liabilities that a debtor must file in any bankruptcy proceeding are really not much more than a form of accrual basis financial statements. The accrual method describes all obligations that have been accrued but not paid by a debtor while itemizing all of a debtor's assets. This is the essence of the accrual method of accounting. The cash method of accounting identifies whether the debtor-in-possession has more or less cash on hand at the beginning or end of a reporting period as time passes. The accrual method of accounting identifies, over a period of time, whether the receivables are increasing or decreasing or if outstanding accounts payable are increasing or decreasing.

Cash method: an accounting method that measures the cash transactions (income and expenses) of an entity

Accrual method: an accounting method that measures all financial transactions of an entity; a debt owed is an accrued expense and an account receivable is accrued income

FACT PATTERN

Which form of accounting would you expect The Lawn Cuttery to utilize?

An operating report must contain an itemization of all receipts and disbursements made by a debtor-in-possession.[26] This is a cash basis representation of the debtor-in-possession's activities. Each bank account maintained by a debtor-in-possession should have its own itemized disbursement schedule included in the monthly operating report. Each disbursement must be identified. It may be sufficient in many cases simply to attach a copy of the debtor-in-possession's check register as an exhibit to the report. The check register will identify the check number, the amount, and the identity of the payee.

A debtor-in-possession should avoid making cash disbursements. If, however, cash disbursements are made, the debtor-in-possession should maintain detailed records of them. The invoices paid or payment receipts should be maintained and itemized in the report so that all transactions conducted by a debtor are accounted for. Otherwise, an examiner, a trustee, a creditor, or the United States Trustee will assume that the cash disbursement was improper.

The report should reconcile, or balance, a debtor-in-possession's bank accounts. This part of the report will disclose the amount on deposit in each account at the beginning and end of a reporting period. Each account should be identified by name, address, and account number.

The accrual portion of an operating report, where required, will identify whether the debtor is or is not generally paying its postpetition debts as they become due. The debtor should disclose debts that are accrued but unpaid and the length of time such debts have been unpaid. Similarly, an aging report of accounts receivable should also be provided.

F.   REVIEWING OPERATING REPORTS

As noted above, an operating report serves as an official record of the debtor-in-possession's postpetition financial affairs. It discloses whether the reorganization is succeeding or failing. Having generally described the contents of an operating report, practical uses of them can now be further illustrated.

---

26. 11 U.S.C. §308 mandates these items in small business operating reports. See also Bankruptcy Rule 2015(2)(3).

A compilation of data from one or more operating reports can provide admissible evidence as to positive or negative trends in a Chapter 11 proceeding. First, total up all receipts for any number of months during the proceeding for which data are desired. Observe whether receipts are increasing or decreasing every month. A calculation might also be made as to the average monthly receipts. Observe the trend. Is it increasing or decreasing? If receipts are rising, the time may have arrived to propose a plan. On the other hand, if receipts are decreasing every month, it might be time to file a motion to convert, especially if the accrued but unpaid expenses are accumulating rapidly.

Second, examine the disbursements. Verify that any insider compensation has been approved by the court, where required, and that the amount paid does not exceed the court-approved amount. If the report discloses that an insider has suddenly received a substantial raise, this may be brought to the attention of the court. If there are substantial cash disbursements, without any verification, this should also be considered evidence of improper management.

Next, review the bank account balances. If the balances at the end of each reporting period are increasing, this may be evidence that the proceeding is succeeding. On the other hand, if the balance is consistently negative or is decreasing from one reporting period to the next, this may be evidence that the proceeding is failing.

The list of accrued but unpaid expenses can be very revealing. Many businesses usually pay their bills 30 to 40 days after receiving them. It is not uncommon to have an entire month of accounts payable accrued and unpaid at any given point in time in the normal operation of any business. This should not be considered a sign of financial difficulty. Thus, if a list of accrued but unpaid expenses is roughly equivalent to a debtor's monthly cash expenses (by reviewing a series of reports these averages can be computed), this should not be construed as a sign of failure. Sometimes, even two months of arrears do not necessarily signify danger. But once a debtor shows three months or more of unpaid postpetition debt, it is time to reconsider the status of the proceeding as a Chapter 11. A debtor's representative should recommend that the matter be converted to a Chapter 7. A creditor's representative may move the court for conversion or the appointment of a trustee or examiner to investigate the status of the proceeding in greater detail. Remember, all unpaid postpetition debts are administrative expenses.[27] The more of them there are, the less will be available for payment of dividends to prepetition unsecured creditors if the proceeding is converted to a Chapter 7.

---

27. See chapter 22 supra.

In a large proceeding sometimes even one or two months of accrued and unpaid expenses can be fatal. In some situations, the delay of even a week in filing a report can result in accrual of additional substantial unpaid expenses without knowledge of the creditors. The best way to prevent this in a large proceeding is to make sure that the Official Creditors' Committee is organized promptly and demand that a debtor provide informal weekly or biweekly reports of operations to the committee. In an appropriate matter, the United States Trustee might undertake such intervention.

The burden of being a Chapter 11 debtor-in-possession is that the debtor becomes an involuntary partner with its creditors. Any effort to conceal the truth from the creditors will ultimately work to the debtor's detriment. Full cooperation and disclosure should be the norm, particularly because the most successful Chapter 11 proceedings are more a process of reconciliation between debtor and creditors than a process of continual adversarial dispute. Full compliance by a debtor-in-possession with all operating rules will only help to increase the chances for a successful outcome to the proceeding.

Summary

Chapter 11 is the most complex, time-consuming, and expensive of all bankruptcy proceedings to prosecute. Chapter 11 is available to any debtor qualified to be a Chapter 7 debtor. A major corporation or the corner store may each file Chapter 11 proceedings.

As is the case with Chapter 13, the goal of a Chapter 11 debtor-in-possession is to obtain court confirmation of a repayment plan. In Chapter 11, the plan is called a plan of reorganization. However, this is where the similarity ends. The process for obtaining confirmation of a Chapter 11 reorganization plan is complex and time-consuming. Further, a Chapter 11 debtor-in-possession is subject to substantially more administrative requirements than a Chapter 13 debtor. The checklist accompanying this chapter outlines these requirements.

The most important administrative requirement placed upon a debtor-in-possession is to file monthly operating reports with the court. The checklist accompanying this chapter outlines the critical elements of an operating report. The forms materials accompanying this text contains a sample operating report approved by the United States Trustee.

The practical effect of the Chapter 11 debtor-in-possession rules is to make the debtor an involuntary partner with its creditors. Cooperation and disclosure are required to be the norm. Full compliance by a debtor-in-possession with all operating rules will only help to increase the chance for a successful outcome to the proceeding.

KEY TERMS

---

accrual method   operating report
cash method   small business debtor
debtor-in-possession
first-day order

CHAPTER 25 CHECKLIST

25.1   CHAPTER 11 ADMINISTRATION —   *Authority*
        DOCUMENTS AND DEADLINES
        25.1.1   Deadline — At Filing

1.	Petition and $1,717 filing fee	Bankruptcy Rules 1002, 1006
2.	Corporate resolution of partnership authorization	Bankruptcy Rule 1004 Official Form B201
3.	List of creditors, unless schedules filed at filing	Bankruptcy Rule 1007(a)(1)
4.	List of 20 largest unsecured claims	Bankruptcy Rule 1007(d)
5.	Corporate debtor — Petition	Bankruptcy Rule 7007.1 Official Form B201A
6.	Individual debtor credit counseling certificate	11 U.S.C. §109(h); 11 U.S.C. §521(b)
7.	Small business debtor financial statements; tax returns	11 U.S.C. §1116(1)

        25.1.2   Deadline — Within 14 Days of Filing

1.	List of equity security holders	Bankruptcy Rule 1007(a)(3)
2.	Statement of Financial Affairs	11 U.S.C. §521(1), Bankruptcy Rule 1007(b)
3.	Schedules of Assets and Liabilities	11 U.S.C. §521(1), Bankruptcy Rule 1007(b)
4.	Statement of Executory Contracts	Bankruptcy Rule 1007(b)
5.	Debtor-in-possession bank accounts	11 U.S.C. §345, consult local rules

6. Attorney statement of   11 U.S.C. §329,
    compensation   Bankruptcy Rule 2016(b)

25.1.3 Deadline — Within 30 Days of Filing

1. Applications to retain   11 U.S.C. §327,
    professionals   Bankruptcy Rule 2014,
                              consult local Rules

2. Applications for   consult local Rules
    insider compensation

3. Commence operating   Bankruptcy Rule
    reports   2015(a)(2), (3); 11 U.S.C.
                              §1116(4)

4. File inventory if   Bankruptcy Rule
    United States Trustee   2015(a)(1)
    requires

25.1.4 Deadline — Within 120   11 U.S.C. §365(d)(4)
        Days of Filing Assume
        Nonresidential Property
        Leases

25.2   OPERATING REPORT — MAJOR FEATURES

25.2.1 Summary of Receipts

25.2.2 Itemization of Disbursements

25.2.3 Identification of Bank Accounts

25.2.4 Reconciliation of Bank Balances

25.2.5 List of Accrued and Unpaid Postpetition Debt

25.2.6 List of Accrued and Uncollected Postpetition Accounts
        Receivable

25.3   UNITED STATES TRUSTEE QUARTERLY FEES

Disbursements/Quarter	Fee
less than $15,000	$325
$15,000 to $75,000	$650
$75,000 to $150,000	$975
$150,000 to $225,000	$1,625
$225,000 to $300,000	$1,950
$300,000 to $1,000,000	$4,875
$1,000,000 to $2,000,000	$6,500
$2,000,000 to $3,000,000	$9,750
$3,000,000 to $5,000,000	$10,400
$5,000,000 to $15,000,000	$13,000
$15,000,000 to $30,000,000	$20,000
$30,000,000 and up	$30,000

DISCUSSION QUESTIONS

1. What distinguishes a Chapter 11 bankruptcy from other bankruptcy proceedings?

2. What documents must a Chapter 11 debtor file with the court? What are the deadlines for filing each document? What is the effect of a failure to file a required document?

3. What rules must a debtor-in-possession comply with regarding the administration of a Chapter 11 estate?

4. What is an operating report? Describe the major features of an operating report.

5. What is the role of the United States Trustee in the supervision of a debtor-in-possession?

PRACTICE EXERCISE

Exercise 25.1

Owen Cash comes to you for advice regarding a possible bankruptcy filing for The Lawn Cuttery, which he recently incorporated. Your supervising attorney examines the financial data and wants to recommend a Small Business Chapter 11 filing. Prepare a memo outlining any special operating rules applicable to a Small Business Chapter 11 debtor conducting business postpetition.

26

Chapter 11: Elements of a Plan

Learning Objectives

- Describe the events and documents involved in the Chapter 11 plan confirmation process

- Describe the time limits relative to filing a Chapter 11 plan, commonly known as the "exclusivity period"

- Describe how claims are classified within a Chapter 11 plan

- Identify the mandatory and permissive elements that must or may be included in a Chapter 11 plan

- Understand the unique Chapter 11 concept of "impaired" claims

A.   CONFIRMATION PROCESS — OVERVIEW

The process of formulating and obtaining confirmation of a Chapter 11 reorganization plan is the most complex process in the Bankruptcy Code. A Chapter 11 reorganization plan is known as a **Plan of Reorganization**. There are a number of steps that must be taken and many rules to apply to achieve confirmation. In a typical situation, this process should take from four to six months. This chapter analyzes the elements of a plan. Chapter 26 infra describes the details of the confirmation process.

Plan of Reorganization: common title of a Chapter 11 reorganization plan

The goal of a Chapter 11 proceeding is to obtain confirmation of a Chapter 11 reorganization plan that will satisfy creditors while retaining assets or continuing the debtor's business. An overview of the entire process will be helpful.

Plan proponent:
entity filing a
Chapter 11 plan

**Disclosure
statement:** a
document filed in
a Chapter 11
proceeding that
describes a debtor-
in-possession's
reorganization
plan, its effect
upon the cred-
itors, the ability of
the plan to be
performed, and a
comparison of the
reorganization
plan's repayment
proposal to the
results likely to be
obtained in a
Chapter 7 pro-
ceeding for the
same debtor

**Prepackaged
bankruptcy:** a
Chapter 11 pro-
ceeding in which a
debtor seeks
Bankruptcy Court
approval of a plan
where votes have
been solicited
before the case has
been filed

**Confirmation
packet:** a group
of documents,
including a Plan of
Reorganization
and a Disclosure
Statement, that are
sent to creditors
when authorized
to solicit votes for
or against a Chap-
ter 11 plan

The first step is to file a reorganization plan. Along with the plan, the **plan proponent** (entity filing the plan) must also file a document known as a **disclosure statement**.[1] A disclosure statement is similar to disclosure documents used in securities transactions. The purpose of a disclosure statement is to tell the creditors everything about the plan and the debtor that may affect the creditors' decision to vote for or against the plan.

Once the plan and disclosure statement have been filed, the next step is a hearing to approve the contents of the disclosure statement.[2] Creditors must receive at least 28 days' notice of the time to object to the disclosure statement.[3] This is an exception to the general rule contained in Federal Rule of Bankruptcy Procedure 2002, requiring 21 days' notice to creditors in most instances.[4] A small business debtor may have a disclosure statement conditionally approved and then combine the disclosure and confirmation hearings. Theoretically, this procedure will shorten the time it takes to confirm a small business Chapter 11 plan (11 U.S.C. §1125(f); see chapter 26 infra). Section 105 of the Bankruptcy Code provides the court with the discretion to conduct combined hearings. This frequently arises in connection with **prepackaged bankruptcy** cases. See chapter 26 infra.[5]

Once the court approves the disclosure statement as containing "adequate information," the plan proponent may then solicit acceptances or rejections (votes) for or against the plan seeking creditor consensus to achieve confirmation.[6] The plan proponent must send all creditors a copy of the plan, a copy of the disclosure statement, a copy of the order approving the disclosure statement, a notice of the hearing on the confirmation of the plan, and a ballot. At least 28 days' notice of the time to object to confirmation must ordinarily be given.[7] Creditors return their ballots to the plan proponent, who files a report with the court summarizing the results of the balloting. This balloting report, along with the original ballots, is filed before the hearing.[8] Samples of these various documents are included on the Forms Disk accompanying this text. The checklist for this chapter summarizes these documents. Collectively, this group of documents is called a **confirmation packet**.

The final step in the process is for the court to hold a confirmation hearing. At the confirmation hearing, the court will either confirm or deny confirmation of the plan.[9] The entire confirmation process is summarized

---

1. 11 U.S.C. §1121; Bankruptcy Rule 3016(b).
2. 11 U.S.C. §1125(b); Bankruptcy Rule 3017(a).
3. Bankruptcy Rules 2002(b), 3017(a).
4. See chapter 5 supra.
5. 11 U.S.C. §105(d)(2)(B)(vi).
6. 11 U.S.C. §1126; Bankruptcy Rule 3017(c). See chapter 27 infra.
7. Bankruptcy Rule 3017(d); 2002(b).
8. Bankruptcy Rule 3018.
9. 11 U.S.C. §1128. See chapter 27 infra.

in the nearby flowchart. The Forms Disk contains a sample plan and disclosure statement. Reference to them will greatly aid in illustrating the concepts introduced in the next two chapters.

B.   TIME TO FILE A PLAN

Section 1121 regulates when a plan may be filed and by who. Unless a trustee has been appointed, only the debtor may file a plan during the 120-day period following the entry of an order for relief.[10] This **exclusivity period** is intended to provide a debtor with breathing room to permit an attempt at reorganization free from the interference that would be caused by a competing plan.

Exclusivity period: a period of time in a Chapter 11 proceeding when only the debtor-in-possession may file a reorganization plan

If a debtor does file a plan within the 120-day exclusivity period, the exclusive period is extended to a date 180 days from the entry of the order for relief. The reason for the extension of the exclusivity period to 180 days is to provide the debtor an opportunity to obtain confirmation of a plan without having to defend against a competing plan at the same time.[11]

> ### *Practice Pointer*
> For example, Flora and Fauna, Inc., files a Chapter 11 on February 13. Flora and Fauna, Inc., has an exclusive right until June 13 (120 days) to file a plan. If a plan is filed by Flora and Fauna, Inc., during this period, whether on day 1 or day 120, the period of exclusivity is now extended to August 12 (180 days).

During the exclusivity period no other party may file a plan. This time period provides Flora and Fauna, Inc., with the opportunity to reorganize its affairs without interference from competing plans of reorganization filed by creditors. On the other hand, if Flora and Fauna, Inc.'s, creditors were to obtain the appointment of a trustee, the exclusivity period would automatically end.

---

10. 11 U.S.C. §1121(b). Recall that the order for relief is entered upon filing a voluntary petition and is the judgment sought by the petitioners in an involuntary proceeding. See chapter 4 supra.
11. 11 U.S.C. §1121(c)(3).

CHAPTER 11 PLAN CONFIRMATION PROCESS

It is possible for a debtor to obtain an extension of either or both of the time periods described above, pursuant to 11 U.S.C. §1121(d). However, such a request must be made during the exclusivity period. The 120-day exclusivity period may not be extended to a date more than 18 months after the order for relief. The 180-day period to obtain confirmation may not be extended to a date more than 20 months after the order for relief. These rules prevent debtors from obtaining indefinite extensions of exclusivity.[12]

There are three events that terminate a debtor-in-possession's period of exclusivity to file a plan. They are the appointment of a trustee, as noted above, the lapse of 120 days after the entry of an order for relief if no plan has been filed, and the lapse of 180 days after the entry of an order for relief if a plan that has been filed has not yet been confirmed.[13]

Small business debtors have been provided with independent exclusivity rules in 11 U.S.C. §1121(e). For a small business, the exclusivity period is 180 days, and in all events, the plan must be filed within 300 days from the order for relief. The court may reduce the time period. The 180-day exclusivity period may be extended upon a showing that it is more likely than not that the court will confirm a plan within a reasonable period of time. Additional extensions may be granted upon a further showing of these elements. The plan must be confirmed within 45 days after it is filed, unless the court extends exclusivity upon the same showing described above.[14] Failure to make this showing within the time periods is cause for dismissal or conversion pursuant to 11 U.S.C. §1112(b)(2).

Once the exclusivity period expires, any party in interest except the United States Trustee may file a reorganization plan.[15] A private trustee may file a plan, the debtor may file a plan, the Official Creditors' Committee may file a plan, or an individual creditor may file a plan. It is for this reason that the party filing a plan is known as the plan proponent. More often than not this will be the debtor.

C.   PLAN CHARACTERISTICS

As a practical matter, the confirmation process generally takes a minimum of four to six months to complete. Because at least 28 days' notice of the time to object is required to be given for each of the disclosure statement

---

12. 11 U.S.C. §1121(d).
13. 11 U.S.C. §1121(c).
14. 11 U.S.C. §1121(e).
15. 11 U.S.C. §1121(c); 11 U.S.C. §307.

and confirmation hearings, and because a debtor must set a ballot deadline, tabulate them, and file a report with the court shortly before the confirmation hearing, it is better practice to separate the disclosure statement and confirmation hearings by at least 60 days so that ample time will exist to vote, to compile the ballots, and to file the report prior to the confirmation hearing. If this will result in the effort at confirmation exceeding the statutory 180-day exclusivity period, the court may extend the period of exclusivity for cause since the debtor is in the process of seeking confirmation of its timely-filed plan.

A confirmed Chapter 11 reorganization plan is in its essence a judicially approved composition agreement. When confirmed, the plan acts as a new contract between the debtor and its creditors. As a result, Chapter 11 is an area of the law where practitioners may exercise some creativity and imagination in the formulation of plans and disclosure statements.

Any reasonable and lawful method of repaying debt can conceivably form the basis of a Chapter 11 plan. The plan may consist of simple repayment to creditors over a period of time from surplus revenues in a manner similar to a Chapter 13 plan, or the plan may involve the refinancing of the debtor's business, call for a sale of the business in whole or part, involve an infusion of investment capital, or may be any combination of all these ideas. The larger a proceeding the more complex the financial concepts will become, but the basic premise is that any reasonable and lawful business method for reorganizing a debtor's financial affairs that can meet with creditor acceptance is a proper foundation for a Chapter 11 plan. Thus, paradoxically, the rules can be highly flexible despite their apparent rigidity.

D.   CLASSIFICATION OF CLAIMS

Section 1122 concerns the classification of claims within a plan. All creditors must be placed within classes. All creditors in a given class must have claims that are substantially similar.[16] For example, a secured creditor and an unsecured creditor may not be included in the same class because these claims are not substantially similar. A priority tax claim may not be classified with unsecured claims. Multiple unsecured claims may be included within the same class. More than one secured claim may also be included in the same class, but it is a better and recommended practice to

---

16. 11 U.S.C. §1122(a).

separately classify each secured claim. The reason for this is that different secured creditors will have different collateral or differing rights regarding the same collateral. As a result each secured claim should be separately classified.

Can The Lawn Cuttery separately classify each of its trucks and specialized equipment into separate classes and propose different treatment for each of them?

Practice Pointer

Claims within a class must be "substantially similar" and the plan must not unfairly discriminate against a particular claim or class of claims.

Section 1122 does not require that all creditors of the same type be placed within the same class. Thus, it is possible to divide substantially similar claims into separate classes. For example, federal tax claims may comprise one class of claims and nonfederal tax claims another class of claims. Similarly, a business may subclassify its unsecured claims into separate classes for suppliers of goods or services, unsecured noteholders, and so on. However, claims may not be classified so as to gerrymander affirmative votes on a plan.[17]

It is specifically possible to create a **convenience class** of creditors.[18] In many Chapter 11 proceedings, there are typically a number of unsecured creditors who are owed relatively small amounts and who are only creditors because the debtor's Chapter 11 filing fortuitously took place when their monthly invoices had not been paid. These creditors are usually owed such relatively small sums that the cost of administering their claims through a plan is likely to be more costly than the claim or dividend. Accordingly, a debtor may create a class of convenience claims and give the class a treatment that would be otherwise impermissible over creditor objection. A debtor may propose that all unsecured claims of less than a fixed amount, such as $500, will be classified as the convenience class and will receive a one-time dividend in discharge of their debts. This dividend may be greater or less than that offered to other unsecured

Convenience class: a group of unsecured claims treated as a class for administrative convenience in a Chapter 11 reorganization plan

---

17. In re Greystone III Joint Venture, 948 F.2d 134 (5th Cir. 1991).
18. 11 U.S.C. §1122(b).

creditors. The plan may also provide that any claimant reducing its claim to qualify for convenience treatment may voluntarily elect to become a member of the convenience class.

For example, Julie's Flying Pig Buttercake Restaurant Inc. has ten unsecured creditors who are owed $100 or less each. Julie's total debt is $150,000. Because it would be uneconomical to write each small creditor a check every three months for four or five years, creation of a convenience class is permitted and its members are paid a one-time dividend on confirmation of the plan in full discharge of the claims included within the class.

FACT PATTERN

After the initial client interview and before filing, Owen immediately goes out and obtains different specialized credit cards from eight of his typical vendors for gas, automotive parts, tractor supplies, and landscaping materials. He charges approximately $200 on each card to establish an account balance with each vendor and to top off his inventory. Can he list these vendors in a convenience class? Would it matter if he had done this six months earlier?

In its essence then, Section 1122 merely requires that a Chapter 11 reorganization plan create classes of claims. This may be as simple as organizing the claims into classes paralleling the distribution scheme described in chapters 22 and 23 supra. Or class creation can be highly complex, involving the creation of separate classes for multiple secured creditors, multiple categories of unsecured claims, and multiple classes of shareholders or bondholders. A Chapter 11 plan for a major corporation can be quite lengthy.

It is good practice to create a separate class for each secured claim. The reason for this is that each secured claimholder usually has either different collateral or different rights with respect to the same collateral than other secured creditors. To the extent that there is different collateral or different rights in the same collateral, the rights of each claimholder may be different in degree or kind.[19] As a result, classification of each secured claim into separate classes will properly account for the differences. With respect to unsecured claims, it is not uncommon to see three classes of unsecured claims within a plan in the form of a convenience class, a trade creditor class, and a class of unsecured noteholders. Insider claims sometimes form a fourth class of unsecured claim. A final class or

---

19. 11 U.S.C. §506. See chapter 22 supra.

classes will be the interests of the equity security holders, the prepetition owners of the debtor.

A reorganization plan is not created in a vacuum. Recall that one function of the Official Creditors' Committee is to negotiate a plan with the debtor so the committee can recommend acceptance to the unsecured creditors.[20] The goal is consensual agreement, a court-approved composition agreement. All parties in interest will save time and money when a debtor negotiates a suitable plan with the Official Creditors' Committee in the first place. The debtor will know what the Official Creditors' Committee will require to recommend that unsecured creditors vote for the plan. On the other hand, the Official Creditors' Committee should be realistic in recognizing just how much "blood" can be squeezed out of the "turnip." Negotiation can result in a less expensive and speedier confirmation process. Every penny saved in administrative expenses is another penny in the pockets of the unsecured creditors. Failure to attempt negotiation of a plan's terms can result in substantial time-consuming and expensive litigation at any step in the confirmation process. The time and expense consumed in litigating these issues can sometimes, ironically, make the reorganization impossible.

E.   MANDATORY PLAN PROVISIONS

Section 1123 is similar to Section 1322 in Chapter 13.[21] Like Section 1322, Section 1123 prescribes the **mandatory** and **permissive elements** of a Chapter 11 plan. The provisions of Section 1123(a) are mandatory and must be included in any Chapter 11 plan. On the other hand, the elements of Section 1123(b) are permissive.

Mandatory element: provisions that must be included in a Chapter 11 or Chapter 13 plan

First, the plan must designate classes of claims and interests. The classes should be organized consistent with Section 1122, as described above. A class of interests represents the interests of the debtor's equity security holders, such as shareholders, partners, or an individual debtor.[22] Second, the plan must specify which of the classes are impaired or not impaired under the plan.[23] What it means to be impaired is the subject of Section 1124 and is discussed below in this chapter.

Permissive element: provisions that may be included in a Chapter 11 or Chapter 13 plan

---

20. See chapter 11 supra.
21. See chapter 24 supra.
22. 11 U.S.C. §1123(a)(1).
23. 11 U.S.C. §1123(a)(2).

Third, the treatment accorded to impaired claims or interests must be described.[24] This is usually the heart of any plan. The plan must tell each class what it is going to receive under the plan.

Fourth, each creditor in the same class must be treated the same, unless a particular creditor agrees to a lesser treatment.[25] In other words, in the negotiation of a plan, a creditor may agree to accept less than the Code entitles it to. This is a practical application of the principle of voluntary subordination, described in chapter 21 supra. The rules are designed for a debtor to propose a minimum performance plan that the court may be required to approve over the objections of virtually all claims by way of the Chapter 11 cramdown procedures discussed in chapter 27 infra.[26] However, a creditor may always voluntarily agree to a lesser treatment of its claim than the Code requires or provides.

Fifth, a plan must provide adequate means for its implementation.[27] That is, the plan must advise each class how the plan will be performed. It is not sufficient to merely promise that creditors are going to be repaid. The plan must describe how the plan will be performed. Section 1123(a)(5) provides a list of ten methods but is not all-inclusive. The list is representative of methods that can be used to perform a plan. Any other reasonable and lawful method of performance devised by a plan's proponent will also be acceptable. Refinancing, sale, periodic repayments, or new investment capital are all acceptable repayment methods, as described earlier in this chapter. Combinations of some or all of these methods can be included in the plan. These are the most common methods proposed for performance of a Chapter 11 reorganization plan. The Code mandates that a method of repayment be provided for, but not what the repayment method must be.

FACT PATTERN

Owen hopes to refinance all of his equipment and vehicles and to stretch out the payment terms for any contracts he cannot restructure.

A debtor can propose to liquidate assets as a Chapter 11 plan performance method.[28] A debtor may choose to liquidate through a Chapter 11 rather than a Chapter 7 for a number of reasons. First, a Chapter 11 may protect the reputation of the debtor's insiders more than a Chapter 7 would. Second, a Chapter 11 debtor remains in control of the business as a debtor-in-possession, rather than a trustee's being appointed to

---

24. 11 U.S.C. §1123(a)(3).
25. 11 U.S.C. §1123(a)(4).
26. 11 U.S.C. §1129(b).
27. 11 U.S.C. §1123(a)(5).
28. 11 U.S.C. §1123(a)(5)(D).

assume control of estate business which a trustee may be ill equipped to handle. There can be situations when this will increase the prospects for creditor dividends. Finally, the Chapter 11 process may sometimes involve less time and expense to liquidate an estate and pay creditors dividends than a Chapter 7 proceeding. For example, if the debtor is in a small specialized industry, management will likely have contacts unavailable to a Chapter 7 trustee that will aid in maximizing the price obtained from a liquidation of assets. Further, if the debtor is in a Chapter 11, the debtor does not have to deal with all the timetables described in chapter 23 supra. The debtor may sell the assets, propose a plan, obtain confirmation, and pay creditors in a fraction of the time that a Chapter 7 proceeding would take, but with exactly the same or better results for creditors.

> ***Would it make sense at this point for Owen to liquidate The Lawn Cuttery and transfer any remaining assets into a new business that he creates?***

FACT PATTERN

Sixth, a plan involving a corporate debtor must provide that the corporation's charter will provide appropriate representation on its board of directors to various classes of shareholders.[29] In most proceedings, compliance with this provision will not be problematic.

Seventh, the plan must be in the interests of the creditors and equity security holders and be consistent with public policy respecting the selection of a debtor's insiders.[30] This means that the plan must identify the postconfirmation insiders of the debtor.

Finally, in Chapter 11 cases for individual debtors, the debtor must commit postpetition earnings for personal services as is necessary for performance of the plan. To aid in implementing this provision, Section 1115 makes the postpetition earnings for personal services property of the estate in a manner similar to Chapter 13.[31]

F. PERMISSIVE PLAN PROVISIONS

Subsection 1123(b) describes the permissive elements of a Chapter 11 plan. Permissive elements are elements that may be included but are

---

29. 11 U.S.C. §1123(a)(6).
30. 11 U.S.C. §1123(a)(7).
31. 11 U.S.C. §1123(a)(8); 11 U.S.C. §1115; 11 U.S.C. §1306. As to Chapter 13, see chapter 24 supra.

not required to be in a Chapter 11 plan. It is nevertheless recommended to include these items within a plan. First, a plan may impair or leave unimpaired a class of claims or interests.[32] Impairment is described below in connection with Section 1124.

Second, a plan may provide for the assumption or rejection of any executory contracts that have not been previously assumed or rejected during the Chapter 11 proceeding.[33] As a practical matter, it is good practice to specifically provide for the assumption or rejection of all executory contracts within a reorganization plan. This may be as simple as a short paragraph assuming all executory contracts not previously assumed or rejected, or exactly the converse. This sort of simple provision appears in the sample plan included on the Forms Disk. Such a clause may be as complex as separately identifying and assuming or rejecting each individual executory contract. Further, it is important for the nondebtor party to an executory contract to know the debtor's intent with regard to assumption or rejection because this will affect the nondebtor party's status as a creditor in the proceeding and thus ultimately the nondebtor party's decision to vote for or against the plan.

FACT PATTERN

Would you recommend that The Lawn Cuttery reject all of its existing executory contracts and simply enter into new contracts for different equipment with different vendors later?

The plan may provide for the settlement or enforcement of any claims that the estate may have.[34] In other words, the plan may act as a settlement agreement of any dispute involving the estate should the plan be confirmed. The plan may also provide for the sale of all or substantially all assets and distribution of the proceeds to claimholders.[35] This is another indication that liquidation is an acceptable method for performance of a Chapter 11 plan.

Section 1123(b)(5) prohibits modification of a security interest in real property that is the debtor's principal residence, but otherwise it permits modification of creditor rights. This provision is identical to that of Section 1322(b)(2) and affects individual debtors in Chapter 11 proceedings (see section 24D supra).

The final permissive provision of Section 1123 is that a Chapter 11 reorganization plan may contain any provision not inconsistent with the

---

32. 11 U.S.C. §1123(b)(1).
33. 11 U.S.C. §1123(b)(2). See also chapter 20 supra.
34. 11 U.S.C. §1123(b)(3).
35. 11 U.S.C. §1123(b)(4).

Bankruptcy Code.[36] However, when a creditor classifies claims, the classifications should follow the scheme and order described in chapters 22 and 23 supra. To act otherwise, absent the consent of any affected creditor, would not be consistent with the provisions of the Bankruptcy Code.

If the Chapter 11 debtor is an individual, the individual's exempt property may not be included in the plan unless the debtor consents.[37] In other words, an individual debtor's exemptions are preserved in Chapter 11. If a debtor wants to voluntarily make exempt property available to perform a plan, this is acceptable. However, the creditors may not force an individual debtor to give up any claimed exemptions in a Chapter 11 plan.

Section 1123(d) permits the charging of interest upon interest if applicable nonbankruptcy law allows it.

G. IMPAIRED CLAIMS

Section 1124 creates a distinction between impaired and unimpaired claims or interests. This concept is unique to Chapter 11. Generally, an **unimpaired claim** is a claim that is being paid according to its prepetition terms on the effective date of the plan. Conversely, a claim not being paid according to its terms on the effective date of the plan is an **impaired claim**. For example, when a class of unsecured claims is scheduled to be paid in full on the effective date of a plan, the class is unimpaired. The **effective date of the plan** is the date defined in the plan as the plan's commencement date. This date may be the date on which the court approves confirmation, or it may be a date on which a specific event is scheduled to occur, such as the close of an escrow in a sale or the funding of a refinancing loan. Although it is not an express requirement of §1123, a plan should always define its effective date.

There is an important difference in treatment accorded to unimpaired versus impaired classes of claims. An unimpaired class of claims is deemed to have accepted a plan whether or not the class votes to accept or reject the plan.[38] This is a major reason why Section 1123 mandates that a plan designate classes of impaired claims.[39] Only impaired classes are entitled to vote for or against confirmation of the plan.

Unimpaired claim: a claim paid according to its terms on the effective date of a Chapter 11 reorganization plan

Impaired claim: a claim not paid according to its terms on the effective date of a Chapter 11 plan

Effective date of the plan: a specific date upon which performance of a Chapter 11 plan begins

---

36. 11 U.S.C. §1123(b)(6).
37. 11 U.S.C. §1123(c).
38. 11 U.S.C. §1126(f). See chapter 27 infra.
39. 11 U.S.C. §1123(a)(3). See discussion supra.

Section 1124 describes three situations that render a class of claims unimpaired. Unless a class satisfies one of the three situations, the class will be impaired. First, a class of claims is unimpaired if the plan provides that the class will be paid in full on the effective date of the plan or that the rights of the class members will be left unaltered by the plan.[40] Simply put, an unsecured claim paid in full or according to its terms on the effective date of the plan is unimpaired. Second, if a plan proposes to continue to pay a creditor its regular installment payments as they become due and there are no defaults, or any defaults are cured on the effective date of the plan, the creditor will be considered unimpaired.[41]

Third, a class of claims is considered unimpaired notwithstanding any contractual provision allowing a creditor to accelerate payment after a default, if the plan cures the default, reinstates the obligation according to its terms, pays to the holder of the claim any consequential damages, and does not otherwise alter the rights of the affected claimholders.[42] This is an extremely important provision because it dramatically affects the rights of debtor and creditors alike. This provision effectively allows a debtor to reinstate any defaulted obligation so long as the creditor is otherwise paid according to the underlying terms of its contract. Not only will the obligation be reinstated, but because the claim or class will be considered unimpaired, the claimant will be deemed to have accepted the plan.

For example, a debtor may reinstate a defaulted trust deed or mortgage obligation through a Chapter 11 plan even if any underlying state law reinstatement period has expired. If the formula of Section 1124(2) is followed by the debtor, the claim will be considered unimpaired and the creditor's acceptance of the plan presumed.

An unsecured obligation may also be affected by Section 1124(2). For example, Marian's Maids, Inc., owes an unsecured loan to the Bank of Nottingham. The due date of the unsecured loan is five years. Three payments are in default and the bank has accelerated the obligation. As long as the Chapter 11 reorganization plan proposes to pay the three defaulted payments and otherwise reinstate the obligation, the claim will not be impaired and will not accelerate. Because the creditor is receiving what it bargained for, it is unimpaired. In each of these situations, the creditor receives exactly what it is entitled to receive under nonbankruptcy law. A creditor receiving all it is entitled to receive is considered to consent to the identical treatment in a plan.

---

40. 11 U.S.C. §1124(1).
41. 11 U.S.C. §1124(2)(A)(B).
42. 11 U.S.C. §1124(2).

Summary

The process of formulating and obtaining confirmation of a Chapter 11 reorganization plan, known as a Plan of Reorganization, is the most complex and time-consuming process in the Bankruptcy Code. The entire process will average four to six months, at a minimum.

The process involves filing a plan and a disclosure statement with the court. The disclosure statement is a history of the debtor-in-possession, an analysis of the proposed plan, and a description of the debtor's ability to perform the plan. The disclosure statement is approved by the court at a disclosure statement hearing. This hearing requires at least 28 days' notice to creditors. When the disclosure statement has been approved, the proponent of the plan may solicit the votes of those creditors entitled to vote. The results of the balloting are filed with the court. The court will hold a confirmation hearing to determine if the plan may be confirmed. The confirmation hearing also requires at least 28 days' notice to the creditors. A checklist of this process is contained in the checklist to this chapter.

A debtor-in-possession has the exclusive right to file a reorganization plan for 120 days following the entry of an order for relief. This exclusivity period can be extended to 180 days if a plan is filed during the initial 120-day period or if a motion for an extension of time is filed during the initial 120-day period. In no event can the exclusivity period extend past 20 months. The exclusivity period terminates if a trustee is appointed. A small business debtor has a 180-day exclusivity period and must have a plan filed within 300 days after the entry of the order for relief, unless the court extends the time period.

Any Chapter 11 reorganization plan must classify the claims of creditors and the interests of the equity security holders (owners of the debtor). All claims within a given class must be similar, such as administrative or priority claims. A convenience class of claims may also be created. Generally, the classification scheme should follow the priorities outlined in chapters 22 and 23 supra.

A Chapter 11 reorganization plan must contain various mandatory provisions. A Chapter 11 plan may also contain various permissive provisions. An outline of the mandatory and permissive plan provisions is contained in the checklist accompanying this chapter. The Forms Disk accompanying this text contains a sample reorganization plan, along with all other basic documents necessary to pursue confirmation.

One of the most important mandatory plan provisions requires designation of impaired classes of claims. Classes of claims that are impaired are entitled to vote to accept or reject the plan. Classes of claims that are unimpaired are deemed to accept the plan. Generally, a class of claims is unimpaired if it is paid in full when the plan is confirmed or if the class is paid according to the terms of the obligation as it existed before the Chapter 11 was filed. Any other claim is unimpaired.

KEY TERMS

confirmation packet   permissive elements
convenience class   Plan of Reorganization
disclosure statement   plan proponent
effective date of the plan   prepackaged bankruptcy
exclusivity period   unimpaired claim
impaired claim
mandatory elements

CHAPTER 26 CHECKLIST

26.1   CHAPTER 11 CONFIRMATION PROCESS

		Prior Notice Required	*Authority*
26.1.1	File a Reorganization Plan	—	11 U.S.C. §1121, Bankruptcy Rule 3016(a)
26.1.2	File a Disclosure Statement	—	11 U.S.C. §1125, Bankruptcy Rule 3016(b)
26.1.3	Disclosure Statement Hearing	28 days of the time to object	11 U.S.C. §1125(b), Bankruptcy Rules 2002(b), 3017(a)
26.1.4	Voting Deadline Set	at disclosure statement hearing	Bankruptcy Rule 3017(c)
26.1.5	Confirmation Hearing	28 days of the time to object	11 U.S.C. §1128, Bankruptcy Rule 2002(b)
26.1.6	Report of Balloting	prior to confirmation hearing	Bankruptcy Rule 3018, consult local rule

26.2   DOCUMENTS SUBMITTED TO CREDITORS   *Rule*
        FOR CONFIRMATION HEARING
        (CONFIRMATION PACKET)

DISCUSSION QUESTIONS

1. Describe the procedure that a plan proponent must follow to obtain confirmation of a Chapter 11 reorganization plan. Identify the essential documents that must be filed with the court during the confirmation process.

2. When may a Chapter 11 reorganization plan be filed? What is the "exclusivity period"?

3. How are claims classified in a Chapter 11 reorganization plan?

4. What elements must be included in a Chapter 11 reorganization plan?

5. What elements may be included in a Chapter 11 reorganization plan?

6. What is an impaired claim? An unimpaired claim? What are the important differences between the two?

PRACTICE EXERCISES

Exercise 26.1
Assume that The Lawn Cuttery files Chapter 11 on January 1. Your supervising attorney asks you to prepare a memo identifying the date on which exclusivity will expire.

Exercise 26.2
Owen Cash wants to propose a plan that favors one supplier over all others. He wants to do this because the closer supplier has offered very favorable terms. Since he won't need the other suppliers, he wants to pay them less or not at all. Prepare a draft of a letter to Mr. Cash advising him whether or not he may propose such a plan.

27

Chapter 11: Plan Confirmation

Learning Objectives

- Describe the requirements of the disclosure statement
- Learn the voting rules and procedures in Chapter 11 plan balloting
- List the conditions for confirmation of a Chapter 11 plan
- Introduce the concept of "cramdown" to confirm a Chapter 11 plan
- Describe how and when a Chapter 11 plan may be modified
- Define the Chapter 11 discharge

A.   DISCLOSURE STATEMENT

Once a debtor-in-possession has formulated and filed a plan, the debtor embarks upon the confirmation process. Any proponent of a plan must follow the same process. A synopsis of this process was described at the beginning of chapter 25 supra. This chapter analyzes the process in greater detail.

When a plan is filed, it generally must be accompanied by a disclosure statement. Votes may not be solicited from creditors until the court approves the disclosure statement's contents.[1] The disclosure statement

---

1. 11 U.S.C. §1125(b); Bankruptcy Rule 3017(d); Bankruptcy Rule 3017.1 applies to small businesses.

hearing is the first step in the Chapter 11 plan confirmation process. Creditors and other parties in interest are entitled to at least 28 days' notice of the time to object to the disclosure statement. A small business debtor may obtain conditional approval of a disclosure statement. Votes can be solicited therefrom and the court may combine the disclosure and confirmation hearings. Theoretically, this procedure will expedite the confirmation process for a small business estate. Section §105(d) of the Bankruptcy Code gives the court discretion to combine the disclosure and confirmation hearings. This is a frequent occurrence in *prepackaged bankruptcy* cases.[2] A disclosure statement must contain information sufficient to enable a creditor or interest holder to determine whether to vote to accept or reject the plan. The Code describes this standard as providing all parties with "adequate information."[3] The disclosure statement should be written in plain English so that anyone can understand its contents. This may be difficult, especially in complex cases, but it is not impossible.

Disclosure statement: a document filed in a Chapter 11 proceeding that describes a debtor-in-possession's reorganization plan, its effect upon the creditors, the ability of the plan to be performed, and a comparison of the reorganization plan's repayment proposal to the results likely to be obtained in a Chapter 7 proceeding for the same debtor

A **disclosure statement** should follow basic journalism principles: "Who, what, where, when, why, and how." A history of the debtor should be included, identifying the causes of the Chapter 11 filing and disclosing all relevant factors that may have contributed to the debtor's financial difficulties.

The disclosure statement should summarize the debtor's progress during the Chapter 11 proceeding. A summary of the most important information from the operating reports can be helpful, particularly as a means of comparing the debtor's actual postpetition results with any relevant projections of future performance provided elsewhere in the disclosure statement. Comparing a debtor's actual Chapter 11 performance with the proposed plan will permit the plan's feasibility to be more rapidly and efficiently assessed by the court and creditors.

The disclosure statement should contain an easy to understand summary of the plan. The summary should describe the practical effect of the plan rather than its technical terms. For example, a disclosure statement for Bonehead Burgers states: "Class 7 creditors will receive dividends equaling 50 percent of the total allowed claims in monthly installments not exceeding 48 months." Without reference to other parts of the plan or disclosure statement this is a confusing statement. The statement would be better stated in the disclosure statement as: "Unsecured creditors will receive payments equal to 50 percent of their claims in monthly payments over four years." A chart summarizing the plan's treatment by class is very helpful. Official Form B25A, included in the Forms Disk, contains such a

---

2. Bankruptcy Rule 2002(b); Bankruptcy Rule 3017(a). See chapter 4 supra. 11 U.S.C. §1125(f) applies to small business debtors, as does Bankruptcy Rule 3017.1. 11 U.S.C.§105(d)(2)(B)(vi).
3. 11 U.S.C. §1125(a)(1).

chart. A disclosure statement should contain a description of how the plan will be performed. For example, if the plan involves a sale of assets or refinancing, describe the essential terms of the sale or refinancing. In a workout situation where claimants will be paid dividends over a period of time from the debtor's surplus revenues, the disclosure statement should contain a **pro forma**. A *pro forma* is a financial projection of revenues and profits that a debtor expects to generate over the life of the plan. Any pro forma should be based upon actual past performance or be able to account in detail for variations from past performance. For instance, it would be imprudent for a debtor that has been in a Chapter 11 proceeding for two years posting annual sales increases of 10 percent to suddenly project annual increases of 25 percent in a plan pro forma without any discussion of the reasons behind the increased sales forecast.

Pro forma: a financial forecast of future performance over a period of time; pro formas are frequently used in Chapter 11 plan practice

The disclosure statement must compare the plan to the likely results if the case were a Chapter 7 proceeding. This is commonly known as a **liquidation analysis**. The reason for this is that one finding that the court must make to confirm the plan is that creditors will receive at least as much as they would receive in a Chapter 7 proceeding.[4] The relevant facts should be shown in the disclosure statement so creditors will be able to utilize the liquidation analysis in determining whether to vote to accept or reject the plan.

Liquidation analysis: portion of a Disclosure Statement comparing a reorganization plan to the results likely to be obtained if the case were a Chapter 7

The disclosure statement should describe the balloting procedure for voting on the plan and how parties in interest may file objections to the plan's confirmation. Some courts also require a description of the cramdown procedures which may permit court approval of the plan over the creditors' objection. See infra this chapter.

A disclosure statement must also include a discussion of the potential material federal tax consequences of a Chapter 11 plan. Presumably, this includes a statement that there are no tax consequences to the plan.

A disclosure statement may and often does discuss additional items. The foregoing covers only the basic elements. For example, if the case involves resolution of a single major dispute that has been resolved, the disclosure statement should address the relevant details. Any factor relating to the required confirmation findings of Section 1129 that may be problematic should be discussed in the disclosure statement. A brief summary of the important items that should be included in a disclosure statement appears in the checklist accompanying this chapter. In small business cases, the court may find and order that the plan provides adequate disclosure. BAPCPA authorized the formulation of a standard form disclosure statement to be used in all small business cases. The purpose of

---

4. 11 U.S.C. §1129(a)(7). See infra this chapter.

developing a standard form is to meet the needs of creditors, the courts, and the United States Trustee in eliciting adequate information while at the same time providing economy and simplicity for small business debtors.[5] Official Form B25A is the standard form Chapter 11 Plan. Official Form B25B is the standard form disclosure statement. They are included in the Forms Disk. Chapter 11 disclosure statements are somewhat similar to registration statements, quarterly reports, or other types of financial reports required by federal or state securities laws. Chapter 11 disclosure statements are specifically exempt from federal or state securities laws regulating the adequacy of such documents. Nevertheless, any governmental official or agency charged with the administration of securities laws may be heard by the Bankruptcy Court on the adequacy of a Chapter 11 disclosure statement. Such an entity does not have a right of appeal or review from the Bankruptcy Court's decision. Parties engaged in seeking approval of a Chapter 11 plan are thus given a "safe harbor" from federal or state securities disclosure laws in connection with the confirmation process.[6]

B. PLAN CONFIRMATION PACKET

When the court approves the disclosure statement, the plan proponent must then send all parties in interest a notice of the confirmation hearing, the plan, the disclosure statement, a ballot, and a notice of the deadline to file ballots.[7] All impaired classes of claims or interests are given the opportunity to vote for or against the plan.[8] The results of the voting are compiled into a report, which is filed with the court prior to the confirmation hearing.[9] Section 1126 contains the provisions governing acceptance of the plan and the balloting procedures. In large reorganizations common to the Southern District of New York or the District of Delaware, plan proponents will typically file a separate motion to approve solicitation and balloting procedures.

---

5. See In re Scioto Valley Mortg. Co., 88 Bankr. 168 (S.D. Ohio 1988). This case includes a detailed list of items that should be included in any Chapter 11 disclosure statement. 11 U.S.C. §1125(f) authorizes the standard form in small business cases, or permits a finding that no disclosure statement will be required where the plan itself provides adequate information.
6. 11 U.S.C. §1125(c), (d), (e); 11 U.S.C. §1145.
7. Bankruptcy Rule 3017(d).
8. 11 U.S.C. §1126(a); Bankruptcy Rules 3017(c), 3017.1(a); Bankruptcy Rule 3018(a).
9. Bankruptcy Rule 3018.

C.   VOTING RULES

A class of claims accepts a plan if, among those voting, a majority of creditors in number and two-thirds in dollar amount of the claims owed to
those voting vote to accept the plan.[10] This is a dual requirement. If less
than a majority of creditors in number or less than two-thirds in dollar
amount among those voting vote to accept a plan, then the class has
rejected the plan and a cramdown procedure will be necessary to confirm
the plan over rejection by one or more impaired classes.[11] To determine
class acceptance, total the number of voting creditors in a class and the
amount of their claims. For example, 12 creditors collectively owed
$12,000 vote on a plan. The class accepts the plan if 7 creditors owed
$8,000 or more vote to accept. If only 6 vote for acceptance, the class
will have rejected the plan (less than a majority). If less than $8,000 in
total dollar amount votes to accept, the class will have rejected the plan,
even if 11 creditors voted to accept the plan (less than two-thirds in
amount). If only 3 creditors in a class vote, but all votes are to accept,
then the class has voted for the plan since a majority in number and two-
thirds in dollar amount of those voting have voted for the plan.

A class of interests, such as shareholders, accepts a plan if two-thirds in
dollar amount of the class of interests accepts the plan.[12] A class of interests accepts a plan if two-thirds of the ownership percentage voting votes
acceptance. The raw number of voters is not relevant in this instance. This
would not be an accurate measure of acceptance by a class of shareholders
in a corporation or partnership. One entity may own 50 percent of all
shares. The only relevant element here is the percentage of shares voted.

The Bankruptcy Code contemplates that an unsuccessful attempt at a
composition agreement may lead to a Chapter 11 filing. This is the subject
of Section 1126(b). For example, Metternich Consulting, Inc., attempts a
composition agreement before a Chapter 11 filing. If Metternich follows
procedures similar to the Chapter 11 confirmation process, presenting the
equivalent of a disclosure statement, plan, and ballot to the creditors in a
manner consistent with the Chapter 11 plan process, then any acceptances to the composition obtained from creditors prior to the Chapter
11 filing may be acceptable as proper ballots.[13] If the debtor can show to
the court that the composition process was treated in a manner similar to a
Chapter 11 proceeding, then prepetition acceptances to the composition

---

10. 11 U.S.C. §1126(a), (c).
11. 11 U.S.C. §1129(b). See this chapter infra for discussion of cramdown.
12. 11 U.S.C. §1126(d).
13. 11 U.S.C. §1126(b). In re Houghton Mifflin Harcourt Publishing Co., 474 B.R. 122 (Bankr.
    S.D.N.Y. 2012).

can be used as acceptances to an identical Chapter 11 plan. This recognizes the fact that debtors attempting to negotiate composition agreements with their creditors are still subject to any legal action taken by nonconsenting creditors, thus sometimes forcing the Chapter 11 filing. Section 1126(b) creates a mechanism that allows and encourages composition agreements by giving them the potential to be confirmable as Chapter 11 plans. An effort at a composition agreement that nonetheless ends up in Bankruptcy Court is often referred to as a **prepackaged bankruptcy:** "A 'prepackaged' plan of reorganization is one where acceptances of the plan have been sought and obtained before the bankruptcy case is even filed. The idea behind prepack plans is to make a Chapter 11 case 'as quick and painless' as possible for creditors and especially for trade creditors."[14]

Prepackaged bankruptcy: a Chapter 11 proceeding in which a debtor seeks Bankruptcy Court approval of a plan where votes have been solicited before the case has been filed

For example, National Wagonworks attempts to negotiate a composition agreement with its creditors and is successful with some but not all creditors. The proposed agreement and its accompanying "disclosure statement" are identical to a Chapter 11 plan and disclosure statement. Sufficient creditors consent to the plan to satisfy the Chapter 11 voting requirements. One creditor, Hupmobile Inc., will not consent and seeks to enforce a writ of execution to seize the assets of National Wagonworks. Because a nonbankruptcy composition agreement cannot be legally enforced against a nonconsenting creditor, National Wagonworks must file a Chapter 11 if it is to prevent the seizure by Hupmobile so the plan can proceed. Section 1126(b) will permit the prompt confirmation of the composition as a Chapter 11 plan that will also bind Hupmobile over its objection. A plan that has been negotiated but has not solicited votes prior to the bankruptcy filing is often referred to as a **prearranged bankruptcy**. This is a further illustration of the fundamental principle that a reorganization plan is in its essence a court-approved composition agreement.

Prearranged bankruptcy: a plan that has been negotiated but has not solicited votes prior to the bankruptcy filing

FACT PATTERN

Would you encourage the filing of a prepackaged bankruptcy for The Lawn Cuttery?

A vote obtained in bad faith or that has been solicited in violation of the Chapter 11 rules may be disallowed. In a prepackaged bankruptcy, a vote solicited before the filing of a petition is not in bad faith if solicited in

---

14. In re Genco Shipping & Trading Limited, 509 B.R. 455 (Bankr. S.D.N.Y. 2014). "A prearranged plan of reorganization contains terms that were negotiated among interested parties prior to the filing of the petition, but acceptances are solicited after the Chapter 11 filing."

compliance with applicable nonbankruptcy law. It is better practice, however, to mirror the Bankruptcy Code requirements as closely as possible.[15]

A class of unimpaired claims is conclusively presumed to have accepted a plan.[16] Thus, if a debtor proposes to pay all creditors in full on the effective date of the plan, all creditors are unimpaired. The votes of creditors will not be a problematic issue at the confirmation hearing. Conversely, a class that will receive nothing under the plan is deemed to have rejected it.[17]

D.   MODIFICATION OF THE PLAN

A plan may be modified at any time before confirmation, as long as the disclosure statement requirements are complied with.[18] After confirmation, modification may be sought for reasons similar to the reasons for seeking modification of a Chapter 13 plan.[19] A debtor may acquire the ability to accelerate a plan's performance, or, conversely, the payments may have to be reduced or the performance period extended. A plan proponent may bring a motion before the court to modify a plan. The court will not permit modification of a confirmed plan if the plan has been **substantially consummated**, except in cases involving individuals.[20] Generally, this means the taking of an irrevocable act in performance of a plan, such as closing an escrow for a sale of the business, completing a refinancing, or repaying a substantial percentage of a promised dividend.[21] A postconfirmation motion to modify a plan must also comply with Section 1125 and provide adequate disclosure. Creditors may modify a prior ballot (that is, change their votes) due to a modified plan.[22]

Substantially consummated: the taking of an irrevocable act in performance of a Chapter 11 plan, such as closing escrow or repaying a substantial portion of a dividend

---

15. 11 U.S.C. §1126(e), (g). Additionally, in a prepackaged bankruptcy, 11 U.S.C. §341(e) provides that the meeting of creditors may not be held if excused by the court upon a showing of cause.
16. 11 U.S.C. §1126(f).
17. 11 U.S.C. §1126(g).
18. 11 U.S.C. §1127(a).
19. 11 U.S.C. §1127(b). See chapter 24 supra.
20. 11 U.S.C. §1127(b); 11 U.S.C. §1101(2); 11 U.S.C. §1127(e).
21. 11 U.S.C. §1101(2).
22. 11 U.S.C. §1127(c), (d).

E.   BALLOTING REPORT

After the balloting is complete and the balloting report is filed with the court, the confirmation hearing takes place.[23] At the confirmation hearing the court will determine whether the requirements for confirmation have been complied with. The standards for confirmation are contained in Section 1129. This is perhaps the most complex and frequently litigated provision of Chapter 11.

F.   CONFIRMATION CONDITIONS

At the confirmation hearing, the court will confirm the plan only if it finds that the plan meets each and every requirement of Section 1129(a). This general principle is identical to that of Section 1325 in Chapter 13, as described in chapter 24 supra. Under Section 1129(a), the court must make 16 findings. If an element has not been complied with, the plan may not be confirmed. Many of the required findings will not be problematic in most proceedings.

First, the court must find that the plan complies with all provisions of the Bankruptcy Code.[24] A plan following the guidelines described in chapter 26 supra will likely be compliant. Second, the proponent of the plan must comply with all applicable provisions of the Bankruptcy Code.[25] This means that the proponent of the plan must be an entity that may file a plan pursuant to Section 1121. Third, the plan must be proposed in good faith and not by any means forbidden by law.[26] A plan designed to accomplish an improper motive or that would be illegal under applicable nonbankruptcy law is probably not a plan proposed in good faith. Fourth, the reasonableness of any fees to be paid to an issuer of securities or for acquiring property under the plan must be approved by the court.[27] Fifth, the court must approve the debtor's postconfirmation management. This will include disclosing all insiders the debtor intends to employ during the life of the plan, including their approximate duties, compensation, and manner of election. In this connection, the court must also find that

---

23. 11 U.S.C. §1128. A Chapter 11 confirmation hearing is treated as a noticed motion. Bankruptcy Rules 3020, 9014.
24. 11 U.S.C. §1129(a)(1).
25. 11 U.S.C. §1129(a)(2).
26. 11 U.S.C. §1129(a)(3).
27. 11 U.S.C. §1129(a)(4).

continuation of such individuals in the employ of the debtor is in the interests of the creditors, equity security holders, and public policy.[28] Sixth, if the debtor's rates are subject to governmental regulation, the Bankruptcy Court must find that any applicable regulatory agency has approved any rate changes provided for in the Chapter 11 plan.[29] Because most debtors do not fall into this category, this provision will rarely apply. Disputes regarding any of the six preceding confirmation requirements arise infrequently.

Seventh, the court must find that as to each impaired class of claims, the individual claimholders have either accepted the plan or will be receiving, on the effective date of the plan, an amount not less than the class would receive in the event the debtor were liquidated under Chapter 7.[30] This is known as the **"best interests of creditors" test**. Unless an impaired class will receive dividends at least equal to a hypothetical Chapter 7 dividend to be paid on the effective date of the plan, the plan cannot be confirmed because it is not in the best interests of creditors. This is why a comparison of the Chapter 11 plan to the results that would be achieved if the proceeding were a Chapter 7 (liquidation analysis) should be included in the disclosure statement. Further, the hypothetical Chapter 7 dividend is the minimum amount that an objecting creditor within a given accepting class must receive for the plan to be confirmable. The mere fact that creditors are assured a minimum dividend, however, does not act to approve the plan over rejection of the plan by a class. Approval of a plan over class rejection requires use of the Chapter 11 cramdown procedures.[31]

> **"Best interests of creditors" test:** the Chapter 11 confirmation requirement that a class of claims receive at least what it would receive if the case were a Chapter 7

For example, Brutus is an unsecured creditor of Wimpy. Wimpy proposes a Chapter 11 plan that will pay unsecured creditors less than they would receive in a Chapter 7 proceeding. Out of sympathy, the unsecured creditors accept the plan as a class. Brutus objects on the ground that he is not receiving a dividend greater than he would receive in a Chapter 7. The plan is not confirmable over Brutus's objection, despite overall acceptance by the class.

Eighth, the court must find that each class has either accepted the plan or is unimpaired.[32] Because unimpaired classes are conclusively presumed to have accepted a plan, their votes are unnecessary and the plan can be confirmed even if they object. A creditor receiving payment in full or the performance it would be entitled to under nonbankruptcy

---

28. 11 U.S.C. §1129(a)(5).
29. 11 U.S.C. §1129(a)(6).
30. 11 U.S.C. §1129(a)(7)(A).
31. See infra this chapter.
32. 11 U.S.C. §1129(a)(8).

law will not be heard to object to the plan's confirmation. A class accepts a plan in accordance with the voting rules described above.

If an impaired class of claims or interests does not accept a plan, the plan will only be confirmable if the debtor can successfully comply with the Chapter 11 cramdown provisions.[33] For example, the plan of Green Acres, Inc., proposes to pay a secured claimholder by returning acreage to the creditor equal to the value of the claim, while Green Acres, Inc., will keep the rest. The secured creditor rejects the plan. Because the creditor is allegedly receiving what it would receive in a Chapter 7, the plan complies with Section 1129(a)(7). However, because the creditor has not accepted the plan and is not unimpaired, the plan cannot be confirmed absent a successful cramdown.

Practice Pointer

The court will be sensitive to claims of artificial impairment, i.e., when a class is designated solely to satisfy the requirement of one impaired class accepting the plan.

Ninth, the court must find that the plan will pay all administrative expenses in full on the effective date of the plan as well as all other nontax priority claims in cash on the effective date of the plan, unless any affected class of priority claim agrees to deferred payments.[34] For example, the priority wage claimants of the Poughkeepsie Polos, a professional polo team, do not agree to receive payment of their priority wage claims on a future date. The Polos must either pay the priority wage claims in full on the effective date of the plan or the plan cannot be confirmed.

Priority tax claims may be paid over a period not exceeding five years from the date of the Order for Relief, so long as all penalties and interest are paid over the period. Secured tax claims may also be paid on this basis.[35] Alternatively, a debtor that can afford to do so and pays an unsecured priority tax claim in full on the effective date of the plan will only need to satisfy the amount of the claim as it existed on the original Chapter 11 filing date. This approach, when feasible, can save payment of

---

33. 11 U.S.C. §1129(b)(1). See infra this chapter.
34. 11 U.S.C. §1129(a)(9)(A), (B).
35. 11 U.S.C. §1129(a)(9)(C). See also 11 U.S.C. §511, codifying the rate of interest to pay on tax claims.

substantial penalties and interest. The Supreme Court has held that a plan proponent may, in appropriate circumstances, allocate the application of dividends to tax claims. For example, the plan proponent may propose to allocate a tax dividend first to any portion of the claim to which a non-debtor may also be liable. This may aid such individuals in avoiding personal liability for the taxes.[36]

Tenth, the court must find that at least one impaired noninsider class has accepted the plan.[37] Thus, if a plan contains only one impaired class and the class rejects the plan, the plan may not be confirmed. In this instance, cramdown will not provide the debtor with a remedy because not every class will have accepted the plan or be unimpaired.[38] Although a class of rejecting impaired claims may be subject to a cramdown, if it is the *only* impaired class, the plan will not be confirmable. Or, stated in another way, there must be at least two impaired classes in a plan, one of which accepts the plan, before the court can consider application of the cram-down provisions to the rejecting impaired class or classes.

Since Robin is described as a "silent" officer in the business, can Owen manufacture a claim owed to her and treat it as impaired? Would this satisfy the confirmation requirement if she is not actively involved in the business?

FACT PATTERN

Eleventh, the court must find that the reorganization is not likely to be followed by further reorganization or liquidation unless the plan so pro-vides.[39] This is commonly known as a **feasibility requirement**. This determination will involve careful analysis of any pro forma or other finan-cial data presented in the disclosure statement to determine the likeli-hood of the debtor successfully performing the promises contained in the plan. This may also involve a determination of the likelihood of a proposed sale or refinancing occurring within a specified period of time. The formula described in chapter 23 supra for analyzing Chapter 13 plans will also apply in Chapter 11 proceedings, albeit on a more complex level when the plan proposes to repay debt over a period of time.

Feasibility requirement: finding that the Bankruptcy Court must make to permit confirma-tion of a Chapter 11 reorganization plan

---

36. United States v. Energy Resources Co., 495 U.S. 545 (1990).
37. 11 U.S.C. §1129(a)(10).
38. 11 U.S.C. §1129(b)(1). Section 1129(a)(8) is the only confirmation requirement that may be overridden by a cramdown procedure according to the plain language of the statute.
39. 11 U.S.C. §1129(a)(11).

Practice Pointer

A feasibility analysis must consider whether the plan has reasonable probability of success. There are no guarantees, and a potential for failure alone will not be enough to upset confirmation.

Twelfth, the court must find that any fees due the court will be paid in full on the effective date of the plan.[40] Thirteenth, plans involving certain types of employee retirement or benefit plans must comply with the provisions of Section 1114. This provision is not likely to be problematic in most cases.[41]

Fourteenth, in a Chapter 11 case for an individual, all postpetition domestic support obligations must be current at the time of confirmation. Fifteenth, also applicable in Chapter 11 cases for individuals, if the holder of an unsecured claim objects, then the debtor must submit all disposable income for a five-year period into the plan unless all creditors can be paid in full sooner. Sixteenth and finally, applicable in all cases, all transfers of property are to be made in accordance with local law.[42]

G.   CHAPTER 11 CRAMDOWN

When there is an impaired class of claims that has not accepted the plan, the Chapter 11 cramdown procedure is available as long as at least one impaired class has accepted the plan. Similar to Chapter 13, when a plan is successfully "crammed down," a Chapter 11 plan may be approved over the dissenting class or classes. Any good Chapter 11 plan will be constructed so as to be able to achieve a successful cramdown upon dissenting classes. Ultimately, the ability to achieve a successful cramdown is the acid test of a Chapter 11 plan. Cramdown litigation is among the most intense in the bankruptcy system.

Cramdown battles can be expensive and time-consuming. As a result, and ironically, they can be counterproductive to the reorganization's successful outcome. The costs of the litigation will increase administrative

---

40. 11 U.S.C. §1129(a)(12).
41. 11 U.S.C. §1114; 11 U.S.C. §1129(a)(13).
42. 11 U.S.C. §1129(a)(14), (15), (16).

expenses which can itself affect plan feasibility. If a cramdown dispute occurs over a lengthy period of time, the underlying facts and circumstances can change. These changes may also impact a plan's feasibility. Although cramdown disputes are unavoidable in many instances, the parties should always endeavor to resolve the dispute through negotiation and not litigation, lest the "victor" be left standing alone in the rubble of the debtor.

For the court to proceed with a cramdown, it must first find that all other elements of Section 1129(a) have been complied with except for Section 1129(a)(8). The plan must comply with all other provisions of Section 1129(a) except plan acceptance by all impaired classes to allow confirmation by cramdown to proceed, although at least one impaired class must consent, required by 1129(a)(10). For a cramdown attempt to succeed, the court must find that the plan does not discriminate unfairly and that the plan is fair and equitable with regard to each class of rejecting impaired claims or interests the plan seeks to cram down.[43] The issue of unfair discrimination is often raised but is rarely found. More frequently, it is the "fair and equitable" standard that creates dispute and that is relied upon by the courts. Fortunately, Section 1129(b)(2) defines the meaning of "fair and equitable" depending upon whether the class of claim to be crammed down is secured, unsecured, or is a class of interest holders.

A plan may be confirmed over rejection by a class of secured claims in one of three instances. First, the plan may be confirmed over rejection by the class if the secured class retains the collateral and will be paid in full over the life of the plan.[44] Second, a Chapter 11 plan may be confirmed over the objection of a class of secured claims if the collateral is to be sold free and clear of liens and the claim is to be paid in full from the proceeds.[45] Third, a plan may be approved over the objection of a class of secured claims if the debtor provides the claimant with the "indubitable equivalent" of its claims.[46] This final method means that if a class of secured claims is given property or cash equal to the full value of the secured claim, the plan may be approved over objection by the class. A substantial body of case law has developed in this area, the analysis of which is beyond the scope of this text. Suffice it to say that as a practical matter many courts view payment in full in cash as the most significant form of indubitable equivalent for payment of a secured creditor's claim. Any other proposal is likely to result in substantial and expensive litigation. For example, Pied Piper, Inc. files Chapter 11 owing its lender,

---

43. 11 U.S.C. §1129(b)(1).
44. 11 U.S.C. §1129(b)(2)(A)(i).
45. 11 U.S.C. §1129(b)(2)(A)(ii).
46. 11 U.S.C. §1129(b)(2)(A)(iii).

Valuation hearing: a hearing held, pursuant to 11 U.S.C. §506, to determine the value of a secured creditor's collateral

Tekbank, $10 million. Pied Piper proposes to transfer stock to Tekbank to satisfy the loan. If Tekbank challenges this valuation, a **valuation hearing** will be required.

FACT PATTERN

Following this same example, could The Lawn Cuttery issue stock to one or more of its creditors to satisfy any of its outstanding debts? Why or why not?

In summary, the concept of cramdown regarding a class of secured claims is simple. If the class is going to be paid the full value of its claims in some manner, which may include a return of its collateral, the plan will generally be confirmable over the claimant's objection. This is the common thread contained in each of the three methodologies to cram down a class of secured claims in Chapter 11.

Absolute priority rule: Prohibition against confirmation of a Chapter 11 reorganization plan if junior classes will receive dividends or retain interests where one or more senior classes are not paid in full and have rejected the plan.

There are two ways to obtain confirmation over rejection of a plan by a class of unsecured claims. The first method is very simple. If the plan proposes to pay an affected unsecured class in full on either the effective date of the plan or over time, the plan will be confirmable.[47] A class that will receive all that it is entitled to will not be heard to complain. Second, if a class of unsecured claims is not going to be paid in full, the court must find that no junior class of claims or interests will retain any interest in any property of the estate.[48] This is commonly known as the **absolute priority rule**. In its essence, this rule means that if the shareholders are proposing to retain an interest in a reorganized debtor, they will not be able to do so unless any rejecting class of unsecured claims is paid in full.

FACT PATTERN

The Lawn Cuttery's proposed Chapter 11 plan lists several unsecured creditors in one class and loans made by Owen to the company in a separate class. Owen plans to pay the unsecured class a zero dividend and to afterward obtain his supplies from other vendors. The plan provides that he will be paid in full for his loans over the next two years. Will these provisions satisfy the confirmation requirements?

A complex issue arises when an operating business proposes to pay its unsecured claimants an amount equal to or greater than the class would

---

47. 11 U.S.C. §1129(b)(2)(B)(i).
48. 11 U.S.C. §1129(b)(2)(B)(ii). See also the Historical and Revision Notes to this subsection.

receive in a Chapter 7 proceeding, but where the interest holders will be retaining an interest in the reorganized debtor. Some cases have permitted this practice, holding that the debtor has in essence "repurchased" the value of the business from the creditors.[49] Other cases do not permit this practice and require payment in full to a rejecting impaired class if any junior class retains any interest in the debtor.[50] Still other cases have adopted a rule that permits a junior class to retain an interest if present and substantial consideration is paid into the plan for the retention of such interest. This is known as the "infusion of new capital" or "new value" exception to the absolute priority rule.[51] In 1988, the United States Supreme Court held that performance of services by an insider to a reorganized debtor (known as sweat equity) will not constitute "new capital" that will permit confirmation by way of cramdown. The Supreme Court in this decision even questioned the continued viability of the "infusion of new capital" rule referred to above.[52]

In Bank of America v. 203 North La Salle Street Partnership, 526 U.S. 434 (1999), the Supreme Court expressly declined to rule definitively on the existence of the new value exception to the absolute priority rule, but did rule that it is insufficient to offer shares in a reorganized debtor solely to the old equity interests. In *La Salle*, the debtor was a limited partnership that owned 15 floors of a high-rise building in Chicago's Loop. The bank was owed approximately $93 million, of which $38.5 million was considered to be unsecured. *La Salle*'s plan proposed to pay the bank the full value of its secured claim but a dividend of only about 16 percent on its unsecured claim and a discharge as to the balance. The source of funding for the plan was to be a $6.125 million infusion of new capital into the partnership. However, only old partners could become partners in the reorganized debtor. As the largest unsecured creditor, the bank objected to the plan, initiating the cramdown dispute. The Supreme Court found on these facts: "[A]ssuming a new value corollary, that plans providing junior interest holders with exclusive opportunities free from competition and without benefit of market valuation fall within the prohibition of §1129(b)(2)(B)(ii)." (526 U.S. 434, 458).

BAPCPA created a statutory exception to the absolute priority rule applicable in individual Chapter 11 cases. If an individual Chapter 11 debtor commits all disposable income into the plan for at least five

---

49. In re Star City Rebuilders, Inc., 62 Bankr. 983 (W.D. Va. 1986).
50. In re Genesee Cement, Inc., 31 Bankr. 442 (E.D. Mich. 1983).
51. Case v. Los Angeles Lumber Prods., 308 U.S. 106 (1939).
52. Norwest Bank Worthin v. Ahlers, 484 U.S. 999 (1988). A debate has raged in the case law ever since. It is beyond the scope of this text to more completely analyze this issue. Readers facing a problem in this area should familiarize themselves with the most recent decisions from their area.

years, then the plan is subject to cramdown over the objection of unsecured creditors. This makes an individual Chapter 11 consistent with the similar requirement applicable in Chapter 13 cases, to the extent that the requirement is equivalent to a five-year applicable commitment period.[53]

Practice Pointer

Whether and to what extent a new value exception exists to the absolute priority rule is the subject of dispute in the case law.

A plan may be confirmed over the objection of a class of interest holders in two circumstances. First, if the affected interest holders are paid any redemption prices to which they may be entitled, the plan may be confirmed over their objection. Second, if no junior interest holder retains any interest in the estate, the plan may be confirmed over rejection by a dissenting class.[54] In essence, the same principles apply to the cramdown of an affected class of interest holders that apply to the cramdown of unsecured claims — payment in full of the interest's value or application of the absolute priority rule to interest holders. Obviously, this provision will only be problematic in a proceeding involving multiple classes of shareholders that will receive dividends; it is not problematic in most common situations.

FACT PATTERN

Would The Lawn Cuttery's plan be acceptable if it were modified to pay the various secured creditors their redemption amounts and for Owen to give up his loan claim?

There may only be one confirmed plan in existence at any given time. If the court is faced with two competing plans, each of which has been accepted by the creditors, the court shall consider the preference of the creditors and interest holders in determining which plan to confirm.[55]

53. 11 U.S.C. §1129(b)(2)(B)(ii). 11 U.S.C. §1129(a)(15), discussed above. See chapter 24 supra.
54. 11 U.S.C. §1129(b)(2)(C).
55. 11 U.S.C. §1129(c).

H. EFFECT OF CONFIRMATION AND CHAPTER 11 DISCHARGE

A confirmed Chapter 11 plan acts as a new contract between the debtor and all of its creditors.[56] Thus, any creditor violating the plan will be in breach of this new contract. Confirmation also revests the debtor with all of the property of the estate free and clear of all liens and interests except as provided for by the plan.[57] Confirmation of a plan also acts to discharge all debts that arose before the date of confirmation except as provided in the plan.[58]

A Chapter 11 discharge is virtually identical to a Chapter 7 discharge except that all Chapter 11 debtors receive a discharge, including corporate and partnership debtors. Debts that are nondischargeable under Section 523 may also be nondischargeable under a Chapter 11.[59] A discharge under Chapter 11 is the only way in which a corporation or partnership may receive a discharge under the Bankruptcy Code.

In certain instances, a Chapter 11 debtor will not be entitled to a discharge under Chapter 11. A debtor liquidating its assets through a Chapter 11 plan that does not plan to continue in business and would not be entitled to a Chapter 7 discharge if the proceeding were a Chapter 7 will not be discharged by the confirmation of a Chapter 11 plan.[60] Thus, a corporate or partnership debtor with a liquidating Chapter 11 plan will not receive a discharge from an unpaid obligation because a corporation or partnership is not entitled to a Chapter 7 discharge.[61] On the other hand, if the debtor is an individual and liquidates all nonexempt assets to pay creditors a dividend through a Chapter 11 plan, the individual will be entitled to a discharge because an individual may receive a Chapter 7 discharge. An individual Chapter 11 debtor does not receive a discharge until all payments under the plan have been completed.[62] A confirmed plan may be revoked by motion made within 180 days after confirmation if the confirmation has been fraudulently obtained.[63]

As a final bit of practical advice, when a plan proposes to pay creditors over a period of time, the creditors should insist upon provisions in the plan requiring regular postconfirmation reports of plan performance. In this manner the creditors will know if the plan is being performed or if

---

56. 11 U.S.C. §1141(a).
57. 11 U.S.C. §1141(b)(c).
58. 11 U.S.C. §1141(d)(1).
59. 11 U.S.C. §1141(d)(2).
60. 11 U.S.C. §1141(d)(3).
61. 11 U.S.C. §727(a)(1). See chapter 14 supra regarding entitlement to a Chapter 7 discharge.
62. 11 U.S.C. §1141(d)(5).
63. 11 U.S.C. §1144.

action should be taken to enforce the debtor's compliance with the plan up to and including revocation of confirmation and conversion of the proceeding to a Chapter 7.

Summary

A basic outline of the Chapter 11 plan confirmation process was provided in chapter 25 supra. This chapter explores this process in greater detail.

The first step in the process is to file a reorganization plan (Plan of Reorganization) and a disclosure statement with the court. The disclosure statement is a history of the debtor and an analysis of the debtor's reorganization plan. The basic contents of a disclosure statement are outlined in the checklist accompanying this chapter.

Before creditors may be given an opportunity to vote for or against the plan, the court must approve the contents of the disclosure statement at a disclosure statement hearing. This hearing requires 28 days' notice to creditors of the time to object. The court will approve the disclosure statement and authorize the plan proponent to solicit ballots to the creditor body if the disclosure statement is found to contain "adequate information" to enable creditors to make an informed decision when voting on the plan. In an electing small business case, the court may conditionally approve a disclosure statement and combine the disclosure and confirmation hearings. Section 105 permits the court to set a combined hearing when it may be appropriate to do so.

Section 1126 of the Bankruptcy Code regulates the voting on a Chapter 11 plan. Each impaired class of claims or interest holders is permitted to vote. A class of claims accepts a plan if a majority in number and two-thirds in dollar amount of those class members voting approve the plan. A class of interest holders accepts a plan if two-thirds in amount or percentage of those class members voting approve the plan. Special provisions permit the court, in some circumstances, to consider ballots obtained by the plan proponent in connection with a prefiling composition agreement (known as a "prepackaged bankruptcy"). A vote found to have been obtained in bad faith may be disallowed. An unimpaired class is conclusively deemed to accept the plan. Conversely, an impaired class that will receive no dividend is presumed to have rejected the plan. The results of the balloting are filed with the court in a report prepared pursuant to Federal Rule of Bankruptcy Procedure 3018.

The final step in the Chapter 11 confirmation process is the confirmation hearing held pursuant to Bankruptcy Code Section 1128. This hearing also requires 28 days' notice to creditors of the time to object. The ballots are sent to creditors with a notice of the confirmation hearing along with the other documents described in checklist 25.2 in chapter 25 supra.

At the confirmation hearing, the court must make 16 findings to confirm a plan. These 16 findings are contained in Section 1129(a) and are outlined in the checklist accompanying this chapter. Many of these findings will not be problematic in most cases. Issues of feasibility and cramdown are commonly the most problematic.

The analysis performed to determine a Chapter 11 plan's feasibility is similar to that described in connection with a Chapter 13 plan, particularly where a Chapter 11 plan offers to make payments to creditors over a period of time from the surplus revenues of an operating business. If the plan involves a different methodology, such as a sale of assets or refinancing loan, the court, in ruling upon the plan's feasibility, will need to determine the debtor's ability to conclude any sale or refinancing.

The issue of a Chapter 11 cramdown will only arise if an impaired class rejects the plan and the court can make all other required confirmation findings. For a plan to prevail in a Chapter 11 cramdown, the court must find that the plan is "fair and equitable" and does not "discriminate unfairly" against a rejecting class. Whether a plan is "fair and equitable" as to a rejecting class will vary depending upon the rejecting class's status as secured, unsecured, or equity security holders. The common thread among these provisions is that if the class is being paid in full or if no junior classes will receive a dividend, then a cramdown may succeed and the plan can be confirmed over the objection of a dissenting class. In an individual Chapter 11 case, the plan is also subject to cramdown if the debtor pays all disposable income into the plan for at least five years. The checklist accompanying this chapter outlines the various cramdown provisions of Bankruptcy Code Section 1129(b)(2). This provision is one of the most complex in the Bankruptcy Code.

As in Chapter 13, a Chapter 11 plan may be modified before or after confirmation. In addition, confirmation can be revoked if it has been fraudulently obtained.

Confirmation of a Chapter 11 plan results in a discharge of the debtor pursuant to Bankruptcy Code Section 1141. Reorganizing corporations and partnerships may obtain a Chapter 11 discharge. This is the only way in which a partnership or corporation may receive a discharge in the bankruptcy system. Liquidating corporations and other business entities may not receive a discharge.

KEY TERMS

absolute priority rule
"best interest of creditors" test

disclosure statement
feasibility requirement
liquidation analysis

prearranged bankruptcy   substantially
prepackaged bankruptcy   consummated
pro forma   valuation hearing

CHAPTER 27 CHECKLIST

| | 2. | The claim is paid in full by sale | 11 U.S.C. §1129(b)(2)(A)(ii) |
| | 3. | The claim receives "indubitable equivalent" | 11 U.S.C. §1129(b)(2)(A)(iii) |

27.3.4 A Plan Is Fair and Equitable to a Class of Unsecured Claims If Either

| | 1. | The class will be paid in full over the life of the plan, or | 11 U.S.C. §1129(b)(2)(B)(i) |
| | 2. | No junior class will retain an interest in the estate | 11 U.S.C. §1129(b)(2)(B)(ii) |

27.3.5 A Plan Is Fair and Equitable to a Class of Interest Holders if Either

| | 1. | The interests are retained or paid in full, or | 11 U.S.C. §1129(b)(2)(C)(i) |
| | 2. | No junior class will retain an interest in the estate | 11 U.S.C. §1129(b)(2)(C)(ii) |

DISCUSSION QUESTIONS

1. What is a disclosure statement? What is its purpose? What essential information should be included in a disclosure statement?

2. Which creditors may vote to accept or reject a Chapter 11 reorganization plan?

3. When is a class of creditors conclusively presumed to have accepted a plan? To have rejected a plan?

4. How does a class of claims accept a plan? How does a class of interests accept a plan?

5. What findings must the court make to confirm a Chapter 11 reorganization plan?

6. How may a plan proponent obtain a cramdown of a Chapter 11 reorganization plan?

7. How may a Chapter 11 plan be modified?

8. What is the scope of a Chapter 11 discharge?

PRACTICE EXERCISE

Exercise 27.1

The Lawn Cuttery operates successfully for five months in Chapter 11. Mr. Cash prepares financial projections, based on the operating results, indicating that a repayment plan can be proposed. Your firm prepares a plan and disclosure statement. The day before you are ready to file the documents, Mr. Cash advises you that last month his fuel expenses increased 25 percent, and all other costs are increasing prices so fast, "it's hard to keep the labels right." Advise Mr. Cash about the potential consequences of submitting inaccurate financial data in a disclosure statement.

28

Chapter 12: Reorganization Proceedings

Learning Objectives

- Describe Chapter 12 and the qualifications to become a Chapter 12 debtor

- Compare Chapter 12 to Chapters 13 and 11

- Understand the unique features of Chapter 12

- Describe the Chapter 12 plan and confirmation process

A.   PURPOSES OF CHAPTER 12

Throughout the 1980s, family farmers were faced with serious economic problems. Many farmers were forced to seek voluntary protection under the Bankruptcy Code to obtain debt relief and protect their family farms. (Recall that a farmer may not be the subject of an involuntary proceeding.)[1] The Bankruptcy Code of 1978, as enacted, did not contain sufficient protection for the unique economic predicament of family farmers. This resulted primarily from the recognition that a family farmer is

---

1. 11 U.S.C. §303(a). See chapter 4 supra.

simultaneously a wage earner and the operator of an increasingly sophisticated business.

Prior to the enactment of Chapter 12, a fundamental problem faced by
many farmers seeking bankruptcy relief was the choice of proceeding.
Many family farmers cannot afford the costs of a Chapter 11 proceeding.
The expeditious and relatively inexpensive procedures of Chapter 13 are
more consistent with an economically pressed farmer's budget. However,
because many farmers owe more than $1,184,200 in secured debt, they do
not qualify to file a Chapter 13.[2] As a result, farmers have had no
alternative but to seek the more complex and expensive Chapter 11 proceeding if a family farm is to be preserved.

However, once a farmer becomes a Chapter 11 debtor-in-possession,
the farmer's frustrations are just beginning. A secured creditor can move
for relief from the automatic stay on the grounds that there is no equity in
the property. The debtor-in-possession farmer can defend by asserting
that the property is necessary for an effective reorganization. The court
invariably orders adequate protection payments to maintain the
automatic stay in effect. If the debtor cannot afford the payments, then
the stay will be relieved and the undesired foreclosure becomes
inevitable.[3]

The problem was even more severe when a bank or cooperative had a
lien on crop proceeds. Such a lien can prevent the family from receiving
even the necessities of life due to the lienholder's rights in cash collateral,
as described in chapter 18 supra.

To counteract each of the above problems, Congress enacted Chapter
12 in 1986 on a temporary basis. BAPCPA made Chapter 12 permanent.
Additionally, the legislation expanded the scope of Chapter 12 to a family
fisherman.

Chapter 12 is essentially a hybrid of Chapters 11 and 13. There are
provisions in Chapter 12 that are virtually identical to the corresponding
provisions in the other reorganization proceedings. There are also a few
provisions unique to Chapter 12. Chapter 12 seeks to provide a family
farmer with the benefits of a Chapter 13, the flexibility and control of a
Chapter 11, and a partial abrogation of the sometimes harsh effects of
the "adequate protection" requirement in the special circumstances of
a family farm. In short, Chapter 12 gives a beleaguered family farmer
a fighting chance to resolve economic problems and retain the family
farm.

---

2. 11 U.S.C. §109(c). See chapters 5 and 24 supra.
3. 11 U.S.C. §362. See chapter 13 supra.

B.   WHO MAY FILE CHAPTER 12

Only a **family farmer** with regular income may be a Chapter 12 debtor.[4] A family farmer with regular income is a family farmer who can afford to make payments under a Chapter 12 plan.[5] Not all family farmers are farmers or families. The term *family farmer* is defined in 11 U.S.C. §101(18). When the Chapter 12 debtor is an individual or individual and spouse, the debtor will qualify for Chapter 12 relief if four conditions are met. First, the proposed debtor must be engaged in a "farming operation." The Code does not define this term but, fortunately, an ample body of case law defining farms has developed from interpretation of the earlier Bankruptcy Act provisions preventing the filing of involuntary bankruptcies against farmers. Generally, a farming operation is one in which primarily crops or herds are raised for purposes of ultimate sale. Hence, a gold mine with a small garden will not be a farming operation. A sheep ranch that discovers gold on the property will likely still qualify as a farming operation.

Family farmer: may be an individual, corporate, or partnership debtor; in the latter two instances, more than 50 percent of the ownership must belong to members of the same family: A qualified family farmer's total debt may not exceed $4,153,150

Second, the proposed debtor's total debt must not exceed $4,153,150. Third, no less than 50 percent of the undisputed liquidated debt must arise from the farming operation, exclusive of the debtor's residence unless it is also the farm. Finally, more than 50 percent of the proposed debtor's and the debtor's spouse's gross income for the year preceding the filing, or each of the second and third years preceding the filing, must be derived from the farming operation.[6] For example, Perry Mason, who visits his farm on weekends but earns only 10 percent of his income from the farm, will not qualify as a family farmer.

A corporation or partnership may also qualify for Chapter 12 relief. There are six requirements for qualification. First, the entity must be a farming operation as described above. Second, more than 50 percent of the stock or equity must belong to members of the same family. Thus, where the Hatfields and McCoys are equal partners, the partnership may not qualify because no single family owns a majority of the stock.

Third, more than 80 percent of the assets must relate to the farming operation. Fourth, the total debt may not exceed $4,153,150. Fifth, at least 50 percent of the total undisputed liquidated debt must be related to the farming operation, exclusive of a dwelling house that is not related to the farm. Finally, if the debtor is a corporation, it must be privately held.[7] If all

---

4. 11 U.S.C. §109(f).
5. 11 U.S.C. §101(19).
6. 11 U.S.C. §101(18)(A). The dollar amounts are subject to adjustment for inflation pursuant to 11 U.S.C. §104(b). The amount shown applies to cases filed on or after April 1, 2016.
7. 11 U.S.C. §101(18)(B). The dollar amounts are subject to adjustment for inflation pursuant to 11 U.S.C. §104(b). The amount shown is the amount effective as of April 1, 2016.

these requirements are satisfied, Green Acres, Inc., may file a Chapter 12 proceeding.[8]

A **family fisherman** is an individual whose debts do not exceed $1,924,550 and 80 percent of which are related to commercial fishing operations, excluding debt on the debtor's personal residence, and from which more than 50 percent of the debtor's income in the year preceding the filing has been earned. A corporation may also qualify as a family fisherman if more than 50 percent of the stock is held by family members, debts do not exceed $1,924,550, and more than 80 percent of the assets and debts are related to the fishing operation.[9]

Family fisherman: may be an individual, corporate, or partnership debtor; in the latter two instances, at least 50 percent of the ownership must belong to the same family: A qualified family fisherman's total debt may not exceed $1,924,550 and at least 80 percent must be related to the fishing operation

C.   COMPARISON TO CHAPTERS 11 AND 13

In examining the general provisions of Chapter 12, it becomes readily apparent that Chapter 12 is no more than a hybrid of Chapters 11 and 13. Many elements of Chapter 12 are borrowed from those proceedings, though there are some unique elements.

There are three basic similarities of Chapter 12 to Chapter 13. First, Chapter 12 imposes an automatic stay in favor of codebtors that is identical to the provision contained in Chapter 13.[10] Second, as in Chapter 13, the debtor's postpetition earnings are property of the estate.[11] Third, a Chapter 12 may be dismissed for many of the identical reasons for which a Chapter 13 may be dismissed or converted.[12] A proceeding may also be dismissed if it appears there is no reasonable likelihood of rehabilitation.[13] However, only the debtor may convert a proceeding from a Chapter 12 to a Chapter 7.[14] This is consistent with the principle that an involuntary proceeding may not be commenced against a farmer.[15]

There are two general similarities between Chapter 12 and Chapter 11. First, a Chapter 12 debtor has duties and powers that are somewhat analogous to those of a Chapter 11 debtor-in-possession.[16] This is so notwithstanding the additional fact that there is also a trustee appointed

---

8. A limited liability company has qualified as a family farmer. In re Sandifer, 448 BR 382 (Bankr. S.C. 2011).
9. 11 U.S.C. §101(19A). This amount is also subject to triannual inflation adjustment pursuant to 11 U.S.C. §104(b).
10. 11 U.S.C. §1201; 11 U.S.C. §1301. See chapter 24 supra.
11. 11 U.S.C. §1207; 11 U.S.C. §1306. See chapter 24 supra.
12. 11 U.S.C. §1208; 11 U.S.C. §1307(a)(1)-(8). See chapter 24 supra.
13. 11 U.S.C. §1208(c)(9).
14. 11 U.S.C. §1208(a).
15. 11 U.S.C. §303(a). See chapter 4 supra.
16. 11 U.S.C. §1203; 11 U.S.C. §1107. See chapter 25 supra.

in every Chapter 12 proceeding. Second, a Chapter 12 debtor-in-possession may be removed for causes identical to the related Chapter 11 provision. A Chapter 12 debtor-in-possession may not, however, be removed from possession on the ground that removal is in the best interests of creditors.[17]

D.   UNIQUE CHAPTER 12 FEATURES

There are three general features of Chapter 12 unique to it. The first of these is the existence of a trustee even though the debtor is the equivalent of a debtor-in-possession.[18] A given district may have a standing Chapter 12 trustee whose duties are analogous to those of a Chapter 13 standing trustee.[19] To the extent that the trustee is not a standing trustee, the trustee's duties are somewhat the same as those of a Chapter 11 trustee with the additional duty that a Chapter 12 trustee has the responsibilities of receiving and disbursing the debtor's Chapter 12 plan payments and that the debtor commences making timely payments under a confirmed Chapter 12 plan. If the debtor owes domestic support obligations, the trustee must also provide notice to the claimholder in a manner identical to a Chapter 7 trustee.[20]

A second unique feature of Chapter 12 is a special definition of *adequate protection* applicable only in Chapter 12. Section 361, regarding adequate protection, does not apply in Chapter 12. This ameliorates the harsh results that were being meted out to farmers in Chapter 11 and Chapter 13 proceedings prior to Chapter 12's enactment. Section 1205(b) retains the common adequate protection methods of periodic payments and additional or replacement collateral, but adds two additional modes of adequate protection. First, customary rent in the community where the property is located may constitute adequate protection. Presumably, this sum might be less than the payments that would be required to service debt on a trust deed or mortgage secured by the debtor's real property. Second, the court has specifically been granted broad equitable discretion to formulate an adequate protection order in Chapter 12.[21] This is supposed to give a family farmer or fisherman a fighting chance.

---

17. 11 U.S.C. §1204; 11 U.S.C. §1104(a)(1). See chapter 11 supra.
18. 11 U.S.C. §1202.
19. 11 U.S.C. §1202(a). See chapter 11 supra.
20. 11 U.S.C. §1202(b), (c); 11 U.S.C. §1226(c). See chapters 11 and 24 supra.
21. 11 U.S.C. §1205(b)(4).

The final unique feature of Chapter 12 permits a sale free and clear of liens if the property sold is farmland, farm equipment, or property used to carry out a commercial fishing operation. This is in addition to the five methods for obtaining approval of a sale free and clear of liens under Section 363(f).[22] For example, Ma and Pa Kettle, Chapter 12 debtors, want to sell their farm for less than the amount of all liens and encumbrances upon it. Unless the affected lienholders consent or are to be paid in full from the proceeds, a sale free and clear of liens would not be permitted in a Chapter 11 or Chapter 7. However, because Chapter 12 specifically permits a sale free and clear of liens of farmland or farm equipment, the sale may take place over the lienholders' objections even though an affected claim may not necessarily be paid in full from the proceeds of the sale.

E.   CHAPTER 12 PLANS AND DISCHARGE

With surprisingly few exceptions, the provisions of Chapter 12 relating to the contents and confirmation of a plan are virtually identical to the related provisions contained in Chapter 13. This is consistent with congressional intent to provide the speed and reduced expense of a Chapter 13 proceeding to family farmers who would otherwise be required to file more complex and expensive Chapter 11 proceedings.

A Chapter 12 plan must be filed within 90 days of commencing the proceeding unless the court extends the period upon finding an extension substantially justified.[23] This is substantially longer than the 14-day period permitted under Chapter 13 but less than the exclusivity period provided to Chapter 11 debtors. Unlike Chapter 11, however, the Chapter 12 plan filing deadline is a mandatory deadline.[24]

Section 1222 is identical to Section 1322, describing the mandatory and permissive elements of a Chapter 12 plan.[25] The one difference from Chapter 13 is that a Chapter 12 plan may modify the rights of a secured claimant secured by the debtor's principal residence. Recall that this is not permitted in Chapter 13.[26] A Chapter 12 plan is subject to the same performance limits (no longer than five years), and on the identical grounds

---

22. 11 U.S.C. §1206; 11 U.S.C. §363(f). See chapter 19 supra.
23. 11 U.S.C. §1221.
24. See chapters 24 and 26 supra.
25. 11 U.S.C. §1222; 11 U.S.C. §1322.
26. 11 U.S.C. §1222(b)(2); 11 U.S.C. §1322(b)(2). See chapter 24 supra.

previously described for Chapter 13 proceedings.[27] A Chapter 12 plan may be modified prior to confirmation in a manner identical to a Chapter 13 plan.[28]

A Chapter 12 confirmation hearing is to be given expedited treatment. The confirmation hearing shall be concluded no longer than 45 days after the plan is filed. A party in interest may object.[29] Except for the expedited treatment accorded the hearing date, this provision is identical to the similar provision in Chapter 13.[30] Note that no disclosure statement is required, nor do creditors vote on the plan. This is identical to Chapter 13.

The standards for confirmation of a Chapter 12 plan are almost identical to the confirmation standards for a Chapter 13 plan.[31] The provisions for the making of Chapter 12 plan payments are essentially identical to the sister provision in Chapter 13. The standards for achieving cramdown of a Chapter 12 plan are identical to the Chapter 13 cramdown provisions. The one difference is that there is no mandatory length for a Chapter 12 plan.

Instead, the plan may be crammed down on unsecured claimants if the debtor pays all disposable surplus income into the plan for at least three years. (This is identical to Section 1325 prior to the 2005 legislation).[32] The effect of confirmation of a Chapter 12 plan is identical to the effect of confirmation in Chapter 11 and Chapter 13 proceedings. The confirmed plan has the status of a binding contract between the debtor and all creditors, those in agreement with and those opposed to the plan. Thus, as with the other reorganization proceedings, a Chapter 12 plan is no more than a judicially approved composition agreement.[33]

On the other hand, a Chapter 12 discharge is analogous to a Chapter 11 discharge and lacks the effect of a Chapter 13 discharge.[34] However, a Chapter 12 debtor may receive an early discharge under the same terms and conditions as a Chapter 13 debtor.[35] Finally, a Chapter 12 plan may be modified after confirmation under the same terms and conditions as a Chapter 13 plan.[36]

---

27. 11 U.S.C. §1222(c); 11 U.S.C. §1322(c). See chapter 24 supra.
28. 11 U.S.C. §1223; 11 U.S.C. §1323. See chapter 24 supra.
29. 11 U.S.C. §1224.
30. 11 U.S.C. §1324. See chapter 24 supra.
31. 11 U.S.C. §1225; 11 U.S.C. §1325. See chapter 24 supra.
32. 11 U.S.C. §1225; 11 U.S.C. §1325. See chapter 24 supra.
33. 11 U.S.C. §1227; 11 U.S.C. §1141(a); 11 U.S.C. §1327(a). See chapters 24 and 27 supra.
34. 11 U.S.C. §1228; 11 U.S.C. §1141. See chapter 27 supra.
35. 11 U.S.C. §1228(b); 11 U.S.C. §1328(b). See chapter 24 supra.
36. 11 U.S.C. §1229; 11 U.S.C. §1329. See chapter 24 supra.

Summary

Chapter 12, commonly known as a family farmer or fisherman reorganization, was enacted into the Bankruptcy Code in 1986 in an effort to provide viable specialized bankruptcy relief to family farmers. Prior to the enactment of Chapter 12, many family farmers failed in bankruptcy reorganizations for three basic reasons. First, many family farmers could not afford the expense of a Chapter 11 proceeding. Second, many family farmers lacked the ability to provide secured creditors with proper forms of adequate protection, as described in Chapter 12 of this text. Third, many family farmers possessed debt in excess of the permissible Chapter 13 amounts. Chapter 12 was enacted to neutralize these problems and, as a result, to provide family farmers with a viable form of bankruptcy relief. The 2005 legislation made Chapter 12 permanent and expanded Chapter 12 to family fishermen.

A family farmer may be an individual, corporation, or partnership. In the latter two instances, more than 50 percent of the ownership must belong to the same family. A qualified family farmer's debt may not exceed $4,153,150. A family fisherman may also be an individual, corporation, or partnership, in a manner similar to farmers, except that the debt limit is $1,924,500.

Chapter 12 is a hybrid of Chapters 11 and 13. The speed and brevity of the Chapter 13 confirmation process are combined with the debtor-in-possession provisions of Chapter 11.

A Chapter 12 debtor has rights similar to a Chapter 11 debtor-in-possession. However, a trustee will always be appointed in a Chapter 12. The functions of a Chapter 12 trustee are similar to those of a Chapter 13 trustee.

Additional methods of providing adequate protection to secured creditors are available to Chapter 12 debtors. Periodic payments, replacement of additional collateral, customary rent in the community, or any equitable order granted by the court may constitute adequate protection.

The elements of a Chapter 11 plan and the findings required for confirmation are identical to Chapter 13, but with three exceptions. See the checklist to chapter 24 for further description. First, a Chapter 12 plan may be filed within 90 days of filing the proceeding. Second, a Chapter 12 confirmation hearing must take place within 45 days of filing the plan. Finally, a Chapter 12 plan, unlike a Chapter 13 plan, may modify the rights of secured creditors of the debtor's residence.

KEY TERMS

family farmer   family fisherman

DISCUSSION QUESTIONS

1. Why was Chapter 12 enacted? What is a family farmer for purposes of Chapter 12?

2. What provisions of Chapter 12 are similar to those of Chapter 13?

3. What provisions of Chapter 12 are similar to those of Chapter 11?

4. What features of Chapter 12 are unique to Chapter 12 proceedings?

PART VI

Review

29

Introduction to Courts and Jurisdiction

Learning Objectives

- Describe bankruptcy jurisdiction
- Define the meaning of the terms "core" and "noncore" proceedings
- Define the meaning of the terms "arising under" and "related to"
- Understand how appeals are taken from a Bankruptcy Court decision to other courts

A.   BANKRUPTCY AND FEDERAL JUDGES

Article III of the United States Constitution creates the federal court system and **federal judges**.[1] Federal judges are distinguishable from other judicial officers by the constitutional requirement that federal judges be provided with two basic protections to ensure their independence: lifetime tenure during good behavior and that their salary not be subject to reduction during their term of office.[2]

The 1978 legislation that enacted the "Bankruptcy Code" gave the newly created Bankruptcy Judges jurisdiction to deal with any matter whatsoever having any relationship to a bankruptcy estate.[3] This was, in

Federal judges:
judges appointed
to the federal
bench pursuant to
U.S. Const., Art.
III, §1, U.S. Const.
Art III, §2

---

1. U.S. Const. art. III.
2. U.S. Const. art. III, §1.
3. 28 U.S.C. §1471, Pub. L. No. 95-598, 92 Stat. 2549 (1978).

essence, a grant of full plenary jurisdiction to Bankruptcy Judges. This broad grant of jurisdiction made Bankruptcy Judges equivalent to full-time federal judges except that their jurisdiction was limited to matters involving bankruptcy proceedings. However, the Bankruptcy Judges created by the 1978 Bankruptcy Reform Act were not given lifetime tenure or the salary protection of full federal judges. Instead, Bankruptcy Judges were given 14-year terms and their salary could be subject to reduction while in office. Rather than serving as Article III judges, the Bankruptcy Judges were created by Congress pursuant to article 1, section 8, of the Constitution, which gives Congress the right to enact bankruptcy laws.[4]

In 1982, in the case of Northern Pipeline Construction v. Marathon Pipeline Company, the Supreme Court reviewed the constitutionality of the Bankruptcy Court system enacted with the Code.[5] In this case, the debtor, Northern Pipeline Construction, filed an adversary proceeding in the Bankruptcy Court to collect an account receivable due from Marathon Pipeline on a turnover theory pursuant to Section 542. In state court, this action would have been a simple debt collection suit not based upon a preference or a fraudulent conveyance or any other subject even remotely involving the Bankruptcy Code. Marathon Pipeline argued that the Bankruptcy Courts were unconstitutional because Bankruptcy Judges were not given the protections provided federal judges under article III of the Constitution and therefore they had no jurisdiction to rule upon matters unrelated to the Bankruptcy Code. In its opinion, the Supreme Court thoroughly analyzed these constitutional issues and ruled that the Bankruptcy Judge and Bankruptcy Court system enacted in 1978 was unconstitutional.

B.   ACTIVITY WITHIN A BANKRUPTCY

To understand Congress's solution to the problem, it is important to review the various levels of a bankruptcy proceeding. First, there is the overall proceeding. This is the type of Chapter proceeding filed: 7, 9, 11, 12, 13, or 15. It should now be obvious that, unlike traditional litigation, a multitude of activities will take place within a bankruptcy proceeding, for the simple reason that all of a debtor's financial affairs are subject to the scrutiny and control of the court. In contrast, a traditional piece of litigation will normally examine only one event or transaction in a vacuum without regard to the parties' other financial affairs.

Within a bankruptcy proceeding, matters will be brought before a Bankruptcy Judge by one of two methods: motion or adversary

---

4. U.S. Const. art. I, §8.
5. 458 U.S. 50 (1982).

proceeding. For example, a sale will generally take place by way of a motion.[6] On the other hand, an action to avoid a preference takes place by way of an adversary proceeding.[7] Adversary proceedings may also arise that will not involve application of the Bankruptcy Code. For example, the collection of an account receivable, while theoretically a turnover complaint, is nothing more than a simple breach of contract dispute to determine the amount due that does not require the application of bankruptcy law.[8]

C.   BAFJA

In 1984, Congress enacted the Bankruptcy Amendments and Federal Judgeship Act ("BAFJA") to be consistent with the Supreme Court's direction.[9] The process thus established is summarized in the accompanying flowchart. Initially, the district courts have original and exclusive jurisdiction over bankruptcies, but Congress may elect to make the jurisdiction nonexclusive. Congress has done this by creating the Bankruptcy Courts.[10] This means that a federal district court or federal Bankruptcy Court may hear a bankruptcy proceeding.

The nonexclusive grant of jurisdiction to the Bankruptcy Court is set forth in 28 U.S.C. §157. Under present law, all bankruptcy proceedings and motions or adversary proceedings occurring within them are referred to Bankruptcy Judges, but any party in interest may request withdrawal of the reference at any time and have the matter referred back to the district court (the article III judge) for disposition.

Practice Pointer
This referral is accomplished by a standing order entered by the district courts referring bankruptcy matters automatically to the Bankruptcy Court.

When the reference is withdrawn, the matter may not be heard by the Bankruptcy Court at all unless all parties in the matter consent or the district court determines in its discretion to reserve jurisdiction with

---

6. See chapters 13 and 19 supra.
7. See chapters 13 and 17 supra.
8. See chapter 15 supra.
9. Bankruptcy Amendments and Federal Judgeship Act of 1984 (BAFJA), Pub. L. No. 98-353 (July 10, 1984).
10. 28 U.S.C. §1334.

the Bankruptcy Court. Further, any Bankruptcy Judge's rulings can be subject to the further approval of a district judge.[11]

BANKRUPTCY JURISDICTION

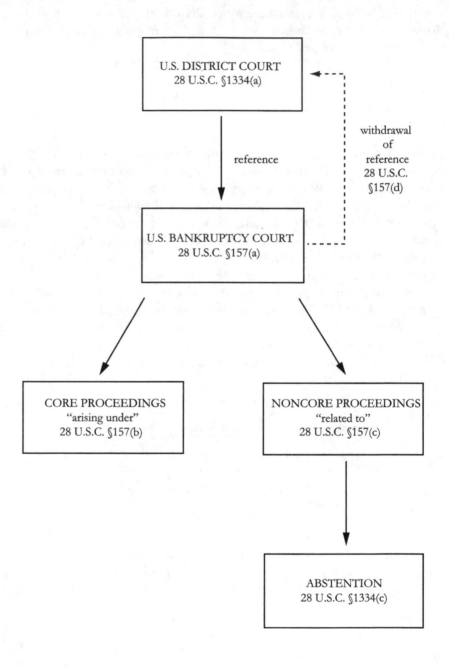

---

11. 28 U.S.C. §157(a), (c), (d).

To distinguish the matters within a bankruptcy proceeding that the Bankruptcy Court may hear, Congress designated proceedings as "core" and "noncore" and relied on the phrases "arising under" or "related to" to define adversary matters within a bankruptcy proceeding.[12]

Bankruptcy Judges have jurisdiction to hear cases filed under Title 11 and may also hear all core proceedings arising within the proceeding and matters "related to" the bankruptcy proceeding.[13]

D. CORE AND NONCORE PROCEEDINGS

Generally, **core proceedings** "arising under" the Bankruptcy Code are those matters that arise by way of motion or adversary proceeding and involve the specific application of one or more provisions of the Bankruptcy Code for their resolution. The matters identified in 28 U.S.C. §157(b)(2) as core proceedings are issues that are generally the subject matter of specific Bankruptcy Code sections. For example, objections to claims, relief from stay motions, motions to assume or reject executory contracts, objections to exemptions, objections to the dischargeability of debts or to the debtor's discharge, preferences, and other uses of the trustee's avoiding powers are all defined as *core proceedings*.[14] The resolution of these issues normally requires the application of specific Bankruptcy Code provisions.

Core proceedings: a matter arising before a Bankruptcy Court that involves the specific application of a Bankruptcy Code provision for its resolution

On the other hand, a matter "related to" a bankruptcy proceeding is a matter that would arise for a debtor whether or not the particular bankruptcy proceeding exists.[15] For example, the debt collection suit filed in *Marathon Pipeline* supra is such a matter. Matters such as these are generally considered **noncore proceedings**. The Bankruptcy Court may hear noncore matters.[16] However, if a party objects to the Bankruptcy Court's hearing of a noncore matter, the Bankruptcy Court must determine whether the matter is a core or noncore proceeding. If the matter is

Noncore proceedings: matters that are related to a bankruptcy proceeding but that do not require specific application of a Bankruptcy Code provision for the matter's resolution

12. 28 U.S.C. §157(b); 28 U.S.C. §1334.
13. 28 U.S.C. §157(b)(1).
14. 28 U.S.C. §157(b)(2).
15. The extent of "related to" jurisdiction has been defined as whether a lawsuit could conceivably have any impact on the bankruptcy estate without the "intervention of yet another lawsuit." In re W.R. Grace & Co., 591 F.3d 164, 172-173 (3d Cir. 2009). See also In re KSRP, Ltd., 809 F.3d 263 (5th Cir. 2015); In re Deitz, 760 F.3d 1038 (9th Cir. 2014); In re National Century Fin. Enters., Inc. Inv. Litigation, 497 Fed. Appx. 491 (6th Cir. 2012); In re Ryan, 276 Fed. Appx. 963, 966 (11th Cir. 2008); Valley Historic L.P. v. Bank of NY, 486 F.3d 831, 836 (4th Cir. 2007).
16. 28 U.S.C. §157(b)(1).

noncore, the Bankruptcy Court must either refer the case to the district court or abstain from further hearing the matter.[17] Personal injury and wrongful death claims are specifically designated as noncore.[18] The practical effect of these provisions is to have a personal injury suit or complex commercial litigation tried in a court other than the Bankruptcy Court in appropriate circumstances.

> **Practice Pointer**
>
> In a noncore matter, the Bankruptcy Court only has the authority to enter findings of fact and conclusions of law.

28 U.S.C. §1334(c) permits the Bankruptcy Court or district court to abstain from hearing a particular matter. If a matter is "related to" the bankruptcy proceeding but would not be heard in the federal court system absent the fact that one of the parties is a debtor in a bankruptcy proceeding, then the Bankruptcy Court or district court may abstain from hearing the matter and will defer to local jurisdiction.[19] A decision to abstain is not reviewable by appeal or otherwise.[20] For example, a trustee seeks to litigate a breach of contract suit in Bankruptcy Court. The defendant moves the court to abstain on the grounds that the claim is noncore and has no independent source of federal jurisdiction. The Bankruptcy Court agrees. This decision may not be appealed.

In Marshall v. Marshall, 547 U.S. 293 (2006), the debtor (commonly known as Anna Nicole Smith) objected to a defamation claim filed in her bankruptcy by her deceased husband's son, Pierce Marshall. In objecting to the claim, she asserted a counterclaim against Pierce, claiming that he tortiously interfered with a gift expected from her deceased husband. The Bankruptcy Court and district courts found judgment for Smith in the amount of $44.3 million. The Ninth Circuit found that matter barred from Bankruptcy Court jurisdiction by a common law exception to bankruptcy jurisdiction barring Bankruptcy Courts from hearing probate or domestic relations matters. The Supreme Court reversed the Ninth Circuit finding that the counterclaim did not seek to probate a will, contest a will, or administer the decedent's estate, and so the Bankruptcy Court had

---

17. 28 U.S.C. §157(b)(3), (b)(4), (c), (d).
18. 28 U.S.C. §157(b)(5).
19. 28 U.S.C. §1334(c)(2).
20. 28 U.S.C. §1334(c)(2).

jurisdiction to hear and to rule upon the counterclaim. The claim objection was a core proceeding. The counterclaim was "related to" claim.[21]

The various circuits within the federal judicial system have been given the power to appoint Bankruptcy Judges in each district. Bankruptcy Judges are appointed by the circuits to 14-year terms.[22]

E.   REMOVAL AND APPEALS

It is possible to remove pending actions from the state court system to the Bankruptcy Court pursuant to 28 U.S.C. §1452. The procedure for removal is contained in Federal Rule of Bankruptcy Procedure 9027.[23] Many times when there is pending litigation at the time a bankruptcy proceeding is filed, the debtor or a creditor will seek to remove the litigation from state court to the Bankruptcy Court. If removal occurs and there is no objection, the Bankruptcy Court will then hear the case.

Appeals from the rulings of a Bankruptcy Court may be made to either the district court in the district where the Bankruptcy Court is located, to the Bankruptcy Appellate Panel ("BAP") for the Bankruptcy Court's particular circuit, or directly to the Court of Appeals for a given circuit.[24] A BAP may be created within a given federal judicial circuit. This panel will be comprised of three Bankruptcy Judges from districts within the circuit. The 1994 Bankruptcy Reform Act makes the establishment of BAPs mandatory unless the judicial council for a particular circuit finds insufficient resources or the likelihood that undue delay would result from establishment of a panel.[25] The BAP will hear all appeals unless the appellant elects, when filing the appeal, or the appellee elects within 30 days after service of the appeal, to have the appeal heard by the district court. In some limited instances, an appeal may be made directly to the circuit if the lower court so certifies.[26] Part 8 of the Federal Rules of

---

21. In Stern v. Marshal, 564 U.S. 462 (2011), the Court held there was no constitutional jurisdiction, and the bankruptcy court also lacked constitutional jurisdiction to rule on the counterclaim. In Executive Benefits Insurance Agency v. Arkison, 573 U.S. — (2014), the Supreme Court held that if the matter is subject to review and entry of findings of fact and conclusions of law by the District Court, then the Bankruptcy Court may hear the matter. In Wellness International Network, Ltd. v. Sharif, 575 U.S. — (2015), the Court held that if all parties consent to jurisdiction by the bankruptcy court, the court may hear the matter.
22. U.S.C. §§151, 152.
23. 28 U.S.C. §1452; Bankruptcy Rule 9027.
24. 28 U.S.C. §158(a).
25. The First and Ninth Circuits have BAP panels. The Second, Third, Fourth, Fifth, Seventh, and Eleventh Circuits do not. The Sixth, Eighth, and Tenth Circuits have BAP panels for limited districts within each circuit.
26. 28 U.S.C. §158.

Bankruptcy Procedure governs appeals. Otherwise, appeals of bankruptcy matters are similar to other federal judicial appeals, including applicability of the Federal Rules of Appellate Procedure. See the nearby flowchart.

BANKRUPTCY APPEALS

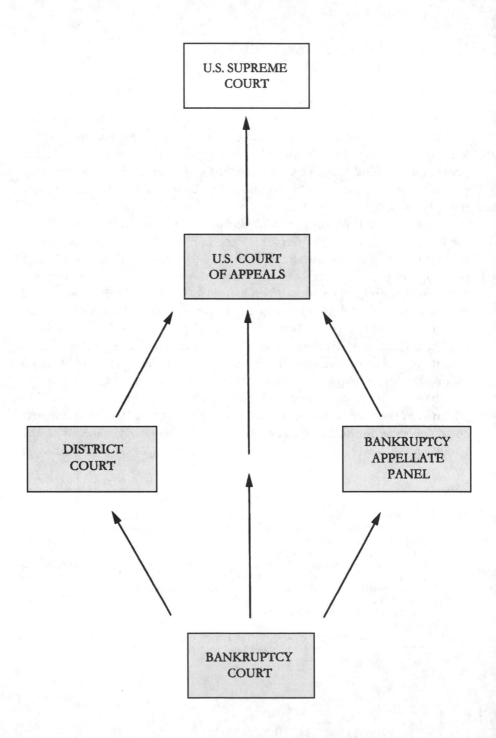

F.   JURY TRIALS

In Granfinanceria, S.A. v. Norberg, the Supreme Court explored the right to a jury trial in adversary proceedings before the Bankruptcy Court.[27] In this case, Norberg, a trustee, sued Granfinanceria to avoid fraudulent transfers. Granfinanceria requested a jury trial. The lower courts held that because suits to avoid fraudulent transfers were not triable by jury under common law and because an action to avoid a fraudulent transfer is a core proceeding, no right to a jury trial existed. The Supreme Court disagreed and reversed.

The Supreme Court held, in essence, that any action to recover money is an action at law for which a Seventh Amendment constitutional right to trial by jury exists. Notwithstanding this decision, the occurrence of a jury trial in the Bankruptcy Court is extremely rare. The 1994 Bankruptcy Reform Act permits the Bankruptcy Court to conduct jury trials if designated to do so by the district court and with the express consent of all parties.[28] Local rules should be consulted to ascertain the procedure in a particular district.

Summary

Federal law confers jurisdiction to hear bankruptcy proceedings on all federal district and Bankruptcy Courts. In some situations, a party may seek removal of a bankruptcy proceeding from a Bankruptcy Court to a federal district court. Normally, however, virtually all bankruptcy proceedings are presided over by the Bankruptcy Courts.

A Bankruptcy Court will always hear core matters. A core matter is any issue whose resolution requires specific application of a Bankruptcy Code provision. A claim objection, an action to avoid a preference, and a motion for relief from the automatic stay are all examples of core proceedings.

On the other hand, a matter arising before the Bankruptcy Court that does not require application of a specific Bankruptcy Code provision for its resolution is known as a noncore matter. A party may request the Bankruptcy Court to abstain from hearing a noncore matter. A decision by the court to abstain is not reviewable by appeal or otherwise. A personal injury action is a good example of a noncore matter.

---

27. 492 U.S. 33 (1989).
28. 28 U.S.C §157(e).

KEY TERMS

core proceedings   noncore proceedings
federal judges

DISCUSSION QUESTIONS

1. What is the difference between a core and noncore proceeding?
   Identify the following as core or noncore proceedings: motion for
   relief from stay; breach of contract claim; preference complaint; objection to claim of exemption; personal injury claim.

2. Describe the higher courts to which a bankruptcy ruling may be
   appealed.

30

Statements and Schedules Tutorial

Learning Objectives

- Prepare the most important pleadings used in bankruptcy practice
- Understand the data contained in the Statements and Schedules

A.   INTRODUCTION

Approximately 95–99 percent of all bankruptcy proceedings filed are individual consumer Chapter 7 or Chapter 13 proceedings. In these cases, the practitioner's most important task is to prepare the information required to be in the Statement of Financial Affairs and the Schedules of Assets and Liabilities, commonly known as the Statements and Schedules, and to complete the applicable Statement of Current Monthly Income and Means-Test Calculation. Performing these tasks well will make the debtor's trip through the bankruptcy system as smooth and uneventful as possible. Proper preparation will also minimize the trustee's effort to administer the case. In an asset proceeding, performing these tasks well will help maximize the estate's recovery because the schedules act as an easy reference guide for the trustee as to the location and value of any assets.[1] Where the debtor's major goal is to satisfy nondischargeable tax claims, well-produced schedules will aid in achieving this result. In a

---

1. See chapter 12 supra.

practice emphasizing bankruptcy law, a paralegal will spend a significant amount of time assisting in the preparation of these documents.

When representing creditors, it is important to carefully read the Statements and Schedules. Because these documents comprise the evidence that allows creditors or the trustee to determine the existence of assets available for liquidation and distribution, raise potential objections to an individual debtor's discharge, or challenge the feasibility of a reorganization, understanding their contents is an important lesson to learn. This chapter is an exercise in learning to prepare and read the Statements and Schedules. This chapter also serves as a review of the Bankruptcy Code and as a final illustration of the Bankruptcy Code's functioning as a system. Chapter 31 is a tutorial about the preparation of the Statement of Current Monthly Income and Means-Test Calculation.

The first group of forms analyzed is collectively referred to as the Schedules.[2] The second form analyzed is known as the Statement of Financial Affairs.[3] These documents are used by all Chapter 7, 11, and 13 debtors.

To simplify the explanation of these forms, we will review them in the context of a statement of facts concerning two hypothetical joint debtors. Each form will then be analyzed, item by item, on the basis of the fact scenario. Chapter 31 utilizes the same scenario.

FACT PATTERN

The Cash fact pattern also provides another example which we can use to help complete and understand the Statements and Schedules.

Where an illustration does not show the entirety of a particular portion of a form this is generally in the interest of space as the omitted material is typically listing information about a particular creditor or transaction. If the answer to any of the lines in any form is "Yes," then complete the information requested for each such payment as shown in the complete copy of Official Forms B106 and B107 in the forms materials.

FACT PATTERN

If a bankruptcy case is filed for The Lawn Cuttery, a similar analysis will need to be done with respect to Official Forms B201, 206A/B-207. Note however that the questions and items are NOT located in the same place in each respective form. This requires a close reading of the nonindividual forms.

---

2. Official Form B106 for individual debtors and Official Form B206 for nonindividuals.
3. Official Form B107 for individual debtors and Official Form B207 for nonindividuals.

Counsel's duty of reasonable investigation as set forth in Section 707(b)(4) alters the relative responsibility for the accurate preparation of the Schedules. Counsel should maintain detailed records to support the contents of the Statements, Schedules, and Statement of Current Monthly Income. The text reflects custom and practice from throughout the country and, where necessary, includes the evolving standards created by BAPCPA.

B.   KEN AND BRETONY BOTTOMLINE

Ken and Bretony Bottomline want to file Chapter 7 without delay. Computer City is threatening to attach their computer, and Lannister Credit is threatening to repossess their Westeros SUV. Only an immediate Chapter 7 filing will prevent a loss of the car to the repossessor.

> ***By comparing the Cash and Bottomline fact patterns, you can see that different information was obtained and different circumstances occurred. Remember to treat each case as unique unto itself when compiling the data necessary to complete the forms.***

FACT PATTERN

Ken and Bretony have lived at 1999 Prince Road in Suffragette City in the Southern District of California in San Diego County for the past two years. Previously, they lived at 45 Coldfish Lane in Frosty Falls, Montana.

Ken has been employed by Stardust, Inc., for two years as a software designer. He receives an annual salary of $78,000. Bretony is currently employed as an assistant manager at the China Girl Tea Shop and receives a monthly salary of $1,000. She has been working at China Girl for three months. For one year before that, she was in a partnership with Kilgore Trout. The name of the partnership was Top O' the Mornin' Irish Tea Co. Top O' the Mornin' went out of business for lack of sales, and all assets were liquidated.

The Bottomlines have three bank accounts: checking and savings accounts at the People's Bank and an IRA account at the Bank of America. The checking account has an average balance of $500. They have savings of $1,000 and a balance of $25,000 in the IRA. The Bottomlines do not have a safe deposit box.

No creditors have attached any assets of the Bottomlines as of the present time. Ken and Bretony hold no property in trust for any third party. No third party holds property in trust for them.

The following suits terminated in the past year: Symphonic Sounds v. Bottomline (judgment for plaintiff) and Dr. Where v. Bottomline (judgment for plaintiff). The following suit is still pending: Williams-Sonoma v. Bottomline. Each suit is for debt collection. The Bottomlines dispute the amount due Williams-Sonoma.

Within the past six months, Bretony has transferred title to an empty lot in Santa Cruz to some old friends, Ozzie and Harriet Oddborn, for no consideration. The lot is valued at $10,000.

The Bottomlines have maintained their own personal records and have kept copies of their tax returns.

The Bottomlines have seen no attorneys in the past year other than our firm. They will be paying us a $2,000 fee for their Chapter 7 filing.

The Bottomlines owe $5,000 in income taxes to the IRS for 2015. They are not entitled to any tax refunds at the present time. They have not received any tax refunds in the past two years.

The Bottomlines do not own their own home. They owe their landlord, Billy Mountain, rent for two months at $1,300 per month. They have a month-to-month lease. They live in their home with their 15-year-old son, Ted. They have cosigned a $7,500 student loan for their 19-year-old daughter, Arya, who is an honors student at the University of the North where she is double-majoring in Drama and Fencing. They owe Lannister Credit $9,600 secured by a 2015 Westeros. The vehicle is worth $15,000. They pay $350 per month, are two payments behind, and have 30 payments remaining. All of their furniture is secured by Repo Recovery Services, to whom the Bottomlines owe $10,000. The furniture is worth $6,000. The debt was not incurred to purchase the furniture. They have a computer worth $1,500.

The Bottomlines have the following unsecured debts:

Computer City	$5,000
Symphonic Sounds	3,000
Dr. Where	500
MasterCard	3,000
Visa	3,000
American Express Green Card	5,000
Macy's	3,000
Wal-Mart	1,500
Capital Ism	2,500
Bank Two	3,000
Sax Baltic Avenue	2,000
Carpet Universe	4,500

By listing the debtors' unsecured debts in this way, it will make it easier to identify what you need to complete the necessary forms later. You should begin to compile a list of the Cashes' unsecured debts.

The Bottomlines have personal wardrobes collectively worth $4,000 at liquidation value. Ken also has a collection of Jerry Garcia ties worth $1,000. They each own a pair of custom WarpSpeed rollerblades, worth $400 a pair. They have no assets other than described. All assets and liabilities are jointly owned or owed. No debts are in dispute except as noted above. They will claim exemptions pursuant to 11 U.S.C. §522(d).

Ken's gross monthly income is $7,000; Bretony's gross monthly income is $1,000. They have provided us with the following approximate monthly expenses:

Rent	$1,300
Utilities (gas and electric)	175
Telephone/cell phone	150
Cable TV	75
Food	1,000
Clothing	100
Laundry	30
Transportation	300
Entertainment	200
Insurance —	
Auto	150
Health	300
Renter's	20
Car payment	350
Internet network fees	50

C. SCHEDULES

Official Forms B106 through 106J-2 for individuals or Official Forms B206-206H for nonindividuals are commonly known as the Schedules of Assets and Liabilities, or colloquially, the Schedules. Along with the Statement of Financial Affairs, Official Form B107 for individuals and Official Form B207 for nonindividuals, the two respective sets of documents are commonly known as the Statements and Schedules. Collectively, the Schedules form an accrual basis form of a financial statement. Debts not paid are in fact accrued debts within generally accepted accounting definitions. In the Schedules, liabilities are listed according to the distribution scheme described in chapters 22 and 23 supra. Assets are segregated between real property, vehicles, all other personal property, and financial assets. The debtor's claim of exemptions is also included in the Schedules. The Schedules will also disclose any executory contracts or leases, codebtors, and the debtor's monthly income and expenses.

The Bottomlines will use the Official Forms applicable to individuals, B106-106J-2 and B107, to complete their Statements and Schedules. We begin with Official Form B101.

Official Form 101

Voluntary Petition for Individuals Filing for Bankruptcy   12/15

The bankruptcy forms use *you* and *Debtor 1* to refer to a debtor filing alone. A married couple may file a bankruptcy case together—called a *joint case*—and in joint cases, these forms use *you* to ask for information from both debtors. For example, if a form asks, "Do you own a car," the answer would be *yes* if either debtor owns a car. When information is needed about the spouses separately, the form uses *Debtor 1* and *Debtor 2* to distinguish between them. In joint cases, one of the spouses must report information as *Debtor 1* and the other as *Debtor 2*. The same person must be *Debtor 1* in all of the forms.

Be as complete and accurate as possible. If two married people are filing together, both are equally responsible for supplying correct information. If more space is needed, attach a separate sheet to this form. On the top of any additional pages, write your name and case number (if known). Answer every question.

Part 1:	Identify Yourself	
	About Debtor 1:	**About Debtor 2 (Spouse Only in a Joint Case):**
1. **Your full name** Write the name that is on your government-issued picture identification (for example, your driver's license or passport). Bring your picture identification to your meeting with the trustee.	Ken First name Middle name Bottomline Last name Suffix (Sr., Jr., II, III)	Bretony First name Middle name Bottomline Last name Suffix (Sr., Jr., II, III)
2. **All other names you have used in the last 8 years** Include your married or maiden names.	First name Middle name Last name First name Middle name Last name	dba Top O' the Mornin' Irish Tea Co. First name Middle name Last name First name Middle name Last name

---

Description

All names by which either debtor has been known or has conducted business during the prior eight years should be listed Part 1, question 2 if any creditor would recognize the debtor only by another name or alias. This is important because creditors need to know all possible names that an account may be listed under for the creditor notice to have meaning.

For example, a creditor of Top O' the Mornin' Irish Tea Co. may not recognize the names Ken and Bretony Bottomline. It may be acceptable for the caption to read "Ken and Bretony Bottomline," but it would be most accurate and informative to note Bretony's prior business name, Top O' the Mornin' (fdba). A creditor may know who Top O' the Mornin' is but not who Bretony is.

> ### *What additional names or aliases should be included in the Cash petition?*

FACT PATTERN

A spouse's maiden or prior married name need not be included unless one or more debts listed are in the spouse's maiden or prior married name.

If a debtor has aliases that creditors have used for billing purposes, such as a business name like Top O' the Mornin', then it would be wise to list this in question 2. However, a nickname need not be included unless it is the name creditors may use in rendering billings.

Official Form 106A/B

Schedule A/B: Property

12/15

In each category, separately list and describe items. List an asset only once. If an asset fits in more than one category, list the asset in the category where you think it fits best. Be as complete and accurate as possible. If two married people are filing together, both are equally responsible for supplying correct information. If more space is needed, attach a separate sheet to this form. On the top of any additional pages, write your name and case number (if known). Answer every question.

Part 1:	**Describe Each Residence, Building, Land, or Other Real Estate You Own or Have an Interest In**

1. Do you own or have any legal or equitable interest in any residence, building, land, or similar property?

☑ No. Go to Part 2.
☐ Yes. Where is the property?

1.1. _____
Street address, if available, or other description

_____

_____
City   State   ZIP Code

_____
County

What is the property? Check all that apply.
☐ Single-family home
☐ Duplex or multi-unit building
☐ Condominium or cooperative
☐ Manufactured or mobile home
☐ Land
☐ Investment property
☐ Timeshare
☐ Other _____

Who has an interest in the property? Check one.
☐ Debtor 1 only
☐ Debtor 2 only
☐ Debtor 1 and Debtor 2 only
☐ At least one of the debtors and another

Other information you wish to add about this item, such as local property identification number: _____

Do not deduct secured claims or exemptions. Put the amount of any secured claims on *Schedule D: Creditors Who Have Claims Secured by Property.*

Current value of the entire property?
$ _____

Current value of the portion you own?
$ _____

Describe the nature of your ownership interest (such as fee simple, tenancy by the entireties, or a life estate), if known.

_____

☐ **Check if this is community property** (see instructions)

Description

Schedule B106A/B itemizes all property of the debtors. Part 1 covers the debtors' real property. Any ownership interest in real estate must be disclosed so that the trustee will be able to ascertain all potential property of the estate.[4] In a typical consumer proceeding where the debtors are renting, the name and address of the rental are not described in this Schedule and so the box "No" is checked. If the Bottomlines owned real estate, the rest of the information called for would be completed for every real property interest owned by either one of them. The lease will be disclosed in Schedule B106G — Executory Contracts and Unexpired Leases infra.

FACT PATTERN

Who holds the interest in the Cash home? What would you need in order to confirm ownership interests?

FACT PATTERN

A similar analysis can be completed for The Lawn Cuttery. Note that in an individual case the initial focus is on real property and vehicles, while in a nonindividual case, the focus is on cash, accounts receivable, and inventory.

Part 2:   Describe Your Vehicles

Do you own, lease, or have legal or equitable interest in any vehicles, whether they are registered or not? Include any vehicles you own that someone else drives. If you lease a vehicle, also report it on *Schedule G: Executory Contracts and Unexpired Leases.*

3. **Cars, vans, trucks, tractors, sport utility vehicles, motorcycles**
    ☑ No
    ☐ Yes

3.1. Make: Lannister Model: Westeros Year: 2015 Approximate mileage: _____ Other information:	**Who has an interest in the property?** Check one. ☐ Debtor 1 only ☐ Debtor 2 only ☐ Debtor 1 and Debtor 2 only ☐ At least one of the debtors and another ☑ **Check if this is community property** (see instructions)	Do not deduct secured claims or exemptions. Put the amount of any secured claims on *Schedule D: Creditors Who Have Claims Secured by Property.* **Current value of the entire property?** **Current value of the portion you own?** $____15,000.00 $____5,400.00

If you own or have more than one, describe here:

3.2. Make: _____ Model: _____ Year: _____ Approximate mileage: _____ Other information:	**Who has an interest in the property?** Check one. ☐ Debtor 1 only ☐ Debtor 2 only ☐ Debtor 1 and Debtor 2 only ☐ At least one of the debtors and another ☐ **Check if this is community property** (see instructions)	Do not deduct secured claims or exemptions. Put the amount of any secured claims on *Schedule D: Creditors Who Have Claims Secured by Property.* **Current value of the entire property?** **Current value of the portion you own?** $_____ $_____

Description

Part 2 of Schedule A/B itemizes the debtors' vehicles and discloses basic information about them, including mileage and whether or not there is

---

4. See chapters 12 and 15 supra.

equity in a vehicle. This will help the trustee easily determine the existence or lack of equity in the vehicle. The "current value of the portion you own" represents equity in the vehicle. The amount here is $5,400 because this is the amount left after subtracting from the $15,000 value the amount of the loan that is due. This information will be disclosed for each and every vehicle owned by a debtor. Line 4 requests the same information for any watercraft owned by a debtor.

How can you determine the value of Owen Cash's truck?

FACT PATTERN

Note that vehicles are not covered until Part 8 on Official Form B206A/B for The Lawn Cuttery filing.

FACT PATTERN

Part 3:	Describe Your Personal and Household Items	
Do you own or have any legal or equitable interest in any of the following items?		Current value of the portion you own? Do not deduct secured claims or exemptions.

6. Household goods and furnishings
Examples: Major appliances, furniture, linens, china, kitchenware
☐ No
☑ Yes. Describe......... Customary household furniture. $ 6,000.00

7. Electronics
Examples: Televisions and radios; audio, video, stereo, and digital equipment; computers, printers, scanners; music collections; electronic devices including cell phones, cameras, media players, games
☐ No
☑ Yes. Describe......... Computer $ 1,500.00

8. Collectibles of value
Examples: Antiques and figurines; paintings, prints, or other artwork; books, pictures, or other art objects; stamp, coin, or baseball card collections; other collections, memorabilia, collectibles
☐ No
☑ Yes. Describe......... Jerry Garcia Tie Collection $ 1,000.00

9. Equipment for sports and hobbies
Examples: Sports, photographic, exercise, and other hobby equipment; bicycles, pool tables, golf clubs, skis; canoes and kayaks; carpentry tools; musical instruments
☐ No
☑ Yes. Describe......... Two pair Warpspeed Roller Blades $ 800.00

10. Firearms
Examples: Pistols, rifles, shotguns, ammunition, and related equipment
☑ No
☐ Yes. Describe......... $

11. Clothes
Examples: Everyday clothes, furs, leather coats, designer wear, shoes, accessories
☐ No
☑ Yes. Describe......... Customary clothing $ 4,000.00

12. Jewelry
Examples: Everyday jewelry, costume jewelry, engagement rings, wedding rings, heirloom jewelry, watches, gems, gold, silver
☑ No
☐ Yes. Describe......... $

13. Non-farm animals
Examples: Dogs, cats, birds, horses
☑ No
☐ Yes. Describe......... $

14. Any other personal and household items you did not already list, including any health aids you did not list
☑ No
☐ Yes. Give specific information. .... $

15. Add the dollar value of all of your entries from Part 3, including any entries for pages you have attached for Part 3. Write that number here ....→ $ 13,300.00

Description

Part 3 of Schedule A/B itemizes personal property. Only those items that most commonly appear in a consumer proceeding appear in the fact memo and only that portion of Part 3 is shown. A complete set of Schedules is included in the Forms materials.

Note that every question requests a "Yes" or "No" response. Every item should be responded to. No item should be left blank. Recall that failure to disclose an asset may be grounds to object to a debtor's discharge.[5]

Item 6 identifies Major appliances, furniture, linens, china, and kitchenware. Provide the total value at liquidation prices.

> ***Recall that Owen made several purchases shortly before filing his last bankruptcy petition. What values would be given to those items in this bankruptcy?***

FACT PATTERN

The same description and comments apply equally to items 7-9 regarding the computer, Jerry Garcia tie collection, the WarpSpeed Roller Blades, and clothing. Notice that item 10 in the illustration has checked "No."

> ***How will you schedule the confederate sword and the Civil War era rifle that Owen left to his dad for safekeeping?***

FACT PATTERN

---

5. See Chapter 14 supra.

Part 4:   **Describe Your Financial Assets**

Do you own or have any legal or equitable interest in any of the following?

Current value of the portion you own?
Do not deduct secured claims or exemptions.

16. **Cash**

Examples: Money you have in your wallet, in your home, in a safe deposit box, and on hand when you file your petition

☐ No

☑ Yes ....

Cash: .... $_____50.00

17. **Deposits of money**

Examples: Checking, savings, or other financial accounts; certificates of deposit; shares in credit unions, brokerage houses, and other similar institutions. If you have multiple accounts with the same institution, list each.

☐ No

☑ Yes ....

Institution name:

17.1. Checking account:	People's Bank	$_____500.00
17.3. Savings account:	People's Bank	$_____1,000.00

18. **Bonds, mutual funds, or publicly traded stocks**

Examples: Bond funds, investment accounts with brokerage firms, money market accounts

☑ No

☐ Yes ....

Institution or issuer name:

_____ $_____

_____ $_____

_____ $_____

19. **Non-publicly traded stock and interests in incorporated and unincorporated businesses, including an interest in an LLC, partnership, and joint venture**

☑ No

☐ Yes. Give specific information about them......................

Name of entity:

% of ownership:

_____ 0%____% $_____

_____ 0%____% $_____

_____ 0%____% $_____

21. **Retirement or pension accounts**

Examples: Interests in IRA, ERISA, Keogh, 401(k), 403(b), thrift savings accounts, or other pension or profit-sharing plans

☐ No

☑ Yes. List each account separately.

Type of account: Institution name:

401(k) or similar plan:	_____	$_____
Pension plan:	_____	$_____
IRA:	Bank of America	$_____25,000.00
Retirement account:	_____	$_____
Keogh:	_____	$_____
Additional account:	_____	$_____
Additional account:	_____	$_____

28. **Tax refunds owed to you**

☐ No

☐ Yes. Give specific information about them, including whether you already filed the returns and the tax years. ....

Federal: $_____

State: $_____

Local: $_____

Description

Part 4 of Schedule B106A/B itemizes a debtor's financial assets. Cash on hand is disclosed in item 16. Item 17 lists funds on deposit. Each and every bank account in the name of a debtor should be disclosed. It is also a good practice to list the last four digits and only the last four digits of any account number.[6] Item 21 discloses the IRA account. Again, it would be good practice to disclose the last four digits of the account number. Item 28 discloses whether or not a debtor is entitled to a tax refund. It is shown here as an example that every item must be responded to. The Bottom-lines are not owed a tax refund.

> ***Should the money that Owen put into his father's safe deposit box be included in his bankruptcy petition? Where would it be disclosed?***

FACT PATTERN

Parts 5-7 of Schedule A/B are not shown. Part 5 discloses any business interests a debtor may have. Since Top O' The Mornin' is no longer in business, the answer to this question is no. The Statement of Financial Affairs has a question about former businesses. See Section D below. Part 6 of Schedule A/B requests disclosures if the debtor has any interests in fishing or farming operations. Part 7 itemizes any other asset not included elsewhere. Part 8, also not shown, totals the value of all preceding parts.

> ***Owen owns and operates The Lawn Cuttery, plows and clears snow during the winter, and sells items online. How and where would his interest in the various business related property be disclosed?***

FACT PATTERN

---

6. FRBP 9037(a)(4).

Official Form 106C

Schedule C: The Property You Claim as Exempt

04/16

Be as complete and accurate as possible. If two married people are filing together, both are equally responsible for supplying correct information. Using the property you listed on *Schedule A/B: Property* (Official Form 106A/B) as your source, list the property that you claim as exempt. If more space is needed, fill out and attach to this page as many copies of *Part 2: Additional Page* as necessary. On the top of any additional pages, write your name and case number (if known).

For each item of property you claim as exempt, you must specify the amount of the exemption you claim. One way of doing so is to state a specific dollar amount as exempt. Alternatively, you may claim the full fair market value of the property being exempted up to the amount of any applicable statutory limit. Some exemptions—such as those for health aids, rights to receive certain benefits, and tax-exempt retirement funds—may be unlimited in dollar amount. However, if you claim an exemption of 100% of fair market value under a law that limits the exemption to a particular dollar amount and the value of the property is determined to exceed that amount, your exemption would be limited to the applicable statutory amount.

Part 1:	Identify the Property You Claim as Exempt

1. **Which set of exemptions are you claiming?** *Check one only, even if your spouse is filing with you.*

☑ You are claiming state and federal nonbankruptcy exemptions. 11 U.S.C. § 522(b)(3)

☐ You are claiming federal exemptions. 11 U.S.C. § 522(b)(2)

2. **For any property you list on *Schedule A/B* that you claim as exempt, fill in the information below.**

Brief description of the property and line on *Schedule A/B* that lists this property	Current value of the portion you own Copy the value from *Schedule A/B*	Amount of the exemption you claim *Check only one box for each exemption.*	Specific laws that allow exemption
Brief description: Lannister Westeros Line from *Schedule A/B*: 3	$ 5,400.00	☐ $ _____ ☑ 100% of fair market value, up to any applicable statutory limit	CCP 703.140(b)(2)(5)
Brief description: furnishings Line from *Schedule A/B*: 6	$ 6,000.00	☐ $ _____ ☑ 100% of fair market value, up to any applicable statutory limit	CCP 703.140(b)(3)(5)
Brief description: computer Line from *Schedule A/B*: 7	$ 1,500.00	☐ $ _____ ☑ 100% of fair market value, up to any applicable statutory limit	CCP 703.140(b)(3)(5)

3. **Are you claiming a homestead exemption of more than $160,375?**

(Subject to adjustment on 4/01/19 and every 3 years after that for cases filed on or after the date of adjustment.)

☑ No

☐ Yes. Did you acquire the property covered by the exemption within 1,215 days before you filed this case?

☐ No

☐ Yes

Part 2:   Additional Page

Brief description of the property and line on *Schedule A/B* that lists this property	Current value of the portion you own *Copy the value from Schedule A/B*	Amount of the exemption you claim *Check only one box for each exemption*	Specific laws that allow exemption
Brief description: Jerry Garcia Ties Line from Schedule A/B: 8	$ 1,000.00	☐ $ _____ ☑ 100% of fair market value, up to any applicable statutory limit	CCP 703.140(b)(3)(5)
Brief description: Roller Blades Line from Schedule A/B: 9	$ 800.00	☐ $ _____ ☑ 100% of fair market value, up to any applicable statutory limit	CCP 703.140(b)(3)(5)
Brief description: clothing Line from Schedule A/B: 11	$ 4,000.00	☐ $ _____ ☑ 100% of fair market value, up to any applicable statutory limit	CCP 703.140(b)(3)(5)
Brief description: checking account Line from Schedule A/B: 17.1	$ 500.00	☐ $ _____ ☑ 100% of fair market value, up to any applicable statutory limit	CCP 703.140(b)(3)(5)
Brief description: savings account Line from Schedule A/B: 17.3	$ 1,000.00	☐ $ _____ ☑ 100% of fair market value, up to any applicable statutory limit	CCP 703.140(b)(3)(5)
Brief description: IRA account Line from Schedule A/B: 21	$ 25,000.00	☐ $ _____ ☑ 100% of fair market value, up to any applicable statutory limit	CCP 703.140(b)(10)(E)
Brief description: _____ Line from Schedule A/B: ___	$ _____	☐ $ _____ ☐ 100% of fair market value, up to any applicable statutory limit	
Brief description: _____ Line from Schedule A/B: ___	$ _____	☐ $ _____ ☐ 100% of fair market value, up to any applicable statutory limit	
Brief description: _____ Line from Schedule A/B: ___	$ _____	☐ $ _____ ☐ 100% of fair market value, up to any applicable statutory limit	
Brief description: _____ Line from Schedule A/B: ___	$ _____	☐ $ _____ ☐ 100% of fair market value, up to any applicable statutory limit	
Brief description: _____ Line from Schedule A/B: ___	$ _____	☐ $ _____ ☐ 100% of fair market value, up to any applicable statutory limit	
Brief description: _____ Line from Schedule A/B: ___	$ _____	☐ $ _____ ☐ 100% of fair market value, up to any applicable statutory limit	

Description

Schedule C, Official Form B106C, is the debtors' claim of exemptions. Each exemption should be itemized and the statute that the debtors select should be identified with particularity, whether the debtors select state exemptions or the federal exemptions, where applicable. Item 1 of Part 1 indicates the selection made. The most probable effective selection for the

Bottomlines is shown.[7] Claim the maximum statutory amount exempt for
each asset subject to an exemption even if there is no apparent equity in
the asset. This will relieve the necessity of later making an amendment
should an issue as to value arise. Note that most of the exemptions
claimed by the Bottomlines include a reference to subsection (5), the
wildcard or catch-all exemption. If the value of an asset exceeds the
amount of a specific exemption (such as a vehicle) the wildcard exemption of (b)(5) acts to exempt any excess up to the exemption limit. Claiming exemptions in this manner is good practice.

FACT PATTERN

*Assuming that the Cashes live in your state, would you recom-
mend that they file using the state or the federal exemptions?
Why?*

The disclosure of an asset's value must be disclosed alongside the
exemption. Note that the form requests the value of an asset to the debtor.
This essentially requests a disclosure of a debtor's equity in the property.
The value of the Westeros car to the Bottomlines is $5,400, the difference
between the market value of $15,000 and the debt owed to Lannister
Credit of $9,600.

FACT PATTERN

*Can the Cashes claim a double exemption in the Ford F150 truck
that they both use as their primarily means of transportation?*

FACT PATTERN

*The Lawn Cuttery, as a corporation, is not entitled to exemp-
tions and thus there is no corresponding Official Form B206C.*

---

7. It may appear that the exemption limit for household goods, furnishings, and wearing
apparel of $12,625 has been exceeded, inasmuch as the value of these assets is $14,900,
including the computer and the checking and savings accounts. (11 U.S.C. §522(d)(3)).
However, recall that each joint debtor may make a claim of exemption, effectively doubling
all the dollar amounts (11 U.S.C. §522(m)) in a state that has not opted out of the federal
exemption scheme. See chapter 10 supra. California has opted out of the federal exemptions
but has enacted them as California law. The subsections correspond to the same subsection
of §522(d).

C. Schedules

Official Form 106D

Schedule D: Creditors Who Have Claims Secured by Property   12/15

Be as complete and accurate as possible. If two married people are filing together, both are equally responsible for supplying correct information. If more space is needed, copy the Additional Page, fill it out, number the entries, and attach it to this form. On the top of any additional pages, write your name and case number (if known).

1. **Do any creditors have claims secured by your property?**
   - ☐ No. Check this box and submit this form to the court with your other schedules. You have nothing else to report on this form.
   - ☑ Yes. Fill in all of the information below.

Part 1:   List All Secured Claims

2. **List all secured claims.** If a creditor has more than one secured claim, list the creditor separately for each claim. If more than one creditor has a particular claim, list the other creditors in Part 2. As much as possible, list the claims in alphabetical order according to the creditor's name.

	Column A Amount of claim Do not deduct the value of collateral.	Column B Value of collateral that supports this claim	Column C Unsecured portion If any

2.1 Lannister Credit

Creditor's Name

Number   Street

City   State   ZIP Code

Who owes the debt? Check one.
- ☐ Debtor 1 only
- ☐ Debtor 2 only
- ☑ Debtor 1 and Debtor 2 only
- ☐ At least one of the debtors and another
- ☑ Check if this claim relates to a community debt

Date debt was incurred _____

Describe the property that secures the claim:

2015 Lannister Westeros

As of the date you file, the claim is: Check all that apply.
- ☐ Contingent
- ☐ Unliquidated
- ☐ Disputed

Nature of lien. Check all that apply.
- ☑ An agreement you made (such as mortgage or secured car loan)
- ☐ Statutory lien (such as tax lien, mechanic's lien)
- ☐ Judgment lien from a lawsuit
- ☐ Other (including a right to offset) _____

Last 4 digits of account number __ __ __ __

$ 15,000.00 $ 9,600.00 $ 5,400.00

2.2 Repo Recovery Services

Creditor's Name

Number   Street

City   State   ZIP Code

Who owes the debt? Check one.
- ☐ Debtor 1 only
- ☐ Debtor 2 only
- ☑ Debtor 1 and Debtor 2 only
- ☐ At least one of the debtors and another
- ☑ Check if this claim relates to a community debt

Date debt was incurred _____

Describe the property that secures the claim:

household furnishings.

As of the date you file, the claim is: Check all that apply.
- ☐ Contingent
- ☐ Unliquidated
- ☐ Disputed

Nature of lien. Check all that apply.
- ☐ An agreement you made (such as mortgage or secured car loan)
- ☐ Statutory lien (such as tax lien, mechanic's lien)
- ☐ Judgment lien from a lawsuit
- ☑ Other (including a right to offset) non-puchase $

Last 4 digits of account number __ __ __ __

$ 10,000.00 $ 6,000.00 $ 0.00

Add the dollar value of your entries in Column A on this page. Write that number here: $_____

Description

Official Form B106D, Schedule D, itemizes secured claims. If there are no secured claims, then check the box "no" on line 1 and proceed to Official Form B106 E/F. If there are secured creditors, complete Part 1 for each and every secured claim as shown. Also list the last four digits of any account numbers that the debtor provides. (These have not been provided in the example.) Frequently, correspondence will be received from creditors requesting account numbers. Including these numbers in the Schedules is helpful. Describe the collateral as succinctly as possible, as shown in the examples, and when the creditor acquired the security interest. List the values as shown. They disclose not only the amount of the debt but establish the existence of equity in an asset subject to a secured claim. Identifying the date when a security interest was acquired will help identify the security interest as a potential preference or as a nonpurchase money lien in consumer goods that may be avoided under Section 522(f)(2). That portion of the form entitled "Nature of Lien" also helps to establish these issues.[8] The Bottomlines' car loan is likely a purchase money security interest. The debt to Repo Recovery is likely a nonpurchase money loan subject to avoidance.

FACT PATTERN

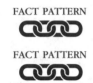

Which of the Cashes' creditors should be listed in Schedule D?

FACT PATTERN

Whether the vehicles obtained by Owen should be included in his bankruptcy case or in The Lawn Cuttery case will depend on the actual ownership interest in the vehicles.

Note that the joint nature of the debts or the existence of a person other than the debtor who may be liable must be disclosed. Finally, if a claim is contingent (such as a pending personal injury claim against a debtor), unliquidated (the amount has not been established) or is otherwise in dispute, this is also noted. These final two points also apply to Schedule B106E/F, discussed below.

Part 2:	List Others to Be Notified for a Debt That You Already Listed

Use this page only if you have others to be notified about your bankruptcy for a debt that you already listed in Part 1. For example, if a collection agency is trying to collect from you for a debt you owe to someone else, list the creditor in Part 1, and then list the collection agency here. Similarly, if you have more than one creditor for any of the debts that you listed in Part 1, list the additional creditors here. If you do not have additional persons to be notified for any debts in Part 1, do not fill out or submit this page.

Name

Number   Street

City   State   ZIP Code

On which line in Part 1 did you enter the creditor? _____

Last 4 digits of account number ___ ___ ___ ___

Description

Part 2 of Schedule D contains space to enter the names of entities a debtor may want to know of the filing, but who are not actually creditors. Part 3 of Schedule E/F is identical but for unsecured claims. Common examples include attorneys for a particular creditor or a collection agency. This would be the place to list Billy Mountain's counsel, if he has one.

---

8. See chapters 10 and 17 supra.

Official Form 106E/F
Schedule E/F: Creditors Who Have Unsecured Claims
12/15

Be as complete and accurate as possible. Use Part 1 for creditors with PRIORITY claims and Part 2 for creditors with NONPRIORITY claims. List the other party to any executory contracts or unexpired leases that could result in a claim. Also list executory contracts on *Schedule A/B: Property* (Official Form 106A/B) and on *Schedule G: Executory Contracts and Unexpired Leases* (Official Form 106G). Do not include any creditors with partially secured claims that are listed in *Schedule D: Creditors Who Have Claims Secured by Property*. If more space is needed, copy the Part you need, fill it out, number the entries in the boxes on the left. Attach the Continuation Page to this page. On the top of any additional pages, write your name and case number (if known).

Part 1:   List All of Your PRIORITY Unsecured Claims

1. Do any creditors have priority unsecured claims against you?
   ☐ No. Go to Part 2.
   ☑ Yes.

2. **List all of your priority unsecured claims.** If a creditor has more than one priority unsecured claim, list the creditor separately for each claim. For each claim listed, identify what type of claim it is. If a claim has both priority and nonpriority amounts, list that claim here and show both priority and nonpriority amounts. As much as possible, list the claims in alphabetical order according to the creditor's name. If you have more than two priority unsecured claims, fill out the Continuation Page of Part 1. If more than one creditor holds a particular claim, list the other creditors in Part 3.

   (For an explanation of each type of claim, see the instructions for this form in the instruction booklet.)

		Total claim	Priority amount	Nonpriority amount
2.1 Internal Revenue Service	Last 4 digits of account number __ __ __ __	$ 5,000.00	$ 5,000.00	$ 0.00

Priority Creditor's Name

When was the debt incurred? _____

Number   Street

As of the date you file, the claim is: Check all that apply
☐ Contingent
☐ Unliquidated
☐ Disputed

City   State   ZIP Code

Who incurred the debt? Check one.
☐ Debtor 1 only
☐ Debtor 2 only
☑ Debtor 1 and Debtor 2 only
☐ At least one of the debtors and another
☐ Check if this claim is for a community debt

Type of PRIORITY unsecured claim:
☐ Domestic support obligations
☑ Taxes and certain other debts you owe the government
☐ Claims for death or personal injury while you were intoxicated
☐ Other. Specify _____

Is the claim subject to offset?
☑ No
☐ Yes

2.2

Priority Creditor's Name

Last 4 digits of account number __ __ __ __ $_____ $_____ $_____

When was the debt incurred? _____

Number   Street

As of the date you file, the claim is: Check all that apply
☐ Contingent
☐ Unliquidated
☐ Disputed

City   State   ZIP Code

Who incurred the debt? Check one.
☐ Debtor 1 only
☐ Debtor 2 only
☐ Debtor 1 and Debtor 2 only
☐ At least one of the debtors and another
☐ Check if this claim is for a community debt

Type of PRIORITY unsecured claim:
☐ Domestic support obligations
☐ Taxes and certain other debts you owe the government
☐ Claims for death or personal injury while you were intoxicated
☐ Other. Specify _____

Is the claim subject to offset?
☐ No
☐ Yes

Description

Part 1 of Official Form B106E/F itemizes Section 507 priority claims.[9] If there are no priority claims, then check the box "No" to the first item and proceed to Part 2. The claim of the IRS is the only priority claim in the example. In this Schedule, as in all of the Schedules, it is more important to place all potential creditors on the list so they receive notice. Notice is more important than precision in the amount. The amounts disclosed

---

9. See chapters 22 and 23 supra.

distinguish between priority and nonpriority portions of a debt. Where dischargeability is an issue, the nonpriority amount is most often dischargeable. When distribution to creditors is the issue, the nonpriority portion of a claim will not receive a dividend until all priority claims have been paid in full.[10]

FACT PATTERN

Owen Cash potentially has three or more priority creditors to include in Schedule E/F. Which creditors would you include in this schedule as a priority creditor?

Often a debtor may not be certain about the exact amount due a particular creditor. When in doubt, insert the debtor's best estimate. A dischargeable debt will remain dischargeable even if an incorrect amount is listed in the Schedules but the creditor has received notice of the proceeding. However, a dischargeable debt may become nondischargeable if it is not listed in the Schedules.[11] Finally, note that the joint nature of the debts or the existence of a person other than the debtor who may be liable must also be disclosed.

---

10. See chapters 14, 22 and 23 supra.
11. 11 U.S.C. §523(a)(3). See chapter 14 supra.

Part 2: **List All of Your NONPRIORITY Unsecured Claims**

3. **Do any creditors have nonpriority unsecured claims against you?**
   ☐ No. You have nothing to report in this part. Submit this form to the court with your other schedules.
   ☑ Yes

4. **List all of your nonpriority unsecured claims in the alphabetical order of the creditor who holds each claim.** If a creditor has more than one nonpriority unsecured claim, list the creditor separately for each claim. For each claim listed, identify what type of claim it is. Do not list claims already included in Part 1. If more than one creditor holds a particular claim, list the other creditors in Part 3. If you have more than three nonpriority unsecured claims fill out the Continuation Page of Part 2.

4.1

American Express Gold Card
Nonpriority Creditor's Name

_____
Number   Street

_____
City   State   ZIP Code

Who incurred the debt? Check one.
☐ Debtor 1 only
☐ Debtor 2 only
☑ Debtor 1 and Debtor 2 only
☐ At least one of the debtors and another

☐ **Check if this claim is for a community debt**

Is the claim subject to offset?
☑ No
☐ Yes

Last 4 digits of account number __ __ __ __

When was the debt incurred? _____

Total claim

$ 5,000.00

As of the date you file, the claim is: Check all that apply.
☐ Contingent
☐ Unliquidated
☐ Disputed

Type of NONPRIORITY unsecured claim:
☐ Student loans
☐ Obligations arising out of a separation agreement or divorce that you did not report as priority claims
☐ Debts to pension or profit-sharing plans, and other similar debts
☑ Other. Specify _credit card_

4.2

Billy Mountain
Nonpriority Creditor's Name

_____
Number   Street

_____
City   State   ZIP Code

Who incurred the debt? Check one.
☐ Debtor 1 only
☐ Debtor 2 only
☑ Debtor 1 and Debtor 2 only
☐ At least one of the debtors and another

☐ **Check if this claim is for a community debt**

Is the claim subject to offset?
☑ No
☐ Yes

Last 4 digits of account number __ __ __ __

When was the debt incurred? _____

$ 2,600.00

As of the date you file, the claim is: Check all that apply.
☐ Contingent
☐ Unliquidated
☐ Disputed

Type of NONPRIORITY unsecured claim:
☐ Student loans
☐ Obligations arising out of a separation agreement or divorce that you did not report as priority claims
☐ Debts to pension or profit-sharing plans, and other similar debts
☑ Other. Specify _unpaid rent_

4.3

Symphonic Sounds
Nonpriority Creditor's Name

_____
Number   Street

_____
City   State   ZIP Code

Who incurred the debt? Check one.
☐ Debtor 1 only
☐ Debtor 2 only
☑ Debtor 1 and Debtor 2 only
☐ At least one of the debtors and another

☐ **Check if this claim is for a community debt**

Is the claim subject to offset?
☑ No
☐ Yes

Last 4 digits of account number __ __ __ __

When was the debt incurred? _____

$ 500.00

As of the date you file, the claim is: Check all that apply.
☐ Contingent
☐ Unliquidated
☐ Disputed

Type of NONPRIORITY unsecured claim:
☐ Student loans
☐ Obligations arising out of a separation agreement or divorce that you did not report as priority claims
☐ Debts to pension or profit-sharing plans, and other similar debts
☑ Other. Specify _judgement_

Description

Schedule B106E/F Part 2 itemizes unsecured claims or creditors. This is normally the longest single Schedule to complete. As with secured claims, it is always best to list the claims alphabetically and to include the last four digits of any account numbers. There are a couple of commonly occurring errors that require further description. A careful review of the fact pattern will reveal that Billy Mountain and Williams-Sonoma are not listed on the specific list of creditors although they otherwise appear in the memo. Oftentimes, when a debtor identifies a lawsuit or overdue rent, a debtor will inadvertently omit these debts from any list of creditors provided to the practitioner. However, these creditors are also unsecured creditors and should be included in Schedule E/F. Omitting these debts from a creditor's list is a frequent error, but one that can affect the debtor's discharge.[12]

All of the comments made with respect to Schedule D supra apply here as well. Most unsecured claims will fall into the category of other given the other categories are limited to student loans or domestic obligations that may not be priority claims. A one-word description such as "goods" or "services" will normally be sufficient to identify the category of other. Three examples are given in the illustration: a credit account, unpaid rent, and a judgment. To file Schedules for the Bottomlines, all of the remaining unsecured claims will also have to be disclosed.

FACT PATTERN

Which of the Cashes' creditors would you include in Part 2 of the Schedule E/F?

Official Form 106G

Schedule G: Executory Contracts and Unexpired Leases   12/15

Be as complete and accurate as possible. If two married people are filing together, both are equally responsible for supplying correct information. If more space is needed, copy the additional page, fill it out, number the entries, and attach it to this page. On the top of any additional pages, write your name and case number (if known).

1. **Do you have any executory contracts or unexpired leases?**
    ☐ No. Check this box and file this form with the court with your other schedules. You have nothing else to report on this form.
    ☑ Yes. Fill in all of the information below even if the contracts or leases are listed on *Schedule A/B: Property* (Official Form 106A/B).

2. **List separately each person or company with whom you have the contract or lease. Then state what each contract or lease is for** (for **example, rent, vehicle lease, cell phone).** See the instructions for this form in the instruction booklet for more examples of executory contracts and unexpired leases.

Person or company with whom you have the contract or lease	State what the contract or lease is for
2.1 Billy Mountain Name Number Street City State ZIP Code	month to month lease for residential real property located at 1999 Prince Road.

---

12. 11 U.S.C. §523(a)(3). See chapter 14 supra.

Description

Any executory contract or unexpired lease is disclosed in Official Form B106G, Schedule G. As in the other forms, if there are no items to disclose, check the box "No" and proceed to the next section. Be specific enough in describing the asset so as to help enable the trustee to determine the effect of the contract or lease as an asset or liability of the estate.[13] The brief description here will likely provide enough information for a trustee to determine whether or not the asset should be administered or abandoned. Also note that the nondebtor party to the contract or lease is also a creditor who needs to be scheduled appropriately on Schedules D, or E/F supra. Recall that the Bottomlines are two months behind in their rent. The unpaid rent would be listed in Schedule E/F.

> ***Are the Cashes a party to any executory contracts or would you check the "No" box?***
>
> ***Once again, whether the executory contracts are held by Owen or The Lawn Cuttery will determine in which petition they should be included.***

FACT PATTERN

FACT PATTERN

---

13. See chapter 20 supra.

Official Form 106H

Schedule H: Your Codebtors

12/15

Codebtors are people or entities who are also liable for any debts you may have. Be as complete and accurate as possible. If two married people are filing together, both are equally responsible for supplying correct information. If more space is needed, copy the Additional Page, fill it out, and number the entries in the boxes on the left. Attach the Additional Page to this page. On the top of any Additional Pages, write your name and case number (if known). Answer every question.

1. **Do you have any codebtors?** (If you are filing a joint case, do not list either spouse as a codebtor.)
   ☐ No
   ☑ Yes

2. **Within the last 8 years, have you lived in a community property state or territory?** (*Community property states and territories* include Arizona, California, Idaho, Louisiana, Nevada, New Mexico, Puerto Rico, Texas, Washington, and Wisconsin.)
   ☑ No. Go to line 3.
   ☐ Yes. Did your spouse, former spouse, or legal equivalent live with you at the time?
       ☐ No
       ☐ Yes. In which community state or territory did you live? _____. Fill in the name and current address of that person.

   _____
   Name of your spouse, former spouse, or legal equivalent

   _____
   Number   Street

   _____
   City   State   ZIP Code

3. **In Column 1, list all of your codebtors. Do not include your spouse as a codebtor if your spouse is filing with you. List the person shown in line 2 again as a codebtor only if that person is a guarantor or cosigner. Make sure you have listed the creditor on *Schedule D* (Official Form 106D), *Schedule E/F* (Official Form 106E/F), or *Schedule G* (Official Form 106G). Use *Schedule D, Schedule E/F, or Schedule G* to fill out Column 2.**

Column 1: **Your codebtor**	*Column 2:* **The creditor to whom you owe the debt** Check all schedules that apply:
3.1 Arya Bottomline Name Number Street City State ZIP Code	☐ Schedule D, line _____ ☑ Schedule E/F, line _____ ☐ Schedule G, line _____

Description

The existence of any codebtor of a debt is described in Official Form B106H, Schedule H. A codebtor for these purposes is someone who is not a debtor in the bankruptcy case. Arya is not a debtor in the bankruptcy case and is a codebtor with her parents. The line item in Schedule E/F where the Bottomlines list University of the North would be the reference to insert here.

FACT PATTERN

Certain debts naturally raise the question of a codebtor, for example, car loans and student loans. A nondebtor may be involved if those debts were incurred while the debtor was single or living at home. Which of the Cashes' debts would you ask about possible codebtors?

FACT PATTERN

It is possible that Owen purchased the company vehicles, and/or leased the equipment, in the company name and signed as the guarantor. If so, The Lawn Cuttery would be included in the corporate filing.

Item 2 needs to be completed only if a debtor lived with a former spouse or equivalent in a community property state with someone other than the debtor in the past eight years. This person would be liable for any unpaid community debts. Since the Bottomlines are both debtors in the case, the answer here is "No."

Official Form 106I

Schedule I: Your Income

12/15

Be as complete and accurate as possible. If two married people are filing together (Debtor 1 and Debtor 2), both are equally responsible for supplying correct information. If you are married and not filing jointly, and your spouse is living with you, include information about your spouse. If you are separated and your spouse is not filing with you, do not include information about your spouse. If more space is needed, attach a separate sheet to this form. On the top of any additional pages, write your name and case number (if known). Answer every question.

Part 1: Describe Employment

1. Fill in your employment information.		Debtor 1	Debtor 2 or non-filing spouse
If you have more than one job, attach a separate page with information about additional employers. Include part-time, seasonal, or self-employed work. Occupation may include student or homemaker, if it applies.	Employment status	☑ Employed ☐ Not employed	☑ Employed ☐ Not employed
	Occupation	software designer	Assistant Manager
	Employer's name	Stardust, Inc	China Girl Tea Shop
	Employer's address		
		Number Street	Number Street
		City State ZIP Code	City State ZIP Code
	How long employed there?	3 months	3 months

Part 2: Give Details About Monthly Income

Estimate monthly income as of the date you file this form. If you have nothing to report for any line, write $0 in the space. Include your non-filing spouse unless you are separated.

If you or your non-filing spouse have more than one employer, combine the information for all employers for that person on the lines below. If you need more space, attach a separate sheet to this form.

	For Debtor 1	For Debtor 2 or non-filing spouse
2. List monthly gross wages, salary, and commissions (before all payroll deductions). If not paid monthly, calculate what the monthly wage would be. 2.	$ 6,500.00	$ 1,000.00
3. Estimate and list monthly overtime pay. 3.	+ $	+ $
4. Calculate gross income. Add line 2 + line 3. 4.	$ 6,500.00	$ 1,000.00

	For Debtor 1	For Debtor 2 or non-filing spouse
Copy line 4 here.. → 4.	$ 6,500.00	$ 1,000.00

5. List all payroll deductions:

		For Debtor 1	For Debtor 2 or non-filing spouse
5a. Tax, Medicare, and Social Security deductions	5a.	$ 1,625.00	$ 250.00
5b. Mandatory contributions for retirement plans	5b.	$	$
5c. Voluntary contributions for retirement plans	5c.	$	$
5d. Required repayments of retirement fund loans	5d.	$	$
5e. Insurance	5e.	$ 300.00	$
5f. Domestic support obligations	5f.	$	$
5g. Union dues	5g.	$	$
5h. Other deductions. Specify: _____	5h.	+ $	+ $
6. **Add the payroll deductions.** Add lines 5a + 5b + 5c + 5d + 5e +5f + 5g + 5h.	6.	$ 1,925.00	$ 250.00
7. Calculate total monthly take-home pay. Subtract line 6 from line 4.	7.	$ 4,575.00	$ 750.00

8. List all other income regularly received:

		For Debtor 1	For Debtor 2 or non-filing spouse
8a. **Net income from rental property and from operating a business, profession, or farm** Attach a statement for each property and business showing gross receipts, ordinary and necessary business expenses, and the total monthly net income.	8a.	$	$
8b. **Interest and dividends**	8b.	$	$
8c. **Family support payments that you, a non-filing spouse, or a dependent regularly receive** Include alimony, spousal support, child support, maintenance, divorce settlement, and property settlement.	8c.	$	$
8d. **Unemployment compensation**	8d.	$	$
8e. **Social Security**	8e.	$	$
8f. **Other government assistance that you regularly receive** Include cash assistance and the value (if known) of any non-cash assistance that you receive, such as food stamps (benefits under the Supplemental Nutrition Assistance Program) or housing subsidies. Specify: _____	8f.	$	$
8g. **Pension or retirement income**	8g.	$	$
8h. **Other monthly income.** Specify: _____	8h.	+ $	+ $
9. **Add all other income.** Add lines 8a + 8b + 8c + 8d + 8e + 8f +8g + 8h.	9.	$ 0.00	$ 0.00
10. **Calculate monthly income.** Add line 7 + line 9. Add the entries in line 10 for Debtor 1 and Debtor 2 or non-filing spouse.	10.	$ 4,575.00 +	$ 750.00 = $ 5,325.00

11. **State all other regular contributions to the expenses that you list in** *Schedule J.*

Include contributions from an unmarried partner, members of your household, your dependents, your roommates, and other friends or relatives.

Do not include any amounts already included in lines 2-10 or amounts that are not available to pay expenses listed in *Schedule J.*

Specify: _____   11. + $ _____

12. **Add the amount in the last column of line 10 to the amount in line 11.** The result is the combined monthly income.

Write that amount on the *Summary of Your Assets and Liabilities and Certain Statistical Information,* if it applies   12. $ 5,325.00

Combined monthly income

13. Do you expect an increase or decrease within the year after you file this form?

☐ No.

☐ Yes. Explain: _____

Description

Official Form B106I, Schedule I, discloses the debtors' place of employ-ment and discloses all sources of a debtors' monthly income, including contributions from another person. Although the fact pattern does not include reference to deductions made from either Bottomline paycheck, the sample Schedule I assumes that 25 percent of their pay is deducted for taxes and additional amounts from Ken's paycheck for family medical coverage. In actual practice, a practitioner will obtain and report the exact amounts since they will be relevant for performance of the means testing calculations in the next chapter.

> *Where the debtor is self-employed, it is important to verify what records he/she is keeping to support the tax and other deductions claimed from the income received.*

FACT PATTERN

> *Recall that there are no corresponding Schedules I and J for nonindividual bankruptcy filings. Moreover, a nonindividual does not receive a bankruptcy discharge.*

FACT PATTERN

Official Form 106J

Schedule J: Your Expenses   12/15

Be as complete and accurate as possible. If two married people are filing together, both are equally responsible for supplying correct information. If more space is needed, attach another sheet to this form. On the top of any additional pages, write your name and case number (if known). Answer every question.

Part 1:   Describe Your Household

1. **Is this a joint case?**

   ☐ No.   Go to line 2.

   ☑ Yes. **Does Debtor 2 live in a separate household?**

   　　☑ No

   　　☐ Yes. Debtor 2 must file Official Form 106J-2, *Expenses for Separate Household of Debtor 2.*

2. **Do you have dependents?**   ☐ No

   Do not list Debtor 1 and   ☑ Yes. Fill out this information for
   Debtor 2.   each dependent..........................

   Do not state the dependents' names.

	Dependent's relationship to Debtor 1 or Debtor 2	Dependent's age	Does dependent live with you?
	Daughter	19	☐ No ☑ Yes
	Son	15	☐ No ☑ Yes
			☐ No ☐ Yes
			☐ No ☐ Yes
			☐ No ☐ Yes

3. **Do your expenses include**   ☐ No
   expenses of people other than   ☐ Yes
   yourself and your dependents?

Part 2:   Estimate Your Ongoing Monthly Expenses

Estimate your expenses as of your bankruptcy filing date unless you are using this form as a supplement in a Chapter 13 case to report expenses as of a date after the bankruptcy is filed. If this is a supplemental *Schedule J*, check the box at the top of the form and fill in the applicable date.

Include expenses paid for with non-cash government assistance if you know the value of such assistance and have included it on *Schedule I: Your Income* (Official Form 106I.)

		Your expenses
4. **The rental or home ownership expenses for your residence.** Include first mortgage payments and any rent for the ground or lot.	4.	$_____1,300.00
If not included in line 4:		
4a. Real estate taxes	4a.	$_____
4b. Property, homeowner's, or renter's insurance	4b.	$_____
4c. Home maintenance, repair, and upkeep expenses	4c.	$_____
4d. Homeowner's association or condominium dues	4d.	$_____

		Your expenses
5.	**Additional mortgage payments for your residence**, such as home equity loans	5. $_____
6.	**Utilities:**	
	6a. Electricity, heat, natural gas	6a. $_____ 175.00
	6b. Water, sewer, garbage collection	6b. $_____
	6c. Telephone, cell phone, Internet, satellite, and cable services	6c. $_____ 275.00
	6d. Other. Specify: _____	6d. $_____
7.	**Food and housekeeping supplies**	7. $_____ 1,000.00
8.	**Childcare and children's education costs**	8. $_____
9.	**Clothing, laundry, and dry cleaning**	9. $_____ 130.00
10.	**Personal care products and services**	10. $_____
11.	**Medical and dental expenses**	11. $_____
12.	**Transportation.** Include gas, maintenance, bus or train fare. Do not include car payments.	12. $_____ 300.00
13.	**Entertainment, clubs, recreation, newspapers, magazines, and books**	13. $_____ 200.00
14.	**Charitable contributions and religious donations**	14. $_____
15.	**Insurance.** Do not include insurance deducted from your pay or included in lines 4 or 20.	
	15a. Life insurance	15a. $_____
	15b. Health insurance	15b. $_____ 300.00
	15c. Vehicle insurance	15c. $_____ 150.00
	15d. Other insurance. Specify: renter's _____	15d. $_____ 20.00
16.	**Taxes.** Do not include taxes deducted from your pay or included in lines 4 or 20. Specify: _____	16. $_____
17.	**Installment or lease payments:**	
	17a. Car payments for Vehicle 1	17a. $_____ 350.00
	17b. Car payments for Vehicle 2	17b. $_____
	17c. Other. Specify: _____	17c. $_____
	17d. Other. Specify: _____	17d. $_____
18.	**Your payments of alimony, maintenance, and support that you did not report as deducted from your pay on line 5,** *Schedule I, Your Income* **(Official Form 106I).**	18. $_____
19.	**Other payments you make to support others who do not live with you.** Specify: _____	19. $_____
20.	**Other real property expenses not included in lines 4 or 5 of this form or on** *Schedule I: Your Income*.	
	20a. Mortgages on other property	20a. $_____
	20b. Real estate taxes	20b. $_____
	20c. Property, homeowner's, or renter's insurance	20c. $_____
	20d. Maintenance, repair, and upkeep expenses	20d. $_____
	20e. Homeowner's association or condominium dues	20e. $_____

21. **Other**. Specify: _____	21. +$	0.00

22. **Calculate your monthly expenses.**

   22a. Add lines 4 through 21.   22a. $ 4,200.00

   22b. Copy line 22 (monthly expenses for Debtor 2), if any, from Official Form 106J-2   22b. $

   22c. Add line 22a and 22b. The result is your monthly expenses.   22c. $ 0.00

23. **Calculate your monthly net income.**

   23a. Copy line 12 (*your combined monthly income*) from *Schedule I*.   23a. $ 5,325.00

   23b. Copy your monthly expenses from line 22c above.   23b. −$ 4,200.00

   23c. Subtract your monthly expenses from your monthly income. The result is your *monthly net income*.   23c. $ 1,125.00

24. **Do you expect an increase or decrease in your expenses within the year after you file this form?**

For example, do you expect to finish paying for your car loan within the year or do you expect your mortgage payment to increase or decrease because of a modification to the terms of your mortgage?

☑ No.

☐ Yes.   Explain here:

Description

Official Form B106J, Schedule J, discloses the debtors' monthly expenses. As in the other Schedules illustrated, only the data contained in the fact memo is shown. The forms materials include the complete form. As with all of the other Schedules, it is best to enter zero for those categories in which the debtor incurs no monthly expense. In an individual Chapter 7, the information in Schedules I and J aids the trustee in determining whether or not an abuse of Chapter 7 exists pursuant to means testing (see chapter 6 supra).[14] Even if they "pass" the means test, their case could still be subject to dismissal for abuse. Notice that when Schedule J is subtracted from Schedule I, the Bottomlines have an excess $1,125 per month. Their practitioner will need to ascertain if they have additional monthly expenses. In a Chapter 13, the data helps determine the feasibility of a Chapter 13 plan.[15]

---

14. See chapters 6 and 8 supra. The Form is included in the Forms Materials.
15. See chapter 24 supra.

How would you determine what value to list for the various expenses when the amounts for that particular liability vary from month to month? What if the debtor is delinquent on a particular utility bill? Does this increase the amount due for purposes of Schedule J?

The information regarding dependents aids creditors and the trustee in determining the reasonableness of the expenses disclosed in Schedule J infra.

If joint debtors are living apart, one of them must complete Official Form B106J-2, Schedule J-2, disclosing the expenses of the debtor not living in the primary household.

D.   STATEMENT OF FINANCIAL AFFAIRS

Official Form 107

Statement of Financial Affairs for Individuals Filing for Bankruptcy   04/16

Be as complete and accurate as possible. If two married people are filing together, both are equally responsible for supplying correct information. If more space is needed, attach a separate sheet to this form. On the top of any additional pages, write your name and case number (if known). Answer every question.

Part 1:   Give Details About Your Marital Status and Where You Lived Before

1. **What is your current marital status?**

   ☑ Married
   ☐ Not married

2. **During the last 3 years, have you lived anywhere other than where you live now?**

   ☑ No
   ☐ Yes. List all of the places you lived in the last 3 years. Do not include where you live now.

Debtor 1:	Dates Debtor 1 lived there	Debtor 2:	Dates Debtor 2 lived there
		☑ Same as Debtor 1	☑ Same as Debtor 1
1999 Prince Road Number Street	From _____ To _____	_____ Number Street	From _____ To _____
Suffragette City CA City State ZIP Code		_____ City State ZIP Code	
		☑ Same as Debtor 1	☑ Same as Debtor 1
45 Coldfish Lane Number Street	From _____ To _____	_____ Number Street	From _____ To _____
Frosty Falls MN City State ZIP Code		_____ City State ZIP Code	

3. **Within the last 8 years, did you ever live with a spouse or legal equivalent in a community property state or territory?** (*Community property states and territories* include Arizona, California, Idaho, Louisiana, Nevada, New Mexico, Puerto Rico, Texas, Washington, and Wisconsin.)

   ☑ No
   ☐ Yes. Make sure you fill out *Schedule H: Your Codebtors* (Official Form 106H).

Description

Part 1 to the Statement of Financial Affairs discloses the debtors' marital status and addresses for the three years prior to the filing. Any earlier addresses are irrelevant. It is always easiest to read the information by listing the most current residence first and proceeding backwards chronologically. It is not usually required to recall exact addresses. An approximate address will generally suffice if the exact information cannot be recalled. Many debtors may not be able to recall all of their exact street addresses. Note that the dates here are incomplete.

It is important to remember that the questions found in Official Form B207 for nonindividuals are not the same or always found in the same place as Official Form B107 for individuals. This requires attention to detail when completing both forms.

Item 3 requests disclosure if a debtor lived with a spouse or legal equivalent in the eight years preceding the filing. This is different from the codebtor disclosures made in Schedule H, supra, because here the only disclosure is the existence of a prior relationship with someone other than a debtor in the case in a community property jurisdiction. The reason for this disclosure is that a former spouse in a community property jurisdiction could have a joint interest in estate property affecting the trustee's rights. See chapters 16 and 19 supra.

Part 2:   Explain the Sources of Your Income

4. **Did you have any income from employment or from operating a business during this year or the two previous calendar years?**
Fill in the total amount of income you received from all jobs and all businesses, including part-time activities.
If you are filing a joint case and you have income that you receive together, list it only once under Debtor 1.

☐ No
☑ Yes. Fill in the details.

	Debtor 1		Debtor 2	
	Sources of income Check all that apply.	**Gross income** (before deductions and exclusions)	**Sources of income** Check all that apply.	**Gross income** (before deductions and exclusions)
From January 1 of current year until the date you filed for bankruptcy:	☑ Wages, commissions, bonuses, tips ☐ Operating a business	$_____	☑ Wages, commissions, bonuses, tips ☐ Operating a business	$_____3,000.00
For last calendar year: (January 1 to December 31, ____) _{YYYY}	☑ Wages, commissions, bonuses, tips ☐ Operating a business	$___78,000.00	☐ Wages, commissions, bonuses, tips ☑ Operating a business	$_____
For the calendar year before that: (January 1 to December 31, ____) _{YYYY}	☐ Wages, commissions, bonuses, tips ☐ Operating a business	$_____	☐ Wages, commissions, bonuses, tips ☐ Operating a business	$_____

5. **Did you receive any other income during this year or the two previous calendar years?**
Include income regardless of whether that income is taxable. Examples of *other income* are alimony; child support; Social Security, unemployment, and other public benefit payments; pensions; rental income; interest; dividends; money collected from lawsuits; royalties; and gambling and lottery winnings. If you are filing a joint case and you have income that you received together, list it only once under Debtor 1.

List each source and the gross income from each source separately. Do not include income that you listed in line 4.

☑ No
☐ Yes. Fill in the details.

	Debtor 1		Debtor 2	
	Sources of income Describe below.	**Gross income from each source** (before deductions and exclusions)	**Sources of income** Describe below.	**Gross income from each source** (before deductions and exclusions)
From January 1 of current year until the date you filed for bankruptcy:	_____ _____ _____	$_____ $_____ $_____	_____ _____ _____	$_____ $_____ $_____
For last calendar year: (January 1 to December 31, ____) _{YYYY}	_____ _____ _____	$_____ $_____ $_____	_____ _____ _____	$_____ $_____ $_____
For the calendar year before that: (January 1 to December 31, ____) _{YYYY}	_____ _____ _____	$_____ $_____ $_____	_____ _____ _____	$_____ $_____ $_____

Description

This item discloses the debtors' income for each of the past two years from employment or trade. "Preceding years" is commonly understood to mean tax years. For instance, in 2017, income for calendar years 2016 and 2015 would be described.

Income earned from sources other than employment is also disclosed here as noted. As the Bottomlines have no other income, Part 2 line 5 is answered "No." All of the questions should be answered even if the answer is "No." For the year of filing, income through the month of filing is disclosed. That information would need to be obtained as would Ken's income in the second year preceding the filing as would any income Bretony earned from Top O' the Mornin'.

FACT PATTERN

Do Owen's online sales constitute income from a source other than employment? Can he argue that the frequency of his sales suggests (or disputes) actual employment?

Part 3:   **List Certain Payments You Made Before You Filed for Bankruptcy**

6. Are either Debtor 1's or Debtor 2's debts primarily consumer debts?

☐ No. **Neither Debtor 1 nor Debtor 2 has primarily consumer debts.** *Consumer debts* are defined in 11 U.S.C. § 101(8) as "incurred by an individual primarily for a personal, family, or household purpose."

During the 90 days before you filed for bankruptcy, did you pay any creditor a total of $6,425* or more?

☐ No. Go to line 7.

☐ Yes. List below each creditor to whom you paid a total of $6,425* or more in one or more payments and the total amount you paid that creditor. Do not include payments for domestic support obligations, such as child support and alimony. Also, do not include payments to an attorney for this bankruptcy case.

* Subject to adjustment on 4/01/19 and every 3 years after that for cases filed on or after the date of adjustment.

☑ Yes. **Debtor 1 or Debtor 2 or both have primarily consumer debts.**

During the 90 days before you filed for bankruptcy, did you pay any creditor a total of $600 or more?

☑ No. Go to line 7.

☐ Yes. List below each creditor to whom you paid a total of $600 or more and the total amount you paid that creditor. Do not include payments for domestic support obligations, such as child support and alimony. Also, do not include payments to an attorney for this bankruptcy case.

7. **Within 1 year before you filed for bankruptcy, did you make a payment on a debt you owed anyone who was an insider?**
Insiders include your relatives; any general partners; relatives of any general partners; partnerships of which you are a general partner; corporations of which you are an officer, director, person in control, or owner of 20% or more of their voting securities; and any managing agent, including one for a business you operate as a sole proprietor. 11 U.S.C. § 101. Include payments for domestic support obligations, such as child support and alimony.

☑ No
☐ Yes. List all payments to an insider.

8. **Within 1 year before you filed for bankruptcy, did you make any payments or transfer any property on account of a debt that benefited an insider?**
Include payments on debts guaranteed or cosigned by an insider.

☑ No
☐ Yes. List all payments that benefited an insider.

Description

Part 3 requires disclosure of loan repayments of $600 or more to a single creditor during the 90 days prior to filing, or payments made to an insider during the year preceding the filing, regardless of amount. This inquiry reveals the potential existence of preferences or sometimes a fraudulent transfer. Recall that, in a consumer proceeding, up to $600 of preferences are essentially permitted, which is why the question is concerned with payments greater than $600. In the example there are no such transfers. Line 6 requests debtors to disclose if their debts are primarily consumer debts. This affects the avoidability of some preferences and may affect the extent to which means testing applies to a debtor.[16] Hence, "None" has been checked. Remember, every question should be answered, even when the answer is "None."

> *What can Owen Cash do about any business debts he might have through his operation of The Lawn Cuttery? Can those debts be listed and discharged through his personal bankruptcy filing?*

FACT PATTERN

Part 4: Identify Legal Actions, Repossessions, and Foreclosures

9. Within 1 year before you filed for bankruptcy, were you a party in any lawsuit, court action, or administrative proceeding?
List all such matters, including personal injury cases, small claims actions, divorces, collection suits, paternity actions, support or custody modifications, and contract disputes.

☑ No
☐ Yes. Fill in the details.

	Nature of the case	Court or agency	Status of the case
Case title Dr. Where v. Bottomline Case number	debt collection	Municipal Court Court Name Number Street City State ZIP Code	☐ Pending ☐ On appeal ☑ Concluded
Case title Symphonic Sounds v. Bottomline Case number	debt collection	Municipal Court Name Number Street City State ZIP Code	☐ Pending ☐ On appeal ☑ Concluded

10. Within 1 year before you filed for bankruptcy, was any of your property repossessed, foreclosed, garnished, attached, seized, or levied?
Check all that apply and fill in the details below.

☑ No. Go to line 11.
☐ Yes. Fill in the information below.

Description

Part 4, Line 9 requires disclosure of all legal actions pending within one year prior to the bankruptcy filing in which the debtor is or has been a party. In the example, only two suits are shown. You would need to add an attachment sheet disclosing the pending suit by Williams-Sonoma. When answering this inquiry, disclose the case number and the court where the litigation is or was pending. To this extent, the example here is incomplete.

Note that this question does not ask merely for those cases in which a debtor may be the defendant. All lawsuits that are pending in which the

---

16. See chapters 5, 17 and 18 supra.

debtor is a *party* when a bankruptcy petition is filed must be disclosed. If the debtor is or has been a plaintiff in a lawsuit, this must also be included in the response. The suit will be an asset of the estate unless it can be exempted or is abandoned by the trustee.[17]

Also remember that a plaintiff in any lawsuit pending against the debtor is also a creditor of the debtor. Often, lawsuits pending against a debtor will be described in the Statement of Affairs but the same information is not included in the Schedules. Remember, when a creditor is suing a debtor, the creditor must be listed on the Schedules if the debtor is to successfully seek and obtain a discharge of the obligation sued upon.[18]

Line 10 asks for the disclosure of any property that has been seized by legal process, garnished, repossessed, foreclosed, or levied within the year prior to the bankruptcy filing. In this example there is no such activity. If, however, a judgment creditor has a wage garnishment or some other type of judgment execution outstanding on a debtor, this action would be described here.

FACT PATTERN

Which items should the Cashes disclose in response to Line 10? Does the termination of utility services fit under this subcategory?

FACT PATTERN

As noted earlier, the vehicle repossessions should be entered in the schedules depending on the actual ownership interest. These transactions could be preferential or fraudulent.[19]

---

11. Within 90 days before you filed for bankruptcy, did any creditor, including a bank or financial institution, set off any amounts from your accounts or refuse to make a payment because you owed a debt?

☑ No

❏ Yes. Fill in the details.

Description

This item requires disclosure of setoffs made during the year preceding the bankruptcy. A setoff might constitute a preference.[20]

---

17. See chapters 15 and 21 supra.
18. 11 U.S.C. §523(a)(3). See chapter 14 supra.
19. See chapters 17 and 18 supra.
20. See chapters 17 and 21 supra.

12. Within 1 year before you filed for bankruptcy, was any of your property in the possession of an assignee for the benefit of creditors, a court-appointed receiver, a custodian, or another official?

☑ No
☐ Yes

Description

Line 12 requires a debtor to identify the existence of any third-party custodian of estate property, including an assignment for the benefit of creditors, so the estate assets may be properly turned over to the trustee or debtor-in-possession.[21]

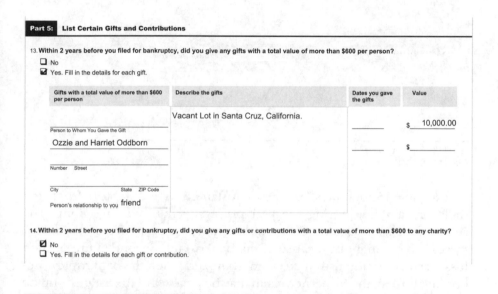

Part 5:	List Certain Gifts and Contributions

13. Within 2 years before you filed for bankruptcy, did you give any gifts with a total value of more than $600 per person?

☐ No
☑ Yes. Fill in the details for each gift.

Gifts with a total value of more than $600 per person	Describe the gifts	Dates you gave the gifts	Value
	Vacant Lot in Santa Cruz, California.	_____	$ 10,000.00
Person to Whom You Gave the Gift		_____	$_____
Ozzie and Harriet Oddborn			
Number Street			
City State ZIP Code			
Person's relationship to you friend			

14. Within 2 years before you filed for bankruptcy, did you give any gifts or contributions with a total value of more than $600 to any charity?

☑ No
☐ Yes. Fill in the details for each gift or contribution.

Description

Part 5, line 13 discloses evidence that may lead to the discovery of fraudulent transfers made by the giving of large gifts.[22] As noted, gifts or contributions in excess of $600 per person should be disclosed. The transfer of the vacant lot to the Oddborns is shown here because this is the best place to disclose it. Situations can arise where the same transaction may apply to more than one question. It is always best to complete every line, even if it may be redundant to do so.

---

21. See chapters 3 and 15 supra.
22. See chapter 18 supra.

Assuming that Owen discloses the sword and gun transfer and the storage of money in his father's safe deposit box, would those "transfers" constitute a gift to his father?

Line 14 discloses charitable contributions in the two years preceding the filing. The Bottomlines do not appear to have given any, but because the information is not specifically included in the memo, this item would have to be double-checked before the form is filed.

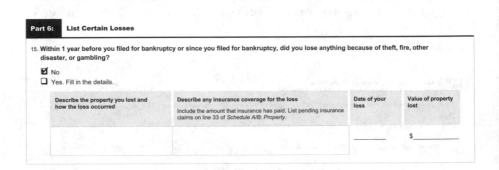

Description

Part 6, Line 15 identifies any losses sustained by the debtors from fire, theft, or gambling during the year preceding the petition's filing. The reason for this disclosure is first to ascertain the existence of "calamity" losses, which might be a cause of the bankruptcy. Second, a fire or theft loss may involve an insurance claim. If unpaid when the bankruptcy proceeding is filed, the insurance claim may be an asset of the estate.[23] In the example, it has been assumed to be no. However, the information is not contained in the memo. Do not assume. All information should be ascertained and completed before filing. Every item must have a completed response. "Unknown" is not a responsive answer to an inquiry that calls for a "Yes" or "No" answer. Recall that if there is a "Yes" response, provide all pertinent data as shown in the responses to the other items.

---

23. See chapter 15 supra.

What information should you schedule in Line 15 for the Cashes?   FACT PATTERN

Part 7:	List Certain Payments or Transfers

16. **Within 1 year before you filed for bankruptcy, did you or anyone else acting on your behalf pay or transfer any property to anyone you consulted about seeking bankruptcy or preparing a bankruptcy petition?**
Include any attorneys, bankruptcy petition preparers, or credit counseling agencies for services required in your bankruptcy.

☐ No
☑ Yes. Fill in the details.

	Description and value of any property transferred	Date payment or transfer was made	Amount of payment
your firm Person Who Was Paid			
Number Street		_____	$____2,000.00
		_____	$_____
City State ZIP Code			
Email or website address			
Person Who Made the Payment, if Not You			

Description

Part 7, Line 16 requires disclosure of payments to attorneys over the past year for legal services pertaining to debt relief. The purpose of these disclosures is to help ensure that the attorneys working on the case do not receive excessive compensation or are not themselves the transferee of a fraudulent transfer.[24] The fee paid in connection with the bankruptcy must be disclosed here as shown. Payments for bankruptcy assistance to persons other than the firm filing the case would be shown here in addition to the fee paid to the firm filing the case which is also disclosed in Official Form B2030, the Disclosure of Compensation of Attorney for Debtor. See chapter 8 supra.

> *Jimmy Bold expressly did not want to be included in the first Cash bankruptcy filing. Would it be necessary to include any payments made to him in this second bankruptcy filing? If so, where would it be entered?*   FACT PATTERN

---

24. See chapters 8 and 18 supra.

17. **Within 1 year before you filed for bankruptcy, did you or anyone else acting on your behalf pay or transfer any property to anyone who promised to help you deal with your creditors or to make payments to your creditors?**
Do not include any payment or transfer that you listed on line 16.

☑ No
☐ Yes. Fill in the details.

18. **Within 2 years before you filed for bankruptcy, did you sell, trade, or otherwise transfer any property to anyone, other than property transferred in the ordinary course of your business or financial affairs?**
Include both outright transfers and transfers made as security (such as the granting of a security interest or mortgage on your property).
Do not include gifts and transfers that you have already listed on this statement.
☑ No
☐ Yes. Fill in the details.

19. **Within 10 years before you filed for bankruptcy, did you transfer any property to a self-settled trust or similar device of which you are a beneficiary?** (These are often called *asset-protection devices*.)

☑ No
☐ Yes. Fill in the details.

Description

Lines 17-19 addresses other transfers of property unless disclosed elsewhere in the form. This evidence may lead to the discovery of fraudulent transfers or preferences made by the granting of a security interest or other transfer of property.[25] All pertinent details, including purpose, identity of transferee, value, and the date of transfer should be concisely disclosed as shown in the example. A practitioner should obtain a copy of any closing statement so it may be made promptly available to a trustee upon the trustee's request. Line 19 will rarely arise in actual practice. Notice that the transfer of the empty lot to the Oddborns could be reported on line 18 instead of the gift as reported in Line 13 supra.

---

25. See chapters 17 and 18 supra.

Part 8:	List Certain Financial Accounts, Instruments, Safe Deposit Boxes, and Storage Units

20. Within 1 year before you filed for bankruptcy, were any financial accounts or instruments held in your name, or for your benefit, closed, sold, moved, or transferred?
    Include checking, savings, money market, or other financial accounts; certificates of deposit; shares in banks, credit unions, brokerage houses, pension funds, cooperatives, associations, and other financial institutions.
    ☑ No
    ☐ Yes. Fill in the details.

21. Do you now have, or did you have within 1 year before you filed for bankruptcy, any safe deposit box or other depository for securities, cash, or other valuables?
    ☑ No
    ◼ Yes. Fill in the details.

22. Have you stored property in a storage unit or place other than your home within 1 year before you filed for bankruptcy?
    ☑ No
    ◼ Yes. Fill in the details.

Part 9:	Identify Property You Hold or Control for Someone Else

23. Do you hold or control any property that someone else owns? Include any property you borrowed from, are storing for, or hold in trust for someone.
    ☑ No
    ◼ Yes. Fill in the details.

Description

Part 8, line 20 discloses all bank accounts closed by the debtor in the year prior to the filing. For any account for which disclosure must be made, complete all the remaining information on the form.

If the debtors have a safe-deposit box or property stored at a self-storage or somewhere other than home, disclose the information on line 21 or line 22, respectively. Otherwise, check the box "None."

> ***Since the safe deposit box actually belongs to Lester and not Owen, would it need to be disclosed in either Line 21 or 22?***

FACT PATTERN

Line 23 requests disclosure of any assets held by the debtor on behalf of a third party. In this example there is no such activity.

Part 10:	Give Details About Environmental Information

For the purpose of Part 10, the following definitions apply:

- *Environmental law* means any federal, state, or local statute or regulation concerning pollution, contamination, releases of hazardous or toxic substances, wastes, or material into the air, land, soil, surface water, groundwater, or other medium, including statutes or regulations controlling the cleanup of these substances, wastes, or material.

- *Site* means any location, facility, or property as defined under any environmental law, whether you now own, operate, or utilize it or used to own, operate, or utilize it, including disposal sites.

- *Hazardous material* means anything an environmental law defines as a hazardous waste, hazardous substance, toxic substance, hazardous material, pollutant, contaminant, or similar term.

Report all notices, releases, and proceedings that you know about, regardless of when they occurred.

24. Has any governmental unit notified you that you may be liable or potentially liable under or in violation of an environmental law?

☑ No
☐ Yes. Fill in the details.

25. Have you notified any governmental unit of any release of hazardous material?

☑ No
☐ Yes. Fill in the details.

26. Have you been a party in any judicial or administrative proceeding under any environmental law? Include settlements and orders.

☑ No
■ Yes. Fill in the details.

Description

Part 10, lines 24-26 ask the debtor to disclose any environmental issues that may affect estate property. This question is required in all cases. The purpose of this question is to bring any environmental issues to the specific attention of the trustee and creditors.

FACT PATTERN

Because The Lawn Cuttery operates several vehicles and potentially utilizes pesticides and/or fertilizers, environmental concerns may be an issue that should be addressed when completing a nonindividual petition for the business.

Part 11: Give Details About Your Business or Connections to Any Business

27. Within 4 years before you filed for bankruptcy, did you own a business or have any of the following connections to any business?

☐ A sole proprietor or self-employed in a trade, profession, or other activity, either full-time or part-time

☐ A member of a limited liability company (LLC) or limited liability partnership (LLP)

☑ A partner in a partnership

☐ An officer, director, or managing executive of a corporation

☐ An owner of at least 5% of the voting or equity securities of a corporation

☐ No. None of the above applies. Go to Part 12.

☑ Yes. Check all that apply above and fill in the details below for each business.

Top 'O the Mornin Irish Tea Shp	Describe the nature of the business	Employer Identification number Do not include Social Security number or ITIN.
Business Name	retail tea sho	EIN: __ __ - __ __ __ __ __ __ __
Number Street	Name of accountant or bookkeeper	Dates business existed
City State ZIP Code		From _____ To _____
Business Name	Describe the nature of the business	Employer Identification number Do not include Social Security number or ITIN.
Number Street		EIN: __ __ - __ __ __ __ __ __ __
City State ZIP Code	Name of accountant or bookkeeper	Dates business existed From _____ To _____

28. Within 2 years before you filed for bankruptcy, did you give a financial statement to anyone about your business? Include all financial institutions, creditors, or other parties.

☑ No

☑ Yes. Fill in the details below.

Description

Part 11, lines 27-28 require a debtor to identify any business ventures in which the debtor has been involved in the four years prior to filing. Any affirmative response requires completing the requested information for each business venture that the debtor has owned.

Summary

It is important in learning the bankruptcy system to know how to effectively prepare and read the most important documents filed at the inception of any bankruptcy proceeding, the Statement of Financial Affairs and Schedules of Assets and Liabilities. These documents are commonly known as the Statements and Schedules. Effective preparation of these documents by the paralegal will expedite an estate's administration. Knowing how to read these documents effectively will permit a creditor's representative to ascertain the potential for a dividend to the creditor or a potential objection to the debtor's discharge.

In effectively preparing the Statements and Schedules, all questions should be answered even when the answer is a simple "no" or "none." All information required to be provided should be provided in as concise a form as possible

In effectively reading the Statements and Schedules, the paralegal should focus on identifying the existence and value of nonexempt assets to determine the potential for unsecured creditors to receive a dividend.

DISCUSSION QUESTIONS

1. What are some of the purposes the Statements and Schedules serve?

2. What should be the concerns of a debtor in effective preparation of the Statements and Schedules?

3. What should be the concerns of a trustee or creditor in effective review of the Statements and Schedules?

4. What are the major differences between an individual Chapter 7 filing and a nonindividual Chapter 7 filing, in terms of the required forms and questions asked?

31

Means Testing Tutorial

Learning Objectives

- Complete the means testing form

A.   INTRODUCTION

The various means testing forms, Official Forms B122A-1-B122C-2, have become as important to individual bankruptcy proceedings as the Statements and Schedules.[1] Officially, for Chapter 7 purposes, known as the Statement of Your Current Monthly Income and the Means-Test Calculation, colloquially these forms have simply become known as the Means Test. As with the Statements and Schedules, a practitioner's most important task is to properly prepare the data required to be included in the form. All commercial bankruptcy software has been programmed to complete the form from data entered by the practitioner. As with the Statements and Schedules, performing this task well will make a debtor's trip through the bankruptcy system as smooth and uneventful as possible. Proper preparation will minimize or eliminate inquiries from the case trustee or the United States Trustee seeking to corroborate the information disclosed in the form. Most of this is accomplished simply by maintaining all the information in the file used to complete and perform the means testing calculations. In a practice emphasizing bankruptcy law, a paralegal will spend a significant amount of time assisting in compiling and organizing the data. If the case trustee or United States Trustee

---

1. Official Forms B122A-B122A-2 are used in Chapter 7 cases, B122B is used in Chapter 11 cases, and Forms B122C-1 and B122C-2 are used in Chapter 13 cases. See chapter 6 supra.

requests the data, it will be at your fingertips and you will be able to respond promptly.

Means testing is not necessary for nonindividual filings because nonindividuals are not eligible to file a Chapter 13 petition.

When a debtor's current monthly income is below the applicable state median income, then it will generally only be necessary to maintain all evidence of income for the six calendar months preceding the filing, the data necessary to perform the current monthly income calculation. When a debtor's current monthly income exceeds the applicable state median income, and a debtor is required to complete Official Form B122A-2 or B122C-2, then all additional backup information should be maintained, including evidence of a debtor's house payment, car payment, and other secured debt. This is in addition to the information required to be supplied to the trustee or United States Trustee in any case (see chapters 4 and 12 supra). However, even in a below median income case, it is good practice to compile and maintain all of the data necessary to fully complete the form. Obtaining and maintaining the necessary data likely falls within counsel's duty of reasonable investigation as set forth in Section 707(b)(4) (see chapter 6 supra).

To maintain consistency, the Bottomlines remain our debtors and all of the facts presented in chapter 30 apply here. Any additional facts are noted in this chapter. The Official Forms analyzed are the Chapter 7 versions, Official Forms B122A-1 and B122A-2. Since approximately 70 percent of all filings are Chapter 7 cases, the Chapter 7 versions of the form are most frequently used in actual practice. Although a few line items change in the Chapter 11 and Chapter 13 versions of the form, the principles and analysis contained in this chapter will apply equally to other versions of the forms. For all purposes, this tutorial uses the median family income figures and allowable deductions for National Standards, local housing allowances, and transportation allowances for the period commencing May 1, 2016.

B.   CURRENT MONTHLY INCOME

Official Form 122A—1

Chapter 7 Statement of Your Current Monthly Income   12/15

Be as complete and accurate as possible. If two married people are filing together, both are equally responsible for being accurate. If more space is needed, attach a separate sheet to this form. Include the line number to which the additional information applies. On the top of any additional pages, write your name and case number (if known). If you believe that you are exempted from a presumption of abuse because you do not have primarily consumer debts or because of qualifying military service, complete and file *Statement of Exemption from Presumption of Abuse Under § 707(b)(2)* (Official Form 122A-1Supp) with this form.

Part 1:	Calculate Your Current Monthly Income

1. **What is your marital and filing status?** Check one only.

   ☐ **Not married.** Fill out Column A, lines 2-11.

   ☑ **Married and your spouse is filing with you.** Fill out both Columns A and B, lines 2-11.

   ☐ **Married and your spouse is NOT filing with you.** You and your spouse are:

   ☐ **Living in the same household and are not legally separated.** Fill out both Columns A and B, lines 2-11.

   ☐ **Living separately or are legally separated.** Fill out Column A, lines 2-11; do not fill out Column B. By checking this box, you declare under penalty of perjury that you and your spouse are legally separated under nonbankruptcy law that applies or that you and your spouse are living apart for reasons that do not include evading the Means Test requirements. 11 U.S.C. § 707(b)(7)(B).

Fill in the average monthly income that you received from all sources, derived during the 6 full months before you file this bankruptcy case. 11 U.S.C. § 101(10A). For example, if you are filing on September 15, the 6-month period would be March 1 through August 31. If the amount of your monthly income varied during the 6 months, add the income for all 6 months and divide the total by 6. Fill in the result. Do not include any income amount more than once. For example, if both spouses own the same rental property, put the income from that property in one column only. If you have nothing to report for any line, write $0 in the space.

		Column A Debtor 1	Column B Debtor 2 or non-filing spouse
2.	**Your gross wages, salary, tips, bonuses, overtime, and commissions** (before all payroll deductions).	$ 6,500.00	$ 500.00
3.	**Alimony and maintenance payments.** Do not include payments from a spouse if Column B is filled in.	$_____	$_____
4.	**All amounts from any source which are regularly paid for household expenses of you or your dependents, including child support.** Include regular contributions from an unmarried partner, members of your household, your dependents, parents, and roommates. Include regular contributions from a spouse only if Column B is not filled in. Do not include payments you listed on line 3.	$_____	$_____

5. **Net income from operating a business, profession, or farm**

	Debtor 1	Debtor 2		Column A	Column B
Gross receipts (before all deductions)	$_____	$_____			
Ordinary and necessary operating expenses	− $_____	− $_____			
Net monthly income from a business, profession, or farm	$_____	$_____	Copy here ➔	$_____	$_____

6. **Net income from rental and other real property**

	Debtor 1	Debtor 2		Column A	Column B
Gross receipts (before all deductions)	$_____	$_____			
Ordinary and necessary operating expenses	− $_____	− $_____			
Net monthly income from rental or other real property	$_____	$_____	Copy here ➔	$_____	$_____

7.	**Interest, dividends, and royalties**	$_____	$_____

	Column A Debtor 1	Column B Debtor 2 or non-filing spouse
8. **Unemployment compensation**	$_____	$_____

Do not enter the amount if you contend that the amount received was a benefit
under the Social Security Act. Instead, list it here: ....↓

    For you.. $ _____

    For your spouse... $ _____

9. **Pension or retirement income.** Do not include any amount received that was a benefit under the Social Security Act.	$_____	$_____
10. **Income from all other sources not listed above.** Specify the source and amount. Do not include any benefits received under the Social Security Act or payments received as a victim of a war crime, a crime against humanity, or international or domestic terrorism. If necessary, list other sources on a separate page and put the total below.		
_____	$_____	$_____
_____	$_____	$_____
Total amounts from separate pages, if any.	+ $_____	+ $_____

11. **Calculate your total current monthly income.** Add lines 2 through 10 for each
column. Then add the total for Column A to the total for Column B.

$ 6,500.00 **+** $ 500.00 **=** $ 7,000.00

Total current
monthly income

Part 2:   Determine Whether the Means Test Applies to You

12. **Calculate your current monthly income for the year.** Follow these steps:

    12a. Copy your total current monthly income from line 11. .... Copy line 11 here➡ $ 7,000.00

            Multiply by 12 (the number of months in a year).   **x 12**

    12b. The result is your annual income for this part of the form.   12b. $ 84,000.00

13. **Calculate the median family income that applies to you.** Follow these steps:

    Fill in the state in which you live.   `CA`

    Fill in the number of people in your household.   `4`

    Fill in the median family income for your state and size of household. ....13. $ 81,837.00

    To find a list of applicable median income amounts, go online using the link specified in the separate
instructions for this form. This list may also be available at the bankruptcy clerk's office.

14. **How do the lines compare?**

    14a. ☐ Line 12b is less than or equal to line 13. On the top of page 1, check box 1, *There is no presumption of abuse.*
           Go to Part 3.

    14b. ■ Line 12b is more than line 13. On the top of page 1, check box 2, *The presumption of abuse is determined by Form 122A–2.*
           Go to Part 3 and fill out Form 122A–2.

Part 3:   Sign Below

By signing here, I declare under penalty of perjury that the information on this statement and in any attachments is true and correct.

✗ _____   **✗** _____
    Signature of Debtor 1   Signature of Debtor 2

Date _____   Date _____
      MM / DD / YYYY   MM / DD / YYYY

If you checked line 14a, do NOT fill out or file Form 122A–2.

If you checked line 14b, fill out Form 122A–2 and file it with this form.

Description

Official Form B122A-1 discloses the debtors' current monthly income.
However, notice the box in the upper right hand corner of the form. If
a debtor's debts are not primarily consumer debts, a debtor is not required
to complete the forms. If a debtor is a disabled veteran, and the indebt-
edness was incurred while on active duty, or if the debtor was a reservist in
the National Guard and meets certain other conditions, the Means Test

will not apply, Instead, the debtor will file Official Form B122A-1Supp, attesting to these facts.[2]

Part 1, line 1 discloses the debtor's filing status. In the example, since the Bottomlines are married and filing jointly, the second box is checked. All succeeding lines will be completed for each debtor as shown.

Line 2 discloses each joint debtor's average monthly income received from all sources in the six calendar months preceding the filing. For Ken, since he receives an annual salary and has been employed for the entire period, his average monthly pay is $6,500. However, if by reviewing all of his payment advices for the entire period, you discover that he received a bonus in one or more months, or overtime, the amount of the bonus and any overtime must also be factored into the calculation. This is why, among other things, it is necessary to obtain payment advices for the entire six-month period. As for Bretony, although she currently receives $1,000 per month, which is disclosed in her Schedule I (see chapter 30 supra), since she has only received the income for three months, her average monthly income over the six-month period is $500.

Depending on when the Cashes file for bankruptcy, Owen's average monthly income may be influenced by other things such as unemployment, a different source of income, or no income.

FACT PATTERN

Line 3 identifies any alimony or maintenance payments. Line 4 applies when a third party other than the debtor regularly contributes to the household expenses.[3] This includes monthly stipends paid by a parent, the pay earned by either child if the pay is contributed to pay household expenses, or if child support received is contributed toward household expenses, and any contributions made by any family member who is not a debtor toward the payment of household expenses. See chapter 6 supra.

Since Les still technically lives in the Cash home, this area will need to be explored to understand whether his contribution(s) have an impact on the household expenses.

FACT PATTERN

---

2. 11 U.S.C. §707(b). See chapter 6 supra.
3. 11 U.S.C. §101(10A). See chapters 6 and 7 supra.

Lines 5 and 6 attempt to segregate gross and net income from the operation of a business or the management of income-producing real property income. If Top O' the Mornin' had been operating within six months of the Bottomline filing, then Bretony would have to complete Line 5.

FACT PATTERN

Again the timing of the Cash bankruptcy filing would determine how much would be reported under line 5.

Line 7 requires disclosure of the described types of income and is self-explanatory. Line 8 applies when either debtor has received unemployment compensation during the relevant period. There does not appear to be any in the example, but it would be prudent to inquire of Bretony as to whether she received any unemployment after the demise of Top O' the Mornin' and if so how much and for what periods.

FACT PATTERN

Note that Robin is no longer working, and depending on the timing of the filing, Owen may not be working. It would be a good idea to check with both regarding unemployment benefits.

Lines 9 and 10 are self-explanatory. Note, however, that payments and benefits received under the Social Security Act are not included as income for purposes of determining current monthly income because receipt of such payments is excluded by the terms of the statute.[4]

Line 11 totals lines 2 through 10 for each debtor. The Bottomlines' combined current monthly income is $7,000.

Part 2 compares the debtors' current monthly income to the median income of a family of similar size in the applicable state to determine whether or not the debtor needs to complete Official Form B122A-2.

Line 12 multiplies the result in Line 11 by 12. The result appears on the form.

Line 13 shows the state where the debtors live, household size, and the applicable median income figure in effect on the filing date. In California, for the period commencing May 1, 2016, the median family income of a family of four is $81,837, the figure that appears in the form.

---

4. Ibid.

For the Cashes, use the median income for your home state.

Line 14 compares the applicable median income to the debtors' annual income. If the debtors' annual income is equal to or less than the applicable median, then abuse is not presumed and the debtors need not complete Official Form B122A-2. If the debtors' annual income exceeds the applicable median income, then the debtors must complete Official Form B122A-2. In the example, the Bottomlines must complete the form as their income of $84,000 exceeds the applicable median income of $81,837.[5]

---

5. 11 U.S.C. §707(b)(7). See chapter 6 supra.

C.   OFFICIAL FORM B122A-2 CHAPTER 7 MEANS TEST CALCULATION

Official Form 122A–2

Chapter 7 Means Test Calculation   04/16

To fill out this form, you will need your completed copy of *Chapter 7 Statement of Your Current Monthly Income* (Official Form 122A-1).

Be as complete and accurate as possible. If two married people are filing together, both are equally responsible for being accurate. If more space is needed, attach a separate sheet to this form. Include the line number to which the additional information applies. On the to p of any additional pages, write your name and case number (if known).

Part 1:	Determine Your Adjusted Income

1. Copy your total current monthly income... Copy line 11 from Official Form 122A-1 here➔ .... $ 7,000.00

2. **Did you fill out Column B in Part 1 of Form 122A–1?**

   ☐ No. Fill in $0 for the total on line 3.

   ☑ Yes. Is your spouse filing with you?

      ☐ No. Go to line 3.

      ☑ Yes. Fill in $0 for the total on line 3.

3. **Adjust your current monthly income by subtracting any part of your spouse's income not used to pay for the household expenses of you or your dependents.** Follow these steps:

   On line 11, Column B of Form 122A–1, was any amount of the income you reported for your spouse NOT regularly used for the household expenses of you or your dependents?

   ☐ No. Fill in 0 for the total on line 3.

   ☐ Yes. Fill in the information below:

State each purpose for which the income was used For example, the income is used to pay your spouse's tax debt or to support people other than you or your dependents	Fill in the amount you are subtracting from your spouse's income
_____	$_____
_____	$_____
_____	+ $_____
Total.	$_____ 0.00

   Copy total here ....➔   — $ ____ 0.00

4. **Adjust your current monthly income.** Subtract the total on line 3 from line 1. $ 7,000.00

Description

Part 1 of Official Form B122A-2, the Means Testing Calculation, is used when a couple is living together but only one spouse files a bankruptcy case. Income of the nonfiling spouse or partner not regularly used to pay the household expenses of the debtor are deducted from income. For example, if Bretony is the only debtor and Ken pays child support to a former spouse on behalf of children that do not live with Ken and Bretony, the amount paid by Ken for child support would be deducted from income in Bretony's Form B122A-2. When there is no spouse, or when the filing is joint, as it is here, the amount inserted in Line 3 is zero.

> *A similar situation would arise in the Cash case if Robin was filing an individual petition, because Owen is paying child support for Lottie.*

D.   DEDUCTIONS — INTERNAL REVENUE EXPENSE STANDARDS

The first group of deductions that debtors may claim from current monthly income are calculated according to Internal Revenue Service collection guidelines, excluding payments for debts. Some of these standards are national, and some are local. There are national standards for day-to-day expenses, local expenses for housing and utilities, local expenses for transportation ownership and operation, and other necessary expenses.[6] The allowable amounts are published on a regular basis. Currently applicable amounts may be found on the United States Trustee Program website: http://www.usdoj.gov/ust. Links may also be found on many local bankruptcy court websites.

---

6. 11 U.S.C. §707(b)(2)(A)(ii)(I).

Part 2:   Calculate Your Deductions from Your Income

The Internal Revenue Service (IRS) issues National and Local Standards for certain expense amounts. Use these amounts to answer the questions in lines 6-15. To find the IRS standards, go online using the link specified in the separate instructions for this form. This information may also be available at the bankruptcy clerk's office.

Deduct the expense amounts set out in lines 6-15 regardless of your actual expense. In later parts of the form, you will use some of your actual expenses if they are higher than the standards. Do not deduct any amounts that you subtracted from your spouse's income in line 3 and do not deduct any operating expenses that you subtracted from income in lines 5 and 6 of Form 122A–1.

If your expenses differ from month to month, enter the average expense.

Whenever this part of the form refers to *you*, it means both you and your spouse if Column B of Form 122A–1 is filled in.

5. **The number of people used in determining your deductions from income**

   Fill in the number of people who could be claimed as exemptions on your federal income tax return, plus the number of any additional dependents whom you support. This number may be different from the number of people in your household. | 4 |

National Standards   You must use the IRS National Standards to answer the questions in lines 6-7.

6. **Food, clothing, and other items:** Using the number of people you entered in line 5 and the IRS National Standards, fill in the dollar amount for food, clothing, and other items. $ 1,509.00

7. **Out-of-pocket health care allowance:** Using the number of people you entered in line 5 and the IRS National Standards, fill in the dollar amount for out-of-pocket health care. The number of people is split into two categories—people who are under 65 and people who are 65 or older—because older people have a higher IRS allowance for health care costs. If your actual expenses are higher than this IRS amount, you may deduct the additional amount on line 22.

People who are under 65 years of age

7a.	Out-of-pocket health care allowance per person	$ 54.00
7b.	Number of people who are under 65	X 4
7c.	**Subtotal.** Multiply line 7a by line 7b.	$ 216.00 Copy here ➔ $ 216.00

People who are 65 years of age or older

7d.	Out-of-pocket health care allowance per person	$ _____
7e.	Number of people who are 65 or older	X ____
7f.	**Subtotal.** Multiply line 7d by line 7e.	$ 0.00 Copy here ➔ + $ 0.00

| 7g. | **Total.** Add lines 7c and 7f.. | $ 216.00   Copy total here ➔ $ 216.00 |

Description

Line 5 reports the number of persons in the household used to determine deductions from income.

Line 6 inserts the allowable amount of expenses under National Standards for food, clothing, household supplies, personal care, and miscellaneous. For a family of four as of May 1, 2016, the amount is $1,509. Line 7 allows a deduction for health care expenses for each member of the household as shown. If there were any members of the Bottomline household 65 or older, for each such person the deduction would rise to $130.

Local Standards You must use the IRS Local Standards to answer the questions in lines 8-15.

Based on information from the IRS, the U.S. Trustee Program has divided the IRS Local Standard for housing for bankruptcy purposes into two parts:

- Housing and utilities – Insurance and operating expenses
- Housing and utilities – Mortgage or rent expenses

To answer the questions in lines 8-9, use the U.S. Trustee Program chart.

To find the chart, go online using the link specified in the separate instructions for this form. This chart may also be available at the bankruptcy clerk's office.

8. **Housing and utilities – Insurance and operating expenses:** Using the number of people you entered in line 5, fill in the dollar amount listed for your county for insurance and operating expenses. .... $ _____623.00_

9. **Housing and utilities – Mortgage or rent expenses:**

9a. Using the number of people you entered in line 5, fill in the dollar amount listed for your county for mortgage or rent expenses.. $ _2,411.00_

9b. Total average monthly payment for all mortgages and other debts secured by your home.

To calculate the total average monthly payment, add all amounts that are contractually due to each secured creditor in the 60 months after you file for bankruptcy. Then divide by 60.

Name of the creditor	Average monthly payment
_____	$_____
_____	$_____
_____	+ $_____
Total average monthly payment	$_____0.00_

Copy here ➜ – $ _____0.00_ Repeat this amount on line 33a.

9c. Net mortgage or rent expense.
Subtract line 9b (*total average monthly payment*) from line 9a (*mortgage or rent expense*). If this amount is less than $0, enter $0. .... $ _____623.00_ Copy here ➜ $ _____623.00_

10. **If you claim that the U.S. Trustee Program's division of the IRS Local Standard for housing is incorrect and affects the calculation of your monthly expenses, fill in any additional amount you claim.** $ _____0.00_

Explain why: _____

11. **Local transportation expenses:** Check the number of vehicles for which you claim an ownership or operating expense.

☐ 0. Go to line 14.
☑ 1. Go to line 12.
☐ 2 or more. Go to line 12.

12. **Vehicle operation expense:** Using the IRS Local Standards and the number of vehicles for which you claim the operating expenses, fill in the *Operating Costs* that apply for your Census region or metropolitan statistical area. $ _____271.00_

Description

Lines 8-10 contain the applicable nonmortgage expense deductions for housing. As of May 1, 2016, the deduction in San Diego County for a family of four is $623 as shown on line 8. Nonmortgage expenses considered in this category include utility expenses.

Line 9 is the applicable mortgage or rental expense deduction. As of May 1, 2016, the allowable amount of deduction in San Diego County for a family of four is $2,411. Because the Bottomlines rent, they do not need to complete the insert at Line 9B. If they owned a home, any mortgage payment would be deducted from the allowance, because the amount may only be accounted for once. See chapter 6 supra. Note also, that the aggregate amount of housing deductions ($3,034) is significantly more than their actual monthly rent of $1,200, and their actual utility expenses of $175. Nonetheless, they are entitled to the entire allowable IRS deduction. For example, at least one court has held that military personnel living on base and having no actual housing expenses may still claim the housing deductions because this is what the statute permits.[7]

FACT PATTERN

You will need to know the actual mortgage and utility expenses for the Cashes to complete this section.

In Line 10, the debtors could disclose additional extraordinary housing or utility expenses. Any such additional expenses must be backed up by appropriate documentation, such as copies of utility bills.

Lines 11 and 12 begin deductions for the costs of transportation or operation of a vehicle. As of May 1, 2016, the allowable operating expense deduction in San Diego County for a family with one vehicle is $271.

---

7. In re Farrar-Johnson, 353 B.R. 224 (Bankr. N.D. Ill. 2006).

13. **Vehicle ownership or lease expense:** Using the IRS Local Standards, calculate the net ownership or lease expense for each vehicle below. You may not claim the expense if you do not make any loan or lease payments on the vehicle. In addition, you may not claim the expense for more than two vehicles.

Vehicle 1	Describe Vehicle 1:	2015 Lannister Westeros

13a. Ownership or leasing costs using IRS Local Standard. .... $ _____471.00_

13b. Average monthly payment for all debts secured by Vehicle 1.
Do not include costs for leased vehicles.

To calculate the average monthly payment here and on line 13e, add all amounts that are contractually due to each secured creditor in the 60 months after you filed for bankruptcy. Then divide by 60.

Name of each creditor for Vehicle 1	Average monthly payment
Lannister Credit	$ _____175.00_
_____ +	$ _____
Total average monthly payment	$ _____175.00_

Copy here ➜   — $ _____175.00_   Repeat this amount on line 33b.

13c. Net Vehicle 1 ownership or lease expense
Subtract line 13b from line 13a. If this amount is less than $0, enter $0. .... $ _____296.00_

Copy net Vehicle 1 expense here ..... ➜ $ __296.00_

Vehicle 2	Describe Vehicle 2:	

13d. Ownership or leasing costs using IRS Local Standard. .... $ _____

13e. Average monthly payment for all debts secured by Vehicle 2.
Do not include costs for leased vehicles.

Name of each creditor for Vehicle 2	Average monthly payment
_____	$ _____
_____ +	$ _____
Total average monthly payment	$ _____

Copy here ➜   — $ _____   Repeat this Amount on line 33c.

13f. Net Vehicle 2 ownership or lease expense
Subtract line 13e from 13d. If this amount is less than $0, enter $0. .... $ _____0.00_

Copy net Vehicle 2 expense here ... ➜ $ ____0.00_

14. **Public transportation expense:** If you claimed 0 vehicles in line 11, using the IRS Local Standards, fill in the *Public Transportation* expense allowance regardless of whether you use public transportation. $ ____0.00_

15. **Additional public transportation expense:** If you claimed 1 or more vehicles in line 11 and if you claim that you may also deduct a public transportation expense, you may fill in what you believe is the appropriate expense, but you may not claim more than the IRS Local Standard for *Public Transportation*. $ ____0.00_

Description

Line 13 deducts the allowable expense for ownership of a vehicle, reduced by the average monthly payment on any debt, since the deduction is limited to the greater of the applicable deduction or the monthly payment, but not both, since to do so would count the same expense twice, identical to the same issue in connection with mortgage payments noted above. See chapter 6 supra. The Bottomlines own one vehicle. The monthly payment shown is the monthly payment as calculated by Line 13b. The practitioner should keep in the file a copy of the contract or a copy of a payment ticket or similar document that evidences the amount of monthly payments and the remaining payments under the contract. This will show how the average monthly debt payment was calculated. The same documentation should be maintained for all secured debts.

FACT PATTERN

What value would be listed for the Cashes?

The Supreme Court has held that an ownership deduction may not be claimed when the debtor owns a vehicle free and clear.[8]

Lines 14 and 15 allow a deduction for using public transportation if a debtor does not own a motor vehicle or if a debtor regularly uses public transportation. For example, a commuter riding the San Diego Trolley from her home in La Mesa to work in downtown San Diego might claim a public transportation deduction.

---

8. Ransom v. FIA Card Services, 562 U.S. 61 (2011). See chapter 6 supra.

Other Necessary Expenses In addition to the expense deductions listed above, you are allowed your monthly expenses for the following IRS categories.	

16. **Taxes:** The total monthly amount that you will actually owe for federal, state and local taxes, such as income taxes, self-employment taxes, Social Security taxes, and Medicare taxes. You may include the monthly amount withheld from your pay for these taxes. However, if you expect to receive a tax refund, you must divide the expected refund by 12 and subtract that number from the total monthly amount that is withheld to pay for taxes.

Do not include real estate, sales, or use taxes. $ 1,875.00

17. **Involuntary deductions:** The total monthly payroll deductions that your job requires, such as retirement contributions, union dues, and uniform costs.

Do not include amounts that are not required by your job, such as voluntary 401(k) contributions or payroll savings. $ 0.00

18. **Life insurance:** The total monthly premiums that you pay for your own term life insurance. If two married people are filing together, include payments that you make for your spouse's term life insurance. Do not include premiums for life insurance on your dependents, for a non-filing spouse's life insurance, or for any form of life insurance other than term. $ 0.00

19. **Court-ordered payments:** The total monthly amount that you pay as required by the order of a court or administrative agency, such as spousal or child support payments.

Do not include payments on past due obligations for spousal or child support. You will list these obligations in line 35. $ 0.00

20. **Education:** The total monthly amount that you pay for education that is either required:
- as a condition for your job, or
- for your physically or mentally challenged dependent child if no public education is available for similar services. $ 0.00

21. **Childcare:** The total monthly amount that you pay for childcare, such as babysitting, daycare, nursery, and preschool.

Do not include payments for any elementary or secondary school education. $ 0.00

22. **Additional health care expenses, excluding insurance costs:** The monthly amount that you pay for health care that is required for the health and welfare of you or your dependents and that is not reimbursed by insurance or paid by a health savings account. Include only the amount that is more than the total entered in line 7.
Payments for health insurance or health savings accounts should be listed only in line 25. $ 0.00

23. **Optional telephones and telephone services:** The total monthly amount that you pay for telecommunication services for you and your dependents, such as pagers, call waiting, caller identification, special long distance, or business cell phone service, to the extent necessary for your health and welfare or that of your dependents or for the production of income, if it is not reimbursed by your employer.

Do not include payments for basic home telephone, internet and cell phone service. Do not include self-employment expenses, such as those reported on line 5 of Official Form 122A-1, or any amount you previously deducted.   + $ 275.00

24. **Add all of the expenses allowed under the IRS expense allowances.**
Add lines 6 through 23. $ 7,476.00

Description

Lines 16-23 of Part 2 permit a debtor to claim deductions based upon the IRS Collection Standards for "Other Necessary Expenses." See chapter 6 supra.

Line 16 permits deductions for taxes that are withheld from pay. The average monthly amount should be computed in the same manner as current monthly income supra. This information will normally be contained on the same payment advices that are used to compute current monthly income. The amount shown is the amount shown in Schedule I of chapter 30 supra.

If Owen is considered to be self employed, it will be necessary to determine what kind of business and personal records he maintains and whether or not you can effectively determine the correct amount of deductions taken. Even if The Lawn Cuttery is incorporated, there may not have been any real change in the records created and maintained since it is still essentially a one person business.

Line 17 allows a deduction for mandatory payroll deductions. Examples include mandatory uniform expenses, union dues, and mandatory 401(k) or similar payments. Voluntary 401(k) or similar contributions, however, are not deductible. The Bottomlines do not have any deductions on this line. Every line should be completed, even if the answer is zero.

Line 18 permits deduction for term life insurance premiums for the debtors only. Premiums paid for nondebtor family members are not deductible. The Bottomlines do not have any life insurance.

Line 19 allows current court-ordered payments to be deducted. The most typical examples are child and spousal support payments. The amount here is zero.

In the Cash case, Owen is obligated to make court ordered child support payments of $125 per week.

Line 20 deducts expenses for employment-required education. For example, a nurse taking a required course to maintain her license may deduct the cost of the course. The same line permits deductions for the education of a physically or mentally challenged child who cannot obtain similar services through public education. The Bottomlines have no such expenses.

Although Owen is essentially self employed, the particular nature of his job could require state, federal, or local licenses, e.g., in his case to use pesticides or certain fertilizers.

Line 21 permits childcare expenses to be deducted. The Bottomlines have no such expense.

Line 22 deducts health care expenses that are not reimbursed by insurance or a health savings account, and are in excess of the health care expense allowances at line 7 supra. There are no such expenses here.

Line 23 allows for telephone and Internet services other than basic telephone and cell phone service to be deducted to the extent the expense is necessary for the health and welfare of the debtor and the debtor's dependents. The amount shown is an aggregate of telephone and Internet expenses shown on Schedule J in chapter 21 supra.

Line 24 is the total of lines 6-23 as shown. Note that the amount is higher than the sum of the deductions from the Bottomlines' paychecks as shown in Schedule I of chapter 30 supra, and their actual monthly expenses shown in Schedule J of chapter 30 supra.

E.   DEDUCTIONS — ADDITIONAL EXPENSE DEDUCTIONS

Section 707(b)(2) permits some additional deductions that are not included within the IRS Collection Financial Standards. Lines 25-31 capture these additional expenses.

Additional Expense Deductions   These are additional deductions allowed by the Means Test.
Note: Do not include any expense allowances listed in lines 6-24.

25. **Health insurance, disability insurance, and health savings account expenses.** The monthly expenses for health insurance, disability insurance, and health savings accounts that are reasonably necessary for yourself, your spouse, or your dependents.

Health insurance $____300.00____

Disability insurance $_____

Health savings account   + $_____

Total $____300.00____   Copy total here ➔ .... $ __300.00__

Do you actually spend this total amount?

☐ No. How much do you actually spend? $_____
☑ Yes

26. **Continuing contributions to the care of household or family members.** The actual monthly expenses that you will continue to pay for the reasonable and necessary care and support of an elderly, chronically ill, or disabled member of your household or member of your immediate family who is unable to pay for such expenses. These expenses may include contributions to an account of a qualified ABLE program. 26 U.S.C. § 529A(b). $__0.00__

27. **Protection against family violence.** The reasonably necessary monthly expenses that you incur to maintain the safety of you and your family under the Family Violence Prevention and Services Act or other federal laws that apply. $__0.00__

By law, the court must keep the nature of these expenses confidential.

28. **Additional home energy costs.** Your home energy costs are included in your insurance and operating expenses on line 8.

If you believe that you have home energy costs that are more than the home energy costs included in expenses on line 8, then fill in the excess amount of home energy costs. $__0.00__

You must give your case trustee documentation of your actual expenses, and you must show that the additional amount claimed is reasonable and necessary.

29. **Education expenses for dependent children who are younger than 18.** The monthly expenses (not more than $160.42* per child) that you pay for your dependent children who are younger than 18 years old to attend a private or public elementary or secondary school. $__0.00__

You must give your case trustee documentation of your actual expenses, and you must explain why the amount claimed is reasonable and necessary and not already accounted for in lines 6-23.

* Subject to adjustment on 4/01/19, and every 3 years after that for cases begun on or after the date of adjustment.

30. **Additional food and clothing expense.** The monthly amount by which your actual food and clothing expenses are higher than the combined food and clothing allowances in the IRS National Standards. That amount cannot be more than 5% of the food and clothing allowances in the IRS National Standards. $__0.00__

To find a chart showing the maximum additional allowance, go online using the link specified in the separate instructions for this form. This chart may also be available at the bankruptcy clerk's office.

You must show that the additional amount claimed is reasonable and necessary.

31. **Continuing charitable contributions.** The amount that you will continue to contribute in the form of cash or financial instruments to a religious or charitable organization. 26 U.S.C. § 170(c)(1)-(2).   + $__0.00__

32. **Add all of the additional expense deductions.**
Add lines 25 through 31. $ 300.00

Description

Line 25 permits deduction of expenses for health insurance, disability insurance, and health savings accounts paid for the debtor or a dependent of the debtor. See chapter 6C supra. Based upon the information provided, the Bottomlines have a $300 monthly health insurance expense.

Line 26 allows debtors to deduct monies paid to support an elderly, chronically ill, or disabled family member of the debtor's household or immediate family who is unable to pay for such expenses. The Bottomlines have no such expense.

> ***The Cashes may or may not have these types of expenses related to Lester's care. This would require more information and investigation.***

FACT PATTERN

Line 27 permits deductions for expenses paid in connection with protecting the debtor's family under the Family Violence Prevention and Services Act. This is a rare deduction. The Bottomlines have no such expense.

Line 28 permits an additional utility deduction for expenses in excess of the applicable IRS allowances, provided that documentation is provided to the case trustee and the documentation justifies the additional expense. The Bottomlines do not have such an expense. Remember, every line must be completed.

Line 29 allows a deduction for education expenses for children under the age of 18, not to exceed $160.42 per month, or $1,925 per year. There are no such expenses present here.

Line 30 allows a deduction of an amount equal to 5 percent of the national standards for food and clothing if the debtor can produce documentation evidencing the additional expense. There are no such facts presented by the Bottomlines. If there were, observe that the national allowances would permit an additional deduction of $52 based upon the amounts in effect as of May 1, 2016.

Line 31 allows deductions for continuing charitable contributions. If the debtors found religion only upon the filing of their case, the deduction is not permissible. There are no such deductions here.

Line 32 is the total of lines 25-31.

F.   DEDUCTIONS FOR DEBT PAYMENT

Deductions for Debt Payment

33. For debts that are secured by an interest in property that you own, including home mortgages, vehicle loans, and other secured debt, fill in lines 33a through 33e.

To calculate the total average monthly payment, add all amounts that are contractually due to each secured creditor in the 60 months after you file for bankruptcy. Then divide by 60.

		Average monthly payment
Mortgages on your home:		
33a. Copy line 9b here .... ➜		$ 0.00
Loans on your first two vehicles:		
33b. Copy line 13b here. .... ➜		$ 175.00
33c. Copy line 13e here. .... ➜		$_____

33d. List other secured debts:

Name of each creditor for other secured debt	Identify property that secures the debt	Does payment include taxes or insurance?	
Repo Recovery Svcs.	personal property	☑ No ☐ Yes	$_____
_____	_____	☐ No ☐ Yes	$_____
_____	_____	☐ No ☐ Yes	+ $_____

33e. Total average monthly payment. Add lines 33a through 33d.	$ 175.00	Copy total here ➜	$ 175.00

34. Are any debts that you listed in line 33 secured by your primary residence, a vehicle, or other property necessary for your support or the support of your dependents?

☐ No. Go to line 35.
☑ Yes. State any amount that you must pay to a creditor, in addition to the payments listed in line 33, to keep possession of your property (called the *cure amount*). Next, divide by 60 and fill in the information below.

Name of the creditor	Identify property that secures the debt	Total cure amount		Monthly cure amount
Lannister Credit	2015 Westeros	$ 700.00	÷ 60 =	$ 11.66
_____	_____	$_____	÷ 60 =	$_____
_____	_____	$_____	÷ 60 =	+ $_____
		Total		$ 11.66

| | | | | $ 11.66 | Copy total here ➜ | $ 11.66 |

35. Do you owe any priority claims such as a priority tax, child support, or alimony — that are past due as of the filing date of your bankruptcy case? 11 U.S.C. § 507.

☐ No. Go to line 36.
☑ Yes. Fill in the total amount of all of these priority claims. Do not include current or ongoing priority claims, such as those you listed in line 19.

Total amount of all past-due priority claims	$ 5,000.00	÷ 60 =	$ 83.33

Description

This portion of the form accounts for a debtor's repayment of secured debt that is contractually due, arrears on secured debt obligations, the payment of priority claims, and the hypothetical payment to a Chapter 13 trustee. The first three are formulaic as set forth in 11 U.S.C.

§707(b)(2)(A)(iii). The last is set forth at 11 U.S.C. §707(b)(2)(A)(ii)(III). See chapters 6, 21, and 24 supra. All of these obligations would have to be paid if the case were a Chapter 13 case. See chapter 24 supra.

Line 33 simply transcribes the average monthly mortgage or vehicle payment reported at line 13 above. Recall that these amounts were deducted from the allowable IRS expense deductions to avoid double counting. Now, they are included. A copy of the debtor's contract, or a payment ticket for a monthly payment should provide the amount of monthly payment and the number of payments remaining. The Bottom-lines' monthly payment is $350. There are 30 payments left and they are two payments behind. For line 33b, multiply $350 by the remaining 30 payments. The result of $10,500 is divided by 60. The amount of $175 is placed at lines 33b. Observe that this is the same amount deducted from the vehicle ownership expense at line 13b. This is necessary to avoid duplicating the expense. See chapter 6D supra.

Line 33d identifies any other secured creditor, the creditor's collateral, and the average payment for the next 60 months. Note that no information has been provided about the payments to El Repo Finance Company. The practitioner would need to obtain the appropriate information to claim this deduction.

Line 34 deducts payments necessary to cure secured debt payments that are in arrears pursuant to an identical formula. Take the amount of the arrears and divide by 60. The answer is placed at line 34 as to Lannister Credit. Observe that the debtors are only permitted to deduct cure payments on secured debt reasonably necessary for the support of the debtor. For example, if the Bottomlines owned a jet ski and were behind on the payments, the cure amounts may not be a permissible expense.

> ***Do the Cashes have any secured debts that are in arrears? Are they reasonably necessary to support the debtors?***

Line 35 permits deductions for the repayment of priority debt. See chapter 21 supra. The Bottomlines owe $5,000 in taxes for 2015. This amount is divided by 60 and the answer is entered on line 35. If there were other priority claims, each would be totaled up and the total divided by 60.

> ***Recall that we previously determined that the Cashes had several priority unsecured debts.***

36. **Are you eligible to file a case under Chapter 13?** 11 U.S.C. § 109(e).
   For more information, go online using the link for *Bankruptcy Basics* specified in the separate
   instructions for this form. *Bankruptcy Basics* may also be available at the bankruptcy clerk's office.

   ☐ No. Go to line 37.

   ☑ Yes. Fill in the following information.

Projected monthly plan payment if you were filing under Chapter 13	$_____ 0	
Current multiplier for your district as stated on the list issued by the Administrative Office of the United States Courts (for districts in Alabama and North Carolina) or by the Executive Office for United States Trustees (for all other districts).	x 5.80	
To find a list of district multipliers that includes your district, go online using the link specified in the separate instructions for this form. This list may also be available at the bankruptcy clerk's office.		
Average monthly administrative expense if you were filing under Chapter 13	$_____ 0.00 Copy total here➜	$____ 0.00

37. **Add all of the deductions for debt payment.**
   Add lines 33e through 36. .... $ 269.99

Total Deductions from Income

38. **Add all of the allowed deductions.**

Copy line 24, *All of the expenses allowed under IRS expense allowances*	$____ 7,476.00	
Copy line 32, *All of the additional expense deductions*	$____ 300.00	
Copy line 37, *All of the deductions for debt payment*	+ $____ 269.99	
Total deductions	$____ 8,045.99 Copy total here ....➜	$ 8,045.99

Part 3:	**Determine Whether There Is a Presumption of Abuse**

39. **Calculate monthly disposable income for 60 months**

39a.	Copy line 4, *adjusted current monthly income*	$____ 7,000.00	
39b.	Copy line 38, *Total deductions*	− $____ 8,045.99	
39c.	Monthly disposable income. 11 U.S.C. § 707(b)(2). Subtract line 39b from line 39a.	$____ -1,045.99 Copy here➜	$____ -1,045.99
	For the next 60 months (5 years).................................		x 60
39d.	**Total.** Multiply line 39c by 60.	$ -62,759.40 Copy here➜	$ -62,759.40

40. **Find out whether there is a presumption of abuse.** Check the box that applies:

   ☑ **The line 39d is less than $7,700*.** On the top of page 1 of this form, check box 1, *There is no presumption of abuse.* Go
   to Part 5.

   ☐ **The line 39d is more than $12,850*.** On the top of page 1 of this form, check box 2, *There is a presumption of abuse.* You
   may fill out Part 4 if you claim special circumstances. Then go to Part 5.

   ☐ **The line 39d is at least $7,700*, but not more than $12,850*.** Go to line 41.

   * Subject to adjustment on 4/01/19, and every 3 years after that for cases filed on or after the date of adjustment.

Description

Line 36 computes a hypothetical monthly payment to a Chapter 13 trustee for a hypothetical five-year Chapter 13 plan. The administrative multiplier for each district is found on the United States Trustee website: http://www.usdoj.gov/ust. The administrative multiplier for the Southern

District of California as of May 1, 2016, is 5.8 percent. To make this cal-culation, however, requires completion of Part 3.

Line 37 totals lines 33 through 36.

Line 38 is the grand total of the debtor's allowable deductions.

G.   DETERMINING WHETHER THE PRESUMPTION ARISES

Part 3 of Official Form B122A-2 provides the final calculations that deter-mine whether or not a debtor's case is or is not presumed abuse.

Line 39a is the current monthly income amount from line 4. Line 39b is the total of all deductions that appears on line 38. Line 39c is the result of subtracting line 39b from line 39a, which for the Bottomlines is a negative amount. When the amount is negative or zero, insert 0 or the negative number in line 50. Multiply the amount in line 50 times 60 to determine how much the debtor can pay over 60 months. When the amount is negative or zero, insert 0 or the negative number in line 39d.

To complete line 36, the hypothetical payment to a Chapter 13 trustee, use the amount appearing in line 39c multiplied by the adminis-trative expense multiplier. For the Bottomlines, the amount will be zero.

Line 40 reports the results in terms of the statutory means testing formula. If the amount on line 39d is less than $7,700, then abuse is not presumed. This is the result for the Bottomlines. If the result is greater than $12,850, then abuse is presumed regardless of the percentage of debt that the Bottomlines can repay.

__What would be the results for the Cashes?__

FACT PATTERN

---

41. 41a. **Fill in the amount of your total nonpriority unsecured debt.** If you filled out *A Summary of Your Assets and Liabilities and Certain Statistical Information Schedules* (Official Form 106Sum), you may refer to line 3b on that form.. $ 36,000.00

                                                                                             x   .25

      41b. **25% of your total nonpriority unsecured debt.** 11 U.S.C. § 707(b)(2)(A)(i)(I).
           Multiply line 41a by 0.25. .... $ 9,000.00 | Copy here➔ | $ 9,000.00

42. **Determine whether the income you have left over after subtracting all allowed deductions is enough to pay 25% of your unsecured, nonpriority debt.**
    Check the box that applies:

    ☑ **Line 39d is less than line 41b.** On the top of page 1 of this form, check box 1, *There is no presumption of abuse.* Go to Part 5.

    ☐ **Line 39d is equal to or more than line 41b.** On the top of page 1 of this form, check box 2, *There is a presumption of abuse.* You may fill out Part 4 if you claim special circumstances. Then go to Part 5.

Part 4:   Give Details About Special Circumstances

43. **Do you have any special circumstances that justify additional expenses or adjustments of current monthly income for which there is no reasonable alternative?** 11 U.S.C. § 707(b)(2)(B).

☐ No. Go to Part 5.

☐ Yes. Fill in the following information. All figures should reflect your average monthly expense or income adjustment for each item. You may include expenses you listed in line 25.

You must give a detailed explanation of the special circumstances that make the expenses or income adjustments necessary and reasonable. You must also give your case trustee documentation of your actual expenses or income adjustments.

Give a detailed explanation of the special circumstances	Average monthly expense or income adjustment
_____	$_____
_____	$_____
_____	$_____
_____	$_____

Part 5:   Sign Below

By signing here, I declare under penalty of perjury that the information on this statement and in any attachments is true and correct.

✗ _____   ✗ _____
   Signature of Debtor 1   Signature of Debtor 2

Date _____   Date _____
     MM / DD   / YYYY   MM / DD   / YYYY

Description

If the result on line 39d is at least $7,700 but less than $12,850, then abuse is presumed only if the percentage that would be repaid to unsecured creditors is at least 25 percent. This calculation is performed on line 41. The Bottomlines' total unsecured debt, for example, is $36,000. Twenty-five percent of this amount is $9,000, an amount that triggers the presumption of abuse without regard to the percentage of debt repaid. Assume, however, that the Bottomlines' unsecured debt was only

$30,000. Twenty-five percent of this amount is $7,500. If the formula determines that they can pay at least $125 per month, then abuse would be presumed.

Part 4 of Official Form B122A-2 provides the opportunity for a debtor to assert additional expense claims that are required for the health and welfare of the debtor or the debtor's family. For example, joint debtors are forced for reasons beyond their control to maintain two households for employment purposes. The additional expenses may be allowable here.[9]

Observe that no abuse is presumed for the Bottomlines because they cannot repay their creditors pursuant to the formula. In common parlance, the Bottomlines have passed the means test. However, also observe that the result of subtracting their Schedule J expenses from their Schedule I income revealed surplus monthly income of $1,125 (see chapter 30 supra). "Passing" the means test only means that abuse is not presumed. If there is a significant amount of actual surplus monthly income appearing on Schedule J, the Bottomlines might be susceptible to a motion for abuse based on the totality of circumstances pursuant to 11 U.S.C. §707(b)(3). See chapter 6E supra.

Summary

Since its introduction in late 2005, means testing has become ubiquitous in individual bankruptcy cases. Proper preparation of the means testing form is as germane to the case as is proper preparation of the Statements and Schedules. As with the Statements and Schedules, proper preparation will minimize inquiries from the case trustee or United States Trustee and will help make a debtor's experience with the bankruptcy system as uneventful as possible.

Understanding that means testing is, ultimately, nothing more than a formula will help to keep the form and its required disclosures in proper perspective.

Just as with the Statements and Schedules, every line of the applicable form must be completed, or the blank spot will result in additional questioning at the meeting of creditors and might require the filing of an amended form. Doing it right the first time will save work in the long run.

A paralegal will also want to make sure that there is sufficient detail in the file to corroborate the debtor's current monthly income, debts, and assets. Copies of the debtor's most recent pay stubs, for example, should be in the file. A copy of a bill from each creditor, including payoff amounts

---

9. In re Graham, 363 B.R. 844 (Bankr. S.D. Ohio 2007).

to secured creditors, and/or a copy of a current credit report should be obtained from the debtor. Copies of all relevant tax returns that a trustee may request should also be obtained. All the debtor's payment advices for the six months preceding the filing should also be maintained. On this last point, when the debtor's current monthly income exceeds the applicable median, the debtor will almost always be required to submit payment advices for the entire six-month period to the United States Trustee.

DISCUSSION QUESTIONS

1. What are the concerns of a debtor in effective preparation of the means testing forms?

2. What are the concerns of a trustee or creditor in effective review of the means testing forms?

32

Researching Bankruptcy Issues

Learning Objectives

■ Identify basic bankruptcy research sources and suggest a methodology for their use

A. TRADITIONAL METHODS

It is impossible for any member of the legal profession to know all of the law: There is simply too much law to know. As a result, the ability to conduct efficient, accurate, and speedy research is a fundamental skill for anyone involved in the legal profession. Knowing where to look for the answer to a question is a paramount concern. No study of the bankruptcy system can be complete without providing a useful method for researching bankruptcy issues. Fortunately, because the Bankruptcy Code is designed to be a self-contained system, an effective methodology for approaching the research of a bankruptcy issue is relatively easy to formulate. The sources described below, used in the order of their description, should produce an answer to even the most complex issue at a minimum of time and effort.

The primary source for answering all bankruptcy questions is the Bankruptcy Code itself.[1] Most basic bankruptcy questions can be answered correctly simply by finding the right Code section.

---

1. U.S.C., Title 11.

The Code is well indexed, and by following the systems approach of this text any practitioner should generally have an easy time establishing a reference point in the Code to commence researching an issue.

It is also important to note a critical difference in statutory research versus research of other sources. Each word of a statute, and often each punctuation mark, has meaning and significance. Each word must be understood to comprehend the full meaning of any Code provision. Careful reading is thus the most useful tool in conducting effective research of this sort.

At the end of each Code section, there is text normally entitled "Historical and Revision Notes." The Historical and Revision Notes contain a capsule description of a particular Code section's legislative history, including the section's derivation from any predecessor section under the Bankruptcy Act. Leading court decisions that interpreted any predecessor Bankruptcy Act section are often referred to in these notes. The analysis discusses the rationale of the cited cases and attempts to indicate if the Code intends to follow or modify the prior law. The analysis is helpful in interpreting the meaning of a particular provision. The Historical and Revision Notes are a valuable secondary source of finding answers to bankruptcy questions. Because these notes are included in many published editions of the Bankruptcy Code, one does not need a second volume to locate them.

The Bankruptcy Code defines the collective rules regulating the collection and distribution of assets to creditors in a bankruptcy proceeding. The Code directs what may or may not be done in a bankruptcy proceeding. However, the Code often does not direct how to implement or use a Code provision within the bankruptcy system. To direct the implementation of a Code provision in the bankruptcy system, the Administrative Office of the United States Courts, in conjunction with the United States Supreme Court, has formulated the "Rules of Practice and Procedure in Bankruptcy," commonly known as the Federal Rules of Bankruptcy Procedure. The Federal Rules of Bankruptcy Procedure direct the method of doing things in a bankruptcy proceeding: What information is required in a form? What should the form look like? How is a motion filed and when? How and when is a creditor claim filed? And so forth. Many basic questions of actual practice that are not contained in the Code are answered by the Federal Rules of Bankruptcy Procedure. The rules should never be overlooked when seeking the answer to a bankruptcy question, particularly a "how to" question.[2]

---

2. 28 U.S.C. §2075. Federal Rules of Bankruptcy Procedure.

Appended to the Federal Rules of Bankruptcy Procedure is a group of forms called "Official and Procedural Bankruptcy Forms." The Official Forms provide guidance as to the content and appearance of the included documents.

In addition to the Federal Rules of Bankruptcy Procedure, each Bankruptcy Court has the power to formulate its own local rules and local forms as long as they are not inconsistent with the Code or the Bankruptcy Rules. Many Bankruptcy Courts have devised their own local rules and local forms, and other Bankruptcy Courts have not. Local rules vary from district to district and can sometimes be the source of answering a practice or procedure question. In addition to local Bankruptcy Court rules, each federal District Court has its own local rules. These also may sometimes help in answering a procedural question. The guidelines of any applicable United States Trustee office will also prove helpful.[3]

The Bankruptcy Courts are a part of the federal court system. The Federal Rules of Civil Procedure and the Federal Rules of Evidence apply in bankruptcy proceedings.

Practice Pointer

Not all of the Federal Rules of Civil Procedure apply to a bankruptcy proceeding. The Bankruptcy Rules specifically cite which rules and which portions of those rules apply in bankruptcy cases.

There are several reporter systems that publish only bankruptcy cases. Cases decided by Bankruptcy Courts, district courts, courts of appeal, and the Supreme Court that relate solely to bankruptcy and bankruptcy-related issues are contained within these reporter systems. The largest reporter system is called the Bankruptcy Reporter and is published by West Publishing Company. Another reporter system is called Bankruptcy Court Decisions (BCD), which is published by CRR Publishing Company. Many of the cases reported in BCD are also included in the Bankruptcy Reporter, but sometimes a case will appear in one system and not in the other. It is acceptable to cite from either set of reporters when writing a brief for a Bankruptcy Court. Sometimes the BCD will release a case before it appears in the Bankruptcy Reporter and vice versa. Collier also publishes a reporter system called Collier Bankruptcy Cases. Many of these

---

3. See chapter 10 supra.

reporter systems have also been incorporated into computer research databases such as LexisNexis or Westlaw.

In addition, there are simplified methods of conducting bankruptcy research through the use of specialized treatises. The bankruptcy system has its own separate treatises. The most commonly used and cited treatise on bankruptcy is Collier on Bankruptcy.[4] Collier's is a multivolume work, organized such that a chapter number in Collier's corresponds to the same numbered Bankruptcy Code section. Thus, Chapter 521 in Collier's corresponds precisely to Section 521 of the Bankruptcy Code. If you want to find the answer to an issue involving exemptions, which is Section 522 of the Bankruptcy Code, you simply look in Chapter 522 of Collier's. There are several other major treatises, but Collier's is cited in court opinions more frequently than any other major work.[5] The publishers of Collier's also publish a major set of practice forms and guides entitled the Collier Bankruptcy Practice Guide. The Guide contains detailed practice tools and sample pleading forms, among other things.

Often a bankruptcy issue will be determined based on existing non-bankruptcy state or federal law. In these situations, one will have to make use of traditional research sources and methods outside the bankruptcy system.

The above are the primary sources of researching a bankruptcy issue, starting with the Code and continuing to the reporter systems. With this relatively small nucleus of materials reviewed in the order described in the checklist accompanying this chapter, most bankruptcy questions can be answered effectively, efficiently, and rapidly.

B.   THE INTERNET

The evolution of the Internet from the mid-1990s, has transformed accessibility to both legal and factual information to assist in conducting legal research or in investigating facts. The availability of online computer research facilities such as Westlaw or LexisNexis makes legal source materials more accessible but does not necessarily make the task of finding applicable case law any easier unless the researcher knows to search under an appropriate word, phrase, or statute.

---

4. Resnick & Sommers, editors-in-chief, Collier on Bankruptcy (16th ed. rev. 2016) (hereafter Collier's).
5. E.g., Norton Bankruptcy Law and Practice 3d (2016).

To this extent, the above methodology can also be used in computer research. First, input the precise Code section or Rule that is the subject of your inquiry. Then narrow your search by selecting an appropriate word or phrase in the universe of cases you have located by Code section. For example, assume that you need to research an issue of the effect of oral misrepresentations in dischargeability litigation (see chapter 13 supra). A word search combining the phrase "oral misrepresentation" and the word "dischargeability" appearing in the same paragraph will be likely to produce a myriad of potentially relevant cases.

In addition to enhancing legal research, the Internet provides an array of bankruptcy research access tools to the fingertips of any person with online access. Many professional bankruptcy organizations have their own websites, the most notable being that for the American Bankruptcy Institute (www.abiworld.org). This site will give you daily news and report important case and legislative developments. The Federal Judiciary Home Page (www.uscourts.gov) will allow you to access any Bankruptcy Court that has created its own website. You can find your local court and place it on your Favorites menu.

> ### *Practice Pointer*
> It is important to remember, however, that all Internet sites are not created equally. It is very important, particularly when looking at Code sections online, to make sure that you are looking at a current version of the statute. Because the Official Forms went through a major revision effective December 1, 2015 and many of the numerical values in the Code were revised effective April 1, 2016, your information could easily be out of date.

Federal Rule of Bankruptcy Procedure 9036 authorizes local rules to permit electronic transmission of notices and documents. Many Bankruptcy Courts now require electronic filing of petitions, a practice that will become commonplace in the near future. All Bankruptcy Courts are being gradually incorporated into what is known as the Electronic Case Filing (ECF) system. Under ECF, all pleadings are filed electronically with the Bankruptcy Court online. All documents filed with a court that has adopted ECF are accessible to attorneys who enroll in the ECF system. Parties in interest may register to receive notices of all pleadings filed in a particular case, making service of process virtually instantaneous.

Use of the Internet is important to comply with the requirements of means testing (see chapter 6 supra) and the other filing requirements imposed by the 2005 legislation. With respect to means testing, the Internet is essential to remain current with the official state median family income and the various IRS expense standards applied in computing the formula. Current links necessary for means testing compliance are located at www.usdoj.gov/ust. Additionally, as counsel's duty of reasonable investigation required by Section 707(b)(4) evolves, the Internet provides rapid access to a debtor's current credit report and sites that provide valuation data for used vehicles (e.g., NADA.com). The Internet also contains websites for approved prepetition credit counselors and postpetition financial management courses required to obtain a discharge in individual cases, as described in chapters 5 and 14 supra.

CHAPTER 32 CHECKLIST

32.1   BANKRUPTCY RESEARCH CHECKLIST
     32.1.1   Bankruptcy Code
     32.1.2   Historical and Revision Notes
     32.1.3   Federal Rules of Bankruptcy Procedure
     32.1.4   Local Rules, Including United States Trustee Guidelines
     32.1.5   Federal Rules of Civil Procedure, Federal Rules of Evidence
     32.1.6   Bankruptcy Reporter Systems
     32.1.7   Bankruptcy Treatises

DISCUSSION QUESTIONS

1. What are the basic resources to utilize in researching a bankruptcy issue?

2. Describe the role that computers can play in conducting bankruptcy research.

Appendix

Noticed Motions and Ex Parte Applications

Common Ex Parte Applications

Application	Code Section or FRBP
Payments to trustees	§1326
Joint Administration	FRBP 1015
Debtor requested conversion	§§706(a), 1112(a), 1208(a), 1307(a)
Debtor requested dismissal	§§1208(b), 1307(b)
Extensions of time	FRBP 9006b
Rule 2004 examinations	FRBP 2004
Deferral of entry of discharge	FRBP 4004(c)
Reopening a closed case	§350(b)
Conditional approval of disclosure statement	§1125; FRBP 3017.1

Common Noticed Motions

Motion	Code Section or FRBP
Dismissal of Chapter 7 as abuse	§707(b)
Compensation of professionals	§§326, 330, 331; FRBP 2016
Enforcement of bankruptcy petition preparer rules	§110

Motion	*Code Section or FRBP*
Dismissal in best interests of creditors	§305
Motion to avoid lien	§522(f)
Objection to claim of exemptions	§522(c); FRBP 4003(d)
Appointment of trustee in involuntary case	§303(g); FRBP 2001
Motion for relief from the automatic stay	§362(d); FRBP 4001
Turnover from debtor	§542; FRBP 7001(1)
Sales of property of $2,500 or more and when there is no co-owner	§363; FRBP 6004
Motion to use cash collateral	§363(c)
Motion to sell property free and clear of liens	§363(f); FRBP 6004(c)
Motion to assume or reject executory contract or unexpired lease	§365; FRBP 6006
Motion to compel abandonment	§554; FRBP 6007
Objection to claim	§502; FRBP 3007
Payment of administrative expenses	§503(a)
Valuation hearing	§506
Motion to dismiss/convert	§1112, 1307
Approval of insider compensation in Chapter 11 cases	FRBP 9014(a)
Extend or reduce exclusivity	§1121
Chapter 11 confirmation hearing	§1128

Note: A noticed motion must normally be served on all creditors, the trustee, and the United States Trustee, except for motions for relief from the automatic stay, which generally require service only upon the debtor, trustee, and any other party with an interest in any property subject to the motion (such as a junior mortgage). An ex parte application is normally served only upon the trustee and the United States Trustee and any party that has requested notice. In all situations, readers should consult any applicable local rules.

Glossary

This glossary has been designed to accomplish two goals. The first is to define basic bankruptcy terms in as succinct a manner as possible. The second is to treat the glossary as a mini-index. At the end of each definition one or more numbers will appear in parentheses. The numbers correspond to the chapter or chapters of the text that contain the primary discussion of the term or phrase defined.

abandon—to remove from property of an estate assets that are burdensome or of inconsequential value to the estate. An asset with no equity or a personal injury claim that has no merit are common examples. Abandonment is governed by Section 554 of the Bankruptcy Code. (21)

absolute priority rule—prohibition against confirmation of a Chapter 11 reorganization plan if junior classes will receive dividends or retain interests where one or more senior classes are not paid in full and have rejected the plan. (27)

accrual method—an accounting method that measures all financial transactions of an entity. A debt owed is an accrued expense. An account receivable is accrued income. (25)

adequate assurance—providing the equivalent of *adequate protection* to the nondebtor party of an executory contract subject to Bankruptcy Code Section 365. A trustee or debtor-in-possession assuming an executory contract must provide the nondebtor party to the contract with adequate assurance of future performance. An assignee of an executory contract must also provide adequate assurance of future performance. Providing adequate assurance includes curing existing defaults and convincing the creditor and the court that future performance will be rendered by the debtor. (20)

adequate protection—a method of protecting a creditor's interest in property of the estate during pendency of the automatic stay. The making of periodic payments or the providing of additional or replacement collateral are methods of adequate protection. Section 361 statutorily defines adequate protection. (13)

Administrative consolidation—when the court consolidates two or more proceedings for less than all purposes. (4)

administrative expenses—generally, all expenses incurred by a bankruptcy estate after a bankruptcy filing. Trustee's fees, auctioneer fees, attorneys' fees, and postpetition rent are common Chapter 7 administrative expenses. (11, 22)

adversary proceeding—a separate lawsuit filed in connection with a bankruptcy proceeding. For example, an action to set aside a preference is commenced as an adversary proceeding. A contested motion will be treated as an adversary proceeding pursuant to Federal Rule of Bankruptcy Procedure 9014. (14)

affiliate—a nondebtor entity owning or controlling 20 percent or more interest in a debtor, or a debtor entity owning or controlling 20 percent or more interest in a nondebtor entity. Section 101(2) of the Bankruptcy Code defines affiliate. (7)

"after notice and a hearing"—a phrase statutorily defined in Section 102(1) of the Bankruptcy Code. Use of this or a similar phrase in any Bankruptcy Code provision triggers the notice requirements of Section 102(1), as placed into practice by Federal Rules of Bankruptcy Procedure 2002 and 9006. Generally, 24-day notice by mail to all creditors and parties in interest is necessary to properly accomplish many bankruptcy procedures. (5)

alleged debtor—the debtor in an involuntary proceeding. (4)

allowed claim—a claim entitled to receive a dividend from a bankruptcy estate. (22)

antecedent debt—a debt incurred or existing before the making of a transfer. (17)

Anti-Assignment Act—a federal statute, 41 U.S.C. §15, that prohibits the assignment of a federal government contract except upon the government's consent. (20)

applicable commitment period—the required length of time for a Chapter 13 repayment plan, dependent upon whether or not the debtor's income is higher or lower than the state median family income. If equal to or higher, the period is five years. If lower, the period is three years. (24)

assignment for the benefit of creditors—the assignment of assets to a third party, in trust, to sell the assets and apply the proceeds to the payment of creditor claims. (2)

assisted person—any person whose debts are primarily consumer debts and whose nonexempt assets are less than $192,450 pursuant to 11 U.S.C. §101(3). Assisted persons are entitled to written retainer agreements and prepetition written disclosures from Debt Relief Agencies pursuant to 11 U.S.C. §§527 and 528. (4)

automatic stay—a statutory bar to the conducting of any collection activity by creditors after a bankruptcy petition has been filed. All litigation involving the debtor as a defendant is stayed. Foreclosures and repossessions are stayed. A creditor may seek relief from the stay in some situations. The automatic stay is one of the three major elements of debtor relief provided by the Bankruptcy Code and is the subject of Bankruptcy Code Section 362. (8, 13)

avoidable preference—a prepetition transfer of estate property in full or partial payment of an antecedent debt, subject to the trustee's avoiding powers. Avoidable preferences are the subject of Bankruptcy Code Section 547. (17)

avoiding powers—the right of a trustee to set aside certain pre- or postfiling transactions that might otherwise be valid under nonbankruptcy law. Preferences, fraudulent transfers, and the ability to set aside unauthorized postpetition transfers are the most common avoiding powers. (15-16)

Bankruptcy Abuse Prevention Consumer Protection Act of 2005 (BAPCPA)—"BAPCPA" is the acronym most commonly used to identify the 2005 amendments to the Bankruptcy Code. (2)

Bankruptcy Act—the name of the bankruptcy laws in effect in the United States between 1898 and September 30, 1979. (1)

bankruptcy alternatives—assignments for the benefits of creditors and composition agreements. (2)

bankruptcy assistance—goods or services provided to an assisted person for the purpose of providing advice, counsel, document preparation, or court appearance in a bankruptcy proceeding. Section 101(4A) of the Bankruptcy Code defines bankruptcy assistance. (4)

Bankruptcy Code—the name of the bankruptcy laws in effect in the United States since October 1, 1979. (2)

bankruptcy petition preparer—a person other than an attorney or an attorney's employee who prepares for compensation a document for filing with the Bankruptcy Court. An unsupervised paralegal may be a bankruptcy petition preparer. Bankruptcy petition preparers are the subject of Bankruptcy Code Section 110. (8)

bankruptcy proceeding—a bankruptcy case filed pursuant to a particular Chapter of the Bankruptcy Code. Bankruptcy proceedings are Chapter 7 liquidations and the various reorganization proceedings provided for by Chapters 9, 11, 12, and 13, as well as cross-border insolvencies under Chapter 15. (2)

bankruptcy systems—the methods developed by societies to resolve the effects of financial crisis between debtors and creditors. (1)

"best interests of creditors" test—The Chapter 11 confirmation requirement that a class of claims receive at least what it would receive if the case were a Chapter 7. (27)

capital asset—an asset used to operate a business, such as equipment or fixtures. (19)

cash accounting—an accounting method that measures the cash transactions (income and expenses) of an entity. (25)

cash collateral—cash, or its equivalent, in which a secured creditor may have an interest. Section 363(c) of the Bankruptcy Code restricts the use of cash collateral absent court approval. (19)

catch-all exemption—consists of any unused portion of federal homestead exemption up to $13,100 in any property of any kind. (10)

Chapter—a specific statutory division of the Bankruptcy Code. Three Chapters contain general rules applicable in all bankruptcy proceedings (1, 3, 5). The remaining six Chapters comprise the specific types of bankruptcy proceedings (7, 9, 11, 12, 13, 15). (2)

Chapter 7—a bankruptcy proceeding in which a debtor seeks to have nonexempt assets liquidated for the payment of dividends to creditors. Chapter 7 is the most common bankruptcy proceeding. (2, 4, 8)

Chapter 11—a reorganization proceeding available to any debtor qualified to be a Chapter 7 debtor. Chapter 11 is the most complex, time-consuming, and expensive of all bankruptcy proceedings. The goal of a Chapter 11 debtor-in-possession is to obtain confirmation of a reorganization plan, a judicially approved composition agreement. (1, 2, 25–27)

Chapter 13—a reorganization proceeding available for individuals with regular income whose unsecured debt is less than $383,175 and whose secured debt is less than $1,149,525. Chapter 13 is the most commonly filed reorganization proceeding. (24)

claim—a right to payment of any kind or a right to performance that may be compensated by damages. Section 101(5) of the Bankruptcy Code defines claim. (7)

claims bar date—a deadline set in a bankruptcy proceeding for creditors to file claims. A claim not filed before expiration of a claims bar date is subordinated to all timely-filed claims. (22)

claims docket—an itemized summary of creditor claims filed in a bankruptcy proceeding. (23)

collateral—an interest in property or other rights held by a secured creditor to secure repayment of a debt. For example, real property is normally collateral for a mortgage or deed of trust. (13, 22)

community claim—a claim enforceable against community property under nonbankruptcy law. Section 101(7) of the Bankruptcy Code defines community claim. (7)

Complaint to Determine Discharge — an adversary proceeding initiated by a trustee or an interested party to entirely avoid a debtor's discharge. Time limitations are found in Fed. R. Bankr. P. 4004. (14)

Complaint to Determine Dischargeability of a Debt — an adversary proceeding initiated by a creditor or debtor to determine the dischargeability of a specific debt pursuant to Bankruptcy Code Section 523(c). A creditor must initiate such a complaint within 60 days of the date first set for the creditors' meeting. A debtor may initiate such a complaint at any time. Time limitations are found in Fed. R. Bankr. P. 4007. (14)

composition agreement — an agreement between a debtor and multiple creditors for the repayment of debt. The various reorganization proceedings of the Bankruptcy Code (Chapters 9, 11, 12, and 13) are judicially approved composition agreements. (1, 2)

confirmation — the act of obtaining court approval of a reorganization plan in the reorganization proceedings of Chapters 9, 11, 12, or 13. A confirmed reorganization plan creates a new binding contract between the debtor and all creditors. (24)

confirmation packet — a group of documents, including a Plan of Reorganization and a Disclosure Statement, that are sent to creditors when authorized to solicit votes for or against a Chapter 11 plan. (26)

consideration — the element of exchange in any contract. (17)

consolidation — a merger, by court order, of two or more related bankruptcy proceedings. Other than a husband and wife, who may file a joint case, consolidation is the only way in which multiple debtors may have their bankruptcy proceedings administered as if they were one debtor. Consolidation can be **substantive**, for all purposes; or, **procedural**, for limited purposes. Consolidation is the subject of Federal Rule of Bankruptcy Procedure 1015. (4)

consumer no asset bankruptcy — a Chapter 7 bankruptcy proceeding for an individual in which there are normally no assets available for distribution to creditors. A consumer no asset bankruptcy is the most common and simplest of all bankruptcy proceedings. (8)

contemporaneous exchange — the presence of consideration in the transfer of property from a debtor to a creditor. A contemporaneous exchange for new value is a defense to a *preference* claim by the trustee. (17)

contested matter — an opposed motion. A contested matter is treated as an adversary proceeding pursuant to Federal Rule of Bankruptcy Procedure 9014. A contested matter is resolved by way of an evidentiary hearing. (14)

convenience class — a group of unsecured claims treated as a class for administrative convenience in a Chapter 11 reorganization plan. A convenience class may receive treatment that the Bankruptcy Code would otherwise prohibit. (26)

conversion — the act of converting a bankruptcy proceeding from one Chapter to another. A typical scenario is a failed reorganization proceeding under Chapter 11 or 13 converted to a liquidation case under Chapter 7. (9, 24)

core proceeding — a matter arising before a Bankruptcy Court that involves the specific application of a Bankruptcy Code provision for its resolution. Bankruptcy Judges have jurisdiction over core proceedings, as described in 28 U.S.C. §157. For example, an action to avoid a preference is a core proceeding. (29)

cramdown — the act of obtaining confirmation of a reorganization plan over the objection of creditors. Different tests or procedures may be utilized to effectuate a cramdown on either secured or unsecured creditors. (24)

Credit bid — the right of a secured creditor to use the debt to bid on the purchase of property. (19)

credit counseling agency — an agency approved by the United States Trustee pursuant to 11 U.S.C. §111, to provide prepetition credit counseling to consumer debtors. (4)

creditor — an entity with a claim arising before the filing of a bankruptcy petition. Section 101(10) of the Bankruptcy Code defines creditor. An entity that a debt is owed to is a creditor. (2, 7)

creditors' meeting — a mandatory hearing, held within 40 days after the entry of an order for relief in any Chapter proceeding. At the meeting of creditors, the trustee and creditors may examine the debtor regarding the assets and liabilities of the bankruptcy estate. Section 341(a) of the Bankruptcy Code mandates the meeting of creditors. (8)

current monthly income — the monthly income of a consumer debtor generally determined by the average of income received from all sources in the six months preceding the filing of a bankruptcy petition, as described in 11 U.S.C. §101(10A). Current monthly income is a key element in determining whether or not a consumer debtor is abusing Chapter 7 pursuant to needs based bankruptcy. (6, 7, 31)

custodian — a third party appointed to administer a debtor's assets under nonbankruptcy law. A court-appointed receiver or assignee for the benefit of creditors are examples of custodians. This term distinguishes bankruptcy trustees from nonbankruptcy fiduciaries. Section 101(11) of the Bankruptcy Code defines custodian. (7, 15)

debt — a liability upon a claim. Section 101(12) of the Bankruptcy Code defines debt. (7)

debt collection — the process of collecting a debt. (1)

debt relief agency—a bankruptcy attorney or bankruptcy petition preparer and any person providing bankruptcy assistance to assisted persons for money or other valuable consideration pursuant to 11 U.S.C. §101(12A). Debt Relief Agencies are subject to written retainer and disclosure requirements of 11 U.S.C. §§527 and 528. (4, 7)

debtor—an entity that owes a debt. The entity filing a voluntary bankruptcy proceeding or against whom an order for relief is entered in an involuntary bankruptcy is known as the debtor. Section 101(13) of the Bankruptcy Code defines debtor. (2)

debtor-in-possession—the fiduciary entity created by a debtor filing a Chapter 11 reorganization proceeding. (8, 11, 25)

debtor relief—what an individual filing personal bankruptcy seeks: a discharge, exemptions, and the benefits of the automatic stay. (1)

disallowed claim—a claim not entitled to receive a dividend from a bankruptcy estate. (22)

discharge—legal relief from personal obligation to satisfy a debt. The subject of Section 524 of the Bankruptcy Code. The discharge is one of the three elements of debtor relief provided for in the Bankruptcy Code, the other two being exemptions and the automatic stay. In certain defined instances a debtor may not be entitled to a discharge. (1, 8)

dischargeable debt—a debt subject to a debtor's discharge. The discharge relieves a debtor from personal liability for the debt. (8, 14)

disclosure statement—a document filed in a Chapter 11 proceeding that describes a debtor-in-possession's reorganization plan, its effect upon the creditors, the ability of the plan to be performed, and a comparison of the reorganization plan's repayment proposal to the results likely to be obtained in a Chapter 7 proceeding for the same debtor. The creditors of a Chapter 11 debtor-in-possession may not vote for or against the reorganization plan until the court approves the contents of the disclosure statement at a disclosure statement hearing. (26, 27)

disinterested person—the subject of Bankruptcy Code Section 101(14). A person who is not creditor, equity security holder, or insider, or who does not have an interest materially adverse to an estate. Only disinterested persons may be employed by a bankruptcy estate or debtor-in-possession. (8)

dismissal—the act of terminating a bankruptcy proceeding, the general effect of which is to restore the parties to their rights and liabilities as they existed prior to the bankruptcy filing. (9, 24)

disposable income—all income not necessary for the maintenance or support of the debtor or a dependent of the debtor. (24)

domestic support obligation — obligations for alimony, support, or maintenance, regardless of when incurred. Section 101(14A) of the Bankruptcy Code defines domestic support obligation. (7)

due process — notice and an opportunity to be heard. (5)

effective date of the plan — a specific date upon which performance of a Chapter 11 plan begins. This date may be a specific date upon which a defined event occurs, such as an order of confirmation becoming final. (26)

Electronic Case Filing (ECF) — the name for online filing of documents with the bankruptcy court and accessibility thereto. A related system known as "Pacer" affords access to review of online court records. (32)

equity or **equity cushion** — the value in an asset over and above that of any liens or encumbrances, such as equity in a home or motor vehicle. (10, 22)

equity security holder — an entity owning an interest in a debtor. The shareholders of a corporate debtor are its equity security holders. The partners of a partnership are its equity security holders. Section 101(17) of the Bankruptcy Code defines equity security holder. (7)

estate — the debtor's property owned at the time of the bankruptcy filing. The estate is created by the filing of a bankruptcy proceeding. The estate is administered by the trustee. (15)

evidentiary hearing — a hearing held to take sworn testimony to permit a Bankruptcy Court to make a decision in a contested matter that is not a separate adversary proceeding. An evidentiary hearing is similar to a trial in a nonbankruptcy environment. A "trial" on a contested motion for relief from the automatic stay is properly called an evidentiary hearing. (5, 13)

ex parte — an application made to the court without notice or with limited notice to limited parties. Ex parte applications are specifically permitted for various ministerial functions. In other circumstances, a legitimate extraordinary circumstance must exist for the court to consider ex parte relief. (5)

examiner — an individual appointed in a Chapter 11 proceeding to conduct an independent investigation of some or all of a debtor's financial affairs. (11)

exclusivity period — a period of time in a Chapter 11 proceeding when only the debtor-in-possession may file a reorganization plan. This period, as provided for in Section 1121 of the Bankruptcy Code, is the first 120 days from the entry of an order for relief. In small business cases, the period is 180 days. This period can be extended. The period terminates upon the appointment of a trustee. (26)

executory contract — contracts for which performance remains due to some extent on both sides. Franchise or license agreements are common executory contracts. Executory contracts are the subject of Bankruptcy Code Section 365. An executory contract may be assumed or rejected. (20)

exempt — free from the reach of creditors or the trustee. (8, 10)

exemptions — statutorily defined property that an individual debtor may protect from administration by a bankruptcy estate. Exempt property is not available for liquidation to pay a dividend to creditors; a debtor may keep exempt property. Exemptions are a primary element of debtor relief. (1, 10)

family farmer — a debtor meeting the filing qualifications for a Chapter 12 proceeding. A family farmer may be an individual, corporate, or partnership debtor. In the latter two instances, more than 50 percent of the ownership must belong to members of the same family. A qualified family farmer's total debt may not exceed $4,153,150. Section 101(18) of the Bankruptcy Code defines family farmer. (28)

family fisherman — a debtor meeting the qualifications for a Chapter 12 proceeding. A family fisherman may be an individual, corporate, or partnership debtor. In the latter two instances, at least 50 percent of the ownership must belong to the same family. A qualified family fisherman's total debt may not exceed $1,924,550 and at least 80 percent must be related to the fishing operation. Section 101(19A) defines family fisherman. (28)

feasibility requirement — finding that the Bankruptcy Court must make to permit confirmation of a Chapter 11 reorganization plan. (27)

federal exemptions — exemptions permitted under federal law, specifically Section 522(d) of the Bankruptcy Code. (10)

federal judges — judges appointed to the federal bench pursuant to U.S. Const., art. III §1, U.S. Const. Art III, §2. (29)

Federal Rules of Bankruptcy Procedure — national rules promulgated to govern practice in all bankruptcy proceedings. (5, 32)

fiduciary — an entity that holds assets in trust for another. A bankruptcy trustee is a fiduciary. (11)

final fee application — an application to approve compensation; required at either the close of the proceeding or when all services to be rendered are complete. (8)

first-day order — common name of critical orders entered within the first day or two of a large corporate Chapter 11 filing. (4, 25)

floating lien — a line of credit from a bank, financial institution, or other lender secured by the existing and after-acquired inventory, equipment, and proceeds of a debtor's business. (17, 18)

fraudulent transfer—a transfer made by a debtor with an intent to hinder, delay, or defraud creditors. A transfer without reasonable or fair consideration made while a debtor is insolvent or that renders a debtor insolvent will also be fraudulent. Fraudulent transfers are the subject of Bankruptcy Code Section 548. Fraudulent transfers are one of the trustee's avoiding powers. (18)

fresh cash rule—portion of a debt incurred by use of a false written financial statement. (14)

fresh start—the phrase most frequently used colloquially to describe the basic elements of debtor relief: discharge, exemptions, and the automatic stay. (8, 10)

gap period claim—a claim arising during the period of time between the filing of an involuntary petition and the entry of an order for relief. (4, 22)

gap period—the common term for the period of time between the filing of an involuntary petition and the entry of an order for relief. (4, 22)

health care business—a business that provides health care services. Special rules apply for a trustee's disposition of health care business records and for the placement of patients in alternative facilities. The court will appoint an ombudsman to speak for the best interests of the patients unless the court can find that such an appointment is not necessary. Section 101(27A) of the Bankruptcy Code defines health care business. (11, 21)

homestead exemption—an exemption permitted in an individual debtor's place of residence. Section 522(d)(1) of the Bankruptcy Code provides a federal homestead exemption. State law also provides homestead exemptions. (10)

impaired claim—a claim not paid according to its terms on the effective date of a Chapter 11 plan. For example, unsecured creditors who are to be paid over an extended period of time are impaired. An impaired class of claims is entitled to vote to accept or reject a Chapter 11 reorganization plan. (26)

insider—generally, an entity in control of a debtor or a debtor's relatives. The definition of an insider will vary depending upon the debtor's identity as an individual, partnership, or corporation. Section 101(31) of the Bankruptcy Code defines insider. (7)

insolvent—an entity is generally insolvent when its liabilities exceed its assets. Section 101(32) of the Bankruptcy Code defines insolvency. (7, 17)

intellectual property—patents, copyrights, and trademarks. Section 101(35A) of the Bankruptcy Code defines intellectual property. (20)

interim fee application—application brought during a bankruptcy proceeding to approve payment of professional compensation. (8)

interim trustee—the trustee appointed by the United States Trustee to administer a bankruptcy estate prior to the meeting of creditors called for by Section 341(a) of the Bankruptcy Code. The interim trustee will become the permanent trustee unless the creditors elect a different trustee at the meeting of creditors. (8)

inventory—any form of personal property that a debtor uses to produce revenue. (17)

involuntary petition—a bankruptcy proceeding initiated by one or more creditors (or general partners of a partnership) by filing a petition seeking the entry of an order for relief; a judgment that the debtor is bankrupt. Section 303 of the Bankruptcy Code governs involuntary petitions. (4)

ipso facto clause—a clause in a contract defining insolvency or a bankruptcy filing as an act of default. These clauses generally are not enforceable in bankruptcy proceedings. (15, 19)

joint case—a bankruptcy proceeding involving an individual and the individual's spouse. (4)

judicial lien—a lien arising by virtue of a court order or judgment. A judicial lien may be a prejudgment writ of attachment or a postjudgment writ of execution. Section 101(36) of the Bankruptcy Code defines judicial lien. (7)

license—an agreement to operate a business or market a product. (20)

licensee—entity to whom a license is issued, the holder of the license. (20)

licensor—entity issuing a license. (20)

lien—a right to property to secure repayment of a debt or the performance of an obligation. A lien may be a judicial, consensual, or statutory lien. Section 101(37) of the Bankruptcy Code defines lien. (7)

liquidation—the sale of an estate's assets to repay creditors. A Chapter 7 bankruptcy is a liquidation proceeding. A Chapter 11 plan may provide for liquidation of the estate rather than reorganization. (2, 25)

liquidation analysis—portion of a Disclosure Statement comparing a reorganization plan to the results likely to be obtained if the case were a Chapter 7. (27)

liquidation value—the value to be obtained from a forced sale of assets. (10)

mandatory element—provisions that must be included in a Chapter 11 or Chapter 13 plan. (24, 26)

market value — the value of an asset, real or personal, sold in the ordinary course of business according to commercially reasonable terms. (10)

means testing — title given to formula contained in 11 U.S.C. §707(b)(2) to determine whether or not a consumer debtor is presumed to be abusing the bankruptcy system by filing a Chapter 7. Abuse is presumed when a debtor's current monthly income exceeds the state median family income and the debtor can repay unsecured creditors at least $128.33 per month over 60 months ($7,700) and a dividend of at least 25 percent or can repay unsecured creditors at least $12,850 over 60 months without regard to the percentage repaid. Where abuse is presumed, the case will be dismissed unless the debtor consents to conversion to Chapter 13. Means testing is sometimes referred to as *needs based bankruptcy*. (6)

median family income — the most current figures provided by the Bureau of the Census as set forth in 11 U.S.C. §101(39A). The amount of median family income determines whether or not a debtor is subject to needs based bankruptcy analysis. (6, 7)

motion for relief from the automatic stay — a motion made by a creditor, pursuant to 11 U.S.C. §362(d), to be freed from the effect of the automatic stay. (5, 13)

needs based bankruptcy — see *means testing*. (6)

new value — the providing of new consideration in a transaction between a debtor and creditor. An avoidable preference will generally not exist where a transaction occurs for new value. This definition is unique to avoidable preferences. (17)

noncapital asset — an asset not used to operate a business. For example, inventory is generally a noncapital asset. (19)

noncore proceedings — matters that are related to a bankruptcy proceeding but that do not require specific application of a Bankruptcy Code provision for the matter's resolution. (29)

nondischargeable debt — a debt not subject to a debtor's discharge; a debtor is not relieved from personal or legal liability for the affected debt. Some types of nondischargeable debts require the filing of a Complaint to Determine Dischargeability of Debt for the debt to become nondischargeable. Nondischargeable debts are described in Bankruptcy Code Section 523(a). (14)

nonpurchase money security interest — a security interest in collateral where the purpose of the loan is other than to purchase the collateral. (10)

nonresidential lease — any real property lease that is not a *residential* lease. A store rental is a common nonresidential real property lease. (20)

notice and a hearing—Bankruptcy Code phrase, which triggers some form of due process, such as a noticed motion, notice of intent, or ex parte application. (5)

notice of intent—the common method of providing notice to creditors, when required, to properly accomplish a bankruptcy procedure. This procedure is also sometimes known as a "notice of intended action." Generally, 24 days' notice by mail upon all creditors and parties in interest is necessary to properly accomplish many bankruptcy procedures. (5)

noticed motion—a motion brought by a party in interest seeking a ruling from the Bankruptcy Court with notice to all interested parties. (5)

Official Creditors' Committee—entity created in a Chapter 11 proceeding to act on the collective behalf of unsecured creditors. (11)

ombudsman—an independent person who may be appointed to serve the best interests of patients in the bankruptcy of a health care business. An ombudsman may also be appointed to report to the court on the protection of personally identifiable information in the sale of customer lists. (11)

operating reports—a regular report of a Chapter 11 debtor-in-possession's postpetition financial activity. Local rules will normally require the filing of monthly reports. (25)

order for relief—a statutory term of art, which signifies that a debtor has filed for bankruptcy relief. (4)

ordinary course of business—generally, normal everyday business transactions. (19, 21)

party in interest—a party with a stake in the outcome of a bankruptcy proceeding. The debtor, creditors, trustee, United States Trustee, and equity security holders are all parties in interest. (11)

permissive element—provisions that may be included in a Chapter 11 or Chapter 13 plan. (24, 26)

person—any kind of entity—individual, corporate, or partnership—except a governmental unit. Section 101(41) of the Bankruptcy Code defines person for purposes of the Bankruptcy Code. (7)

personally identifiable information—information that may generally be used to contact or locate an individual, such as name and address, Social Security number, date of birth, and other similar information. Section 101(41A) of the Bankruptcy Code defines personally identifiable information. (11)

petitioning creditors—creditors initiating an involuntary petition against a debtor. (4)

plan—a Chapter 13 plan. (24)

Plan of Reorganization — common title of a Chapter 11 reorganization plan. (26)

plan proponent — entity filing a Chapter 11 plan. (26)

postpetition transfer — a transfer of estate property after a bankruptcy filing that is made without court approval or is not otherwise authorized by the Bankruptcy Code. An unauthorized postpetition transaction may be avoided by a bankruptcy trustee. Postpetition transactions are the subject of Bankruptcy Code Section 549. (18)

Prearranged bankruptcy — A plan that has been negotiated but has not solicited votes prior to the bankruptcy filing. (27)

preference — a transfer of property or an interest in property to a creditor, on the eve of bankruptcy, in full or partial satisfaction of debt to the exclusion of other creditors. A preference meeting certain defined conditions will be avoidable by a bankruptcy trustee. (17)

prepackaged bankruptcy — a Chapter 11 proceeding in which a debtor seeks Bankruptcy Court approval of a plan where votes have been solicited before the case has been filed. (27)

prepetition credit counseling — counseling that a debtor must receive from a credit counseling agency as a prerequisite to seeking individual bankruptcy relief. (4)

Priming loan — administrative loan with priority over existing prepetition secured debt. (21).

priority claim — a claim given priority over other unsecured claims. Section 507(a) of the Bankruptcy Code describes priority claims. Tax claims and certain wage claims are common priority claims. (22)

pro forma — a financial forecast of future performance over a period of time. Pro formas are frequently used in Chapter 11 plan practice. (27)

pro rata — a distribution to creditors within a given class on a proportional basis. (23)

professional — an attorney, accountant, auctioneer, appraiser, and the like. A professional rendering services to a bankruptcy estate must be approved by the court for the services to be compensable. The fees of a professional rendering services to a bankruptcy estate are subject to court approval by way of a fee application as described in Bankruptcy Code Sections 330 and 331. (8)

proof of claim — the filing of a formal written claim by a creditor in a bankruptcy proceeding. A proof of claim must always be filed in a Chapter 7 proceeding for a claim to be entitled to receive a dividend. It is always wise to file a proof of claim on behalf of a creditor. (22)

property of the estate — property subject to administration by a bankruptcy trustee for the distribution of dividends to creditors. (15, 24)

purchase money security interest — a security interest in collateral when the purpose of the loan is to purchase the collateral. (10)

reaffirmation agreement—a debtor's agreement to remain legally liable for repayment of a debt otherwise dischargeable in a bankruptcy proceeding. For a debt to be legally reaffirmed, strict compliance with the provisions of Bankruptcy Code Section 524 is required. (8)

receivable—a right to payment, whether or not such right has been earned by performance. (17)

redemption—a right given a Chapter 7 consumer debtor to pay a lump sum to a secured creditor in an amount equal to the value of any collateral. A valuation hearing may be necessary to determine the adequacy of the redemption amount. Section 722 of the Bankruptcy Code permits redemption. (22)

regular income—income sufficient and stable enough to support performance of a Chapter 13 plan by an individual. Regular income is not limited to wages or salary. Pension, Social Security, and commission income may all constitute regular income for Chapter 13 purposes. (5)

reorganization—a bankruptcy proceeding where a debtor seeks confirmation of a plan that will repay creditors while permitting the debtor to retain assets or continue in business. The proceedings permitted by Chapters 9, 11, 12, and 13 of the Bankruptcy Code are reorganization proceedings. (2, 24)

reorganization plan—a repayment plan prepared according to the requirements of Chapter 11 of the Bankruptcy Code. (26)

replacement value—the price a retail merchant would charge for property of that kind considering the age and condition of the property at the time value is determined. (10)

residential real property—real property in which a debtor resides. A real property lease is a lease in which the debtor resides in the premises. (20)

Rule 2004 Examination—an extended examination of any person pursuant to Federal Rule of Bankruptcy Procedure 2004 regarding one or more aspects of a debtor's financial affairs. A Rule 2004 Examination is similar to a deposition in nonbankruptcy proceedings. (8)

sale free and clear of liens—a sale held pursuant to 11 U.S.C. §363(f). Such a sale seeks court approval to sell liened property over the objection of any lienholder. (19)

Schedules of Assets and Liabilities—a fundamental bankruptcy pleading consisting of a prioritized and itemized list of a debtor's assets (property) and liabilities (debt). (4, 30)

secured creditor—a creditor with collateral that may satisfy part or all of the creditor's allowed claim. (22)

security—commercial documents used to evidence an ownership interest in an entity, among other things. Section 101(49) of the Bankruptcy Code defines security. (7)

security agreement—an agreement creating a security interest. A security interest is a consensual lien created by agreement. Section 101(50) of the Bankruptcy Code defines security agreement. (7)

serial filing or serial bankruptcy—a debtor who files a second (or third) bankruptcy proceeding after dismissal of one or more prior proceedings. (5, 13)

setoff—the common law right of a creditor to balance mutual debts with a debtor. (18)

single asset real estate—real property that encompasses a single property or project and that generates substantially all the gross income of a debtor and on which no substantial business is conducted other than operation of the property and activities thereto, not including residential real property with three or fewer units. Single asset real estate is defined in Bankruptcy Code Section 101(51B). (7)

small business debtor—a Chapter 11 debtor with liquidated debts not in excess of $2,566,050 who elects treatment as a small business debtor, excluding a debtor whose primary activity is owning and operating real estate. Small business debtors are defined in Bankruptcy Code Section 101(51D). (11, 25)

solvent estate—an estate capable of paying all claims in full and returning assets to the debtor. (23)

spendthrift trust—a trust containing a clause precluding invasion of the trust assets to satisfy the debts of a beneficiary. (15)

stacking—individual joint debtors claiming state and federal exemptions. (10)

Statement of Financial Affairs—a fundamental bankruptcy pleading consisting of a questionnaire concerning a debtor's financial affairs. (4, 30)

Statement of Intention—a notice to be given, within 30 days after a filing, to the holders of collateral securing the repayment of consumer debt. The debtor must advise any affected creditor of the debtor's intention regarding the collateral. The debtor may reaffirm the contact, redeem or return the collateral, or avoid the lien under specific defined circumstances. (22)

Statements and Schedules—common name of the Statement of Financial Affairs and Schedules of Assets and Liabilities filed by any debtor within the bankruptcy system. These pleadings will be the most important initial pleadings in any bankruptcy proceeding. (4, 30)

statutory lien—a lien created by operation of law other than a court order. A state law mechanic's lien is a statutory lien. Section 101(53) of the Bankruptcy Code defines statutory lien. (7, 16)

strip-off/strip-down—ability to avoid the unsecured portion of an otherwise secured debt in some circumstances in Chapter 13 cases. (22, 24)

strong arm clause—the trustee's rights as a super-creditor, which are contained in the Bankruptcy Code Section 544. (16)

subordination—the relegation of a claim to a lesser status than it is otherwise entitled to under the Bankruptcy Code. A creditor may consent to subordination or the court may order subordination for equitable reasons. Subordination is the subject of Section 510. (22)

substantially consummated—the taking of an irrevocable act in performance of a Chapter 11 plan, such as closing escrow or repaying a substantial portion of a dividend. (27)

substantially contemporaneous—an exchange taking place in the ordinary course of business. (17)

Substantive consolidation—when the court consolidates two or more proceedings for all purposes. (4)

surplus monthly income—amount of monthly income available to repay unsecured creditors pursuant to means testing. (6)

30/30/30 rule—time periods within which a motion for relief from the automatic stay must be resolved, as described in Bankruptcy Code Section 362(e). (13)

transfer—any means that may be devised to dispose of property or an interest in property. This is an intentionally broad definition. Section 101(54) of the Bankruptcy Code defines transfer. (7, 17)

trustee—a fiduciary appointed by the United States Trustee to administer a bankruptcy estate. (2, 11)

turnover complaint—the right of a bankruptcy trustee under 11 U.S.C. §542 to recover property of an estate in the possession of the debtor or other third party. A trustee generally obtains a turnover by filing a turnover complaint. (15)

undersecured creditor—a secured creditor whose collateral is worth less than the total amount of its allowed claim. (22)

unimpaired claim—a claim paid according to its terms on the effective date of a Chapter 11 reorganization plan. For example, if a debtor-in-possession pays all unsecured claims in full on the effective date of a plan, the claims are unimpaired. An unimpaired class of claims will be deemed to have accepted a Chapter 11 plan. (26)

United States Trustee—a division of the Department of Justice responsible for monitoring the administration of bankruptcy estates. (11)

unlisted debt—a debt not included in a debtor's schedules. (14)

valuation hearing—a hearing held, pursuant to 11 U.S.C. §506, to determine the value of a secured creditor's collateral. (22, 27)

venue—the proper Bankruptcy Court (federal district) in which a bankruptcy proceeding should be commenced. Generally, venue is where the debtor resides or where the debtor business's primary business address or assets are located. Venue may be changed by a motion of a party in interest. (4)

voluntary petition—a bankruptcy proceeding initiated by a debtor filing a petition for relief. Most bankruptcy proceedings are voluntary. (4)

Table of Cases

Table of Statutes

Uniform Commercial Code

Miscellaneous State Statutes

English Statutes

Other

Table of Federal Rules of Bankruptcy Procedure

Table of Secondary Authorities

Report of the Commission on the Bankruptcy Laws of the United States, H.R. Doc. No. 137, 82d
    Cong., 1st Sess., pt. I, ch. 17 (1973), 11
Riesenfeld, Evolution of Modern Bankruptcy Law, 31 Minn. L. Rev. 401 (1947), 6–7, 9–11

S. Rep. No. 989, 95th Cong., 2d Sess. 81 (1978), 151
S. Rep. No. 989, 95th Cong., 2d Sess. 94 (1978), 142

Uniform Fraudulent Transfer Act, 7A U.L.A. 7 (West Supp. 2012), 287

Wolf, Neal, The Enterprise Bankruptcy Law of the People's Republic of China, Bankruptcy Strate-
    gist Vol. 25 No. 9 (July 2008), 12

www.abiworld.org, 571
www.census.gov, 399
www.uscourts.gov, 17, 571
www.usdoj.gov/ust, 549

Index